TWELFTH EDITION

Introduction to the Foundations of American Education

TWELFTH EDITION

Introduction to the Foundations of American Education

JAMES A. JOHNSON
Northern Illinois University

VICTOR L. DUPUIS
Pennsylvania State University

DIANN MUSIAL
Northern Illinois University

GENE E. HALL
University of Nevada, Las Vegas

DONNA M. GOLLNICK
National Council for the Accreditation of Teacher Education

ALLYN AND BACON
Boston ■ *London* ■ *Toronto* ■ *Sydney* ■ *Tokyo* ■ *Singapore*

Executive Editor: Stephen D. Dragin
Development Editor: Linda Bieze
Production Supervisor: Joe Sweeney
Editorial Assistant: Barbara Strickland
Marketing Manager: Kathleen Morgan
Editorial-Production Service: Omegatype Typography, Inc.
Manufacturing Buyer: Megan Cochran
Cover Administrator: Linda Knowles
Electronic Composition: Omegatype Typography, Inc.

A Pearson Education Company
75 Arlington Street
Boston, MA 02116

Internet: www.ablongman.com

Between the time Website information is gathered and published, some sites may have closed. Also, the transcription of URLs can result in typographical errors. The publisher would appreciate notification where these occur so that they may be corrected in subsequent editions.

Library of Congress Cataloging-in-Publication Data

Introduction to the foundations of American education / James A. Johnson . . . [et al.]. — 12th ed.
p. cm.
Includes bibliographical references and index.
ISBN 0-205-32387-1 (alk. paper)
1. Education—Study and teaching—United States. 2. Education—United States. 3. Educational sociology—United States. 4. Teaching—Vocational guidance—United States. I. Johnson, James Allen.
LB17 .I59 2002
370'.973—dc21 2001022106

Printed in the United States of America

10 9 8 7 6 5 4 3 2 RRD-OH 06 05 04 03 02

Credits for photos appear on page 594, which constitutes a continuation to the copyright page.

Coverage of Interstate New Teacher Assessment and Support Consortium (INTASC) Standards for Beginning Teacher Licensing and Development

INTASC Standards		Text Chapter/Page Number
STANDARD 1	Central concepts, tools of inquiry, and structures of the subject being taught.	**Chapter 1:** 18, 19, 24, 26–29 **Chapter 15:** 527–537, 562–568
STANDARD 2	Children's learning and intellectual, social, and personal development.	**Chapter 3:** 113–121, 129 **Chapter 9:** 349, 360 **Chapter 10:** 386, 390, 392, 393, 395–396, 397, 402 **Chapter 11:** 408–409 **Chapter 13:** 464, 466, 471, 473, 477 **Chapter 14:** 496
STANDARD 3	Student differences in their approaches to learning and adaptations for diverse learners.	**Chapter 4:** 148–151 **Chapter 9:** 348–351 **Chapter 13:** 467–468, 480
STANDARD 4	Instructional strategies for students' development of critical thinking, problem solving, and performance skills.	**Chapter 4:** 161 **Chapter 7:** 299 **Chapter 10:** 381–385, 387 **Chapter 11:** 428–429 **Chapter 14:** 504, 505–509, 510–512
STANDARD 5	Individual and group motivation and behavior for positive social interaction, active engagement in learning, and self-motivation.	**Chapter 7:** 288 **Chapter 10:** 426 **Chapter 12:** 442–444 **Chapter 14:** 500, 501, 502, 503
STANDARD 6	Effective verbal, nonverbal, and media communication techniques for inquiry, collaboration, and supportive interaction in the classroom.	**Chapter 4:** 151–154 **Chapter 14:** 509–518
STANDARD 7	Instructional planning based on knowledge of subject matter, students, the community, and curriculum goals.	**Chapter 4:** 148–151 **Chapter 8:** 313–316 **Chapter 11:** 410–429 **Chapter 12:** 438–439, 441 **Chapter 13:** 474–484 **Chapter 14:** 504–509 **Chapter 15:** 558–560
STANDARD 8	Formal and informal assessment strategies for intellectual, social, and physical development of the learner.	**Chapter 5:** 197, 200 **Chapter 9:** 356–357 **Chapter 11:** 427 **Chapter 12:** 442 **Chapter 15:** 525, 537–555, 560–561
STANDARD 9	Reflection to evaluate effects of choices and actions on others.	**Chapter 1:** 30–36 **Chapter 9:** 353, 357–361 **Chapter 12:** 451–455
STANDARD 10	Relationships with school colleagues, parents, and agencies to support students' learning and well-being.	**Chapter 1:** 36–37 **Chapter 15:** 561

National Council for the Accreditation of Teacher Education (NCATE) Professional Standards		
NCATE Standards		**Text Chapter/Page Number**
STANDARD 1	Candidate knowledge, skill, and dispositions	**All Chapters**
STANDARD 2	Assessment system and unit evaluation	**Chapter 9:** 356–357 **Chapter 15:** All **All Chapters:** Journal entries and portfolio development activities
STANDARD 3	Field experiences and clinical practice	**All Chapters:** School-based experience activities
STANDARD 4	Diversity	**Chapter 1:** 8–9, 17 **Chapter 2:** All **Chapter 3:** All **Chapter 4:** All **Chapter 5:** 231–247, 266–267, 270 **Chapter 7:** 282–301 **Chapter 8:** 327–333 **Chapter 9:** 348–351 **Chapter 10:** 397–402 **Chapter 13:** 468–469
STANDARD 5	Faculty qualifications, performance, and evaluation	**Chapter 1:** All **Chapter 15:** All
STANDARD 6	Governance and resources	**Chapter 8:** 317–321

CONTENTS

INTASC Standards Table v

NCATE Standards Table vi

List of Features xxi

Preface xxiii

PART ONE

The Profession of Teaching xxx

Viewing Education through Professional Lenses 1

1 Teaching as a Profession

Education in the News: No Crisis, but Trouble on the Way 3

Learner Outcomes 4

Today's Teachers 5
The Importance of Teachers to Society 6
The Public View of Teachers and Schools 6
Who Teaches? 8
Teachers Needed 12

Teaching as a Profession 18
Characteristics of a Profession 18
Quality Assurance Continuum 20
Professional Responsibilities 24

Debate
Should Nationally Certified Teachers Be Paid More? 25

Professional Dilemma
Who Is Cheating Now? 30

Reflecting on One's Practice 30

Relevant Research
Making Meaning of the Educational Portfolios 35

Working with Colleagues, Other Professionals, and Students' Families 36
Participating in the Profession 37

Global Perspectives
Education International 42

Challenges Affecting Teachers 42
Salaries 42
Working Conditions 47

Beginning and Continuing a Teaching Career 47
Becoming Licensed 48
Searching for a Teaching Position 49
Remaining a Teacher 50

Summary **51**
Discussion Questions **52**
Journal Entries **52**
Portfolio Development **52**
School-Based Experiences **53**
Websites **53**
Notes **54**
Bibliography **54**

Appendix 1.1: State Teacher Licensure Offices **56**
Appendix 1.2: Professional and Religious Education Associations: A Selected List **58**

PART TWO
School and Society 60
Viewing Education through Sociological Lenses **61**

2 Diversity in Society

Education in the News: Little Newcomers in a Strange Land 63
Learner Outcomes 63
Culture and Society 65
Characteristics of Culture 65
Dominant or Mainstream Culture 65
Microcultural Groups 66
Diversity and Education 67
Assimilation 68
Cultural Pluralism 69
Cultural Choice 70
Socioeconomic Status **71**
Social Stratification 72
Class Structure 72
Poverty 73
Ethnicity and Race 75
Race 75
Ethnicity 76
Ethnic Diversity 76
Relevant Research
Development of Racial and Gender Identity 78
Gender 78
Differences between Females and Males 78

Global Perspectives
Poverty, Illiteracy, and School Attendance in China 81

Sexual Orientation 81

Language 82
Language Diversity 82
Dialectal Diversity 83

Professional Dilemma
Communicating with Parents of English Language Learners 84

Exceptionalities 84
Inclusion 85

Debate
Are Too Many Kids Labeled Gifted? 86

Cultural Differences 88
Disproportionate Placements 88

Religion 88
Religious Pluralism 88
Religion in Schools 89

Geography 90
Rural Communities 90
Suburban Communities 91
Urban Communities 92

Cultural Identity 93
Intragroup Differences 93
Biculturalism and Multiculturalism 93

Summary 94
Discussion Questions 96
Journal Entries 96
Portfolio Development 96
School-Based Experiences 97
Websites 97
Notes 98
Bibliography 99

3 Schools Facing Social Challenges

Education in the News: Racial Gap in Schools Splits a Town Proud of Diversity 101

Learner Outcomes 101

Groups in Society 103
Power and Domination 103
Ethnocentrism 105
Prejudice and Discrimination 106

Today's Families 108
Parenting 109

Professional Dilemma
What If He Has Two Mommies? 110

Latchkey Children 110
Homeless Students 112
Abuse 112

Today's Youth 113
Who Is This Generation? 114
Challenges of Youth Culture 116

Democracy and Schooling 122
Equality and Education 122

Relevant Research
Conflict of Liberal Discourse and Self-Interest 124

Roles of Schools 125
Purposes of Schools 127

Debate
Can Retention Be Good for a Student? 130

Whose Schools? 132

Global Perspectives
Universal Values 133

Democratic Schools 133

Summary 135
Discussion Questions 136
Journal Entries 136
Portfolio Development 137
School-Based Experiences 137
Websites 137
Notes 138
Bibliography 139

4 Education That Is Multicultural

Education in the News: Internet at School Is Changing Work of Students—and Teachers 141

Learner Outcomes 142

Undergirding Tenets 143
Diversity 144
Social Justice and Equality 145

Global Perspectives
Antiracist and Multicultural Education 146

Culture of the School 146
Traditions 147
Hidden Curriculum 147

Culturally Relevant Teaching 148
Building on Cultural Context 148
Centering the Cultures of Students 149
Validating Student Voices 151

Debate
Should We Correct Students' Grammar All the Time, Every Time? 153

Educational Challenges 154
The Challenge of Technology and Equity 155
The Challenge of Gender-Sensitive Education 157

Relevant Research
Boys and Girls in Performance-Based Science Classrooms 159

The Challenge of Language Diversity 159

Teachers as Social Activists 161
Thinking Critically 161
Practicing Equity in the Classroom 162

Professional Dilemma
Harassment in Schools 163

Teaching for Social Justice 163
Involving Communities and Families 164

Summary 165
Discussion Questions 166
Journal Entries 166
Portfolio Development 166
School-Based Experiences 167
Websites 167
Notes 168
Bibliography 169

PART THREE

Governance and Support of American Education 170

Viewing Education through Organizational Lenses 171

Organizing and Paying for American Education

Education in the News: Study: School Choice Popular; Academic Results Are Unclear 173

Learner Outcomes 174

The Structure of the American Education System 175
The Organization of Schools 176
Organization of the School District 180
Organization of Education at the State Level 182
The Federal Government's Role in Education 186
Other Types of Education Agencies 189
Choice: Increasing Options along with Uncertain Outcomes 190
Issues Related to Organization and Structure 195

Professional Dilemma
What Is the Appropriate Role for Teachers When the Politics Get Rough? 197

The Financing of Education: Sources of Funds and the Move from Equity to Adequacy 200
A System of Taxation and Support for Schools 201

Relevant Research
Reform of School Finance in Michigan 206

Debate
Has Student Fund-Raising Gone Too Far? 208

Education Spending 210
Perennial School Finance Issues 213
Accountability 215

Global Perspectives
International Comparisons in Spending for Schools 219

Summary 220
Discussion Questions 222
Journal Entries 222
Portfolio Development 223
School-Based Experiences 223
Websites 223
Notes 224
Bibliography 225

Legal Foundations of Education

Education in the News: Prayers Are Heard at Football Games Despite Ruling 227

Learner Outcomes 227

Legal Aspects of Education 229
Legal Provisions for Education: The U.S. Constitution 229
Church and State 231
Segregation and Desegregation 239
Equal Opportunity 244

Professional Dilemma
What Will You Do If a Child in Your Classroom Has AIDS? 247

Teachers' Rights and Responsibilities 248
Conditions of Employment 248
Academic Freedom 254
Liability for Negligence 256

Students' Rights and Responsibilities 258
Students' Rights as Citizens 259

Debate
Should Teachers and Support Staff Be Able to Suspend Students? 262

Students' Rights and Responsibilities in School 265

Relevant Research
Zero Tolerance, Zero Sense 272

Global Perspectives
Legal Aspects of Education in Other Countries 272

Summary 274
Discussion Questions 275
Journal Entries 275
Portfolio Development 276
School-Based Experiences 276
Websites 276
Notes 277
Bibliography 277

PART FOUR

Historical Foundations of Education 278

Viewing Education through Historical Lenses 279

7 Antecedents of American Education

Education in the News: Quintilian Defines "An Ideal Teacher" 281

Learner Outcomes 281

The Beginnings of Education (to A.D. 476) 282

Global Perspectives
Educational Ideas Borrowed from around the World 283

Non-Western Education 283
Western Education—The Greeks 285
Western Education—The Romans 287

Relevant Research
School Violence 288

Education in the Middle Ages (476–1300) 289
The Dark Ages (400–1000) 289
The Revival of Learning 290

Professional Dilemma
Can a Knowledge of History Help to Improve Multicultural Education? 291

Education in Transition (1300–1700) 291
The Renaissance 292
The Reformation 292

Modern Period (1700–Present) 294
The Age of Reason 294
The Emergence of Common Man 295

Debate
Should Kids Read *Goosebumps*? 296

Summary 300
Discussion Questions 301
Journal Entries 301
Portfolio Development 302
School-Based Experiences 302
Websites 302
Notes 302
Bibliography 303

8 The Important Role of Education in Our Developing Nation

Education in the News: Why Study History? 305

Learner Outcomes 306

Providing Education in the New World 307
Colonial Education 307
The Struggle for Universal Elementary Education 309

Global Perspectives
Educational Transplantation from Europe 310

The Need for Secondary Schools 311
Aims of American Education 313

Relevant Research
Critiquing Historical Sources 314

History of Federal Involvement 316
Preparation of Teachers 317

Global Perspectives
European Beginnings of Teacher Training 317
Evolution of Teaching Materials 321

Debate
Should NEA Affiliates Help Get Rid of Bad Teachers? 322

Education for Diverse Populations 327
Education of African Americans 327
Education of Women 331

Global Perspectives
Maria Montessori 332

Private Education in America 333

Professional Dilemma
Can a Teacher Both Defend and Criticize Past and Present Schools? 334

Summary 336
Discussion Questions 337
Journal Entries 337
Portfolio Development 338
School-Based Experiences 338
Websites 338
Notes 339
Bibliography 339

Using Recent History to Improve Student Learning

Education in the News: Is History Knowable? 341
Learner Outcomes 342
More Students and Bigger Schools 342
The Rapid Growth of the Educational Enterprise 342
School District Consolidation 343
Growth of Programs 345

Debate
Should Seat Belts Be Mandatory on School Buses? 346

Relevant Research
Student Homework 349

A Developing Profession 351
The Increasing Complexity of the Educational Enterprise 351

Recent Trends in Education 357
New Emphases in Education 358

Global Perspectives
Jean Piaget 360

Professional Dilemma
How Can the Busy Teacher Keep Up with Historical and Contemporary Research? 362

Global Perspectives
Educators' Worldwide Responsibility 363

Summary 366
Discussion Questions 367
Journal Entries 367
Portfolio Development 368
School-Based Experiences 368
Websites 368
Notes 369
Bibliography 369

Appendix 9.1: Important Dates in the History of Western Education 370

PART FIVE
Philosophical Foundations of Education 374

Viewing Education through Philosophical Lenses 375

10 Philosophy: The Passion to Understand

Education in the News: The Cheating Game 377

Learner Outcomes 378

Structure and Methodology of Philosophy 378
The Branches of Philosophy 379
Thinking as a Philosopher 381

Professional Dilemma
Should Ethics Be Taught in Public Schools? 384

Schools of Philosophy and Their Influence on Education 385
Idealism 386

Relevant Research
Teaching for Critical Thinking 387

Realism 389
Pragmatism 392
Existentialism 393

Debate
Should Schools Sell Cola Companies Exclusive Rights? 394

Eastern Ways of Knowing 397

Global Perspectives
The Fabric of Eastern Ways of Knowing 399

Native North American Ways of Knowing 400

Summary 402
Discussion Questions 403
Journal Entries 403
Portfolio Development 403
School-Based Experiences 403
Websites 404
Notes 404
Bibliography 405

11 Educational Theory in American Schools: Philosophy in Action

Education in the News: A Wake-Up Call 407

Learner Outcomes 407

Authoritarian Educational Theories 410
Perennialism 410
Essentialism 412

Debate
Should Today's Education Be Relevant to Tomorrow's Job Market? 413

Behaviorism 416
Positivism 418

Nonauthoritarian Educational Theories 419
Progressivism 419
Reconstructionism 421
Humanism 423
Constructivism 425

Professional Dilemma
Should I Use Homogeneous or Heterogeneous Ability Grouping? 426

Relevant Research
Developing Authentic Assessments 427

Global Perspectives
Looking beyond the Boundaries 429

Summary 430
Discussion Questions 430
Journal Entries 431
Portfolio Development 431
School-Based Experiences 431
Websites 431
Notes 432
Bibliography 432

12 Building an Educational Philosophy

Education in the News: Authors Add Character to Curriculum 435

Learner Outcomes 436

Using Philosophy in the Classroom 438
Classroom Organization 438

Debate
Is Environmental Education Scaring Our Kids to Death? 440

Motivation 442

Relevant Research
The Three C's of Safe Schools: Cooperation, Conflict Resolution, and Civic Values 443

Discipline 445

Professional Dilemma
Should You Use Authentic Assessment to Grade Students? 447

Classroom Climate 448

Using Philosophy Beyond the Classroom 451
Teachers as Change Agents 451
Teachers as Leaders 453

Global Perspectives
The World as Classroom 455

Summary 455
Discussion Questions 457
Journal Entries 457
Portfolio Development 457
School-Based Experiences 457
Websites 458
Notes 458
Bibliography 459

PART SIX

Student Programs, Teacher Practices, and Standards-Based Education and Assessment 460

Viewing Education through Program Development Lenses 461

13 Designing Programs for Learners

Education in the News: Charter Schools Working Together 463

Learner Outcomes 463

Types of Curriculum Design 464
Separate Courses Design 464
Fused Courses Design 465

Core Courses Design 466
Activity Courses Design 466

Students Served by the Curriculum 467
Terminal Students 467
College-Bound Students 468
Vocational–Technical Students 468
Destination Unknown 468
Nontraditional Students 468

Purposes of Curriculum 469
General Education 469
Exploratory Education 471
Education for Career 472

Alternative Curriculum Programs 474
Charter Schools 474

Debate
Are Charter Schools Eroding Support for Public Schools? 475

Effective Schools 477
School Vouchers 478
Outcomes-Based Education 478
Private Industry 479
Essential Schools 480
Magnet Schools 480

Relevant Research
Do Magnet Schools Boost Achievement? 481

Home-Based Schools 481
The Comer Model 482

Global Perspectives
Schools of Reconciliation in Northern Ireland 483

Putting Change in Perspective 484
Assessing the Magnitude of Change 484

Professional Dilemma
"I've Been There, Seen That, Done That Before" 485

Restructuring Schools 486
Transforming Schools 486

Summary 487
Discussion Questions 488
Journal Entries 488
Portfolio Development 488
School-Based Experiences 488
Websites 488
Notes 489
Bibliography 489

14 Providing Instruction

Education in the News: Program Recognizes Teachers' Extra Efforts 491

Learner Outcomes 491

Organizing Teachers to Provide Instruction 492
School Organization 493

Global Perspectives
German Education 494

Graded and Nongraded Schools 495
Arrangements for Staff 497
Instructional Scheduling 498

Relevant Research
Block Scheduling Can Enhance the School Climate 499

Organizing Students 500
Class Size for Management and Grouping 500
Grouping Philosophy 500

Professional Dilemma
Adjusting the Attitude of Learners 502

Instructional Practices 503
Goals for Learning 503

Models of Learning 504
Mastery Model 505
Individualized Models 505
Thinking Skills Model 506
Hunter Model 507
Teacher Expectation and Student Achievement Model 508
4Mat Model 508

Instructional Technology 509
Classroom Learning Centers 510
Educational Television 511
Computer Technology in Education 512
Personal Computers 513

Debate
Should School Computer Labs Be Phased Out? 515

Summary 519
Discussion Questions 520
Journal Entries 520
Portfolio Development 520
School-Based Experiences 520
Websites 520
Notes 521
Bibliography 521

Appendix 14.1: Domains of Learning 522

15 Standards-Based Education and Assessment

Education in the News: High-Stakes Testing: They're Here and They're Not Going Away 525

Learner Outcomes 525

Standards-Based Education 527
Differing Conceptions of Standards 527
Differing Uses of Standards 530
Differing Sources of Standards 530
Three Types of Standards 531
An Example of National Performance Standards 533
Standards Frameworks 534

The Debate over Setting Standards 535
The Ongoing Debate over the Value of Standards 535

Global Perspectives
Australia Is Exploring a New Approach to Education Reform 537

The Changing Face of Assessment 537
What Is Assessment? 538
Purposes for Assessment 539
Authentic Contextualized Assessment 541
Methods of Authentic Assessment 543

Relevant Research
A Case Study of Alternative Assessment: Student, Teacher, and Observer Perceptions in a Ninth Grade Biology Classroom 545

Designing Authentic Performance Assessments 546
Professional Aspects of Good Assessments 551
The Ups and Downs of Testing 552

Professional Dilemma
What Is the Proper Way to Prepare for High-Stakes, State-Mandated Tests? 555

Debate
Should States Determine the Specifics of Education Standards? 556

Bringing Standards to the Classroom: A True Story 557
A School District Moves to Standards-Based Education 558
Assessing Student Learning in Standards-Based Education 560
Supporting Teachers and Students in Implementing Standards-Based Education 561
Standards-Based Education as a Paradigm Change 567

Summary 569
Discussion Questions 570
Journal Entries 571
Portfolio Development 571
School-Based Experiences 571
Websites 572
Notes 572
Bibliography 573

Epilogue: Education in the Twenty-First Century

Debate
Will Public Education Survive the Next Century? 575

Name Index 577

Subject Index 581

LIST OF FEATURES

EDUCATION IN THE NEWS

No Crisis, but Trouble on the Way 3
Little Newcomers in a Strange Land 63
Racial Gap in Schools Splits a Town Proud of Diversity 101
Internet at School Is Changing Work of Students—and Teachers 141
Study: School Choice Popular; Academic Results Are Unclear 173
Prayers Are Heard at Football Games despite Ruling 227
Quintilian Defines "An Ideal Teacher" 281
Why Study History? 305
Is History Knowable? 341
The Cheating Game 377
A Wake-Up Call 407
Authors Add Character to Curriculum 435
Charter Schools Working Together 463
Program Recognizes Teachers' Extra Efforts 491
High-Stakes Testing: They're Here and They're Not Going Away 525

DEBATE

Should Nationally Certified Teachers Be Paid More? 25
Are Too Many Kids Labeled Gifted? 86
Can Retention Be Good for a Student? 130
Should We Correct Students' Grammar All the Time, Every Time? 153
Has Student Fund-Raising Gone Too Far? 208
Should Teachers and Support Staff Be Able to Suspend Students? 262
Should Kids Read *Goosebumps*? 296
Should NEA Affiliates Help Get Rid of Bad Teachers? 322
Should Seat Belts Be Mandatory on School Buses? 346
Should Schools Sell Cola Companies Exclusive Rights? 394
Should Today's Education Be Relevant to Tomorrow's Job Market? 413
Is Environmental Education Scaring Our Kids to Death? 440
Are Charter Schools Eroding Support for Public Schools? 475
Should School Computer Labs Be Phased Out? 515
Should States Determine the Specifics of Education Standards? 556
Will Public Education Survive the Next Century? 575

PROFESSIONAL DILEMMA

Who Is Cheating Now? 30
Communicating with Parents of English Language Learners 84

What If He Has Two Mommies? 110
Harassment in Schools 163
What Is the Appropriate Role for Teachers When the Politics Get Rough? 197
What Will You Do If a Child in Your Classroom Has AIDS? 247
Can a Knowledge of History Help to Improve Multicultural Education? 291
Can a Teacher Both Defend and Criticize Past and Present Schools? 334
How Can the Busy Teacher Keep Up with Historical and Contemporary Research? 362
Should Ethics Be Taught in Public Schools? 384
Should I Use Homogeneous or Heterogeneous Ability Groupings? 426
Should You Use Authentic Assessment to Grade Students? 447
"I've Been There, Seen That, Done That Before" 485
Adjusting the Attitude of Learners 502
What Is the Proper Way to Prepare for High-Stakes, State-Mandated Tests? 555

RELEVANT RESEARCH

Making Meaning of the Educational Portfolio 35
Development of Racial and Gender Identity 78
Conflict of Liberal Discourse and Self-Interest 124
Boys and Girls in Performance-Based Science Classrooms 159
Reform of School Finance in Michigan 206
Zero Tolerance, Zero Sense 272
School Violence 288
Critiquing Historical Sources 314
Student Homework 349
Teaching for Critical Thinking 387
Developing Authentic Assessments 427
The Three C's of Safe Schools: Cooperation, Conflict Resolution, and Civic Values 443
Do Magnet Schools Boost Achievement? 481
Block Scheduling Can Enhance the School Climate 499
A Case Study of Alternative Assessment: Student, Teacher, and Observer Perceptions in a Ninth Grade Biology Classroom 545

GLOBAL PERSPECTIVES

Education International 42
Poverty, Illiteracy, and School Attendance in China 81
Universal Values 133
Antiracist and Multicultural Education 146
International Comparisons in Spending for Schools 219
Legal Aspects of Education in Other Countries 272
Educational Ideas Borrowed from around the World 283
Educational Transplantation from Europe 310
European Beginnings of Teacher Training 317
Maria Montessori 332
Jean Piaget 360
Educators' Worldwide Responsibility 363
The Fabric of Eastern Ways of Knowing 399
Looking beyond the Boundaries 429
The World as Classroom 455
Schools of Reconciliation in Northern Ireland 483
German Education 494
Australia Is Exploring a New Approach to Education Reform 537

PREFACE

The twelfth edition of *Introduction to the Foundations of American Education* is the product of the collaborative effort of five professional educators, each bringing his or her particular and general knowledge, both practical and scholarly, to the field of education and teaching. This team approach enriches the text by enlisting each author's valuable perspectives on a variety of educational topics, issues, events, and people. This edition uses the metaphor of a camera lens to give students a helpful way to study and interpret educational issues pertinent to schools, students, and the teaching profession.

As you know, a camera's zoom lens enables the photographer to view the world from different perspectives. Some lenses use tinted filters to clarify a scene or to enhance a particular view. Also, you can adjust the view through a camera lens to bring certain things into sharper focus. In this book, we use the wide-angle foundations of education lens to view education as a community of teachers and learners immersed in a complex system of institutions, norms, beliefs, social mores, laws, and instructional and assessment practices. The wide-angle lens helps us see underlying causes, examine issues of justice and equality, view education through big ideas, ask basic questions, clarify assumptions, and assess structures. This perspective is the basis of the six parts that comprise the overall structure of the book. The wide-angle view places the six sections in perspective, while the zoom ability focuses in on particular big ideas and questions in each chapter.

Thus, students can examine each of the foundation areas in depth as the different lenses bring it into sharper focus. We hope, as they use this text, that students will react to each of the six different parts with the particular lens perspective that we offer.

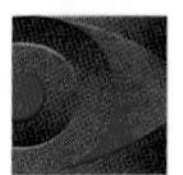

NEW FEATURES OF THE TWELFTH EDITION

As always, we present all major areas of the foundations of education—essential knowledge for anyone to become an informed and successful educator. In addition to the traditional foundation areas of history, philosophy, and sociology, we include the equally essential areas of school organization, finance, law, and curriculum. Specifically, this edition includes:

- A **completely new opening chapter** that describes new teacher licensing expectations, including INTASC and NCATE standards, to give students a clear picture of the steps they need to take to become licensed teachers

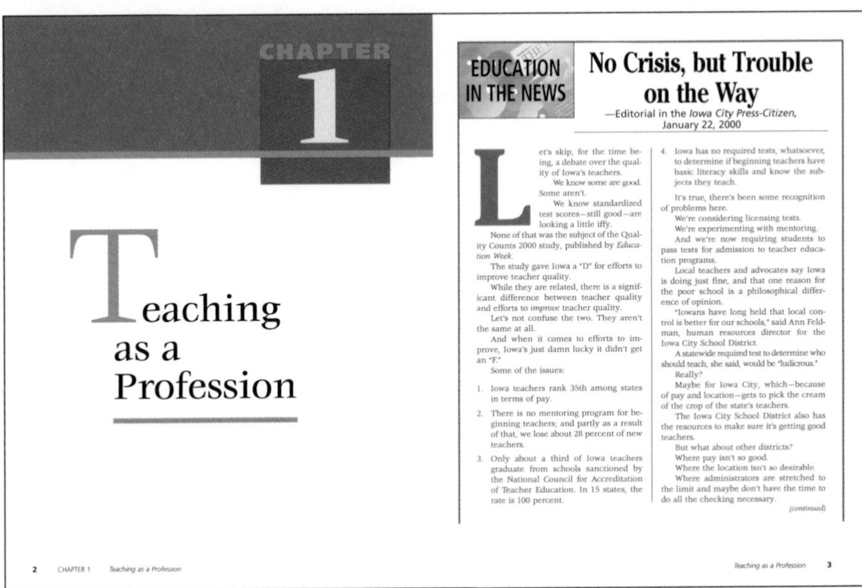

CHAPTER 1

Teaching as a Profession

EDUCATION IN THE NEWS

No Crisis, but Trouble on the Way

—Editorial in the *Iowa City Press-Citizen*, January 22, 2000

Let's skip, for the time being, a debate over the quality of Iowa's teachers.

We know some are good. Some aren't.

We know standardized test scores—still good—are looking a little iffy.

None of that was the subject of the Quality Counts 2000 study, published by *Education Week*.

The study gave Iowa a "D" for efforts to improve teacher quality.

While they are related, there is a significant difference between teacher quality and efforts to *improve* teacher quality.

Let's not confuse the two. They aren't the same at all.

And when it comes to efforts to improve, Iowa's just damn lucky it didn't get an "F."

Some of the issues:

1. Iowa teachers rank 35th among states in terms of pay.
2. There is no mentoring program for beginning teachers; and partly as a result of that, we lose about 28 percent of new teachers.
3. Only about a third of Iowa teachers graduate from schools sanctioned by the National Council for Accreditation of Teacher Education. In 15 states, the rate is 100 percent.
4. Iowa has no required tests, whatsoever, to determine if beginning teachers have basic literacy skills and know the subjects they teach.

It's true, there's been some recognition of problems here.

We're considering licensing tests.

We're experimenting with mentoring.

And we're now requiring students to pass tests for admission to teacher education programs.

Local teachers and advocates say Iowa is doing just fine, and that one reason for the poor school is a philosophical difference of opinion.

"Iowans have long held that local control is better for our schools," said Ann Feldman, human resources director for the Iowa City School District.

A statewide required test to determine who should teach, she said, would be "ludicrous."

Really?

Maybe for Iowa City, which—because of pay and location—gets to pick the cream of the crop of the state's teachers.

The Iowa City School District also has the resources to make sure it's getting good teachers.

But what about other districts?

Where pay isn't so good.

Where the location isn't so desirable.

Where administrators are stretched to the limit and maybe don't have the time to do all the checking necessary.

(continued)

2 CHAPTER 1 *Teaching as a Profession*

Teaching as a Profession 3

- **Standards-based education, high-stakes testing, performance assessments,** and **authentic assessments** presented in the new Chapter 15 to help preservice teachers become conversant in various ways to assess student learning
- An **Education in the News feature** to open each chapter, giving a published news report to help readers see the currency and relevance of chapter content
- **Learner Outcome Statements** at the beginning of each chapter to help readers know the expected outcomes they will demonstrate after reading a chapter—a concept that will carry over into their professional practice
- A focus in each chapter on the **Big Ideas** that shape thinking in these foundation areas to help readers see the bigger picture of how what they are studying will apply in classroom practice
- A **Debate** feature in each chapter, in which two educators write about opposing sides of an issue related to the chapter topic; readers also have an opportunity to register their opinions on each issue at the book's Companion Website
- **Key Terms and Concepts** defined in marginal glossaries to aid reading comprehension

DEBATE

Should Nationally Certified Teachers Be Paid More?

YES

Jeanne Serven is nationally certified in the field of Early Adolescence/English Language Arts. A 25-year teaching veteran, she's currently on loan to the Illinois State Board of Education, where she works to help improve the quality of teaching and learning. She can be reached at Jaserven@aol.com.

Traditionally, experienced teachers in search of professional salaries have had three options: 1) Get as much education as the pay scale rewards. 2) Move to a "rich" school district in the suburbs. 3) Leave the classroom to go into administration.

It's high time to add a fourth option for teachers who continually improve their practice and meet the highest standards set by their profession: Provide financial rewards for nationally certified teachers.

I teach in a small, rural school district in Illinois. I have a master's degree, 25 years of teaching experience, and I'm at the top of my salary scale. I make $33,987.

Now, I'm not inclined to move to the suburbs or become an administrator. I'm interested in being the best teacher I can be for my students.

So four years ago, I applied for national certification in Early Adolescence/English Language Arts. For months, I collected student work, videotaped my teaching, put together a professional portfolio, and examined the instruction in my classroom.

Then I analyzed and reflected on what I saw. In the process, I improved the instruction in my classroom and boosted the level of student learning.

Unlike most evaluations of teacher performance, the national board evaluation process was fair and equitable. Evaluators are practicing classroom teachers in the same content areas and grade levels as the candidates they're evaluating.

The strength of the process lies in the requirement for actual classroom documentation and evidence, rather than personal recommendations. It's an assessment based on standards developed by classroom teachers.

NO

Elizabeth Ahlgren is the chair of the math department at Morse High School in San Diego. She's a local building rep, treasurer of the San Diego Teachers Association, and a member of the California Teachers Association State Council of Education. She can be reached at eahlgren@morsehs.com.

National certification is an arduous, time-consuming, and expensive voluntary process designed to "establish high and rigorous standards for what accomplished teachers should know and be able to do." And it may have great value for those who choose to go through it. But paying more to those who succeed has precious little value for the profession, teachers, and students.

- *Paying nationally certified teachers more will promote elitism, not a stronger teaching profession.* Some argue that national certification elevates teaching and makes teachers professionals, like doctors and lawyers. That's nonsense.

What really makes us professionals? Professional wages that attract people to the field and keep them there, and professional working conditions that make it easy for educators to do their jobs well.

What good is it to pay a few experienced teachers more money when new teachers don't earn enough to be able to afford to stay in the profession?

Paying new teachers better salaries would be a far better way to support the profession. So would supporting new teachers in their classrooms with mentoring, adequate instructional materials, and high quality professional development activities.

If the goal is a top quality teacher in every classroom, providing "bonuses" to a few senior teachers won't do much to achieve it.

- *Paying nationally certified teachers more will help a few teachers at the expense of the many.* All teachers—not just candidates for national certification—should engage in rich collegial discussions, take the time to reflect on and improve lessons, and maintain a professional portfolio.

Teaching as a Profession 25

In addition, popular features carried over from the previous edition include:

- **Professional Dilemma** features that provide opportunities to analyze real-life problems that preservice teachers will encounter in their classrooms
- Summaries of published research studies in **Relevant Research** features to model the use of research for preservice teachers
- **Global Perspectives** sections in each chapter to provide preservice teachers with a better understanding of international educational practices and how they compare to practices in the United States
- **School-Based Experiences, Journal Entries, Portfolio Development,** and **Websites** to visit at the end of each chapter, providing tools for the students' growth as professional educators

Teachers must become lifelong learners to maintain and improve their teaching skills throughout their careers.

licensure differ from state to state. For this reason, if you plan to teach in a state different from the one in which you are going to school, you may want to contact that state directly for licensure information. Information on licensure requirements is available on the websites of state licensing agencies; for a list of agencies and contact information, see Appendix 1.1 at the end of this chapter. The certification officer at your institution should be able to provide you with licensure information and details about seeking a license in another state.

The initial license allows a new teacher to practice for a specified period of time, usually three to five years. This period in a teacher's career is called induction. On completion of successful teaching during that period and sometimes a master's degree, a professional license can be granted. Most states require continuing professional development throughout the teacher's career and periodical renewal of the license, typically every five years.

performance-based licensing
A system of licensing professionals based on the use of multiple assessments that measure the applicant's knowledge, skills, and dispositions to determine whether he or she can perform effectively in the profession.

States traditionally required candidates to take specific college courses, complete student teaching, and successfully pass a licensure examination for a license. Most states are now in the process of developing **performance-based licensing** systems. They will not be specifying courses to be completed; instead, they indicate the knowledge, skills, and sometimes dispositions that candidates should possess. Future decisions about granting a license will depend on the results of state assessments based primarily on licensure test scores.

portfolio
A compilation of works, records, and accomplishments that teachers and teacher candidates prepare for a specific purpose to demonstrate his or her learnings, performances, and contributions.

Concerned about the limitations of standardized tests and their predictability of successful classroom practice, more than thirty states are participating in a consortium to develop performance-based licensure standards and assessments. The ten principles of the Interstate New Teacher Assessment and Support Consortium (INTASC) have been adopted or adapted for licensure by many states. These ten principles describe what teachers should know and be able to do in their first few years of practice. You should be developing this knowledge and skills in the college program in which you are currently enrolled. Some states are requiring teachers to submit **portfolios,** which are scored by experienced teachers, as evidence of teaching effectiveness before granting the professional license. The portfolios that you begin to compile during your teacher

22 CHAPTER 1 *Teaching as a Profession*

STUDENT WEBSITES

The Companion Website at http://www.ablongman.com/johnson, available to all users of the text, features online practice tests, links to websites discussed in the book, a discussion area based on the Journal Activities in the book, and an activity for each segment of the Allyn & Bacon Interactive Video for Foundations of Education and Introduction to Teaching (described below).

Beginning in January 2002, a PIN-protected Interactive Companion website will be available to all students who purchase the text new. This website offers a robust collection of materials to help students get the most out of *Introduction to the Foundations of American Education:* online practice tests, interactive activities, audio and video clips, and numerous links to websites related to virtually every topic discussed in the book.

SUPPLEMENTS FOR THE INSTRUCTOR

A full array of instructional supplements rounds out the book's package:

- **Instructor's Resource Manual**—correlates chapter outline, learner outcome statements, lecture notes, and all supplements
- **Test Bank and Journal Activity Masters**—scores of objective, essay, and performance-based assessment items for each chapter, plus reproducible journal activities
- **Computerized Test Bank**—for Windows and Mac platforms
- **CourseCompass**—an exclusive computerized course management system

- **Allyn & Bacon Interactive Video for Foundations of Education and Introduction to Teaching**—actual classroom footage to bring alive the concepts discussed in the text
- **Allyn & Bacon Foundations of Education Transparencies**—a set of 100 acetate transparencies that illustrate many text concepts
- **Allyn & Bacon Digital Media Archive CD-ROM for Education, 2001 Edition**—color images, video and audio clips, and weblinks to enhance your in-class presentations on text concepts

THE AUTHOR TEAM

James A. Johnson, professor of education emeritus at Northern Illinois University, has been an educator for more than thirty-five years, serving as a public school teacher, teacher educator, and university administrator. He has been coauthor of twelve editions of *Introduction to the Foundations of American Education,* as well as author or coauthor of a dozen other college textbooks.

Victor L. Dupuis, professor emeritus of curriculum and instruction and Waterbury Professor of Secondary Education at Pennsylvania State University, continues a professional career that began forty-five years ago. Currently, he serves as a private consultant in areas of staff development, Native American education, and curriculum development and evaluation with Dupuis Associates. He has also taught social studies and English and served as a school district curriculum director and teacher educator. In addition to coauthoring all twelve editions of this text, he has published widely in the areas of curriculum and instruction and Native American literatures.

Diann Musial, professor of leadership and educational policy and Northern Illinois University Presidential Teaching Professor, has served in elementary school administration and in industry as a researcher and director of training in addition to her work as a teacher educator. Her consulting activities include work with public and private school districts, and she has coauthored the last five editions of this text. Additionally, she is coauthor of *Classroom 2061: Activity Assessments in Science Integrated with Mathematics and Language Arts* (SkyLight Professional Development, 1995) and *Teaching Science for Deep Understanding* (SkyLight Professional Development, 2002).

Gene E. Hall, dean of the College of Education at the University of Nevada at Las Vegas (UNLV), has served for more than thirty years as a teacher educator, researcher, and university administrator. He is active in assisting teacher education institutions in their efforts to become nationally accredited. He is also internationally known for his research on change process in schools and their organizations. He is the lead architect of the widely used Concerns-Based Adoption Model (CBAM), which organizational leaders and staff developers employ in studying and facilitating the change process. In addition to coauthoring the last four editions of this text, he is coauthor of *Implementing Change: Principles and Potholes* (Allyn & Bacon, 2001).

Donna M. Gollnick is senior vice president of the National Council for the Accreditation of Teacher Education (NCATE), where she oversees all accreditation activities. She is also president of the National Association for Multicultural

Education (NAME) and is a recognized authority in multicultural education. In addition to her work in teacher accreditation, she has taught in secondary schools and coauthored the last three editions of this text. She is also coauthor, with Philip C. Chinn, of *Multicultural Education in a Pluralistic Society,* Sixth Edition (Merrill, 2002).

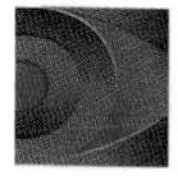

ACKNOWLEDGMENTS

We are sincerely grateful to the many colleagues, reviewers, and editors who have helped us over the years to make this text the most popular and widely used book in the field. We thank our publisher, Allyn and Bacon, for its continued support over the years, and for enabling us to deliver the message that we, as professional educators, deem crucial for the preparation of teachers. In particular, we thank Steve Dragin, our series editor, for his support and assistance. A special word of thanks to Linda Bieze, our developmental editor, for her professional effort with this text. She has provided the needed polish for the rough edges and kept our lofty goals in perspective for students and the field of education. We also sincerely thank the following reviewers:

Rose Adesiyan, Purdue University, Calumet
Charles Alberti, Bemidji State University
Morris L. Anderson, Wayne State University
James Binko, Towson University
Saundra Bryn, Arizona State University, West
Perry Castelli, Troy State University
William "David" Cauble, Western Nebraska University
Alan Dean, University of Rio Grande
Joan Dengel, Edinboro University of Pennsylvania
Dorothy Engan-Barket, Mankato State University
Geneva Gay, University of Washington
John Georgeoff, Purdue University
Frank Guldbrandson, University of Minnesota–Duluth
Thomas M. Gwaltney, Eastern Michigan University
Hurst Hall, Northwestern State College
Bruce Hill, Triton College
Mary E. Huba, Iowa State University
Michael James, Connecticut College
Monica Janas, College of Charleston
Michael H. Jessup, Towson University
Kristi Johnson, Marymount University
Kathryn W. Linden, Purdue University
Mary Ann Manos, Bradley University
William R. Martin, George Mason University
Paul M. McGhee, Morehead State University
Theodore Meyers, University of Memphis
Jane A. Newburger, Cazenovia College
James E. Newby, Howard University
Carolyn O'Grady, Gustavus Adolphus College

Thomas R. Oswald, North Iowa Area Community College
Richard L. Perez, Glendale Community College
Eugene T. W. Sanders, Bowling Green State University
Tyll van Geel, University of Rochester
Paul Wagner, University of Houston, Clear Lake
David E. Washburn, Bloomsburg University of Pennsylvania
Thomas H. Williams, West Virginia Wesleyan College
Wayne Willis, Morehead State University
John R. Zelazek, Central Missouri State University

TWELFTH EDITION

Introduction to the Foundations of American Education

PART 1

CHAPTER 1
Teaching as a Profession

The Profession of Teaching

Viewing Education through Professional Lenses

A lens metaphor is particularly useful in thinking about teaching, teachers, and the profession of teaching. A lens can be used to focus on certain spots, and the light that passes through a lens can contain a broad spectrum of colors. Both of these characteristics of lenses—focal point and broad spectrum—are easily applied to examining essential aspects of teaching as a profession. First of all, consideration needs to be given to the question "What do we focus on?" Chapter 1 begins with a close-up focus on teachers, society's concerns about the quality of teachers, and the teacher's working conditions, including salaries. The second half of the chapter broadens the focus to more of a landscape view of the profession. The role of the teachers' unions and that of professional associations are described, and some of the contemporary issues that the profession is engaging are introduced.

Keep in mind as you read this text that, throughout, the most critical focal point is on learning. Student learning must be the focus of all the teacher's teaching. Learning is at the center of district, state, and federal efforts to evaluate and improve the quality of education and schooling. Learning to teach must be the focal point for you as you read this text and as you continue your teacher preparation program. Assessment of your learning and ultimately that of your students will be the key to your success as a teacher.

In your reading and study, whether up close and personal or taking a broad look at the horizon, the focus is on learning. As an aspiring teacher, you are now focusing on learning what the job of teaching entails and what you need to do to become a teacher. Answers to these and related questions about the profession of teaching are the topics of Chapter 1.

The following questions will help you focus your learning as you read Chapter 1:

1. How do teachers and community members feel about the importance of teachers in having high levels of student learning?
2. What are key characteristics of the working conditions for teachers?
3. What are typical salaries and benefits for teachers?
4. In what areas are there most likely to be position openings for new teachers?
5. Are there ways for outstanding teachers to receive extra recognition and reward?
6. If you were asked to prepare a portfolio about your potential to be an outstanding teacher, what would you include?
7. What are the names and functions of the various specialty and job-related associations that are available to teachers?

CHAPTER 1

Teaching as a Profession

No Crisis, but Trouble on the Way

—Editorial in the *Iowa City Press-Citizen,* January 22, 2000

Let's skip, for the time being, a debate over the quality of Iowa's teachers.

We know some are good. Some aren't.

We know standardized test scores—still good—are looking a little iffy.

None of that was the subject of the Quality Counts 2000 study, published by *Education Week.*

The study gave Iowa a "D" for efforts to improve teacher quality.

While they are related, there is a significant difference between teacher quality and efforts to *improve* teacher quality.

Let's not confuse the two. They aren't the same at all.

And when it comes to efforts to improve, Iowa's just damn lucky it didn't get an "F."

Some of the issues:

1. Iowa teachers rank 35th among states in terms of pay.
2. There is no mentoring program for beginning teachers; and partly as a result of that, we lose about 28 percent of new teachers.
3. Only about a third of Iowa teachers graduate from schools sanctioned by the National Council for Accreditation of Teacher Education. In 15 states, the rate is 100 percent.
4. Iowa has no required tests, whatsoever, to determine if beginning teachers have basic literacy skills and know the subjects they teach.

It's true, there's been some recognition of problems here.

We're considering licensing tests.

We're experimenting with mentoring.

And we're now requiring students to pass tests for admission to teacher education programs.

Local teachers and advocates say Iowa is doing just fine, and that one reason for the poor school is a philosophical difference of opinion.

"Iowans have long held that local control is better for our schools," said Ann Feldman, human resources director for the Iowa City School District.

A statewide required test to determine who should teach, she said, would be "ludicrous."

Really?

Maybe for Iowa City, which—because of pay and location—gets to pick the cream of the crop of the state's teachers.

The Iowa City School District also has the resources to make sure it's getting good teachers.

But what about other districts?

Where pay isn't so good.

Where the location isn't so desirable.

Where administrators are stretched to the limit and maybe don't have the time to do all the checking necessary.

(continued)

State standards—whether in testing or anything else—aren't designed for districts already doing well.

They're designed for districts that need help.

And let's get rid of this nutty idea that we have local control of our schools.

Federal and state mandates on what schools have to do—and can't do—would fill a book.

And a very large book, at that.

School districts also are limited in how much money they can raise.

And the money they're allowed to spend is a direct result of legislative action.

Local control?

That's a myth. Let's forget about it.

We're doing OK right now. There's no teacher crisis in Iowa.

But a bubble is about to catch up to us when a large group of teachers—who started in the '60s and '70s—retires.

And *that* is going to present problems.

Do we need to change?

Yes.

And we need to do it now, before we have problems.

LEARNER OUTCOMES

After reading and studying this chapter, you will be able to

1. Identify the characteristics of professions and develop arguments for or against declaring teaching a profession.
2. Articulate the role demographics play in determining teacher supply and demand and identify areas in which teachers will be in high demand over the next decade.
3. Identify sources of evidence to show that you are developing the knowledge, skills, and dispositions outlined in the INTASC standards.
4. Outline the professional responsibilities of a teacher as viewed by the public, parents, and professional colleagues.
5. Identify some of the challenges that affect teachers and not other professionals and clearly articulate why you plan to pursue a teaching career.
6. Identify the basic requirements for the initial teaching license in the state in which you plan to teach, including the type of tests and other assessments that will be required. ■

If you are are reading this text, you must have already decided that you want to teach or you are exploring the possibility of teaching as a career. The authors of this textbook view teaching as a profession that is critical to the well-being of society. Many young people indicate that they have chosen teaching because they care about children and youth. Although teaching requires caring, it also requires competence in the subject being taught and in the teaching of that subject. Teachers' knowledge and skills should lead to the ultimate goal of successful teaching: student learning. Parents and policymakers alike agree that effective teachers help children and youth to learn.

Standards and assessments are critical in quality assurance for professions such as teaching. The teaching profession includes at least three stages of quality assurance, beginning with the teacher preparation program in which you are now or will be enrolled. Next, state licensing systems give the public assurance that teachers are qualified and competent to help students learn. The third stage of continuing professional development is tied to retaining the state license and seeking national certification. Each of these stages is accompanied by assessments of performance to determine whether individuals are qualified for the important job of teaching.

Teaching is a challenging, complex, and demanding profession that draws from the many diverse groups in the United States.

Reflection is one of the important characteristics of successful teachers. Professionals who reflect on and analyze their own teaching are involved in a process that is critical to improving both teaching and student learning. Individuals who are making either a lifelong or short-term commitment to teaching should consider the responsibilities and expectations of a teaching career. In this chapter you will begin exploring the realities of what it means to be a teacher.

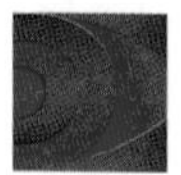

TODAY'S TEACHERS

More than 3.1 million teachers provide the instructional leadership for public and private schools in the United States. Most of today's new teachers must meet rigorous national and state standards for entering the profession that did not exist a decade ago. Requirements for entering teacher education programs in colleges and universities are now higher than admission requirements for most other professions. Grade point averages of 3.0 are becoming more common for admission; tests and other assessments must be passed before admission, at the completion of a program, and for state licensure. Not everyone can teach. The teaching profession is becoming one that attracts the best and brightest college students into its ranks.

If America's education goals are to be realized, our schools will need to recruit, hire, and develop the largest, best-prepared, and most diverse generation of teachers this nation has ever known.

Recruiting New Teachers

Teacher candidates in colleges and universities today are very diverse in age and work experience. Some of you are 18 to 22 years old, the traditional age of college students, but more of you are nontraditional students who are older and have worked for a number of years in other jobs or professions. Some of your classmates may have worked as teachers' aides in classrooms for years. Others may be switching careers from the armed forces, engineering, retail management, or public relations. Welcome to a profession in which new teachers represent such diverse work experiences as well as varying educational and economic backgrounds.

FIGURE 1.1 GREATEST INFLUENCE ON STUDENT LEARNING

A recent survey of 2,525 adults nationwide found that of the choices shown at right, more than half of respondents say the quality of teachers is the greatest influence on student learning.

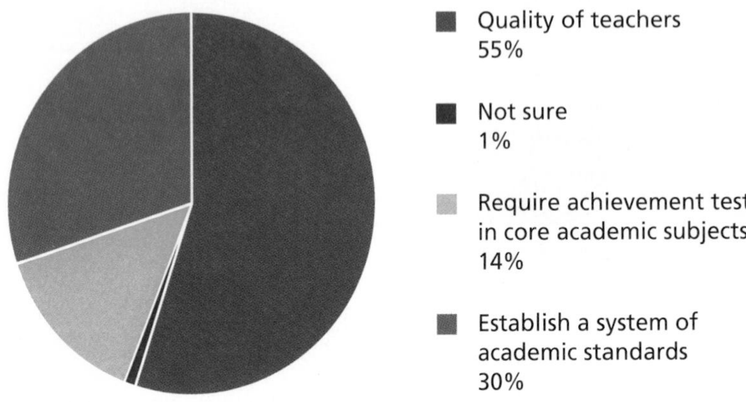

Source: Recruiting New Teachers, Inc., as reported in *Education Week,* February 24, 1999, p. 4.

THE IMPORTANCE OF TEACHERS TO SOCIETY

Society has great expectations for its teachers. "Nine out of ten Americans believe the best way to lift student achievement is to ensure a qualified teacher in every classroom," according to a 1998 national survey.[1] More than half of the respondents in another national survey said that the quality of teachers is the greatest influence on student learning (see Figure 1.1). In addition to guiding students' academic achievement, teachers have some responsibility for students' social and physical development. They are expected to prepare an educated citizenry that is well informed about the many issues that are critical to maintaining a democracy. Teachers are asked to prepare children and youth with the knowledge and skills necessary to work in an **information age.** They help students learn to work together and try to instill the values that are critical to a just and caring society.

Teaching is one of the most important careers in a democratic society. Although critics of our education system sometimes give the impression that there is a lack of public support for schools and teachers, the public now ranks teaching as the profession that provides the most important benefit to society. Public perceptions of the importance of teaching have improved over the past fifteen years.[2] In fact, respondents to a 1998 survey placed teachers first by more than a 3:1 margin over physicians, nurses, businesspeople, lawyers, journalists, politicians, and accountants as shown in Figure 1.2.

THE PUBLIC VIEW OF TEACHERS AND SCHOOLS

Nine of ten Americans believe that the best way to improve student achievement is to have qualified teachers.[3] Teachers and the public agree that the quality of the teaching staff is of primary importance in selecting a school.[4] Parents and students know who the effective teachers are in a school. Some parents do everything possible to ensure that their children are in those teachers' classes. At the same time they know the teachers who do not help students learn and steer their children into other classes if at all possible. They clearly know the value of an effective teacher to the potential academic success of their children.

information age
A period in which society must deal with vast amounts of changing information.

The annual Phi Delta Kappa/Gallup Poll survey on the public's attitudes toward public schools asks respondents to grade schools in both their local area and the nation as a whole. Nearly half of the public gave their local schools an A or B in 2000, somewhat higher than in the previous fifteen years, as shown in Figure 1.3. Teachers rate schools higher than the general public; 64 percent of the teachers in the survey graded schools as an A or B, compared with 49 percent of the general public. Interestingly, both teachers and the public grade their own schools higher than other schools; only 25 percent of them rated other schools as an A or B.

Curiously, the public and teachers do not agree on all of the changes necessary to improve schools, as shown in Table 1.1. Teachers would like to see more parent involvement, whereas the public sees discipline and stricter rules as most important. They agree on having more teachers and/or reducing class size. Over half of the respondents in another survey were concerned about student drug use, school violence, student drinking, lack of parental involvement, teenage pregnancy, and students' lack of basic skills. They were less concerned about large classes and poor-quality teachers. Latino and African American

FIGURE 1.2 PROFESSIONS THAT PROVIDE THE MOST BENEFIT TO SOCIETY ACCORDING TO SURVEY RESPONDENTS

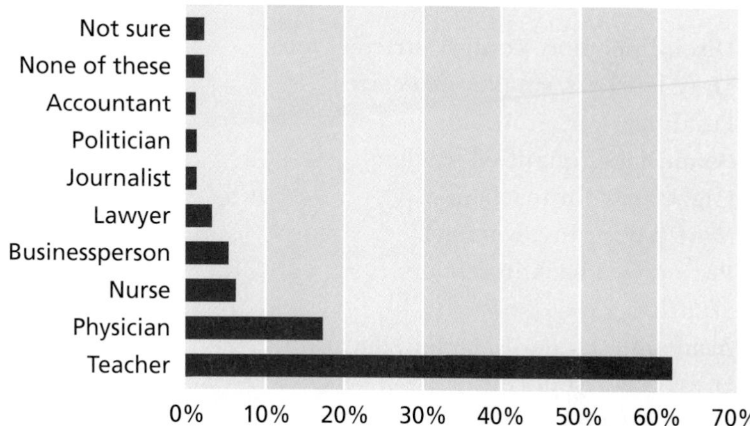

Source: Based on data from Recruiting New Teachers, Inc., *The Essential Profession: A National Survey of Public Attitudes toward Teaching, Educational Opportunity and School Reform.* Belmont, MA: Author, 1998.

No nation can remain free which does not recognize the importance of education. Our public schools are the backbone of American life and character.

Samuel M. Lindsay

FIGURE 1.3 GRADES GIVEN THE LOCAL PUBLIC SCHOOLS BY THE PUBLIC

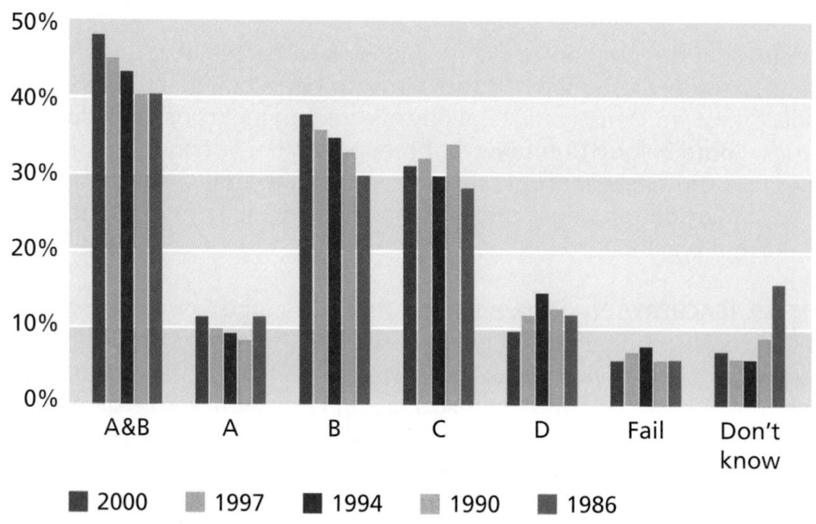

Source: Based on data from Carol A. Langdon and Nick Vesper, "The Sixth Phi Delta Kappa Poll of Teachers' Attitudes toward the Public Schools," *Phi Delta Kappan, 81*(8) (April 2000).

TABLE 1.1 WHAT WOULD YOU CHANGE TO IMPROVE THE PUBLIC SCHOOLS IN YOUR COMMUNITY?

	Public (percent)	Teachers (percent)
Discipline/more control/stricter rules	12	6
More teachers/smaller class size	10	12
Funding	5	8
Better/more qualified teachers	7	*
Higher pay for teachers	3	5
More parent involvement	3	18
Prayer/God back in schools	4	*
Security	4	*
Academic standards/better education	3	2
Dress code/uniforms	3	*
More/updated equipment/books/computers	2	3
Curriculum/more offered	2	*

Source: Adapted from Carol A. Langdon, and Nick Vesper, "The Sixth Phi Delta Kappa Poll of Teachers' Attitudes toward the Public Schools," *Phi Delta Kappan, 81*(8) (April 2000) pp. 607–611.

respondents were more likely than others to find the lack of teacher quality a serious and widespread problem. Respondents also affirmed the desire to "keep the guarantee of a free public education for every child."[5]

WHO TEACHES?

Teachers represent the diversity of the nation. However, white females are overly represented in the teaching force, particularly in early childhood and elementary schools. They are Democrats, Republicans, and members of the Reform and other parties. Some belong to unions, but others don't. Therefore, it is impossible to generalize about teachers or other educators in the United States. However, some of the similarities and differences among teachers may help you to understand the current teaching profession.

PROFILE OF U.S. TEACHERS The United States has 2.7 million public school teachers, 400,000 private school teachers, and 932,000 college and university faculty members. Over 60 percent of the teachers work at the elementary school level. In addition to teachers, 411,000 administrative and education professionals plus 1.25 million teachers' aides, clerks and secretaries, and service workers staff the nation's public schools. Another million education-related jobs include education specialists in industry, instructional technologists in the military, museum educators, and training consultants in the business world. Altogether, there are approximately five million educators in the United States, making education one of the largest professions in the country.

In addition to being passionate about helping learners, teachers are good managers and take time to work with their colleagues.

Nearly 75 percent of the nation's public school teachers are women. The percentage of male teachers is higher in grades 9–12, where 46 percent of the teachers are men. Men are even better represented in vocational schools, making up 63 percent of the teachers.

The percentage of white teachers is 86.5, having increased by 2.4 percent during the past thirty years, while the number of white students in schools today is 62.7 percent. Only 7 percent of the teachers are African American; 6 percent are Latino, Asian American, or American Indian. To further exacerbate the differences between the racial composition of students and that of the teaching force, projections show the teaching force becoming more white over the next decade.

The median age of teachers in 1996 was 44, higher than it has been for the past forty years. This graying of the teaching force will lead to large numbers of retirements over the next ten years, resulting in the need to replace two million teachers. This means that there are, and will be, plenty of openings. Three-fourths of the teachers are married; 12 percent are single; and another 12 percent are widowed, divorced, or separated.

More than half of the nation's teachers have a master's degree or higher; 2 percent have doctorates. Given the just-described demographics of age and formal education, at this time, in general, very experienced teachers are staffing our classrooms. Sixty-five percent of the teachers have been full-time teachers for more than ten years; 30 percent of the teachers have over twenty years of full-time teaching experience. Public school teachers are older and more likely to have advanced degrees than are private school teachers. Other differences between teachers who work in public and private schools are shown in Figure 1.4.

Instead of asking why women lag behind men in mathematics, we might ask the following: Why do men lag behind women in elementary school teaching, early childhood education, nursing, full-time parenting, and like activities? Is there something wrong with men or with schools that this state of affairs persists?

Nel Noddings

ACADEMIC QUALITY OF TEACHERS AND OTHER PROFESSIONALS Of all the factors in schooling that influence student learning, the quality and caliber of teachers have the greatest effect on student learning. Academically able teachers know the subjects they teach at a depth that allows them to draw on their **knowledge base** for examples and representations to help students learn. They are excited

knowledge base
Information that is supported by empirical research, disciplined inquiry, informed theory, and the wisdom of practice.

Most teachers enter and remain in their profession because of a desire to work with young people.

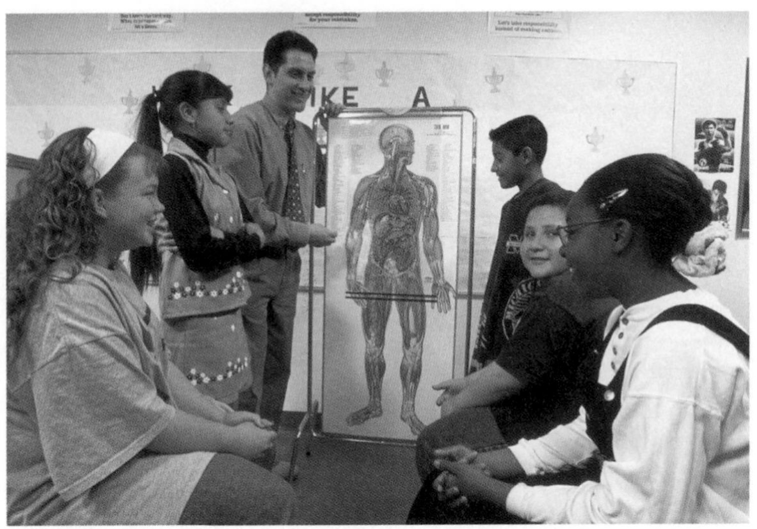

about the subjects that they teach, continue to study the subject throughout their careers, and instill excitement about the subject in their students.

However, a number of critics do not believe that most teachers are academically competent. Reports released during the past twenty years on the quality of education have often bashed teachers, reporting that they are the least academically able of college graduates. The facts challenge these unfounded perceptions of the nation's teachers. Of the high school seniors who take the SAT or ACT, those who indicate that they plan to major in education do have lower test scores than those who are planning to major in other fields. However, many of the high school seniors who declared teaching as their goal do not pursue that goal or do not successfully complete an education program.

FIGURE 1.4 DIFFERENCES BETWEEN PUBLIC AND PRIVATE SCHOOL TEACHERS

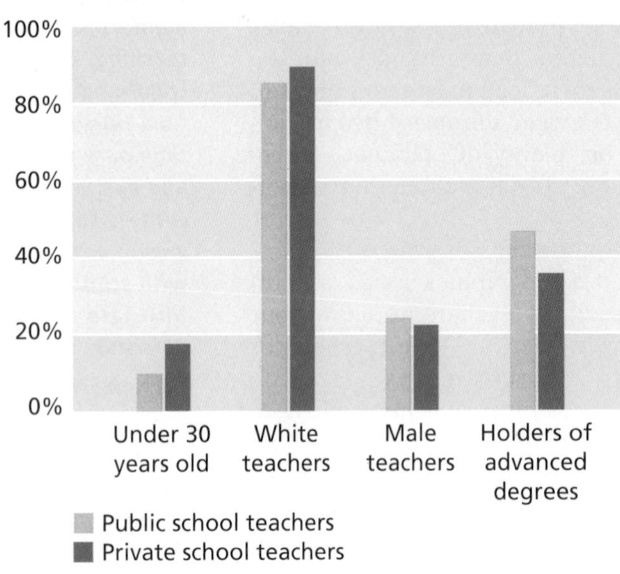

Source: Based on data from the National Center for Education Statistics, U.S. Department of Education, *Digest of Education Statistics, 1999,* NCES 2000-031. Washington, DC: Author, 2000.

Researchers at the Educational Testing Service and American College Testing, Inc. examined the SAT and ACT scores of teacher candidates who had taken teacher licensure tests before admission to teacher education programs or before being licensed by a state. They found that candidates pursuing a license to teach a subject at the secondary and/or middle school level generally have college admissions test scores similar to those of all college students majoring in that academic area. Teacher candidates in mathematics and science have substantially higher SAT scores than all other college graduates. At the same time, teacher candidates in physical education, special education, and elementary education continue to have lower SAT and ACT scores than other college graduates.[6]

Studies of academic prowess show that teachers perform at about the same level as other professionals. Teachers scored relatively high on measures of prose, document, and quantitative literacy tasks in a comparison with lawyers, electrical engineers, accountants, auditors, computer systems analysts, marketing professionals, financial managers, physicians, personnel and training professionals, social workers, and education administrators and counselors.[7] No significant differences were found between female and male teachers or between elementary and secondary teachers. Teachers are as academically able as members of other professions that are often perceived as more prestigious.

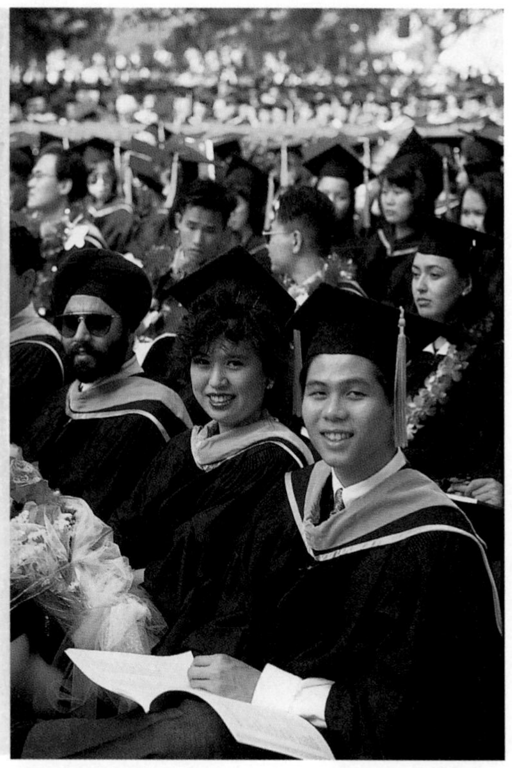

Two hundred thousand new teachers graduate from college each year. About one-third of them will not take teaching jobs, and another one-third will leave teaching after a few years.

RETENTION IN THE PROFESSION A high percentage of teachers who begin working in a classroom decide that teaching is not the profession they wish to pursue. Nearly 20 percent of the new teachers hired in a year are not teaching three years later. Unfortunately, teachers who had scored in the top quartile of test takers on college admissions tests left the profession during this period at a rate that was twice that of other teachers.

Teachers leave the classroom for a number of reasons. Some decide to return to school full time for an advanced degree. Others decide to pursue another career that might be more satisfying for them or pays a higher salary. Other factors for leaving teaching are related to poor working conditions in schools, including a lack of administrative support, perceived student problems, and little chance for upward mobility.

Like all other professionals, teachers become accomplished with experience. Most states do not grant a professional license to teachers until they have worked for at least three years. Teachers cannot seek national certification from the National Board for Professional Teaching Standards (NBPTS) until they have taught for three years. When teachers leave the profession in their first few years of practice, schools are losing an important developing resource. Induction and mentoring programs for new teachers increase the number who remain in the classroom. Good professional development programs for teachers—in other words, **induction** programs—also help to retain new teachers. When you search for your first teaching job, check whether the school district provides induction, mentors, and professional development. They are services that help teachers to improve their skills as well as the chances of being successful teachers and remaining as teachers over a longer period of time.

The common teacher is not common at all. He (or she) is bulging with talent, with energy, and with understanding. What we human teachers have to give, ultimately, is ourselves—our own love for life, and for our subject, and our ability to respond to the personal concerns of our students.

Terry Borton, *Reach, Touch, Teach*

induction
The first one to three years of full-time teaching.

TEACHERS NEEDED

Many factors influence the number of teachers that a school district needs annually. The number of students in schools, the ratio of teachers to students in classrooms, immigration patterns, and migration from one school district to another influence the demand for teachers. The supply of teachers depends on the numbers of new teachers licensed, teachers who retired the previous year, and teachers returning to the work force.

Sometimes the supply is greater than the demand, but projections for the next decade indicate a demand for new teachers beyond the number that are being prepared in colleges and universities. Overall, the United States does not have a teacher shortage. The problem is the distribution of teachers. School districts with good teaching conditions and high salaries do not face teacher shortages. However, inner cities and rural areas too often do not have adequate numbers of qualified and licensed teachers. There also are greater shortages of teachers in parts of the country with increasing populations, such as states in the Southwest.

TEACHER SUPPLY The supply of new teachers in a given year consists primarily of two groups: new teacher graduates and former teacher graduates who were not employed as teachers in the previous year. Not all college graduates who prepared to teach actually teach. Of 1992–1993 college graduates who prepared to teach, only 51 percent had worked in K–12 public school in the four years after graduation.

Nearly half of the teachers hired by the typical school district are first-time teachers. One-third are experienced teachers who have moved from other school districts or from other jobs within the district. Experienced teachers reentering the field make up the remainder of the new hires. Unfortunately, not all teachers who are hired have been even minimally prepared to teach before they take charge of a classroom, as shown in Figure 1.5. Over one-fourth of newly hired teachers are not qualified for the beginning license to teach. Some new hires do not have a license; others have a temporary, provisional, or emergency license.

FIGURE 1.5 TYPE OF TEACHING LICENSE HELD BY TEACHERS WITH THREE YEARS OR LESS EXPERIENCE

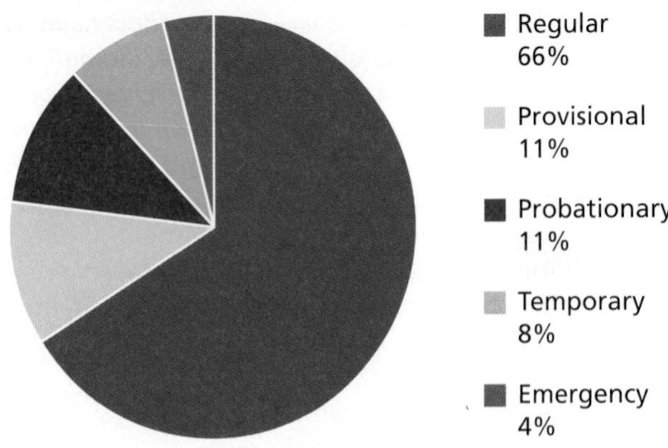

Source: Based on data from the National Center for Education Statistics, U.S. Department of Education, *The Condition of Education 2000.* Washington, DC: Author, 2000.

NEW TEACHERS Over half of the new teachers who are hired annually just graduated from college. Seventeen percent of the first-time teachers were substitute teachers in the previous year, which is the path to entering teaching in a number of districts that have many more applicants than openings. Others beginning their teaching careers had worked in nonteaching roles or outside of education in the previous year. Two percent of the new teachers were engaged in homemaking or childrearing.

A growing number of new teachers are not recent college graduates. They are applicants who are changing careers, such as retirees from the military or business careers. These older new teachers with years of work experience often have completed alternative pathways into teaching in school-based graduate programs that build on their prior experiences.

Still other new teachers have no preparation to teach; some do not even have a college degree. More often they have a degree in an academic area such as chemistry or history but have not studied teaching and learning or participated in clinical practices in schools. A number of states and school districts allow these individuals to teach with only a few weeks of training in the summer. Participants in these programs are more likely to be dissatisfied with their preparation than are teachers who have completed regular or nontraditional programs for teacher preparation. They often have difficulty in planning the curriculum, managing the classroom, and diagnosing students' learning needs, especially in their first years of teaching. Individuals who enter the profession through this path leave teaching at a higher rate than other teachers.

RETURNING TEACHERS A number of licensed teachers drop out of the profession for a period of time but return later in life. Over one-fifth of the new hires each year are these teachers. Thirty percent of the returning teachers were substitute teachers in the previous year; 15 percent were working in education but not in teaching roles. Others were working outside of education, attending college, or engaged in homemaking or childrearing. Therefore, when you finish your teacher education program, you will be competing for teaching positions not only with other new graduates but also with experienced teachers who are returning to the classroom or moving from one school district to another.

TEACHER DEMAND The demand for teachers in the United States varies considerably from time to time, from place to place, from subject to subject, and from grade level to grade level. One of the major factors related to the demand for teachers is the number of school-age children, which can be projected into the future on the basis of birth rates. For example, enrollment of 5- to 17-year-olds increased from 31.2 to 52.2 million between 1984 and 1997, a 16 percent increase. It is projected to increase another 4 percent by 2009, to 54.2 million.

The number of school-age children in the United States is expected to increase to 54.2 million by 2009.

FIGURE 1.6 DEMAND FOR K–12 CLASSROOM TEACHERS PROJECTED THROUGH 2009

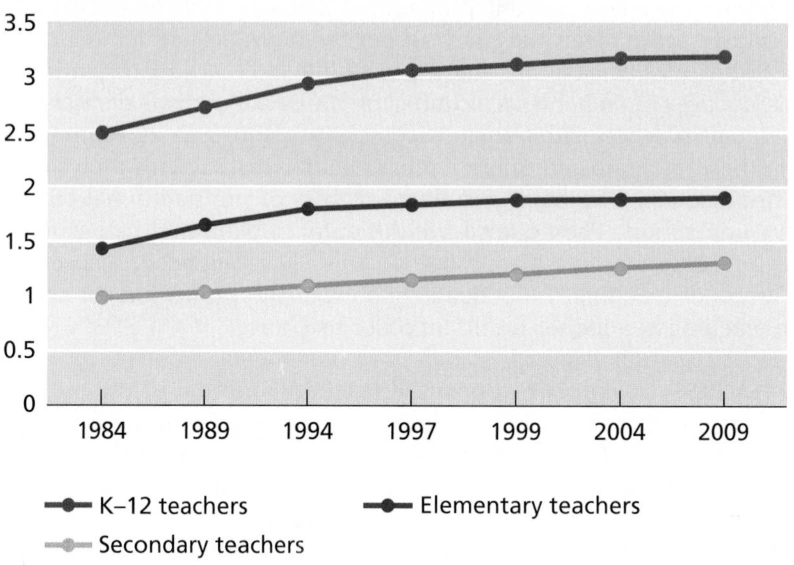

Source: Debra E. Gerald and William J. Hussar, *Projections of Education Statistics to 2009.* Washington, DC: National Center for Education Statistics, U.S. Department of Education, 1999.

The increase in the number of students will require additional teachers, as shown in Figure 1.6. Many teachers will be retiring over the next decade, raising even further the number of new and reentering teachers needed to staff the nation's schools. As you plan your teaching career, you may want to consider a number of other factors that influence the demand for teachers. They may influence decisions you make about the subjects that you will teach and the area of the country in which you will teach.

STUDENT-TO-TEACHER RATIOS Obviously, one measure of a teacher's workload is the number of students taught, that is, class size. The number of students taught by a teacher varies considerably from school to school and from state to state. Elementary teachers generally have more students in a class than secondary teachers, but secondary teachers will have five to seven classes per day. Figure 1.7 shows student-to-teacher ratios in public and private schools.

The demand for teachers has increased, in part, because some states and school districts are limiting the student-to-teacher ratio, especially in the primary grades. In large school districts, lowering the student-to-teacher ratio by even one student creates a demand for many more teachers. State initiatives to reduce the ratio have an even greater impact on the number of teachers needed. California, for example, began providing financial incentives to schools that limited the student-to-teacher ratio to 20:1 for grades K–3 in 1996, leading to a serious shortfall of qualified teachers who had completed programs leading to state licensure.

LOCATION OF THE SCHOOL DISTRICT Even within a given metropolitan area, one school district may be growing rapidly, building new schools, and hiring new teachers because of new housing developments while the neighboring school district is closing schools and reducing its number of teachers. Nevertheless, the greatest shortages are usually in urban schools with large proportions of low-income and culturally and linguistically diverse populations. Some teachers do not want to teach in large urban school districts because of poor working conditions in many schools and relatively low salaries as compared to schools in the wealthier suburbs. Many other teachers believe that teaching in a large city is challenging and fulfilling with many advantages.

FIGURE 1.7 STUDENT-TO-TEACHER RATIOS IN ELEMENTARY AND SECONDARY PUBLIC AND PRIVATE SCHOOLS

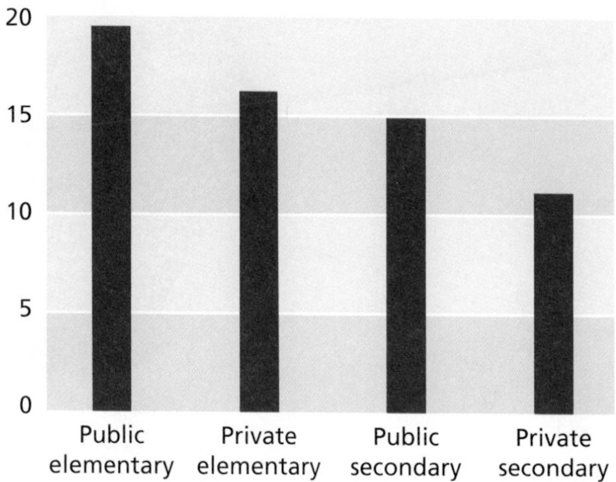

Source: Based on data from Debra E. Gerald and William J. Hussar, *Projections of Education Statistics to 2009.* Washington, DC: National Center for Education Statistics, U.S. Department of Education, 1999.

Urban schools are more likely than others to be staffed by unprepared teachers who have not met the qualifications for a state license. New inexperienced teachers are disproportionately represented in the schools that need the best teachers available. Attrition rates for new teachers in these districts are often 30–50 percent in the first five years of teaching, leading to the constant need for replacements. To address this problem, some states have scholarships and loan-forgiveness programs to encourage teacher candidates to work in these high demand areas.

Student enrollment also varies depending on the part of the country, as shown on the map in Figure 1.8. By 2009, increases over 15 percent are expected in Arizona, Idaho, Nevada, and New Mexico; decreases are expected in most midwestern and northeastern states. Student enrollment in the District of Columbia, Maine, North Dakota, and West Virginia is projected to decrease by 7 to 12 percent.[8]

Almost all teachers can find a teaching position if they are willing to move to a place where jobs are available. One of the problems is that new teachers often want to remain close to home, which is more likely to be in small towns and suburban areas. To attract teachers to areas with teaching shortages, some school districts are offering signing bonuses and paying moving expenses. Others are exploring strategies to offer teachers housing and favorable mortgages.

TEACHING FIELD SHORTAGES Teacher shortages are more severe in some fields than others. For instance, the number of students diagnosed with disabilities has increased considerably over the last decade and now totals more than five million. As a percentage of the total public school enrollment, the number of students requiring special education has risen to nearly 13 percent. Consequently, most school districts report the need for more special education teachers.

A critical shortage of bilingual teachers also exists. The need for bilingual teachers is no longer limited to large urban areas and the southwestern states. Immigrant families with children have now settled in cities and rural areas across the Midwest and Southeast. The projected demographics for the country indicate

FIGURE 1.8 PROJECTED CHANGE IN GRADES K–12 ENROLLMENT IN PUBLIC SCHOOLS, BY STATE: FALL 1997–FALL 2009

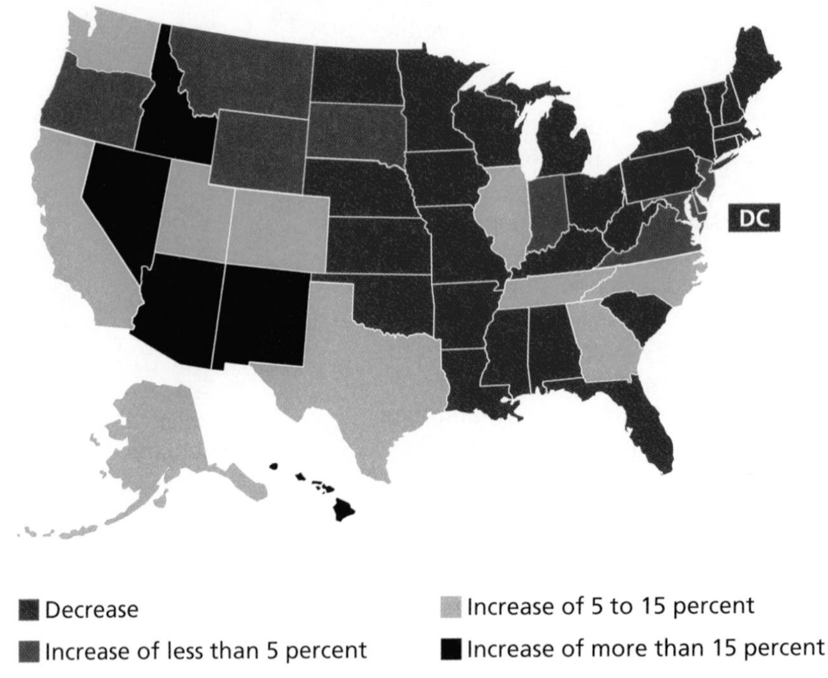

Source: Debra E. Gerald and William J. Hussar, *Projections of Education Statistics to 2009.* Washington, DC: National Center for Education Statistics, U.S. Department of Education, 1999.

a growing number of students with limited English skills, requiring more bilingual and English as a Second Language (ESL) teachers than are available today.

Licensed mathematics and science teachers are prime candidates for job openings in many school districts. One of the problems in secondary schools, especially, is that teachers may have a state license but too often not in the academic area that they are assigned to teach. The National Commission on Teaching and America's Future reported that

- Nearly one-fourth (23 percent) of all secondary teachers do not have even a college minor in their main teaching field. This is true for more than 30 percent of mathematics teachers.
- Among teachers who teach a second subject, 36 percent are unlicensed in that field and 50 percent lack a minor.
- Fifty-six percent of high school students taking physical science are taught by out-of-field teachers, as are 27 percent of those taking mathematics and 21 percent of those taking English. The proportions are much higher in high-poverty schools and in lower-track classes.
- In schools with the highest minority enrollments, students have less than a 50 percent chance of getting a science or mathematics teacher who holds a license and a degree in the field he or she teachers.[9]

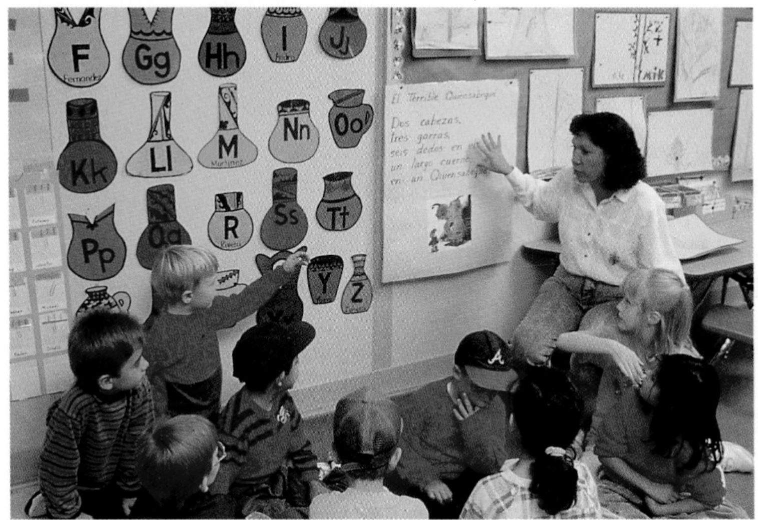

Bilingual teachers are in short supply throughout the United States—especially in southern and western states. What employment opportunities does this need present? What challenges does the growing population of students with limited English proficiency (LEP) present to teachers?

Teachers receive these out-of-field assignments when teachers with the appropriate academic credentials are not available. Sometimes the assignments are made to retain teachers whose jobs have been eliminated as enrollments shift and schools are closed. The tragedy is that students suffer as a result. It is difficult to teach what you do not know.

TEACHERS FROM DIVERSE RACIAL, CULTURAL, AND LINGUISTIC BACKGROUNDS Although the student population becomes more racially, ethnically, and linguistically diverse, the teaching pool is becoming less so. Thirty-seven percent of public school students in grades 1–12 were members of racial and ethnic minority groups in 1998; less than 15 percent of the nation's public school teachers are from the same groups. The number of Latino students is rapidly increasing, pulling almost even with the number of African American students in the 2000 census. The racial and panethnic composition of the student population and teaching force is shown in Figure 1.9.

Having teachers from different ethnic and cultural backgrounds is important to the majority of people in the United States.[10] Most school districts are seeking culturally diverse faculties, but districts with large culturally diverse populations are aggressively recruiting teachers from diverse backgrounds. The federal government and some states provide incentives to colleges and universities to support the recruitment of a more diverse teaching force. Another implication of the demographics of increasing

FIGURE 1.9 **THE RACIAL AND PANETHNIC COMPOSITION OF THE STUDENT POPULATION AND TEACHING FORCE IN PUBLIC SCHOOLS**

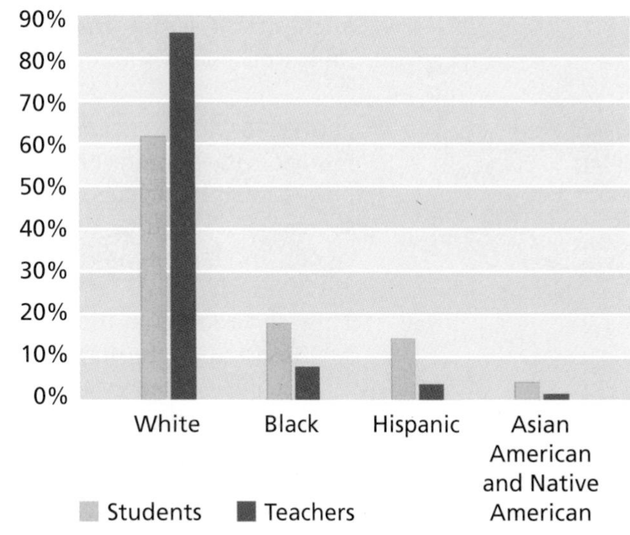

Sources: Based on data from (1) National Center for Education Statistics, U.S. Department of Education, *The Condition of Education 2000.* Washington, DC: Author, 2000. (2) National Center for Education Statistics, U.S. Department of Education, *Digest of Education Statistics, 1999.* Washington, DC: Author 1999.

student diversity is that all teachers need to become skilled at teaching in diverse schools and classrooms.

TEACHING AS A PROFESSION

Teaching is a profession laden with risk and responsibility that requires a great deal from those who enter it.

John I. Goodlad

Historically, law, medicine, architecture, and accountancy have been considered professions, but teaching and nursing have been classified as semiprofessions. This distinction is based in part on the prestige of the different jobs as reflected in the remuneration received by members of the profession. Although teaching salaries remain lower than those of other professionals in most parts of the country, most teachers probably consider themselves professionals. A piece of good news is that over the past decade the prestige of teaching has risen. Most teachers have master's degrees and continue to participate in professional development activities throughout their careers. For the most part they manage their professional work, designing and delivering a curriculum during a school year. They develop their own unique teaching styles and methods for helping students learn. In this section we will explore the factors that determine a profession and a professional and demonstrate that teaching itself is evolving into a full-fledged profession.

CHARACTERISTICS OF A PROFESSION

Professionals provide services to their clients. Their work is based on unique knowledge and skills grounded in research and practice in the field. Professions require their members to have completed higher education, usually at the advanced level. The competence of most professionals is determined in training by **authentic assessments** in real settings. Traditionally, they have had control of their work with little direct supervision.

PROFESSIONAL KNOWLEDGE One of the characteristics of a profession is that its members have some generally agreed upon knowledge bases for their work. This professional knowledge has evolved from research and practice in the field. Researchers are finding that teachers who have prepared to teach are more successful in classrooms than are those who only have a degree in an academic discipline. These competent and qualified teachers are key to student learning. They also remain in the classroom for longer periods of time.

First and foremost, teachers must know the subjects that they will be teaching. Secondary teachers often major in an academic area that they later will teach so that they learn the structure, skills, core concepts, ideas, values, facts, and methods of inquiry that undergird the discipline. They must understand the discipline well enough to help young people learn it and apply it to the world in which they live. If students are not learning a concept or skill, teachers must be able to relate the content to the experiences of students to provide meaning and purpose.

authentic assessments An assessment procedure that uses real-world situations to assess students' ability to encounter those situations successfully, using journals, drawings, artifacts, interviews, and so on.

Elementary and middle school teachers usually teach more than one subject. A growing number of states and some colleges are requiring these teacher candidates to major in an academic area or have a concentration in one or more academic areas. Middle school teachers may teach one or two subjects, sometimes team teaching with others whose academic preparation is in other subjects. Ele-

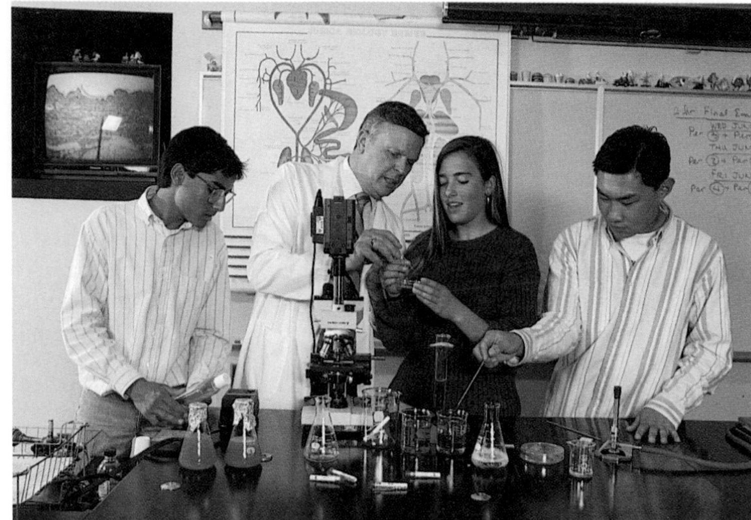

Each teaching discipline has unique requirements and knowledge bases needed for certification.

mentary teachers, by contrast, often teach reading, English language arts, social studies, mathematics, and science in a self-contained classroom with few or no outside professional resources to assist them. In many schools they are also expected to help students develop healthy lifestyles and an appreciation for music and art. To begin to have the academic knowledge to teach requires more than four years of college for many teacher candidates.

One of the primary cornerstones of the field of teaching is knowledge about teaching and learning and the development of skills and **dispositions** to help students learn. Therefore, teacher candidates study theories and research on how students learn at different ages. They must understand the influence of culture, language, and socioeconomic conditions on learning. In addition, they have to know how to manage classrooms, motivate students, work with parents and other colleagues, assess learning, and develop lesson plans built on the prior experiences of fifteen to thirty or more students in the classroom. Teaching is a very complex field. There are seldom right answers that fit every situation. Teachers must make multiple decisions throughout a day, responding to individual student needs and events in the school and community.

Qualified teachers have also had the opportunity to develop their knowledge, skills, and dispositions with students in schools. These field experiences and clinical practice (that is, student teaching or an internship) should be accompanied by feedback and mentoring from experienced teachers who know the subject they teach and how to help students learn. Work in schools is becoming more extensive in many teacher education programs. Some teacher candidates participate in yearlong internships in schools, ending in a master's degree. Others work in professional development schools in which higher education faculty, teachers, and teacher candidates collaborate in teaching and inquiry. In both of these cases, most, if not all, of the program is offered in the school setting.

It is the knowledge about teaching and learning, translated into student learning in the classroom, that makes up the professional knowledge for teaching. It should not be surprising that people who begin to teach without this professional knowledge and the accompanying experiences for honing their skills in classrooms have difficulty in managing classrooms and teaching effectively.

dispositions
The values, commitments, and professional ethics that influence beliefs, attitudes, and behaviors.

STANDARDS Standards are an important part of professions. They define, in part, what professionals should know and be able to do. They indicate the core values of the profession and the essential, agreed upon knowledge and skills that professionals should have. Members of the profession develop standards to guide training, entry into the profession, and continuing practice in the profession. States also develop standards that define the minimal expectations to practice the profession in a particular state.

Standards and standards-based education are prevalent at all levels of education today. To finish your teacher education program, you are likely to have to meet professional, state, and institutional standards that outline what you should know and be able to do as a novice teacher. When you begin teaching, you will be expected to prepare students to meet state or district standards. Assessments are designed to determine whether students meet the P–12 standards at the levels expected. Most states require teacher candidates to pass standardized tests at a predetermined level before granting the first license to teach. Some states require beginning teachers to pass **performance assessments** based on standards in the first three years of practice to receive a professional license.

Standards developed by the profession can be levers for raising the quality of practice. When used appropriately, they can protect the least advantaged students from incompetent practice.[11] Some educators view standards as a threat, especially when a government agency or other group holds individuals or schools to the standards, making summative judgments about licensure or approval. Others use standards as powerful tools for changes in a profession or in school practices. Standards and related assessments are discussed in greater detail in Chapter 15.

QUALITY ASSURANCE CONTINUUM

One of the roles of professions and their standards is to provide quality control over who enters and remains in the profession. Most other professions, such as law, medicine, and dentistry, require candidates to graduate from an accredited professional school before they are even eligible to take a licensing examination to test the knowledge and skills necessary to practice responsibly. Some professions also offer examinations for certification of advanced skills, such as the CPA exam for public accountants, or for practice in specialized fields such as pediatrics, obstetrics, or surgery. The same quality assurance continuum now exists for teaching. Figure 1.10 depicts a comprehensive quality assurance system for teaching that includes complementary sets of standards and assessments for initial teacher preparation, state licensure, national board certification, and continuing professional development.

ACCREDITATION Do you know whether the teacher education program you are in is a part of an accredited institution? Your college or university is probably accredited by one of six regional accrediting bodies that apply standards to the university as a whole by reviewing its financial status, student services, and the general studies curriculum. However, professional accreditation in teacher education is granted to the school, college, or department of education that is responsible for preparing teachers and other educators. Fewer than half of the 1,300 institutions that prepare teachers are accredited by the profession's accrediting agency, the National Council for Accreditation of Teacher Education (NCATE). Professional accrediting bodies accredit nearly all of the institutions

performance assessment
A comprehensive assessment system through which candidates demonstrate their proficiencies in the area being measured.

FIGURE 1.10 THE PROFESSIONAL CONTINUUM AND QUALITY ASSURANCE IN TEACHING

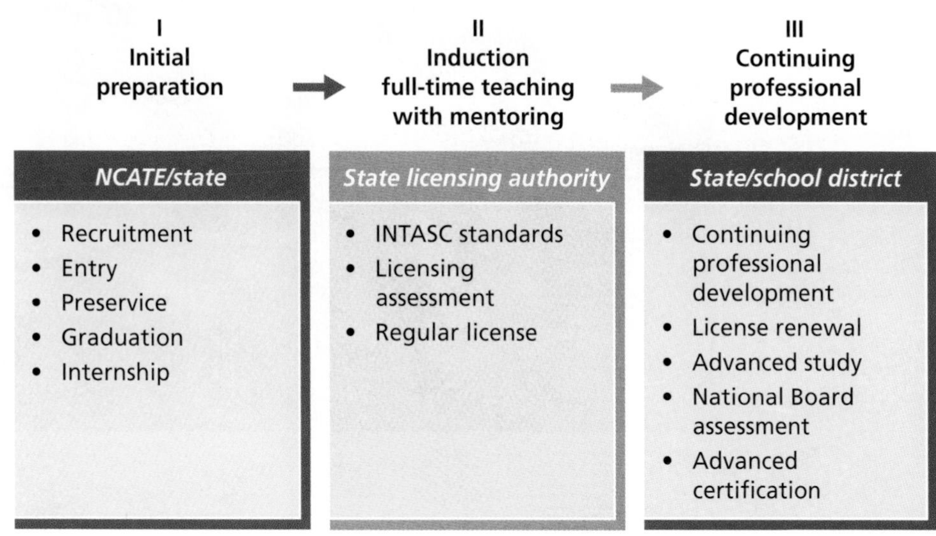

that prepare physicians, architects, veterinarians, dentists, and lawyers. In most states these professionals must have graduated from accredited schools to sit for state licensing tests. However, fewer than five states require all of their teacher education programs to be nationally accredited. To check on the accreditation status of your institution, visit NCATE's website at www.ncate.org.

Accreditation can be the momentum for improvement in the profession, often provoking real change in the preparation of professionals. NCATE's standards, for example, hold schools of education responsible for the quality of the educators who complete programs. They expect the faculty to prepare candidates to meet professional and state standards as shown through successful practice in schools. Field experiences and clinical practice in schools must be designed for teacher candidates to develop the knowledge, skills, and dispositions necessary to help all students learn.

Accreditation provides assurance to the public that graduates of programs are qualified and competent to practice. The proportion of accredited schools, colleges, and departments of education in a state has been found to be the best predictor of the proportion of well-qualified teachers in a state.[12] Since well-qualified teachers are the strongest predictor of student achievement on national achievement tests, accreditation is an important first step of a quality assurance system in the education field.

LICENSURE State licensure is the second step of a quality assurance system for professionals. To practice as a physician, nurse, lawyer, architect, or teacher, you must be granted a license from a state agency. A license to teach usually requires completion of a state-approved teacher education program and passing a standardized test of knowledge. A growing number of states requires teacher candidates to major in an academic area rather than in education. In addition, student teaching or an internship must be completed successfully. Requirements for

Teachers must become lifelong learners to maintain and improve their teaching skills throughout their careers.

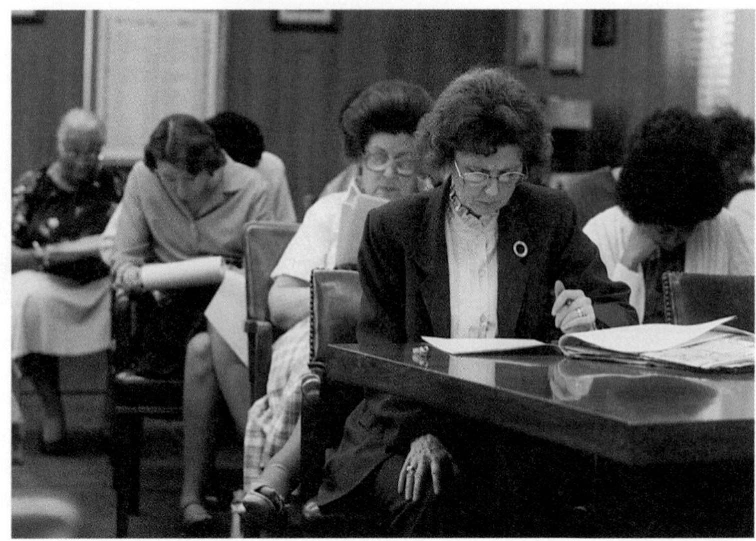

licensure differ from state to state. For this reason, if you plan to teach in a state different from the one in which you are going to school, you may want to contact that state directly for licensure information. Information on licensure requirements is available on the websites of state licensing agencies; for a list of agencies and contact information, see Appendix 1.1 at the end of this chapter. The certification officer at your institution should be able to provide you with licensure information and details about seeking a license in another state.

The initial license allows a new teacher to practice for a specified period of time, usually three to five years. This period in a teacher's career is called induction. On completion of successful teaching during that period and sometimes a master's degree, a professional license can be granted. Most states require continuing professional development throughout the teacher's career and periodical renewal of the license, typically every five years.

performance-based licensing
A system of licensing professionals based on the use of multiple assessments that measure the applicant's knowledge, skills, and dispositions to determine whether he or she can perform effectively in the profession.

portfolio
A compilation of works, records, and accomplishments that teachers and teacher candidates prepare for a specific purpose to demonstrate his or her learnings, performances, and contributions.

States traditionally required candidates to take specific college courses, complete student teaching, and successfully pass a licensure examination for a license. Most states are now in the process of developing **performance-based licensing** systems. They will not be specifying courses to be completed; instead, they indicate the knowledge, skills, and sometimes dispositions that candidates should possess. Future decisions about granting a license will depend on the results of state assessments based primarily on licensure test scores.

Concerned about the limitations of standardized tests and their predictability of successful classroom practice, more than thirty states are participating in a consortium to develop performance-based licensure standards and assessments. The ten principles of the Interstate New Teacher Assessment and Support Consortium (INTASC) have been adopted or adapted for licensure by many states. These ten principles describe what teachers should know and be able to do in their first few years of practice. You should be developing this knowledge and skills in the college program in which you are currently enrolled. Some states are requiring teachers to submit **portfolios,** which are scored by experienced teachers, as evidence of teaching effectiveness before granting the professional license. The portfolios that you begin to compile during your teacher

INTASC Principles
What Teachers Should Know and Be Able to Do

1. The teacher understands the central concepts, tools of inquiry, and structures of the discipline(s) he or she teaches and can create learning experiences that make these aspects of subject matter meaningful for students.
2. The teacher understands how children learn and develop, and can provide learning opportunities that support their intellectual, social, and personal development.
3. The teacher understands how students differ in their approaches to learning and creates instructional opportunities that are adapted to diverse learners.
4. The teacher understands and uses a variety of instructional strategies to encourage students' development of critical thinking, problem solving, and performance skills.
5. The teacher uses an understanding of individual and group motivation and behavior to create a learning environment that encourages positive social interaction, active engagement in learning, and self-motivation.
6. The teacher uses knowledge of effective verbal, nonverbal, and media communication techniques to foster active inquiry, collaboration, and supportive interaction in the classroom.
7. The teacher plans instruction based on knowledge of subject matter, students, the community, and curriculum goals.
8. The teacher understands and uses formal and informal assessment strategies to evaluate and ensure the continuous intellectual, social, and physical development of the learner.
9. The teacher is a reflective practitioner who continually evaluates the effects of his/her choices and actions on others (students, parents, and other professionals in the learning community) and who actively seeks out opportunities to grow professionally.
10. The teacher fosters relationships with school colleagues, parents, and agencies in the larger community to support students' learning and well-being.

Each of these ten principles is accompanied in the full INTASC document with knowledge, dispositions, and performance expectations for candidates. INTASC content standards also have been developed for teachers of the arts, English language arts, mathematics, science, social studies, elementary education, and special education. INTASC standards can be accessed from the web at www.ccsso.org/intasc/html.

education program could evolve into the documentation that you will later need to submit for your first professional license.

ADVANCED CERTIFICATION Advanced certification has long been an option for many professionals but is relatively new for teaching. The National Board for Professional Teaching Standards (NBPTS) was established in 1987 to develop a system for certifying accomplished teachers. The first teachers were certified in 1995; by 2000 over 4,800 experienced teachers had been board certified. The number of teachers seeking national certification continues to increase. Nearly 10,000 teachers were preparing documentation for certification in 2000.

The National Board standards outline what teachers should know and be able to do as accomplished teachers. Nationally certified teachers

1. Are committed to students and their learning.
2. Know the subjects they teach and how to teach those subjects to students.
3. Are responsible for managing and monitoring student learning.
4. Think systematically about their practice and learn from experience.
5. Are members of learning communities.

The process for becoming nationally certified is time-consuming and requires at least a year. Why then do teachers seek national certification? For one thing, it is a recognition of accomplishment by one's peers that is self-fulfilling. Nationally certified teachers are aggressively being recruited by some school districts. Some school districts and half of the states pay an extra salary stipend that can be several thousand dollars annually to nationally certified teachers.

Your current teacher education program should be providing the basic foundation for future national certification. Teachers must have taught for at least three years before they are eligible for national certification. The process requires the submission of portfolios with samples of student work and videotapes of the applicant teaching. In addition, the teachers must complete a number of activities at an assessment center. Experienced teachers score the various assessment activities. Many teachers do not meet the national requirements on the first try but report that the process is the best professional development activity in which they have participated. Overwhelmingly, teachers report that they have become better teachers as a result. More and more parents in the future will likely request a nationally certified teacher in the classrooms of their children.

PROFESSIONAL RESPONSIBILITIES

Being a professional carries responsibilities for practice. Professionals in most fields regulate licensure and practice through a Professional Standards Board controlled by members of the profession rather than the state government. Professional Standards Boards for teaching currently exist in about one-fourth of the states; other agencies have this responsibility in the remaining states. Not only do these boards set standards for licensure, but they also have standards and processes for monitoring the practice of teachers. They usually have the authority to remove a teacher's license for cause.

DEVELOPING PROFESSIONAL COMMITMENTS AND DISPOSITIONS Successful teachers exhibit dispositions that facilitate their work with students and parents. Teachers' values, commitments, and professional ethics influence interactions with students, families, colleagues, and communities. They affect student learning, motivation, and development. They influence a teacher's own professional growth as well. Dispositions held by teachers who are able to help all students learn include:

1. Enthusiasm for the discipline(s) she or he teaches and the ability to see connections to everyday life.
2. A commitment to continuous learning and engagement in professional discourse about subject matter knowledge and children's learning of the disciplines.
3. The belief that all children can learn at high levels.

DEBATE

Should Nationally Certified Teachers Be Paid More?

Jeanne Serven is nationally certified in the field of Early Adolescence/English Language Arts. A 25-year teaching veteran, she's currently on loan to the Illinois State Board of Education, where she works to help improve the quality of teaching and learning. She can be reached at Jaserven@aol.com.

Traditionally, experienced teachers in search of professional salaries have had three options: 1) Get as much education as the pay scale rewards. 2) Move to a "rich" school district in the suburbs. 3) Leave the classroom to go into administration.

It's high time to add a fourth option for teachers who continually improve their practice and meet the highest standards set by their profession: Provide financial rewards for nationally certified teachers.

I teach in a small, rural school district in Illinois. I have a master's degree, 25 years of teaching experience, and I'm at the top of my salary scale. I make $33,987.

Now, I'm not inclined to move to the suburbs or become an administrator. I'm interested in being the best teacher I can be for my students.

So four years ago, I applied for national certification in Early Adolescence/English Language Arts. For months, I collected student work, videotaped my teaching, put together a professional portfolio, and examined the instruction in my classroom.

Then I analyzed and reflected on what I saw. In the process, I improved the instruction in my classroom and boosted the level of student learning.

Unlike most evaluations of teacher performance, the national board evaluation process was fair and equitable. Evaluators are practicing classroom teachers in the same content areas and grade levels as the candidates they're evaluating.

The strength of the process lies in the requirement for actual classroom documentation and evidence, rather than personal recommendations. It's an assessment based on standards developed by classroom teachers.

National certification is an arduous, time-consuming, and expensive voluntary process designed to "establish high and rigorous standards for what accomplished teachers should know and be able to do." And it may have great value for those who choose to go through it. But paying more to those who succeed has precious little value for the profession, teachers, and students.

Elizabeth Ahlgren is the chair of the math department at Morse High School in San Diego. She's a local building rep, treasurer of the San Diego Teachers Association, and a member of the California Teachers Association State Council of Education. She can be reached at eahlgren@morsehs.com.

■ *Paying nationally certified teachers more will promote elitism, not a stronger teaching profession.* Some argue that national certification elevates teaching and makes teachers professionals, like doctors and lawyers. That's nonsense.

What really makes us professionals? Professional wages that attract people to the field and keep them there, and professional working conditions that make it easy for educators to do their jobs well.

What good is it to pay a few experienced teachers more money when new teachers don't earn enough to be able to afford to stay in the profession?

Paying new teachers better salaries would be a far better way to support the profession. So would supporting new teachers in their classrooms with mentoring, adequate instructional materials, and high quality professional development activities.

If the goal is a top quality teacher in every classroom, providing "bonuses" to a few senior teachers won't do much to achieve it.

■ *Paying nationally certified teachers more will help a few teachers at the expense of the many.* All teachers—not just candidates for national certification—should engage in rich collegial discussions, take the time to reflect on and improve lessons, and maintain a professional portfolio.

YES | NO

Like anyone who has gained additional expertise, I'd like to be rewarded. The additional money that my national certification could earn would provide an incentive for me to stay in my rural school. Is it fair for rural and urban students to lose some of their best teachers because of the system's inability to reimburse them adequately for their efforts?

I realize there are some obstacles to overcome. First, the funding for raises for nationally certified teachers would have to come from the state. It can't be left to individual districts with varying abilities to pay.

Second, the National Board for Professional Teaching Standards must push to offer certification in every teaching field as quickly as possible. By 2003, 17 certificates will be available, covering 82 percent of the profession. (For details, call 800/532-1813.)

Finally, educators must understand that paying more for nationally certified teachers won't close the door to recognition of expertise in the profession.

Instead, it will create more options for experienced teachers, more mentors for new teachers, more mentors for those who wish to achieve national certification, and more spokespeople for the profession.

Encouraging more teachers to become nationally certified will create better teachers in all schools and reward them for their knowledge and skills in the classroom. Since, as a recent report notes, "what teachers know and do is the most important influence on what students learn," national certification will pay off. And our students will reap the dividends.

Source: Should Nationally Certified Teachers Be Paid More? *NEA Today* (April 1998): 47.

And all teachers should be compensated for the work they do—not for what they did in the past, not for what they plan to do, and not for the titles they hold.

In San Diego, nationally certified teachers become mentor teachers and are compensated for the hours they spend working with other teachers, not for their new credential.

Why not pay all teachers for the work they do now—for the time they donate to activities crucial to school and student success, like curriculum development, student tutoring, and participation in school site councils?

And there's a question of fairness to consider: Is a bonus for nationally certified teachers fair to those with second jobs, young children, or dependent parents, who can't afford to take the time and spend the money—$2,000 at last count—to apply for national certification. Do they deserve less than those who can afford to be involved in the certification process?

- *Paying nationally certified teachers more will not improve student learning.* Paying a stipend to those who successfully attain national certification may lure a few more teachers into attempting national certification. But it's not going to make much of a dent in efforts to improve learning in America's public schools.

To improve student learning in this country, all of us need to go to work every day and do our best to help as many students as we can.

That's why most of us chose to teach in the first place—and why a divisive pay raise for nationally certified teachers doesn't add up.

WHAT'S YOUR OPINION?

Should nationally certified teachers be paid more?

Go to **www.ablongman.com/johnson** to cast your vote and see how NEA readers responded.

4. Valuing the many ways in which people seek to communicate and encouraging many modes of communication in the classroom.
5. Development of respectful and productive relationships with parents and guardians from diverse home and community situations, seeking to develop cooperative partnerships in support of student learning and well-being.

One of the characteristics of a profession is the acceptance of a statement of ethics that professionals are expected to uphold. A number of professional associations have codes of ethics for individuals in a particular role, such as the spe-

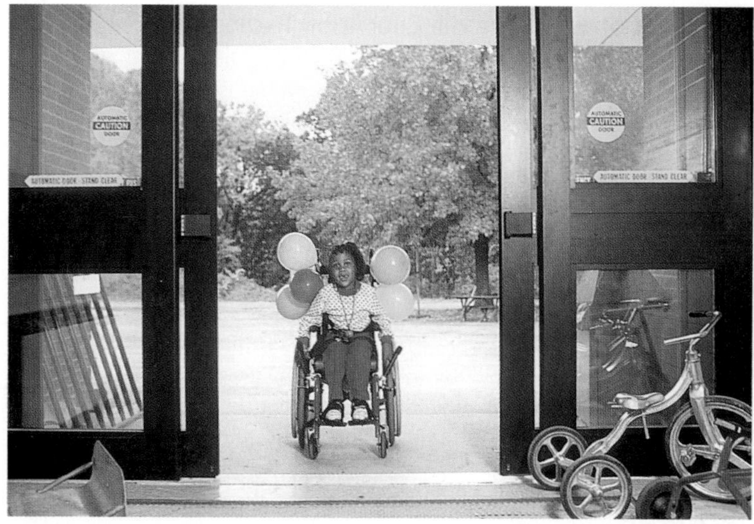

Given the trend to include students with disabilities in general education classrooms, it is likely that some of your students will have special needs, no matter what grade or subject you teach.

cial education teacher. Professional standards boards apply a code of ethics as they investigate complaints against teachers and other educators, sometimes removing one's license because of infractions. The code of ethics adopted by the largest organization of teachers, the National Education Association (NEA), outlines the critical values and behaviors expected of practicing teachers.

Teacher candidates have made some of these professional commitments when they decide to be a teacher. Your teacher education program should help you to further develop these dispositions and commitments and learn new ones. They are usually assessed as you work in classrooms with students and families.

FOCUSING ON STUDENT LEARNING Recent research is finding that the quality of teachers accounts for more variation in student learning than do other school factors such as class size. Parents have always known this fact, seeking the best teachers for their children when possible. In addition, most people believe that all children can learn; 68 percent of the respondents in a recent survey indicated

Every student deserves a competent and highly qualified teacher.

PREAMBLE

The educator, believing in the worth and dignity of each human being, recognizes the supreme importance of the pursuit of truth, devotion to excellence, and the nurture of the democratic principles. Essential to these goals is the protection of freedom to learn and to teach and the guarantee of equal educational opportunity for all. The educator accepts the responsibility to adhere to the highest ethical standards.

The educator recognizes the magnitude of the responsibility inherent in the teaching process. The desire for the respect and confidence of one's colleagues, of students, of parents, and of the members of the community provides the incentive to attain and maintain the highest possible degree of ethical conduct. The Code of Ethics of the Education Profession indicates the aspiration of all educators and provides standards by which to judge conduct.

The remedies specified by the NEA and/or its affiliates for the violation of any provision of this Code shall be exclusive and no such provision shall be enforceable in any form other than the one specifically designated by the NEA or its affiliates.

PRINCIPLE I

COMMITMENT TO THE STUDENT

The educator strives to help each student realize his or her potential as a worthy and effective member of society. The educator therefore works to stimulate the spirit of inquiry, the acquisition of knowledge and understanding, and the thoughtful formulation of worthy goals.

In fulfillment of the obligation to the student, the educator—

1. Shall not unreasonably restrain the student from independent action in the pursuit of learning.
2. Shall not unreasonably deny the student's access to varying points of view.
3. Shall not deliberately suppress or distort subject matter relevant to the student's progress.
4. Shall make reasonable effort to protect the student from conditions harmful to learning or to health and safety.
5. Shall not intentionally expose the student to embarrassment or disparagement.
6. Shall not on the basis of race, color, creed, sex, national origin, marital status, political or religious beliefs, family, social or cultural background, or sexual orientation, unfairly—
   a. Exclude any student from participation in any program
   b. Deny benefits to any student
   c. Grant any advantage to any student
7. Shall not use professional relationships with students for private advantage.
8. Shall not disclose information about students obtained in the course of professional service unless disclosure serves a compelling professional purpose or is required by law.

PRINCIPLE II

COMMITMENT TO THE PROFESSION

The education profession is vested by the public with a trust and responsibility requiring the highest ideals of professional service.

In the belief that the quality of the services of the education profession directly influences the nation and its citizens, the educator shall exert every effort to raise professional standards, to promote a climate that encourages the exercise of professional judgment, to achieve conditions that attract persons worthy of the trust to careers in education, and to assist in preventing the practice of the profession by unqualified persons.

In fulfillment of the obligation to the profession, the educator—

9. Shall not in an application for a professional position deliberately make a false statement or fail to disclose a material fact related to competency and qualifications.
10. Shall not misrepresent his/her professional qualifications.
11. Shall not assist any entry into the profession of a person known to be unqualified in respect to character, education, or other relevant attribute.
12. Shall not knowingly make a false statement concerning the qualifications of a candidate for a professional position.
13. Shall not assist a noneducator in the unauthorized practice of teaching.
14. Shall not disclose information about colleagues obtained in the course of professional service unless disclosure serves a compelling professional purpose or is required by law.
15. Shall not knowingly make false or malicious statements about a colleague.
16. Shall not accept any gratuity, gift, or favor that might impair or appear to influence professional decisions or action.

Adopted by the NEA 1975 Representative Assembly

that most children are capable of learning demanding academic subject matter and should be required to meet a common set of academic standards. This sentiment received the strongest support from Latino (79 percent) and African American (71 percent) respondents.

You should be familiar with the academic standards for P–12 students when you accept your first teaching assignment. Students will be expected to meet the standards at a level deemed appropriate by the state or school district and are tested for knowledge on standardized tests. The results from these tests appear in local newspapers; schools within a state are ranked on the basis of how well students perform on these tests. Principals and teachers often are held responsible for test scores, sometimes losing their jobs if scores do not improve or high scores are not retained.

Policymakers who have promoted the use of standardized tests to measure learning may not realize that the tests alone provide very limited information about student learning. Although tests may measure some slice of students' knowledge, they tell little about their ability to think critically or solve problems and provide little, if any, evidence about their ability to apply the knowledge in appropriate settings. Although some states and districts use multiple performance assessments to determine student learning, most of the public and policymakers focus on test scores listed on the reports brought home by students and reported in newspapers. The unfortunate result is that many teachers are teaching to the tests and ignoring content that otherwise would be taught.

PROFESSIONAL DILEMMA

Who Is Cheating Now?

Testing is pervasive in our educational system today. Many school districts and states require students to pass tests to move from one grade to another grade. They must pass tests to graduate from high school and to enter most colleges and universities. Teacher candidates must pass numerous standardized tests to be licensed.

Not only are students and teacher candidates tested regularly and often, but their schools and universities also are held accountable for their performance on these tests. The aggregated results are published in newspapers and on websites. Schools and colleges are ranked within a state. Some are classified as low performing and lose part of their public funding. In some schools teachers' and principals' jobs depend on how well their students perform on these standardized tests.

The standardized tests that are being used in elementary and secondary education are supposed to test for evidence that students are meeting state standards. For the most part they are paper-and-pencil tests of knowledge in a subject area. Although the state standards are advertised as being developed by teachers and experts, many educators argue that many of the standards expect knowledge and skills that are developmentally inappropriate at some grade levels. In areas such as social studies, recall of specific facts that cover spans of hundreds of years is not an uncommon requirement.

It probably comes as no surprise that some teachers are teaching to the test, taking weeks out of the curriculum to coach students for the test. Too often, teachers and administrators are taking inappropriate steps to ensure higher scores. Test questions have been shared with students before the test. Students have been given additional time to complete a test. Low-performing students have been asked to stay at home on test days; high-performing students who are sick on test day are begged to come in anyway. As a result, teachers and principals are losing their jobs in cheating scandals across the country.

- What ethical issues are involved when educators interfere with the testing process?
- What are the limitations of standardized testing for high-stakes decisions about grade promotion, graduation, and teacher licensure?
- Why are standardized tests so pervasive in today's society?
- How would you respond if you knew that a teacher in your school was cheating in the way that he or she is preparing students for upcoming tests?

Teacher candidates themselves are not free from this testing mania. Most states require passing standardized tests to be eligible for a license. Most teacher education programs include multiple assessments of teaching performance, including the ability to help students learn. By the time you begin your first teaching assignment, you should have strategies for assessing student learning and adjusting your teaching to ensure that students are learning. With experience, you will develop a repertoire of knowledge and skills on which you can draw to help students learn—the ultimate goal of teaching. Chapter 15 is devoted to descriptions of standards, assessment approaches, and emerging issues.

REFLECTING ON ONE'S PRACTICE

It is interesting, and perhaps useful to educators, to note that physicians proudly claim to "practice" medicine throughout their careers. Many people have suggested that teachers should borrow this concept and also proudly undertake to "practice" teaching throughout their careers. This interpretation of the word *practice* implies that teachers, like physicians, should constantly strive to improve their performance—something that all good teachers do. This section attempts to provide you with a few practical suggestions as you prepare to "practice" your profession as a teacher.

SYSTEMATIC OBSERVATION AND JOURNALING As you proceed through your teacher education program, you should seize every opportunity to observe a wide variety of activities related to the world of education. For instance, in addition to the observation and participation assignments that you will have as part of the formal teacher education program, you should seek out opportunities to visit and observe a wide variety of classrooms. You should also attempt to find summer employment that allows you to work with children or youth.

INFORMAL NOTE TAKING One of the most common ways to collect information is by writing down your observations—in other words, taking notes. Note taking can be done in a variety of ways. For instance, when you go into your classroom, you could start by writing a brief description of the setting, such as the physical appearance of the room, the number of students, the teaching devices available, and so on. You can then systematically describe each of the things you observe. The more detail you can record, the more you will learn from the observations. Create a list of questions before you begin any given observation. If you are interested in how a teacher motivates students during a particular lesson, write down the question "What techniques does the teacher use to help motivate students?" Then record your observations under that question.

STRUCTURED OBSERVATIONS Observations that are conducted according to a predetermined plan are often referred to as **structured observations.** As your college or university sends you out into schools for various laboratory experiences, you will probably be provided with guidelines that will help structure your observations. In fact, some colleges have developed written structured observation forms that will guide you when participating in clinical experiences. We also recommend that you create your own structured observation forms around the questions that particularly intrigue you. In other words, if you are especially interested in classroom diversity, devise your own structured observation form to remind you to look for details concerning that particular topic the next time you are in a classroom. In fact, it might be fun for you to create some structured observation forms that you can use with the professors in your college classes. The more aware you are of what you are looking for as you observe a classroom, the more you are likely to learn about that particular topic.

OBSERVATION INSTRUMENTS You might find it difficult to believe, but literally hundreds of structured observation instruments have been devised to help educators collect more valid data about classrooms. These observation instruments range from quite simple devices to extremely complex systems that require computers for analysis. Generally, however, they fall into two basic categories—structured interviews and **classroom analysis systems.**

STRUCTURED INTERVIEWS Structured interviews consist of a series of specific questions that are asked of a respondent as well as some provision for recording the

structured observations
Observations that are conducted according to a predetermined plan.

classroom analysis systems
Clearly defined sets of procedures and written materials that educators can use to analyze the interaction between teachers and students.

respondent's answer. You could prepare a series of important questions that you would like to ask a principal, teacher, student, parent, or anyone else connected with the educational enterprise. You must make sure that these questions are not ambiguous and that the respondent will clearly understand what you are asking. You can then seek out a number of respondents and interview them with the same structured interview technique. Obviously, the more people you survey through such a technique, the more representative your data will be for the population in general. If you ask only one teacher the question "What is the single best discipline technique that you use in your classroom?" you will glean only one idea; if you ask 100 teachers the same question, you will obtain much more representative data about effective discipline techniques that teachers use.

When doing a structured interview, you must be very careful to record your respondent's answers accurately. It is best to use a tape recorder, which you simply let run during your interview. In this way you obtain a complete record of the answers and can go back and listen to it many times later on. You can also write down your respondent's answers, but it may be difficult for you to record answers accurately and completely.

During the last fifty years, as researchers have attempted to understand more objectively what takes place in schools, they have created many systems to study classroom activity. In general, these classroom analysis systems come in two types: quantitative and qualitative. Quantitative systems use well-defined categories and coding procedures to count the occurrence of different teacher and student behaviors. Qualitative systems are more open-ended or descriptive.

ANALYSIS OF PRACTICE AND REFLECTION Once you have collected observations of teaching, children, classrooms, and schools, it is very important to take time to think about what you have seen. There are several techniques for systematically analyzing your observations, but equally important is taking time to reflect on the analyses. In our rush to get everything done, we frequently fail to take time to examine our experiences and impressions. However, being serious about finding time for thoughtful reflection is an important part of becoming an excellent teacher, and there are some processes that can be helpful.

REFLECTIVE JOURNALING Educators at all levels have come to realize that learners profit greatly from thinking reflectively about, and then writing down, what they learn in school. This process is called reflective journaling. If you are not now required to keep a journal in your teacher education program, we strongly recommend that you start doing so. If you are required to keep a journal, we urge you to take this assignment seriously, because you will learn much in the process.

There is no one way to go about keeping a journal. All you need is something to write on and the will to write. A spiral notebook, a three-ring binder, or a computer works fine. Preferably at the end of each day (and at the very least once each week), briefly summarize your thoughts about and reactions to the major things you learned. It will probably be useful to spend more time thinking and reflecting and to write down only a brief summary. We believe that your journal should be brief, reflective, candid, personal, and preferably private—something like a personal diary. It is best if you can be perfectly honest in your journal and not worry about someone evaluating your opinions.

When you start to work in schools, you will discover (if you have not already done so) that teachers in elementary and secondary schools are using journaling more and more with their students. There is something about thinking and then writing down our thoughts about what we have learned that helps us internalize, better understand, and remember what we have been taught.

At the end of each chapter in this book, we offer you several suggestions for entries in your journal. We sincerely hope that you will do reflective journaling in your remaining teacher education program.

SUMMARIZING EDUCATIONAL INFORMATION Regardless of the technique you use to record your educational observations, it is imperative that you take the time to study them. The best way to study is to reread your recorded data many times. Once you have become thoroughly familiar with the content of your recorded data, you are ready to begin summarizing your findings. This requires an open mind. You should strive to disregard any previous prejudices you may have had on the topic. Remember that your goal is to understand objectively the data from your observations. It is sometimes helpful to talk with fellow students about your findings. This type of peer brainstorming will frequently allow you to see data from a slightly different and perhaps more objective viewpoint. In fact, you might want to team up with classmates who are making the same observations using the same data collection technique so that you all have the same frame of reference. Your goal in summarizing your information is to draw accurate conclusions from the data you have collected.

FORMING HYPOTHESES Once you have condensed and summarized your data, you are ready to draw conclusions and form hypotheses, or tentative interpretations, based on your observations. For example, if one of your original questions was "What techniques do teachers use to motivate their student?" you will obviously develop hypotheses to answer that particular question. The hypotheses that you form at this stage in your development as an educator make worthwhile all the effort you make to verify for yourself some of what you have probably been reading and hearing in your college classes. In addition, your hypotheses are the basis on which you will eventually pattern your own teaching style.

TESTING YOUR CONCLUSIONS Every belief, conclusion, or hypothesis that you develop as an educator should be considered tentative. In other words, it is important to formulate such beliefs at this point in your career, but you need to keep an open mind about them and continually revalidate them. The teacher who is constantly attempting to improve is also constantly forming new or modified beliefs, hypotheses, and conclusions about teaching. That is why it is critically important for you and all educators to observe and analyze classroom activity continually in an ongoing effort to understand more fully this very complex field.

PORTFOLIO DEVELOPMENT As you move through your teacher education program and on into your career as a teacher, you will find that you have been collecting stacks, boxes, and files of information and "stuff" related to you, your teaching, and the accomplishments of the students you have taught. If you are like most teachers, you will not know for sure what to do with all of it, yet you will be reluctant to throw any of it away. Our advice is that you be very careful about discarding material until you have organized a folio and anticipated the needs of various portfolios that you might have to prepare. A *folio* is an organized compilation of all the products, records, accomplishments, and testimonies of a teacher and his or her students. Imagine the folio as being a large file drawer with different compartments and file folders. Some of the material that is included is related directly to you and your background. Other items or artifacts are things that others have said about you. And some are examples of projects that your students have completed.

A *portfolio* is a special compilation assembled from the folio for a specific occasion or purpose, such as a job interview or an application for an outstanding teacher award. The portfolio might also be used by you and your professors throughout your teacher education program to document your performance in meeting state, professional, and institutional standards. Portfolios are required in some states as evidence that you should be granted a professional teaching license after the first few years of actual work in classrooms. Portfolios will also be required for national board certification later in your career. The folio can be organized around three major categories of items—background and experience, attestations, and products and outcomes—as shown in Table 1.2. Let's look at each of these three categories.

Many pieces of factual information about you belong in your folio. Demographic information, where you attended school, the states where you are licensed to teach, and the record of your work experience are examples of these factual items. When organizing your folio, you will identify areas in which you should aim to add information. Now is the time to anticipate some of the material that you might need in preparing a particular portfolio in the

TABLE 1.2 Types of Information and Artifacts to Include in a Professional Folio

Background and Experience	Attestations	Products and Outcomes
Facts	Recognition by others	Works of others based on your teaching
Demographics	Awards	Examples of student work
• Age	Honorary society memberships	Photographs of your classroom
• Birth date	Letters from	Student test scores
• Marital status	• Students	Videotape/audiotape of lessons
Education	• Parents	Grant proposals funded
• Degrees	• Professors	Student awards
• Institutions	• Employers	Effects of leadership
Education platform/philosophy	• Colleagues	• Committee reports
Professional credentials	Newspaper articles about you	• School/class awards
Work experience	TV segments about you	• Curriculum developed
Current role and responsibilities	Committee assignments	• Projects completed
Multicultural experiences	Elected offices	Subordinates who have been recognized or promoted
Special skills		• Lesson plans
• Languages		• Authored curriculum
• Art/music		• Media productions
Community service		• Written reflection
• Volunteer work		

RELEVANT RESEARCH

Making Meaning of the Educational Portfolios

STUDY PURPOSE/QUESTION: Can portfolios be used to help students make meaning of their experiences and provide an opportunity for an assessment of their work?

STUDY DESIGN: The research focused on the use of portfolios in two different projects. A kindergarten teacher studied the process she used throughout a school year in which her class developed portfolios of their "best" work and interacted with adults about the portfolios at the end of the year. In the second project, teacher candidates prepared portfolios that included entries that they believed represented themselves as teachers.

STUDY FINDINGS: The kindergarten teacher was surprised at the items that the children in her class selected as their best work; the students' selections were different from those the teacher would have selected as their best. "In the children's minds, 'best work' meant work that represented the people, objects, and events that were of most interest and importance to them" (p. 592). The teacher, by contrast, was looking for examples that showed learning and growth. For the students the portfolio activity was a "powerful learning tool"; it served as an authentic assessment for the teacher.

The portfolios presented by the teacher candidates varied greatly in their presentation and contents. The candidates found the preparation of portfolios to be a potent learning experience because the open-ended format allowed them to discover the meaning of their experiences. A content analysis of the portfolios and candidate questionnaires indicated that candidates learned what was expected, though at different levels. The project also helped them to synthesize and reflect on their learning to develop a cohesive teaching philosophy.

IMPLICATIONS: Educational portfolios are "those that merge assessment with learning—the kind of learning that involves deep understanding, reflectivity, and multiple dimensions, including the moral and ethical." The researcher identified four essential elements of these portfolios. First, they allow for individuals to make their own meaning of their experiences. The contents to be included are clear but not prescriptive. The second essential element is that the contents and their meaning can be shared and discussed with others who matter. The portfolios have much more meaning when they are used for learning purposes, not assessments. Third, the process of preparing a portfolio occurs over a period of time. Finally, the portfolios are developed and presented in a context that is supportive of reflection and moral deliberation. Faculty and teachers who are designing portfolio activities should be clear about the purposes. Portfolios that are used for summative assessments are not always those that promote learning.

Source: Vicki Kubler LaBoskey, "Portfolios Here, Portfolios There . . . Searching for the Essence of 'Educational Portfolios,' " *Phi Delta Kappan, 81*(8) (April 2000): 590–595.

future. For example, when you apply for most teaching positions, a prospective employer will want to know the kinds of experiences you have had in schools and classrooms with diverse students. If you do not currently have any examples in your folio, plan to add some related experiences as your teacher education program unfolds. Your professors may expect to see evidence that you are meeting standards such as INTASC or those of a specialty professional association.

The occasions on which other people recognize your contributions and achievements are called *attestations.* Awards, letters of commendation, newspaper articles, elected positions, and committee memberships are examples of attestation items to keep in your folio.

Through your efforts as a teacher candidate and teacher, students complete assignments, produce plays, achieve on examinations, and receive awards. In this part of the folio, compile the works and successes of the people you have worked with, along with photographs and video records of your classroom and student projects. You may want to include videotapes of your teaching with a description of your classroom context and analysis of your teaching. Also include copies of your best lesson plans, committee reports, grant proposals, and other products that have resulted from your leading the efforts of others.

PREPARING A PORTFOLIO When the need arises to prepare a portfolio, such as for use in documenting that you meet standards or in your interview for a teaching position, you will be delighted that you did the advance work with your folio. Time always seems too short when a special portfolio needs to be developed. But when you do the folio work along the way, you will find it relatively easy to pull specific examples and documents to fit a particular job interview or to make final application for a teaching award. Also, when you develop the folio with the broader array of items suggested in Table 1.2, you will be able to prepare a higher-quality presentation of your accomplishments.

PORTFOLIO DEVELOPMENT TASKS To help you in beginning your folio, we have included at the end of each chapter several suggestions under the heading "Portfolio Development." These suggestions anticipate some of the items that you may need to include in future portfolio presentations; we have selected topics and tasks that are important to you at this early point in your teacher education program.

WORKING WITH COLLEAGUES, OTHER PROFESSIONALS, AND STUDENTS' FAMILIES

Teaching today requires working with colleagues in a number of activities. In the classroom teachers may team teach or plan with other teachers who are teaching the same grade or subject. Teams work together to plan curriculum and assessment activities. Teachers support each other through professional development activities and peer evaluations in a number of schools. Special educators, bilingual educators, school psychologists, and other professionals serve as resources to teachers in planning for individualized student learning as well as physical and emotional development.

Support personnel in schools include custodians, secretaries, principals, other administrators, and parent or community liaison people. These support personnel can be very helpful to teachers in maintaining a positive learning environment, understanding the community, and contacting families. They can serve as resources in planning events and making appropriate contacts in the community.

Teachers are also expected to work with families in support of student learning. Parental involvement is no longer limited to parent and teacher conferences scheduled periodically during a school year. Teachers and other school officials

Teachers often organize events for students to exhibit and demonstrate their work to parents and others.

contact parents to confer about students and to prevent potential problems that could interfere with learning.

PARTICIPATING IN THE PROFESSION

One of the rewarding aspects of becoming a teacher is the opportunity to work with other well-educated and highly dedicated professionals. There are many types of professional organizations and associations that teachers can join. In most school districts, teachers are represented by a teachers' organization or union that is responsible for negotiating contracts and setting working conditions. These organizations and associations have become major influences in the development of national education policy; in the determination of state policies, laws, and rules and regulations related to schooling; and (at the local level) in curriculum decisions and labor contract negotiations. At all of these levels, teachers are actively involved and are responsible participants as well as part of the membership that works with the resultant policy decisions and the curriculum products.

Teachers have opportunities to become involved in professional/specialty associations as well. These associations deal directly with developing student and teacher standards, the design of curriculum, innovation in teaching, improving instructional processes, and so forth. They provide teachers with the opportunity to work with other teachers who have like concerns and interests; they also enable teachers to participate in various professional leadership activities. Some specialty organizations focus on teaching specific subjects or grade levels such as science teaching, mathematics teaching, English teaching, reading, middle school, and early childhood education. These associations usually have national, state, and local chapters. Clearly, teachers profit from membership and participation in both professional organizations and professional/specialty associations. In this section we briefly describe each of these types of professional organizations and present a sampling of their activities.

TEACHER UNIONS Most teachers join local, regional, and national organizations as a bargaining force to improve working conditions. The National Education Association (NEA) and the American Federation of Teachers (AFT) are the major two unions for teachers. Some teachers have chosen to join other state or local organizations that are not affiliated with the NEA or the AFT but operate similarly to a union. The unions provide a number of services for their members, leadership on a number of professional issues, and a political presence at the local, state, and national levels. This section presents some background on the two major unions.

NATIONAL EDUCATION ASSOCIATION (NEA) The National Education Association is by far the largest teachers' organization, with 2.5 million members, including teachers, administrators, clerical and custodial employees, higher educational faculty, and other school personnel. Teacher education candidates may join the NEA's Student Program. More than a million teacher education candidates have joined the student group since it was formed in 1937. You may wish to explore the advantages of joining this organization on your campus.

The NEA is committed to advancing public education. The organization was founded in 1857 as the National Teachers' Association (NTA). In 1870 the NTA united with the National Association of School Superintendents, organized in 1865, and the American Normal School Association, organized in 1858, to form the National Education Association. The organization was incorporated in 1886 in the District of Columbia as the National Education Association and was chartered in 1906 by an act of Congress. The charter was officially adopted at the association's annual meeting of 1907, with the name *National Educational Association of the United States.*

The Representative Assembly (RA) is the primary legislative and policymaking body of the NEA. NEA members of state and local affiliates elect the

The National Education Association is the largest professional association for teachers in the United States; the American Federation of Teachers is another major teachers' union. These two organizations may decide to become one union in the future.

9,000 RA delegates who meet annually in early July to debate issues and set policies. The president, vice-president, and secretary-treasurer are elected at the annual RA. The top decision-making bodies are the Board of Directors and the Executive Committee. An executive director has the primary responsibility for implementing the policies of the association. Standing committees and ad hoc committees carry out much of the work of the association

Given its long history of advocacy of teaching as a profession, it should not be surprising to learn that the NEA sponsors many professional initiatives designed to disseminate best practices, facilitate teacher leadership, and empower teachers to reform schools. The NEA has organized to provide professional help in student assessment and accountability; professional preparation, state licensure, and national certification; and governance and member activities. The NEA also initiated in 1954, along with four other associations, the accrediting body for teacher education, NCATE, and continues today to provide leadership through appointments to NCATE's governance board and Board of Examiners, the practitioners who visit college campuses to apply the standards. These and other program areas offer an array of activities and initiatives to further advance teacher professionalism.

Members of the NEA receive its newsletter, *NEA Today,* and have access to numerous other publications and products, including publications that are available on-line through its professional library. Recent reports from the association address diversity, portfolios, student assessment, school safety, cooperative learning, discipline, gender, inclusion, reading and writing, and parent involvement. Handbooks by experienced teachers are helpful resources for new teachers.

AMERICAN FEDERATION OF TEACHERS (AFT) The second largest teachers' union is the American Federation of Teachers, with national headquarters in Washington, D.C. It was organized in 1916 by teachers in Winnetka, Illinois, to establish an organization to meet their needs and to create a strong union affiliation. The Chicago Teachers' Federation preceded the AFT, being established in 1897 and affiliating with the American Federation of Labor (AFL) in 1902.

AFT membership has grown steadily. The late Albert Shanker, who was the president from 1964 until his death in 1997, is given much of the credit for the growth and success of the AFT, including its national involvement in political discussions related to education. In 1965 membership was at 110,500; by 2000 membership exceeded one million. The organization of the AFT includes a president, numerous vice-presidents, a secretary-treasurer, and administrative staff. The membership serves on standing committees and council committees.

Since its inception, the AFT has boasted of its affiliation with the AFL, and later the AFL-CIO. The AFT has stressed that organized labor was an important force in establishing our system of free public schools and that it has actively supported school improvement programs. Affiliation with organized labor gives the AFT the support of the more than 15 million members of the AFL-CIO. Support from local labor unions has often worked to the advantage of local AFT unions in their efforts to gain better salaries and improved **fringe benefits** from local boards of education.

fringe benefits
Provisions for medical and life insurance, medical care, retirement, and/or professional education.

The AFT has diverse resources available to its members. Lobbying and political action activities support a number of professional issues in addition to bargaining issues at the local, state, and national levels. Its publications include the journal *American Educator.* Jointly with the NEA, the AFT conducts the QUEST conference to convene the leadership of both organizations to discuss professional issues. The Educational Research and Dissemination Program helps to make selected findings from recent research on classroom management and effective teaching available to teachers

STATE AND LOCAL TEACHER ORGANIZATIONS The state and local affiliates of the NEA and the AFT are the power bases of the organizations. Although the local association of teachers has the highest priority in the organization, its strength lies in the solidarity of numbers and services and resources provided by the state and its regional administrative offices. Local elections for the role of bargaining agent among competitive teacher groups remain the most important step in the process for organizing teachers in a district, whether or not the local teachers' organization is affiliated with a state or national group.

For the most part, teachers participate directly in the affairs of local organizations. Solutions to the problems at hand are primarily the concern of local teachers' organizations. The influence of these groups could be weakened without the support and resources of strong state and national parent organizations. At the same time local organizations sometimes become indifferent about their national and state affiliations.

Leadership at the national level views the problems and differences in beliefs among local organizations as a viable part of the democratic process rather than as divisive. From the many geographic locations, grassroots local teacher organizations may rise through the state associations to the national level or from the local organizations directly to the national level. Decisions related to national policy are then made by majority vote, with attention paid to input from all levels—local, state, and national. In some instances, local organizations have severed relations with their state and national affiliates when the members felt that their particular needs were not well met. Because the power of the state and national organizations is reduced somewhat each time a local organization withdraws from its state and/or national affiliation, state organizations are compelled to pay careful attention to the particular needs of local teachers' association affiliates.

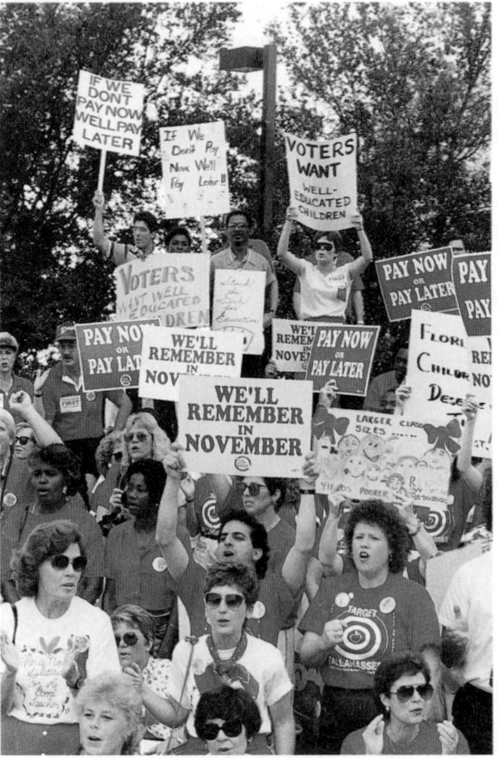

Political action committees of professional teacher organizations encourage teachers to participate in the political life of their local, state, and national communities.

POLITICAL ACTION Both the NEA and AFT have political action committees and governmental relations departments. Political action committees are engaged in action to elect political candidates who are sympathetic to education and teachers' issues. They monitor elected officials' voting records on education bills and analyze the platforms of new candidates. They actively participate in the election campaigns of the president, governors, and key legislators. Although the unions have traditionally supported Democratic candidates, they now are somewhat less partisan, endorsing candidates who support education and teacher issues that the association values, regardless of the candidates' political affiliation.

The state and national political action committees of the two associations have a common aim: to promote education by encouraging teachers to participate in the political life of their local, state, and national communities. These committees throughout the states are responsible for recommending political endorsements to their respective boards of directors. Union leaders believe that their political clout pays off for education. In terms of support of future political candidates, teachers' unions remain consistent in their claims that they will support those who seem to favor public education. Governmental relations departments monitor the federal administration's actions that affect public education, and they have been vehement in their opposition to funding cuts in public education programs.

PROFESSIONAL ASSOCIATIONS Teachers may join, participate in, and provide leadership for many professional associations that focus on their chosen professional interests. These associations are organized around academic disciplines and specific job assignments, such as science teaching, mathematics teaching, special education, school psychology, and reading. They also relate to broad-based curriculum movements such as writing across the curriculum, cooperative learning, and multicultural education.

Over 500 organizations focusing on some aspect of education exist in the United States. They typically have websites, publish professional journals, sponsor conferences, establish standards, and work to advance the field they represent. A number of them have reduced membership fees for college students. A selected list of professional organizations with website addresses is found in Appendix 1.2 at the end of this chapter.

PHI DELTA KAPPA INTERNATIONAL The professional organization Phi Delta Kappa International (PDK) is one of the largest and most highly regarded organizations for educators in the world. Today it is open to all educators, although in its earlier years women were not allowed to join. It publishes excellent professional material, including the journal *Phi Delta Kappan,* a newsletter, *Fastback* booklets on timely educational topics, research reports, books, and various instructional materials. The organization also sponsors many surveys, research projects, grants, awards, conferences, training programs, and trips. Local PDK chapters bring together teacher candidates, higher education faculty, and local teachers and administrators. You may want to consider a student membership and become involved in your local chapter. Visit PDK's website (www.pdkintl.org).

RELIGIOUS EDUCATION ASSOCIATIONS National and regional religious education associations are under denominational or interdenominational control. These organizations may represent sectarian schools attended by students who prefer them to public schools or secular private schools. Some religious groups or clubs supplement the public or private school program by offering educational activities for youth and adults. Examples of religious organizations include the Association of Seventh-Day Adventists Educators, Catholic Biblical Association of America, Council for Jewish Education, National Association of Episcopal Schools, Association of Christian Schools International, and Religious Education Association. Appendix 1.2 includes the website addresses of some of these organizations.

GLOBAL PERSPECTIVES: Education International

In January 1993 Education International (EI) officially replaced the World Confederation of Organizations of the Teaching Profession (WCOTP), which had worked vigorously to improve the teaching profession and educational programs around the world. EI has united more than 240 national educator unions and professional associations from around the world. This new organization brings together more than twenty million elementary, secondary, and college and university staff people. In the United States this merger brings the NEA and the AFT together under a world umbrella. The EI is focusing its efforts on improving the quality of education throughout the world, upgrading education employee working conditions and compensation, fighting for adequate educational funding, sharing curricula, safeguarding human rights, fighting for gender equality, and building stronger educational organizations.

CHALLENGES AFFECTING TEACHERS

The working conditions for many teachers have not always been good. Fortunately, they have improved measurably in recent years, and the following sections will show some of the ways in which these improvements are coming about. This information represents more good news for those who are preparing for careers in the education field.

SALARIES

Salaries vary considerably from state to state and from school district to school district. The average teacher salary in the United States in 1998–1999 was $40,582. Table 1.3 shows average teacher salaries in each state, beginning with the top salary of $51,584 in Connecticut to the low of $28,552 in South Dakota. As you can see from Table 1.3, salaries in most northeastern states are higher than those in other parts of the country. One reason for the higher salaries is a difference in the cost of living from one area to another. It is more expensive to live in a number of the northeastern states, Alaska, Hawaii, and large urban areas. However, cost of living alone does not explain the differences. Connecticut and school districts such as Rochester, New York, view teachers as professionals, have high expectations for them, support them through mentoring and professional development, use multiple assessments to determine teacher effectiveness, and pay salaries commensurate with those of other professionals.

TABLE 1.3 AVERAGE PUBLIC SCHOOL TEACHER SALARIES IN DECLINING ORDER BY STATE, 1998–1999

State	Average Salary	State	Average Salary
Connecticut	51,584	Vermont	36,800
New Jersey	51,193*	Tennessee	36,500
New York	49,437*	North Carolina	36,098
Pennsylvania	48,457	Florida	35,916
Michigan	48,207*	Alabama	35,820
District of Columbia	47,150*	Kentucky	35,526
Alaska	46,845	Texas	35,041
Rhode Island	45,650	Arizona	35,025*
Illinois	45,569	Iowa	34,927
California	45,400*	Maine	34,906
Massachusetts	45,075*	Missouri	34,746
Delaware	43,164	South Carolina	34,506
Oregon	42,833	West Virginia	34,244
Maryland	42,526	Idaho	34,063
Indiana	41,163	Wyoming	33,500
Wisconsin	40,657	Utah	32,950*
Ohio	40,566	Nebraska	32,880
Hawaii	40,377	Louisiana	32,510
Georgia	39,675	New Mexico	32,398
Minnesota	39,458	Arkansas	32,350*
Nevada	38,883	Montana	31,356
Washington	38,692	Oklahoma	31,149*
Colorado	38,025*	Mississippi	29,530
Virginia	37,475*	North Dakota	28,976
Kansas	37,405	South Dakota	28,552
New Hampshire	37,405		

*estimated

Source: National Education Association. *Rankings & Estimates: Rankings of the States 1999 and Estimates of School Statistics 2000.* Washington, DC: Author.

SALARY DIFFERENCES Each board of education is an agent of the state and is therefore empowered to set salary levels for employees of the school district it governs. Each school system usually has a **salary schedule** that outlines the minimum and maximum salary for several levels of study beyond the bachelor's degree and for each year of teaching experience. For example, a beginning teacher with a bachelor's degree may be paid $23,000, and one with a master's degree may be paid $27,000. Teachers with twenty years of experience may be paid $50,000 to $76,000, depending on the school district in which they are employees. Beginning teacher salaries range from $33,162 in Alaska to $19,146 in North Carolina.

salary schedule A printed and negotiated schedule that lists salary levels based on years of experience and education.

Some people may argue that teachers are paid less because they do not work year-round. However, they earn less than other professionals even when the number of weeks worked during a year is taken into account. Teachers between twenty-two and twenty-eight years of age earned an average $7,894 less in 1998 than other college-educated adults of the same age. By age forty-four to fifty, they earned $23,655 less than their counterparts in other occupations.[14] The difference is even greater between teachers with master's degrees and others with master's degrees; these teachers earned $43,313, compared to $75,824 earned by nonteachers. Salaries also lag behind those in other countries even though the workloads of U.S. teachers are usually heavier, as shown in Figure 1.11.

The relatively poor salaries of teachers can become a deterrent for those who would like to teach. Some people argue that raising teachers' salaries will make no difference in the quality of the teaching force. Experiences in states such as Connecticut are contradicting those arguments. Higher salaries are attracting teachers to the state even though candidates must meet performance assessments required for licenses at high levels. As a result, students in the state's classrooms are also performing at higher levels.

FIGURE 1.11 UPPER SECONDARY SCHOOL TEACHER SALARIES AROUND THE WORLD

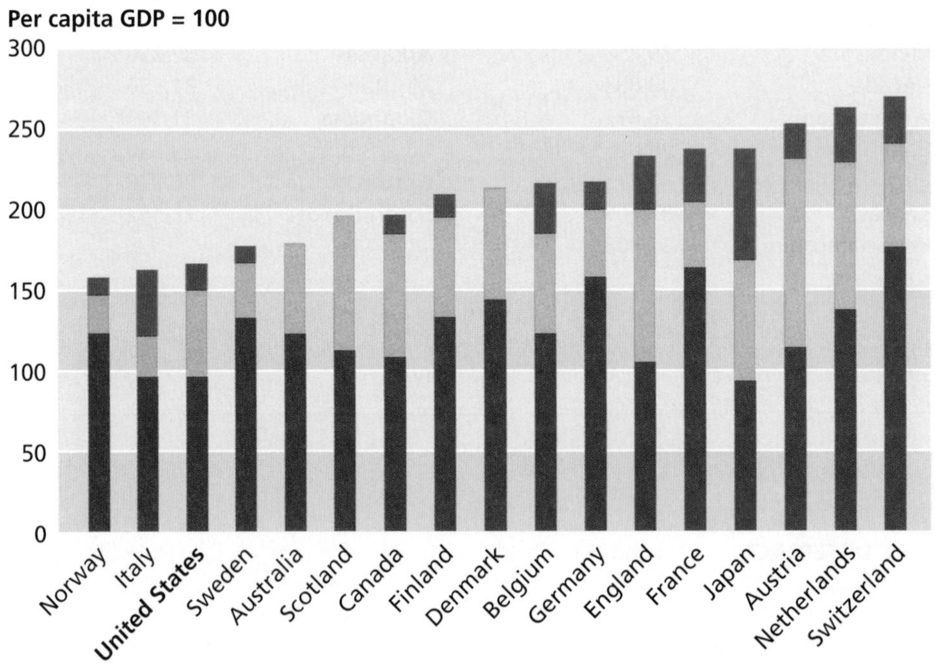

Source: F. Howard Nelson and Timothy O'Brien, *How U.S. Teachers Measure Up Internationally: A Comparative Study of Teacher Pay, Training, and Conditions of Service* (Washington, D.C.: American Federation of Teachers, 1993), p. 99. Reprinted from National Commission on Teaching and America's Future, *What Matters Most: Teaching for America's Future.* New York: Author, 1996.

The organization Recruiting New Teachers found that more than 75 percent of the public supported raising teachers' salaries. Over half of the respondents in this survey indicated that they would choose teaching as a career if they were guaranteed an annual income of $60,000. Further, they would recommend teaching as a career for members of their family if the salary was at this level.[15] These findings suggest that the pool of available teachers would be much larger if teachers' salaries were higher. With the pending shortage of teachers over the next few years, higher salaries will probably be needed to attract and retain the professionals we would like to have teaching the nation's children.

SALARIES AND INFLATION Although the average teacher's salary of $39,347 may sound good to a beginning teacher, experienced educators believe that their purchasing power has remained relatively unchanged over the years. The average teacher salary has increased from around $10,000 in the mid-1970s to nearly $40,000 today, but inflation has caused the constant-dollar average teacher salary to increase only around $1,000. Of course, teacher salaries vary greatly from place to place; in some school districts, salaries have risen considerably since the 1970s, even when corrected for inflation.

FRINGE BENEFITS Almost all full-time teachers receive fringe benefits that, when added to their basic salary, constitute their total compensation package. When you pursue your first teaching position, you will want to inquire about these benefits as well as the salary. Although the salary is usually of first concern to a teacher, the fringe benefits are equally important over the long term. Fringe benefits vary from school to school but frequently include some type of insurance benefits—hospitalization insurance, medical/surgical coverage, and major medical insurance. Somewhat less frequently, a teacher's medical insurance also includes dental care and prescription drugs; it may include coverage of eyeglasses and other types of less common medical services. Benefits often include a group life insurance policy as well.

Many school districts also provide some type of professional liability insurance for their teachers. In fact, some states require by law that all school districts do so. The liability insurance covers teachers and other educators who may be sued for not providing appropriate services or other abuse of professional responsibilities.

Full-time public school teachers should be eligible for retirement benefits as part of their total compensation package. These benefits vary from state to state. In some states teachers receive a combination of state teacher retirement and social security retirement. In other states a teacher's retirement may depend totally on a state program and be divorced entirely from the federal social security retirement system. It is sometimes possible for teachers who move from state to state to transfer their retirement benefits to the state in which they ultimately retire. A teacher's retirement package is an extremely important part of the total compensation package and needs to be well understood by everyone entering the profession.

School districts also provide special leave provisions for teachers. Leave policies should clearly indicate the number of days available with pay for personal illnesses, emergencies, and deaths. Some school systems allow a day or so of personal leave for special situations. Professional development leave may be available in some school districts to support the continuing education of teachers, but

Instead of moonlighting at a second job, some teachers earn extra pay by coaching school athletic teams or sponsoring student organizations.

the availability of such leave varies greatly from district to district. Some school districts make it very difficult for teachers to participate in professional organizations and state and national activities.

EXTRA INCOME Because of relatively low teachers' salaries, a relatively large number of teachers must seek extra income to support themselves and their families adequately. Extra income is sometimes available for taking on additional responsibilities within the school; these might include coaching athletic teams or sponsoring student organizations. Teaching summer school is another possibility for many teachers.

Although most teachers arrange for their salary to be paid in equal payments throughout the year, the summer months are often available for seasonal jobs such as working at youth camps, tutoring, and painting houses. Unfortunately, some teachers must still engage in **moonlighting,** or working a second job during the school year. The AFT found that 39 percent of its members were working second jobs to make ends meet. These teachers are more likely to be under forty years of age and have less than fifteen years of teaching experience. Nearly 90 percent of the moonlighters are white, and more than half are male.

moonlighting
Holding a second job, outside regular teaching hours, in addition to the primary job of teaching.

RECRUITMENT INCENTIVES The increasing shortage for teachers is leading to a number of innovative strategies for recruiting teachers. Job fairs are held in areas where there is an apparent surplus of teachers so that school districts from areas of shortage can interview prospective applicants. Technology is being used in innovative ways too. For example, the Clark County School District in Las Vegas,

Nevada, will ship overnight a video telephone to an applicant so that he or she can be interviewed without having to travel to Las Vegas. In March 2000 the federal government began offering teachers 50 percent discounts on vacant homes in economically distressed neighborhoods. This program, which has also been offered to police officers, gives teachers an economic incentive to live and teach in low- and middle-income school districts. At the time, Federal Housing Administration chief Andrew Cuomo stated, "A good teacher can make a great neighbor as a mentor, an inspiring role model, and as a living link between the classroom and the community."[16]

WORKING CONDITIONS

Almost everyone feels better about his or her work when the environment is supportive and conducive to high-quality output. The same is true for teachers and students. Like other factors in education, working conditions differ greatly from school to school. Within a single school district the conditions can change dramatically across neighborhoods. Some schools are beautiful sprawling campuses with the latest technology. In others toilets are backed up, paint is peeling off the walls, classes are held in storage rooms, and administrators are repressive. Most teachers who begin their careers in the second type of setting either aggressively seek assignments in other schools as soon as possible or leave the profession.

Teachers do work under very different conditions from those of most other professionals. Secondary and middle school teachers usually work with students in forty-five- to fifty-five-minute time periods with brief breaks between classes. Elementary and early childhood teachers are usually in self-contained classrooms in which they have few breaks, often having to supervise students during recesses. They have little time during the school day to work with colleagues or to plan for the next lesson or next day. Although teachers work in schools an average of 7.3 hours daily, teachers are involved in work related to teaching an average of 49 hours per week. In many schools teachers have limited access to telephones or computers for support in their work.

One of the problems is aging school facilities that desperately need to be replaced. Recent federal legislation is providing some support for replacement and renewal of schools. With the student population growing dramatically over the next decade, additional resources will be required to provide working conditions that support student learning. Public support will be needed to use taxes for these purposes.

BEGINNING AND CONTINUING A TEACHING CAREER

It is never too early to begin thinking about becoming licensed and finding a job. You can ensure that you take the appropriate courses and participate in activities that provide experiences for becoming licensed and being successful in your early years of teaching. One of the steps will be to collect and organize the materials that may be required for performance assessments throughout your teacher education program, job applications, and future renewal of your license.

BECOMING LICENSED

Teachers must obtain a license before they can legally teach in public schools. Each state determines its own licensure requirements. Although requirements may be similar from state to state, unique requirements exist in many states. You will need to check the requirements for the state in which you plan to work to ensure that you have completed an appropriate program and to determine the assessments that will have to be completed.

LICENSURE TESTS Most states require teacher candidates to pass one or more standardized tests at a specified level to be eligible for the first license to teach. Written assessments are required in forty-five states, the District of Columbia, and other U.S. territories. Forty-one states require basic skills tests; many institutions require these tests to be passed before a candidate is admitted into teacher education programs. Thirty-one states require candidates to pass tests in both professional pedagogical and content or subject-matter knowledge. The cutoff scores that determine passing are set by states and vary greatly. Teacher candidates who do not pass the test in one state may be able to pass in another state that has a lower cutoff score.

Assessments for initial teacher licensure are required in all states except Alabama, Idaho, Iowa, North Dakota, South Dakota, Utah, Vermont, Washington, and Wyoming. Ohio and Connecticut require a full range of assessments, including portfolios and classroom observations. Indiana, Florida, and Kentucky are developing performance assessments beyond standardized tests for use in making decisions about initial and continuing licensure. Oregon and Washington expect teachers to show evidence of positive effects on student learning in their first years of teaching to receive a professional license.

An increasing number of states are requiring future teachers to major in an academic area rather than education. Courses in education, field experiences, and student teaching or an internship are completed along with the academic major to become eligible for a license when the program is completed. Do you know the requirements for a license in the state in which you are attending school?

ALTERNATIVE LICENSURE Some states have developed alternative licensure opportunities for people who wish to become teachers. In some states anyone with a bachelor's degree in just about any major may begin teaching with some type of provisional certificate. These teachers may be introduced to teaching and learning in intensive programs of a few weeks before they are responsible for a classroom. Some school districts do assign mentors to these teachers during their first year of practice, and the teachers are usually required to take education courses to retain their licenses over time. These alternative routes to licensure have come under considerable criticism from teachers and the teacher education establishment because they do not recognize the importance of learning about teaching and learning and practicing under the supervision of an experienced teacher before beginning to teach.

Alternative routes are often designed to facilitate midcareer changes from other professions, such as business or the military, into the teaching profession. Candidates in these programs often participate in yearlong internships in which they are mentored by experienced teachers and work collaboratively with both

Volunteering to work with children or working as a paid teacher aide can give you valuable on-the-job experience.

higher education and school faculty in taking courses and working with students. These alternative route programs are available at many colleges and universities.

SEARCHING FOR A TEACHING POSITION

Teacher education candidates should begin thinking about employment early in their college careers. A helpful resource is the *Job Search Handbook for Educators* from the American Association for Employment in Education (www.aaee.org); it may be available in your college's job placement office. This handbook contains suggestions for preparing your résumé, cover letters, and letters of inquiry; it also provides excellent practical suggestions for improving your interviewing techniques. Information on teacher supply and demand in different fields is included in the handbook as well.

School districts would like applicants to present evidence that responds to the following questions. Portfolios with illustrations of performance are very helpful in this process.

1. Can the candidate do the job? Does the candidate have the necessary academic background? Can the candidate provide evidence that his or her students learned something? Does he or she know how to assess learning? Is he or she sensitive to the needs of diverse children? Can the candidate respond well to individual differences? How strong is he or she in regard to community activities?
2. Will the candidate do the job? What interview evidence does the candidate provide that communicates a professional commitment to getting the job done?
3. Will the candidate fit in? Is this candidate a good match for the needs of the district and the student needs as identified? How will the candidate work with other teachers and staff?
4. Will the candidate express well what he or she wants in a professional assignment? Does the candidate have personal and professional standards of his or her own?

5. Does the district's vision match the candidate's vision? Understanding the expectations of both the district and the candidate is critical if the candidate is to be successful.

Many state agencies that are responsible for teacher licensing and school districts have job openings listed on their websites. If you have a specific state and school district in mind, these job listings should be helpful in determining the possibilities and narrowing your search.

REMAINING A TEACHER

Teaching improves dramatically during the first five years of practice. Often teachers hone their skills alone as they practice in their own classrooms and take advantage of available professional development activities. A more promising practice is the assignment of mentors to new teachers to assist them in developing their skills during the early years of practice. Teachers who do not participate in an induction program, who are dissatisfied with student discipline, or who are unhappy with the school environment are much more likely to leave teaching than are their peers.[17]

Continuing professional development is one of the ongoing activities of career teachers. Often teachers return to college for a master's degree that may help to increase their knowledge and skills related to teaching and learning and the subjects they teach. They learn new skills such as the use of the Internet to help students learn. They learn more about the subjects they teach through formal courses, reading on their own, exploring the Internet, working in related businesses in the summers, or traveling. They ask colleagues to observe their teaching and provide feedback for improving their work. They seek advice from other teachers and professionals with whom they work.

Experienced teachers see teaching as a public endeavor. They welcome parents and others to the classroom. As cooperating teachers and mentors, they become actively engaged with higher education faculty in preparing new teachers. They become researchers as they critically examine their own practice, testing various strategies to help students learn, and sharing their findings with colleagues in faculty and professional meetings.

RENEWAL OF LICENSES Most states require teaching licenses to be renewed periodically. A professional license is usually not granted until after two or three years of successful practice. Some states require a master's degree; a few require the successful completion of a portfolio with videotapes of teaching that are judged by experienced teachers. To retain a license throughout one's career, continuing professional development activities may be required.

NATIONAL CERTIFICATION The ultimate recognition of teaching by one's colleagues can be gained by national certification through the process designed by the National Board for Professional Teaching Standards. Some states and school districts support teachers in this effort through financial aid for preparing for the assessment process; some will even pay the assessment fee, which is over $2,000. Nationally board certified teachers are often compensated above the normal salary schedule. Teachers who have participated in this process report that it is the best professional development activity in which they have ever participated, leading to improved teaching and student learning. The national board license must be renewed every ten years.

SUMMARY

TODAY'S TEACHERS

This chapter has briefly introduced you to the teaching profession. Although it sometimes appears that teachers are under constant public attack, most U.S. citizens believe that teaching is the most important profession in society. They believe that qualified teachers are critical in improving student achievement and that they deserve higher salaries than they are usually paid.

You are free to rise as far as your dreams will take you. Your task is to build the future of this country and of our world. You are our new global citizens.

Geraldine A. Ferraro

Critics of teachers and teacher educators often stereotype teachers as academically inferior to other college graduates, but recent research shows that secondary teachers score at about the same level on college admission tests as academic majors in the same field. Teachers are disproportionately white and female. The average age of teachers is older than it has been for the past forty years, which will lead to a growing number of retirements over the next decade.

The total school enrollment is projected to increase throughout the next decade. The growing number of students is likely to result in a teacher shortage unless many more teachers are produced and the large numbers of teachers who have been prepared, but are not teaching, return to the classroom. This need for teachers may lead to hiring more teachers who are not adequately prepared. This shortage will disproportionately affect students from families with low incomes in urban and rural areas, who often have to settle for new teachers and teachers without regular teaching licenses.

TEACHING AS A PROFESSION

Although teachers do not yet earn salaries comparable to those of other professionals, teaching is evolving into a full profession that sets its own standards and monitors the practice of its members. National accreditation, state licensure, and national board certification make up the three stages of a quality assurance system to ensure the preparation and licensure of competency. As members of a profession, teachers are expected to have dispositions that support work with students and families and adhere to the profession's code of ethics.

Successful teachers are reflective about their work, as shown in their ability to gather, analyze, and use data to improve their teaching. These teachers have a natural curiosity about their work and are continually searching for better answers to the problems they face. Beginning in their teacher education programs, teachers write in reflective journals, collect and organize information and data, and compile information from these folios into portfolios for specific purposes such as performance assessments and job applications.

CHALLENGES AFFECTING TEACHERS

Teachers face a number of challenges that most other professionals do not experience. For one, their salaries are lower than those of most other college graduates even when they are adjusted for the shorter working year. Teaching allows for few breaks during a work day, limited access to telephones and computers on the job, and little release time during the school day for professional development activities.

BEGINNING AND CONTINUING A TEACHING CAREER

Most states require teachers to pass basic skills tests, subject matter tests, and professional pedagogical tests to be eligible for a state license. In addition, teachers normally complete teacher education programs in four or five years and are sometimes required by the state to have a grade point average of 2.5 to 3.0. A few states also require the successful completion of portfolios or evidence of a positive effect on student learning before a professional license is granted.

DISCUSSION QUESTIONS

1. What are the characteristics of a profession? What are your arguments for recognizing teaching as a profession or not?
2. Why do shortages of teachers exist in some subjects and not others?
3. What should national accreditation tell you about your teacher education program?
4. What is national board certification and why is it important in a teacher's career?
5. Of what value are journals, folios, and portfolios in preparing to teach?
6. What support should school districts provide to teachers in the induction years to encourage retention in the profession beyond three years?

JOURNAL ENTRIES

1. Record your thoughts about the teaching profession—its strengths and weaknesses, your interest in teaching as a career, and your excitement and doubts about working in the profession.
2. Think about teaching as compared to other well-established professions such as law, medicine, and architecture. Record your thoughts and arguments about teaching being a profession.
3. After visiting the website of the professional organization that represents your teaching field, write your impressions of the organization, the benefits membership might have for you, and reasons for joining or not joining the organization now and in the future.

PORTFOLIO DEVELOPMENT

1. Your first folio development task is to find and organize the many materials, artifacts, and records that you currently have. If you are like most of us, the bits and pieces are stored in several different locations. Examples of term papers, transcripts, awards, letters of recognition, and journals for trips are scattered. Take some time now to find and begin organizing these materials. Organize them by categories such as those listed in Table 1.2. Keep in mind the ultimate purpose of developing this folio. At various points in the future, you will be drawing items out of the folio to develop a portfolio for completion of student teaching or to apply for a teaching position or national certification.

2. The U.S. Department of Education now publishes each year a national teacher education report card, which includes information about all teacher education institutions in your state. Review the performance of candidates on state licensure tests in your field at your institution and other institutions in your state. Reflect on why there are differences in performance across institutions and whether state licensure tests are an appropriate measure of teaching competence.

SCHOOL-BASED EXPERIENCES

1. Ask several of the teachers in a school in which you are observing how they are involved in their teachers' union and other professional associations. Analyze why some teachers are more involved than others.
2. Begin making a list of the teaching challenges that you observe as you visit schools. Discuss the challenges that you had not expected when you initially thought about teaching as a career and how those challenges are now influencing your decision.

WEBSITES

1. <www.abacon.com/education/johnson> The home page for this textbook contains a wealth of enrichment material to help you learn more about the foundations of education.
2. <www.abacon.com> The website for Allyn and Bacon, the publisher of this book and many other books in the field of education, includes online practice tests, answers to frequently asked questions, and more.
3. <www.nea.org> The National Education Association's website includes information about membership, services, issues, educational facts, meetings, legislation, and publications.
4. <www.aft.org> The website of the American Federation of Teachers includes information on membership, educational issues, meetings, legislative activities, and publications.
5. <www.rnt.org> The website of Recruiting New Teachers, Inc. includes information about becoming a new teacher and offers a number of handbooks for people who are considering teaching as a career, including *Take This Job and Love It! Making the Mid-Career Move to Teaching.*
6. <www.ncate.org> A list of institutions with teacher education programs accredited by NCATE and information about becoming a teacher are available on this website. It also includes links to state agencies and their licensure requirements.
7. <www.nbpts.org> The website for the National Board for Professional Teaching Standards includes information on the process for seeking national board certification as well as the board's standards, assessments, and publications.
8. <www.ccsso.org/intasc.html> This website houses the INTASC standards for general teacher education and specific subject fields that are being adapted as performance-based licensure standards by many states.
9. <www.nasdtec.org> Information on licensure requirements and state agencies that are responsible for teacher licensing are available on this website of the National Association of State Directors of Teacher Education and Certification.

10. <www.edweek.org> The website of *Education Week* includes statistics on education and articles from this popular weekly newspaper.
11. Several websites provide information about teaching opportunities, including <www.nationjob.com/education>, <www.Teachers-Teachers.com>, and, for overseas opportunities, <www.fowt.com>

NOTES

1. Recruiting New Teachers, Inc. *The Essential Profession: A National Survey of Public Attitudes Toward Teaching, Educational Opportunity and School Reform.* Belmont, MA: Author, 1998.
2. Ibid.
3. Ibid.
4. Carol A. Langdon and Nick Vesper, "The Sixth Phi Delta Kappa Poll of Teachers' Attitudes toward the Public Schools," *Phi Delta Kappan, 81*(8) (April 2000), pp. 607–611.
5. Recruiting New Teachers, Inc., ibid.
6. Drew H. Gitomer, Andrew S. Latham, and Robert Ziomek. *The Academic Quality of Prospective Teachers: The Impact of Admissions and Licensure Testing.* Princeton, NJ: Educational Testing Service, 1999.
7. Barbara A. Bruschi, and Richard J. Coley, *How Teachers Compare: The Prose, Document, and Quantitative Skills of America's Teachers.* Princeton, NJ: Educational Testing Service, 1999.
8. Debra E. Gerald, and William J. Hussar, *Projections of Education Statistics to 2009.* Washington, DC: National Center for Education Statistics, U.S. Department of Education, 1999.
9. National Commission on Teaching and America's Future. *What Matters Most: Teaching for America's Future.* New York: Author, 1996.
10. Recruiting New Teachers, Inc., ibid.
11. Linda Darling-Hammond, "Teaching for America's Future: National Commissions and Vested Interests in an Almost Profession," *Educational Policy, 14*(1) (January and March 2000): 162–183.
12. National Commission on Teaching and America's Future, ibid.
13. Recruiting New Teachers, Inc., ibid.
14. "Who Should Teach? The States Decide." *Education Week, XIX*(18) (January 13, 2000) pp. 8–9.
15. Ibid.
16. Richard Wolf, quoted in Paul Leavitt, "Capitol Roundup," *USA Today,* March 13, 2000.
17. "Who Should Teach? The States Decide," ibid.

BIBLIOGRAPHY

American Association for Employment in Education. *The Job Search Handbook for Educators.* Evanston, IL: Author, published annually.

Bruschi, Barbara A., and Coley, Richard J. *How Teachers Compare: The Prose, Document, and Quantitative Skills of America's Teachers.* Princeton, NJ: Educational Testing Service, 1999.

Langdon, Carol A., and Vesper, Nick. "The Sixth Phi Delta Kappa Poll of Teachers' Attitudes Toward the Public Schools," *Phi Delta Kappan, 81*(8) (April 2000), pp. 607–611.

National Association of State Directors of Teacher Education and Certification (NASDTEC). *The NASDTEC Manual 1998–1999: Manual on the Preparation and Certification of Educational Personnel.* (4th ed.). Dubuque, IA: Kendall-Hunt, 1998.

National Board for Professional Teaching Standards. *What Teachers Should Know and Be Able to Do.* Detroit, MI: Author, 1989.

National Commission on Teaching and America's Future. *What Matters Most: Teaching and America's Future.* New York: Author, 1996.

Recruiting New Teachers, Inc. *The Essential Profession: A National Survey of Public Attitudes toward Teaching, Educational Opportunity and School Reform.* Belmont, MA: Author, 1998.

U.S. Department of Education. *The Initial Report of the Secretary on the Quality of Teacher Preparation.* Washington, DC: Author, 1999.

U.S. Department of Education, National Center for Education Statistics. *The Digest of Education Statistics.* Washington, DC: Author, 1999.

APPENDIX 1.1

STATE TEACHER LICENSURE OFFICES

Alabama
<www.alsde.edu>

Alaska
<www.educ.state.ak.us>

Arizona
<www.ade.state.az.us>

Arkansas
<www.arkedu.state.ar.us>

California
<www.ctc.ca.gov>

Colorado
<www.cde.state.co.us>

Connecticut
<www.state.ct.us/sde>

Delaware
<www.doe.state.de.us>

District of Columbia
<www.k12.dc.us>

Florida
<www.firn.edu>

Georgia
<www.gapsc.com

Hawaii
<www.K12.hi.us>

Idaho
<www.sde.state.id.us>

Illinois
<www.isbe.state.il.us>

Indiana
<www.state.in.us/psb>

Iowa
<www.state.ia.us/educate>

Kansas
<www.ksbe.state.ks.us>

Kentucky
<www.kde.state.ky.us>

Louisiana
<www.doe.state.la.us>

Maine
<http://janus.state.me.us/education/homepage.htm>

Maryland
<www.msde.state.md.us>

Massachusetts
<www.doe.mass.edu>

Michigan
<www.mde.state.mi.us>

Minnesota
<www.educ.state.mn.us>

Mississippi
< www.mdek12.state.ms.us >

Missouri
< www.dese.state.mo.us >

Montana
< www.metnet.state.mt.us >

Nebraska
< www.nde.state.ne.us >

Nevada
< www.nsn.k12.nv.us/nvdoe >

New Hampshire
< www.ed.state.nh.us >

New Jersey
< www.state.nj.us/education >

New Mexico
< www.sde.state.nm.us/divisions/ais/licensure/index.html >

New York
< www.highered.nysed.gov/tcert >

North Carolina
< www.dpi.state.nc.us >

North Dakota
< www.state.nd.us/espb >

Ohio
< www.ode.ohio.gov >

Oklahoma
< www.sde.state.ok.us >

Oregon
< www.ode.state.or.us >

Pennsylvania
< www.cas.psu.edu/pde.html >

Rhode Island
< www.state.ri.us/manual/data/queries/stdept_.idc?id = 46 >

South Carolina
< www.state.sc.us/sde >

South Dakota
< www.state.sd.us/deca/deca.htm >

Tennessee
< www.state.tn.us/education/lic_home.htm >

Texas
< www.sbec.state.tx.us >

Utah
< www.usoe.k12.ut.us/cert >

Vermont
< www.state.vt.us/educ >

Virginia
< www.pen.k12.va.us >

Washington
< www.access.wa.gov >

West Virginia
< www.state.wv.us >

Wisconsin
< www.dpi.state.wi.us >

Wyoming
< www.k12.wy.us >

APPENDIX 1.2

PROFESSIONAL AND RELIGIOUS EDUCATION ASSOCIATIONS: A SELECTED LIST

American Alliance for Health, Physical Education, Recreation, and Dance (AAHPERD)
<www.aahperd.org>

American Association of Physics Teachers (AAPT)
<www.aapt.org>

American Comparative Literature Association (AGLA)
<www.acla.org>

American Council on the Teaching of Foreign Languages (ACTFL)
<www.actfl.org>

American Federation of Teachers (AFT)
<www.aft.org>

American Library Association (ALA)
<www.ala.org>

American Speech-Language-Hearing Association (ASHA)
<www.asha.org>

Association for Advancement of Health Education (AAHE)
<www.aahperd.org/aahe>

Association for Childhood Education International (ACEI)
<www.acei.org>

Association for Education in Journalism & Mass Communications (AEJMC)
<www.ukans.edu/~acejmc/STUDENT/PROGLIST.HTML>

Association for Educational Communications and Technology (AECT)
<www.aect.org>

Association for Supervision and Curriculum Development (ASCD)
<www.ascd.org>

Association of Christian Schools International (ACSI)
<www.acsi.org>

Council for Exceptional Children (CEC)
<www.cec.sped.org>

Education International (EI)
<www.ei-ie.org/main/english/index.html>

International Reading Association (IRA)
<www.reading.org>

International Society for Technology Education (ISTE)
<www.iste.org>

International Technology Education Association (ITEA)
<www.itea.org>

Interstate New Teacher Assessment and Support Consortium (INTASC)
<www.ccsso.org/intasc/html>

Modern Language Association of America (MLA)
<www.mla.org>

Music Teachers National Association (MTNA)
<www.mtna.org>

National Art Education Association (NAEA)
<www.naea-reston.org>

National Association for Bilingual Education (NABE)
<www.nabe.org>

National Association for the Education of Young Children (NAEYC)
<www.naeyc.org>

National Association for Gifted Children (NAGC)
<www.nagc.org>

National Association for Multicultural Education (NAME)
<www.inform.umd.edu/name>

National Association for Sports and Physical Education (NASPE)
<www.aahperd.org/naspe>

National Association of Biology Teachers (NABT)
<www.nabt.org>

National Association of Episcopal Schools (NAES)
<www.naes.org>

National Board for Professional Teaching Standards (NBPTS)
<www.nbpts.org>

National Business Education Association (NBEA)
<www.nbea.org>

National Catholic Educational Association (NCEA)
<www.ncea.org>

National Council for Accreditation of Teacher Education (NCATE)
<www.ncate.org>

National Council for the Social Studies (NCSS)
<www.ncss.org>

National Council of Teachers of English (NCTE)
<www.ncte.org>

National Council of Teachers of Mathematics (NCTM)
<www.nctm.org>

National Education Association (NEA)
<www.nea.org>

National Middle Schools Association (NMSA)
<www.nmsa.org>

National Science Teachers Association (NSTA)
<www.nsta.org>

Phi Delta Kappa
<www.pdkintl.org>

Teachers of English to Speakers of Other Languages (TESOL)
<www.tesol.org>

PART 2

CHAPTER 2
Diversity in Society

CHAPTER 3
Schools Facing Social Challenges

CHAPTER 4
Education That Is Multicultural

School and Society

Viewing Education through Sociological Lenses

In Part Two you will examine schools and society through the lens of sociology.

The big ideas that are addressed in the first chapter of this section are diversity, culture, and microcultural groups. They provide the sociological lens for examining differences and similarities of students in schools and the communities in which they live.

The second chapter in this section zooms in to examine the meaning of group membership in society, the changing family structure, the challenges of youth, the purposes of schools, and equality in education. One of the big ideas in this chapter is democracy and the equal participation of citizens.

The concluding chapter of this sociological review of education focuses on the provision of education that is multicultural. One of the moral and ethical responsibilities of educators is the provision of social justice to help all students learn.

The following questions will help you to focus your learning as you read in Part Two:

1. Why is culture important in knowing a group of people?
2. How do race, ethnicity, gender, and socioeconomic status interact in society to result in discrimination and inequity?
3. What impact do society and culture have on the education process?
4. What is the relationship between power and discrimination?
5. How do schools contribute to the socialization of children and youth?
6. Whose values are taught in schools?
7. What factors influence the subculture of a school?
8. What roles do diversity, equality, and social justice play in the delivery of education that is multicultural?
9. What are the purposes and characteristics of culturally relevant teaching?
10. How do schools interact with the culture of students and communities to promote or limit student learning?
11. What is the digital divide and why do educators worry about it?

CHAPTER

2

Diversity in Society

EDUCATION IN THE NEWS

Little Newcomers in a Strange Land

By Daniel Yi, *Los Angeles Times,* September 8, 2000

Kathleen Lui's elementary school students were tightly wrung coils of anxiety on their first day of school.

Most kids are. But these newcomers to University Park Elementary in Irvine, young students just learning English, had special reason.

New country, new school, new classmates, new teacher, new language. There is only so much pressure a child can take.

"You have something of a challenge," Ahiroshi Nagasaki, a UCI pharmacological researcher who moved from Japan five months ago, told his 6-year-old twins, Sayuko and Yukako, in Japanese. "But you have to go through it."

They didn't seem convinced. Neither did their classmate, Yasmin Seghatoleslami, 6. The Iranian girl clung to her mother's arm as her parents prepared to leave after the morning orientation.

"Mama, please don't go," she pleaded in Farsi. "I'm afraid."

Sepideh Seghatoleslami gently patted her daughter's dark hair, reassuring her.

Yasmin is not usually shy, the mother later explained. The family moved from Iran recently, and adapting to the new surroundings has been a challenge.

"She left her self-confidence in Iran," said Seghatoleslami, 30. "But this is good for her, to see new things, new cultures."

University Park Elementary gives a whole new meaning to "fitting in." More than a third of the school's 630 students speak a language other than English at home. The school district counts more than 50 languages among its pupils. Those who are not fluent enough in English spend a year in an English Language Development class like Lui's before they can join in the regular curriculum.

Lui teaches first-, second- and third-graders, and in 10 years she has seen almost the entire world pass through her classroom: Chinese, Czechs, Estonians, Finns, Iranians, Japanese, Koreans, Vietnamese, and this year a lively pair of Russian sisters adopted by an Irvine couple.

"It's amazing, isn't it?" said Lui, herself a picture of diversity. She is Japanese Hawaiian, and her husband is of Sicilian and Chinese descent.

On Thursday, she faced her new crop of students, 20 children ages 6 through 10: nine Korean speakers, seven Japanese, the Russian sisters, the initially reluctant Yasmin and a Mandarin speaker.

LEARNER OUTCOMES

After reading and studying this chapter, you will be able to

1. Describe culture and some of its characteristics.
2. Identify the dominant culture in the United States and explain its impact on people who are not members of the dominant culture.

(continued)

3. Understand three theories and ideologies that describe ways in which schools respond to students who do not have ancestral roots in Western Europe.
4. Identify microcultural groups to which students belong and indicate why some are more important to their cultural identity than others.
5. Describe the value of teachers' being bicultural or multicultural. ■

The United States today is diverse. More than a million new immigrants annually are introducing new religions, languages, and ways of thinking and acting to areas of the country that previously lacked the rich diversity of urban areas. **Diversity** is broadly defined to include class, ethnicity, race, religion, language, gender, sexual orientation, ability, age, and geographic locations. Educators will need to learn to incorporate the history, experiences, and perspectives of diverse groups into their teaching and to draw on students' diversity to help students learn.

Children learn how to think, feel, speak, and behave through the **culture** in which they are raised. Their parents, teachers, and other adults in the neighborhood and the churches, synagogues, and mosques they attend teach the culture and model the cultural norms. When schools use a different language or linguistic patterns from those used in the home, dissonance between schools and homes occurs. When students never see themselves in textbooks or stories, the culture of their families and communities is denigrated. As a result, students too often learn that their own culture is inferior to the official culture of the school. To teach effectively, teachers need to know the cultures of their students and be able to draw on their cultural histories and experiences to help them learn. Each of us belongs to a number of different microcultural groups within our culture. Not only are we African American, Navajo, German American, or Korean American; we are also males or females, heterosexual or homosexual, Christian or Buddhist, middle class or poor, young or old. Our behaviors in these groups are influenced by the culture in which we are raised and later live, and they may differ from one culture to another. For example, different cultures have different expectations for men and women that are influenced by ethnicity, religion, and socioeconomic status. Membership in these microcultural groups, the interaction across groups, and society's view of the group are critical factors in determining one's cultural identity. When we meet new people, we usually identify them immediately by their sex and race and maybe their ethnicity. We will not know their religion and its importance to them unless they are wearing clothing identified with a specific religion. We don't know the importance of their ethnicity, religion, language, or socioeconomic status to their identity. Therefore, we need to be very careful about stereotyping students and their families solely on the basis of factors that can be easily identified. Culture is far too important to ignore in providing education that serves all students.

diversity
The wide range of differences among people, families, and communities based on their cultural and ethnic backgrounds.

culture
Socially transmitted ways of thinking, believing, feeling, and acting within a group of people that are passed from one generation to the next.

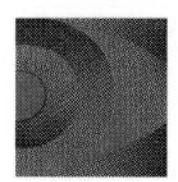

CULTURE AND SOCIETY

Society is composed of individuals and groups that share a common history, traditions, and experiences. Culture provides the blueprint for how people think, feel, and behave in society. A culture imposes rules and order on its members by providing patterns that help them know the meaning of their behavior. Members of the same cultural group understand the subtleties of their shared language, nonverbal communications, and ways of thinking and knowing. But they often misread the cultural cues of other groups, a problem that can lead to miscommunications and misunderstandings.

People around the world have the same biological and psychological needs, but the ways in which they meet these needs are culturally determined. The location of the group, available resources, and traditions have a great influence on the foods eaten, grooming and clothing patterns, teaching and learning styles, and interactions of men and women and parents and children. The meaning and celebration of birth, marriage, old age, and death depend on one's culture. Culture affects all aspects of people's lives, from the simplest patterns of eating and bathing to the more complex patterns of teaching, learning, and caring for those who are less fortunate.

CHARACTERISTICS OF CULTURE

Culture is learned, shared, adapted, and dynamic. People learn their culture through **enculturation.** Parents and other caretakers teach children the culture and the acceptable norms of behavior within it. Individuals internalize cultural patterns so well and so early in life that it is difficult for them to accept that there are different, but just as appropriate, ways of behaving and thinking. When people live and actively participate in a second culture, they begin to see more clearly their own unique cultural patterns. Understanding cultural differences and learning to recognize when students do not share your own cultural patterns are critical steps in the provision of an equitable learning environment. Therefore, it is important to learn about your own culture as well as others.

Culture is not static. It is dynamic and continually adapted to serve the needs of the group. Individuals and families adapt their culture as they move from one section of the country to another or around the globe. The conditions of a geographic region may require adjustments to the culture. Technological changes in the world and society can also lead to changes in cultural patterns.

DOMINANT OR MAINSTREAM CULTURE

The dominant culture in the United States is that of white, middle-class Protestants whose ancestors immigrated from western Europe. Today, the dominant culture is composed primarily of business managers/owners and professionals who are college educated.

The legal system, democratic elections, and middle-class values have their underpinnings in institutions and traditions of Western Europe. Historically, it has been the male members of the group who have dominated the political system and related government positions of authority. Policies and practices have

enculturation
The process of learning the characteristics of the culture of the group to which one belongs.

been established and maintained both to maintain the advantages of the dominant culture and to limit the influence of other cultural groups.

What are some of the characteristics of the dominant culture today? Universal education and literacy for all citizens are valued. Mass communications, which have been enhanced by technology and electronic networks, influence people's view of themselves and the world. A job or career must be pursued for a person to be recognized as successful. Fun is usually sought as a relief from work. Achievement and success are highly valued and are demonstrated by the accumulation of material goods such as a house, car, boat, clothes, and vacations.

Individualism and freedom are core values that undergird the dominant culture in the United States. Members believe that individuals should be in charge of their own destiny or success.[1] Freedom is defined as having control of one's own work and families with little or no interference by others, especially by government. Members of the dominant group rely on associations of common interest rather than strong kinship ties. They believe in absolute values of right and wrong rather than in degrees of rightness and wrongness.

Members of this group identify themselves as American. They do not see themselves as primarily white, Christian, English speaking, middle class, male, or heterosexual. Many middle-class Catholics and Jews share values and behaviors similar to those of the dominant group, as do a number of middle-class African Americans, Hispanics, Native Americans, and Asian Americans. Many low-income families also hold the same values, but do not have the income to support a similar lifestyle. The mass media and international communications systems are contributing to the development of a universal culture that mirrors the dominant U.S. culture. Some people worry that the positive aspects of other cultures are losing ground as television and movies teach a common culture.

microcultural groups
Distinct groups to which everyone belongs that are influenced by society and their own cultures.

MICROCULTURAL GROUPS

Cultural identity is not determined by ethnicity and race alone. As shown in Figure 2.1, individuals are members of multiple **microcultural groups.** They are female or male and members of specific socioeconomic, religious, language, geographic, and age groups. In addition, mental and physical abilities help define who we are. It is membership in these microcultural groups that determines our cultural identity.

FIGURE 2.1 CULTURAL IDENTITY IS BASED ON MEMBERSHIP IN MULTIPLE MICROCULTURAL GROUPS THAT INTERACT WITH ONE ANOTHER

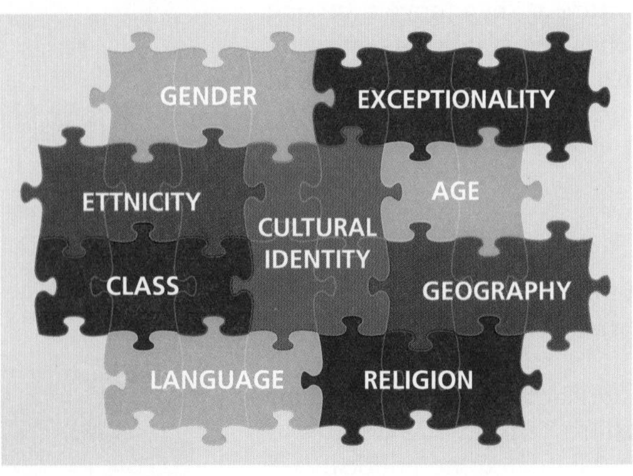

Students in U.S. schools are among the most diverse in the world. At the beginning of this century, one-third of the students in the nation's schools were young people of color. They will make up 40 percent of the school population by 2020 and half of the population by 2050. They are already the majority in schools in California, Texas, and the nation's largest cities. The native language of schools is not limited to English. Some school districts can identify more than 100 languages used in the homes of their students. Religious diversity has also increased beyond the traditional Judeo-Christian heritage as immigrants from Asia, Africa, and the Middle East bring their religious traditions to the mix. In addition, a greater number of students with disabilities are now active participants in schools and society.

The relationship of an individual's group memberships to the dominant culture may have a great influence on how individuals perceive themselves and are viewed by others. Because of the importance of power relationships between groups in discussions of diversity and equality, educators should understand how they themselves are centered in this dialogue. Educators need to know which groups they belong to and what influence those memberships have on their own identity. A critical self-examination may be helpful in the identification of otherness and difference that pervades a culturally diverse society. Later in this chapter we will look in some detail at several microcultural dimensions and their significance in U.S. education.

DIVERSITY AND EDUCATION

Many people in this country celebrate the differences among groups and the contributions that they have made to society. Others worry that these differences will lead to a divided society. The differences sometimes lead to misunderstandings, stereotypes, and even conflicts, yet members of diverse groups can also learn what they have in common, develop common interests, and learn to appreciate and value their differences.

Individuals from diverse groups have challenged the monocultural, universalist view of the world and society that has guided the country's laws and practices. They question the curriculum taught in schools, colleges, and universities. They ask why so many Hispanics drop out of school, why students in poverty attend dilapidated and filthy schools with few licensed teachers who have majored in the subjects they are teaching, why so many young African American men are in jail, why single mothers do not earn enough to stay out of poverty, and why so few students with disabilities are in general education courses.

Diversity raises concerns about equality and inequality in society and schools. Concerned educators are exploring the intersections of race, ethnicity, gender, and class as they relate to individual and group identity. They work to overcome the stratification based on race, able-bodiness, language, gender, and socioeconomic status that tracks students into special education, gifted programs, advanced placement courses, and low-level, uninteresting, academically unchallenging courses. Educators who believe that all students can learn understand that the cultural backgrounds and experiences of their students must be respected and reflected in all aspects of the education process.

As an educator, you will encounter during your career students from diverse ethnic, racial, religious, age, and economic groups and with different physical and mental abilities. The translation of this reality into educational practice leads to different strategies and outcomes. Ethnographic studies provide valuable information about how teachers and schools interact with students in the learning process. Researchers have discovered that schools often use teaching strategies

Today's classroom reflects the diversity in U.S. society. Students may look similar, but come from different cultural backgrounds and experiences in their lives.

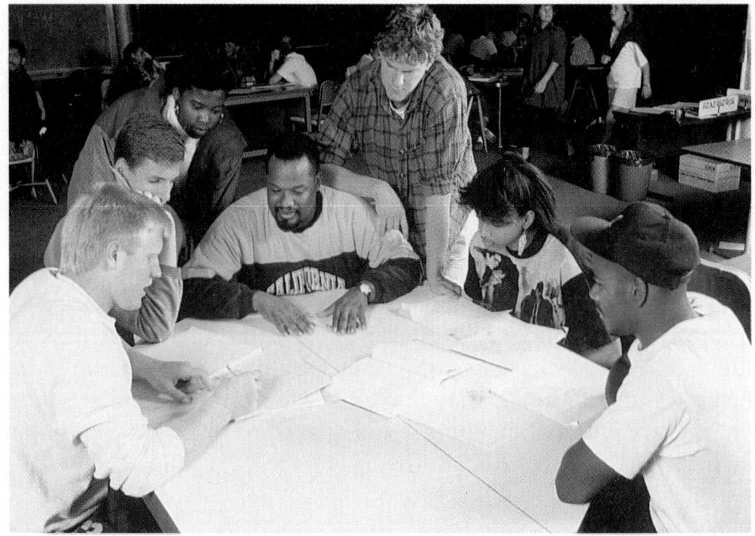

that differ from those that are effective at home, particularly as they relate to language and learning styles.

Over time, the relationship of groups to society has been described differently by sociologists, politicians, philosophers, and educators. These differing descriptions have led to the development of policies and practices that range along a continuum from promotion to condemnation of group differences. Assimilation, cultural pluralism, and cultural choice are the subjects of three prevalent theories and ideologies.

ASSIMILATION

Assimilation is a process by which an immigrant group or culturally distinct group is incorporated into the mainstream culture. The group either adopts the culture of the dominant group as its own or interacts with it in a way that forges a new or different culture that is shared by both groups. Members of a group experience a number of stages in this process.

The first step involves learning the cultural patterns of the dominant group. The speed at which group members become acculturated is usually enhanced by interactions in settings such as work, school, and worship. In many cases previous cultural patterns are shed—either enthusiastically or grudgingly—and those of the dominant group are adopted. Native languages and traditions can be lost within a few generations. These steps are usually required by society for an individual to attain some modicum of financial success or achievement of the good life in the United States.

The final stage of assimilation is structural assimilation.[2] At this stage members of the immigrant or culturally distinct group interact with the mainstream group at all levels, including marriage. They no longer encounter prejudice or discrimination and share equally in the benefits of society.

assimilation
A process by which an immigrant or culturally distinct group is incorporated into the dominant culture.

At the beginning of the twentieth century, the melting pot theory emerged as a description of how immigrants contributed to the evolution of a new American culture. This theory described the egalitarian state that is central to the national rhetoric. Many immigrants believed that the prejudices and inequities they had experienced in their native countries would not exist in the United States and that they would become valued members of the dominant society. Although many European immigrants did merge into the mainstream, people of color were prevented from "melting"—becoming structurally assimilated—by racist ideology. Racism has prevented Native, African, Hispanic, and Asian Americans from becoming structurally assimilated for generations.

Assimilation remains the guiding principle in most schools. **Acculturation,** or learning of the dominant culture through immersion, is the prevailing strategy. School success usually depends on how well students are able to adjust to the dominant culture that permeates the curriculum and school activities. Their own unique cultural experiences and patterns are not recognized, valued or used in the teaching and learning process.

The poor academic performance of many students of color and from low-income families is sometimes explained by a cultural deficit theory in which students and their families are blamed for their failures. A problem, this theory suggests, may be that these students have not been socialized to think and act like children of the dominant culture. Proponents of this theory blame the educational deficiencies of the home environment and such factors as single parents, teenage mothers, and inadequate child-rearing practices. The provision of equal educational opportunity is a policy response to this theory. Compensatory programs are offered to help students overcome both their educational and cultural deficiencies by making them more like students from the dominant culture. The perception exists that these families do not value education, as manifested by the lack of books in their homes or lack of participation of parents in schools. However, education is valued in most communities. The problem is more likely the lack of financial resources and inability to take off work to meet with school officials. Some teachers and school leaders have become very creative in overcoming these problems.

CULTURAL PLURALISM

Cultural pluralism exists in societies in which the maintenance of distinct cultural patterns, including languages, is valued and promoted. Groups may be segregated, but they participate somewhat equally in politics, economics, and education. In some cases groups have been able to establish and maintain their own political, economic, and educational systems.

Cultural pluralism in its ideal form does not exist in the United States at this time. Although diversity does exist, parity and equality between groups do not. For example, some Native American nations do have their own political and educational systems, but they do not share power and resources equally with the dominant group. Some immigrant groups choose to maintain their native culture, religion, and language. This goal is more likely to be attained if families live in communities where there is a fairly large concentration of others from a similar cultural background; Little Italy, Chinatown, Harlem, East Los Angeles, and Amish and Hutterite communities provide these settings. Often, culturally distinct groups have been forced into segregated communities because of discriminatory housing patterns.

The implementation of cultural pluralism in schools requires the recognition of the multiple cultures that make up society. Rather than the dominant culture's being centered in the classroom and school, the cultures of the particular group or groups served by the school are the predominant focus of the curriculum.

acculturation
The process of learning the cultural patterns of the dominant culture.

cultural pluralism
The maintenance of cultures parallel and equal to the dominant culture in society.

Identification with an ethnic group helps students sustain and enhance the culture of their group. However, students are sometimes caught between their ethnic culture and the dominant culture, leading to conflicts between students and their parents.

Examples include the Afrocentric and Native-centric programs that exist today in some urban areas and tribal-controlled schools. Also, some ethnic and religious groups have maintained their culture and history in private schools. The Amish and Hutterites, for example, operate their own schools to prevent the destruction of their cultures by the dominant group. Jewish and Islamic private schools promote religious study and practices; the rules of the religion guide student and teacher behavior.

Public schools generally teach only the dominant culture. The faculty might not represent the diversity of the students in the school and might have little, if any, knowledge about the cultures represented or personal experience with them. Students who are from low-income families or from ethnic, racial, religious, or language groups other than the dominant culture often do not achieve well academically.

A cultural difference theory helps explain the differential achievement of students of diverse backgrounds. Disjunctures in cultural patterns between the home and school may prevent academic success. Schools that focus only on the dominant culture expect all participants to operate as if they are members of the culture. This practice gives an advantage to students from the dominant group because the language and expected behaviors are the same as, or very similar to, those in their homes and communities. Students from other ethnic, racial, language, socioeconomic, and religious groups must reject their own cultural patterns or become bicultural to be successful at school. Some parents and communities have responded by establishing their own private or charter schools that reflect their own culture.

Schools in a culturally pluralistic society are staffed by a diverse teaching force that at a minimum represent the cultures of students. Teachers from the same cultural backgrounds as students should understand the language patterns of students. Teachers from different cultural backgrounds would be expected to know the multiple cultural patterns of communication and learning and be able to use them to help students learn.

cultural choice
The freedom to choose and adapt the characteristics from one's own and other cultures in developing one's own cultural identity.

CULTURAL CHOICE

Cultural choice is the freedom to choose and adapt the characteristics that determine one's cultural identity. As the twenty-first century dawns, cultural diversity in the United States is increasing. Some immigrants plan to assimilate into the dominant culture as soon as possible. They choose to adopt the new culture and shed the old. Others do not want to shed their unique cultural identity and patterns in order to be successful members of society. Many learn to be bicultural and bilingual, bridging two cultures and learning when it is appropriate to use the patterns of each. Others do not have a choice. Ideally, we could choose to assimilate, maintain our native culture, or become bicultural or multicultural and function effectively in more than one cultural group. Society would support these cultural choices and not value one choice over another or discriminate on the basis of group membership.

Unfortunately, this description does not match reality for large segments of the population. Most people of color, such as African Americans, are acculturated, but discrimination has prevented them from becoming structurally assimilated even if they choose that route. Strong identity and affiliation with their cultural group has been necessary as a source of solidarity in the effort to combat existing inequities and to obtain adequate housing and education. Although members of some cultural groups may be able to live almost solely within their distinct cultural milieu, most are forced to work within the dominant culture. Those who choose to assimilate might not be accepted by the dominant group but might also be rejected by the group into which they were born.

Equality across groups does not yet exist, but it continues to be a value espoused by society. Discrimination against groups prevents their members from having cultural choices. As the barriers to equality are reduced, there is likely to be greater individual choice and mobility across groups. We will move toward an open society in which cultural background determines who we are but is not the basis for discrimination. Cultural differences will be respected and encouraged to flourish.

Schools that value cultural choice consciously avoid the dominance of a single culture. Such schools integrate the contributions and histories of diverse groups—particularly those represented in the school, but not limited to them—throughout the curriculum. Bilingualism and bidialectalism prevail in classrooms as well as halls. Students are the center of instruction, and teachers utilize students' cultural patterns to promote learning. Students learn to operate comfortably in both their own and other cultures, including the dominant culture. Equality is manifested in the equal participation of all groups in courses and extracurricular activities, as well as in comparable achievement on academic assessments.

SOCIOECONOMIC STATUS

Most people want the "good life," which includes a decent job, affordable housing, good health, a good education for their family members, and periodic vacations. One way to estimate the good life is **socioeconomic status,** which is the primary determinant of the standard of living families are able to maintain. It also has a great impact on one's chances of attending college and attaining a job that ensures material comfort throughout life.

socioeconomic status
The economic condition of individuals based on their income, occupation, and educational attainment.

Socioeconomic status (SES) serves as a criterion to measure the economic condition of individuals. It is determined by one's occupation, income, and educational attainment. Wealth and power are other important factors that affect the way one is able to live, but these data are difficult to measure through census data. We often can guess families' socioeconomic status if we know such things as where they live, the type of car they drive, the schools attended by their children, and the types of vacations they take.

SOCIAL STRATIFICATION

Most societies are characterized by **social stratification,** in which individuals occupy different levels of the social structure. Wealth, income, occupation, and education help define these social positions. However, high or low rankings are not based only on SES criteria. Race, age, gender, religion, and disability can contribute to lower rankings as well. Although members of most ethnic groups can be found at all levels of the socioeconomic status scale in the United States, those from Western European backgrounds have a disproportionately high representation at the highest levels.

Social mobility remains one of the core values of the dominant culture. We are told that hard work will lead to better jobs, higher income, and a better chance to participate in the good life. We read the Horatio Alger stories of individuals who were born in poverty but through hard work became wealthy as a corporate president, prestigious publisher, successful writer, athlete, or entertainer. Although dramatic upward mobility continues to occur, the chances of moving from poverty to riches, no matter how hard one works, are rare. Individuals who are born into wealthy families are much more likely to become wealthy than are those born into families living under the poverty level. They are also much more likely to attend good schools, finish college, and find high-paying administrative jobs. They are raised with those expectations and usually meet them.

CLASS STRUCTURE

The combined wealth of the world's 225 richest people is the same as the annual income of the poorer half of the world population.

The State of the World Atlas, 1999

The population can be divided into distinct classes to study inequities in society as well as the characteristics of individuals and families at these different levels. One of the early categorization systems identified the population as lower, middle, and upper class, with finer distinctions in each of the three groups. The "underclass" is the label sometimes given to the portion of the population that lacks a stable income and is persistently in poverty.

Individuals who do manual work for a living are sometimes described as the "working class." When farm laborers and service workers are included in the working class, this group represents 41 percent of the employed population. Most members of this class have little control of their work. Many of the jobs are routine, mechanical, and not challenging. Work sometimes is sporadic and affected by an economy in which employees face layoffs, replacement by robots and advances in technology, part-time work, and unemployment as jobs move to locations with cheaper labor. Fringe benefits such as vacation time and health plans are often limited. The education required for working-class jobs is usually less than that for many middle-class positions, except for skilled and crafts workers who have had specialized training and may have served apprenticeships. Even these skilled workers, however, work as long and hard as others, often working overtime and holding two jobs to make ends meet.

social stratification Levels of social class ranking based on income, education, occupation, wealth, and power in society.

The middle class is large. Most people who don't perceive themselves as poor or rich define themselves as middle-class. Annual middle-class incomes range from $30,000 to $80,000, encompassing 38 percent of the population. It includes both blue-collar and professional/managerial workers. For most of the middle class, $80,000 would be the top of their earning potential, and this is often possible only because both spouses work. Families in this class have very different lifestyles at the opposite ends of the income continuum. The clerical workers, technicians, and salespeople in the group have less control of their jobs than the professionals, managers, and administrators who often supervise them. These workers tend to have somewhat better fringe benefits than do members of the working class. These professionals expect to move beyond $80,000 in their careers. Forty-one percent of the population now earns over $80,000 annually.

Many professionals, managers, and administrators receive incomes that are above $50,000, placing them in the upper middle class. They have become the affluent middle class, but they often believe that their condition is universal rather than unique. They often think that most of the U.S. population shares the same affluence, advantages, and comforts. A $50,000 salary in a neighborhood where most families earn over $150,000 seems low; in another neighborhood a family making $50,000 would be considered well off. The professionals are men and women who have usually had to obtain professional or advanced degrees. They include teachers, lawyers, physicians, college professors, scientists, and psychologists. Excluding teachers, most earn far above the middle-class median per capita income of $47,060. Successful executives and businesspeople are the managers and administrators in this group. These workers usually have more autonomy over their jobs and working conditions than working- and lower-middle-class workers.

The upper class consists of wealthy and socially prominent families. The income and wealth of members of this class are on a far higher plane than those of the other classes, and the gap is growing. For example, in 1980 corporate chief executive officers earned 42 times as much as their manufacturing employees; by 1990 they earned 85 times as much; and by 1998 the multiple had grown to 419.[3] These great differences contribute to limited interactions with members of other classes. Children in this class rarely attend public schools, which isolates them from other social classes. Probably the greatest assimilation of lifestyles and values occurs among members of ethnically and culturally diverse groups who attain upper-class status.

POVERTY

The U.S. government has established a poverty index that sets a conservative ceiling on poverty. Using this threshold, which is an annual income of $17,404 for a family of four, 35.6 million persons are in poverty—13.3 percent of the population. There are many myths about people who are poor. One is that they do not work. In reality, many work in full-time jobs that pay such low wages that they cannot pull their families out of poverty.

Children, the elderly, women, and minorities suffer disproportionately from poverty. The percentage of children living in poverty in the United States is more than double that of most other major industrialized nations, even though the United States has the highest gross domestic product per capita. Many industrialized nations have succeeded in reducing child poverty levels to below 5 percent.[4] This tragedy is reflected in an increase in the number of homeless families and students over the past decade.

Just because a child's parents are poor or uneducated is no reason to deprive the child of basic human rights to health care, education, proper nutrition.

Marian Wright Edelman

FIGURE 2.2 Children and Adults Living below the Poverty Level in the United States

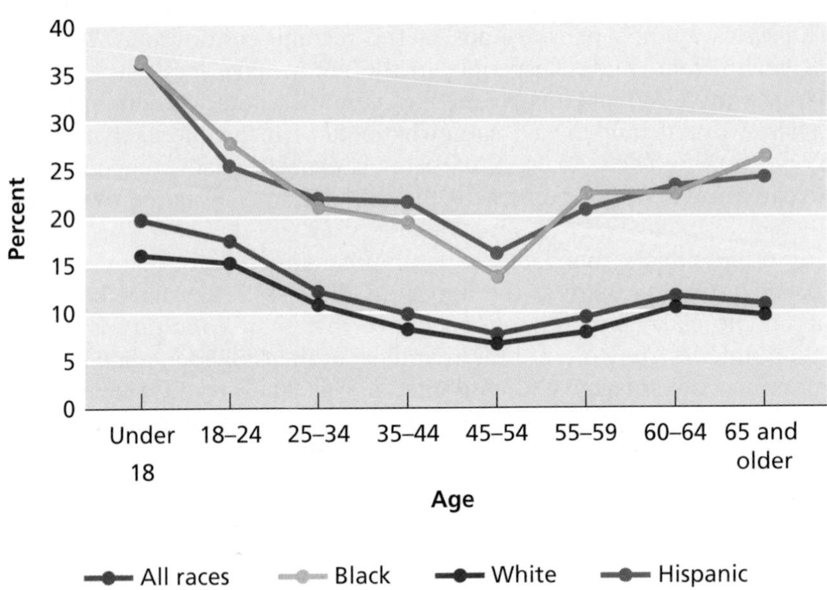

Source: U.S. Census Bureau, *Statistical Abstract of the United States: 1999.* Washington, DC: U.S. Government Printing Office, 1999.

FIGURE 2.3 Percent of Population in Poverty by Racial and Ethnic Group

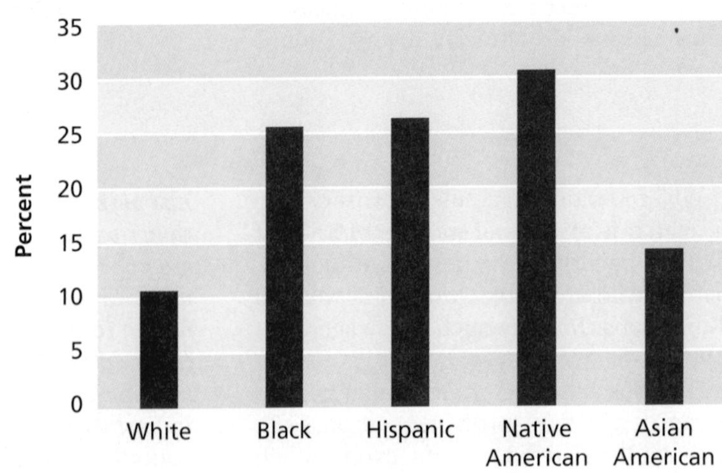

Source: U.S. Census Bureau, *Statistical Abstract of the United States: 1999.* Washington, DC: U.S. Government Printing Office, 1999.

Although 69 percent of the population living below the poverty level are European American, they represent only 11 percent of all European Americans in the country. The percentage of other racial groups in poverty is much higher, as shown in Figure 2.2 and 2.3. The median income of European Americans remains greater than other racial groups. African American families earn 61 percent as much as whites; Hispanic families earn 60 percent as much as whites. And although this income disparity decreases when one compares two-income families with the same level of education, it does not disappear. Women who work full-time year round also encounter discriminatory practices that keep their incomes at 74 percent that of men.

ETHNICITY AND RACE

National origin is an important part of identity for many individuals. Native American tribes are the only indigenous **ethnic groups** in the United States; therefore, more than 99 percent of the U.S. population, or their ancestors, came from somewhere else at some time during the past 500 years. Many people can identify a country of origin, although the geographical boundaries may have been moved since their ancestors immigrated. A growing number of people have mixed heritage, with ancestors from different parts of the world.

Although many people now identify themselves by their panethnic membership (for example, as African American or Asian American), race remains a political reality in U.S. society. It has become integrally interwoven into the nation's policies, practices, and institutions, including the educational, economic, and judicial systems. The results are that whites have advantages that are reflected in higher achievement on tests and higher incomes as adults. The issue of race encompasses personal and national discussions of affirmative action, immigration, desegregation, and a color-blind society. Race and ethnicity may be linked, but they are not the same. Both influence one's cultural identity and status in society.

RACE

Race and gender are among the first things one notices when one meets another person. Race provides "clues about *who* a person is."[5] These clues are often based on stereotypes against which people are supposed to "act out their apparent racial identities; indeed we become disoriented when they do not."[6] Race is used to explain differences in behavior, language, and socioeconomic standing. Ideas about race are created from one's own experiences in his or her racial group and with other groups. They are informed by reflections of racial differences in the news, in movies and music, and on television. And ideas about race are reflected in policies and actions of judges, teachers, legislators, police, and others who are in charge of institutions that affect people's lives.

Skin color is a signifier of race but does not capture the meaning of race. Many people have mixed racial backgrounds that place them along a continuum of skin color; they might not be obviously white, black, brown, or otherwise easily identifiable as one race or another. Historically, state laws declared the official race as nonwhite if a small percentage of one's racial heritage was other than white. The official message was, and continues to be, that white is the ideal and that anything else, including small percentages of other races, is less than ideal. This example is one of many ways in which race affects our everyday lives and becomes an integral part of our identity, whether we like it or not. Although race is no longer accepted as a scientific tool for distinguishing groups of people, it continues to be used to sort people in society.

People of color usually identify themselves by their race or ethnic group and are usually identified as such by others. They are confronted with their race almost daily in encounters with employers, salespeople, and colleagues or as they watch the evening news. Whites, on the other hand, are seldom confronted with their race; in fact, many see themselves as raceless. White has become the norm against which others are classified as *other.* As a result, many whites are unable

I have a dream my four little children will one day live in a nation where they will not be judged by the color of their skin but by the content of their character.

Martin Luther King, Jr.

ethnic group
Group based on the national origin (that is, a country or area of the world) of one's family or ancestors in which members share a culture and sense of common destiny.

to see that they have been privileged in society. Their silence contributes to the maintenance of racist society.

ETHNICITY

National origin is the primary determinant of one's ethnicity. Ethnic group members share a common history and a "sense of peoplehood, culture, identity, and shared languages and dialects."[7] They identify with the ethnic group and share "a common set of values, political and economic interests, behavioral patterns, and other culture elements that differ from those of other groups in society."[8] Identification with an ethnic group helps sustain and enhance the culture of the group. Ethnicity is strongest when members have a high degree of interpersonal associations with other members and share common residential areas.

Ethnic cohesiveness and solidarity are strengthened as members organize to support and advance the group, fight discrimination, and influence political and economic decisions that affect the group as a whole. In the 1960s these struggles with the dominant culture led to the calls for changes in institutions like schools, colleges, and government programs to support equality across ethnic groups. During this period, African, Hispanic, Asian, and Native Americans called for recognition of their ethnic roots in the school curriculum. By the 1970s European ethnic groups, especially those of southern and eastern European origins, had also joined this movement. Ethnic studies programs were established in colleges and universities to study the history, contributions, and experiences of U.S. ethnic groups that had traditionally been excluded.

ETHNIC DIVERSITY

The U.S. Census Bureau reports population data on the five racial and ethnic groups shown in Figure 2.4. Within each of these broad classifications exist numerous ethnic groups with identities and often loyalties that are linked to specific countries. Many families trace their heritage to specific countries (for example, Poland or Korea) and/or tribes (for example, Lakota or Ibo). Many U.S. citizens whose ancestors emigrated either voluntarily or involuntarily identify themselves as German, Vietnamese, Hmong, Croatian, Russian, Punjabi, Argentinean, Mexican, Lebanese, or Ethiopian American. Beginning with the 1990 census, people were asked to identify themselves by their ethnic origin. Sixty percent identified with a single ancestry, 30 percent with multiple ancestries, and 5 percent as solely American.[9] The 2000 census included a new category for individuals whose racial and/or ethnic heritage represents more than one group; people are no longer forced to choose one group membership over another.

FIGURE 2.4 PANETHNIC AND RACIAL COMPOSITION OF THE U.S. POPULATION

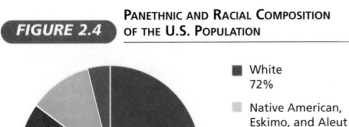

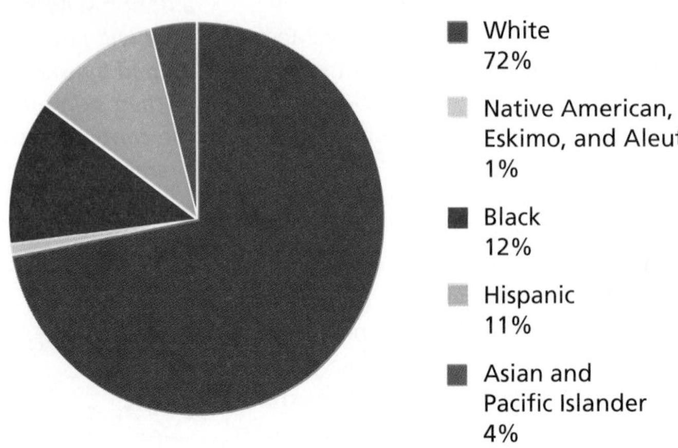

Source: U.S. Census Bureau, *Statistical Abstract of the United States: 1999.* Washington, DC: U.S. Government Printing Office, 1999.

The Census Bureau's broad classifications do not accurately describe the ethnic diversity of the United States. There are more than 500 Native American tribes. Asian Americans include recent immigrants and people whose ancestors immigrated from countries as diverse as India, Korea, Japan, and the Philippines. Hispanics include people from Mexico, Central American countries, Puerto Rico, Cuba, Spain, and South American countries. Although Africans continue to emigrate to the United States, most African Americans have long historical roots in this country; many have ancestors not only from Africa but from Europe and Native American tribes. European Americans range from Western Europeans who may have lived in the United States for several hundred years to those from Eastern Europe who immigrated in large numbers at the beginning of the twentieth century to recent immigrants from Russia and other former Soviet countries.

In describing the United States, many people proudly refer to it as being a land of immigrants who left their original homelands because of economic hardships or political repression. However, this picture is only partially true. The groups that are most oppressed in this country are those who are indigenous or whose ancestors entered the country involuntarily. Native Americans were here long before Europeans and others appeared. They suffered greatly as the foreign intruders took over the land, almost annihilating the population. The U.S. government admitted the near genocide of a people only in 2000, when the head of the Bureau of Indian Affairs apologized for "the agency's legacy of racism and inhumanity that included massacres, forced relocations of tribes and attempts to wipe out Indian languages and cultures."[10]

The ancestors of most African Americans were brought by slave traders as a commodity to be sold. They were not even treated as full humans until well into the nineteenth century. Not until late in the twentieth century did Africans begin to immigrate to the United States in any significant numbers. The Mexican Americans in the Southwest were inhabitants of lands that were annexed as part of the spoils for winning the Spanish American War; they did not immigrate. Today, many Mexicans would like to immigrate to this country but, prevented by immigration laws, cross the border illegally to obtain jobs and have a better chance for economic stability. However, illegal immigrants constantly face possible deportation, loss of everything they have gained in this country, and separation of children and parents or husband and wife.

Who can immigrate or be admitted as a refugee is determined by Congress. Immigration policies have prevented or severely limited the immigration of some groups while favoring others. For example, people with either Chinese or Japanese heritage have been excluded at different times. Individuals fleeing Communist regimes have often been granted refugee status, but others have found it very difficult to obtain such status when fleeing regimes supportive of the United States, even though those regimes were dictatorships with numerous human rights violations. Immigration quotas historically were heavily weighted toward Western Europeans; beginning in 1965, however, immigration became more open to people from other countries. As a result, the numbers of Hispanic and Asian Americans coming to the United States have grown dramatically.

Schools are early recipients of the growing number of new immigrants. Immigrants today are settling beyond urban areas of California, Florida, Illinois, New Jersey, New York, and Texas. States that have had limited ethnic diversity in the past—among them Arkansas, Iowa, Montana, and Nebraska—are becoming home to students from other countries.

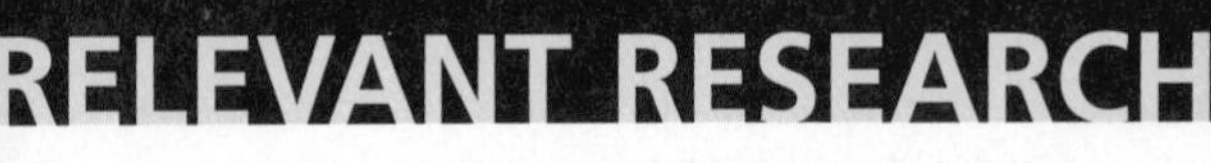

RELEVANT RESEARCH

Development of Racial and Gender Identity

STUDY PURPOSE/QUESTIONS: The question of how working-class white males and females construct their gender and racial identity was the focus of this study.

STUDY DESIGN: Lois Weis conducted an ethnographic study in a high school located in a city where the major factory had recently closed. She collected data from students, teachers, and other school personnel in classrooms, study halls, and the cafeteria, and in extracurricular activities.

STUDY FINDINGS: The study findings indicate that the vast majority of the young white working-class males in the study believed that they would have wives and families in the future. Their descriptions of females exhibited an assumed male superiority in which females were both "other" and inferior. Weis found that their male identity was "dependent upon the construction of women as unable to take care of themselves monetarily and as having full responsibility for the day-to-day activities of children." The school appeared to offer no "sustained challenge to the vision of male dominance."

The identities of these young men were also based on their construction of race. The goodness of white was always contrasted with the badness of black. Black men were constructed as overly sexualized individuals from whom white women must be protected. The white males in this study elaborated "their own sexuality in relation to Blacks. Black men and women [were] the foil against which they set up their own heterosexuality." On the other hand, white females did not develop their identities in relationship to blacks.

IMPLICATIONS: White working-class males tend to construct their sense of their own gender and racial identity according to their perceptions of superiority over females and persons of color. These white males set up negative stereotypes of these groups in opposition to their own perceived positive attributes.

Source: Michelle Fine, Lois Weis, and Linda C. Powell, "Communities of Difference: A Critical Look at Desegregated Spaces Created for and by Youth," *Harvard Educational Review* 67 (2) (Summer 1997): 247–284.

GENDER

Males and females are culturally different even when they are members of the same socioeconomic, ethnic, and religious group. The ways they think and act are defined in part by their gender identity. The two groups are often segregated at social gatherings, employed in different types of jobs, and expected to behave in a stereotypical fashion.

DIFFERENCES BETWEEN FEMALES AND MALES

Learning the gender of a baby is one of the important rites of parenthood. However, the major difference between boys and girls is the way adults respond to them. There are few actual physical differences, particularly before puberty. It is primarily the socialization process in child rearing and schools that determines gender identity and the related distinctive behaviors.

Some researchers attribute differences in mathematical, verbal, and spatial skills to different hormones that affect specific hemispheres of the brain. However, recent studies show that females and males are performing more alike, suggesting that the previously observed gender differences are not biologically determined. For example, there are no differences in quantitative abilities until the age of ten and then only slight differences that sometimes favor girls and sometimes favor boys in the middle school years. Males do perform better in high school, but the differences are declining as female students become more interested in mathematics. Gender differences in spatial abilities are declining, and one's abilities in this area can be improved with training. There no longer appear to be gender differences in verbal abilities.[11]

We know of no culture that has said, articulately, that there is no difference between men and women except in the way they contribute to the creation of the next generation.

Margaret Mead

By age two, children realize that they are a girl or boy; by five or six, they have learned their gender and stereotypical behavior.[12] In most cultures boys are generally socialized toward achievement and self-reliance, girls toward nurturance and responsibility. However, anthropologists have documented variations in the behaviors of males and females from culture to culture. In this country there are differences in the expectations and behaviors of the two genders that are rooted in different groups' ethnicity, religion, and socioeconomic level.

A major difference between males and females is how they are treated in society. Society generally places men in positions of superiority, as evidenced by their disproportionate holding of the highest status and highest-paying jobs. Many times this relationship extends into the home, where the father and husband may both protect the family and rule over it. Sometimes this relationship leads to physical and mental abuse of women and children.

Although 90 percent of all women in the United States today will work outside the home at some time, society's view of them as inferior has contributed greatly to the current patterns of discrimination that keep many women in low-prestige and low-paying jobs. The jobs in which women are concentrated are

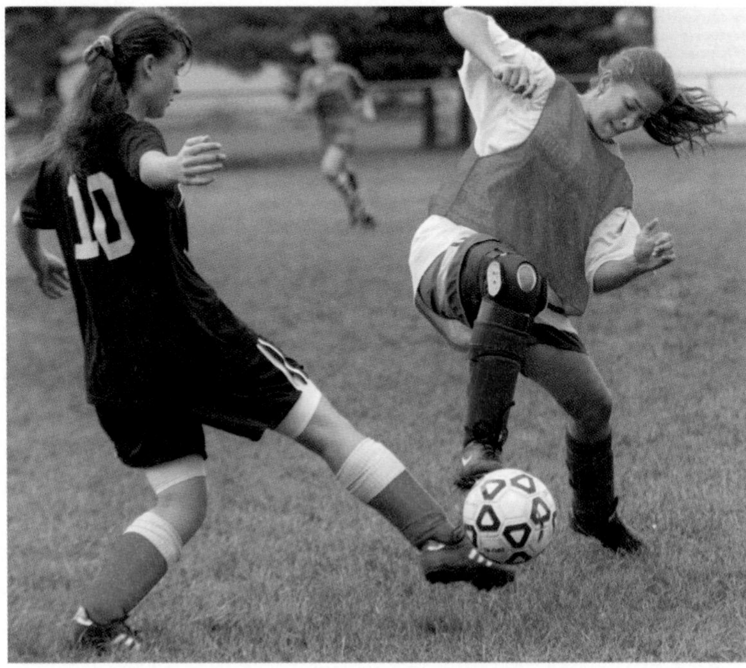

Title IX prevents discrimination in education programs based on sex. Schools must make provisions for girls and young women to participate in intramural, club, and interscholastic sports.

those that naturally extend their role as nurturers and helpers: nursing, teaching, and secretarial work. Job and wage discrimination is a critical issue for women, especially today when a large number of families are headed by women without the advantage of a second income. Women earn less than men throughout their life span, as shown in Figure 2.5. And families headed by single women are more likely to be in poverty than any other group; more than 35 percent of the persons in these families fall below the official poverty level. As barriers to professional education and employment are broken, the number of women in traditionally male occupations has increased. For example, the number of female physicians increased from 6.5 percent in 1950 to 26 percent in 1998; female attorneys and judges increased from 4 to 27 percent; and female principals increased from 20 percent in 1982 to 45 percent in 1998.

Young women sometimes appear ambivalent, especially in relation to education and family relations. Some undervalue themselves and become passive and self-sacrificing. This pattern may lead them into unwanted pregnancies and unfulfilling relationships. As a result, a disproportionately large number of these women drop out of school, limiting their ability to earn a decent income. Thus, they and their children are likely to be forced into poverty at least temporarily.

Schools often reinforce behavior that is stereotypically gender specific. Girls are expected to be quiet, follow the rules, and help the teacher. Boys and young men are expected to be more rowdy and less attentive. Many working-class males develop patterns of resistance to school and its authority figures because schooling is perceived as feminine and as emphasizing mental rather than manual work.

Many males are also not well served by the current socialization patterns. Some do not fit neatly in the dominant culture's stereotypical vision of maleness.

FIGURE 2.5 AVERAGE MALE AND FEMALE INCOMES BY AGE

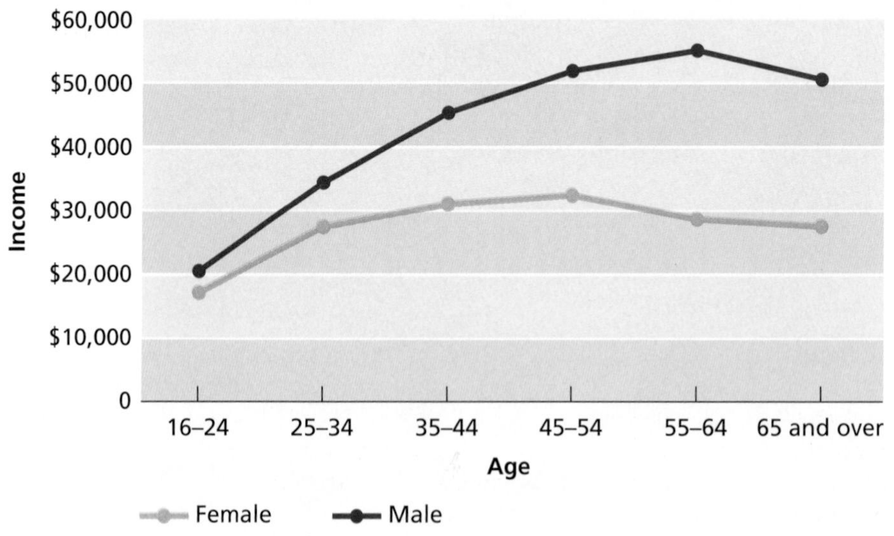

Source: U.S. Census Bureau, *Statistical Abstract of the United States: 1999.* Washington, DC: U.S. Government Printing Office, 1999.

Society has not been very tolerant of deviation from traditional masculine roles. Although much progress has been made over the past two decades, men still may be ridiculed for having "female characteristics" such as a high voice or nonaggressive behavior. Some men would feel more comfortable working as preschool teachers, nurses, or librarians—traditionally female careers—but may have learned that those jobs are inappropriate for "real men."

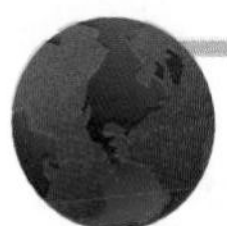

GLOBAL PERSPECTIVES: Poverty, Illiteracy, and School Attendance in China

Illiteracy among the Chinese is high. Nineteen percent of the 6- to 14-year-old children do not attend school; 56 percent of them are girls; 84 percent of the students not attending school live in rural areas. Families encourage young men to attend school and prepare for a college education; they will be expected to care for parents in their old age. The education of young women is valued less; they will eventually marry and move into another family. Sometimes, young people must work. In China's Hubei Province, for example, the population has completed an average of 4.5 years of school; 16 percent of the 8.5 million people living in the province are illiterate or semiliterate. Thirty-eight percent of the women in rural areas are illiterate, compared to 15 percent of the rural men and 6 percent and 19 percent of the men and women, respectively, who live in cities.[13]

In 1986 China passed a law requiring compulsory school attendance, but some rural families don't appear to know of the requirement. And the employers who hire the young people ignore it. The 1992 Law on the Protection of the Rights and Interest of Women has not been effectively implemented.

To encourage attendance by females and reduce their dropout rates, some school officials and teachers in Hubei Province have initiated visits to the homes of students, informing them about the compulsory attendance law and encouraging parents to support their children's education. Teachers and school administrators sometimes use part of their own salaries to pay the school fees for students whose families cannot afford to pay them. Some school districts have been able to waive these fees for students from low-income families. However, not all schools have taken on the challenge of increasing rates of attendance for either boys or girls.[14] Much work is left to provide equality for females in China and many other parts of the world.

SEXUAL ORIENTATION

Many cultural groups place high value on heterosexuality and denigrate or outlaw homosexuality. However, sexual orientation is established early in life. It is not learned in adolescence or young adulthood, nor is it forced on others by immoral adults. The majority of gay adults report feeling different from other children before they entered kindergarten.[15] It has been estimated that 5 to 10 percent of the population is homosexual.

Gays and lesbians often face discrimination in housing, employment, and many social institutions, as evidenced when schools and universities prohibit the establishment of gay student clubs. Some states still have laws on the books that make it illegal to engage in homosexual relations. Homophobia, as expressed in harassment and violence against gays and lesbians, is tolerated in many areas of the country. As a result of these prejudices and discriminatory practices, many gays and lesbians hide their homosexuality and have established their own social clubs, networks, and communication systems to support each other.

Isolation and loneliness are the experiences of many gay and lesbian youth. If gays and lesbians openly acknowledge their sexual orientation, they are likely to be harassed and face reprisals from peers and school officials. Structures within the schools do not provide them the same kind of support that is available to other students. Educators often know little about this group and have had few or no contacts with gays or lesbians who are out. Students in the classroom also may be the children of gay and lesbian parents. Without a better understanding of homosexuality, teachers may find it difficult to work effectively with gay and lesbian students or with the children of homosexual parents.

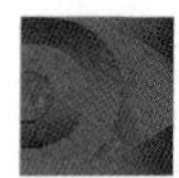

LANGUAGE

The Jewish people have been in exile for 2,000 years; they have lived in hundreds of countries, spoken hundreds of languages and still they kept their old language, Hebrew.

Isaac Bashevis Singer

Language interacts with our ethnic and socioeconomic background to socialize us into linguistic and cultural communities. Children learn their native language by imitating adults and their peers. By age five they have learned the syntax of language and know the meaning of thousands of words.

When there are cultural similarities between speaker and listener, spoken messages are decoded accurately. When the speaker and listener differ in ethnicity and/or class, miscommunication may occur. Even within English, a word, phrase, or nonverbal gesture takes on different meanings in different cultural groups and settings. Educators need to recognize that miscommunications between them and students may be due to inaccurate decoding rather than lack of ability.

LANGUAGE DIVERSITY

English is not the native language for over 30 million Americans. Spanish, Italian, and sign language are the most common languages other than English. Another complicating factor is that a growing number of new immigrant students enter U.S. schools with no or very limited school experiences in their home countries.

The length of time required to learn English varies. Most students become conversationally fluent within two or three years.[16] However, young people may require five to seven years to reach the proficiency necessary for success in academic subjects such as social studies and English. Students who are conversationally fluent may be immersed in English-only classrooms without appropriate support to ensure that they can function effectively in academic work. The result: These students may fall farther behind their classmates in conceptual understanding of the concepts being taught.

As immigrants assimilate into the dominant culture of the United States, their native language is often replaced by English within a few generations. The native language is more likely to be retained when schools and the community value bilingualism. As commerce and trade have become more global, professionals and administrators have realized the advantages of knowing the com-

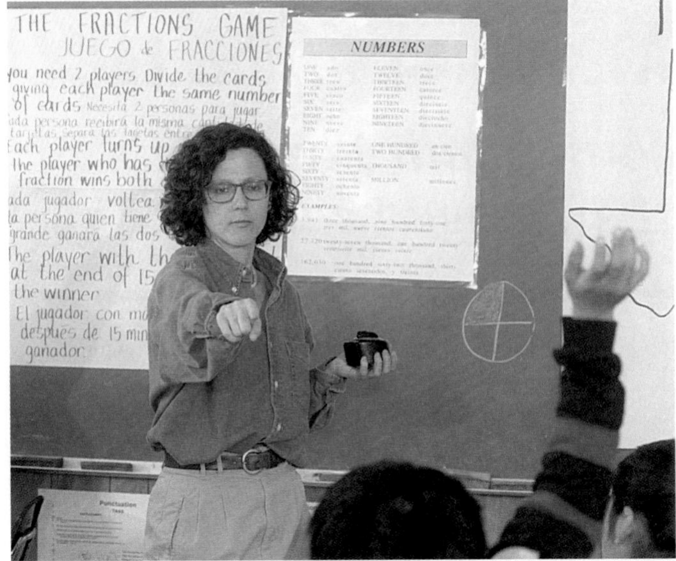

Bilingual education uses both the native languages of students and English in classrooms to ensure that students learn the academic concepts being taught.

petitor's culture and language. They are encouraging their children to learn a second language at the same time that many of our educational policies are discouraging native speakers from using two languages. The call for English-only usage in schools, in daily commerce, on street signs, and on official government documents highlights the dominance of English desired by some citizens.

American Sign Language (ASL) is officially recognized as a language with a complex grammar and well-regulated syntax. It is the natural language that has been developed and used for communication among individuals who are deaf. As with oral languages, children learn ASL very early by imitating others who use the language. To communicate with the hearing, many individuals who are deaf also use signed English, in which the oral or written word is translated into a sign. ASL is a critical element in the identity of people who are deaf. The language can be more important to their cultural identity than their membership in a particular ethnic, socioeconomic, or religious group.

DIALECTAL DIVERSITY

Standard English is the dialect used by the majority of dominant group members for official or formal communications. However, numerous regional, local, ethnic, and class (or SES) dialects are identifiable across this country. Each has its own set of grammatical rules that are known to its users. Although each dialect serves its users well, standard English is usually viewed as more credible in schools and the work world. Television news anchors, reporters, and talk show hosts use standard English. Although teachers may be bidialectal, most use standard English as the example that should be emulated by students.

Many Americans are bidialectal or multidialectal in that they use standard English at work but use their native or local dialect at home or when they are socializing with friends. Social factors have an influence on which dialect is appropriate in a specific situation. At one time, students were not allowed to use a dialect other than standard English in the classroom. Today, students are usually allowed to use their dialects but are encouraged to learn standard English, which

PROFESSIONAL DILEMMA

Communicating with Parents of English Language Learners

At least 13 percent of all people over five years old in the United States use a language other than English at home. Many parents who do not speak English fluently are reluctant to visit schools because of their limited English skills. The reasons for not meeting with teachers are not that parents do not care about their children and their education. This dissonance is further exacerbated by the inability of most teachers to understand the language and culture of parents. Parents often are embarrassed and misunderstood by school officials. They sometimes cannot attend school events or conferences because they are working and employers will not give them the time off. Or they may have young children at home who cannot be left alone while the parent goes to school.

How then can teachers communicate with parents about their children and their social and academic development in school? Teachers might know only English and the parents only Spanish, Farsi, French, Japanese, Hmong, or Swahili. Even if the teacher were to go to the student's home, communications would be limited and possibly misinterpreted. Written notes or phone messages in English would have to be translated by parents, or for them by the child, placing the burden again on the family.

Some schools have hired bilingual teachers and aides who can help bridge the language differences. When the number of bilingual education professionals is limited, schools may hire community liaisons who work with parents and teachers to bridge language and cultural differences. These community liaisons may accompany teachers on home visits and parents on school visits. These approaches may begin to affirm the diversity of a community and help it to move away from a cultural deficit approach in which students' cultures and languages are not valued and must be compensated. Students are the benefactors when families and educators work together to promote student learning and social development.

1. How will you communicate with parents who speak a language different from your own?
2. How will you learn about the resources available in your school district to assist you in working with families whose primary language is not English?
3. How can you ensure that you don't misunderstand parents when their language and culture are different from your own?
4. What responsibility do teachers have to understand and become comfortable in a culture other than their own?

will provide them with an advantage when they seek employment in the dominant culture.

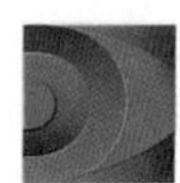

EXCEPTIONALITIES

More than twenty-five million people in the United States have a severe disability. Individuals with a disability are often labeled by society as mentally retarded, learning disabled, speech impaired, visually impaired, hearing impaired, emotionally disturbed, behaviorally disturbed, or physically impaired. Those with physical disabilities can readily be recognized by their use of a cane, braces, wheelchair, or sign language. Some individuals are labeled very early in their

Students with disabilities are usually mainstreamed or included in general education classrooms along with students who do not have disabilities. All students benefit from this arrangement, with improved outcomes for students with disabilities and an enhanced appreciation for diversity among all students.

school careers as mentally retarded or emotionally disturbed and are placed in special programs that may prepare them for self-sufficiency but sometimes limit their potential. Critics of labeling declare this system to be demeaning and stigmatizing.

Fewer than 30 percent of students with disabilities receive a regular high school diploma. Seventeen percent of the students who have been in special education take courses at the postsecondary level; another 15 percent enroll in vocational programs. Unemployment for persons with disabilities is higher than among any other group.[17]

Nondisabled people often react with disdain to individuals with disabilities and view them as inferior. But like all other individuals, people with disabilities want to be recognized as persons in their own right. They have the same needs for love and the same desire to be successful as the nondisabled. Instead, society has historically not accepted them as equals. Some individuals with severe disabilities are placed in institutions out of the sight of the public. Others are segregated in separate schools or classes. Too often, they are rejected and made to feel inept and limited in their abilities.

Schools, which should be part of the solution, have often contributed to the problems of students with disabilities. Most classrooms are not physically designed to accommodate the special needs of all students. Chalkboards are too high for students in wheelchairs. Desks do not usually accommodate wheelchairs, and special ramps and elevators are often nonexistent. However, special equipment such as computers and amplification devices can make participation in learning possible for many students who were not given that opportunity in the past.

INCLUSION

inclusion
The integration of all students, regardless of their background or abilities, in all aspects of the educational process.

Inclusion is the practice of fully integrating all students into the educational process, regardless of their race, ethnicity, gender, class, religion, physical or mental ability, or language. Students see themselves represented in the curriculum as well as in classes for the gifted. Historically, inclusion referred primarily to the integration of students with disabilities with able-bodied students in

DEBATE

Are Too Many Kids Labeled Gifted?

YES

Patti Bricker coordinates the gifted and ESL programs for the South-Western City Schools in Grove City, Ohio, and serves as president of the Gifted Coordinators of Central Ohio. An educator with more than twenty years of experience, Bricker is an active member of the South-Western Education Association. She can be reached at **Bricke1@aol.com.**

As a coordinator of services for gifted students, I spend a great deal of time meeting with parents who are upset that their child isn't labeled gifted.

I patiently explain that parents and teachers confuse well-behaved, good students with gifted ones all the time.

I tell parents that just because their daughter gets all *A*s, follows the rules, and achieves at an above-average level doesn't mean she's gifted.

I tell them that just as their son's academic weaknesses don't make him learning disabled, his strengths don't necessarily make him gifted.

Then I try to help them understand what giftedness means. I explain that a truly gifted child has the potential to demonstrate exceptional ability, ability that far exceeds what's typical for that child's age.

I explain that a truly gifted child thinks differently when it comes to problem-solving, applying knowledge to new situations, and making connections. Like a gifted athlete, a student gifted in mathematics, for example, can perform extraordinary feats when innate ability is coupled with appropriate nurturing.

I explain to parents and teachers that labeling children gifted when they're not can have serious negative consequences.

Some kids may get stuck with a label that will set them up for failure. Once labeled, the kids who can't do the work expected of gifted students may suffer a loss of confidence that makes it harder—not easier—for them to live up to their potential.

In addition, when students with a wide range of ability levels are included in classes for gifted students, the curriculum for those classes is diluted.

NO

Roberta Kaplan Braverman teaches gifted and talented students at the Laurel Hartford School for fifth and sixth graders in New Jersey. An NEA activist, Braverman is vice president of the New Jersey Association for Gifted Children. She can be reached at **BraveMOM@aol.com**

Too many kids are *not* labeled gifted. In fact there are too few students identified as gifted, and those who are don't get the services they deserve.

Today's gifted students are an endangered species, hovering close to extinction because some believe equal opportunity means everyone should get exactly the same education.

I say put the pleasing—but rhetorical—notion that "all kids are gifted" aside. Not all kids can be rocket scientists. Those who can deserve an appropriately challenging education.

Gifted students, by definition, represent the top 5 to 10 percent of learners. Traditional ways to identify gifted students—through test scores, demonstrated mastery, and nominations by peers, teachers, and parents—don't go far enough.

With training, educators can—and must—find the gifted students who aren't teacher-pleasers, the kids who act out because they're bored, and the females and minorities who are often just overlooked.

Once identified, this larger group of gifted students must have access to services that help them reach their awesome potential. That's not happening today for a few key reasons:

- Heterogeneous grouping, cooperative learning, dumbed-down textbooks, padded scores on standardized tests, and standards interpreted as ends in themselves have all contributed to trap gifted students in one-size-fits-all classes.
- Teachers, overwhelmed with the span of students' abilities in very mixed classes, are teaching below the middle. Gifted students get less teacher time and attention and are often recruited to tutor less able classmates. Many are bored.
- Classroom teachers don't routinely pretest and compact the curriculum for gifted students because they haven't been required or trained to do so.

YES NO

The result is one-size-fits-all service, which benefits the kids in the middle the most. When that happens, the truly gifted students are not getting the education they need and deserve.

Finally, if we place kids who aren't truly gifted into the gifted program, we mislead parents and teachers about the true definition of giftedness. That leads to a continued cycle of disappointment, disillusionment, and general distrust in the school system.

So what about the kids who are gifted in nonacademic ways? Since the advent of Howard Gardner's multiple intelligences, it has become popular to assume a "strength" equals "giftedness." This seems nonproductive. We're identifying too many students because the definition is too broad.

In Ohio, we're required to identify students as "gifted" in the nonacademic areas of creativity and visual and performing arts, in addition to cognitive ability and specific academic subjects. Students identified in nonacademic areas usually receive no gifted services. What's the point?

To fix what's broken, we need to streamline our identification process so that we're getting the very top students in particular domains. We need to train teachers to recognize and nurture exceptional ability. Then we can design quality programming to meet students' individual needs.

In the final analysis, it's in everyone's best interest to be realistic about giftedness, a phenomenon that defines just 3 percent of our population.

After all, how many Michael Jordans, Pavarottis, and Einsteins do you know?

Source: Are Too Many Kids Labeled Gifted? from *NEA Today,* January 1998, p. 43.

- And yet research shows that gifted students often know more than 80 percent of the content to be taught in an academic year—before it starts.
- As financing public schools becomes increasingly difficult, the academically gifted are seen as the least needy group. Budget cuts almost always eliminate programs for the gifted first.

The myth prevails that these students will make it on their own. The truth: We're in danger of producing a population of underachievers, performing far below their abilities, perhaps forever turned off to education.

To educate more gifted students better, teachers need training to recognize and work with this talented population. A top staff development priority: management skills to accommodate mixed ability classes.

In addition, schools need to make pretesting, pacing plans, enriched curriculum, and flexible schedules available for gifted students.

It's not important whether students are pulled out of or supported in regular classes by specialists, labeled or not labeled gifted. It's critical that those with academic talent get an appropriate education.

Developing leaders and problem solvers to guide us through the next century should be our goal. The notion that "too many kids are labeled gifted" is stifling our students—and our future.

WHAT'S YOUR OPINION?

Are too many kids labeled gifted?

Go to **www.ablongman.com/johnson** to cast your vote and see how NEA readers responded.

general education classrooms and schools. Inclusion of all students requires collaboration among the adults who work with students with disabilities. Team teaching includes a special educator and a regular teacher, often accompanied by a teacher's aide. The team individualizes instruction for each student. At times students with disabilities may be pulled out of the classroom for special services; but these special sessions should be limited and should be used only to meet complex individual needs.

Researchers are finding improved student outcomes for students with disabilities and nondisabled students who are in the same classrooms. Nondisabled students also receive positive benefits: Inclusion helps them to become more tolerant of others, to appreciate diversity, and to be more responsive to the needs of others.[18]

CULTURAL DIFFERENCES

Individuals with similar disabilities often find comfort and security with one another. Those who are hearing impaired share a language that is used by only a few of the hearing; the language provides them with a strong sense of community. In some cities many visually impaired individuals continue to live in the community near a school for the blind, where they can be close to potential work settings and provide support to each other. Individuals with mental retardation sometimes share group homes in which they can support one another and develop a degree of self-reliance. In these settings they establish patterns of communication and behavior that are natural to them, but may seem odd to nonmembers.

DISPROPORTIONATE PLACEMENTS

Some disabilities are linked to membership in one or more other microcultural groups. Individuals labeled as mentally retarded or emotionally disabled disproportionately are from low-income families. Low-income children are also overrepresented in classes for seriously emotionally disturbed students. Middle-class students are more likely to be classified as learning disabled. This pattern is also found in the placement of males and students of color in special education and gifted classes. African American and Native American students are overrepresented in many of the special education classes for mentally and emotionally disturbed students, as are males in general. On the other hand, Hispanic, African, and Native American students are underrepresented in gifted and talented programs. Educators need to monitor the reasons for their referrals of students to be tested for placement in these classes and provide equity in the delivery of education services.

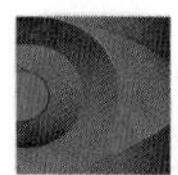

RELIGION

Religion can have a great influence on the values and lifestyles of families and can play an important role in the socialization of children and young people. Religious doctrines and practices often guide beliefs about the roles of males and females. They also provide guidance regarding birth rates, birth control, child rearing, friendships, and political attitudes.

By age five, children are able to generally identify their family's religious affiliation. Although 88 percent of the population regard their religious beliefs as very or fairly important; less than half attend a religious service on a weekly basis.[19] However, strong religious perspectives are reflected in the daily lives of many families.

RELIGIOUS PLURALISM

Religious pluralism flourishes in this country. There are 1,600 to 2,000 different religious groups in the United States today.[20] Members of religions other than those with a Judeo-Christian heritage are increasing as more immigrants arrive from Asia and the Middle East. Other families declare themselves atheists or simply do not participate in an organized religion. Still others live in cults that are established to promote and maintain a religious "calling." Some religious groups believe that their religion is the only correct and legitimate view of the world. Other groups recognize that the differences have grown out of different historical experiences and accept the validity of diverse groups. At the same time, every major religion endorses justice, love, and compassion as virtues that most individuals and nations say they are trying to achieve.[21]

Public schools cannot advance a religion, but neither can religion be ignored in the curriculum. Diverse religious beliefs should be acknowledged and respected in classrooms and schools.

Although they are not as dominant as earlier in U.S. history, Protestants are still in the majority with 59 percent of the population. Two percent of the population is Jewish, and 27 percent is Catholic. Eight percent do not indicate a preference. Within each of the major religious groups, there are distinct denominations and sects that have the same general history but may differ greatly in their beliefs and perspectives on the correct and appropriate way to live. These Western religions are compatible with the values of the dominant culture; they usually promote patriotism and emphasize individual control of life.

With the influx of immigrants from Asia, Africa, and the Middle East over the past few decades, religious diversity among the population has increased further with the introduction of non-Western religions such as Islam, Hinduism, and Buddhism. The interaction of these faiths with Western religions and their impact on mainstream society have yet to be determined. In the meantime students from diverse religious backgrounds will appear in classrooms. Teachers will need to learn to respect these differences if they are going to serve the students and community well.

Some religious groups, such as the Amish and Hutterites, are very closed. They establish their own communities and schools to help maintain the religion, foster mutual support, and develop group cohesiveness. Members of groups such as the Mormons promote primary relationships and interactions with other members of the same faith. Most social activities are linked to religion, and institutions have been developed to reflect and support the religious beliefs. In many rural areas the church is the center of most social and community activities. Many religions expect their members to spend much of their nonworking hours in church and charity activities. For many people religion is the essential element that determines their cultural identity.

RELIGION IN SCHOOLS

The First Amendment of the U.S. Constitution, which requires the separation of church and state, is a cornerstone of American democracy. When it comes to schools, however, there is disagreement about the meaning of the amendment. Public schools cannot advance a religion, but they also cannot inhibit religion. While schools must be neutral to religion, their policies and practices must protect the religious liberty rights of students. Religion cannot be ignored in the curriculum; it should be acknowledged and taught about when appropriate.

Families appear satisfied with schools when they reflect the values that are important in their religion. However, schools may be attacked when the curriculum, assigned readings, holidays, school convocations, and graduation exercises are perceived to be in conflict with religious values. Many court cases over the past century have helped to sort out these issues.

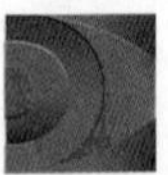

GEOGRAPHY

Communities and their schools differ from one region of the United States to another. Children and families may suffer culture shock in moving from one region to another. People behave differently, dress differently, and like different things even if they are from the same religious and ethnic backgrounds.

Over the past thirty years, many individuals and families have migrated from the Northeast and Midwest to states in the South and West. By 2010 60 percent of the U.S. population will live in the South and West, compared to 48 percent in 1970. One-fourth of the population will live in California, Florida, and Texas alone. The population in rural areas of the upper Midwest is currently older than in other parts of the country; but by 2010 one-fifth of Florida's population will be over sixty-five years old, and 15 percent of the population in Arizona, Arkansas, Pennsylvania, and West Virginia will be retired.[22]

An examination of differences among rural, suburban, and urban communities captures some of the geographic variation. However, differences among communities are also found as one crosses the Northwest, Southwest, Midwest, South, and Northeast. Within these regions states have their own cultural uniqueness. The geography of a state like Colorado, for example, tends to promote the development of different cultural patterns among populations in the flat farmlands, urban centers, and mountains.

RURAL COMMUNITIES

Rural schools are often the center of rural life. Values tend to be conservative, and the immediate rural family tends to remain a cohesive unit. Schoolchildren may travel long distances to school, and social interactions at school provide community links beyond family. By urban and suburban standards, rural families live long distances from one another. To the rural family, however, the distances are not great, and there is a feeling of neighborliness. The social structure is less stratified than in more populous geographical areas, and everyone tends to know everyone else.

Workers in rural areas generally are poorly paid for their work, earning about three-fourths of the wages paid in urban areas. Although housing costs may be lower, other expenses are not much different. As a result, 17 percent of the rural population live in poverty,[23] although the rural poor are invisible to most people. Poverty is disproportionately high on Native American reservations but also exists on the Midwestern plains, Western ranches, and farms across the country.

Employment in manufacturing is limited in rural areas. However, increasing numbers of urban and suburban dwellers are choosing to live in the country and commute to their employment in the more populous metropolitan areas. Those who have settled in the rural areas are generally young and well educated. They are fleeing the complexities of city life to acquire self-reliance and self-confidence, to return to a physically healthier environment, or simply to be able to own an affordable home. In some instances this exodus to the country has

Children in farming communities usually experience aspects of life that are foreign to most city and suburban students.

caused problems for rural schools, because the newcomers' values have clashed with those of the rural community. Family living habits and expectations for school programs differ, and some newcomers demand increased social services. In many rural communities it takes a considerable length of time for newcomers to be accepted into the social structure.

Despite the pivotal role of rural schools in rural life, these schools face real difficulties. Too often there are teacher shortages that result in the staffing of schools by teachers without a license or with limited academic background in the subject being taught. Teachers in rural areas sometimes feel isolated, especially if they are not from the area. As ethnic diversity increases in these areas, teachers will be confronted with cultures and languages to which they may have had little or no exposure.

SUBURBAN COMMUNITIES

Nearly half of the U.S. population now lives in the suburbs. An increasing number of households will consist of retirees and owners of vacation homes. The suburban population has become more diverse as middle-class families of color have moved away from cities. It is becoming even more ethnically and linguistically diverse as new immigrants settle in the suburbs. The most dramatic change in the suburbs, however, is that poverty now exists there as well as in cities and rural areas. The National Center for Children in Poverty reports that 20 percent of suburban children under six years old live in families with incomes below the poverty level.

Suburbs are characterized by single-family homes, shopping centers, and space for parks and recreation activities. Funding for schools has traditionally been better in the suburbs than in other areas. As a result, most suburban schools are in good condition; some boast sprawling, beautiful, and technologically advanced campuses. Teachers are licensed and generally teach the subjects that they are qualified to teach. Students outperform their rural and urban counterparts on achievement tests, and more suburban students than students from other areas attend college. Safety is usually not a concern for students, parents, or teachers. With changing demographics in the suburbs, however, these conditions may begin to change—particularly in suburban areas close to major cities.

Suburban taxpayers sometimes are unwilling to pay adequately for the education of children in poverty. Retirees sometimes fight school bond issues that are needed to support public education. Already a growing number of middle- and upper-middle-class parents in the suburbs are choosing private schools.[24]

URBAN COMMUNITIES

Urban areas are usually rich in educational and entertainment resources such as libraries, museums, theaters, professional sports, colleges, and universities. The urban population is ethnically and racially diverse, although some residential areas remain segregated. In many cities people of color constitute the majority of the urban population. The foreign-born population is larger in cities than the national average of 7.9 percent: Foreign-born people are 59.7 percent of the population in Miami, 38.4 percent in Los Angeles, and 28.4 percent in New York City.[25]

Class differences are evident across urban neighborhoods. Low-income families and families in poverty are often isolated in neighborhoods with few resources; inadequate police protection; and poorly maintained parks, schools, and public areas. Children who live in an underserved section of a city are often restricted by it, having few contacts outside the area. Their opportunities to participate in the educational and entertainment resources of the city are very limited.

Although there are many single-family homes in a city, many children live in multifamily condominiums, apartments, and projects. Some city residents live comfortably by U.S. standards, but a disproportionate number of urban residents are economically oppressed. One of the reasons for high poverty rates among most groups in cities is the lack of academic credentials that qualify workers for better-paying jobs. The jobs that in other communities may be open to teenagers are filled by adults for whom no other options are available. The result is high unemployment among youth from oppressed groups. Crime rates in many low-income neighborhoods exceed the national average. There are higher infant mortality rates, lower access to adequate health care, and five times as many AIDS cases[26]—all factors that are common when people have inadequate incomes to support themselves and their families.

Public funding for city schools may be similar to that in other areas, but families in many urban neighborhoods are unable to contribute to schools at the same level as many suburban parents. Parents have less time to volunteer for school and community involvement or fund-raising projects. They often have more than one job; in some cases they are caught in their own addictions and maladies exacerbated by the stress of poverty, violence, and lack of community support.

Many urban middle-class and upper-middle-class families opt for private schools over public schools. African Americans make up 33 percent of central city school populations, and Hispanic students are 22 percent. A disproportionately high percentage of students are foreign-born or first-generation immigrants with limited English proficiency. Bilingual education and federally funded programs such as Title I for students from low-income families help to meet the needs of urban schools. Low-income students in urban areas are less likely to complete high school on time, although they complete postsecondary degrees at the same rates as their suburban and rural counterparts.[27] There are severe teacher shortages in urban schools. As a result, many teachers have not completed a teacher education program and are working on emergency licenses. A large percentage of teachers in city schools have had little or no preparation in the subjects that they are assigned to teach; this problem is particularly severe for mathematics and science. Perhaps this is a major reason why urban students perform less well on national achievement tests.

CULTURAL IDENTITY

The interaction of memberships in multiple microcultures determines one's cultural identity. However, each microcultural membership is weighted differently. Membership in a particular microculture can greatly influence the membership in another group. For example, some religions have strictly defined expectations for women and men that will control their behavior as adolescents, newlyweds, and married couples. Membership in some of the microcultural groups may have little impact on how individuals see themselves, while other microcultural identities such as race and gender are very important.

Others' perceptions of one's group memberships also have an influence on cultural identity. In a racist and sexist society some individuals are viewed as inferior to others. In the United States discrimination has strongly affected the cultural identity of some females, individuals with disabilities, persons of color, gays, and lesbians.

Cultural identity is dynamic and may change over time. For example, the behavior and values of a married female with two young children may be greatly influenced by her ethnic, religious, and class background. If she divorces, aspects of her identification as a woman at a different class level may become more important determinants of her own identity than they previously were.

INTRAGROUP DIFFERENCES

There are many differences within the same microcultural group. For example, all women belong to the same gender microculture but not to the same ethnic, religious, or socioeconomic group—all of which have an impact on how women see themselves as females and how they are treated by society. For example, socioeconomic status has a great impact on how families are able to live. Individuals from the same ethnic group may have very different language and behavioral patterns as well as lifestyles as a result of their socioeconomic status. Educators must be careful not to stereotype students based on a single observable microcultural membership.

BICULTURALISM AND MULTICULTURALISM

Individuals who have competencies in and can operate successfully in two or more different ethnic or language groups are bicultural or multicultural, and are often multilingual as well. Having proficiencies in different cultural groups has advantages in today's global economy. Fluency in two or more languages is a requirement for a growing number of jobs at different income levels. Being bicultural does not lead to rejection of the primary cultural identification. It does allow a broad range of abilities on which one can draw as needed.

Many individuals who are not members of the dominant culture become bicultural to attend school, work, and participate effectively in their own ethnic communities. Different behaviors and language or dialects are expected in the two settings. To be successful on the job usually requires proficiency in the ways of the dominant group. Because most schools reflect the dominant society, many students of color or from low-income families are forced to adjust if they are going to be academically successful. On the other hand, many European Americans find almost total congruence between the culture of their family, schooling, and work. Partly for this reason, many do not participate in groups different from their own and do not comprehend the value of becoming competent in two or more cultures and languages.

SUMMARY

CULTURE AND SOCIETY

The way individuals behave and think is determined by their culture. Culture is so pervasive in life that people often are not aware that their actions and thoughts are culturally determined. Culture is learned, shared, adapted, and dynamic. Although characteristics and contributions of diverse cultural groups are reflected in U.S. society, the dominant cultural group (white, Protestant, heterosexual, middle-class European Americans) has had the greatest impact on societal values and behavioral expectations. The interactions of culture and society are critical elements when one studies students, families, communities, and schools.

DIVERSITY AND EDUCATION

Several theories have evolved to describe the nature of diversity in the United States. Assimilation was the predominant theory during the twentieth century. To be successful in society, newcomers and other visibly distinct groups were expected to shed their cultural identities and adopt those of the dominant group. In a culturally pluralistic society, by contrast, distinctive cultural patterns are valued, promoted, and treated as equal to the dominant culture. Cultural choice allows individuals, families, and groups to maintain their own cultures, assimilate into the dominant society, or be bicultural or multicultural. Each of these theories has been translated into educational strategies that guide a school's curriculum and the interactions of students and teachers.

SOCIOECONOMIC STATUS

The way students and their families live is greatly affected by their socioeconomic status, which is determined by one's income, wealth, occupation, income, and educational attainment. Social stratification gives some groups more advantage and prestige in society than others based not only on socioeconomic status, but also on membership in ethnic, racial, gender, language, religious, and ability groups. Forty-one percent of the population comprises the working class who do manual and service work for a living. Thirty-eight percent of the U.S. population falls into the middle class, which is primarily made up of white-collar and professional workers. Thirteen percent of the population lives in poverty even though many of them work full or part-time. Women and persons of color suffer disproportionately from not earning wages and salaries at the same level as members of the dominant group.

ETHNICITY AND RACE

The United States is becoming increasingly ethnically and racially diverse, in part as a result of immigration from Asia, Mexico, Central America, and the Middle East. Many people continue to identify others by their observable racial characteristics or language, often leading to stereotyping and discrimination against members of a racial or language group. Race or ethnicity is the primary cultural identification for many people of color and new immigrants, but many European Americans see themselves as raceless.

GENDER

Although research over the past few decades finds few differences between females and males, differences in economic status, jobs, and educational attainment continue to exist. These economic and social differences are being gradually reduced over time, but women, especially those who are single heads of households, are much more likely to live in poverty. Neither males nor females are well served by the traditional stereotypes of their abilities and roles in the workforce, families, and society. Many educators are not aware of their actions in classrooms that perpetuate these stereotypes. Many are also not knowledgeable about homosexuality and how to appropriately support gay and lesbian students.

LANGUAGE

A growing number of English language learners are found in schools across the country, even in Midwestern rural and small town schools that previously had limited diversity. Although students can become conversant in a second language within a few years, it usually requires five to seven years to become academically competent in a second language. In addition, a number of students use a dialect that is not Standard English in their home environments. To ensure that all students learn at high levels, teachers should respect the dialects and languages of students and their families as they are used appropriately in helping students become competent in Standard English.

EXCEPTIONALITIES

Today's teachers are likely to have students with disabilities in their classrooms many times over their careers. Like members of other underserved groups in society, students with disabilities are often labeled and stereotyped in ways that are not conducive to learning and that do not support the belief that all students can learn. A disproportionately large number of disabled students do not finish high school or attend college. Too often, they are not made to feel comfortable in schools and necessary services are not available to them. Students from low-income families, students of color, and young men are more likely to be labeled mentally retarded or emotionally disabled, resulting in disproportionately large numbers being placed in special education classes.

RELIGION

Religious diversity in the United States is expanding to include religions other than Christianity and Judaism as Asian, African, and Middle Easterners immigration grows. Although public schools cannot advance a religious doctrine, they are built on a Protestant tradition and often include artifacts of Christianity. Families with other religious backgrounds seldom see their traditions and values reflected in the public schools and often feel discriminated against because of their religion.

GEOGRAPHY

As the population shifts and ages, teachers may have to move to a different part of the country than that in which they grew up to find desirable employment. Cultural traditions and values differ from one region of the country to another and may require some adjustments. Differences within the same region exist in communities and schools located in rural, suburban, and urban areas.

CULTURAL IDENTITY

Individuals belong to numerous microcultural groups, which determine their unique cultural identity. The groups that appear to be the most important in cultural identity are race, ethnicity, gender, and class or socioeconomic status. To many, religious affiliation is very important in determining cultural patterns and behaviors. One's language, disability, or sexual orientation may also be essential in the determination of cultural identity. Membership in one microcultural group may be so important that it influences membership in all of the others.

DISCUSSION QUESTIONS

1. Why do we often not recognize our own cultural patterns?
2. Why is it important to help students learn their own cultural background and heritage?
3. How have theories describing diversity impacted on the educational process in the past decade?
4. How do race, ethnicity, gender, and socioeconomic status interact to affect students in schools?
5. What will be the differences in the populations with which you will work if you teach in a school in an urban, suburban, or rural area?

JOURNAL ENTRIES

1. Write an autobiographical description of how membership in the microcultural groups described in this chapter has contributed to your own cultural identity. The description should indicate why membership in one or more groups is especially important in the identification of who you are.
2. Describe an experience that you have had with members of another culture that has influenced how you think about that cultural group. How have your impressions changed over time as you have had experiences with other members of that group?

PORTFOLIO DEVELOPMENT

1. Develop an outline of the microcultural memberships (race, ethnicity, language, gender, socioeconomic class, religion, ability, and geographic location) of the students in a class that you are observing at the P–12 level. What are the intragroup differences within the ethnic groups represented in the class? Develop a plan for learning more about the groups that are different from your own.

2. Contrast educational practices that have evolved to support different theories related to diversity. Develop an argument for incorporating those practices into your own teaching.

SCHOOL-BASED EXPERIENCES

1. In a school with students from diverse language backgrounds, interview a teacher about the strategies that are used to ensure that students do not fall academically behind because their native language is not English.
2. Through interviewing students and reviewing materials used in the classroom that you are observing, determine how cultural differences are reflected in the curriculum and activities of the school.

WEBSITES

In addition to the sites listed here, we encourage you to search the web using key words such as "culture," "race," "socioeconomic status," "poverty," "homelessness," "gender research," and "rural statistics." Search also under specific ethnic groups such as "Italian American," "African American," "Lakota," or "Japanese," and specific religious groups such as "Pentacostal," "Seventh-Day Adventist," or "Islam."

1. <www.aauw.org> The website of the American Association of University Women includes discussions of issues, government policies, and research related to education and equity for girls and women.
2. <www.adl.org> The Anti-Defamation League fights anti-Semitism, bigotry, and extremism. Its website includes information on religious freedom, civil rights, and the Holocaust as well as resources for teachers on fighting hate.
3. <www.cec.sped.org> The Council for Exceptional Children is dedicated to improving educational outcomes for individuals with exceptionalities, students with disabilities, and/or the gifted. The website identifies resources to help professionals obtain conditions and resources necessary for effective professional practice.
4. <www.ComingTogether.com> This website focuses on children with disabilities and their families. It contains stories by mothers, fathers, and teachers who are dealing with the realities that accompany disability. Its goal is to unite, inspire, and give courage to families that include children or adults with disabilities.
5. <www.doi.gov/bureau-indian-affairs.html> The website of the Bureau of Indian Affairs includes information on the bureau's projects.
6. <www.edc.org/womensequity> The website of the Women's Educational Equity Association provides information about Title IX and women's equity issues, including links to additional resources.
7. <www.fiu.edu/~escotet/> This site offers access to international, multicultural, cross-cultural, and intercultural development education. It links the user to more than 5,000 news sources from or about all five continents with special emphasis on Latin America and the Caribbean. All menus are in English and Spanish.
8. <www.glsen.org> The website of the Gay, Lesbian, and Straight Education Network provides resources and updates for ending bias against gays in schools and society.

9. <www.lulac.org> The League of United Latin American Citizens advances the economic condition, educational attainment, political influence, health, and civil rights of the Hispanic population of the United States.
10. <www.ncai.org> The National Congress of American Indians works to inform the public and Congress on the governmental rights of Native Americans and Alaska Natives. The website includes a directory of tribes in the United States.
11. <www.now.org> The National Organization for Women is a women's advocacy group that supports legislation for equity and candidates who support women's rights and equity. They actively fight against sexual discrimination and harassment.
12. <www.nul.org> The National Urban League has sought to emphasize greater reliance on the unique resources and strengths of the African American community to find solutions to its own problems. It has strong roots in the community, focused on the social and educational development of youth, economic self-sufficiency, and racial inclusion.
13. <www.splcenter.org> The Southern Poverty Law Center combats hate, intolerance, and discrimination through education and litigation against hate groups. It publishes *Teaching Tolerance,* which is available at no cost to teachers, and numerous other teaching resources.

NOTES

Unless otherwise indicated, the data reported in this chapter are from the U.S. Census Bureau, *Statistical Abstract of the United States: 1999.* Washington, DC: U.S. Government Printing Office, 1999.

1. R. N. Bellah, R. Madsen, W. M. Sullivan, A. Swidler, and S. M. Tipton, *Habits of the Heart: Individualism and Commitment in American Life.* New York: Harper & Row, 1985, 23.
2. Milton M. Gordon, *Assimilation in American Life: The Role of Race, Religion, and National Origins.* New York: Oxford University Press, 1964.
3. Sarah Anderson, John Cavanagh, Chuck Collins, Chris Hartman, and Felice Yeskel, *Executive Excess 2000: Seventh Annual CEO Compensation Survey.* Washington, DC: Institute for Policy Studies and United for a Fair Economy, August 2000.
4. " 'Children' Progress Elsewhere," *U.S. News & World Report* (August 28, 1995): 24.
5. Michael Omi and Howard Winant, *Racial Formation in the United States from the 1960s to the 1990s.* New York: Routledge, 1994, 59.
6. Omi and Winant, 1994, 59.
7. James A. Banks, *Teaching Strategies for Ethnic Studies.* 6th ed. Boston: Allyn and Bacon, 1997, 13.
8. Banks, 13.
9. U.S. Bureau of the Census, 1990 Census of Population Supplementary Reports. *Detailed Ancestry Groups for States.* CP-S-1-2. Washington, DC: U.S. Government Printing Office, October 1992.
10. Kelley, M. (September 8, 2000). Indian affairs head makes apology. Associated Press.
11. Myra Sadker, David Sadker, and Susan Klein, "The Issue of Gender in Elementary and Secondary Education," in Gerald Grant, ed., *Review of Research in Education,* vol. 17. Washington, DC: American Educational Research Association, 1991.
12. Jessie Bernard, *The Female World.* New York: Free Press, 1981, 4.
13. Dali Tan and Dawei Tan, *Keeping Chinese Girls in School: Effective Strategies from Hubei Province.* Washington, DC: American Association of University Women Educational Foundation, 1995.
14. Dali and Dawei, 1995.

15. Francis Mark Mondimore, *A Natural History of Homosexuality.* Baltimore: Johns Hopkins University Press, 1996.
16. W. P. Thomas and Virginia P. Collier, *School Effectiveness for Language Minority Students.* Washington, DC: National Clearinghouse for Bilingual Education, 1997.
17. U.S. Department of Education, National Center for Education Statistics, *Digest of Education Statistics 1999.* Washington, DC: U.S. Government Printing Office, 1999.
18. Dorothy Kerzner Lipsky and Alan Gartner, "Inclusion, School Restructuring, and the Remaking of American Society," *Harvard Educational Review 66* (4) (Winter 1996): 762–796.
19. Gallup Organization, "Gallup Poll: How Important Would You Say Religion Is in Your Own Life?" Princeton, NJ: Author, August 2000.
20. Charles R. Kniker, "A Journey with Strangers: Understanding the Religious Right and Its Impact upon American Education," *Religion and Education 23* (2) (Fall 1996): 25–30.
21. Gary Orfield and Holly J. Lebowitz, eds., *Religion, Race and Justice in a Changing America.* New York: Century Foundation, 1999.
22. Joint Center for Housing Studies at Harvard University, *The State of the Nation's Housing: 1996.* Cambridge, MA: Author, 1996.
23. Sue Books, "The Other Poor: Rural Poverty and Education," *Educational Foundations 11* (1) (Winter 1997): 73–85.
24. Jonathan Kaufman, "Suburban Parents Shun Many Public Schools, Even the Good Ones," *Wall Street Journal* (March 1, 1996).
25. *Improving Student Performance in the Inner City* (Policy and Research Report). Washington, DC: The Urban Institute, 1996.
26. *Improving Student Performance.*
27. U.S. Department of Education, National Center for Education Statistics, *Urban Schools.* Washington, DC: U.S. Government Printing Office, 1996.

BIBLIOGRAPHY

Anti-Defamation League. *Religion in the Public Schools: Guidelines for a Growing and Changing Phenomenon.* Rev. ed. New York: Author, 1996.

Banks, James A. *Teaching Strategies for Ethnic Studies.* 6th ed. Boston: Allyn and Bacon, 1997.

Beykont, Zeynep F., ed., *Lifting Every Voice: Pedagogy and Politics of Bilingualism.* Cambridge, MA: Harvard Education Publishing Group, 2000.

Fine, Michelle; Weis, Lois; Powell, Linda C.; and Wong, L. Mun. *Off White: Readings on Race, Power, and Society.* New York: Routledge, 1997.

Gollnick, Donna M., and Chinn, Philip C. *Multicultural Education in a Pluralistic Society.* 6th ed. Columbus, OH: Merrill, 2001.

Mishel, Mishel; Bernstein, Lawrence Jared; and Schmitt, John. *The State of Working America, 1998–99.* Ithaca, NY: ILR Press, 1999.

Mondimore, Francis Mark. *A Natural History of Homosexuality.* Baltimore: Johns Hopkins University Press, 1996.

Orfield, Gary, and Lebowitz, Holly J., eds. *Religion, Race and Justice in a Changing America.* New York: Century Foundation, 1999.

Pugach, Marleen C. *On the Border of Opportunity: Education, Community, and Language at the U.S.-Mexico Line.* Mahwah, NJ: Lawrence Erlbaum Associates.

Rose, Stephen J. *Social Stratification in the United States: The New American Profile Poster.* New York: New Press, 2000.

Smith, Dan. *The State of the World Atlas.* New York: Penguin Reference, 1999.

Sullivan, Andrew. *Virtually Normal: An Argument about Homosexuality.* New York: Vintage, 1995.

"Symposium: Ethnicity and Education." *Harvard Educational Review 67* (2) (Summer 1997): 169–349.

Tilly, Charles. *Durable Inequality.* Berkeley, CA: University of California Press, 1999.

CHAPTER

3

Schools Facing Social Challenges

EDUCATION IN THE NEWS

Racial Gap in Schools Splits a Town Proud of Diversity

By Kate Zernike

The New York Times, August 4, 2000

Set above the leafy banks of the Hudson River, this cluster of villages north of New York City has long cultivated a reputation as an idyll of diversity and tolerance. Blacks and whites mingle easily in the shops lining the quaint main street. Interracial families seek out the town as a place where they can live without incident.

The charge, then, hit right at the heart. Armed with previously unreleased statistics broken down by race, a group of parents, black and white, accused the school district of systemic segregation: steering blacks away from honors classes and into special education, disciplining blacks at disproportionate rates, allowing test scores of blacks to lag far behind those of whites for a decade.

The release of the numbers divided the community in a way most people here thought nothing ever could. White parents defended the schools, pointing the finger at what they called deviancy and neglect in black families.

While some black parents said the statistics confirmed the discrimination they suspected, others denounced the group's report as perpetuating painful stereotypes. In the tension, car windows were smashed and sidewalk confrontations erupted.

The conflict here offers a cautionary tale. Closing the gap between black and white achievement has become the nation's thorniest education challenge. Impressed by success in Texas, many states hope to do what the parents here did: release scores by race. California began doing so this year; New York, Connecticut, Massachusetts and Florida all recently announced plans to do so.

This places a new onus on diverse and well-off suburban communities like this, which have long been able to disregard poor performance by blacks in averages lifted by higher scores of whites. The idea, state officials say, is that exposing the disparity forces school districts to seek to eliminate it. But Nyack's experience suggests that the path from releasing numbers to improving schools can be exceptionally rough terrain, that merely acknowledging the existence of a gap, even in well-meaning communities, is a process filled with pain and controversy.

LEARNER OUTCOMES

After reading and studying this chapter, you will be able to

1. Understand that middle-class and wealthy whites have advantages and benefits in society because they are members of the dominant group.

(continued)

2. Understand that students are living in many different family arrangements and that educators should not stereotype student behavior or academic potential on the basis of their family structures.
3. Understand that young people need caring adults to help them maneuver through the tribulations and challenges of childhood and the teenage years.
4. Understand that schools play an important role in the socialization of today's children and youth.
5. Understand that educational equality requires that all students learn and are represented proportionately in advanced placement and special education classes. ■

In a democracy all citizens are called on to fully participate with the aim of promoting the common good. To ensure the participation of most citizens, power must be shared somewhat equally across groups in society. The United States describes itself as the premier model of a democratic society but is in fact governed primarily by the majority of the citizenry that have power. Others are not privy to the same or similar benefits; in many instances they have given up on equal participation in society, not even voting in elections—the basic right to choose one's representatives in a democracy. Nevertheless, most citizens continue to espouse the nation as a democracy with the goal of greater equality and prosperity for all. As a result, one of the goals for schooling is to prepare students to engage in and promote the ideals of a democracy.

Power provides economic, educational, and political advantages for individuals and groups. Although democracy has undergirded the political rhetoric in the United States for more than two hundred years, elected representatives at almost any level of government do not include men and women in equal numbers; nor do they reflect the ethnic, racial, religious, language, economic, or age diversity that actually exists in the nation. There are significant differences in the education levels, types of jobs, and family incomes across racial and ethnic groups and between men and women. Children in low-income families suffer disproportionately from limited access to the best teachers, the best instruction in schools, good nutrition, safe environments, and community support and caring for their well-being. In other words, power is not equally distributed across the nation's citizens.

Individuals are often identified by their group membership. They are classified on forms as black, Hispanic, Asian American, Native American, or white. They speak English or another language. They are Buddhist, Islamic, Jewish, Catholic, Protestant, or nonbelievers. They are from the South, New England, the Pacific Northwest, Mexico, or somewhere else outside of the United States. They are wealthy, or middle-class, or poor. They are children, youth, middle-aged, or old. In many cases the group membership is the critical determinant of power in society rather than individual potential and hard work. Membership in some groups provides access to college, good jobs, and higher standards of living. Society raises barriers against members of other groups, making it difficult for many of its members to finish high school and find a job that will adequately support a family.

What is the nature of groups in a democratic society? How do interactions with members of groups different from one's own influence one's ability to achieve a democratic state supportive of egalitarian ideals? Finally, how do schools contribute to the maintenance of society and help students engage in and promote the ideals of a democracy? We will address the big ideas of group membership, power, and democracy in this chapter.

GROUPS IN SOCIETY

A democratic society struggles with how to support individuality and yet develop a consciousness of shared concerns and actions that promote **equality**—the state of being neither inferior nor superior. This challenge is paramount in a society such as the United States, which includes many groups that affect and are affected by political, social, and economic systems.

Some individuals are members of a group because of birth characteristics such as race or gender. Others belong to groups in which the members share the same national origin, native language, economic circumstances, religious affiliation, and/or residence in a specific geographic region. Of course, each individual belongs to numerous groups or microcultures. At the same time, people often interact with members of different groups in school, work, or social settings. People also may interact with others around common interests such as environmental concerns, school funding, moving drug dealers from the block, or day-care support.

Different members of U.S. society view the importance of group membership differently. Many European Americans, especially the Protestant middle class, do not identify themselves by their racial, ethnic, gender, religious, or socioeconomic group. To many of these people, white, Christian, and middle-class constitute the norm against which others are defined. Therefore, many such people do not distinguish themselves from the larger society and often do not acknowledge the advantage that membership in these groups has provided them. On the other hand, people whose ancestral roots are outside of Europe, or who are recent immigrants, are more likely to identify themselves and be identified by others on the basis of their ethnicity, race, language, or religion. They or other members of their group have experienced **discrimination:** practices that exclude them from equal access to housing, jobs, or educational opportunities, or unfair treatment by store clerks or police officers. Their common history and experiences reinforce a group identity that is distinct from mainstream society.

Having experienced discrimination, members of excluded groups can describe differential power relations among groups. Members of groups who do not experience discrimination, however, have a more difficult time acknowledging that differences in power and advantage exist. As a result, rights based on group membership versus those of individuals are debated on college campuses, in board meetings of corporations, by politicians, and in many formal and informal neighborhood meetings. These discussions focus on programs that are perceived to favor a group other than one's own—programs such as affirmative action, bilingual education, or equal funding for male and female athletes, for example. An examination of power relationships and experiences with differences should highlight the struggles inherent in a democratic society.

equality
The state of being neither inferior nor superior.

discrimination
Individual or institutional practices that exclude members of a group from certain rights, opportunities, or benefits.

POWER AND DOMINATION

In 1916 John Dewey described a democratic society as one in which all of its members are able to share its benefits on equal terms.[1] Nearly ninety years later,

Teacher–student relationships, as with many others in U.S. society, are defined by one person having power over others.

many persons of color, limited English speakers, women, persons with disabilities, gays and lesbians, people with low incomes, and people affiliated with religions other than Protestantism have still not experienced equality with members of the **dominant group.** Why has the United States not yet been able to achieve the egalitarian ideal that should characterize democracy? The primary factor is the inequitable power relationships that exist across groups.

Schools provide an example of institutions in which power relationships have been developed and maintained. Students' work and class rules are determined by teachers. Teachers are evaluated, and disciplined when necessary, by principals who report to a superintendent of schools. The rules and procedures for managing schools traditionally have been established by authorities who are not directly involved with the school and who may not even live in the community served by the school. Parents, especially in economically disadvantaged areas, often feel powerless in the education of their children.

Not only do power and domination characterize political and economic systems, they also influence relations within the family, between the sexes, among racial groups, and among members of many religious traditions. The father figure traditionally has been all powerful. Instead of shared relations between males and females, husbands and wives, and parents and children, one sometimes dominates the other. In these power relationships someone or some group is viewed as inferior to another. It is no accident that politics, religions, and businesses have been controlled primarily by men. Until recently, they were the group more likely to be socialized to be in charge. Although this pattern is beginning to disintegrate in some families and groups, it remains so prevalent that it is often not questioned; it has been accepted as the natural way of behaving. As a result, when women are harassed, wives or children are beaten, and disproportionate numbers of African American young men are jailed, many members of the society do not react.

dominant group
The cultural group that has the greatest power in society; sometimes referred to as the mainstream culture or group. In the United States the dominant group is composed primarily of people from a European background who are Protestant, middle-class, not disabled, heterosexual, and male.

Many people with power in U.S. society believe that they have this status because of their individual abilities and accomplishments. They usually give no credit to their membership in the dominant group. For example, most whites do not think they have an advantage over members of other racial and ethnic groups. On the other hand, many people of color perceive whites as having excessive influence.[2] There appears to be a large gap in the perceptions of power between the different groups in society.

Power not only allows domination over the powerless, it also allows access to societal benefits such as good housing, tax deductions, the best schools, and social services. It is not an asset that the powerful are willing to give up or readily share with those whom they see as less deserving. A more equitable sharing of resources for schools would guarantee that all students, regardless of income or ethnic background, would have qualified teachers, sufficient books and other instructional resources, well-maintained buildings and playgrounds, and access to high-level academic knowledge. Such equality does not exist across schools that students attend today. The great disparities between schools for advantaged and underserved students have been described graphically in Jonathan Kozol's book, *Savage Inequalities: Children in America's Schools:*

> New Trier's physical setting might well make the students of Du Sable High School envious. The *Washington Post* describes a neighborhood of "circular driveways, chirping birds and white-columned homes." It is, says a student, "a maple land of beauty and civility." While Du Sable is sited on one crowded city block, New Trier students have the use of 27 acres. While Du Sable's science students have to settle for makeshift equipment, New Trier's students have superior labs and up-to-date technology. One wing of the school, a physical education center that includes three separate gyms, also contains a fencing room, a wrestling room and studios for dance instruction. In all, the school has seven gyms as well as an Olympic pool. . . .
>
> The youngsters, according to a profile of the school in *Town and Country* magazine, "make good use of the huge, well-equipped building, which is immaculately maintained by a custodial staff of 48."
>
> It is impossible to read this without thinking of a school like Goudy, where there are no science labs, no music or art classes and no playground—and where the two bathrooms, lacking toilet paper, fill the building with their stench.[3]

ETHNOCENTRISM

Our actions, values, thoughts, and patterns of learning are shaped by our culture. Most of the time, we are not aware of the power of our cultural upbringing. This phenomenon often leads to **ethnocentrism,** in which members of a group view their culture as superior to all others—and perceive persons from other cultural groups as strange and unusual. Ethnocentrism is sometimes promoted in emotional calls for patriotism, especially at times when a country is involved in a political conflict with another country. The other country is often denigrated by name-calling based on negative stereotypes of its citizens.

Ethnocentrism is not limited to relations with other nations; it occurs often between groups within the United States. For example, homosexuals are victims of abuse by radio talk show hosts and some religious groups. Members of some religious groups believe that their cultural values and lifestyles are the only correct ones; they do not tolerate alternative beliefs. Historically, many members of the dominant culture have believed that their culture is superior to those with non-European roots. Ethnocentrism extends beyond individuals' views of their culture, and has led to discriminatory policies and practices that favor members of the dominant group.

ethnocentrism The belief that members of one's own group are superior to the members of other groups.

One of the manifestations of ethnocentrism is the inability to accept differences among groups as natural and appropriate. The values and behaviors of the dominant group become the norm against which others are measured. The dominant group often treats the differences as deficits that must be overcome through education and special programs.

When differences are translated into a deficit model, groups that are not accepted as part of the dominant culture are expected to give up their culture to be accepted. Schools and other institutions marginalize members of these groups because their differences are not valued. These attitudes are translated into compensatory education for children of poverty, transitional bilingual education for students with limited English proficiency, and special education for students with disabilities.

If teachers believe that all students can learn and that teachers can ensure that learning occurs, they must confront their own ethnocentrism. Often teachers do not recognize that they subtly, and sometimes overtly, transmit feelings of superiority over students and their cultural groups—both through curriculum content and through classroom interactions. To be effective, teachers need to think about differences as part of this nation's rich cultural history.

PREJUDICE AND DISCRIMINATION

Every American ought to have the right to be treated as he would wish to be treated, as one would wish his children to be treated. This is not the case.

John F. Kennedy, June 11, 1963

Power relationships between groups appear to influence young people's perceptions of themselves and of the members of other groups. One of the struggles of youth is the construction of self, including identification and affiliation with one's gender and a racial or ethnic group. This process appears to be integrally tied to identifying "otherness," which involves assigning characteristics and behavior to members of other groups to distinguish them from oneself. The construction of "others" places them either in a dominating or submissive role relative to the individual. This construction is often dependent on stereotypes that are promoted among peers and reinforced by society.

Not only do our perceptions of others affect how we see ourselves in relationship to them; these perceptions also have an influence on the treatment of many groups by society. **Prejudice** is a preconceived negative attitude against members of an ethnic, racial, religious, or socioeconomic group that is different from one's own. This prejudice sometimes extends to people with disabilities or of a different sexual orientation. Such negative attitudes are based on numerous factors, including information about members of a specific group that is stereotypical and many times not true. The prejudiced individual often has had little or no direct social contact with members of the other group.

An individual's prejudice may have a limited negative impact on members of the other group. However, these attitudes are passed on to children through the **socialization** process—the process through which children learn the social norms of their culture. Also, prejudiced attitudes can be transferred into discriminatory behavior that prevents members of a group from being interviewed for a job, joining a social club, or being treated like other professionals. Prejudices are too often reinforced by schools in which a disproportionate number of students in low-achieving tracks are from low-income families and in which students in special education are English language learners. Because of this situation in schools, some students form stereotypes of their low-income and foreign-born peers as academically inferior. Through this process, too, many students from low-income families and ethnic minority groups are prevented from gaining the skills and knowledge necessary to enter college or an apprentice trade.

prejudice
Preconceived negative attitude toward the members of a group.

socialization
The process of learning the social norms of one's culture.

INSTITUTIONAL DISCRIMINATION In addition to individual prejudice and discrimination, society has historically discriminated against members of powerless groups. The individuals who control and oversee our institutions are primarily members of the dominant culture. They tend to be ethnocentric in feeling that their culture is superior to others, even though they have rarely experienced other cultures and have little knowledge about them. Laws and systems that promote and support the dominant culture have been designed to help maintain its superiority and the power of its members. "English only" laws that prevent official documents and communications from being printed or spoken in any language other than English represent but one example of these efforts. Such practices have often become institutionalized in state and federal laws, the judicial system, schools, and other societal institutions. They have become so ingrained in the system that it is difficult to recognize them unless one is directly affected by the discriminatory policies.

RACISM An assumption of superiority is at the center of **racism,** in which members of a racial group believe that they are innately better than members of other groups. Racism is not a topic that is easily discussed in most classrooms. It is intertwined with the lived experiences of many and evokes emotions of anger, guilt, shame, and despair. Most people have learned that the United States is a just and democratic society. Therefore, it is difficult to confront the contradictions that support racism. Nevertheless, in U.S. society this way of thinking and acting can be observed in policies and practices developed primarily by leaders from the dominant group. It is important to acknowledge the advantages, as well as the damage, caused by racism in order to overcome its negative impact on society.

Racism is so universal in this country, so widespread and deep-seated, that it is invisible because it is so normal.

Shirley Chisolm

Students and adults go through stages of racial identity as they address issues of discrimination and their own racial identification.[4] Teachers should recognize that students will be moving back and forth across the stages outlined in Table 3.1 in their struggle to know themselves. One of the first steps in this process is to begin to confront one's own racial identity. How close is one to reaching an internalization or autonomy stage? If educators have not struggled with issues of racism, how it affects their lives, and how they may contribute to its perpetuation, it will be impossible for them to develop antiracist classrooms.

racism
The conscious or unconscious belief that racial differences make one group superior to another, leading to discriminatory actions that limit the opportunities for members of the perceived inferior group to share in the same benefits of society.

SEXISM AND OTHER ISMS Women of all racial and ethnic groups, people with disabilities, gays, lesbians, persons with low incomes, the elderly, and the young also suffer from discrimination and their lack of power in society. Many individuals are members of more than one of these powerless groups. For example, a low-income Hispanic woman may be triply harmed as a result of racism, classism, and **sexism**—cultural attitudes and practices that devalue women. This woman's chances of reaching a standard of living to be comfortable in this nation are severely limited by her circumstances and group membership.

Sexism has contributed to limited participation of female students in advanced mathematics and sciences—areas that could improve young women's chances for attending and being successful in college. Women's wages remain lower than men's, contributing to poverty in one-third of the households headed by women in this country. Gays and lesbians continue to face legal discrimination in many areas of the nation. The young and elderly disproportionately face poverty. Equality has not been achieved when great disparity in jobs, incomes, and access to quality education continues to exist among groups.

sexism
The conscious or unconscious belief that men are superior to women and subsequent behavior and action that maintain the superior, powerful position of males.

TABLE 3.1 DEVELOPMENT OF RACIAL IDENTITY

Black Racial Identity	White Racial Identity
Preencounter: African American individuals have assimilated into the mainstream culture, accepting many of the beliefs and values of the dominant society, including negative stereotypes about blacks.	*Contact:* White individuals are not aware of themselves as racial beings and are oblivious to acts of individual racism. They have a color-blind view of race and racism.
Encounter: African Americans usually enter this stage when they are confronted directly by a racist act such as rejection by white peers or racial slurs or attacks. They are then forced to confront their own racial identity.	*Disintegration:* Whites usually enter this stage as a result of some experiences with race that lead to the recognition that race does matter, that racism exists, and that they are white. They may show empathy when blacks experience racial discrimination, but often fail to understand their anger.
Immersion–Emersion: One's identification as an African American becomes paramount. At first this identification is manifested in anger against whites, but it evolves into a growing knowledge base about African American history and culture. The result of this exploration is an emerging security in a newly defined and affirmed sense of self.	*Reintegration:* Individuals believe consciously or unconsciously that whites are superior to people of color.
Internalization: Individuals begin to build coalitions with members of other nonwhite or nondominant groups and to develop relationships with whites who respect and acknowledge them.	*Pseudoindependence:* One begins the intellectual process of learning about and fighting against racism. One begins to understand that whites have responsibility for maintaining or eliminating racism.
Internalization–Commitment: Individuals are able both to maintain and to move beyond their personal racial identity—to be concerned with African Americans as a group.	*Immersion–Emersion:* Individuals begin to grasp the need to challenge racism. They often experience feelings of guilt and shame for the racist ideas that they believed in the past.
	Autonomy: White individuals have abandoned cultural, institutional, and personal racism. They have a more flexible view of the world, their own whiteness, and other racial groups. They value and seek out cross-racial/cultural experiences.

Sources: "Black Racial Identity" column is based on the five stages of black racial identity developed by W. E. Cross, Jr. and described in Beverly Daniel Tatum, "Talking about Race, Learning about Racism: The Application of Racial Identity Development Theory in the Classroom," *Harvard Educational Review, 62* (1) (Spring 1992): 1–24. "White Racial Identity" column is based on the six stages of white racial identity developed by J. E. Helms and described in Robert T. Carter, "Is White a Race? Expressions of White Racial Identity," in Michelle Fine, Lois Weis, Linda C. Powell, and L. Mun Wong, eds., *Off White: Readings on Race, Power, and Society.* New York: Routledge, 1997.

TODAY'S FAMILIES

Families in the United States have changed dramatically in recent decades. In the 1950s the norm was a working father and a mother at home with two or more school-aged children. Today only 68 percent of children aged eighteen or younger live in families with both parents. Families today include mothers working while fathers stay at home with the children, single-parent families, families with two working parents, remarried parents, childless marriages, families with adopted children, gay and lesbian parents, extended families, grandparents parenting grandchildren, and unmarried couples with children.

The average age of parents is older than in the past; couples now marry six years later on average than they did in the 1950s. More than 80 percent of today's young people age eighteen to twenty-four years old have never been married. Most men and women have worked for a number of years before marrying; a few (under 2 percent) never marry. Half of the population that marries later divorces and remarries. The median age of marriage is twenty-four for females and twenty-six for males; when they remarry after a divorce, the median ages are 34.5 and 37.4, respectively. Seven of ten children under age nineteen are living with two parents, even though one may be a stepmother or stepfather. Almost one-fourth live with a single mother; others live with a single father, grandparents, or other guardian.

Thirty percent of children under 18 years of age live in families without two traditional heterosexual parents. However, these nontraditional families provide the love and support necessary to raise children.

Families are smaller today, with an average total of 3.18 members. Families of color have higher birthrates than white families. The average age of people of color is younger than that of whites; thus, a larger percentage of women of color are of childbearing age. African Americans are currently the largest non-European group in the United States, but by the year 2025 nearly one-fourth of school-aged children will be Hispanic.

Ideally, it would be an advantage for children to have two caring and loving parents, but it is not essential. After reviewing research on the diversity of families, Frank Furstenberg concluded that

> Family structure explains a relatively small amount of the variation in key outcomes of success such as educational attainment, mental health, or problem behavior, especially when single-parenthood does not expose children to poverty, conflict, and instability. Yet, we cannot gainsay the fact that in American society, where economic and social support for families of all types is meager, children are more likely to be disadvantaged when they grow up in a single-parent household. The reverse is just as true: children are more likely to grow up in a single-parent household when they are disadvantaged. Mounting evidence suggests that disadvantage breeds family instability by undermining confidence in marriage, necessitating improvised and impermanent arrangements, and restricting access to good neighborhoods, schools, and social services.[5]

Educators should avoid labeling a child as dysfunctional because he or she does not live with both parents. Too often, teachers develop a self-fulfilling prophecy about students in nontraditional families rather than maintaining—and demonstrating—high expectations for their success in school.

PARENTING

Most parents want what's best for their children, but there is no simple guidebook for steering children through the complex terrain that they will have to

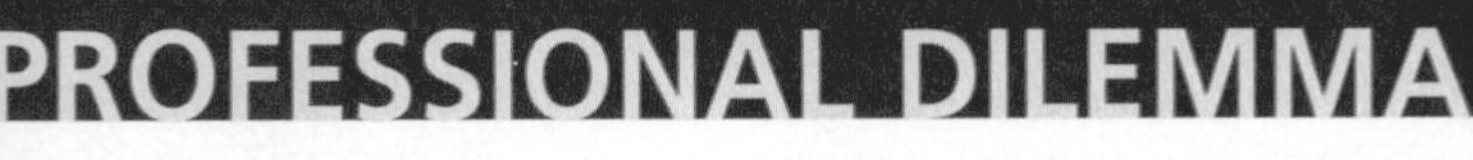

PROFESSIONAL DILEMMA

What If He Has Two Mommies?

In the 1950s most students came from families with both a mother and a father. In the subsequent forty years, more and more students have been raised by single mothers and now by a growing number of single fathers. Some students do not live with either parent but stay instead with relatives or in a foster home. As society becomes more tolerant of a variety of family structures and as adults become more open about their sexual orientation, teachers will also be introduced to lesbian and gay parents who may be living with a partner or separated from a partner.

The curriculum in most schools, especially at the preprimary and elementary levels, is often developed around the family—a nuclear family with a mother, father, and siblings. But for decades now, schools have been populated with students whose families do not fit that model. The curriculum and instructional materials seldom mirror the diversity of families, which may include parents with special needs, interracial parents, single parents, gay and lesbian parents, and foster parents.

The dilemma for teachers extends beyond the curriculum. They must figure out how to value and respect the diversity of families. Otherwise, both students and parents will feel ignored and isolated from the school setting. Teachers may also have to help other students develop an understanding of the diversity. Sometimes students respond to such differences in negative and hurtful ways. Teachers will need to develop strategies for confronting homophobic behavior from the outset.

- How could a primary teacher introduce gay and lesbian parents into a reading lesson?
- What are different ways in which teachers are likely to learn that some of their students have gay or lesbian parents?
- How should a teacher with strong views against homosexual relationships approach the reality of having the children of gays and lesbians in the classroom?
- How can a school develop a climate of acceptance of all students regardless of the structure and nature of the families in which they live?

navigate to grow up. Often parents draw from their own experiences as children and adults, but they did not face the same pressures from peers and the mass culture that today's students find. To increase students' chances of making it safely through childhood and adolescence, teachers and parents need to work together, setting high standards and helping young people meet them.

With the growing female influence in the family, the typical family structure is no longer as patriarchal as it once was. Many families are less autocratically controlled by adults and have become more egalitarian in the way they operate. In the past, nurturing children was the primary responsibility of mothers. Today more fathers are actively involved in parenting as well.

LATCHKEY CHILDREN

Most single parents work outside the home; and in many two-parent families, both parents work. Unless working parents have been lucky enough to arrange a flexible schedule that allows them to be home when their children are not in school, they are not available to care for their children, especially during the period immediately after school. The result is children of all ages left to care for themselves after school. Young children in these families have been referred to as latchkey children, because they often wear a house key around their neck.

Only 5 percent of K–5 students and 26 percent of students in grades 6–8 have to care for themselves after school. Parents provide supervision after school for over half of the students in this age range. Other children stay with adults other than their parents or attend center-based programs, as shown in Figure 3.1. Children from low-income families are more likely to stay with relatives than other children; they are also less likely to care for themselves after school than children in families with higher incomes.

One-fifth of the children in kindergarten through fifth grade attend afterschool programs with adult supervision and guidance on first aid, nutrition, health, homework, and being on their own at home. These programs are sometimes available at the child's school, or they may be organized by local houses of worship in cooperation with community groups. Young children may learn how to get home from school safely, how to use the telephone and be familiar with emergency telephone numbers, what to do in case of fire, how to deal with strangers, and how to use their time wisely. Often parents must pay a fee for their children to participate in these programs. Unfortunately, some families cannot afford the cost of such care.

Educators should be sensitive to the realities faced by children left alone after school. Children sometimes are frightened to be at home alone, especially when they have no siblings. The process of traveling from school to home can be dangerous and scary in neighborhoods where drugs are being sold and peers are

FIGURE 3.1 **BEFORE- AND AFTER-SCHOOL CARE: PERCENTAGE OF CHILDREN IN GRADES K–8 WHO RECEIVED VARIOUS TYPES OF CARE BEFORE AND AFTER SCHOOL: 1999**

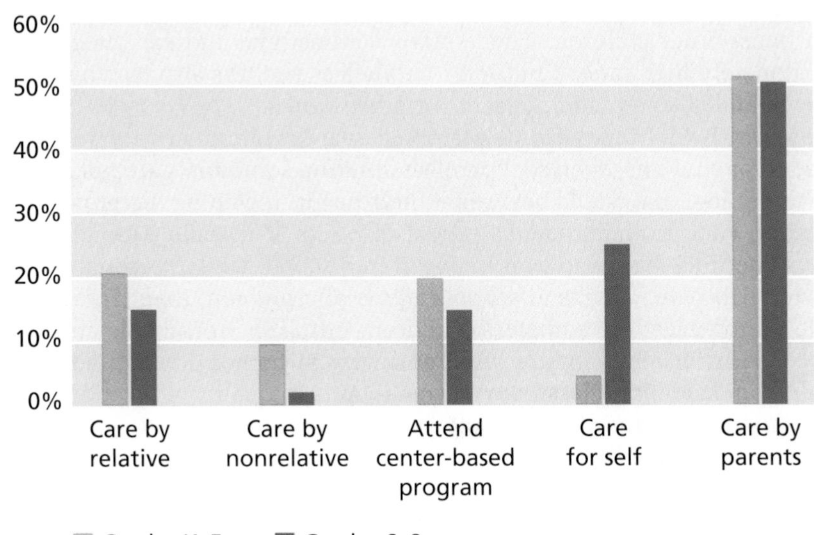

Source: U.S. Department of Education, National Center for Education Statistics, *The Condition of Education 2000,* NCES 2000-062. Washington, DC: U.S. Government Printing Office, 2000.

tempting each other to misbehave. Adolescents may be tempted to experiment with chemicals and sex while adults are not around. Television often becomes the babysitter, providing children with the opportunity to learn from educational programs—or from pornography. In almost all cases children are thankful (although grudgingly at some ages) for caring adults who can provide supervision and assistance.

HOMELESS STUDENTS

Increasing numbers of Americans are an illness, an accident, a natural disaster, or a paycheck away from becoming homeless.

Anonymous

The National Law Center on Homelessness and Poverty estimates that more than 700,000 people in the United States are without shelter on any given night and that up to 2 million people will be homeless at some point during a year. Nearly forty percent of the homeless are families with children; 25 percent of the homeless in cities are young people under the age of eighteen. Single men are nearly half of the homeless population; single women make up 14 percent of the homeless.[6] Like the adult homeless, homeless young people live in shelters, in abandoned buildings, and on the street. However, "in most cases, homelessness is a temporary circumstance—not a permanent condition."[7]

The increase in homelessness since the late 1970s is due to two factors: There is a shortage of affordable rental housing, and poverty has increased. Working people make up approximately one-fifth of the homeless. Their wages are not adequate to provide food, clothing, and housing. A full-time minimum wage job often does not provide enough income for a family to rent a one-bedroom unit at fair market prices.

Homelessness is devastating to families. Only 28 percent of the minor children of homeless parents live with the homeless parent;[8] children may be placed in foster care or left with relatives or friends. Children who live in shelters and on the streets suffer from inadequate health care. They may be surrounded by diseases such as whooping cough and tuberculosis. They are not always inoculated against common childhood diseases, making them more susceptible to illness than most other children. They suffer from asthma and ear infections at disproportionately high rates. Children in homeless shelters also face hypothermia, hunger, and abuse by their parents or other adults.

The Stewart B. McKinney Homeless Assistance Act eliminated the residency requirement for students; even so, homeless children sometimes are not allowed to attend the school that would best serve their needs, including the provision of transportation back to the student's school of origin if feasible. Homeless students are sometimes forced to wait to enroll in a school while personal records are collected. However, access to schools is less of a problem than it was in the past. The percentage of homeless children enrolled in school, including preschool, nearly matches that of children living in homes. Today's advocates focus more on students' classroom success. A high-quality education offers homeless children a chance for academic and economic success. To ignore them because they do not have a home or are not well groomed deprives them of the opportunity to rise above their current circumstances. They need more, not less, of our attention as educators.

ABUSE

Domestic violence is often hidden or ignored by society. One-third of the females murdered in this country are killed by a spouse, ex-spouse, or boyfriend. Only 4 percent of male murder victims are killed by someone they knew intimately. This number has dropped by 60 percent since 1976, although the number of murdered women has remained about the same.[9] Physical violence against women and girls is near an epidemic level in some countries. A report on domestic violence by UNICEF indicates that up to half of the females in some countries have been abused by a family member or boyfriend. Over 60 million females have been killed by their own families either deliberatively or through neglect.[10] Domestic violence has become the primary cause of homelessness for women with children. Nearly half of homeless women and children are fleeing abusive relationships.

Most children have probably been faced with angry parents who raise their voices or may even spank them. But every year at least one of every hundred of the nation's children is the victim of serious abuse and/or neglect by parents, caretakers, or relatives. Abuse accounts for about 10 percent of the emergency room treatments of children under age seven. Approximately 1,300 children die annually as a result of abuse and neglect. Nearly three million suspected cases are reported annually to authorities. Parents or caretakers are the murderers of 57 percent of the children under 12 years old who are killed every year.[11] Neglect is the cause of half of the reported abuse cases; one in four is the result of physical abuse, usually by males; and sexual abuse is reported in 12 percent of the cases. Males are more likely to be the perpetrators of physical and sexual abuse. Sexual abuse is an especially insidious form of child abuse. At least 16 percent of girls and 10 percent of boys are sexually abused before they are eighteen years old. The sensational news stories report sexual abuse of children by strangers. In most cases, however, the abuser will likely be a parent or trusted family friend.

Children and youths who are abused or neglected may arrive at school hungry, bruised, and depressed. They may arrive early at school and seem to have little desire to leave the safety of the school. These children, like all others, need teachers who are caring, retain high expectations for them, and can provide hope for the future. School and other social service professionals may be the only adults available to support abused youngsters.

When old enough, many abused youths run away from home, choosing to confront possible abuse on the streets rather than the known abuse at home. Abused children make up a large proportion of the adults seeking psychological and mental health treatment. For many of these children, the negative experiences and conditions of their childhood become the foundation for crime.[12] The young people have learned abuse from the adults who were closest to them.

TODAY'S YOUTH

Young people face numerous challenges as they mature to adulthood. Changing family structures, alteration of what was once a societal set of expected values, and increased pressures to grow up quickly and be adult all have contributed to the difficulty of this period. Many students are able to draw on the support of friends, family, religion, and inner strength to resist being drawn into negative responses. Others find their own ways of countering circumstances over which they appear to have no control.

The love and care of adults helps children and youths make a safe passage through childhood and adolescence. Teenagers are trying to figure out who they are and how they fit into the family, neighborhood, school, and larger world. They are searching for answers, but in their own ways. One of the challenges for parents, caretakers, educators, and youth workers is to encourage sound choices among the unlimited possibilities while avoiding excessive interference.

WHO IS THIS GENERATION?

The number one thing young people in America—indeed young people around the world—have going for them is their sense of honesty, morality, and ethics. Young people refuse to accept the lies and rationalizations of the established order.

Dick Gregory

The great majority of U.S. teenagers are not the dangerous, drug-using, sexually promiscuous, and nonproductive adolescents of the common stereotypes. Young people might not always agree with the adults with whom they interact, and sometimes they even break the rules; but they finish high school and attend college at higher rates than in the past. And in many other respects, today's teens are more like their counterparts of past generations than different from them.

Many teens, especially inner-city youths, report that the messages they receive about themselves in the media and in schools are usually negative ones such as "You aren't worth anything."[13] They feel that adults and communities no longer care about them. This feeling seems to be validated by poor funding of the schools, parks, and community centers needed to assist youths in many low-income communities. In a study of neighborhood-based organizations for youths in three urban areas, researchers found that communities saw youths in one of three ways: as resources to develop, as problems to be managed, or as adults-in-waiting. The most successful programs were youth-based organizations in which the adult leaders believed that young people are resources to develop.[14]

Respect on the part of adults is critical in helping youths to develop self-esteem. Teenagers don't always have appropriate adult support at home; their parents may be too tired or too busy or may have too many problems themselves to care adequately for their children. For many teens, then, schools and neighborhood organizations are the primary sources of adult supervision and guidance. And teens need a "caring adult who recognizes a young person as an individual and who serves as a mentor, coach, gentle but firm critic, and advocate."[15] Yet many inner-city youths see school "as a place that has rejected and labeled them by *what they are not* [for example, not college-bound] rather than by *what they are.*"[16]

Junior high and high school students are becoming more ethnically, racially, linguistically, and religiously diverse. Many rural, urban, and suburban schools are becoming home to new immigrants from around the world; one of the fastest-growing ethnic group is that of Asian Americans. Also, children and youths are more likely to live below the poverty level than any other age group. The conditions in which low-income students live differ greatly from those of students in middle-class and upper-middle-class communities, which in turn are also becoming more isolated one from another.

Although there remain neighborhoods in which most families are from the same ethnic group, many areas are diverse. Public housing units and shopping centers often include families from different national, ethnic, racial, and language groups. Young people in these neighborhoods interact with peers from other groups to confront the street and its dangers as well as to pursue common interests.

Today's teenagers have complex identities that are influenced by their peers, parents, teachers, neighborhoods, and community and religious leaders. Their identity is also influenced by their ethnic membership and the interaction of that membership with the dominant society. Out-of-school experiences are at least as important in these youngsters' development as are school experiences. It is within these multiple contexts that young people define themselves as, for example, Latino, older sister, daughter, Catholic, smart, and athlete.

ECONOMIC REALITIES A 1996 study of young people and voting found that young people are not apathetic and cynical, but that they are realistic about the economic realities in which they live. Today's youth, the study reported,

> are the first generation that does not expect to exceed their parents' standard of living. They have already borne substantial responsibility caring for younger siblings, and this shows up in their sharp concern for children and for younger generations. They do not expect that they can keep their own children protected as they were protected. They do not expect to be able to afford an education for their children. This generation does expect that they will need to support their own parents in retirement. They do not expect that Social Security will exist for their own retirement.[17]

Although they may be worried and somewhat pessimistic about their future economic conditions, they continue to seek out postsecondary education to improve their job and career opportunities. In 1998 66 percent of high school graduates entered college immediately after graduation as compared to 49 percent of the graduates in 1972.[18]

Many young people begin to work while they are in high school. Nearly 40 percent of sixteen- to nineteen-year-old high school students are working. There is evidence of a strong positive link between working in high school and obtaining a job after graduation. After-school jobs are particularly beneficial to students from low-income families who do not have family or school connections to help them find employment. Eight to ten years after high school, people who worked as teenagers earn more than their counterparts who did not.[19] Unfortunately, many students who could derive long-term benefits from working while in high school—those in inner-city areas—have limited access to jobs. The lack of employment opportunities contributes to low self-esteem and to pessimism about the future and the value of school. In addition, in communities in which there is high unemployment, many young people do not get opportunities to learn how to work either through their own experiences or through the modeling of working adults.

RESILIENCY Many young people overcome disastrous childhood and adolescent experiences and go on to become successful workers, professionals, and community leaders. These individuals' personal attributes give them strength and fortitude and help them confront overwhelming obstacles that seem designed to prevent them from reaching their potential. This ability to overcome devastating conditions in one's environment is **resiliency.** Resilient students are usually social, optimistic, energetic, cooperative, inquisitive, attentive, helpful, punctual, and on task. Richard Sagor suggests that educators design four types of educational experiences to help students develop resiliency:

- Provide students with authentic evidence of academic success (competence);
- Show them that they are valued members of a community (belonging);
- Reinforce feelings that they have made a real contribution to their community (usefulness); and
- Make them feel empowered (potency).[20]

resiliency
The ability to overcome overwhelming obstacles to achieve and be successful in school and life.

CHALLENGES OF YOUTH CULTURE

Adults usually regard teenagers as too young to have the benefits of adulthood. They expect teenagers to enjoy youth, begin dating, develop friendships, plan for their future—and learn how to behave like responsible adults. At the same time, many adults see adolescents as teenage mothers, welfare queens, gang members, drug abusers, and killers. Young people are bombarded by messages about themselves in music, movies, books, and television. Other potent influences are the circumstances in which teenagers live, which may include drugs, violence, and the lack of adult support. Young people must sort through all these influences as well as the messages given by significant peers and adults in their lives. This section explores some of the challenges with which most teens struggle and about which they make decisions, whether alone or with help from others.

SEXUALITY The defining of one's **sexuality**—one's nature as a sexual being—begins in the early teens and continues throughout life. Coming to terms with one's sexuality often involves some turmoil both within oneself and with parents and caretakers during the teen years. Many young women will also be confronted with the danger of sexual assault. While trying to develop intimate relations with young men, they may fear them. The development of a healthy sexual self is a complicated process.

The definition of self for many young women is influenced by perceptions of cultural expectations as reflected on magazine covers and movie screens around the world. Rejection is to be avoided at all costs, perfection in all walks of life is achievable, and slim is beautiful.

Many teenagers associate sex itself with the freedom and sophistication of adulthood. The decision about having sex is one that causes much consternation among youths. Their uncertainty is fueled by the mixed messages they receive from parents, teenage friends, religious doctrines, the media, and older adult friends. At the same time that one medium glamorizes sex, other voices tell teenagers that sex is sinful and that abstinence before marriage is the only moral option.

Girls and women often connect sex with being accepted, being attractive to another, and being loved. Many boys and men, by contrast, link sex with status, power, domination, and violence—a far cry from the loving relationship that many females have envisioned. Thus, ideal sexuality for men and women differs. These different perceptions of what is correct and acceptable behavior place both sexes in jeopardy. Women may be sexually attacked; men may be arrested for sexual harassment or rape.

Rape is most often the reason for the sexual activity of young girls. Six of ten girls fourteen years old and younger report rape as a sexual experience, and it is the only experience for 43 percent of those who have had sexual relations at that age.[21] Although adolescents may be more sexually active than in past generations, sex is not always a voluntary choice for young women.

Teenage sex is not, however, as rampant as many believe. The sexual activity of both teenage females and teenage males is decreasing. A 1995 study showed that the percentage of teenage males ages fifteen to nineteen who had had sexual intercourse declined from 60 percent in 1988 to 55 percent in 1995. The study also found that teenagers were becoming more responsible about sex and using contraceptives more often.[22]

sexuality
The character of a sexual self—how a person sees herself or himself and what choices one makes regarding sexual activity.

Concurrently, there has been a decline in teenage births. Junior high students are not producing babies at the high rate that media reports would sometimes have the public believe. In fact, 98 percent of junior high girls reach the age of fifteen without becoming pregnant. One out of ten teens becomes pregnant or causes pregnancy; one out of twenty-five actually becomes a parent; and one in forty becomes a parent without being married.[23] Teenage males are not fathering the babies of most teenage females. Instead, two-thirds of teen pregnancies are the result of sexual relations between teenagers and men over 20.[24]

Poverty appears to be the most important factor in determining who teenage mothers will be. Of pregnant teenage girls, 83 percent are in poverty. Eighty-five percent of unmarried teenage mothers are from low-income families. "Early motherhood is a survival strategy by young women from indigent, chaotic families which often attracts resources from family, public agencies, and men that would not otherwise have been available."[25] To reduce teenage pregnancy, we may need to reduce poverty in these families. Certainly, pregnancy has much less to do with age and ethnicity than with poverty.

Many teenage parents, especially mothers, are forced to take on adult responsibilities much earlier than society expects of its youth. Too often, teenage mothers are forced to fend for themselves under poverty conditions. Their own parents can provide little or no support, and the fathers of their children are often absent and not contributing financially.

Teenagers are becoming more responsible about their sexual activity and are learning to use contraception to reduce the risk of pregnancy and the transmission of AIDS and other venereal diseases. School programs such as sex education and health clinics are helpful, but they are not always supported by families and communities. Educators should be aware that the teen years are traumatic for many young people as they struggle with the development of their sexuality. Teenagers' apprehensions and activities related to sex may affect their school behavior and their ability to perform satisfactorily in school.

DROPPING OUT Students drop out of high school and college for different reasons, but dropping out at either level is harmful to young people in the long term. In the United States over 25 percent of all persons twenty-five or older have not completed high school. However, the dropout rate is less for younger people, as shown in Figure 3.2. The dropout rate has gradually decreased over the past three decades. In 1998, 88 percent of all eighteen- to twenty-four-year-olds had

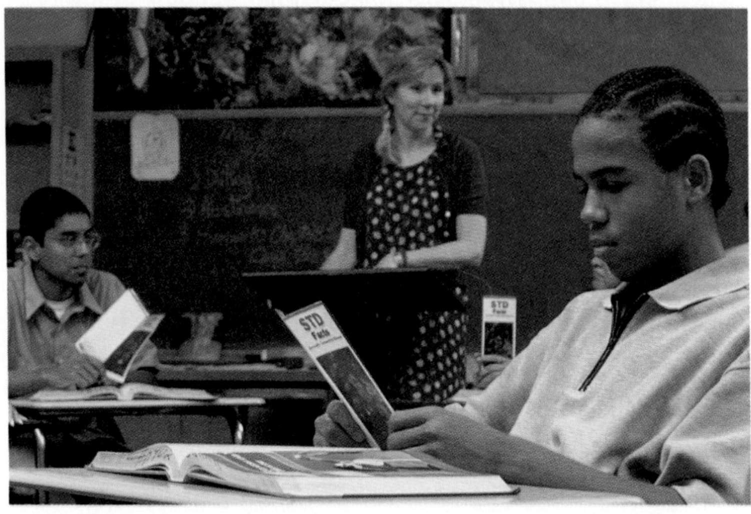

Motivated by the AIDS epidemic, many schools now offer programs that promote awareness of sexually transmitted diseases.

FIGURE 3.2 DROPOUT RATES BY RACIAL OR ETHNIC GROUP

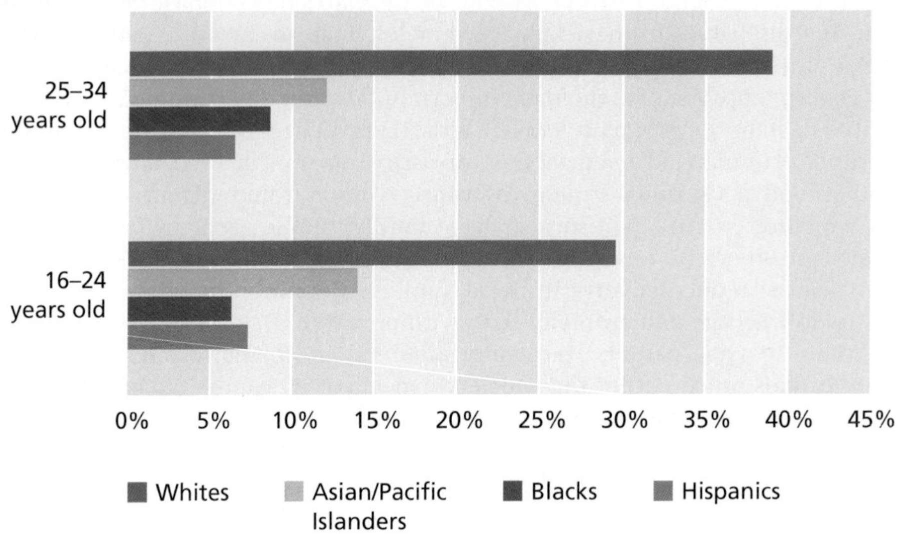

Source: U.S. Department of Education, National Center for Education Statistics, *The Condition of Education 1999,* NCES 2000-009; and *Digest of Education Statistics 1999.* Washington, DC: U.S. Government Printing Office, 1999.

completed high school or GEDs. About 5 percent of students in the tenth to twelfth grades drop out each year—a figure that has fluctuated only slightly for nearly twenty years.

Hispanic students continue to have a fairly high dropout rate. In 1998 30 percent of Hispanic teenagers had dropped out of high school in the previous year. Hispanic students who speak English well are more likely to complete high school than are students whose English proficiency is limited. The largest proportion of Hispanic dropouts are immigrants who never attended U.S. schools; many had not completed more than elementary school in their countries of birth. Although first- and later-generation Hispanics graduate at higher rates than immigrants, they are still two to three times more likely to drop out of school than peers from other ethnic groups. More Mexican Americans drop out of high school than other Hispanics.[26]

Students from low-income families drop out of high school at a rate seven times greater than that of students from middle- and high-income families. Students whose parents did not finish high school are three times as likely not to complete high school as those whose parents did graduate. More females finish high school than males, and a greater percentage of students without disabilities complete high school than students with disabilities.[27] Students who complete high school are more likely than dropouts to be employed. Eighty-five percent of high school graduates are in the labor force as compared to 65 percent of dropouts.

Talented high school graduates who do not seek postsecondary training represent another type of dropout. Just over half of the students who enter 4-year colleges graduate. The underdeveloped talent of these students represents a substantial loss to society.

DRUGS One of the questions with which many teenagers struggle is whether to experiment with nicotine, alcohol, and other drugs. Although not as glamorized in films and advertisements as in the past, drinking and smoking are still associated with independence and adult behavior. Teens use drugs for different reasons. Sometimes biological predispositions or psychological problems trigger drug use. In other cases social pressures, family problems, or self-hate lead young people to drugs.

The public worries about drug use. In the 2000 Phi Delta Kappa/Gallup Poll of the Public's Attitudes Toward Public Schools, respondents ranked the use of drugs as the fifth greatest problem behind the lack of financial support for schools, lack of discipline, overcrowding, and fighting/violence/gangs.[28] Parents worry particularly about drug usage that may lead to chemical dependency in the future. **Chemical dependency,** such as addiction to drugs, alcohol, or tobacco, is one of the causes of social and academic problems among youths. People are judged to be dependent when they find that their need for the chemical substance is constant and they can no longer control their use. Dependency can be difficult to overcome and often requires professional treatment.

chemical dependency The habitual use, either for psychological or physical needs, of a substance such as drugs, alcohol, or tobacco.

A large percentage of teenagers do try one or more drugs; alcohol is the favorite, being used more than twice as often as other drugs. Figure 3.3 shows the percentages of high school seniors who have used alcohol, marijuana, and other

FIGURE 3.3 PERCENTAGE OF HIGH SCHOOL SENIORS WHO REPORTED USING ALCOHOL OR ILLEGAL DRUGS ANY TIME DURING THE PREVIOUS YEAR

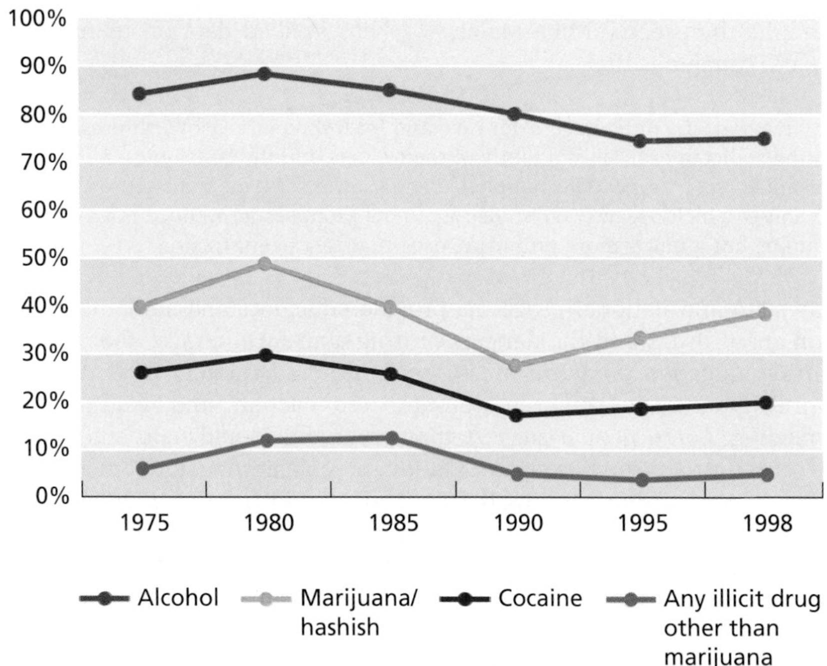

Source: U.S. Department of Education, National Center for Education Statistics, *Digest of Education Statistics 1999*. Washington, DC: U.S. Government Printing Office, 1999.

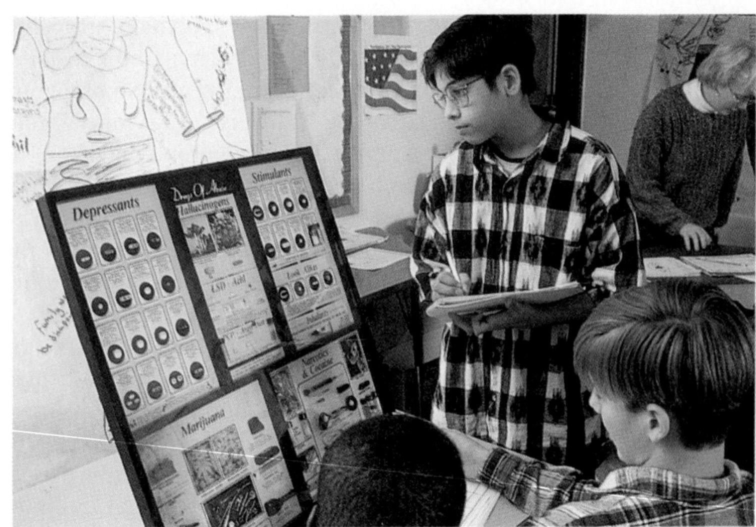

Programs to prevent and reduce drug and alcohol abuse in schools focus on educating students, as well as on forming community self-help groups and involving specially trained police officers to instruct students.

illicit drugs. Although the rate of usage is higher than the public may find acceptable, current usage by seniors is down from what it was in the mid-1970s and throughout most of the 1980s. Students who plan to attend college are less likely to use drugs. Male teenagers are only slightly more likely than females to use drugs other than marijuana.[29]

Teens under age eighteen use illegal drugs other than marijuana less than any other age group in the U.S. population. Figure 3.4 graphs usage of some drugs by different age groups showing that drug use is much more prevalent among adults than teens. Mike Males, who has studied data on teenagers for many years, concludes that

> The large majority of teenagers, for now and for unknown reasons, are resisting both the addicted examples of many of their elders and the histrionics of the official anti-drug crusade. The national turning away of American youths from drug abuse, which began two decades ago, now promises to produce not a drug-abstaining but a much more promising drug-managing generation.[30]

Many state and national programs provide educators and students with information about drugs and the dangers of drug abuse. Generally, the most successful drug education programs are those that are adequately funded, involve parents and students, are taught by well-prepared teachers, and avoid preaching and moralizing. Some people suggest that programs should help students understand and control normal experimentation, in which the majority of teenagers participate, as well as emphasizing the perils of self-destructive addiction.

VIOLENCE Television news reports, newspapers, and politicians all proclaim that the nation is becoming more violent, and they present numerous examples to make the point. It is certainly true that the United States is the most violent industrialized nation in the world. For example, twenty million teenagers between the ages of fifteen and nineteen live in the United Kingdom, Canada, Australia, Germany, France, and Italy; in 1990 300 of these young people were murdered, whereas 3,000 of the United States' seventeen million teenagers were killed. During that same year, 30 of Japan's teens were involved in murders.[31] The rate of adult murders in the United States, too, is seven times higher than in other industrialized nations.[32]

A 1994 Gallup poll found that U.S. adults think that youths commit more than three times as much violent crime as they actually do. Fourteen percent of those arrested for murder are fifteen- to eighteen-year-olds. The greatest increases in arrests since 1969 have been for drunk driving, drug abuse, and larceny/theft. Forty-three percent of people arrested for murders are eighteen- to twenty-four-year-olds; over half of those arrested for rape are over 25 years old. Almost 80 percent of serious and nonserious crimes are committed by males; murder victims are also more likely to be males.

Another myth is that most youths who are murdered are killed by their peers in gang shootings and other conflicts. In fact, two-thirds of slain youths in the United States are victims of adult-perpetrated crime. Youths are the predominant perpetrators of street violence, but adults are the aggressors in home violence. Young people (twelve to nineteen years old) are nearly four times as likely to be victims as those over thirty-five.

FIGURE 3.4 **CURRENT DRUG USE BY TYPE OF DRUG AND AGE GROUP: 1997**

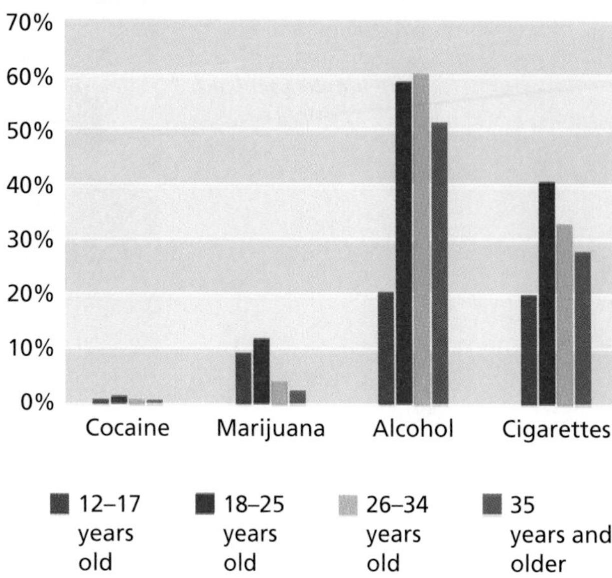

Source: U.S. Census Bureau, *Statistical Abstract of the United States: 1999.* Washington, DC: U.S. Government Printing Office, 1999.

Crime is related more directly to poverty than to the age of the criminal. At all age levels, persons with low incomes are more likely than persons with higher incomes to commit crimes. They are also more likely to be the victims of violent crimes. One reason for the higher crime rate for burglary and auto theft among teens is that a larger proportion of teens than of adults live in poverty. Low-income teenagers commit crimes at about the same rate as adults who live in poverty. At the same time, most people in poverty do not commit crimes.

Gangs involve more students than ever. A 1995 survey of law enforcement agencies found a total of 23,388 gangs and nearly 700,000 gang members in the United States. There are gangs in all states and in most large cities; a growing number of smaller cities and rural areas are also becoming homes to gangs.[33] There are some female gangs, but most gangs are made up of young men. For youths of both sexes, gangs can provide a sense of place and a feeling of importance as well as a strong identity structure. Gangs often provide a discipline that has been missing from the experience of many young people. Most gangs are not violent, but those that are violent are territorial.

Suicide is another form of violence that affects the student population. However, the suicide rate for teenagers is lower than that for people between the ages of 20 and 54; there are 12 suicides for every 100,000 teens. Whites are more likely to commit suicide than nonwhite groups, and males take their own life nearly five times as often as females. Suicide attempts are often calls for help. Teachers should be alert for signs that may suggest the need for a referral to other professionals.

Gangs involve more school-age students than ever before. Schools are trying to combat gang and other youth violence through conflict resolution and other programs that help students learn to handle problems.

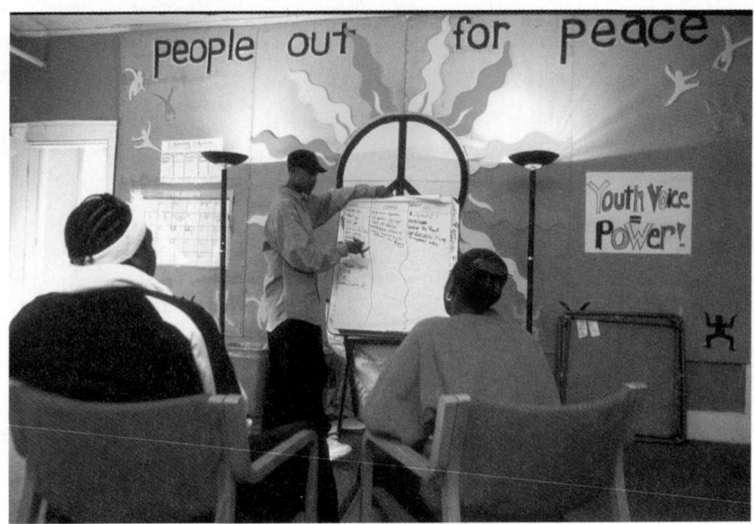

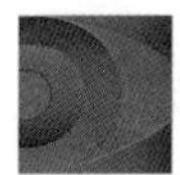

DEMOCRACY AND SCHOOLING

Children learn to function in society through the process called socialization. Parents and families are usually the primary socialization agents, especially in the early years of a child's life. Children also learn culturally appropriate behaviors through religious training, the community, and even television. On the child's entrance in school, whether as an infant or at age six, teachers and other school personnel take on socializing roles during a large portion of the student's waking hours. At this point, the family shares the teaching function with professionals in schools.

Schooling and educators in a liberal democratic society face numerous tensions, in part because there is no one agreed-upon way to educate students. There is a strain between the public rights mandated by democratic principles and the private rights demanded by capitalist markets. Democracy calls for equality, while capitalism adapts to inequality. A liberal education for all is the goal of one; preparation for work is the goal of the other. Public schools tend to heed both sides and simultaneously promote some of both. Teachers confront these tensions in their schools and in the communities that have an influence on their work. Some of these issues are elaborated in this section.

EQUALITY AND EDUCATION

meritocracy
A system based on the belief that individuals' achievements are based on their own personal merits and hard work and that the people who achieve at the highest levels deserve the greatest social and financial rewards.

Although equality is an espoused goal of democracy, its meaning differs from one person to another. Many believe that each individual has an equal chance at success, which is often measured by the dominant group in terms of wealth and accumulated material goods. This system of **meritocracy** is built on the idea that with hard work, diligence, and persistence, an individual should be able to finish school, attend college, and obtain a well-paying job. Poverty and discrimination are obstacles to be overcome by individuals.

A problem with the meritocracy approach is that not all individuals begin the game of life from the same starting line. Whites from the middle class and above start with advantages such as membership in the dominant culture, sufficient family income to support a college education, decent housing, adequate health care, and good schools with qualified teachers. In reality the children of the wealthy have a much greater chance of being wealthy in their adulthood than do the children of low-income families. The powerful are able to ensure that their advantages are inherited by their children. Therefore, equality of opportunity could begin to be realized only if the children from powerless groups were provided the same or similar advantages.

You learn about equality in history and civics, but you find out life is not really like that.

Arthur Ashe

Critics of the public rhetoric on equality charge that U.S. institutions and political and economic systems are rigged to support the privileged few rather than the pluralistic majority. Both the shrinking middle class and the widening gap between wealth and poverty contribute to this problem. Nevertheless, some people still think that a more equitable society is not only desirable but also possible to achieve. Resources could begin to be more fairly distributed if all workers received a decent wage. The application of civil rights laws and a drastic reduction of discriminatory practices would contribute greatly to the provision of fairness and justice in the distribution of societal benefits. In the same spirit, schools should question whether their policies and practices are equitable. One step in this investigation might be an examination of whether gifted and talented programs and honors programs are accessible to students from diverse cultural groups.

If a society accepts equality as one of its primary goals, its members must be active participants in achieving the goal. A truly egalitarian society will not accept the needless human suffering and exploitation that are reflected in homelessness; an inadequate minimum wage; or schools that are dangerous, unsafe, and/or inadequately staffed. Such a society must also confront and eliminate racism, sexism, and other forms of discrimination.

EQUAL EDUCATIONAL OPPORTUNITY One way to address equality in the educational system is to offer **equal educational opportunity:** to provide to all students, regardless of their backgrounds, similar opportunities to learn and to benefit from schooling. The dilemma in this approach is the question of what constitutes equal educational opportunity. On the surface it would seem that all students should have access to high-quality teaching, small classes, up-to-date technology, college preparatory courses, a building that supports learning, and a safe environment. In reality most equal educational opportunity programs have struggled with overcoming educational deficiencies of underserved students by providing compensatory or remedial programs to reduce the educational gaps that have given advantaged students a head start. Most policymakers and educators have not addressed the other factors that would provide equal opportunity.

Even when the school has the latest technology, is clean and well maintained, and is staffed by qualified professionals, equal opportunity is not automatically guaranteed. Many other factors need to be considered. What percentages of students in advanced mathematics and science classes are female and students of color? Who are the students who make up the college preparatory and advanced placement classes? Who is assigned to or chooses a general or vocational track? Who is referred to special education classes? Who has access to the best teachers? Who participates in which extracurricular activities? If the percentages of students from diverse groups in these various school settings are somewhat proportional to their representation in the school population as a whole, equal educational opportunity may be approaching the goal of its supporters.

equal educational opportunity Access to similar education for all students regardless of their cultural background or family circumstances.

RELEVANT RESEARCH

Conflict of Liberal Discourse and Self-Interest

STUDY PURPOSE/QUESTIONS: How do middle-class parents think about schooling and school structures that support equality?

STUDY DESIGN: The researchers used an interpretive mode of inquiry in which interviews provided the data source. In a Midwestern university town where eight of the thirteen elementary schools were segregated by social class, the researchers selected twenty middle-class families to participate in the study. In all cases the mothers volunteered to be interviewed.

STUDY FINDINGS: Although the narratives and positions of the twenty participants varied, a number of patterns did emerge. The mothers verbally supported socially inclusive and integrated ideals of education. At the same time they worked with school officials to ensure that their own children received the advantages to which they thought they were naturally entitled. "The mothers in this study felt their children would gain from stratified and segregated, rather than equitable and inclusive school structure, [but] they were not comfortable taking an openly elitist, conservative position on schooling" (p. 590).

IMPLICATIONS: The liberal support for inclusivity of the participants in this study was in conflict with their overt efforts to guarantee that their own children received advantages. This dilemma often makes it very difficult to initiate reforms for equality. Many families whose children have traditionally had the advantages of programs for "gifted" students and other tracking practices are unwilling to give up those programs and practices to ensure that all students have access to a challenging curriculum.

Source: Ellen Brantlinger, Massoumeh Majd-Jabbari, and Samuel L. Guskin, "Self-Interest and Liberal Educational Discourse: How Ideology Works for Middle-Class Mothers," *American Educational Research Journal, 33* (3) (Fall 1996): 571–597.

OPPORTUNITY TO LEARN STANDARDS Schools today are expected to provide all students the opportunity to learn the skills outlined in national standards for mathematics, science, English, the arts, foreign languages, history, geography, civics, and economics. The provision of remediation for the underserved is no longer the focus. The expectation is that all students can learn. The general public also expects U.S. students to achieve better on international tests than students in any other part of the world. However, one may wonder whether opportunity to learn actually means the ability to perform well on some tests. More optimistically, national standards could help to prevent students from being tracked into courses and programs that limit their access to higher-level knowledge. They could even encourage critical thinking and the ability to view the world and academic subjects from multiple perspectives.

EQUALITY OF RESULTS Some theorists and educators would argue that we must not stop at just providing the opportunity to learn. Opportunity to learn places the burden on individuals, in that they choose whether to take advantage of the opportunity. But if the goal is to ensure equality of results, teachers would be expected to develop strategies for helping all students learn at a high level. They would start their careers with the disposition or belief that all children, regardless of their group memberships and environmental circumstances, are capable of learning. Students who were not performing well academically or otherwise would become the intellectual challenges for the teacher or, even better, for a team of teachers and other support personnel. The goal would become developing strategies to ensure learning rather than simply moving students to a different class to accommodate their limitations (and limit their chances for success in school).

ROLES OF SCHOOLS

Schools play many roles in society. Not only do they prepare students to be contributors to society, they also reflect society's high ideals (universal education) and bad practices (differential opportunity based on race and income). One's philosophical and political perspectives determine how one views the roles of schools. The following questions help clarify some different perspectives on the goals of schools:

1. Should schools present themselves as a model of our best hopes for society and as a mechanism for remaking that society in the image of those hopes?
2. Should schools focus on adapting students to the needs of society as currently constructed?
3. Should schools focus primarily on serving the individual hopes and ambitions of their students?[34]

In other words, should schools be supportive primarily of democratic equality, social efficiency, or social mobility? Advocates of democratic equality view education as a public good in which all students should be exposed to a liberal arts education and should learn to be productive citizens in a democracy. Proponents of social efficiency believe that schools should serve the private sector by preparing students for future jobs; this goal has probably been the most dominant in the past. However, many people now see promoting social mobility as a more important role of schools. People with this perspective view education as an asset that can be accumulated and used for social competition. Credentials are more important than what is learned; the purpose is to gain a competitive advantage over others so as to secure a desirable social position.

REPRODUCTION Traditionally, schools are expected to reproduce the cultural, political, social, and economic order of society. However, theorists differ in their views of how schools actually perform this reproduction role. Functionalism, conflict theory, and resistance theory provide contradictory descriptions of how schools carry out their reproductive role for society.

Functionalists view schools as important in supporting technological development, material well-being, and democracy. Since the release of the federal report *A Nation at Risk* in 1983, most reports calling for the reform of schools have referred to the need for an educated workforce. A less explicit message of those reports is that schools should socialize students for their roles as workers. Schools should also provide equal educational opportunity for all students and be a primary step for improving their social and economic status.

Conflict theorists also view schools as reproductive of society, but in ways less noble than those described by functionalists. The conflict theorists conclude that schools have been structured to maintain the power and dominance of the individuals and groups that benefit most from the current system. Rather than being benevolent institutions that provide all students an equal chance to succeed, schools legitimize existing inequities. Advantages depend greatly on ascribed characteristics. Students whose parents graduated from college are much more likely to graduate from college; students whose parents never finished high school are themselves more likely not to finish high school. The academic tracking systems in many schools reinforce this unequal distribution. The number of middle-class students in college preparatory and advanced placement courses is disproportionately high relative to the total school population. The number of males and students of color in special education classes is disproportionately high; students of color and those from low-income families are underrepresented in gifted and talented programs. It appears to these critics that one group is being groomed for management positions in the labor market while the second group is being prepared to labor under the direction of the first. Thus, schools provide neither equal educational opportunity nor a chance to improve one's status to any appreciable degree (except in rare individual cases).

Over the past decade researchers working on resistance theory have investigated the interactions of students and teachers as schools carry out their reproduction function. These researchers have found that reproduction is not an automatic process that is implemented with systematic precision. Students sometimes resist domination by school authorities. They do not readily accept their inferiority status. Seth Kreisberg describes student resistance:

> Students resist doing homework and delay the beginning of classes. They develop intricate systems of cheating and psyching out teachers. They smoke cigarettes and marijuana in school bathrooms and sell drugs in school stairwells. They are opinionated with teachers and wear clothes that offend adults. They refuse to participate in some classes and organize to change unfair rules.[35]

The resistance theory suggests much more interaction in the reproduction process than has been explained by the previous two theories. It also allows for the possibility that people can change the system of reproduction by encouraging the development of schools that are not based on domination and submission and that actually model democracy. Through the process of resistance, students can become active participants who help define and redefine schools.

RECONSTRUCTIONISM Some educators believe that schools are able to do more than just reproduce society. They believe that schools do not need merely to reflect the inequities that prevail in the broader society; rather, schools can reconstruct or transform society. Reconstructionist educators believe that all students can learn at a high level regardless of their race, ethnicity, gender, or socioeconomic status. And they argue that education can make more of a difference in the lives of students than it currently does.

To implement a reconstructionist approach, classrooms and schools become democratic settings in which both students and teachers are active learners and participants. Students study problems confronting society and learn how to confront practices that are inequitable to some students. Teachers and other school personnel actively work with the community to overcome inequities and injustices to students and their families. Social justice, human rights, human dignity, and equity are critical values that guide the work of reconstructionism. In the reconstructionist process the school itself should become a model of democracy that leads, rather than follows, societal practices.

PURPOSES OF SCHOOLS

Shortcomings in the current education system are related to one's perception of the purposes of schooling. Depending on the speaker and the times, the reasons for schools' problems differ. Sometimes people point to the poor quality of the curriculum, the teachers, or the preparation of teachers. At other times too much bureaucracy in the school system is the culprit. Some observers blame school problems on poverty, discrimination, and privilege in society. Some identify economic conditions, changing family values, or the gap between schools and families as the root cause of the lack of learning. To others, the fundamental problem is a lack of agreement about the desired outcomes of schools.

School boards, educators, parents, and communities have their own beliefs about the basic purposes of schools and the reasons for current problems in schools. These beliefs often draw ammunition from national reports calling for the reform of education. Through such reports and through discussions and debates among individuals and groups, U.S. society continually refines and redefines ideas about the purposes of schools. The five purposes described below are only a sampling of those most often mentioned by educators and the public. Most schools address each of these purposes, but in any given school, one purpose may receive more prominence than others at a given time.

CITIZENSHIP Educators, parents, and policymakers agree that schools should help students become *good citizens.* There is less agreement about how schools should do this. In some schools, especially elementary schools, students receive a grade or rating on their "citizenship" within the classroom. Historically, students have taken a civics or government course or have studied citizenship issues in another social studies course. The focus in citizenship education or in civics and government courses is usually on the structure of the United States' political system and on treasured documents such as the Constitution and Bill of Rights. Patriotism and loyalty to the United States are implicit values that often undergird both these courses and the school's hidden curriculum. A limitation of this patriotic approach is that students might not get the opportunity to grapple with the problems and

Citizenship education in public schools implicitly values patriotism and loyalty to one's country.

issues that are inherent in democratic society. Students may learn the civic values but never be pushed to discuss why inequities remain in society.

Preparation for citizenship cannot be taught in a single course. The school should work to develop democratic citizens who respect others; believe in human dignity; are concerned about and care for others; and fight for justice, fairness, and tolerance. Dewey also believed that good citizenship involves participating in the making of laws as well as obeying them. Education should help students develop habits of mind that will bring about social changes without introducing disorder.[36] Students will learn through practice how to be active, involved citizens. What better place to model democratic practice and equitable participation than in our schools?

READINESS FOR THE WORKFORCE A major concern expressed in a number of national reports on education has been the quality of the workforce, which includes growing numbers of women and people of color at all levels. Many observers blame schools for not providing students with the skills and behaviors necessary to participate in today's economy. Some employers report that many young people do not read, write, or compute at the level needed for the jobs available. In response these employers have sometimes established their own training programs to teach basic literacy.

There is a lack of agreement about the nature of these necessary skills, especially in an economy in which the greatest growth in jobs will be in the service areas, where people of color and women have disproportionately high representation. Most high schools prepare students either to attend college or to get a job soon after graduation. Many areas of the country have vocational high schools to teach occupational skills. Many school districts have also established magnet schools with single purposes, including career preparation in the arts; health fields; computing; and service areas such as foods, hotels, and tourism. A serious dilemma is the overrepresentation of low-income students, students of color, and females in nonacademic tracks.

Educators, policymakers, and the business community debate the "real" purpose of schools. Is it to help students learn a trade, or learn how to learn, or learn

Many students begin preparing for a job by taking vocational courses in high school or at postsecondary vocational schools.

how to take orders and follow the rules? This question is particularly important when conditions change as rapidly as they do in today's society. The vocation for which one is prepared initially may become obsolete within a few years. Perhaps students should be prepared to think, adjust to change, and be active participants in their life's work. They need to be able to handle change and to adapt to new occupations and situations.

ACADEMIC ACHIEVEMENT Media reports of student scores on achievement tests often highlight schools' ability to offer students a strong academic background. Some school districts base their reputations on how well their students perform and how many are admitted to colleges. In some communities parents will camp out overnight to be first in line to enroll their children in a preschool that will provide the jump start needed for success on future tests to ensure admission in prestigious colleges and universities.

Countries and their education systems are compared through student scores on international tests. When the scores of U.S. students fall below those of students in other countries, parents and policymakers become concerned. Concern about performance in reading, writing, and mathematics periodically leads to a back-to-basics movement in which the traditional academic subjects are emphasized. "Frills" such as the development of self-esteem, hobby activities, and any other areas that take time away from academic study are condemned as a misuse of public funds. In response, some states and school districts have increased the length of the school day so that students have more time to learn academic subjects. One of the related debates is whether to promote students if they have not achieved at the expected level.

The attention to academic achievement in the 1990s focused on the development of national standards in the arts, English, health, mathematics, physical education, social studies (including civics, geography, and history), and science. Many schools have revised their curricula to be standards-based. Test publishers have revised standardized tests used by states and school districts to reflect these standards. One of the principles that undergirds the work on standards and assessments is the belief that *all* students can learn. Low-income students, students of color, and females are expected to learn at the high levels historically expected of middle-class white males. School systems' reputations—and sometimes their state funding—are dependent on how well students perform.

SOCIAL DEVELOPMENT One of the reasons that parents send their children to school is to give them the opportunity to develop interpersonal skills by interacting with other students. In this process students learn to respect others; they also learn a set of rules for working appropriately with peers and adults. Although there is usually not a course to teach skills in social development, appropriate behavior is constantly reinforced by teachers and other school personnel in the classroom and on the playground.

Teachers can give students opportunities to work with students from diverse cultural backgrounds and to learn about those differences in the process. Teachers can encourage interactions across groups through cooperative learning activities in which students from different groups are placed together. Other team projects allow teachers to place together students who might not seek each other out otherwise. A part of teaching is helping students to learn to work together positively.

Today's technology also opens many possibilities for interactions with students and adults in cultures beyond school boundaries. Internet and two-way

DEBATE

Can Retention Be Good for a Student?

Gwendolyn Malone, a fifth grade teacher in rural Clarke County, Virginia, is president of the 133-member Clarke County Education Association. A teacher for five years when she wrote this piece, Malone works at Cooley Elementary. She can be reached at maloneg@clarke.k12.va.us.

A child recently reached my fifth grade classroom without the ability to read even at a first grade level.

The child had been systematically promoted with his peers for years in the hopes that he would eventually pick up the necessary reading skills.

Every other student in the class knew the child couldn't read. The embarrassment was so painful the child cried every single time I called on him.

If this child had been retained at the primary grade level, he might have learned to read. He might have avoided years of humiliation. And he might have been more prepared for upper elementary skills, including risk-taking, guessing, context clueing, and the use of prior knowledge.

Social promotion set this child up for repeated failure, low self-esteem, and a high risk of becoming a drop-out statistic. Retention might have prepared this child for academic success.

For most struggling children, retention provides the opportunity to refresh, relearn, and acquire new skills that help them move to the next grade level.

Most important, if framed properly, retention gives students self-confidence and an "I can do this" attitude that's likely to boost their academic achievement for years to come.

But if grade retention is to be successful, educators must:

- Stop sitting back and hoping against all odds that children, if promoted, will eventually absorb the skills they need. It won't happen.
- Nip the problem in the bud by retaining students early in their school careers.

Kids get an essential educational foundation in kindergarten, first, and second grade. If they don't have a grasp of the basics at this age, they shouldn't be permitted to move on.

Philip Bowser, a past National Association of School Psychologists "school psychologist of the year," is an NEA activist in Roseburg, Oregon. Bowser can be reached at pbowser@orednet.org.

Imagine going to your physician with an illness. The doctor says, "There's an old treatment for your condition. At best, it helps only one in 10 who get it, but no one can predict which one.

"That one person will experience a little bit of relief for a short period of time," the doctor continues, "but then the problem will return. Everyone will have negative side effects, some of which can be severe, some lifelong."

The illness is underachievement. The treatment—if educators practice full disclosure—is grade retention.

It's easy to understand the appeal of holding back a student who fails to meet benchmarks. Retention can take a student from the bottom of a class to somewhere nearer the middle. That seems like progress, doesn't it?

The problem is that students are compared to the grade placement, not to their peers. The students have "caught up" to the wrong group!

Most likely, the learning problems that contributed to the original retention decision will persist, and the retained students, in a year or two, will be back at the bottom of the class.

As a districtwide school psychologist, I follow retained students for a few years. In my experience, grade retention is a dangerous gamble.

But you don't have to take my word for it. The research shows that:

- Retained students rarely make significant academic progress in the retained year.
- First or second graders who show improvement over nonretained, underachieving peers quickly lose that advantage. The two groups soon perform the same academically, but the retained group develops measurable mental health problems.
- A single retention increases a student's probability of dropping out by 21 to 27 percent.

I'd like to call these three grades simply "primary grades," stop grading students in them, and instead provide a list of skills each child must master and knowledge they must acquire before advancing to third grade.

- Establish a way of transitioning students into the next higher grade when they're ready.

If children have mastered third grade skills or if retained children have "caught up," then they shouldn't have to remain in an unproductive or unchallenging setting. They should be moved within that academic year to an academically appropriate or age-appropriate level.

When kids see that there's a way out of a situation they don't like, they'll take it. Retained students will see the incentive to learn and be promoted with their peers.

Students who are retained early on with support and nurturing tend to feel better about themselves and enjoy school more than those who reach the later elementary levels not only unprepared but ashamed that other students are aware of their deficiencies.

Students who are promoted without the academic skills they need become embarrassed, hurt, angry, and defensive. That makes it even harder for them to catch up.

It would be easier, more academically sound, and even more economical to prevent dropouts by retaining these children in the primary grades.

Let's give these students what they need—a hand up, not a hand-out.

Source: Can Retention Be Good for a Student? from *NEA Today,* March 1998, p. 43.

- The stigma of retention damages self-concept and creates a negative attitude toward school to a much greater degree than most educators predict beforehand or recognize later.
- The most common retainee is a nonwhite male, small of stature, from a low-income family, with parents uninvolved in schooling.
- "Old for grade" adolescents are at increased risk for substance abuse, earlier sexual activity, behavioral problems, and emotional distress.

Those who frame the problem as a choice among grade retention, social promotion, or low academic standards don't see the variety of existing remedies with stronger therapeutic force and fewer side effects.

What if school districts took the cost of extending a student's career an extra year—on average, $5,000—and used the money for effective prevention and remediation programs?

What if teachers had decent class sizes and adequate time to reflect and plan individualized instruction?

What if schools involved parents earlier, gaining their support for additional tutoring, cross-grade groupings, and summer school?

Wouldn't these solutions be more effective than running kids through the same course of instruction that has already proven inadequate?

When parents and teachers decide to retain, they do so in the dark, in spite of ample evidence that they will be adding a significant risk factor to the life of a child. To me, that's not a chance worth taking.

WHAT'S YOUR OPINION?

Can retention be good for a student?

Go to **www.ablongman.com/johnson** to cast your vote and see how NEA readers responded.

video connections allow students in rural New Mexico to talk directly with students in inner-city Chicago or in Tokyo, Japan. Many teachers have developed these linkages themselves with the assistance of other knowledgeable teachers they have met in college classes and at professional meetings.

CULTURAL TRANSMISSION Schools around the world are expected to transmit the culture of their nation to young people so that they can both maintain it and pass it on to the next generation. Schools have often approached this task by teaching history with an emphasis on important events and heroes. This emphasis helps children learn the importance of patriotism and loyalty. Formal and informal curricula reflect and reinforce the **values** of the national culture—the principles, standards, or qualities the culture endorses.

These national values and rules are so embedded in most aspects of schooling that most teachers and students do not realize they exist. The only exceptions may be students who do not belong to the dominant culture or whose families have recently immigrated. In these cases students and families quickly learn that schools might not reflect or support aspects of their culture that differ from the culture of the dominant group. This dissonance between schools and families is most noticeable when students are from backgrounds other than western European ones. Students from religious backgrounds that have not evolved from a Judeo-Christian heritage are also likely to question the culture that is being transmitted at school. The challenge for educators is to transmit the national culture while including the richness and contributions of many who are not yet accepted as an integral part of that culture. In this way schools begin to change and expand the national culture.

WHOSE SCHOOLS?

Schools are microcosms of the societies that create them, and the dominant social values that prevail in a society will prevail in its schools.

Jing-Qui Liu

Although schools are expected to transmit the culture of the United States to the younger generation, educators do not agree on *whose* culture. Is there really a national or common culture that the diverse racial, ethnic, language, and religious groups in the country accept? Dialects, behaviors, and values vary within the same cultural group as well as across groups whose members live in different regions of the country. Cultural differences are even experienced by people who move from rural areas to the city or vice versa.

How can schools begin to accommodate all of these differences? Some conservative politicians and popular talk show hosts argue that schools should ignore diversity. These observers believe that all students should learn the common heritage and adopt the national culture as their own. In this approach, students who are not members of the dominant group are expected to leave their native language or dialect and other cultural characteristics at the school doorstep.

Multicultural theorists and educators argue that the diversity of students enriches the school community. They believe that cultural differences should be valued and integrated throughout the curriculum and all activities of the school. In this approach, teachers draw on the cultural backgrounds and experiences of students to teach academic knowledge and skills.

WHOSE VALUES? Parents' choices of private schools, home schooling, or segregated schools have been based in part on the values that parents believe schooling can impart. Although schools usually do not offer a course in which values are explicitly presented and discussed, values implicitly influence the formal and informal curriculum. Curricula usually support the current ideological, political, and economic order of U.S. society. For example, individualism is much more highly regarded than the rights of the group. The Protestant work ethic is evident in society's expectation of hard work and in the general belief that someone who works hard will be successful in life. Although these values might seem uncontroversial, they can be the cause of extensive debate and emotional pleas at meetings with groups of parents, school board meetings, and community forums.

values
Principles, standards, or qualities that are considered worthwhile or desirable.

Some parents are concerned that the curriculum does not reflect their religious values; often, they think that their religion is purposefully denigrated in schools. These concerns are expressed most frequently by members of some fundamentalist Christian communities but also by Amish and Hutterite communities and by some Jewish, Muslim, and other non-Christian families and communities. On the other hand, atheists believe that religious values, especially Christian ones, pervade the school curriculum.

The emphasis on individualism and competition that is prevalent in many schools is not compatible with the cooperative patterns practiced by Native American tribes and in many Hispanic and African American communities. These differences can lead to conflict between parents and schools and between groups within a community. The courts have often been asked to sort through these value issues. Parents turn to the courts when they believe that schools have acted inappropriately. They may also believe either that the schools do not have a democratic process in which they can be heard or that the majority of the community will not support their petitions. School prayer, creationism, the banning of books, sex education, and segregation are among the areas that have been tested in the courts.

Because parents and other groups in a community may vehemently disagree about the values to be reinforced in schools, teachers should be aware of their own values. Knowing their own values as well as those of the families represented in the school should help teachers prepare for potential conflicts. Expectations can vary greatly from one community or school to another.

GLOBAL PERSPECTIVES: Universal Values

One might wonder whether a diverse population can ever reach agreement on the values to be taught in schools. But one K–12 school in Lucknow, India, has been promoting diverse students' emotional and spiritual growth as well as academic excellence for nearly forty years. The City Montessori School has 19,000 students in fifteen branches in a city with more than 1.5 million people and two very influential religious groups: Hindu and Muslim. Students learn and are expected to practice what the faculty and parents define as "universal values." As described by Carolyn Cottom, these include "kindness, compassion, cooperation, responsibility, and other such values rooted in the world's religions."[37]

The school's approach integrates these universal values with excellence, global understanding, and service. In daily reflection times, students use texts and stories from many religions. They "visit India's holy places—Hindu, Sikh, Buddhist, Muslim, Christian, Jewish, Baha'i, and Jain—in order to learn tolerance for one another."[38] They also have exchange programs with schools in more than twenty countries. Students are expected to provide service to local communities and villages.

In developing this approach, those involved have drawn on effective practices from around the world. The school takes its teaching philosophy and its name from the Italian educator Maria Montessori. The mentoring aspect of teaching comes from Russia. The universal values are not those of one religious group but are basic to many religions. They also are the values of humanitarians around the globe, whether or not they are religious.

DEMOCRATIC SCHOOLS

When common schools were first established in the United States, one of their overarching goals was to "promote the character traits required for a democracy."[39] In many schools preparation for citizenship has been limited to a civics course and

In democratic classrooms, teachers and students work collaboratively in the teaching and learning process.

is no longer a theme that influences classroom work or school activities. A number of educators, however, have established democratic classrooms and schools that are grounded in the following conditions necessary for a democracy:

1. The open flow of ideas, regardless of their popularity, that enables people to be as fully informed as possible.
2. Faith in the individual and collective capacity of people to create possibilities for resolving problems.
3. The use of critical reflection and analysis to evaluate ideas, problems, and policies.
4. Concern for the welfare of others and the common good.
5. Concern for the dignity and rights of individuals and minorities.
6. An understanding that democracy is not so much an ideal to be pursued as an idealized set of values that we must live by and that must guide our life as a people.
7. The organization of social institutions to promote and extend the democratic way of life.[40]

Democratic schools reflect democratic structures and processes and include a curriculum that provides students with democratic experiences. These schools require students, teachers, parents, and community members to be active participants in the educational process. Equity undergirds the structure of democratic schools. All students have access to all programs. Tracking, biased testing, and other practices that deny access to some students are eliminated. The emphasis on grades, status, test scores, and winning is replaced with cooperation and concern for the common good. Those involved in this democratic project also work toward the elimination of inequities in the broader community as well as in the school.

A democratic curriculum encourages multiple perspectives and voices in the materials used and the discussions that ensue. It respects differences in viewpoints. It does not limit information and study to the areas chosen by members of the dominant group. It includes discussions of inequities in society and challenges students and teachers to engage actively in eliminating them.

Establishing a democratic classroom or school is not an easy undertaking. There sometimes is resistance from colleagues and parents; some people believe that teachers should be all-knowing authoritarians so as to exert control over their students. Those who want schools to prepare students for social efficiency are supportive of stratified systems using grades and test scores to sort students into tracks that prepare them for future jobs. Supporters of schooling as a route to social mobility expect competition to determine which students deserve the greatest rewards; for example, acceptance in the gifted program and admission to a prestigious college. Democratic schools, on the other hand, support equity, equal access, and equal opportunity for all students.

SUMMARY

GROUPS IN SOCIETY

Group membership is important in schooling because many students come from families and communities that do not share the culture that is taught and reinforced in school policies, practices, and expectations. U.S. society is based primarily on the cultural traditions of western Europe. Through historical and political developments, whites have been socialized to view themselves as superior to the members of other racial groups. This power differential is also found in relations between males and females and between individuals who are relatively wealthy and those in poverty. Individual achievement is highly valued in the dominant culture.

TODAY'S FAMILIES

Students in schools today come from very diverse families. Although a majority of children live with their mother and father, many live with single parents, grandparents, adoptive parents, foster parents, gay or lesbian parents, or relatives. Some have no home; others live in unsanitary, unsafe, and/or abusive conditions. Because many parents work and are not at home at the end of the school day, large numbers of students are on their own for several hours before adults are available to supervise them. Thus, teachers and parents need to work together to guide students safely through childhood and adolescence.

TODAY'S YOUTH

Most teenagers are not the incorrigibles that are often hyped in the media. Teens are struggling with economic and social realities that can prove dangerous when wrong or inappropriate decisions are made. These struggles are often related to sexuality and drug experimentation. The greater poverty suffered by young people today contributes to some of them dropping out of school and engaging in violent acts. However, many young people exhibit amazing resiliency, which allows them to overcome economic and social hardships to finish school and become productive adults.

DEMOCRACY AND SCHOOLING

In the meritocratic system that undergirds the U.S. economic and political system, society assumes that success is the well-earned result of ability and hard work. Individuals who are not successful are blamed for their lack of ability or desire. Proponents of this view believe that discrimination no longer exists, and they resent policies and practices that grant rights to members of a group rather than to individuals. Critics of meritocracy believe that greater equality could be achieved in society through a more equal distribution of resources, the serious application of civil rights laws, and a drastic reduction in discriminatory practices against the members of powerless groups. Educators debate the value of equal educational opportunity programs, national educational standards, and efforts to monitor the equality of results so as to promote greater equality in schools. At the beginning of the twenty-first century, schools are still far from providing equality for all students.

Theories of functionalism, conflict, and resistance provide different descriptions of the role of schools in reproducing culture and society. Reconstructionism suggests that schools can transform society by serving as model democratic and equitable institutions. Schools serve many purposes, including the development of citizenship, preparation for work, the development of academic and social competence, and the transmission of the culture to another generation. Although most parents would agree with these purposes, they may disagree about the values that undergird the curriculum and teaching practices.

Democratic schools and classrooms involve parents, students, teachers, administrators, and community members as partners in the design and delivery of education. Teachers draw on resources that represent diverse voices and perspectives. The policies and practices of schools promote equity for all students, abandoning practices that sort students and give privilege to those from advantaged backgrounds.

DISCUSSION QUESTIONS

1. Why is it so difficult for middle-class whites to acknowledge that their group membership historically and currently places them in a privileged position?
2. Provide examples of discriminatory practices against females, African Americans, non–native English speakers, Native Americans, the disabled, the elderly, and/or homosexuals that have become institutionalized in the educational system.
3. How have families changed over the past fifty years? What impact have these changes had on schools?
4. What kind of adult support do teenagers need as they cope with the challenges of adolescence?
5. Why do many adults have very negative impressions of teenagers? How accurate are those negative impressions?
6. Contrast meritocracy and equality. What characteristics in society would be indicators that equality exists across groups in this country?
7. How do functionalists and reconstructionists expect schools to implement the purposes outlined in this chapter?
8. How can teachers bridge the value differences between various groups in the community? What curriculum content could spark debates in the community?

JOURNAL ENTRIES

1. Describe the privileges or lack of privileges that you have had as a result of your membership in specific ethnic, racial, gender, economic, and religious groups. Why have these privileges been extended to or withheld from you?

2. Describe your perceptions of students that you would teach in an inner-city school in a large metropolitan area as compared to students in a wealthy suburban area. How do you think your perceptions might influence your academic expectations for the two groups of students?
3. Write a summary of what democracy means to you. What importance do the *common good* and *equality* receive in your description?

PORTFOLIO DEVELOPMENT

1. Write a paper that *(a)* describes a classroom that operates on democratic principles and *(b)* contrasts it with traditional classrooms. The description should include the setup of the room, the interaction between the teacher and students, and the interactions of students, among other characteristics.
2. Select a school or community in which there has been debate regarding the values to be reflected in the curriculum. Analyze the fundamental differences between the groups in a paper, chart, or pictorial format. Identify strategies that could have prevented the conflict.

SCHOOL-BASED EXPERIENCES

1. In one of your next observations of a class in a school, identify and record the written and unwritten rules that guide the interactions of students with each other and with the teacher. These rules are part of the informal curriculum. What values do they reinforce?
2. During one of your next visits to a school, observe how students interact with individuals from cultural backgrounds different from their own. You could make these observations not only in the classroom but in the halls, at the principal's office, and during extracurricular activities. Are students interacting across ethnic, racial, gender, and socioeconomic groups? What is the nature of the interactions? How has the school encouraged positive, productive interactions? Students, teachers, and parents could be helpful informants in your data gathering; ask them for their perceptions.

WEBSITES

To find websites with useful information on the relationships between schools and groups in a democratic society, try searching under key words such as "citizenship," "democratic schools," "homeless students," "child abuse programs," "gangs," and "dropout prevention."

1. <www.childrensdefense.org> The website of the Children's Defense Fund (CDF) includes data about the status of children in the United States. It also includes information on the CDF's programs and activist work.
2. <nch.ari.net> The website for the National Coalition for the Homeless has information bulletins on homelessness in the United States.
3. <www.calib.com> The National Clearinghouse on Child Abuse and Neglect Information's website serves as a national resource for professionals seeking information on the prevention, identification, and treatment of child abuse and neglect.
4. <www.preventchildabuse.org> This website includes resources for professionals and others who are fighting child abuse.

5. <www.naacp.org> The website of the National Association for the Advancement of Colored People addresses issues of school desegregation, fair housing, employment, and voter registration, as well as elections, health, and equal economic opportunity.

NOTES

Unless otherwise indicated, the data reported in this chapter are from the U.S. Census Bureau, *Statistical Abstract of the United States: 1999.* Washington, DC: U.S. Government Printing Office, 1999.

1. John Dewey, *Democracy and Education: An Introduction to the Philosophy of Education.* New York: The Free Press, 1916, 99.
2. Tom W. Smith, *Taking America's Pulse II: Survey of Intergroup Relations.* New York: The National Conference for Community and Justice, 2000.
3. Jonathan Kozol, *Savage Inequalities: Children in America's Schools.* New York: Crown, 1991, 65.
4. J. E. Helms, ed., *Black and White Racial Identity: Theory, Research and Practice.* Westport, CT: Greenwood Press, 1993.
5. Frank F. Furstenberg, Jr., "Family Change and Family Diversity," in Neil J. Smelser and Jeffrey C. Alexander, eds., *Diversity and Its Discontents: Cultural Conflict and Common Ground in Contemporary American Society.* Princeton, NJ: Princeton University Press, 1999, 147–165.
6. U.S. Conference of Mayors, *A Status Report on Hunger and Homelessness in America's Cities: 1998.* Washington, DC: Author, 1998.
7. National Coalition for the Homeless, "How Many People Experience Homelessness?" (NCH Fact Sheet #2). Washington, DC: Author, 1999, 1.
8. Urban Institute, *Homelessness: Program and the People They Serve* (Summary Report of the Findings of the National Survey of Homeless Assistance Providers and Clients). Washington, DC: Author, 1999.
9. U.S. Department of Justice, Bureau of Justice Statistics, *Homicide Trends in the U.S.: 1998 Update.* Washington, DC: U.S. Government Printing Office, 1998.
10. UNICEF, *Domestic Violence: An Epidemic.* New York: Author, 2000.
11. American Psychological Association, "Facts about Violence." Washington, DC: Author, 2000.
12. Mike A. Males, *Framing Youth: 10 Myths about the Next Generation.* Monroe, ME: Common Courage Press, 1999.
13. Shirley Brice Heath and Milbrey W. McLaughlin, *Identity and Inner-City Youth: Beyond Ethnicity and Gender.* New York: Teachers College Press, 1993.
14. Heath and McLaughlin, 1993.
15. Heath and McLaughlin, 1993, 61.
16. Heath and McLaughlin, 1993, 4.
17. The Heinz Family Foundation, "Democracy Project Interim Report." Philadelphia: Author, 1996.
18. U.S. Department of Education, National Center for Education Statistics, *The Condition of Education 2000* (NCES 2000-062). Washington, DC: U.S. Government Printing Office, 2000.
19. Duncan Chaplin and Jane Hannaway, "High School Employment: Meaningful Connections for At-Risk Youth." Washington, DC: The Urban Institute, 1996.
20. Richard Sagor, "Building Resiliency in Students," *Educational Leadership 54* (1) (September 1996): 39.
21. Males, 1999.
22. Freya L. Sonenstein, Leighton Ku, Laura Duberstein Lindberg, Charles F. Turner, and Joseph H. Pleck, "New Data on Sexual Behaviors of Teenage Males: Sexual Activity Declines, Contraceptive Use Increases from 1988 to 1995." Washington, DC: The Urban Institute, May 1997.
23. Mike A. Males, *The Scapegoat Generation: America's War on Adolescents.* Monroe, ME: Common Courage Press, 1996.

24. Males, 1999.
25. Males, 1999, 185.
26. U.S. Department of Education, National Center for Education Statistics, *The Condition of Education 1999* (NCES 2000-009). Washington, DC: U.S. Government Printing Office, 1999.
27. National Center for Education Statistics, *Dropout Rates in the United States: 1995.* Washington, DC: U.S. Department of Education, 1997.
28. Lowell C. Rose and Alec M. Gallup, "The 32nd Annual Phi Delta Kappa/Gallup Poll of the Public's Attitudes Toward the Public Schools." Bloomington, IN: Phi Delta Kappa, 2000.
29. U.S. Department of Education, National Center for Education Statistics, *The Condition of Education 1997* (NCES 1997-388). Washington, DC: U.S. Government Printing Office, 1997.
30. Males, 1996, 183.
31. World Health Organization, *World Health Statistics Annual 1993.* Geneva: Author, 1995.
32. Males, 1996.
33. James H. Burch II and Betty M. Chemers, *A Comprehensive Response to America's Youth Gang Problem.* Washington, DC: Office of Juvenile Justice and Delinquency Prevention, March 1997.
34. David F. Labaree, "Public Goods, Private Goods: The American Struggle over Educational Goals," *American Educational Research Journal 34* (1) (Spring 1997): 81.
35. Seth Kreisberg, *Transforming Power: Domination, Empowerment, and Education.* Albany, NY: State University of New York Press, 1992, 17.
36. Dewey, 1916.
37. Carolyn Cottom, "A Bold Experiment in Teaching Values," *Educational Leadership 53* (8) (May 1996), 54.
38. Cottom, 1996, 56.
39. Labaree, 1997, 67.
40. James A. Beane and Michael W. Apple, "The Case for Democratic Schools," in Michael W. Apple and James A. Beane, eds., *Democratic Schools.* Alexandria, VA: Association for Supervision and Curriculum Development, 1995.

BIBLIOGRAPHY

Apple, Michael W., and Beane, James A. *Democratic Schools.* Alexandria, VA: Association for Supervision and Curriculum Development, 1995.

Cantor, Ralph; Kivel, Paul; Creighton, Allan; and the Oakland Men's Project. *Days of Respect: Organizing a Schools-Wide Violence Prevention Program.* Alameda, CA: Hunter House, 1997.

Children's Defense Fund. *The State of America's Children Yearbook 2000.* Washington, DC: Author, 2000.

Chomsky, Noam, and Barsamian, David. *The Common Good.* Monroe, ME: Common Courage Press, 1998.

Davidson, Ann Locke. *Making and Molding Identity in Schools: Student Narratives on Race, Gender, and Academic Engagement.* Albany, NY: State University of New York Press, 1996.

Fine, Michele; Weis, Lois; Powell, Linda C.; and Wong, L. Mun. *Off White: Readings on Race, Power, and Society.* New York: Routledge, 1997.

Freire, Paulo. "The Adult Literacy Process as Cultural Action for Freedom," *Harvard Educational Review, 1* (4): 480–498.

Koppelman, Kent L. *Values in the Key of Life: Making Harmony in the Human Community.* Amityville, NY: Baywood, 2001.

Kozol, Jonathan. *Ordinary Resurrections: Children in the Years of Hope.* New York: Crown, 2000.

Males, Mike A. *Framing Youth: 10 Myths about the Next Generation.* Monroe, ME: Common Courage Press, 1999.

Touraine, Alain. *What Is Democracy?* Boulder, CO: Westview Press, 1998.

CHAPTER

4

Education That Is Multicultural

EDUCATION IN THE NEWS

Internet at School Is Changing Work of Students—and Teachers

By Kenneth J. Cooper, *The Washington Post,* September 5, 2000

As students across the country trundle back to class, they are taking their seats in schools more wired than ever before and huddling around desktop computers in small groups more often. Then they are tapping into the Internet to complete their assignments.

Fully 95 percent of the nation's public schools are now connected to the Internet. By comparison, less than half the nation's households are.

The wiring of America's schools—originally conceived as a way to bridge the "digital divide" that isolates poor children and to transmit advanced courses to rural schools—is also changing the way teachers teach and students learn. Quite possibly, it may be increasing how much students learn, particularly average and shy ones, educational technology experts say.

While there are no published studies to verify those preliminary conclusions, and most schools suffer from shortages of tech-trained teachers and classroom computers, specialists are pleased with the initial results.

"There is nothing that says technology will improve student achievement, but we believe that it does because it meets so many different learning styles," says Cindy Bowman, an education professor at Florida State University.

Two-thirds of public school teachers say they now employ computer applications in lessons, and at least 30 percent use the Internet, according to an Education Department survey. And students at every grade level this school year will exchange e-mails with "keypals" in foreign countries, take "virtual field trips" to museums and historic sites or research the range of academic subjects on the Internet.

Education technology specialists say there is preliminary evidence that the students who may learn more using the Internet include "visual learners," average students, disabled ones, students not fully proficient in English and shy ones who shrink from joining classroom discussion.

"There's a growing body of evidence that many learners do blossom with interactive media more than they do face to face," says Chris Dede, a professor of learning technologies at Harvard University.

In the opinion of Dede and other experts, the Internet can also alter the learning experience for all students.

Rather than studies being linear and sequential—one page or textbook chapter after another—researching a topic on the World Wide Web can lead students to spontaneous discoveries of related information drawn from more than one academic subject, similar to browsing through open stacks in a library.

(continued)

The technology-driven changes penetrating schools across the country mean the most adept teachers do less lecturing, and change from classroom know-it-all to learning coach who guides students to what they need to know.

So far, schools in prosperous suburban districts have advanced the most in tapping the educational potential of the Internet. Those schools are better able to bear the cost of training teachers as well as purchasing computers and wiring classrooms.

LEARNER OUTCOMES

After reading and studying this chapter, you will be able to

1. Discuss the importance of diversity, equality, and social justice in delivering high-quality education for *all* students.
2. Describe the hidden curriculum, the culture that is reflected in the hidden curriculum, and the messages this curriculum sends to students from diverse backgrounds.
3. Identify teaching practices that are culturally relevant.
4. Describe and contrast approaches for teaching students who are learning English.
5. Provide examples of teaching for social justice and discuss the role of social justice in schools and classrooms. ■

Diversity, equality, and social justice are the perspectives through which education that is multicultural is developed. Provision of social justice and equality is a moral and ethical responsibility of educators; the goal is to help all students learn and reach their potential, regardless of their socioeconomic status, ethnicity, race, language, gender, religion, and ability or disability. Teachers and administrators view all aspects of education—including the hidden curriculum, staffing patterns, discipline, and extracurricular activities—through these perspectives to ensure that the needs of diverse students are an integral part of the education process.

Curriculum and instructional practices in education that is multicultural value diversity, draw on the cultural experiences of students, include multiple ways of learning and viewing the world, and support democracy and equity in classrooms and schools. Education that is multicultural reflects more than the dominant society; it reflects the diversity of the community, country, and world. In culturally relevant teaching, teachers believe that all students can learn and place students at the center of teaching, building on their cultural backgrounds and experiences to develop meaningful learning experiences. Constant vigilance about the content and delivery of academic subjects is required.

multicultural education
An educational strategy that incorporates the teaching of exceptional and culturally diverse students, human relations, and the study of ethnic and other cultural groups in a school environment that supports diversity and equal opportunity.

Many educators have mistakenly thought that **multicultural education** is only for students who are not members of the dominant group in society. Rather, it is for all students regardless of their microcultural memberships. It is as important for students and teachers of European Protestant backgrounds as it is for those from ethnic and cultural groups that have traditionally faced discrimination in society. All content should be multicultural and should be presented through the viewpoints of many different groups to help students understand that there is more than one perspective on the interpretation of events and facts.

Too many educators have thought they were "doing" multicultural education simply by including information about groups other than their own in a lesson. This additive approach is evident in black history and women's history months or in highlighted sections in textbooks that discuss, for example, Japanese Americans. In some schools attention to multiculturalism begins and ends with tasting ethnic foods and participating in ethnic festivals. Although these activities can contribute to the development of education that is multicultural, they are side attractions and do not represent an integrated curriculum and school environment.

In education that is multicultural, all teaching is culturally relevant, and classrooms and schools are models of democracy and **equity.** This effort requires educators to

1. Place the student at the center of the teaching and learning process;
2. Promote human rights and respect for cultural differences;
3. Believe that all students can learn;
4. Acknowledge and build on the life histories and experiences of students' microcultural memberships;
5. Critically analyze oppression and power relationships to help students understand racism; sexism; classism; and discrimination against persons with disabilities, gays, lesbians, the young, and the aged;
6. Critique society in the interest of social justice and equality; and
7. Participate in collective social action to ensure a democratic society.[1]

Although you should begin to struggle with these issues now, the process of learning about others and reflecting on one's attitudes and actions in these areas is a lifelong activity.

UNDERGIRDING TENETS

For centuries, women, people with low incomes, and members of oppressed ethnic and religious groups have fought for an education equal to that available to members of the dominant group. In the nineteenth century courageous educators established schools to serve some of these students, often encountering opposition from the community at the time. Eighty years ago educators at the Intercultural Service Bureau in New York City were fighting for the incorporation of intercultural education into the curriculum to increase knowledge about new immigrants and to eliminate the prejudice against them. In 1954 the Supreme Court declared separate-but-equal education for black and white students illegal in the *Brown* v. *Board of Education* case. The civil rights struggles in the 1960s laid the groundwork for new curriculum content about African Americans, Hispanics, Native Americans, and Asian Americans. Attention to equity for women, individuals with disabilities, and limited-English speakers soon followed.

Equality is the heart and essence of democracy, freedom, and justice.

A. Philip Randolph

equity
The state of fairness and justice across individuals and groups; it does not imply the same educational strategies across groups but does expect equal results.

These events became the foundation for education that is multicultural. Two core beliefs about schooling and society guide the development of education that supports democracy for all. One is the belief that cultural diversity is a national strength that should be valued and promoted. Another is that social justice and equality remain viable goals for society and should be modeled in classrooms and schools. In this section we will examine these two major tenets on which multicultural education is built.

DIVERSITY

There has been a great amount of public and academic discussion of multiculturalism in recent years. Editorials, national news programs, radio talk shows, and debates among college students and faculty periodically focus on the importance of diversity in society and in the curriculum. Simply put, the argument on one side is that the recognition and promotion of cultural and ethnic diversity will strengthen the nation. The other side argues that the promotion of diversity will divide the nation and lead to even greater conflict among groups. This second group also argues that the Western tradition is denigrated as diversity is highlighted.

The claim that multicultural education will divide the nation suggests that the nation is already united.[2] Campaigns for members of Congress, governors, and mayors include debates about immigration, provision of services to undocumented workers and their children, English-only policies, and gay rights. Multiculturalists argue that "multicultural education is designed to help unify a deeply divided nation rather than to divide a highly cohesive one."[3] They believe that individuals should have the opportunity to learn more about each other and to interact on an equal basis in schools and society. They believe that members of diverse groups can maintain their ethnic and cultural diversity while developing together a common civic culture. An outgrowth of these debates has been the establishment of general education requirements for ethnic, women's, and/or global studies in colleges and universities. Most states also expect teacher education candidates to study diversity and to be able to incorporate it into their teaching. The national accrediting agency for teacher education programs in colleges and universities, NCATE, has required the inclusion of multicultural content in teacher education curricula since 1978. Most of the developing state and national standards for preschool through high school curricula include references to diversity.

What does the public think of incorporating diversity into the curriculum of our schools? A survey of the National Conference for Community and Justice found that

> On the whole, the data suggest that cultural diversity is hardly a foreign or unfamiliar concept in contemporary American society. Asked "How important do you think it is that people from different groups learn to understand and appreciate the lifestyles, tastes, and contributions of each other's groups?" 67% of those surveyed nationwide said such understanding and appreciation is "very important," while another 25% feel it is "important." Across the board, roughly nine in ten people in all diverse groups surveyed endorse this concept, including 91% of whites.
>
> As a counterpart question, survey participants were also asked about the desirability of "teaching all students about the racial, ethnic, and cultural groups that make up America today." A substantial 57% say they find it "very desirable" and another 31% "somewhat desirable," while only 9% deem such education "undesirable," adding up to an 88% mandate from the adult public. Again, roughly nine in ten respondents endorse the teaching of cultural diversity in the nation's schools.

Social justice calls for people to help others who are not as advantaged as they are.

These results indicate that whatever negative perceptions groups have about each other, many of the prerequisites of tolerance and inter-group cooperation are present in today's America: respect for the differences among us and a commitment to increased understanding of those differences.[4]

The public not only believes that diversity should be incorporated in the curriculum but also that teachers in a school should represent different cultural groups.[5] A diverse student body and faculty make it possible for students not only to learn about others, but also to interact in authentic settings with people from different backgrounds. The Internet has opened opportunities for students in schools with limited diversity to become acquainted with people from diverse backgrounds in other parts of the country and world.

SOCIAL JUSTICE AND EQUALITY

Peace, prosperity, freedom, and justice traditionally have defined the good society for Americans.[6] But what is meant by *justice* in a society that places so much emphasis on individualism and the freedom to be left alone? Justice itself is related to fairness, moral rightness, and equity. Our judicial system is designed to guarantee legal justice for individuals and groups. Social justice, on the other hand, focuses on how we help others in the community who are not as advantaged as we are. In fact, most religions measure the quality of a society by the justice and care it gives to the downtrodden—the homeless, the sick, the powerless, the uneducated.[7]

Justice can never be done in the midst of injustice.
Simone de Beauvoir

The ethic of social justice, especially as it relates to the teacher–student relationship, is essential in the profession of teaching, along with other moral commitments. Social justice in education requires schools to provide all students equal access to a high-quality education. Practices that perpetuate current inequities are confronted and strategies for eliminating them employed. The acceptance of social justice as a moral and ethical responsibility of educators and schooling is critical in the provision of education that is multicultural.

As we discussed in Chapter 3, schools reflect the inequities of the broader society. As you reflect on the inequitable conditions in most schools, ask yourself the following questions:

- How fair is it for some students to attend school in dilapidated, foul-smelling, crowded buildings while others attend classes in beautiful buildings with future-oriented technology and well-groomed grounds?
- How fair is it for wealthier students to have the most experienced and best-qualified teachers, who also earn the highest of all teaching salaries?
- How fair is it that wealthier students are exposed to an intellectually challenging curriculum and experiences while many low-income students do not even have advanced placement classes offered in their school?
- How fair is it that students of color, especially males, and students with disabilities or limited English proficiency are pulled out of regular classes and isolated in segregated classes during much of the school day?
- How accurate are curricula and pedagogy that do not reflect the rich plurality of the people, histories, experiences, and perspectives of the groups that make up the United States and world?

These are among the numerous questions that educators ask themselves if they are serious about providing social justice in schools. The promise of a democratic society has been that all students have a fair chance to learn and succeed. Instead, the current system supports the same inequities that exist in society. The already advantaged students normally continue to be advantaged over students in low-income areas from the day they enter school. A theory of social justice suggests that school systems give those students with the fewest advantages the most advantages in their education and schooling to begin to ensure an equal and fair playing field. The goal might be to use the best-funded and most successful schools as the norm for all schools, with the least advantaged receiving the greatest resources for their education.

GLOBAL PERSPECTIVES: Antiracist and Multicultural Education

Even people who advocate changing schools to reflect democracy and equality sometimes disagree about the appropriate educational strategy. In the United Kingdom the debate between antiracists and multiculturalists began to flourish in the 1970s after the release of several national reports on immigrants and race relations. The differences between the two groups went beyond the label for what is called *multicultural education* or *education that is multicultural* in the United States. The supporters of antiracist education focused on the structure of the education system and on power relationships between the dominant Anglo society and the powerless immigrant groups. The primary emphasis of the advocates for multicultural education was on the content of the curriculum. Finally, in the 1990s, a synthesis of the two approaches evolved in which the strategy for social justice is an education that is antiracist *and* multicultural.[8]

CULTURE OF THE SCHOOL

The school itself is a cultural system that differs from the family and broader community in which people participate. Despite individual differences in ability, rate of learning, and personal interest, most students are subjected to the same type

Competition in regional athletics and other extracurricular activities often reflects the traditions of a school's culture.

of instruction. The school rules regulate classroom behavior as well as determine acceptable dress and speech. Common rituals are found in athletics, extracurricular clubs, graduation exercises, and school social events. The signs and emblems of the school culture are displayed in school songs, colors, and cheers.

TRADITIONS

Traditions in the school culture are associated with regional influences; the social structure of a community; and location in a rural, urban, or suburban area. Some schools are influenced greatly by the religion of the children's families, others by the presence of a large military base.

Regional interests may influence the sports activities that are fueled through school spirit. In the Midwest, for example, basketball is the favored sport. In other parts of the country, fierce athletic competition may be associated with football, swimming, wrestling, or gymnastics. Rural schools often emphasize Future Farmers of America clubs, agricultural programs, and 4-H clubs—activities that are usually not found in urban schools.

Schools with long histories have developed lasting traditions that are transferred from generation to generation. Some graduates retain lifelong feelings of pride about their schools. For others the memories are of mediocrity and of never being challenged.

HIDDEN CURRICULUM

All schools offer a formal curriculum that includes coursework in numerous academic areas. In addition, there is a **hidden curriculum** that is seldom discussed and sometimes not acknowledged by educators. It includes the rules that guide the work of the school. This informal curriculum defines the behaviors and attitudes expected of both students and teachers. It is political in that it signifies which students are privileged by promoting their cultural values and patterns. Yet according to convention, schools designate the teacher as the expert and grant the teacher authority to rule over students. Critical theorists argue that these practices help to maintain the status quo and current inequities in society.

hidden curriculum
The norms and values that define expectations for student behavior and attitudes and that undergird the curriculum and operations of schools.

For most students from the dominant culture, the hidden curriculum reinforces behaviors expected by their families. These students fit fairly easily into the school culture. Students from different cultural backgrounds, however, may find school practices foreign and even contradictory to what they learn at home. The emphasis on competition between students is an example of one set of cultural assumptions being valued over another. Some students need to be taught the "rules" of competition to participate fully in the learning process.[9]

The informal curriculum could become more equitable and supportive of democratic principles if educators acknowledged that many school policies and practices are discriminatory in that they promote and reinforce only the dominant culture. Teachers who recognize their own prejudices and discriminatory practices in teaching and classroom management are able to develop strategies for eliminating them.

CULTURALLY RELEVANT TEACHING

All people have preferred learning and teaching styles that are embedded in their cultural background and experiences. Until teachers learn to recognize these differences and develop a repertoire of different strategies for teaching subject matter, some students will be deprived of appropriate assistance in the learning process. However, making generalizations about culturally diverse learners is often very dangerous. Teachers need to be thoughtful about the role that culture—values, behaviors, language—play in learning; at the same time teachers must avoid characterizing all students who appear to share the same ethnicity or class as being the same.

At first glance it might seem that handling diversity in a classroom would be much easier if teachers could just pick up a recipe book that clearly stated what instruction would be effective for students from a specific group. The problem with this approach is that not only are there differences across ethnic and cultural groups, but there are also many differences among members within the same group. The intragroup differences may be based on socioeconomic level, religion, language, and degree of assimilation. Therefore, descriptions of a group usually do not apply to all members of that group. The generalizations in the recipe book would lead to **stereotyping** and prejudging students.

Just like teaching itself, culturally relevant teaching is complex. A teacher cannot determine the learning styles, prior knowledge, or cultural experiences of students by simply knowing that they are from a specific ethnic group or socioeconomic level. The teacher will need to observe and listen to students and their parents as well as assess student performance to develop the most effective teaching strategy. Culturally relevant teaching validates the cultures of students and communities. As a result, students begin to feel that teachers care about them, which is a first step in building a foundation for trust between teachers and students. Effective teachers incorporate "authentic, meaningful experiences and materials, which are linked to children's lives, into classroom practice and co-curricular activities."[10]

stereotyping
The attribution of common traits, characteristics, and behavior to a group of people without acknowledgement of individual differences within the group.

BUILDING ON CULTURAL CONTEXT

Understanding the cultures of students and drawing on them to teach the subject matter are vital in effective teaching. Students usually can determine rather quickly whether the teacher values them and their cultures. To demonstrate a respect for the students' background and experiences, teachers should be able to help students see the relationship between the subject matter and the world in which they live. Students should be able to see themselves in the representations (that is, books, examples, word problems, and films) used by teachers. If the teaching style and representations are based totally on the culture of the teacher, it will be difficult to convince students that their cultures are as valued as the teacher's culture.

Use of students' prior knowledge and experiences with the subject matter is also critical. Students make sense of information in different ways. Therefore, the teacher must be able to teach the same concept by explaining it in different ways, relating it to something meaningful in the student's life and demonstrating it with multiple representations. For most beginning teachers, repertoires are rather limited; with experience, good teachers are able to draw on many different strategies to take advantage of each student's learning style and cultural patterns.

A child miseducated is a child lost.

John F. Kennedy

It is important to know what kind of knowledge, skills, and commitments are valued in the students' cultures. Some students rebel against academic study and school authority as a form of resistance against the values of dominant society and its institutions. For example, some white working-class families value common sense and working with one's hands. They place less value on "book learning" than most middle-class families. Understanding these differences should help the teacher develop different strategies for presenting and discussing the subject matter.

Some of the conflict in student–teacher interactions results from lack of information and understanding about cultural differences in oral and nonverbal communications. Communicating is like other aspects of culture. People usually think that the way that they communicate with other members of the culture is "normal." They don't realize that there are many other ways to communicate that make as much sense as their own but that they have just not had the opportunity to experience them. As long as people interact only with members of the same culture, they use the same cultural cues for whose turn it is to speak, the meaning of a raised eyebrow, or the seriousness of a statement.

Often teachers do not realize that they and their students are reading cultural cues differently. Students may even be punished for responding inappropriately when they may have read the teacher's intent differently based on their own cultural experiences. Recognizing that miscommunications may be based on cultural differences is the first step in improving cross-cultural communications. A next step is to be able to admit that one is part of the problem. Next is the development of alternate means for communicating and understanding the messages from other cultures.

One approach is to systematically teach the communication patterns of the dominant culture to students who are not members of that culture. In this strategy the students' communication patterns are still valued, but they learn when it is to their advantage to use the communication patterns of the dominant group. In other words, they begin to become bicultural. However, teachers who also learn to function effectively in more than one culture will most often gain respect from students and will begin to genuinely model a multicultural pedagogy.

CENTERING THE CULTURES OF STUDENTS

A major dimension of education that is multicultural is the integration of principles of diversity and equality throughout the curriculum. The curriculum for all academic areas should reflect these principles. Adding a course on ethnic studies

Teachers must be able to transcend their own cultural backgrounds to develop learning experiences that build on the cultural backgrounds of all their students.

Pluralism in the curriculum is not a matter of trivial pursuit, nor is it primarily about self-esteem. . . . It's about truth.

Asa Hilliard

or women's studies to the curriculum is an easy way to introduce students to the culture, history, and experiences of others; but it is not enough. The additive approach—including a unit on one or another group sporadically during the year—suggests that these groups are not an integral part of society. They are somewhat interesting to study, but they are not really a part of the whole picture. As a result, the curriculum places the culture, values, history, and experiences of the dominant group at the center. The implicit message is that the dominant culture is the most important in society and that other cultures do not count or are certainly not as important. But many students will learn more if their cultures are integral to the curriculum. As they learn within their own cultural context, they see themselves and their cultures valued by the teacher and school authorities.

One-third of the students in our nation's schools do not see themselves, their families, or their communities in the curriculum. It is not only students of color who seldom find themselves at the center of the curriculum; the curriculum does not normally include information on or the stories of women, people with disabilities, English language learners, families in poverty, the elderly, or members of religions that are not Judeo-Christian. An inclusive curriculum begins to reflect the reality of our multicultural world rather than just the piece of it that belongs to the dominant group. For example, learning science and mathematics would be enhanced for Native American and other students if the knowledge and traditions of various Native American tribes or nations were incorporated into the curriculum. Researchers Sharon Nelson-Barber and Elise Estrin report that

> Many American Indian students have extensive knowledge of mathematics and science knowledge that is rooted in naturalist traditions common to Native communities and arrived at through observation and direct experience. Because many Indian communities follow traditional subsistence lifestyles, parents routinely expose their offspring to survival routines, often immersing the children in decision-making situations in which they must interpret new experiences in light of previous ones. Unfortunately, a majority of teachers recognize neither Indian students' knowledge nor their considerable learning strategies. Thus, not only is potentially important content knowledge ignored but well-developed ways of knowing, learning, and problem solving also go unrecognized.[11]

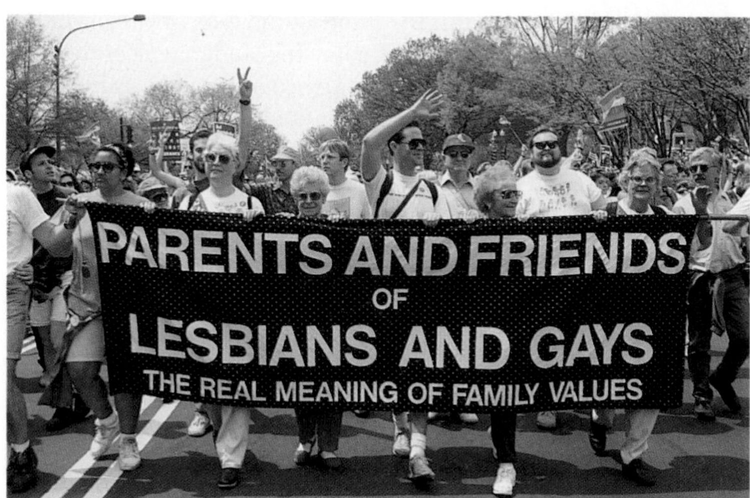

Teaching for social justice helps students struggle with social problems and discrimination that many people face daily.

Some parents and communities have become so upset at schools' unwillingness to respect and validate their own cultures that they have established charter or private schools grounded in their own, rather than the dominant, culture. Afrocentric schools exist in a number of urban areas. Some Latino and Native American groups have set up schools in which they are at the center of the curriculum. Jewish, Islamic, Black Muslim, Lutheran, Catholic, Amish, and other schools reinforce the values, beliefs, and behaviors of their religions in private schools across the country. Single-sex schools focus on developing the confidence, academic achievement, and leadership skills of young women by using their learning styles and cultural experiences. Schools in some urban areas have been designed for African American young men to validate their culture and develop their self-esteem, academic achievement, and leadership capacities to confront the hostile environment that they face in their interactions with the dominant society.

No matter how great or how limited the ethnic diversity is in a school or whose culture is centered in the curriculum, the curriculum should be multicultural. For example, rural white students should have the same opportunities to view the world and subject matter from multicultural and global perspectives as students in diverse urban settings. Because students in some schools do not have opportunities to interact directly with members of diverse groups, the curriculum often becomes their primary source for the exploration of diversity, social justice, and related issues.

VALIDATING STUDENT VOICES

In a democratic classroom all participants must have a **voice**—the right and opportunity to speak and be heard as an equal. Teachers must not dominate the dialogue. Students, especially low-income students and students of color, see teachers as representing the dominant cultural group and as not being open to hearing other perspectives represented by their cultures.

voice
The right and opportunity to speak and be heard as an equal.

Yet including student voices in the classroom dialogue is not always easy. Students usually have limited experience of active participation in their own learning. When the classroom climate begins to include student voices, they may express anger and be confrontive; they may even test the limits of the type of language that can be used and the subjects that can be broached. Allowing student voices to be an integral part of classroom discourse often tests the patience of teachers as they and their students figure out how to listen and contribute to the learning process. At the same time, tolerance, patience with one another, and the willingness to listen will develop as student voices contribute to the exploration of the subject matter.

Respect for differences is key in affirming student voices. For many educators this affirmation requires relinquishing the power that they have traditionally had as the voice of authority with the *right* answers. Class time can no longer be monopolized with teacher talk. The meaningful incorporation of student voices requires the development of listening skills and the validation of multiple perspectives, languages, and dialects. It should allow students to participate in the dialog through speaking, writing, and artistic expression. It should allow them to use the modes of communicating with which they feel the most comfortable while teaching them other modes as well.

The wise person can see a question from all sides without bias. The foolish person can see a question only from one side.

Confucius

Teachers can also affirm student voices by encouraging students to relate the subject matter to their own realities or lived experiences. Because most teachers have very limited experiences in other cultures, they must expand their knowledge about them. Students can become active participants in helping others learn about their cultures and everyday experiences. Teachers can facilitate learning activities to guide students in teaching each other. If teachers are not able to help students see the relationship of the subject matter to their own lives, they may not be able to help students learn. Listening to student voices and being able to adjust teaching strategies appropriately will help make teachers effective.

The affirmation of student voices requires that educators listen to the voices of *all* students. It is particularly important to hear the voices of students of color, low-income students, girls and young women, English language learners, and students with disabilities. The formal and hidden curricula have always validated the voices of the dominant groups. One of the goals of multicultural education is to validate the voices and stories of others too. Teachers must ensure that these voices are not drowned out again in their classrooms. The stories or narratives of others will increase the knowledge and tolerance of differences. Many

Many educators must learn to relinquish their traditional role as the single voice of authority in order to allow student voices to be heard.

DEBATE

Should We Correct Students' Grammar All the Time, Every Time?

YES

Donna Angle teaches English at Willow Run Project Education, an alternative high school in Michigan. She is also an adult education teacher and community college instructor in the Ypsilanti area. A prolific writer, Angle has written five novels and many freelance newspaper and magazine articles.

We have a problem. Too many high school students can't write. They get good grades in English, but they can't tell a sentence fragment from a ham on rye. They graduate, toddle off to college, enroll in Composition 101, then stare, aghast, at their first *D* papers.

"But, but," young Misty Dawn Wunderkind protests, "my English teacher said I'm a wonderful writer!"

Misty may have wonderful ideas, but her mechanics are appalling. She begins with a capital letter and ends with a period two pages later. There's no punctuation, except for apostrophes in all plural nouns, possessive or not. When it comes to verb tenses, she shifts faster than a race car driver.

Who am I to complain? As you may have guessed, I teach English. I correct errors that others have ignored and search for those elusive ideas last seen wandering aimlessly through Gobbledy-Gook National Forest.

It wouldn't hurt to resurrect the practice of calling attention to all writing errors. Let's tell the students what's wrong, why it's wrong, and how to fix it.

"But all those marks will overwhelm students," someone is bound to say. "Why don't we pick a focus for the assignment—say, capitalization—and only mark that? We can get the other stuff later."

But later rarely comes. Misty goes right on making errors and believes that everything is fine. Why shouldn't she? Nobody ever disabused her of that notion.

"But I don't have time to do all that grading," someone else might say. "I have 30 students (or 40 or 90)."

That's a legitimate problem. Writing teachers should have fewer students. Unfortunately, it's the rare administrator who recognizes the wisdom of paring down class size.

In the meantime, we still have work to do. My students write a lot. It takes time to grade their work, but that's what I signed up for.

NO

Katherine Wright Knight teaches high school English in Little Rock, Arkansas. A local and state NEA leader, Knight sits on NCATE's Board of Examiners and presents dozens of professional development workshops to other teachers. She can be reached at wrightknight@aristotle.net.

It can be more destructive than constructive to attempt to correct every grammatical error students make in speech or writing.

Take a second to imagine teaching a Ghandi or a King. What do you think would have happened if every time young Martin put forth an effort to speak, he was interrupted? What if all his ideas had been rewritten by a mentor or teacher? What if every time he spoke, someone had corrected every error—or perceived error—in content, word choice, or grammatical usage?

Is it possible he might have become stifled, strangled, unnerved, or shy? His self-esteem and fervor might well have been devastated. He might never have become the man so many of us knew and loved.

It's not any different with the students we have in our classrooms.

Several years ago, I had a student I'll call Nataki. She was unable to orally articulate a complete thought. Sometimes, it was a struggle for me to sit through her rambling—even when she was just asking a question.

But what purpose would it have possibly served, if I had stopped Nataki every time she made a mistake? How would the other students have perceived her? How would she have perceived herself? And what would Nataki and the other students have thought of me?

Realistically, it's not possible to correct years of damage, poor home teaching, or poor schooling during one speech. Instead, I offered Nataki an opportunity to improve her skills. We met weekly to practice, and I gave her practice materials for the summer and for her remaining high school years.

I offered Nataki an individual plan for a problem that interfered with effective communication. It deserved an individual strategy.

YES | NO

I have put together packets for my students about grammar, punctuation, and sentence structure. They are concise for quick reference and explain when to use a semi-colon, how to use "table" as three parts of speech, and what agreement means.

Students write first drafts, I read and mark them, and they revise. Some people grumble about the extra work, but if they do it, they improve.

"Oh, my kids make grammar errors, and the spelling isn't perfect, but that's what computers are for," another teacher might say. "Besides I couldn't burst Misty Dawn's balloon. She feels so good when she gets an *A*. After all, are the mechanics all that important?"

Yes. Good ideas get lost in incoherence. English is a wonderful language if it's used well, but it's going to degenerate into lip-plucking gibberish if we aren't careful.

"But all those red marks!" another teacher says. "You know what they told us in ed psych about red ink!"

I have yet to see a student suffer a nervous breakdown over a marked-up paper. Besides, along with corrections, I always give praise.

As one young man rather indelicately put it, "I don't give a bleep if the ink's red. A mistake's a mistake. Show me how to fix it."

As for Misty Dawn's feel-good *A,* she'll feel better about a good paper. Let's give her the skills to write it.

Source: Should We Correct Students' Grammar All the Time, Every Time? *NEA Today,* November 1998, p. 47.

A blanket policy—"correct students all the time, every time"—won't work for a lot of reasons:

- Learning can't occur where there is no encouragement and no respect. Too often, students believe we have no respect for what they believe, what they say, and who they are. We need to show them otherwise.
- It's important not to interrupt the message and the messenger if you want complete thoughts or the best ideas. You know what I mean if you've ever been in the middle of a comment when the phone rings.

  Constant corrections hurt more than students' self-esteem. A student's ideas—when interrupted abruptly, frequently, or rudely—may be lost forever. That shouldn't happen in a place where teaching and learning occurs.
- Students will learn more when we offer them the opportunity to correct their own mistakes. And they'll learn from their peers—if they learn in an environment where they can correct each other without fear of embarrassment or intimidation.
- Students shouldn't be treated as blank slates. They bring a wealth of resources to the language arts classroom that can be tapped. When teachers are trained to tap into students' creativity, enthusiasm, and depth of feeling—not turn it off—they'll be stunned by how much learning will take place.

A final note to the unbelievers: Nataki graduated with honors and is now in medical school.

WHAT'S YOUR OPINION?

Should we correct students' grammar every time?

Go to **www.ablongman.com/johnson** to cast your vote and see how NEA readers responded.

students will learn to value both their own culture and that of others. In the process teachers and students will also learn that they have much in common.

EDUCATIONAL CHALLENGES

The challenges in delivering education that is multicultural are many. The diversity of the U.S. student population is growing differently than in the past. By the time you start teaching, approximately one-third of students in schools across the nation will be from ethnic groups other than European. By 2020 more than 45 percent of the school-age population will be students of color. Because many teacher candidates have either no or limited experience with the ethnic and religious groups represented in their classrooms, they will face the unknown. The ideals of diversity, equality, and social justice will require that these teachers engage in continuous learning about and with these communities.

Education is not preparation for life; education is life itself.

John Dewey

In some schools, of course, teachers may still face fairly homogeneous student populations with little exposure to diversity and the multicultural nature of the country as a whole. But even with limited ethnic diversity, most schools will have males and females from different religious and economic backgrounds. The ethic of social justice is just as important in these settings as in those with great ethnic and language diversity. To provide a well-rounded and balanced curriculum for these students, teachers will need to work harder at bringing different perspectives to presentations and discussions. They will need to develop innovative strategies for providing direct exposure to diversity and issues of equality.

THE CHALLENGE OF TECHNOLOGY AND EQUITY

Information technology is influencing the way many of us live and work today. We use the Internet to look and apply for jobs, shop, conduct research, make airline reservations, and explore areas of interest. We use e-mail and the Internet to communicate instantaneously with friends and business associates around the world. Computers are commonplace in homes and the workplace. However, usage is not as widespread as we might expect. Members of oppressed groups are much less likely to have access to the knowledge, equipment, and skills necessary to compete successfully in an information society.

Although the number of Internet users is growing exponentially each year, most of the world's population does not have access to computers or the Internet. Only 6 percent of the population in developing countries are connected to telephones.[12] Although more than 94 percent of U.S. households have a telephone, only 42 percent have personal computers at home and 26 percent have Internet access.[13] The lack of what most of us would consider a basic communications necessity—the telephone—does not occur just in developing nations. On some Native American reservations only 60 percent of the residents have a telephone. The move to wireless connections may eliminate the need for telephone lines, but it does not remove the barrier to equipment costs.

information technology
Computer, software, telecommunications, and multimedia tools that are used to input, store, process, and communicate information.

Who has Internet access? Fifty percent of the children in urban households with an income over $75,000 have Internet access, compared with 2 percent of the children in low-income, rural households.[14] Nearly half of college-educated people have Internet access, compared to 6 percent of those with only some high school education. Forty percent of households with two parents have access; 15 percent of female, single-parent households do. Thirty percent of white households, 11 percent of black households, and 13 percent of Hispanic households have access. Teens and children are the two fastest-growing segments of Internet users.[15] The **digital divide** between the populations who have access to the Internet and information technology tools is based on income, race, education, household type, and geographic location. Only 16 percent of the rural poor, rural and central city minorities, young householders, and single-parent female households are connected.[16]

digital divide
The difference in access to technology tools and the Internet between those with economic advantages and those without.

Another problem that exacerbates these disparities is that African Americans, Hispanics, and Native Americans hold few of the jobs in information

FIGURE 4.1 **INTERNET CONNECTIONS BY CONCENTRATION OF STUDENTS FROM LOW-INCOME FAMILIES AS DETERMINED BY THE PERCENTAGE OF STUDENTS ELIGIBLE FOR FREE OR REDUCED-PRICE LUNCH**

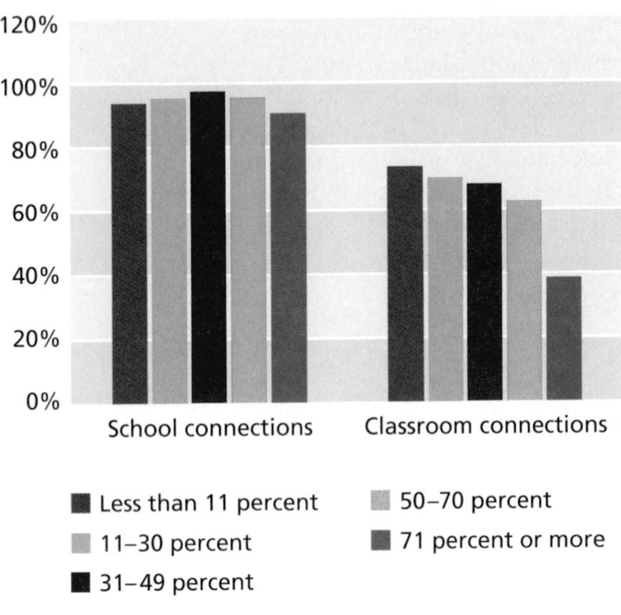

Source: U.S. Department of Education, National Center for Education Statistics, *Advanced Telecommunications in U.S. Public Schools Surveys, 1994–1999.* Washington, DC: U.S. Government Printing Office, 2000.

technology. Women hold about 20 percent of these jobs and are receiving fewer than 30 percent of the computer science degrees. The result is that women and members of the most oppressed ethnic groups are not eligible for the jobs with the highest salaries at graduation. Baccalaureate candidates with degrees in computer science were offered the highest salaries of all new college graduates in 1998 at $44,949.

Do similar disparities exist in schools? More than 90 percent of all schools in the country are wired with at least one Internet connection. The number of classrooms with Internet connections differs by the income level of students. Using the percentage of students who are eligible for free lunches at a school to determine income level, we see that nearly twice as many of the schools with more affluent students have wired classrooms as those with high concentrations of low-income students, as shown in Figure 4.1. Thus, the students who are most unlikely to have access at home also do not have access in their schools, increasing the divide between groups even further.

Access to computers and the Internet will be important in reducing disparities between groups. It will require greater equity across diverse groups whose members develop knowledge and skills in computer and information technologies. The field today is overrepresented by white males. Schools will need to develop strategies for encouraging females, African Americans, Hispanics, Native Americans, and people with disabilities to participate in courses and experiences that help them develop the analytical, problem-solving, and creative skills necessary for jobs in this field. One of the problems may be that classes are not culturally relevant for many students. The American Association of University Women, for example, reports that girls are finding programming courses dull and uninviting and electronic games violent and unchallenging.[17] If the Internet is not being used in schools and communities to address the problems faced in those communities, it is not authentic or culturally relevant to students or their families.

The information superhighway offers unprecedented opportunities for educators to create collaborative learning environments that will stimulate critical thinking skills and academic excellence among all students.

Jim Cummins and Dennis Sayers, *Brave New Schools*

Even more important, the Internet can open up access to knowledge beyond the official knowledge of dominant society. In a society that promotes equality, access should be available to all students, regardless of their family's incomes, but it also should be available to adults in libraries and community centers. The Children's Partnership, an advocacy group for children, has identified the following five key characteristics of a positive information society. It

1. Is community driven and meets real community needs;
2. Overcomes major content barriers facing the underserved;

Most schools are now wired to the Internet, but a digital divide still exists between schools in low-income and other areas.

3. Provides people to help;
4. Offers online content that is easy to use;
5. Is sustainable.[18]

If computers and the Internet are to be used to promote equality, they will have to become accessible to populations that cannot currently afford the equipment, which needs to be updated every three years or so. However, access alone is not enough. Students will have to be interacting with the technology in authentic settings. As technology becomes a tool for learning in almost all courses taken by students, it will be seen as a means to an end rather than an end in itself. If it is used in culturally relevant ways, all students can benefit from its power.

THE CHALLENGE OF GENDER-SENSITIVE EDUCATION

In the past most girls and young women were prepared for the traditional female roles of wife and mother rather than the male roles of wage earners and heads of households. They were encouraged to choose the lower-paying "women's jobs" such as teacher, nurse, child care worker, librarian, or health care worker. When they had to become the primary wage earner because of the loss of a husband through divorce or death, women were at a significant disadvantage. They lacked the required skills or experiences necessary for jobs in which they could earn a wage high enough to maintain a comfortable living. Over the past twenty-five years many women have broken through the traditional patterns. For instance, over 40 percent of the graduates from medical and law schools today are women. Men, on the other hand, are still not as likely as females to work in jobs that were traditionally women's.

The rigid definitions of gender roles that remain in some jobs, schools, religions, and ethnic groups limit the options and potential of both males and females. Men and women do not prepare for all professions at the same rate. Only 36 percent and 25 percent of the graduates in dentistry and theology, respectively, are women. Fewer than 30 percent of the computer science degrees and 16 percent of the engineering degrees are earned by women. Even though more women are entering high-income professions that historically were dominated by men, women are overrepresented at the other end of the income scale. Thirty-five percent of all households headed by women live below the poverty level, compared to 13 percent of the total population.

Schools have played an important role in helping more young women realize their potential during this period. Still, not all teachers and other school personnel are sensitive to gender differences that make a difference in learning. In some classrooms, students are separated and sorted by gender, reinforcing the stereotypical gender roles. Boys are expected to behave in one way, girls in another. Boys are expected to excel in sports competition, computer science, mathematics, and science. Girls are expected to perform better in English, reading, writing, and social studies.

If gender equity existed, females and males would be expected to participate at nearly the same rates in all courses, sports, and jobs. Let's look at some of today's realities.

- Girls and boys enroll in mathematics and science at about the same rate, but girls are more likely to stop with Algebra II and less likely to take physics.
- Girls do not participate at the same rates as boys in computer courses; they are more likely to be in data entry and word processing courses.
- Girls enroll in English at higher rates than boys; boys are more likely to be in remedial English courses.
- Both boys and girls from low-income families or ethnic backgrounds other than European are more likely to be in remedial classes than are affluent white students.
- Girls are more likely to be in gifted classes, but they drop out of them at higher rates than boys do.
- Boys and girls are involved in advanced placement and honors courses except for physics at about the same rate.
- Girls earn equal or higher grades in all subjects.
- Males score higher on SAT and ACT tests used for college admission.[19]

To promote gender equity, females should be encouraged to be involved in mathematics, science, and computer science. Males should be encouraged to participate in areas in which they are underrepresented: the fine arts, foreign languages, advanced English, and the humanities.

A gender-sensitive education provides equity to boys and girls, young women and young men. It does not mean that males and females are always treated the same. Different instructional strategies may be needed for the two groups to ensure participation and learning. Understanding cultural differences among females and males will be important in developing appropriate teaching strategies. Not all girls and young women respond to instruction in the same way. Their other microcultural groups intersect with their femaleness in determining their interaction with teachers and effective instructional strategies. Culturally relevant teaching will affirm students' cultures and experiences in ways to promote learning for all students.

Teachers in gender-sensitive classrooms monitor interactions among girls and boys as well as their own interactions with the two sexes. They intervene when necessary to equalize opportunities between the sexes. If boys are not performing as well in language arts as girls or girls are not performing as well in mathematics, the challenge is to develop approaches that will improve their performance.

Different educational strategies that draw on students' cultural strengths may be needed to equalize performance in knowledge and skill development for

RELEVANT RESEARCH

Boys and Girls in Performance-Based Science Classrooms

STUDY PURPOSE/QUESTIONS: Do middle school girls and boys share equally in hands-on activities in science classes? Do performance behaviors account for changes in attitudes about science?

STUDY DESIGN: The researchers observed six middle school science classes in five schools twice a month, each month, for one academic year. Observers recorded students' behaviors as they worked with other students on hands-on activities. The number of male and female students was nearly equal and included European Americans, African Americans, Hispanic Americans, and Asian Americans.

STUDY FINDINGS: Boys and girls both exhibited leadership behaviors as shown in providing instructions to other members of the group or explaining a science concept. These leadership behaviors were predictors of positive science attitudes at the end of the year. Students who provided leadership had higher perceptions of their science abilities at the end of the year. Even with girls providing leadership at the same level as boys, girls' perceptions about their science abilities dropped over the school year. Boys' perceptions of their abilities did not change. These perceptual differences did not have any real effect on grades or abilities. The involvement of girls in the hands-on activities did differ from the boys' involvement. Boys tended to manipulate the equipment more than girls did, relegating the girls to following the boys' directions. Possibly because they were not actively engaged in the science activity, girls sometimes became bored with the activity, not fully participating. Thus, the performance-based science classes did not guarantee equal participation in the science activity. Nevertheless, involving students actively in science learning does promote positive attitudes about science.

IMPLICATIONS: Developing science activities that are hands-on and performance-based helps to develop positive attitudes about science for both boys and girls. However, teachers need to figure out how to help boys learn to share the science activity more equitably with girls rather than controlling the equipment, shutting girls out of direct involvement in the activity. Otherwise, girls become bored and may develop a perception that they are not as capable in science as the boys. Since boys seem to shut girls out of these activities, teachers might sometimes group girls together to conduct the performance-based activities so that have opportunities to manipulate the equipment themselves.

Source: Jasna Jovanovic and Sally Steinbach King, "Boys and Girls in the Performance-Based Science Classroom: Who's Doing the Performing?" *American Educational Research Journal,* 35 (3) (Fall 1998): 477–496.

girls and boys. Although competitive strategies are effective for many white boys, most girls and boys from other racial groups are more successful in collaborative settings. Instruction should include hands-on laboratory experiences, collaborative learning, practical applications, group work, and authentic learning to build on the learning styles of different students. The goal is to help both boys and girls learn the subject matter. Teachers will need to draw on multiple teaching strategies to reach this goal.

THE CHALLENGE OF LANGUAGE DIVERSITY

A growing number of immigrant students are populating schools in large cities. Even small cities and rural areas are now home to immigrant families and their children. The number of English language learners in Omaha, Nebraska, for example, increased from 500 in 1992 to over 3,000 in 2000. The percentage of the U.S. population that is foreign born is now at the same level it was at the beginning of the twentieth century—almost 14 percent. In 1980 immigrants came primarily from Europe and Canada. Today they come from Mexico, the Philippines, Vietnam, Cuba, China, India, El Salvador, the Dominican Republic, Canada, and Korea/South Korea.

Differences between the languages used at home and at school can lead to dissonance between students, their families, and school officials. Many students who enter school with limited English skills are not only trying to learn a second language but also adjusting to a new culture. This is particularly true for recent immigrants.

The dropout rate for English language learners is two to two and a half times as great as for other students of the same age. Those who are most likely to drop out of school do not feel that they are part of the broader school culture.[20] According to the National Association for the Education of Young Children, the problem for young children is

> the feeling of loneliness, fear, and abandonment children may feel when they are thrust into settings that isolate them from their home community and language. The loss of children's home language may result in the disruption of family communication patterns, which may lead to the loss of intergenerational wisdom; damage to individual and community esteem; and children's potential nonmastery of their home language or English.[21]

The NAEYC urges teachers to encourage "the development of children's home language while fostering the acquisition of English."[22] But not everyone agrees with NAEYC and other education association that support **bilingual education.** Members of Congress, state legislators, and local school board members debate strategies for teaching English language learners.

The debate centers on whether to use students' native languages in instruction. Many school districts and some states require bilingual education if a specific number of students who speak the same native language are enrolled in a school. This approach, of course, requires teachers who are fluent in both English and the native language. There are at least six different approaches to teaching academic content to English language learners.[23]

bilingual education
An education strategy that uses English and the native language of students in classroom instruction.

English as a second language (ESL)
An education strategy for teaching English to speakers of other languages without the use of the native language for instruction.

Sheltered instruction, newcomer programs, and transitional bilingual education approaches are assimilationist in that they are designed to integrate students into the dominant or mainstream culture. Although the native language may be used for instruction early in the program, the goal is to move to English-only instruction as soon as possible, usually between one and four years. In sheltered instruction teachers teach the academic subjects at the same time that they are teaching English to students. The newcomer programs are designed for new immigrants who have limited or no experience with English and often have limited literary skills in their native language. These programs sometimes exist within a school; some school districts have one or more schools for new immigrants. The most successful programs are those in which students attend for as much as four years.[24] Teachers in these two approaches should have knowledge and skills in **English as a second language (ESL).**

In transitional bilingual education, academic subjects are taught in the native language as students learn English. Gradually, more and more of the instruction is conducted in English. After a few years students in transitional bilingual education move into classes with instruction in English only. Developmental bilingual education, by contrast, supports bilingualism and literacy in both English and the native language. Both English and the native language have equal status, and both are used for instructional purposes.

Two immersion language programs use a second language for instruction and help students to understand and appreciate a second culture while maintaining their own native culture and language. Foreign/second language immersion is designed for English speakers who want to learn a second language in a classroom in which Spanish, French, Japanese, Farsi, or another language is used for instruction. Two-way immersion is used to develop bilingualism in all students as language training is integrated with academic instruction. Classes usually have an equal number of English speakers and speakers of another language.

As a school decides the appropriate approach for teaching English language learners, parents must be involved in the discussions and decisions. Together, educators and parents will have to decide whether they want to promote bilingualism among all students or only among the English language learners. Is the goal for English language learners to become competent in both English and their native language or to move into English-only instruction as soon as possible? Each approach has learning implications for students and cost implications for school systems.

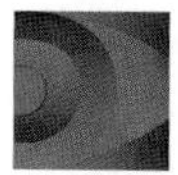

TEACHERS AS SOCIAL ACTIVISTS

Education that is multicultural requires educators to be active participants in the educational process. Social justice, democracy, power, and equity become more than concepts to be discussed in class; they become guides for actions in the classroom, school, and community. Educators become advocates not only for their own empowerment, but for that of students and other powerless groups.

Never doubt that a small group of thoughtful, committed citizens can change the world. Indeed it is the only thing that ever has.

Margaret Mead

THINKING CRITICALLY

Educators who think critically ask questions about why inequities are occurring in their classroom and school. They wonder why girls are responding differently to the science lesson than boys. But they don't stop with wondering; they explore and try alternatives to engage the girls in the subject matter. They realize that teaching equitably does not mean teaching everyone the same way. (Nor, however, does it mean using thirty different lesson plans tailored to the individual learning style and cultural background of each student.) Teaching equitably may mean helping students function effectively in multiple cultural settings used by the students in the classroom. Teachers who think critically are able to draw on their vast repertoire of strategies to build on the diverse cultural backgrounds and experiences of the students, acknowledge the value of that diversity, and help them all learn.

Critical thinkers are able to challenge the philosophy and practices of the dominant society that are not supportive of equity, democracy, and social justice. They are open to alternative views; they are not limited by narrow parochialism that is based on absolutes and the notion of one right way. They question content for accuracy and biases, and they value multiple perspectives. They seek explanations for the educational meanings and consequences of race, class, and gender.

PRACTICING EQUITY IN THE CLASSROOM

Caring and fairness are two qualities that students praise when describing successful teachers. Students know whether teachers view them as very special or as incompetent or worthless. Teacher perceptions may be based on personal characteristics of the student; sometimes they are based on group membership. A teacher may feel that homeless children who smell and arrive in dirty clothes have little chance of success. Teachers may pity children from one-parent homes and blame their lack of academic achievement on their not having two parents. Teachers may ignore English-language learners until they learn English and can communicate. Are these fair practices?

A school that provides an education that is multicultural will not tolerate such unjust practices by teachers. Both the classroom and the school will be models of democracy in which all students are treated equitably and fairly. In such a school, teachers and instructional leaders confront their own biases and develop strategies for overcoming them in their own interactions with students and colleagues. They learn to depend on one another for assistance, both in developing a culturally relevant curriculum and in ensuring that students are not subject to discrimination. As a result, students learn to respect differences and to interact within and across ethnic and cultural groups as they struggle for social justice in the school and the community.

Teachers sometimes give more help to some students than to others. They might praise some students while tending to correct and discipline others. Their expectations for academic success may differ depending on students' family income or ethnic group. However, most teachers do not deliberately set out to discriminate against certain students, especially in any harmful way. The problem is that everyone has been raised in a racist, sexist, and classist society in which the biases are so embedded that it is difficult for people to recognize anything other than the very overt signs. Teachers often need others to point out their discriminatory practices.

A good pattern to begin to develop even now, early in your teacher education program, is to reflect on your practice and the practice of teachers whom you observe. Among the questions that you might ask are:

- Are students from different gender, economic, and ethnic groups treated differently? What are the differences?
- Are there fewer discipline and learning problems among the students who are from the same background as the teacher? What is contributing to the differences?
- Do the least advantaged students receive the most assistance from the teacher? What are the differences in the instruction given to various students?
- How are the students' cultures being incorporated into the curriculum and instruction?

A key to ensuring that interactions with students are equitable is the ability to recognize one's own biases and make appropriate adjustments. Educators must be able to admit that they sometimes make mistakes. An ability to reflect on one's mistakes and why they occurred should lead to better teaching.

PROFESSIONAL DILEMMA

Harassment in Schools

Tyrone approaches you after school one day complaining that other students are calling him "sissy" and "faggot." He asks you for help, but you are not sure how to respond. You tell him you will do what you can but in the meantime he should try to avoid those particular students. You tell him that the other students probably don't mean to be hurtful.

You have not heard this taunting, but you begin to listen for signs of it in class and the halls. You discover that a small group of boys not only are calling names in whispers at the beginning of class, but also are pushing and shoving Tyrone in the hall. But it is not just Tyrone they are harassing. They make sexual comments to some of the girls in class as well. Then they laugh and high-five each other to celebrate their power over other students.

What do you do? Too often in the past, educators ignored such actions that tormented students who might be gay, small in stature, smart, or academically behind others. The actions of the bullies were chalked up to "boys being boys." However, harassment is not an activity to be taken lightly. Courts are holding schools responsible for not stopping harassment against other students. A helpful resource for educators, "Protecting Students from Harassment and Hate Crimes: A Guide for Schools," is available from the U.S. Department of Education; it can be downloaded from the web at www.ed.god/pubs/Harassment/.

1. What is your responsibility as an educator to confront and eliminate the harassment that you have observed?
2. What should you say to the boys who are the perpetrators of the taunts and pushing?
3. Where should you go for assistance in handling this problem?
4. How should you interact with the parents of the perpetrators and the victims of harassment in your classroom and school?
5. How can you ensure a safe environment for all students in your classroom?

TEACHING FOR SOCIAL JUSTICE

Culturally relevant teaching helps students struggle in class with social problems and issues that many students face daily in their lives both within and outside of school. Racism, sexism, classism, prejudice, and discrimination are felt differently by students of color than by members of the dominant group. Anger, denial, guilt, and affirmation of identity are critical parts of learning about and struggling with the pernicious practices that permeate most institutions. Although it is sometimes difficult to discuss these issues in classrooms, they are confronted in a system based on diversity and equality.

> ***Washing one's hands of the conflict between the powerful and the powerless means to side with the powerful, not to be neutral.***
>
> Paulo Freire

Most students of color, females, low-income students, students with disabilities, and gay students have probably already experienced discrimination in some aspect of their lives. They may have not acknowledged it, or they may be very angry or frustrated by it. On the other hand, many students from the dominant group have never experienced discrimination and often do not believe that it exists. In most cases they do not see themselves as advantaged; they do not think that they receive any more benefits from society than anyone else. These students will have a difficult time fighting social injustices if they have neither experienced them nor become aware of their existence. Are they receiving a good education if they are never exposed to the injustices that do exist or helped to confront their own biases?

In teaching for social justice, teachers help students understand the inequalities, oppression, and power struggles that are the realities of society. But this kind of teaching does not stop there. It provides hope for a world that is more equitable and socially just. Students and teachers become engaged in confronting injustice and working to remove the obstacles that prevent equality as an academic subject is studied. Maxine Green writes:

> To teach for social justice is to teach for enhanced perception and imaginative explorations, for the recognition of social wrongs, of sufferings, of pestilences wherever and whenever they arise. It is to find models in literature and in history of the indignant ones, the ones forever ill at ease, and the loving ones who have taken the side of the victims of pestilences, whatever their names or places of origin. It is to teach so that the young may be awakened to the joy of working for transformation in the smallest places, so that they may become healers and change their worlds.[25]

Students learn to apply the knowledge and skills they are learning to a local, regional, or global issue. The learning becomes authentic as it is related to the world that students care about. Students may take on community projects that examine pollution in their neighborhoods, political stances in their regional area, or the cost of food in their neighborhood versus another part of town. Students and teachers who tackle social justice as an integral part of their classroom work are providing education that is multicultural and reconstructionist. They are doing more than learning about the world. They are also working toward making it better for those who are least advantaged.

INVOLVING COMMUNITIES AND FAMILIES

It takes a whole village to educate a child.

Nigerian folk saying

In the delivery of multicultural education, parents and the community are the essential resources on which an educator must draw to understand the cultural context in which students live. It will be impossible to develop meaningful learning experiences for students if the teacher cannot relate to the real-life experiences of students who come from different ethnic, racial, and income backgrounds than the teacher.

Few beginning teachers will have had direct involvement in multiple cultural communities. Therefore, they must be open to continuing to learn about cultural differences and must depend on parents, students, and other community members to assist them. Many parents, especially those from powerless groups, are not comfortable in the school setting. Rather than waiting for them to come to a parent–teacher meeting or conference on their own, it is often necessary for the teacher to approach these parents in a nonthreatening setting. A trusting relationship in which both teachers and parents work together for the benefit of the child is key. A growing number of schools have parent advocates or liaisons who can assist the teacher in working with parents and communities. These individuals can help educators work effectively in communities with which they have little background or experience.

Learning to function effectively in several cultural communities requires participants to be comfortable with their own background. They also should understand the possible privilege they may have had in society because of their race, gender, sexual orientation, or socioeconomic status. Teachers who are most suc-

Families and the community are essential resources to help teachers understand the cultural context in which their students live.

cessful in helping students from diverse cultural backgrounds learn are those who "struggle to confront their own histories, hear the dissonance in their own profession, and begin to construct working alliances with colleagues, parents, and communities to meet the needs of all students," note Cochran-Smith and Lytle.[26] Teachers who provide education that is multicultural may begin to face these challenges in college, as beginning teachers, or after years in the classroom.

SUMMARY

UNDERGIRDING TENETS

Education that is multicultural is based on the principles of democracy, social justice, and equality. The goal is to ensure that all students participate equally in the education system. It values the cultural diversity of students as reflected in their gender and ethnic, racial, language, religious, and socioeconomic backgrounds. Educators strive for the provision of educational equality in which all students are provided challenging and stimulating learning experiences.

CULTURE OF THE SCHOOL

The school itself is a cultural system with its own rules and traditions. In addition to the formal curriculum of courses, a hidden curriculum defines acceptable behaviors and attitudes for students. In a culturally diverse school, the hidden curriculum often reflects the diversity of the dominant society rather than the multiple groups in the school population.

CULTURALLY RELEVANT TEACHING

Culturally relevant teaching occurs in schools that are multicultural. Teachers incorporate the culture of students into the curriculum. They use representations and examples from the cultures of the students as well as those from the dominant society. The cultures of students' families and the community are valued and reflected in all aspects of instruction. Students' voices that are usually silenced in the classroom become an important part of classroom dialog.

EDUCATIONAL CHALLENGES

Educators face many challenges in delivering education that is multicultural. Bridging the digital divide between students who have access to computers and the Internet and those who do not is one of the challenges faced by educators in providing equity and social justice. Other challenges include the delivery of gender-sensitive education that draws on different educational strategies to help male and female students perform at the highest possible levels no matter the subject area. Strategies for teaching English language learners vary according to the goals of a school and community.

TEACHERS AS SOCIAL ACTIVISTS

The four or five years that students spend in college to prepare for teaching only begin to ready them to work with students who are culturally diverse or to be able to deliver education that is multicultural. Beginning and experienced teachers will continue to learn about diversity, social justice, and equality and their implications for teaching and learning. Students, parents, and communities will be valuable resources in this learning process. Most educators will find it a lifelong and worthwhile endeavor.

DISCUSSION QUESTIONS

1. What conditions and practices existing in schools suggest that social justice is not a principle that undergirds the educational system?
2. What are the potential benefits and perceived dangers of allowing student voices to be an integral part of instruction?
3. Why is multicultural education just as important for students who are members of the dominant group in society as for those who are members of powerless groups?
4. How can teaching be made culturally relevant?
5. What are the differences between transitional bilingual education, developmental bilingual education, and immersion bilingual programs?

JOURNAL ENTRIES

1. Think about your high school and college experiences. How have they helped you clarify your thinking about racism, sexism, and classism in society and/or in schooling? Have they reinforced stereotypes? Or have they helped you understand how race, gender, and class affect many policies and practices that impact one's life? Write your conclusions in your journal.
2. Discuss your perceptions of being a teacher who is a social activist. Do you think that is an appropriate role for a teacher? Why or why not?

PORTFOLIO DEVELOPMENT

1. Develop a culturally relevant lesson plan on a topic that you will be teaching. Describe the cultural context for the students to whom the lesson will be taught.
2. For the subject and level that you plan to teach, design a lesson in which you introduce social justice.

SCHOOL-BASED EXPERIENCES

1. As part of an early field experience activity in your teacher education program, gather a minimum of five observational sets of data on a student of color in a classroom. In particular, look for the nature of the interaction between the student and the teacher, the communication patterns with one or two other students, the oral classroom participation patterns, and the student's engagement with the subject matter.
2. Visit an inner-city school and a rural or suburban school and observe how student voices are incorporated in classes. Record the nature of the dialogue between students and teachers and among students; be able to describe the degree of equality across the voices and whether any significant patterns of differences emerged.

WEBSITES

For information on many dimensions of multicultural education, search the web using words such as "bilingual education," "Individuals with Disabilities Act (IDEA)," "English as a Second Language programs," "English-only laws," "censoring books," and "performance assessment." Several particularly useful sites are listed below.

1. <www.ascd.org> The website of the Association of Supervision and Curriculum Development includes a number of resources related to teaching diverse students and multicultural education.
2. <www.bigmyth.com> This website has a collection of cross-cultural world creation myths that can be used to compare cultures around the world.
3. <www.cal.org> The website of the Center for Applied Linguistics provides resources for scholars and educators who use the findings of linguistics and related sciences in identifying and addressing language issues.
4. <www.cec.sped.org/home.htm> The home page of the Council for Exceptional Children provides information on this association for parents, educators, and others interested in special education and disability issues.
5. <www.curry.edschool.virginia.edu/go/multicultural/> The Multicultural Pavilion Teacher's Corner is the name of this home page, which links teachers and others who are struggling with issues related to multicultural education.
6. <www.nabe.org> The website of National Association for Bilingual Education, which promotes educational excellence and equity through bilingual education, includes legislation, policies, and research related to language diversity.
7. <www.nameorg.org> The website of the National Association for Multicultural Education (NAME) connects users to others who are working in the field of multicultural education.
8. <www.nccj.org> The National Conference of Community and Justice is a human relations organization dedicated to fighting bias, bigotry, and racism in the United States. It promotes understanding and respect among all races, religions, and cultures through advocacy, conflict resolution, and education.
9. <www.pta.org> The website of the National Parent Teacher Association includes information on building home–school relationships.
10. <www.rethinkingschools.org> This website was designed by a group of teachers who wanted to improve education in their own classrooms and schools as well as to help shape school reform that is humane, caring, multiracial, and democratic.

11. <www.sonoma.edu/cthink/> This website was developed by the Critical Thinking Community (CTC) for educators, students, and the general public. It provides information about critical thinking, theory and practice, concepts, definitions, techniques for learning and teaching, and classroom exercises.
12. <www.teachingforchange.org> The website of NECA promotes social and economic justice through transformative, high-quality education for all learners.

NOTES

1. Donna M. Gollnick and Philip C. Chinn, *Multicultural Education in a Pluralistic Society*. 5th ed. New York: Macmillan, 2001.
2. James A. Banks, "Multicultural Education: Development, Dimensions, and Challenges," *Phi Delta Kappan 75* (1) (September 1993): 55–60.
3. Banks, 23.
4. National Conference of Christians and Jews, *Taking America's Pulse: A Summary Report of the National Conference Survey on Inter-Group Relations*. New York: Author, 1994, 9.
5. Recruiting New Teachers, Inc., *The Essential Profession: A National Survey of Public Attitudes toward Teaching, Educational Opportunity and School Reform*. Belmont, MA: Author, 1998.
6. Robert N. Bellah, Richard Madsen, William M. Sullivan, Ann Swidler, and Steven M. Tipton, *The Good Society*. New York: Vintage Books, 1991.
7. Bellah et al.
8. Peter Figueroa, "Multicultural Education in the United Kingdom: Historical Development and Current Status," in James A. Banks and Cherry A. McGee Banks, eds., *Handbook of Research on Multicultural Education*. New York: Macmillan, 1995, 778–800.
9. Lisa Delpit, *Other People's Children: Cultural Conflict in the Classroom*. New York: New Press, 1995.
10. American Association of Colleges for Teacher Education, *Culturally Responsive Teachers Inform the Reform Agenda: Recommendations for Policy and Practice*. Washington, DC: Author, 1998.
11. Sharon Nelson-Barber and Elise Trumbull Estrin, "Bringing Native American Perspectives to Mathematics and Science Teaching," *Theory into Practice, 34* (3) (Summer 1995): 174–185.
12. Worldwatch Institute, *State of the World 2000*. New York: W. W. Norton, 2000.
13. U.S. Department of Commerce, *Falling through the Net: Defining the Digital Divide*. Washington, DC: U.S. Government Printing Office, 1999.
14. The Children's Partnership, *Online Content for Low-Income and Underserved Americans: The Digital Divide's New Frontier*. Santa Monica, CA: Author, 2000.
15. U.S. Department of Commerce, 1999.
16. The President's Information Technology Advisory Committee, *Resolving the Digital Divide: Information, Access, and Opportunity*. Arlington, VA: National Coordination Office for Computing, Information, and Communications, 2000.
17. American Association of University Women (AAUW), *Tech-Savvy: Educating Girls in the New Computer Age*. Washington, DC: Author, 2000.
18. The Children's Partnership, 2000, p. 6.
19. AAUW, 2000.
20. David L. E. Watt, Betty Roessingh, and Lynn Bosetti, "Success and Failure: Stories of ESL Students' Educational and Cultural Adjustment to High School," *Urban Education 31* (2) (May 1996): 200.
21. National Association for the Education of Young Children, *Responding to Linguistic and Cultural Diversity—Recommendations for Effective Early Childhood Education*. Washington, DC: Author, 1996.
22. NAEYC, 1996.

23. Fred Genesee, ed., *Program Alternatives for Linguistically Diverse Students.* Washington, DC: Center for Research on Education, Diversity and Excellence, 1999.
24. Genessee, 1999.
25. Maxine Greene, "Introduction: Teaching for Social Justice," in William Ayers, Jean Ann Hunt, and Therese Quinn, eds., *Teaching for Social Justice.* New York: New Press, 1998, p. xlv.
26. Marilyn Cochran-Smith and Susan L. Lytle, "Interrogating Cultural Diversity: Inquiry and Action." *Journal of Teacher Education 43* (2) (March–April 1992): 104–115.

BIBLIOGRAPHY

American Association for University Women. *Gender Gaps: Where Schools Still Fail Our Children.* New York: Marlowe & Co., 1999.

American Association for University Women. *Tech-Savvy: Educating Girls in the New Computer Age.* Washington, DC: Author, 2000.

Anti-Defamation League. *Hate Hurts: How Children Learn and Unlearn Prejudice.* New York: Author, 2000.

Ayers, William; Hunt, Jean Ann; and Quinn, Therese, eds. *Teaching for Social Justice.* New York: New Press, 1998.

Brisk, Maria Estela. *Bilingual Education: From Compensatory to Quality Schooling.* Mahwah, NJ: Lawrence Erlbaum, 1998.

Cloud, Nancy; Genesee, Fred; and Hamayan, Else. *Dual Language Instruction: A Handbook for Enriched Education.* Washington, DC: Center for Research on Education, Diversity and Excellence, 2000.

Corson, David. *Language Policy in Schools: A Resource for Teachers and Administrators.* Mahwah, NJ: Lawrence Erlbaum, 1999.

Cummins, Jim and Sayers, Dennis. *Brave New Schools: Challenging Cultural Illiteracy.* New York: St. Martin's Press, 1997.

Delpit, Lisa. *Other People's Children: Cultural Conflict in the Classroom.* New York: New Press, 1995.

Fletcher, Scott. *Education and Emancipation: Theory and Practice in a New Constellation.* New York: Teachers College Press, 2000.

Gollnick, Donna M., and Chinn, Philip C. *Multicultural Education in a Pluralistic Society.* 5th ed. New York: Macmillan, 1997.

Grant, Carl A., and Sleeter, Christine E. *Turning on Learning: Five Approaches for Multicultural Teaching Plans for Race, Class, Gender, and Disability.* Columbus, OH: Merrill, 1996.

Hollins, Etta R., and Oliver, Eileen I. *Pathways to Success in School: Culturally Responsive Teaching.* Mahwah, NJ: Lawrence Erlbaum,1999.

Ladson-Billings, Gloria. *The Dreamkeepers: Successful Teachers of African American Children.* San Francisco: Jossey-Bass, 1994.

Multicultural Perspectives: The Magazine of the National Association for Multicultural Education.

Rethinking Schools. A newsletter on teaching for equity and social justice published by Rethinking Schools.

Rethinking Schools. *Rethinking Our Classrooms: Teaching for Equity and Justice.* Milwaukee: Author, 1994.

Shor, Ira. *When Students Have Power: Negotiating Authority in a Critical Pedagogy.* Chicago: The University of Chicago Press, 1996.

Sleeter, Christine E. *Multicultural Education as Social Activism.* Albany, NJ: State University of New York Press, 1996.

Teaching Tolerance. *Responding to Hate at School.* Montgomery, AL: Author, 1999.

Tharp, Roland; Estrada, Peggy; Dalton, Stephanie S.; and Yamauchi, Lois A. *Teaching Transformed: Achieving Excellence, Fairness, Inclusion, and Harmony.* Washington, DC: Center for Research on Education, Diversity and Excellence, 2000.

Thorne, Barrie. *Gender Play: Girls and Boys in School.* New Brunswick, NJ: Rutgers University Press, 1997.

PART 3

CHAPTER 5
Organizing and Paying for American Education

CHAPTER 6
Legal Foundations of Education

Governance and Support of American Education

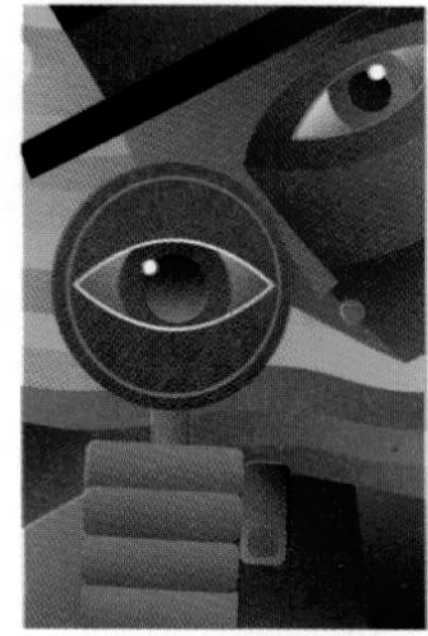

Viewing Education through Organizational Lenses

In Part Three you will view schools and the U.S. system of education through three different filters or wavelengths of light. The first is structural, the focus being on how schools and school districts are organized.

The second filter that is applied in this part places the focus on the financing of education. Money has to be found to operate all the schools, which means taxation in a variety of forms.

With the third filter we will view schools in terms of the laws of the land. Schools are legally constituted entities. As professionals, teachers and administrators must know and understand how laws, policies, and court cases delimit what they can, should, and must do.

The following questions will help you to focus your learning as you read Part Three:

1. What are the role and authority of the school principal? Who supervises the school principal?
2. Who is in charge of the school district: the superintendent or the school board?
3. Does a school district have to do what the state department of education says? Can the federal government tell schools what to do?
4. Property taxes have been the major source of revenue for schools. What is wrong with this?
5. Which three amendments to the U.S. Constitution provide the legal basis for public schools?
6. Can public funds be used to support students in parochial schools?
7. How is equal opportunity addressed in U.S. law?
8. Do school students in the United States have the same rights as adult citizens?
9. What protections, if any, do nontenured teachers have?
10. Is it legal for teachers to strike?
11. Do teachers and school administrators have to obtain a search warrant before they can search a student?

CHAPTER

5

Organizing and Paying for American Education

EDUCATION IN THE NEWS

Study: School Choice Popular; Academic Results Are Unclear

By Lori Aratani
Mercury News Staff Writer

Americans choose what car they drive, what stores they shop in—and now a growing number of families are taking a free-market approach to choosing what school their children attend.

One in four students nationwide is now going to a school outside his or her neighborhood, whether it's a public magnet program, a charter campus or a private school, according to a report released today by researchers with a California-based education think tank. But researchers with Policy Analysis for California Education said enthusiasm for choice isn't necessarily translating into the academic achievement that advocates promise.

"From breakfast cereals to SUVs, consumers demand choices in a democratic society," said Bruce Fuller, lead author of the report, "School Choice: Abundant Hopes, Scarce Evidence of Results." "But as market dynamics are used to energize school reform, we have yet to see solid evidence of achievement gains."

The report comes at a time when choice programs are rapidly expanding but research on their effectiveness remains scant.

Polls indicate strong public support for school choice programs. And politicians are once again offering vouchers and charter schools as solutions to the nation's education ills. . . . George W. Bush recently unveiled a voucher program using federal money to help low-income students who attend failing schools. [Former] President Clinton has voiced strong support for charter schools.

FIVE TYPES OF CHOICE

The PACE report examined the effects of five types of choice: magnet schools, charter schools, open enrollment, vouchers and tax-credit programs. Of the five, vouchers is the smallest. California offers three of the five choices to residents: open enrollment, magnet and charter schools. An initiative to establish a publicly funded voucher program was soundly defeated in 1993, although there are movements to bring the issue back to the ballot.

Though choice programs have been around for almost three decades, their popularity has leaped in recent years. Between 1993 and 1999, the number of students participating in choice programs increased from 9.7 million to 13.6 million, including students who attend private schools.

But, according to the report's authors, poor families continue to be left behind, even in programs that are targeted at low-income students. Part of the problem may be that they lack the know-how to explore options, said Luis Huerta, the report's

(continued)

co-author. In the case of vouchers, the payments often don't cover the full cost of private or parochial education, which may preclude poor families from participating.

The PACE report is timely because educators and legislators are searching for ways to restore public faith in the nation's education system. Many view choice programs as a tool to give parents more say in how their children are educated. Others view the programs as a way of injecting competition into a public school system that they say has grown stagnant and unresponsive to change. Advocates of vouchers, for example, think competition from private schools will force public campuses to improve or be shut down.

As the report says: "The demand for school choice is irresistible: wider options for parents and a more diverse array of schools."

Among some of PACE's key findings:

- Suburban parents appear fairly satisfied with their neighborhood campuses. Even in voucher programs targeted at low-income families, the poorest families remained in their neighborhood schools.
- Of the five programs examined, research has shown significant academic gains only among students who attend magnet schools. While some studies have found achievement gains among voucher students, researchers said it's unclear whether those gains are tied to the program or to the characteristics of families who choose to accept vouchers. Researchers found those families are more likely to be involved in their child's education.
- Evidence shows that parents are more satisfied with a charter school they have chosen than they were with their neighborhood school.

LEARNER OUTCOMES

After reading and studying this chapter, you will be able to

1. Describe the organizational structure of schools, school districts, and the authority relationships among schools, states, and the federal government.
2. Analyze pro and con arguments presented for increasing school choice.
3. Describe the relationship of teachers to their principal and how the responsibilities of the principal relate to those of the school district superintendent and the school board.
4. Summarize the key sources of funding for public schools and issues related to over-reliance on any one of these sources.
5. Describe the underlying theme related to the large number of states that have court cases dealing with school finance.
6. Compare the spending for public schools in the United States with other developed countries. ■

Several big ideas are developed in this chapter. The first addresses the American education system structure. Although complex, there is an explainable pattern to school organization. On top of the local pattern is the organization of education within each state. The federal government also influences the way in which schools operate, and so a brief description of its involvement in and influence over schooling is presented. Another big idea developed in this chapter deals with the complexity of school finance. Key elements and critical issues in the financing of education make up the second topic. The funds to finance schooling come from several different sources. Each of these sources brings with it certain advantages and particular problems.

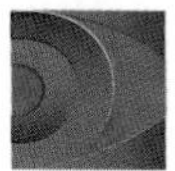

THE STRUCTURE OF THE AMERICAN EDUCATION SYSTEM

Descriptions of the U.S. education system generally start at the "top" of the organization chart, with the U.S. Department of Education; move "down" through the state structures; and ultimately arrive at the school district and school levels. This top-down approach reflects, in an organizational sense, the fact that it is easier to understand the pieces when you first have a view of the whole. Also, the top-down approach indicates that there are more authority and responsibility the further up one is in the structure. In many ways this is true.

However, in education, unlike many businesses, the "bottom" is composed of professionals (teachers and principals) who know as much or more about their business as those who are more removed from the day-to-day life in classrooms. Therefore, teachers and principals correctly argue, they should have a great deal of say in determining what happens with their students on a day-to-day basis. Our decision to start this chapter with a description of schools, rather than at the federal level, is in some ways making a symbolic statement that teachers can be viewed as being at the top.

To avoid many of the problems implied in a vertical (top-down) picture of the education system, some theorists have advocated a horizontal perspective, as is represented in Table 5.1. One important emphasis of this horizontal policy-to-practice continuum is that for education to improve, the agencies and people at each point along the continuum have to do their job well. A second critical feature is that all have to trust people and agencies at other points along the continuum. This means, for example, that teachers have to develop an understanding of the functions and purposes of other parts of the system. Teachers cannot stay isolated in their classrooms, unaware of the issues and expectations of the school, school district, and the state. At the other end of the continuum, it is important that policymakers learn more about the work of teachers and what goes on in schools.

TABLE 5.1 THE POLICY-TO-PRACTICE CONTINUUM IN THE U.S. EDUCATION SYSTEM

Federal	State	Intermediate	District	School	Classroom
President	Governor	Director	Superintendent	Principal	Teacher
Congress	Legislature	Board	Board	Site council	Students
Secretary	Chief state school officer			Teachers	
U.S. Department of Education	State department of education		District office staff		

Another important organizational concept to keep in mind is the difference between line and staff relationships. In any organization some people will have the job of being supervisors, bosses, honchos, managers, or directors. Other people will report to these persons. The supervisor typically has the authority, at least to some degree, to direct, monitor, and evaluate the work of the subordinate. When one person has this type of authority over another, there is a **line relationship.** But when there is no formal supervisory authority of one person over the other, they have a **staff relationship.** This distinction becomes important in education because in many instances it is not clear or absolute who has the authority or responsibility to direct the work of others. For example, teachers, as professionals, can legitimately claim more independence than can employees of other organizations. But teachers are not completely free to do whatever they want. If they were, the system of education would break down, at least as it is experienced by the students who must move through it.

THE ORGANIZATION OF SCHOOLS

The basic building block of the U.S. education system is the school. To an amazing extent schools are organized in the same way in each state. In fact, schools are organized pretty much the same in other countries too.

Each school consists of a set of classrooms, with corridors for the movement of students, and a central office. There will be one or more large spaces for a cafeteria and gymnasium/auditorium. The school will have outside spaces for a playground, staff parking, and a driveway for dropping off and picking up students. Wherever you go, you will find this basic architecture.

This typical design of schools is frequently criticized for resembling an egg crate. If you viewed a school building with the roof off, you would see that it resembled an egg carton: a series of cells or pockets with routes running between them. Some educational critics see this architecture as interfering with the need to introduce new educational practices. For example, the walls restrict communication between teachers and channel the flow of student traffic.

Even when a school is built with modest attempts to change the interior space, teachers and students are able to preserve the egg-crate concept. For example, you may have seen an elementary school that had an open-space design. Instead of self-contained classrooms, there might be an open floor plan equivalent in size to three or four classrooms. However, if you observed the arrangement of furniture, bookshelves, and screens, you probably noted that teachers and students had constructed zones and areas that were equivalent to three or four self-contained classrooms.

We are not criticizing teachers for how they have adapted to new school architectures; rather, we are pointing out how the organization of the space parallels the activity of the people who use it. There are many good reasons for organizing schools around self-contained classrooms. And in the case of the open-space concept, the noise from three or four teachers and 90 to 120 children can be so disruptive that little learning can occur. One key to the successful use of open-space plans, then, is to be sure the building is designed in ways that control and dampen noise.

The physical arrangement of a school into classrooms has organizational as well as instructional implications. For example, it is easy for teachers to be isolated in their classrooms. This geographic isolation contributes to their not knowing about or becoming engaged with issues that are affecting the whole school.

line relationship
An organizational arrangement in which a subordinate is directly responsible to a supervisor.

staff relationship
An organizational arrangement in which one party is not under the direct control or authority of another.

The principal is responsible for the actions of all school personnel, as well as working with committees of parents and teachers.

Geographic isolation can affect the school as a whole too. The school staff might not be aware of community concerns or of what is going on in other schools across the district. It is important that teachers and administrators make deliberate efforts to learn about other parts of the education system. This need to see the bigger picture is especially true for the school principal.

THE ROLES AND RESPONSIBILITIES OF PRINCIPALS The principal is in charge of the school. In law the principal is the final authority at the school. The principal is typically responsible for instructional leadership, community relationships, staff (including teachers, secretaries, and custodians), teacher selection and evaluation, pupil personnel, building and grounds, budgets, administration of personnel, provisions of contracts, administration of the attendance center office, and business management. The principal is in a line relationship with the school district superintendent. In larger school districts the principal may have an intermediate supervisor, such as an assistant superintendent or a director of elementary or secondary education.

Principals' tasks and responsibilities are expanding. For example, there is a push to increase teacher participation in making school decisions. And there is a movement to increase parent and community involvement in school decisions. Both of these trends have led to the creation of teams or committees of teachers and parents to work with the principal. Working with these committees places new demands on the principal's time and generates new expectations for the types of leadership skills a principal needs to possess or develop.

ASSISTANT PRINCIPALS In larger elementary schools and in most junior high schools, middle schools, and high schools, there will be one or more additional administrators. Normally, they are called assistant principals, although sometimes in high schools they are titled vice principals. Large high schools will have several assistant or vice principals and some other administrators that have "director" titles, such as director of athletics and director of counseling. These administrators share in the tasks of the principal and provide additional avenues of communication between teachers, students, staff, parents, community, and the district office. In elementary schools the job differentiation between the assistant principal and the principal will be less clear, and both administrators will be a part of most operations. In the high school setting, specific roles and tasks will frequently be assigned to the different assistant principals. For example, one assistant principal might handle discipline. Another example would be the evaluation of teachers. In most districts each teacher must be observed formally. This activity takes more time than the principal will have available, so the assistant principal(s) will observe some teachers. Normally, the principal will concentrate on observing the new teachers because it is the principal who makes the recommendation on rehiring beginning teachers.

DEPARTMENT HEADS AND TEAM LEADERS In elementary schools there will normally be another, less formal level of leadership: grade-level or team leaders. These are full-time teachers who assume a communication and coordination role for their grade level(s) or team. In junior high schools and high schools there will be department chairs. Normally, the departments will be organized around the major subject areas (mathematics, science, English, and social studies) and the cocurricula (athletics and music). Teachers will be members of one of the departments, and there will be regular meetings to plan curriculum and to facilitate communication. In middle schools the leaders of interdisciplinary teams will likely serve in the same way. In each case these department heads or team leaders will meet with the principal from time to time and meet regularly with their teachers.

TEACHERS The single largest group of adults in the school is the teachers. A typical elementary school will have from fifteen to thirty-five teachers, and there will be more than one hundred in a large high school. Teachers are busy in their classrooms working with their students, and this is where the egg-crate architecture of schools can be a problem. Unless special mechanisms are used, such as team leaders or department chairs, it is very easy for individual teachers to become isolated from the school as a whole. The self-contained classroom architecture and the work of attending to twenty to forty students in the classroom give each teacher little time or opportunity to communicate with other adults. As a consequence, the principal and all the teachers need to work hard with the other members of the school staff to facilitate communication. All must make an effort to work together to continually improve the school.

Some school districts have developed new roles for master teachers; for example, each Douglas County Colorado school has a Building Resource Teacher (BRT) who is responsible for staff development.

SCHOOL SUPPORT STAFF A school has other personnel that support the administrators and teachers. One of the most important of these supporting roles is filled by the school secretary. Every teacher and principal will advise you to be sure to develop a good working relationship with the school secretary, who is at the nerve center of the running of the school. When a student has a problem, when a teacher needs some materials, when the principal wants a piece of information from the files, or when a student teacher wants to know about parking a car, the first person to contact is the school secretary. Another important resource to the school are the custodians. How clean your classroom and school are will depend on the efforts of the custodians, and they also can be helpful to teachers in locating supplies and moving furniture. Keep in mind that they observe and talk with students. Frequently, custodians and other support staff will know about something that is going on before the teachers do. Cafeteria workers are another group of adult workers in the school who can make a positive difference in how the school feels and functions.

THE SCHOOL ORGANIZATION CHART All of the personnel described above work in the school building. Their working relationships can be pictured in an **organization chart,** as shown in the bottom part of Figure 5.1. The principal is the single line authority for all of these adults *and* for all of the students! Most experts on organizations will advocate that no more than five to seven people should be directly supervised by one administrator. Yet in nearly all schools the principal will be responsible for a minimum of thirty adults and several hundred students. In very large schools the principal may have two hundred adults to supervise. As you can see, the simple picture of top-down direction for education breaks apart when one considers the wide array of tasks and the sheer number of people at work in each school. There have to be a number of structures for arranging the relationships among the varied role groups and facilitating coordination and communication.

organization chart
A graphic representation of the line and staff relationships of personnel in a school, school district, or other type of organization.

WHEN TO TALK TO WHOM When teachers have an idea about the school or want to try something different, it is important for them to talk with their principal. If

FIGURE 5.1 A School Organization Chart

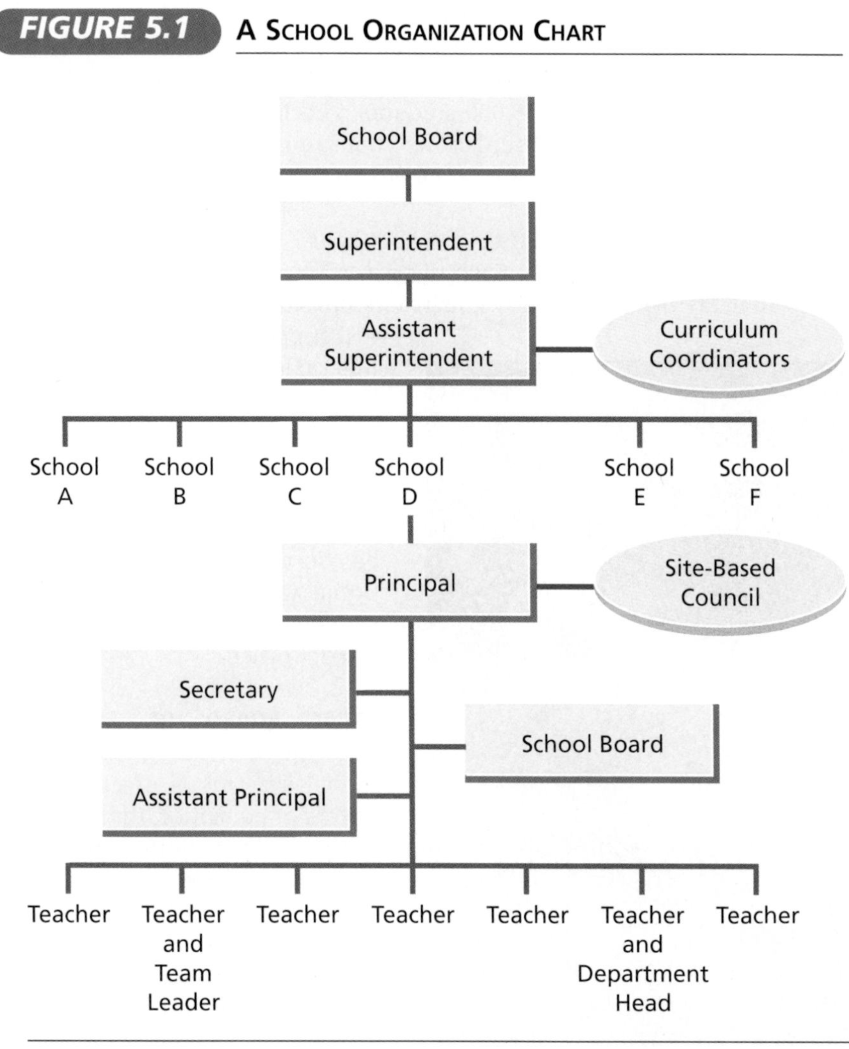

there are department heads or team leaders, then the first discussions should be with them. In any organization, including schools, it is normal protocol to talk first with the person at the next level above. When there is a concern or problem, it is important to use the official administrative system—to contact the principal. If this method fails and there is a serious problem, then a teacher may continue up the line by contacting the principal's supervisor: the assistant superintendent or the superintendent. If there is a serious disagreement, then a teacher may file a grievance through procedures outlined in the negotiated contract. In any instance it is wise for a beginning teacher, or one who is new to the system, to seek advice from experienced colleagues before taking action. In addition to knowing the system, one must know how the system works; colleagues and principals can be helpful in this regard.

ORGANIZATION OF THE SCHOOL DISTRICT

Public schools in the United States are organized into school districts, which have similar purposes but widely different characteristics. Some districts provide only elementary education; others provide only high school education; still others provide both elementary and secondary education. Approximately 26 percent of the districts have fewer than 300 pupils, and their total enrollments make up about 1.3 percent of the national enrollment. Only 1.1 percent of the districts have an enrollment in excess of 25,000 students, yet these districts enroll about 28 percent of the total student population. Thousands of school districts have only 1 school campus; in comparison, a few urban districts have as many as 500 schools.

The school district is governed by a school board, and its day-to-day operations are led by a superintendent. Each district will have its own district office that houses an array of administrative, instructional support, financial, and clerical support staff. As the state and federal levels of government have become active in setting educational agendas, there has been a concomitant response at the district level in the form of an ever increasing list of tasks that must be accomplished. These additional tasks have brought more functions and personnel to the district office.

About 92 percent of the public school boards in the United States are elected by popular vote; about 7 percent are appointed.

LOCAL BOARD OF EDUCATION

Legal authority for operating local school systems is given to local boards of education through state statutes. The statutes prescribe specifically how school board members are to be chosen and what duties and responsibilities they have in office. The statutes also specify the terms of board members, procedures for selecting officers of the board, duties of the officers, and procedures for filling any vacancies. Local citizens serving as school board members are official agents of the state.

About 92 percent of the school boards in the United States are elected by popular vote; most members are elected in special nonpartisan elections. About 7 percent are appointed. The percentage of appointed school boards is higher in school districts enrolling more than 25,000 pupils; yet even in three-fourths of these larger districts the board members are elected.

Normally, teachers may not be board members in the districts where they teach; however, they may be board members in districts where they live if they teach in different districts. The trend for more teachers to become board members most likely results from the goal of professional associations to secure seats on school boards.

POWERS AND DUTIES OF SCHOOL BOARDS The powers and duties of school boards vary from state to state; the school codes of the respective states spell them out in detail. School boards' major function is the development of policy for the local school district—policy that must be in harmony with both federal and state law. Boards have only those powers granted or implied by statute that are necessary to carry out their responsibilities. These powers usually include the power to act as follows:

- Obtain revenue
- Maintain schools
- Purchase sites and build buildings
- Purchase materials and supplies
- Organize and provide programs of studies
- Employ necessary workers and regulate their services
- Admit and assign pupils to schools and control their conduct

Some duties of school boards are mandatory, while others are discretionary. Some duties cannot be delegated. If, for example, a board is given the power to employ teachers, the board must do this; the power may not be delegated—even to a school superintendent. Boards can delegate much of the hiring process to administrators, however, and then act officially on administrative recommendations for employment. An illustration of a discretionary power left to the local board is the decision whether or not to participate in a nonrequired school program—for example, a program of competitive athletics. Another illustration of discretionary power is the decision to employ only teachers who exceed minimum state certification standards.

Powers and duties granted to a board of education are granted to the board as a whole, not to individual members. An individual member of a board has no more authority in school matters than any other citizen of the community unless the school board legally delegates a task through official action to a specific member; in those instances, official board approval of final actions is necessary. A school board, as a corporate body, can act officially only in legally held and duly authorized board meetings, and these meetings usually must be open to the public. Executive or private sessions may be held, but ordinarily only for specified purposes such as evaluating staff members or selecting a school site. Usually, any action on matters discussed in private session must be taken officially in an open meeting.

SUPERINTENDENT OF SCHOOLS One of the primary duties of the local board is to select its chief executive officer, the superintendent. There is one notable

In Florida two-thirds of the school district superintendents are elected.

exception to the general practice of selection of the superintendent by school boards. In a few states, especially in the Southeast, school district superintendents are elected by the voters. In these situations school superintendent selection is a political process just like that used for the election of mayors, county commissioners, some judges, and others. In either case, whether named by the board or elected by the people, the superintendent is responsible for the day-to-day operations of the school district, responding to school board members' interests, planning the district's budget, and defining long-term aspirations for the district. The superintendent is expected to be visible in the community and to provide overall leadership for the district.

THE CRITICAL IMPORTANCE OF LEADERSHIP The importance of leadership by the superintendent and board members cannot be overemphasized. The quality of the educational program of a school district is influenced strongly by the leadership that the board of education and the superintendent provide. Without the communication and support of high expectations by boards and superintendents, high-quality education is not likely to be achieved. Curriculum programs over and above state-required minimums are discretionary. For a school district to excel, the local authorities, board members, and the superintendent must convince their communities that specified school programs are needed and desirable.

CENTRAL OFFICE STAFF The superintendent of schools works with a staff to carry on the program of education. The size of the staff varies with the school district; of course, some kind of organization is necessary. Many school systems use a line and staff organization like that shown in Figure 5.2.

In this pattern, line officers hold the administrative power as it flows from the local board of education down to the pupils. Superintendents, assistant superintendents, and principals are line officers vested with authority over the people below them on the chart. Each person is directly responsible to the official above and must work through that person in dealing with a higher official. This arrangement is frequently referred to as the chain of command.

Administrative staff members are shown in Figure 5.2 as branching out from the direct flow of authority. Staff includes librarians, instructional supervisors, guidance officers, transportation officers, and others. They are responsible to their respective superiors but have no authority over teachers. They assist and advise others from their special knowledge and abilities. Teachers are generally referred to as staff even though they are in the direct flow of authority. However, their authority in this arrangement prevails only over pupils.

ORGANIZATION OF EDUCATION AT THE STATE LEVEL

In certain countries, such as Taiwan, the national constitution specifies responsibility for education; but the U.S. Constitution does not specifically provide for public education. As will be explained in Chapter 6, however, the Tenth Amendment has been interpreted as granting this power to the states. As a consequence, the states are the governmental units in the United States charged with the responsibility for education. Local school districts then receive through state law their empowerment to administer and operate the school system for their communities. State legislatures, within the limits expressed by the federal Constitution and by state constitutions, are the chief policymakers for education. State

FIGURE 5.2 TYPICAL SCHOOL DISTRICT LINE AND STAFF ORGANIZATION

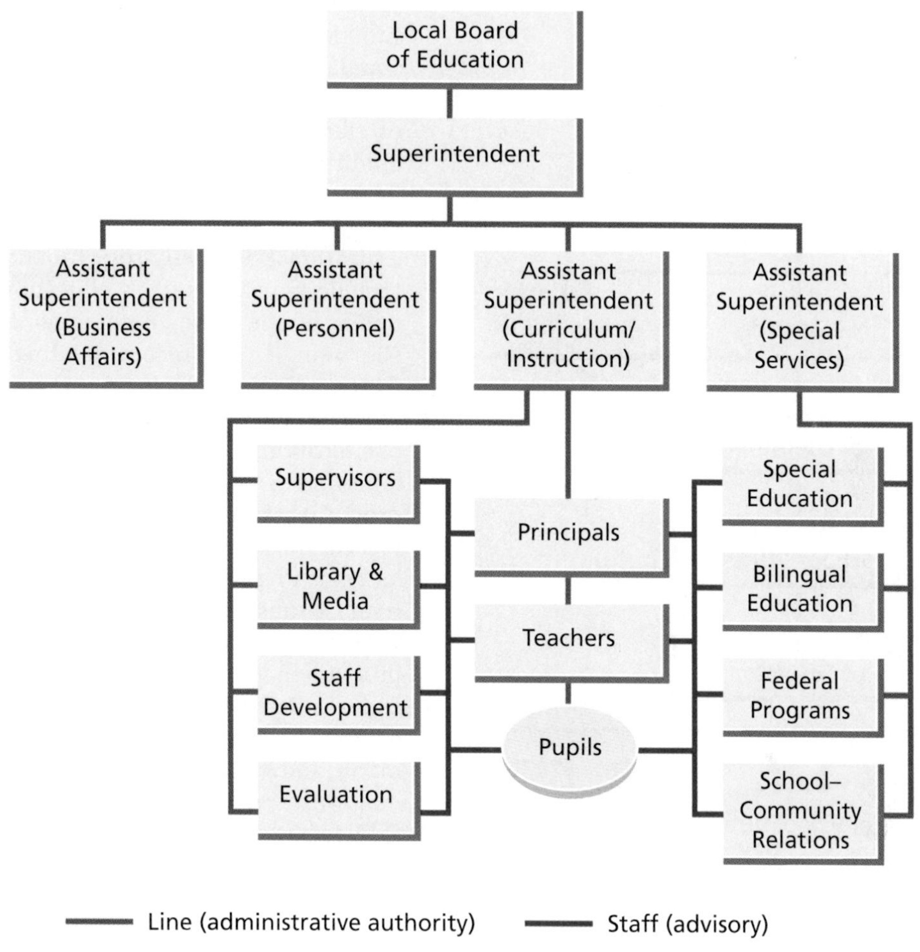

legislatures grant powers to state boards of education, state departments of education, chief state school officers, and local boards of education. These groups have only the powers granted to them by the legislature, implied powers from the specific grant of power, and the necessary powers to carry out the statutory purposes. The responsibilities and duties of intermediate units are also prescribed by the state legislatures. Figure 5.3 shows a typical state organization for education.

Stability, continuity, and leadership for education can come from the state board. However, as identified in Figure 5.3, many other individuals and groups are increasingly likely to engage in education issues. For example, many legislators have established records of heavy influence on the direction of education. Through their initiatives new laws may affect any and all parts of the education system. There are "education governors" as well. Many state leaders have been very involved in supporting and attempting to shape education in their states. Suffice it to say, numerous participants and agencies and many kinds of influences have impacts on the shape and direction of the U.S. education system.

FIGURE 5.3 Typical Structure of a State Education System

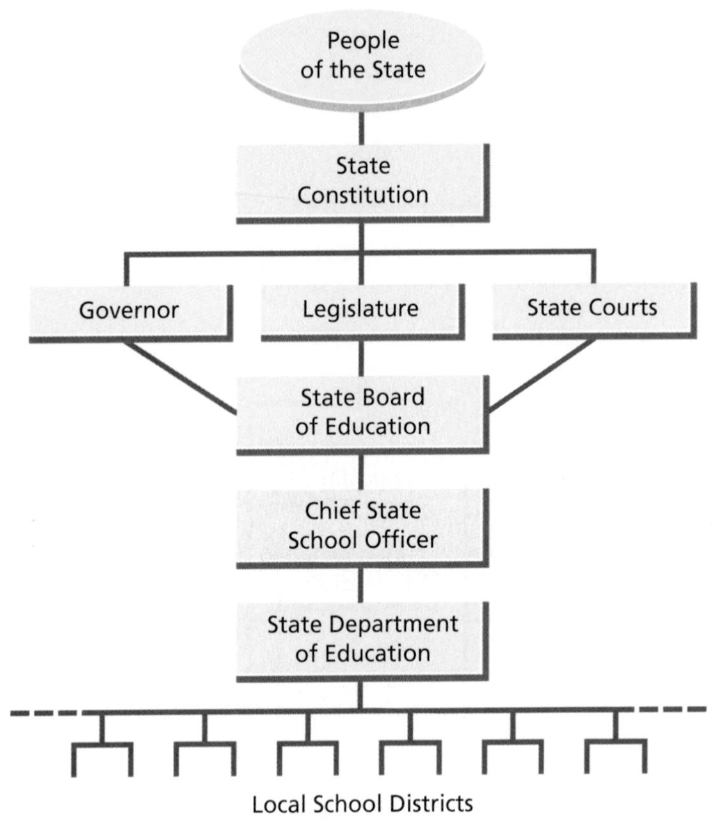

STATE BOARDS OF EDUCATION State boards of education are both regulatory and advisory. Some regulatory functions are the establishment of standards for issuing and revoking teaching licenses, the establishment of standards for approving and accrediting schools, and the development and enforcement of a uniform system for gathering and reporting educational data. Advisory functions include considering the educational needs of the state, both long- and short-range, and recommending to the governor and the legislature ways of meeting these needs. State boards of education, in studying school problems and in suggesting and analyzing proposals, can be invaluable to the legislature, especially since the legislature is under pressure to decide so many issues. A state board can provide continuity for an educational program that ordinary legislative procedures don't accommodate. A state board can also coordinate, supplement, and even replace study commissions appointed by a legislature for advising on educational matters. These commissions frequently include groups studying textbooks, finance, certification, school district reorganization, school building standards, and teachers' education.

Each state's constitution specifies the division of authority and responsibility among the legislature, the state board of education, and the governor.

STATE BOARD MEMBERSHIP Members of state boards of education get their positions in various ways. Usually, they are appointed by the governor, with confirmation by the senate; or they may be elected by the people, the legislature, or local school board members in a regional convention—also with confirmation by the senate. The terms of members of state boards of education are usually staggered to avoid a complete changeover at any one time. Board members usually serve without pay but are reimbursed for expenses. The policies of nonpayment and staggered terms are considered safeguards against political patronage.

CHIEF STATE SCHOOL OFFICERS Every state has a chief state school officer, commissioner of education, or superintendent of public instruction. Currently, nineteen of these officers are elected by the people, twenty-seven are appointed by the state board of education, and four are appointed by the governor.

Arguments advanced for electing the chief state school officer hold that, as an elected official, the person will be close to the people, responsible to them, and free from obligations to other state officials. An elected person will also be independent of the state board of education. Opponents of the election method argue that this method keeps the state department of education in partisan politics, that an elected official is obligated to other members of the same political party, and that many excellent candidates prefer not to engage in political contests. Those who advocate that the chief state school officer should be appointed by a state board of education claim that policymaking should be separated from policy execution, that educational leadership should not rest on the competence of one elected official, and that this method enhances the state's ability to recruit and retain qualified career workers in education.

Opponents of appointment by a state board of education claim mainly that an appointed chief school officer will not be responsible to the people. The principal objection to gubernatorial appointment is the inherent danger of the appointee's involvement in partisan politics. Another perspective on this issue is that an elected state school officer is legally an "official" of the state, whereas an officer appointed by a state board of education is generally an "employee," not a legal official.

The states are the governmental units in the United States charged with the primary responsibility for education.

STATE DEPARTMENTS OF EDUCATION The state government carries on its activities in education through the state department of education, which is directed by the chief state school officer. These activities have been classified in five categories: operational, regulatory, service, developmental, and public support and cooperation activities. Operational activities are those in which the state department directly administers schools and services, such as schools for the blind. Regulatory activities include making sure that teacher license standards are met, that school buses are safe, and that curricular requirements are fulfilled. Service activities include advising and consulting, disseminating research, and preparing materials (on state financial aid, for example). Developmental activities are directed to the improvement of the department itself and include planning, staffing, and research into better performance for the operational and regulatory as well as the service functions. Public support and cooperation activities involve public relations, political activities with the legislature and governor, and relations with various other governmental and nongovernmental agencies.

STATE LEGISLATURES State legislatures are generally responsible for creating, operating, managing, and maintaining state school systems. The legislators are the state policymakers for education. State legislatures create state departments of education to serve as professional advisors and to execute state policy. State legislatures, though powerful, also operate under controls. The governors of many states can veto school legislation as they can other legislation, and the attorney general and the state judiciary system, when called on, will rule on the constitutionality of educational legislation.

State legislatures make decisions about how education is organized in the state; certification standards and tenure rights of teachers; programs of study; standards of building construction for health and safety; financing of schools, including tax structure and distribution; and compulsory attendance laws.

FIGURE 5.4 INFLUENCES ON LEGISLATIVE DECISION MAKING

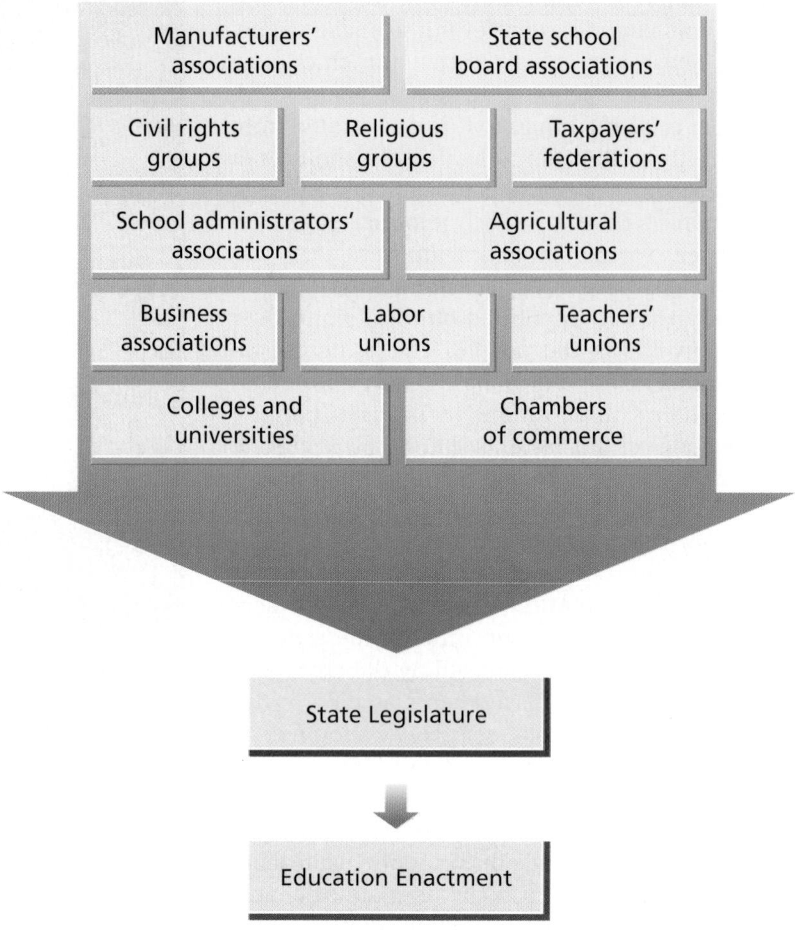

State legislatures, in their legislative deliberations about the schools, are continually importuned by special-interest groups. These groups, realizing that the legislature is the focus of legal control of education, can exert considerable influence on individual legislators. Some of the representative influential groups are illustrated in Figure 5.4.

Education is not mentioned in the U.S. Constitution.

It is not uncommon for more than a thousand bills to be introduced each year in a state legislative session. Many of these bills originate with special-interest groups. In recent years state legislatures have dealt with educational bills on a wide range of topics, including accountability, finance, textbooks, adult basic education, length of the school year, legal holidays, lotteries, teacher and student testing, no-pass-no-play policies, and school standards of various sorts.

THE FEDERAL GOVERNMENT'S ROLE IN EDUCATION

Under the Tenth Amendment to the U.S. Constitution, education is a function of the states. In effect, states have the primary responsibility for education, although the schools are operated by local governmental units commonly called school districts. But although the states have the primary responsibility for education and the schools are operated at the local level, the federal government has an ever increasing involvement in education. In the 1960s and 1970s the rationale for this interest and involvement was linked to national security and solving social problems. In the early 1990s the rationale was based on economic competitiveness. In the late 1990s the focus shifted to standards and testing, as well as concerns about funding of the crumbling infrastructure of schools. The result of this federal involvement has been the establishment of federal agencies, programs, and laws that address various aspects of the U.S. education system.

LEADERSHIP The federal government has historically provided leadership in education in specific situations, usually in times of need or in crises that could not be fully addressed by the leadership in states or local school districts. In the 1980s the time was right for more active leadership on the part of the federal government, such as moves to establish national priorities in education and to raise major issues. *A Nation at Risk,* the report prepared by the National Commission on Excellence in Education, was published in 1983.

That report was not a mandate, nor was funding recommended; but it did provide recommendations to be considered by states and local school districts. Identifying national educational issues and encouraging forums on these issues at the state and local levels, along with soliciting responses, are appropriate federal activities. Other activities include research on significant national educational issues and dissemination of exemplary practices.

The federal government also includes the Department of Education, which directly operates some education programs, funds special projects, and provides financial aid to states and local school districts.

THE U.S. DEPARTMENT OF EDUCATION In October 1979, then President Jimmy Carter signed legislation creating a cabinet-level federal agency, the Department of Education. The Department of Education took on the functions of the U.S. Office of Education, which was created in 1953 as a unit within the Department of Health, Education, and Welfare. The first-ever unit of education in the federal

In the last thirty years, the federal government has increased its activity in and leadership of education.

government, established in 1867 through the diligent efforts of Henry Barnard, was also called the Department of Education. Later, it was called the Office of Education (1869); at another time it was the Bureau of Education within the Department of the Interior. In 1939 the Office of Education became a part of the Federal Security Agency, which in 1953 became the Department of Health, Education, and Welfare, wherein the U.S. Office of Education was assigned until the new department was created in 1979.

The latest version of the Department of Education, in contrast with the first (1867) Department of Education, has the potential for becoming a powerful agency. The original 1867 department had the following stated purpose:

> To collect such statistics and facts as shall show the condition and progress of education in the several States and Territories, and to diffuse such information respecting the organization and management of schools and school systems, and methods of teaching as shall aid the people of the United States in the establishment and maintenance of efficient school systems, and otherwise promote the cause of education throughout the country.

There is no question that offering aid and awarding grants are effective ways to influence the goals of education nationally. However, there is continuing debate about whether the offices of the federal government should have a stronger or weaker influence on education. Some maintain that the socioeconomic forces of society are not contained within local school districts or state boundaries, and therefore that direct federal intervention is needed. Others advocate dissolution of the department, insisting that education is a state responsibility.

It was within this political–educational context that the new Department of Education was created. Those who favored creating a new department felt that education was too important to be lost in the gigantic Department of Health, Education, and Welfare. Opponents took the position that a national Department of Education would result in more federal control and standardization.

In the short life of the U.S. Department of Education, the influencing of education has continued to be based primarily on the use of grants and aid. However, the first several secretaries of education have been strong spokespersons for particular education agendas. For example, former secretaries William Bennett and Lamar Alexander were strong advocates for choice and voucher plans. The secretaries of education and their staffs also set funding priorities within the constraints laid down by Congress. As described next, there is a wide array of federal programs and involvement in education both within the Department of Education and within other federal agencies.

EDUCATIONAL PROGRAMS OPERATED BY THE FEDERAL GOVERNMENT The federal government directly operates some school programs. For example, the public school system of the District of Columbia depends on Congress for funds. The Department of the Interior has the educational responsibility for children of national park employees, for Samoa (classified as an outlying possession), and for the trust territories of the Pacific, such as the Caroline and Marshall Islands. Many of the schools on Native American reservations are financed and managed through the Bureau of Indian Affairs of the Department of the Interior. Twenty-five of these schools have become what are called contract schools, in which the tribe determines the program and staff but the Bureau of Indian Affairs supports the schools financially. The Department of Defense is responsible for the Military Academy at West Point, the Naval Academy at Annapolis, the Coast Guard

Academy at New London, and the Air Force Academy at Colorado Springs. The Department of Defense also operates a school system for the children of the military staff wherever members are stationed. The instruction supplied in the vocational and technical training programs of the military services has made a big contribution to the education of our nation as well.

CATEGORICAL AID Another strategy for federal involvement in education is **categorical financial aid.** These funds are granted to be used for a specific purpose, such as compensatory education for the disadvantaged, bilingual education, education for people with disabilities, or vocational education. Categorical aid is accompanied by strict rules and regulations designed to ensure that the aid is used for the purposes intended by Congress. The intended uses of these funds evolve from year to year as Congress and society perceive new needs.

OTHER TYPES OF EDUCATION AGENCIES

The organization of the U.S. education system that has been described so far has been in a straight line. We have described how education is organized from bottom to top (or is it top to bottom?). Obviously, the whole system is not this simple. There are many related agencies and organizations that are important as well. Some of them that will play a more direct role in your work as a teacher are highlighted here.

INTERMEDIATE UNITS The **intermediate unit** of school organization, which may consist of one or more counties, functions between the state department of education and the local school districts. These units have different names in different states. For example, in some states, such as New York and Colorado, they are called BOCES (Boards of Cooperative Educational Services); in Texas they are called Regional Service Centers; and in California, County Education Offices.

A fundamental purpose of the intermediate unit is to provide two or more local districts with educational services that they cannot efficiently or economically provide individually; cooperative provisions for special education and vocational–technical education have been very successful. Other services that intermediate units can provide include audiovisual libraries, centralized purchasing, in-service training for teachers and principals as well as other school workers, health services, instructional materials, laboratories, legal services, and special consultant services. The in-service dimension of the intermediate units has escalated in some states in recent years, stimulated by educational reform.

REGIONAL EDUCATIONAL LABORATORIES The Regional Labs are a federal creation. In 1965, as part of the Elementary and Secondary Education Act, authorization and funding to establish a new type of educational agency was initiated. The nation was divided into geographic regions, each consisting of three to seven states, and a new type of education agency was established to serve each of these regions. The purpose of these Regional Educational Laboratories is to link education personnel in schools, school districts, and state agencies with the latest findings from research and development efforts. Each lab conducts its own education research and curriculum development efforts. It also consults with educators, conducts training sessions, and organizes regional conferences. A list of the names and locations of these regional laboratories can be found at the website for the Office of Educational Research and Improvement (OERI).

categorical financial aid
Funds that are targeted by the policymakers to be used for specific purposes.

intermediate unit
A level of school organization between the state and the local district.

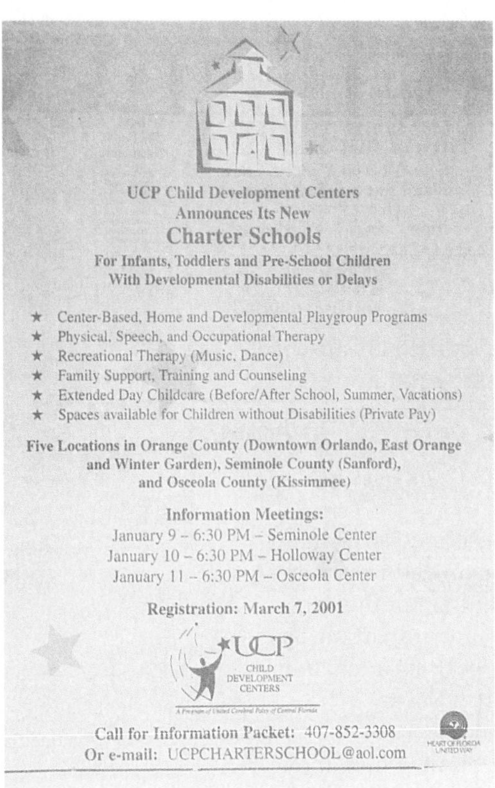

Charter schools are increasingly available as an alternative to regular public schools.

NATIONAL R&D CENTERS Another important resource for educators has been the National Educational Research and Development (R&D) Centers. These, too, were established under President Lyndon Johnson's Great Society program, more specifically the Elementary and Secondary Education Act of 1965. For the first time in the history of the United States there was a national commitment to ongoing support for research in education. To address this goal, a set of multidisciplinary research and development centers were established. Each of these R&D centers is based at a major university and receives multiyear funding. Names and locations of the current set of national R&D centers are available also on the OERI website.

FOUNDATIONS The preceding agencies and organizations involved in education receive public funding (tax dollars). There are also private funds that support a large number of activities in public schools, including an impressive array of foundations. Foundations are not hamstrung by government regulations, so they are more able to support experimentation and novel educational activities. Some foundations are large and widely known, such as the Kellogg Foundation. Others are smaller or target their funding to particular states or particular topics. For example, the Hogg Foundation in Texas invests mainly in that state and primarily supports issues related to mental health. A very promising foundation in the Midwest is the Ewing Marion Kauffman Foundation in Kansas City. One of its novel projects is Project Choice, in which eighth graders and their parents sign a contract that the student will graduate from high school on time and drug free. If the student fulfills the contract, the Kauffman Foundation supports the student in going to college.

CHOICE: INCREASING OPTIONS ALONG WITH UNCERTAIN OUTCOMES

The newspaper article from the San Jose *Mercury News* that was introduced at the beginning of this chapter foreshadows one of the hottest education topics across the United States: school choice. In the past parents had no say in the determination of the public school their child would attend. Children were assigned to a school by the school district. Now there are increasing numbers and types of alternatives to the traditional neighborhood public school. Nearly one in four students is exercising some form of choice within public and/or private schools. The problem for many parents now is not whether they have a choice but which one of the alternatives will be best. In the following paragraphs a number of these choices are briefly described. Many of these options are being installed within public school districts, while other of the alternatives are found in private schools. Most of these options bring the opportunity for increased parent and student involvement in school decision making. All represent, in some way, a break with the traditional public school and classroom structures. The creation of choices also means that there is now competition between the alternatives, which some believe will lead to more efficiencies and effectiveness. However, the research to date, though limited, does not provide clear evidence of a trend toward higher student achievement. The findings do indicate that upper-income and more educated families are more likely to exercise choice.[1,2]

SITE-BASED DECISION MAKING (SBDM) **Site-based decision making (SBDM),** also known as school-based management (SBM), emerged in the school restructuring movement of the 1980s. SBDM permits an individual school within a district to be more involved in decisions related to the educational operations of that school—for example, budgeting, personnel, and curriculum. The increase in decision-making authority may be granted by the school board or the state. An example of the latter is the Kentucky Education Reform Act, which includes a mandate for SBDM in all public schools in the state.

The SBDM concept came about in part through educational reform recommendations for greater participation of teachers in governance at the local school level. Parents' demands to have more say in the education of their children were also a factor in promoting school-based management. Two objectives of school-based management are to reduce school district regulatory control of individual schools and to empower teachers with the opportunity to participate in making decisions for their schools.

School-based management is based on two fundamental beliefs: the belief that those who are most affected by decisions ought to play a significant role in making those decisions and the belief that educational reform efforts will be most effective and long-lasting when carried out by people who feel a sense of ownership and responsibility for the process.

Researchers have observed that successful SBDMs take a great deal of effort. They require that schools and school districts *(a)* work with union officials to remove constraints; *(b)* create an instructional guidance system for curriculum and instruction reform; *(c)* establish a budget for professional development and training at both the district and school levels; *(d)* implement building and districtwide computer networks that allow schools to access information; *(e)* promote information sharing across schools, districts, and states; and *(f)* encourage experimentation by means of compensation systems.[3]

MAGNET SCHOOLS Many school districts have been pressured by citizens and ordered by the courts to equalize the proportions of different racial groups in each school. One response, especially by large urban school districts such as those in Houston and Kansas City, has been to develop special academic programs and custom-designed facilities that will attract all students; hence the name *magnet* schools. There are elementary, middle, and high school magnets. The program may emphasize the performing and visual arts, or math and science, or the liberal arts. Whatever the theme, the faculty, curriculum, and all students in the magnet school are there because of their interest in the school's theme.

CHARTER SCHOOLS A relatively new approach to providing communities with alternative schools that are supported by public funds is charter schools. These schools come into existence through a contract with either a state agency or a local school board. The school establishes a contract, or charter, that lays out how the school will operate in exchange for receiving public funding. Charter schools have greater autonomy than regular public schools and will be released

site-based decision making (SBDM)
A school governance process that gives greater voice to teachers, parents, and community representatives around school policies.

FIGURE 5.5 ESTIMATED DISTRIBUTION OF SCHOOL SIZE FOR CHARTER SCHOOLS AND ALL PUBLIC SCHOOLS

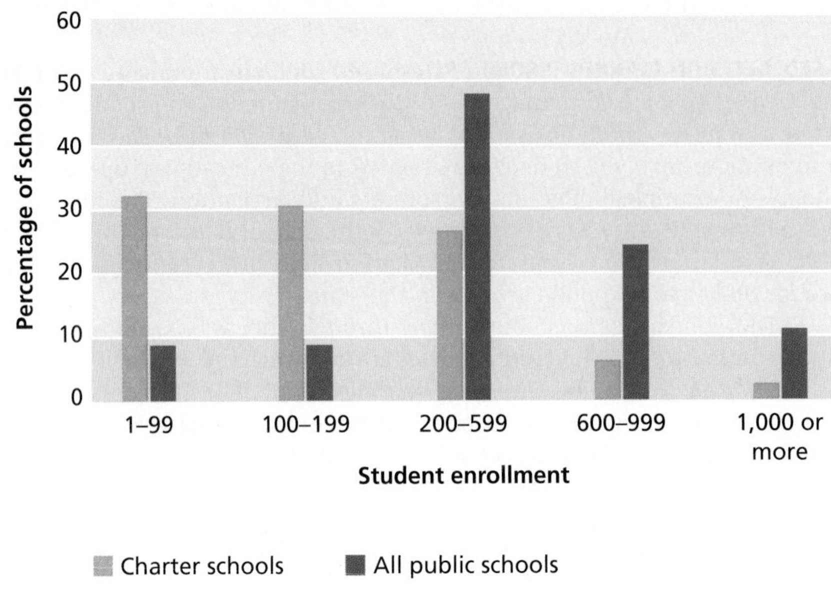

Source: U.S. Department of Education, Office of Educational Research and Improvement, *The State of Charter Schools 2000.* Washington, DC: Author, 2000.

from various district and state regulations. However, charter schools are still held accountable for student learning and, in most settings, having a diverse student body. There has been geometric growth in the number of charter schools since the first one was established in Minnesota in 1992. As of 1999, thirty-six states and the District of Columbia had passed legislation to permit the establishment of charter schools. For the 1998–99 school year 250,000 students were enrolled, representing 0.8 percent of all public school students.[4] However, as can be seen in Figure 5.5, charter schools tend to have significantly smaller enrollments than public schools.

YEAR-ROUND SCHOOLS The normal school year of nine to ten months with the full summer off is often criticized. One concern is that students will forget too much over the summer. Critics point out that the current school year was put into place back in the 1800s, when most people lived on farms and the children were counted on to perform summer chores. One interesting solution is the year-round school. This is not an extended school year in that students attend school for more days. Rather, year-round schools spread the time in school across twelve months. One way a school may do this is by having multiple "tracks" of six to eight weeks. During any one cycle, one-fourth to one-third of the students will be on vacation and the others will be attending classes. In this way students have more frequent but shorter times away from school. An additional advantage is that the school site can handle more students on an annual basis.

VOUCHERS Without a doubt, the most controversial choice alternative is school vouchers. At its simplest, a voucher program issues a check or a credit to parents that can be used to send their child to a private school. Most voucher programs are funded with state tax dollars. However, some voucher programs are funded by private foundations and occasionally individuals. For example, in the Edgewood Independent School District in San Antonio, Texas, a group of business executives is putting up $50 million over ten years for vouchers for low-income families to attend any private school or even public schools in other school districts. For the publicly financed programs there are restrictions on who is eligible, as in Florida, where the state plan allowed vouchers to be used only after the state had designated the public school as a failing school. Typically, the amount of a voucher would be equivalent to the amount the public school received for each student, in other words, $4,000–$5,000. The debates center on the use of public dollars to support private schools. The most serious point of contention comes into play when it is possible for the voucher funded with state education money to be used to pay for a child to attend a religious school. This raises very real constitutional questions about the separation of church and state, which are discussed in detail in Chapter 6. The National Education Association has been very active in opposition to voucher programs, since it sees this choice as undermining public education. A useful summary of pros and cons about vouchers is presented in Table 5.2.

TABLE 5.2 VOUCHER PROS AND CONS

Critics argue that:	Supporters argue that:
Only the most motivated students will use vouchers, increasing the segregation of students by race, economic status, and parents' educational background.	Low-income parents should be able to choose private schools over poorly performing public schools.
Vouchers weaken the public schools by diverting resources from them.	Increased competition from voucher schools will force public schools to improve, or risk closure.
Lack of accountability and quality control at voucher schools is a misuse of public money.	Private schools are unburdened by bureaucracy and regulations that hamstring the public school system.
Spending public money on religious education is unconstitutional.	Private schools provide more tailored services at a lower cost.
Transportation problems and difficulties in providing adequate information to all parents will make voucher systems inequitable.	Voucher systems allow parents more influence over their children's education.
Property taxes will rise as state aid to local districts is lost.	Voucher programs emphasize educational choices, not requirements dictated by the government.
Vouchers will increase overall costs. Private schools, like any other government contractor, will become even more dependent on and demanding of public funds, causing more spending.	Vouchers expand options for low-income parents, enhancing their feelings of empowerment and inclusion in society.
Vouchers do not really equalize the playing field, since no voucher program so far provides enough money for poor children to be able to attend the most expensive private schools.	

Source: What We Know about Vouchers: The Facts behind the Rhetoric. San Francisco: WestEd, 1999.

TABLE 5.3 The Increase in the Number of Public and Private Schools over Time

Elementary and Secondary Schools in the United States

Characteristics	1980–81	1987–88	1990–91	1995–96	1996–97	1997–98
All elementary and secondary schools	106,746	110,055	109,228	114,811	—	116,910
All public schools	85,982	83,248	84,538	87,125	88,223	89,508
All private schools	20,764	26,807	24,690	26,686	—	27,402

— = data not available.

Source: U.S. Department of Education, National Center for Education Statistics, *Digest of Education Statistics 1999*. Washington, DC: Table 5, page 14.

PRIVATE, PAROCHIAL, AND INDEPENDENT SCHOOLS Alternative structures of schools exist outside the public school system too. These range from elite secondary schools (mainly in the Northeast), to dynamic alternative schools for high school dropouts, to church-supported schools, to schools that are operated for profit. As can be seen in Table 5.3, there is a gradual increase in the number of private schools.

INDEPENDENT SCHOOLS Private education, which preceded public education in the United States, continues to be available as an alternative to the public schools.[5] Private schools are increasingly being referred to as independent schools. One source of information on these schools is the Council for American Private Education (CAPE), a coalition of fourteen private school organizations. Another is the National Association of Independent Schools (NAIS). The following description of independent schools is based on an NAIS publication.[6]

An **independent school** is a nonprofit institution governed by a board of trustees that depends almost entirely on private funds—tuition, gifts, grants—for its financial support. Most independent schools are accredited by their regional accrediting group and by state departments of education. All must meet state and local health and safety standards as well as the mandatory school attendance laws. Unlike public schools, independent schools are not involved in or part of large, formal systems. They do, however, share many informal contracts among themselves and with public schools. The vast majority offer programs that prepare students for college.

Independent schools vary greatly in purpose, organization, and size, and they serve students from all racial, religious, economic, and cultural backgrounds. Some are progressive and innovative; some are conservative and traditional. They are both large and small, day and boarding, single-sex and coeducational. Independent schools have been an integral part of our nation's educational resources since colonial times.

independent school
A nonprofit, nonpublic school that is governed by a board of trustees.

Because each independent school is free to determine and practice its own philosophy of education, spirit and environment vary from school to school, even though schools may display similar organizational structures and educational programs. This diversity among independent schools is one of their most distinctive characteristics.

GOVERNANCE OF INDEPENDENT SCHOOLS Each independent school is incorporated as a nonprofit, tax-exempt corporation and governed by a board of trustees that selects its own members, determines the school's philosophy, selects the chief administrative officer, and bears ultimate responsibility for the school's resources and finances. The chief administrator responsible for the day-to-day operation of the school may be called the headmaster, headmistress, president, or principal. The head's duties are comparable to those of a public school superintendent.

ISSUES RELATED TO ORGANIZATION AND STRUCTURE

So far this description of how the U.S. education system is organized and works has been free of discussion of issues, problems, conflicts, and ambiguities. But pick up a newspaper or watch the television news, and you will quickly be confronted with one or more of the debates about what education *should* be doing or *should not* be doing. The following is a short list of hot topics and issues related to school organization.

ISSUE: LOCAL CONTROL An important and unique feature of education in the United States is a belief in **local control:** a belief that educational decisions should be made at the local level rather than at the state or national level. The rationale is that people at the local level, including teachers and parents, know what is best. Those who advocate more federal and state involvement argue that education is a responsibility of all of society. The mobility of the population and the interdependence of social elements have undermined the traditional concept that local people should have the sole voice in determining the directions of education. Some also argue that national survival requires centralized policies and programs laid down by states and the federal government.

The underlying questions have to do with power, authority, and what is best for students and society. The issue of local control has been more hotly debated in recent years as the states have assumed more control over curriculum, statewide testing, and school funding. Local control advocates are also concerned about the increasing involvement of the federal government in education. For example, many people interpreted President Bill Clinton's call for national testing as a move toward a single federal exam that would be applied to all states, schools, and students.

CHALLENGING LOCAL CONTROL Local control is challenged each time a decision by a local board or a local school district is taken to the courts. As is discussed in Chapter 6, many court decisions dealing with the relationship between religion and the public school or with desegregation have been in response to local control. In most states, courts today are tending to rule that local control, combined with the traditional system of financing education, has resulted in inequality of educational opportunity rather than equality.

local control
Educational decision making by citizens at the local level rather than at the state or national level.

CENTRALIZATION IS THE ALTERNATIVE TO LOCAL CONTROL We have come full circle; education in large cities is already centralized, and many of these large districts are trying to solve some of their problems by decentralization. Frequently, a centralized authority does not respond well to citizens' needs and demands. Ex officio boards and councils for local community or neighborhood schools, which advise officials on large city or county boards, represent efforts to keep some form of local control in the large centralized systems.

ISSUE: SCHOOL CHOICE IN PUBLIC SCHOOLS In most school districts parents have little or no choice as to which public school their children attend. The school district makes the decision, usually based on where the children reside. Since the 1970s, however, there has been a movement toward parents' having a choice. Some districts may include one or two alternative schools such as charter schools or magnet schools that parents can choose. In some districts, such as Cambridge, Massachusetts, all families list their top three schools; then the public authorities make assignments, balancing individual preferences against the state's interest in preventing overcrowding and in ensuring ethnic diversity within each school. Studies to date do not indicate that students show greater achievement when there is choice. However, parental satisfaction is higher. Choice is being pursued the most by parents who take an intense interest in their children's success at school. The issue, then, is one of equity and opportunity for children whose parents are not actively pursuing the available alternatives because children who do not choose, and schools that are not chosen, could be left behind.[7]

ISSUE: THE REVAMPING OF SCHOOL BOARDS One consequence of the increased involvement of the state and federal levels, as well as the school community, in education is that school boards now have less say and less control. In many ways they are in a crossfire among all the other interests. The interests of people serving on school boards have shifted; many more board members now focus on a particular agenda or topic, rather than maintaining a balanced view and districtwide policy perspective. School boards are increasingly seen as an impediment to school reform rather than as a source of support. As a result, there are increasing calls for redefinition of the roles, powers, and responsibilities of school boards. In response, some mayors of large cities are moving to have more control over schools and school boards. For example, Chicago's Mayor Richard Daley petitioned the Illinois legislature to give him control over the city's failing schools. Now, instead of being run by an elected school board, Chicago schools are run by a professional board appointed by the mayor and accountable to him. One national commission report has suggested that state officials should consider disbanding school boards and developing new structures.[8] On the other side of the debate are those who point out that school boards are the *local* communities' representatives in the educational system. The loss of school boards would further undercut local control and the opportunity for community participation in basic democracy.

Politics will be most intense around competition for scarce resources such as money and time. Politics can be intense around philosophical and ideological views also.

ISSUE: POLITICS IN EDUCATION So far in this chapter we have provided information about the formal structures of public education at the local, state, and federal levels. Although these organizational structures illustrate the line and staff relationships, there is another set of relationships that is important to consider and understand. Each of these levels is involved in politics—the politics of education. For example, local school districts are likely to be interested in federal educational programs and grants, so they will contact members of Congress to express their opinions. The purpose is to influence representatives' understanding of local needs and their actions on relevant legislation. That is politics, par-

PROFESSIONAL DILEMMA

What Is the Appropriate Role for Teachers When the Politics Get Rough?

The education accountability movement of the last decade has demanded that teachers and school administrators make serious efforts to change the way schools operate and to implement new approaches to help students learn. Policymakers, business leaders, and citizens at large have demanded that schools "reform" and "restructure." As is discussed in Chapter 15, schools are now expected to implement curriculum standards and to administer newly created tests of student learning. Yet major changes in the structure and operation of schools are difficult to accomplish. It is hard for teachers to give up or change what they have been doing. It takes a great deal of time to work through the process that is necessary to develop a consensus among teachers, administrators, and parents about how a school should be restructured and what it should become. It also takes several years to work out the kinks when trying something new.

Suppose that after you had spent three years discussing and then two years implementing a major restructuring of your school and saw that it was working with students, a newly elected majority on the school board demanded that you return to the old way. As a teacher, what would you do?

This is not a hypothetical question. In one recent example, after more than three years of broad-based discussions involving teachers, administrators, students, parents, and community members, one school district's school board approved new performance-based graduation requirements for one of its high schools. The new requirements were based on student accomplishments rather than on seat-time. In fact, the high school had received national recognition for its efforts.

In November of the second year of implementation, three conservative members were elected to the five-member school board. A major theme in their election campaign was an attack on the new graduation requirements, which they promised to remove. In January the new majority on the school board proceeded to implement its campaign promise. Although students from the school, parents, and school staff members asked that the board not do this, or that the board at least allow the new graduation requirements to be optional, the board voted three to two to return to the traditional requirements. Remember that there were now students in their second year of high school who had been told that they were expected to meet the new graduation requirements.

The school board did not stop there. In the same month, January, the board terminated the superintendent, who was viewed as a very able educator by most and was well known and respected nationally. By the end of the school year several school principals and teachers had taken positions elsewhere, and the district was running advertisements nationwide for principals and teachers who held "traditional" educational values. This might sound like an extreme case, but similar events have happened in other school districts, and similar cases will happen in one form or another during your years as an educator.

If you were a teacher in a school district where something like this occurred, what would you do? Your colleagues, the school, your students, and the innovative program have been challenged. It is clear that there is the potential for casualties, including your job. Of course, your actions will depend partly on which side of the issue you are on. Either way, what will you do?

- Will you speak out or wait for others to do so?
- What will you tell your students?
- Will you support your principal publicly or leave the principal on his or her own?
- How do you think you would feel the next time you were asked to invest four or five years in designing and implementing a major change in your school?

tisan and nonpartisan. (Partisan politics are associated with political parties.) The same activities take place at the state level. Local school districts and professional associations follow closely what is happening in their state legislature.

Special-interest groups are organizing to influence local school board elections by using fund raising, mass communication, and grassroots campaigning.

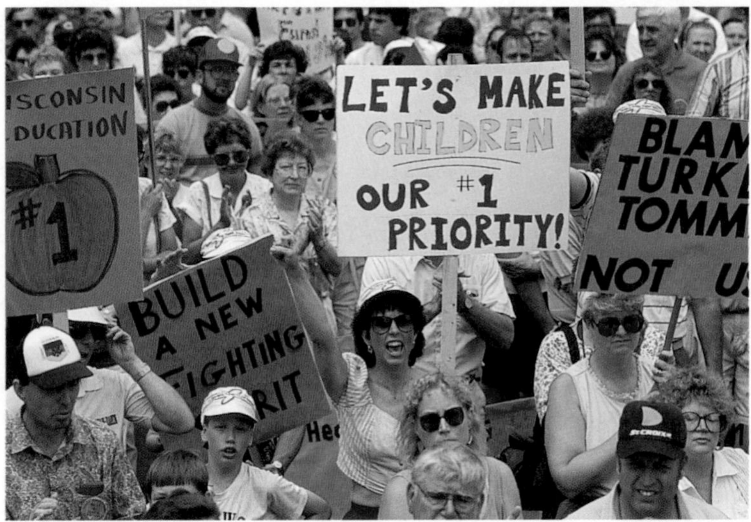

These groups do not hesitate to let members in the legislature know their opinions or to urge action. It is not unusual for local school superintendents and board members to lobby their senators and representatives in person. These contacts with federal and state agencies are representative of political action. There are many other types of education politics that you need to be aware of as well.

THE INCREASING VOLATILITY OF ELECTION POLITICS One common example of politics in education is found in school board elections. The individuals who serve on the school board can make a major difference in what you can and cannot do as a teacher. Take, for example, the concerted efforts of the Religious Right to increase their voice in school matters by influencing school board elections. Religious Right groups are skilled at orchestrating campaigns to elect school board members who are favorably disposed to their agendas, which include demanding curriculum changes, challenging sex education programs, pushing for prayer in the classroom, and purging reading lists in libraries. These groups' political strategies are good examples of what politics are about. They are well organized and use state-of-the-art combinations of fund raising, mass communication, and old-fashioned door-to-door campaigning. Since there tends not to be much interest in school board elections, a relatively small number of people (say, the membership of one or two churches) voting as a block can swing an election. The definition of what is fair in politics is not always clear. For example, the Religious Right has been criticized for running "stealth" candidates. In other words, the candidates do not say explicitly what they believe and what they plan to do if elected. Still, they are using the democratic process to influence policy and practice.

POLITICS AT THE SCHOOL DISTRICT LEVEL The people who are likely to be involved in politics at the local level include school board members, superintendents, and community members. Politics begin for prospective board members when they decide to run for the school board. As President John F. Kennedy said, "The first thing you need to be is elected."

The motives expressed by those seeking board membership appear to be honorable. The encouragement to run for the school board by friends and neighbors, current school board members, and family members seems innocuous. In school district elections, however, depending on the circumstances and issues, bitterness and resentment can occur. The healing, when and if it happens, is likely to take place through the political process of talking about interests and needs.

SCHOOL BOARD POLITICS Board members are expected to be accountable to their public constituency. However, some board members feel that they should be accountable to the entire community, while others feel that they should be accountable only to a specific segment of the community. The two positions are not compatible and may bring about strife among board members and within the community. Political activity is the likely result.

Most school districts have at-large elections for board members. At-large elections allow the entire electorate to vote for each candidate or each board member who is running for reelection. A disadvantage of at-large elections is that there is less chance of a minority candidate winning a seat.

There are other political issues that board members and the public may view as emotional and difficult to deal with. Among them may be firing a superintendent, having a strike, closing schools, opening a school-based clinic that provides sexual advice and contraceptives to teenagers, raising taxes, reducing staff and educational opportunity, busing students, admitting a child with AIDS, desegregating schools, and tolerating consistently losing athletic teams. Such issues are divisive and can result in political havoc until resolved. An additional area of political tension can develop between city government and the school district.[9]

THE SUPERINTENDENT AND BOARD POLITICS The superintendent is the chief executive officer of the school district. The superintendent's formal power comes from the board of education, but he or she also gains power through access to various sources of information. In relation to education politics, the control of information is power.

Generally, boards are considered to be policymakers, and superintendents implement the policies. Cooperative development of specific policies helps to establish the roles of both the board of education and the superintendent. However, specific educational (and other) issues can precipitate strenuous debate between the superintendent and the board and among board members. It is likely that the public will also wish to express its opinions.

THE SUPERINTENDENT AND STAFF POLITICS In addition to dealing with the board, the superintendent also works with a staff to carry on the education programs. Figure 5.2 on page 183 illustrates a typical school district's organization. The superintendent interacts directly with assistant superintendents and principals. Depending on the school district policy, the superintendent may also interact directly with the teachers' union representatives in collective bargaining. The superintendent may also be the negotiator for the school district in bargaining with the representatives of the noncertified employees, including secretaries and custodians. The more contacts the superintendent has, particularly if those contacts are controversial, the greater the potential for political activity among the staff—commonly referred to as "office politics." The staff has power in that it can also control information. The staff can initiate and spread rumors, which will in time spread to the community. Enter dirty politics, full of intrigue and maneuvering. A school district that is involved in such political activities will suffer until the issues are resolved, which may involve dismissing personnel.

SCHOOL-BASED MANAGEMENT: LOCAL COUNCILS AND POLITICAL ACTIONS Politics are a part of school-based management, or site-based decision making, too. Community members who serve on a site council are likely to have different perspectives and opinions about what the school should be doing. The principal and teachers may have other ideas. If the members of the council are honest and sincere and, after serious debate, are willing to compromise, positive decisions can be made. But if some members come with a narrow agenda—such as firing the principal—political infighting is likely to occur within the council, particularly if the members are deeply entrenched and are not open to modification of their positions. The only way decisions will be reached in all cases will be through the political processes of negotiation and bargaining.[10]

POLITICS: NEITHER POSITIVE NOR NEGATIVE Although many of the examples presented here might appear to be negative, keep in mind that politics are neither good nor bad. Instead, politics are the way that all organizations work. There will always be areas of disagreement in educational organizations. People have varying interests that must be talked about. In many cases there will be basic differences in points of view, but a decision has to be made for the organization to move ahead. This is where political skill becomes a special strength for teachers and school administrators. Those who are skillful in talking with all parties and negotiating areas of agreement make significant contributions. Rather than judging "politics" as bad, successful teachers learn to understand how politics work and develop the skills to contribute to and influence the political process. Closing the classroom door guarantees that your positions and ideas will not be considered. Learn more about organizations and political processes and you will see politics as fascinating and, yes, fun.

THE FINANCING OF EDUCATION: SOURCES OF FUNDS AND THE MOVE FROM EQUITY TO ADEQUACY

The whole people must take upon themselves the education of the whole people and must be willing to bear the expense of it.
John Adams

When the financing of education is considered, the first question asked by many is "How much? How much do I have to pay, and how much do schools receive?" In the last decade, two other questions have sharpened the discussions about education finance: "Does each school have the same amount of funding?" This is the "equity" question. "Is there sufficient funding so that all students can achieve?" This is the "adequacy" question. The equity question was at the center of many school funding law suits in the 1980s and early 1990s. In 1989 a decision of the Kentucky Supreme Court brought the adequacy question to the front. That court decision held that every child in the state had the right to an "adequate" education. The direct consequence of that decision was passing of the Kentucky Education Reform Act (KERA) by the state legislature. The significance of KERA is that it did not deal solely with equalizing spending by each school district, that is, equity. KERA went further by specifically connecting funding with implementation of school and curriculum reforms, specifying student outcomes and development of a statewide strategy for assessing academic achievement. Now questions related to the financing of education have to deal with all three questions: How much? Is there equity in the distribution? And are the resources adequate so that all students can achieve the identified outcomes? These finance questions are explored in the remainder of this chapter.

This examination of the financing of public education begins with a close look at the different sources of funds and how these sources are organized into a comprehensive system of taxation. The next major topic is a description of how the funds are distributed to school districts and schools. The description of school finance ends with a discussion of accountability and the introduction of a number of issues and dilemmas that are the subject of continuing analysis and debate.

FIGURE 5.6 THE PUBLIC EDUCATION DOLLAR: REVENUES BY SOURCE: SCHOOL YEAR 1996–97

(Total revenues: $305 billion)

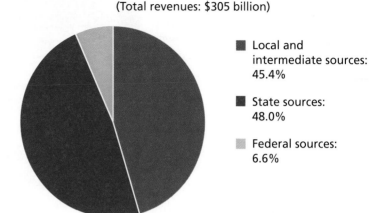

- Local and intermediate sources: 45.4%
- State sources: 48.0%
- Federal sources: 6.6%

Source: U.S. Department of Education, National Center for Education Statistics, *Common Core of Data, National Public Education Financial Survey.*

A SYSTEM OF TAXATION AND SUPPORT FOR SCHOOLS

Money to support education comes from a variety of taxes paid to local, state, and federal governments. These governments in turn distribute tax money to local school districts to operate the schools. The three principal kinds of taxes that provide revenue for schools are property taxes, sales or use taxes, and income taxes. The property tax is generally a local tax, while the sales tax generally is a state and local mix, and the income tax is collected at the state and federal levels. More than $337 billion of revenues were raised by local, state, and federal governments to fund public education in the 1999 fiscal year.[11]

Each type of tax is a part of a system. Each individual kind of tax has advantages and disadvantages, yet it is unlikely that any one of these taxes used by itself for education will be the answer. In evaluating a system of taxes, one should consider the varying ability of citizens to pay, the economic effects of the taxes on the taxpayer, the benefits that various taxpayers receive, the total yield of the tax, the economy of collection, the degree of acceptance, the convenience of paying, the problems of tax evasion, the stability of the tax, and the general adaptability of the system. It is apparent that systems of taxation are complicated; each is an intricately interdependent network.

Figure 5.6 diagrams the percentages of revenues school systems nationwide receive from federal, state, and local sources. As you can see, public education is primarily funded by local and state sources of revenue.

PROPERTY TAXES AND LOCAL REVENUE The **property tax** has been the primary source of local revenue for schools. It is based on the value of property, both real estate and personal. Real estate includes land holdings and buildings such as homes, commercial buildings, and factories. Personal property consists of automobiles, machinery, furniture, livestock, and intangibles such as stocks and bonds. The property tax has both advantages and limitations.

property tax
A tax based on the value of property, both real estate and personal.

PROPERTY TAXES: ADVANTAGES AND LIMITATIONS The main advantage of the property tax is its stability. Although the tax tends to lag behind changes in market values,

A local school district can impose the highest possible property taxes and still not be able to offer a program comparable to what a wealthier neighboring district offers under a lower rate of taxation.

it provides a steady, regular income for the taxing agency. Also, property is fixed; that is, it is not easily moved to escape taxation, as income might be.

The property tax has numerous limitations, however. It can have a negative impact on housing: It tends to discourage rehabilitation and upkeep because both of these would tend to raise the value of the property and therefore its taxes. The tax is often a deciding factor in locating a business or industry. And it is likely not to be applied equally on all properties.

DETERMINING THE VALUE OF PROPERTY One problem with the property tax lies in the potential unfairness of inconsistent property assessments. In some areas assessors are local people, usually elected, with no special training in evaluating property. Their duty involves inspecting their neighbors' properties and placing values on them. In other areas sophisticated techniques involving expertly trained personnel are used for property appraisal. In either circumstance assessors are likely to be subject to political and informal pressures to keep values low to keep tax rates low.

The assessed value of property is usually only a percentage of its market value. This percentage varies from county to county and from state to state. Attempts are made within states to equalize assessments or to make certain that the same percentage of full cash value is used in assessing property throughout the state. In recent years attempts have been made to institute full cash value for the assessed value. For the property tax to be a fair tax, equalized assessment is a necessity.

ASSESSED VALUATIONS AND THE QUALITY OF EDUCATION Limited tax rates for **current expenses** and limitations on indebtedness point out further the significance of assessed valuation as a factor in determining the quality of an educational program. A local school district can be making the maximum effort, taxing to the limit, and still not be able to offer a program comparable to what a wealthier neighboring district offers under a medium effort. The effort made by a local school district indicates the value that the citizens place on education; yet equal effort does not produce equal revenue, equal expenditures per pupil, or equal opportunity, that is, adequacy.

current expenses
Expenditures for daily operations and maintenance of schools.

PROPERTY TAX: PROGRESSIVE OR REGRESSIVE Property tax is most generally thought of as a **progressive tax**—that is, one that taxes according to ability to pay; the more wealth one has in property, the more one pays. But because assessments may be unequal and because frequently the greatest wealth is no longer related to real estate, the property tax can be regressive. **Regressive taxes,** like sales and use taxes, are those that affect low-income groups disproportionately. There is some evidence to support the contention that people in the lowest-income groups pay a much higher proportion of their income in property taxes than persons in the highest-income groups.

INEQUITIES OF THE PROPERTY TAX: WHAT THE COURTS HAVE SAID Significant support for schools across the nation has been provided by the property tax. However, as has been described, because of schools' heavy dependence on property taxes for financing, enormous discrepancies in resources and quality have built up between schools located in rich and poor communities.

To illustrate the school finance consequences of differences in local wealth, look at a simple example. A school district having assessed property valuations totaling $30 million and a responsibility for educating 1,000 pupils would have $30,000 of assessed valuation per pupil. Property taxes are calculated on the basis of assessed valuations, so a district with a high assessed valuation per pupil is in a better position to provide quality education than is one with a low assessed valuation per pupil. If school district A has an assessed valuation of $90 million and 1,000 pupils, for example, and school district B has an assessed valuation of $30 million and 1,000 pupils, a tax rate of $2 per $100 of assessed valuation would produce $1.8 million for education in district A and only $600,000 in district B. School district A could therefore spend $1,800 per pupil, compared with $600 per pupil in school district B, with the same local tax effort.

THE PERSPECTIVE OF THE COURTS ON TAXATION AND EDUCATION Can the property tax continue to be the primary base for financing schools? This question was asked of the U.S. Supreme Court in *San Antonio (Texas) Independent School District* v. *Rodriguez* (1979). Keep in mind that the U.S. Constitution does not mention education, so any litigation has to be based on indirect connections. In *Rodriguez* the challenge was initiated under the Equal Protection Clause of the Fourteenth Amendment. This clause prohibits state action that would deny citizens equal protection. The U.S. Supreme Court, in a five-to-four decision, reversed the lower court decision in *Rodriguez* and thus reaffirmed the local property tax as a basis for school financing. Justice Potter Stewart, voting with the majority, admitted that "the method of financing public schools . . . can be fairly described as chaotic and unjust." He did not, though, find it unconstitutional. The majority opinion, written by Justice Lewis F. Powell Jr., stated, "We cannot say that such disparities are the product of a system that is so irrational as to be invidiously discriminatory." Justice Thurgood Marshall, in the dissenting opinion, charged that the ruling "is a retreat from our historic commitment to equality of education opportunity."

Another part of the opinion in *Rodriguez* addressed the role of the states in supporting public education:

> The consideration and initiation of fundamental reforms with respect to state taxation and education are matters reserved for legislative processes of the various States, and we do no violence to the values of federalism and separation of pow-

progressive tax
A tax that is scaled to the ability of the taxpayer to pay.

regressive tax
A tax that affects low-income groups disproportionately.

> ers by staying our hand. We hardly need add that this Court's action today is not to be viewed as placing its judicial imprimatur on the status quo. The need is apparent for reform in tax systems which may well have relied too long and too heavily on the local property tax. And certainly innovative thinking as to public education, its methods, and its funding is necessary to assure both a higher level of quality and greater uniformity of opportunity. These matters merit the continued attention of the scholars who already have contributed much by their challenges. But the ultimate solutions must come from the lawmakers and from the democratic pressures of those who elect them.

These comments in *Rodriguez* foreshadowed the continuing string of school finance suits that have been filed in most states.

STATE SOURCES OF REVENUE AND AID On the average in the United States, the states provide about 48 percent of the fiscal resources for local schools. This money is referred to as state aid, and within most states all or a major portion of this money is used to help achieve equality of opportunity.

The main sources of tax revenue for states have been classified by the Department of Commerce in four groups: sales and gross receipt taxes, income taxes, licenses, and miscellaneous. Sales and gross receipt taxes include taxes on general sales, motor fuels, alcohol, insurance, and amusements; income taxes include both individual and corporate; licenses include those on motor vehicles, corporations, occupations, vehicle operators, hunting, and fishing. The miscellaneous classification includes property taxes, taxes on severance or extraction of minerals, and death and gift taxes. The two largest sources of state revenues are sales and income taxes.

SALES AND INCOME TAXES Sales and income taxes are lucrative sources of state revenue, and it is relatively easy to administer both. The sales tax is collected bit by bit, in a relatively painless way, by the vendor, who is responsible for keeping records. The state income tax can be withheld from wages; hence, collection is eased. Income taxes are considered *progressive taxes* because they frequently are scaled to the ability of the taxpayer to pay. Sales taxes are *regressive;* they affect low-income groups disproportionately. All people pay the sales tax at the same rate, so people in low-income groups pay as much tax as people in high-income groups. Part of the advantage of sales taxes and income taxes is that they can be regulated by the legislature that must raise the money.

Charitable gambling, such as church bingo, is permitted in forty-six states.

GAMING: A NEW SOURCE OF REVENUE In 1964 New Hampshire implemented a lottery. By 1998 thirty-seven states were operating lotteries. Legalized gambling in its many forms, from casinos and riverboats to horse racing, has become the newest source of state and local revenues. Gambling is an indirect source of revenue in the sense that it is not seen as a direct tax on citizens; instead, the revenues come through taxes on the games. In 1997 gamblers bet a record $50.89 billion. Income for states from lotteries grew from $978 million in 1980 to $16 billion in 1997. In fifteen states part or all of the net proceeds from the lottery is allocated to education. In some states, such as California, the original intent was that these funds would be used for educational enhancements. But within three years of the California lottery's implementation, in a tight budget year, the California legislature incorporated the lottery funds into the base education budget.

An early study of the Florida lottery found the same thing. In the 1989–90 school year, the level of state funding for education decreased, and approximately 56.8 percent of the lottery proceeds was used as a substitute for existing resources. The findings from the study also indicated that there was equity in the distribution of the funds. Clearly lotteries and other games represent a potential new source of funds for education.[12] It also is clear that without careful wording in the original statutes and continuous monitoring, these funds may merely become another revenue stream to fund the general budget, rather than being set aside for educational enhancements.

RECENT CHALLENGES TO SCHOOL FINANCE WITHIN THE STATES The number of court cases related to school finance has increased in recent years. Some states have had new suits initiated, while others are continuing to struggle to respond to earlier court decisions and directives. In all, nearly forty states have experienced or are experiencing court cases that deal with school finance.

THE STATE PERSPECTIVE ON TAXATION AND EDUCATION Equal protection challenges have been, or are currently being, made at the state level. In some states the plaintiffs have emphasized a claim of equal protection; in others the focus has been on specific language in the education clause. In all cases the issue is whether the state has fulfilled its constitutional obligation to provide for education. The answer by the state supreme courts in some states has been that education is not a fundamental right, and that as long as there is provision for a minimally adequate education, the equal protection clause is met. In *Serrano* v. *Priest* (1971) the California Supreme Court was called on to determine whether the California public school financing system, with its substantial dependence on local property taxes, violated the Fourteenth Amendment. In its six-to-one decision the California court held that heavy reliance on unequal local property taxes "makes the quality of a child's education a function of the wealth of his parents and neighbors." Furthermore, the court declared, "Districts with small tax bases simply cannot levy taxes at a rate sufficient to produce the revenue that more affluent districts produce with a minimum effort." Officially, the California Supreme Court ruled that the system of school financing in California was unconstitutional but did not forbid the use of property taxes as long as the system of finance was neutral in the distribution of resources. Within a year of *Serrano* v. *Priest,* five other courts—in Minnesota, Texas, New Jersey, Wyoming, and Arizona—ruled similarly.

STATES' RESPONSIBILITY TO GUARANTEE EQUAL EDUCATIONAL OPPORTUNITY In 1989 and 1990 several state supreme courts made significant decisions about school finance. In a number of states the education finance systems were knocked down by the courts, and the state legislatures were directed to remedy the wrongs.

In Montana, in *Helena Elementary School District* v. *State* (1989), the Montana Supreme Court ruled that the state's school finance system violated the state constitution's guarantee of equal educational opportunity. The state's constitution article mandates that the state establish an educational system that will develop the full educational potential of each person. In 1990 the court delayed the effects of its decision to allow the legislature time to enact a new finance system.[13]

The Kentucky Supreme Court ruled that the entire system of school governance and finance violated the state constitution's mandate for the provision of an efficient system of common schools throughout the state (*Rose* v. *The Council for Better Education Inc.,* 1989). The Kentucky Supreme Court's opinion stated that

> The system of common schools must be adequately funded to achieve its goals. The system of common schools must be substantially uniform throughout the

RELEVANT RESEARCH

Reform of School Finance in Michigan

STUDY PURPOSE/QUESTIONS: As different states restructure the financing of schools in response to court and legislative actions, there is a need to examine the results. This study examined the effects of changes in the financing of schools in Michigan.

STUDY DESIGN: The study analyzed data about pupils, education funding in each school district, property wealth, property tax rates, and state aid payments.

STUDY FINDINGS: In March 1994 the Michigan voters voted two to one in favor of raising the state sales tax from 4 percent to 6 percent to fund schools, thereby reducing the reliance on local property taxes. A related goal in this school finance reform was to reduce the funding disparity between school districts with high and low assessed property values.

One clear result of the Michigan reform was a cut in property taxes for school operations by nearly 50 percent. As for the second goal, to increase equity in per-pupil funding across the state, the study found that pupils in the lowest-revenue districts have received a 30 percent increase in real dollars, while students in the highest-revenue district have seen nearly a 4 percent decrease. Over the next several years the gap between highest- and lowest-funding districts will continue to narrow, and the lowest per-pupil funding for any district will be $5,800.

IMPLICATIONS: This study suggests that it is possible to shift the burden of the financing of schools away from heavy reliance on the property tax. A second important implication is that state financing strategies can be established that narrow the funding gap by raising the bottom, while not severely impacting the districts that have had higher levels of per-pupil funding.

Source: Henry Prince, "Michigan's School Finance Reform: Initial Pupil-Equity Results." *Journal of Education Finance 22* (4) (Spring 1997), 394–409.

> state. Each child, *every child,* in this commonwealth must be provided with an equal opportunity to have an adequate education. Equality is the key word here. The children of the poor and the children of the rich, the children who live in poor districts and the children who live in the rich districts must be given the same opportunity and access to an adequate education. This obligation cannot be shifted to local counties and local school districts.

The court directed the state legislature to develop a new educational system, which was adopted as the Kentucky Education Reform Act (KERA) in 1990.

Throughout the 1990s there continued to be suits, court actions, and legislative initiatives regarding how best to address funding inequities for public schools. Further, earlier court decisions have been revisited. For example, in a turnaround of earlier decisions, in 1994 the State Supreme Court of Arizona ruled that the state's property tax–based school financing system was unconstitutional because it created wide disparities between rich and poor school districts. As has been true in other states, the court left it up to the legislature to rectify the problem.

Undoubtedly, changes are occurring in the state provisions for financial support for education. Equal expenditures per pupil might not, because of other factors, ensure equal opportunity; but equal expenditures per pupil do, in fact, enhance the likelihood of equal opportunity.

ENTREPRENEURIAL EFFORTS TO FUND EDUCATION The combination of tight budgets, increasing enrollments, and demands for better educational services is pressuring school, school district, and state officials to search for new funding sources. Some sources that were highly controversial in the past, such as the lottery, have now become a regular part of the main revenue stream. Other potential new sources of funds are now being considered, debated, and utilized.

ADVERTISING: A NEW SOURCE OF REVENUE School districts have found that they can raise money by selling space for advertising. In Colorado Springs, District 11, for example, soft drinks and fast foods are advertised on the sides of school buses. Other school districts are seeking corporate sponsorships to support music and sports programs. For example, the Denver Public Schools solicited $500,000 from four companies to sponsor education programs and ran the companies' ads on school buses and at the district's main football stadium. One school district near the Dallas–Fort Worth International Airport is even selling space for advertising on the rooftops of district buildings to catch the eye of travelers on incoming flights.

Commercialism in classrooms is expanding rapidly. For example, in the 1998–99 school year more than 150 school districts signed exclusivity deals with one of the cola companies.

MORE STUDENT FEES Expanded use of student fees, especially for noncore subjects and extracurricular activities, is prevalent. Fees for enrollment, gym clothes, yearbooks, and lab equipment have become standard. Fees for student parking are becoming routine as well. For parents with more than one child in a secondary school, these fees can total more than $500 a year. Through various fees a large high school can increase its revenues by $50,000 to $250,000 annually, which can add up to $1 million in four years. Participation in an athletic program means more fees. For example, in the 1996–97 school year, each student athlete in the Eanes, Texas, school district paid a $100 fee.

MORE FUND-RAISING SCHEMES The entrepreneurial spirit seems to have no bounds once school and school district administrators jump on the capitalist bandwagon. Bake sales and parent booster groups are routine compared to some of the more innovative approaches being tried around the United States. For example, several school districts in California sent students home with forms their parents could

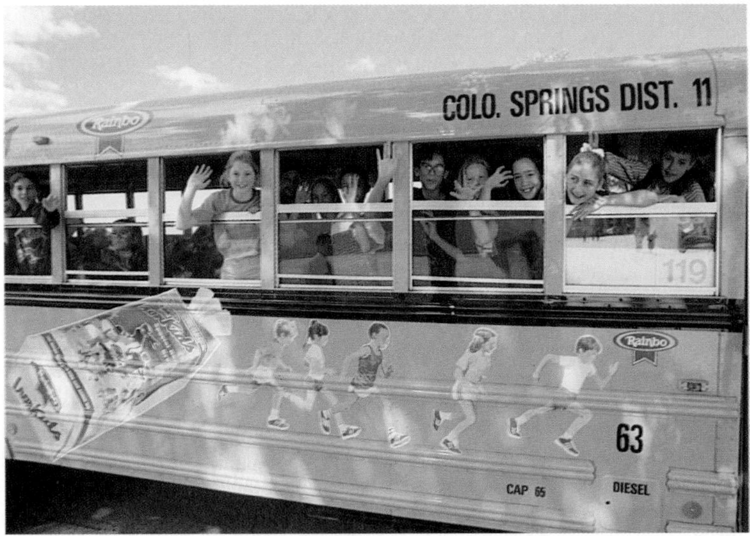

A newfound source of financial support for schools is advertising, although accepting this type of funding is a topic of intense debate.

DEBATE

Has Student Fund-Raising Gone Too Far?

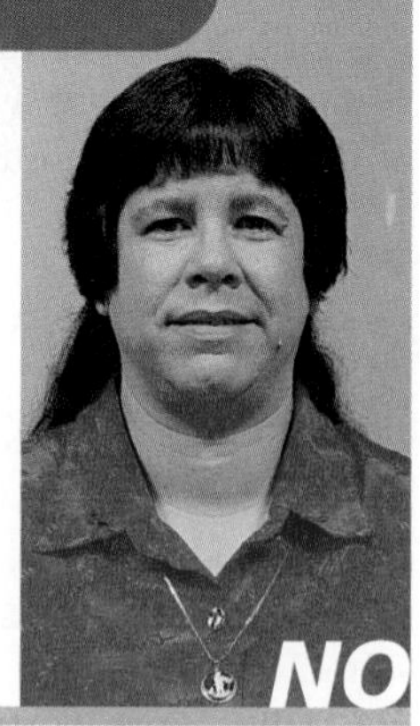

Mary Neff is an English teacher at Odessa High School in western Texas. A twenty-one-year teaching veteran and NEA activist, Neff co-edits her local NEA newsletter in Ector County and has held local NEA office. Neff currently serves on her school district's policy and planning committee.

I know student fundraising is getting out of hand when:

- I cover a class for a fellow teacher, and, as her students enter my room, they immediately ask me if I sell anything to eat.

- Anxious teenagers plead with me to please buy a cookbook, candy bar, ham, fruit box, posters, even manure to fertilize my lawn.

- Students go beyond raising money for an academic competition across the state and, instead, raise funds to go to Disneyland.

- One of my seniors takes a school-sponsored cruise to the Bahamas. On the day they are to explore the islands, the student can't find his boarding pass and has to remain on the ship. For this, he misses three days of school.

- An 11-year-old New Jersey boy, last seen going door-to-door selling wrapping paper for a school fund-raiser, is found murdered.

These events—and particularly this recent tragedy—should give us all pause. What are we really asking children to do when they're handed the "opportunity" to raise money for extras? What are we really selling?

Some say the real-world experience students gain from fundraising—and the travel it buys—builds character and broadens horizons.

But I often wonder if the students in Japan are out selling stationery and smoked sausage in the evenings. Are we, in America, so bereft of character-building opportunities that we must ask our children to go door-to- door?

My fantasy is a complete school year without fundraisers. Who would miss the bags of candy, brochures full of merchandise, lost or stolen collection envelopes, and teachers-turned-bill collectors?

Clorinda Graziano teaches instrumental music at Frank Borman Middle School in Phoenix, Arizona. An NEA activist, she's served as chair of her local negotiations team for three years. Last year, Graziano helped her band students raise $160,000 so they could march in the New Year's Day Parade in London.

I have fond memories of selling Girl Scout cookies when I was in the third grade and going door-to-door with my mother raising money for various charities.

My biggest fundraising education came in high school, helping raise money for band and chorus annual trips. It's amazing to me, as I think back now, how much I learned from those experiences.

I learned about bookkeeping, banking, ordering, marketing, dealing with salespeople, budgeting, responsibility, working as a group, goal-setting, and achievement—all "real-life" skills.

If we didn't raise the money, we didn't go—that was the bottom line. That was a tremendous lesson to learn at a young age.

All the skills I learned as a student fundraiser have helped me immensely as a music instructor. Our schools always need money for something that's outside the spectrum of what the school district can provide.

Almost all of the handbell and handchime sets at individual schools are paid for through music student or PTA fundraisers. Students' summer music camp tuitions are routinely funded by candy sales.

By far the biggest fundraising project I've been involved in was our effort to send 104 junior high band students and chaperones to London to march in last year's New Year's Day Parade.

Each student and chaperone had to earn $1,525 to go. With more than 70 percent of our students on free or reduced-price lunch, there aren't a lot of families with extra money to shell out every time their children want something. We either help them earn their own way, or they can't go.

So we helped. We set up individual accounts for each student. What they raised was credited toward their own trip.

YES / NO

I would welcome back the lost time and energy spent raising money. My time is better spent preparing for instruction. Students' time is better spent in the classroom and in after-school clubs that pursue interests, not dollars.

We should rely more on booster clubs made up of parents and patrons who raise money to supplement the activities that are important to them. And we should establish clearer priorities for our school systems and the communities that fund them.

Asking a community to finance any and all activities and materials that are not covered by the school budget is grossly unfair to everyone. We need to accept the simple fact that if it's not in the budget, perhaps we won't get it.

And perhaps we don't need it. Maybe we shouldn't raise money for unlimited student travel and laptops to keep athletic statistics, while at the same time issuing paperback books held together with rubber bands.

When we tell taxpayers they have to pay an additional $25 in property taxes, maybe we can understand why they rebel.

After all the fruit cakes, greeting cards, and bumper stickers they've already bought, why should they have a clear picture of what the public schools are trying to accomplish?

Let's face it: We are slowly bleeding money out of our communities to finance frills and dubious endeavors.

If you ask our school patrons what their goals for our schools are, I don't think a trip to Never-Never Land would be high on the list.

Source: "Has Student Fundraising Gone Too Far?," *NEA Today* (February 1998): 43.

Students sold candy, washed cars, held carnivals, sponsored volleyball tournaments, and more.

It paid off. Going to London was a great experience for all of us.

I know the students took the trip more seriously because they worked so hard to go, and because so many people had cared enough about them to send them on the trip of a lifetime.

I was amazed to hear so many parents tell me how much the fundraising had brought their families together. That unexpected benefit really boosted students' self-esteem.

Student fundraising does so much more than just raise money for school projects. It would be a shame if the appalling murder of a New Jersey boy while soliciting fundraising orders door-to-door forces an end to all student fundraising efforts.

It's not the school's fault that the child was alone, selling in a neighborhood to people he didn't know.

Schools have been trumpeting the message—"don't sell by yourself, don't sell to strangers, don't sell in strange neighborhoods"—for years. Plus, the child's parents should have known where he was on a Saturday afternoon and should have gone over the rules with him in advance.

A few unfortunate and preventable incidences shouldn't curtail the opportunities of all.

There are too many lifetime skills that can be learned and experiences gained to simply end student fund-raising. What's at stake is much more than just a few dollars.

WHAT'S YOUR OPINION?

Has student fundraising gone too far?

Go to **www.ablongman.com/johnson** to cast your vote and see how NEA readers responded.

sign to switch their long-distance telephone carrier. The school's parent–teacher association would receive 10 percent of the long-distance payment from each family. If the students signed up friends, neighbors, and relatives, the school would gain more revenue. Projections were that through this mechanism a large school could gain as much as half a million dollars a year.

Del Oro High School in Loomis, California, tested a novel way of raising money to support its sports teams. At one fall football game three cows are turned loose on the football field for "cow-chip bingo." The field is marked off in one-yard squares and chances are sold. The owner of a square where a cow makes a "deposit" wins.

QUESTIONS ABOUT FUND-RAISING EFFORTS Given the special place and role of schools in society, important questions are being raised about the appropriateness of many

State aid for education is classified for general or categorical use, and general aid is often administered through a foundation program that will fund each school district up to a foundation level of education required per pupil.

of these newer fund-raising efforts. Equity is one important issue. Schools in wealthy communities can raise more money than schools located in poor communities. If an important goal is to provide equal educational opportunity for all students, then the unequal distribution of funds and equipment is once again an issue. A second important question has to do with children being exposed to advertising in schools. A recent report by Consumers Union points out how the underfunding of schools has led to students being a captive audience for marketers.[14] Many educators are concerned that students are impressionable, unsophisticated as consumers, and easily influenced. In the school context many students will have difficulty distinguishing advertising from lesson messages. Because of budget pressures, however, schools and school districts will likely continue to develop their commercial bent.

FIGURE 5.7 **THE PUBLIC EDUCATION DOLLAR: CURRENT EXPENDITURES BY FUNCTIONS, 1996–97 SCHOOL YEAR**

(Current expenditures: $270 billion)

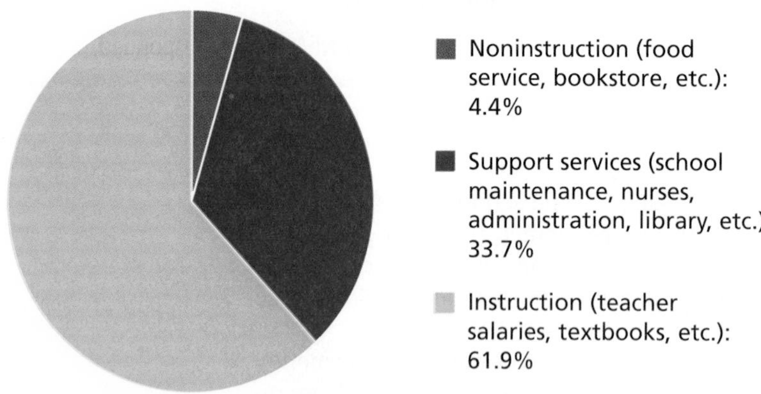

Source: U.S. Department of Education, National Center for Education Statistics, *Common Core of Data, National Public Education Financial Survey.*

EDUCATION SPENDING

Once funds for education are collected at the local, state, and federal levels, they are distributed to schools and school districts. Some of the funds are targeted by state and federal governments for specific activities and programs, but most decisions about allocations of funds are determined by each school district. In general, teachers and principals have little say about how monies will be spent.

The overall pattern of distribution of the public education dollar is shown in Figure 5.7. By far the largest proportion of the expenditures (61.9%) is directly related to instruction, teacher salaries being the major expense. One-third of the education dollar goes to support services, an amount that includes much of the expenses for operating the school district office.

Another frequently used statistic for examining and comparing school districts and states is per-pupil expenditure. For the 1997–98 school year the national average was $6,189 per pupil. However, the range of expenditures across states varies by thousands of dollars. For example, the lowest per-pupil expenditures were in Alabama ($4,849), Arizona ($4,595), Arkansas ($4,708), Idaho ($4,721), Mississippi ($4,288), South Dakota ($4,669), Tennessee ($4,937), and Utah ($3,969). The highest per-pupil expenditures were in Alaska ($8,271), Connecticut ($8,904), the District of Columbia ($8,393), and New York ($8,852). As can be seen in Figure 5.8, over the last thirty-plus years there has been a consistent trend of greater per-pupil expenditures each year.[15]

STATE AID State aid for education exists largely for three reasons: The state has the primary responsibility for educating its citizens; the financial ability of local school districts to support education varies widely; and personal wealth is now less related to real property than it once was. State aid can be classified as having general or categorical use. *General aid* can be used by the recipient school district as it desires; *categorical aid* is earmarked for specific purposes. Categorical aid may include, for example, money for transportation, vocational education,

FIGURE 5.8 **CURRENT EXPENDITURE PER PUPIL IN AVERAGE DAILY ATTENDANCE IN PUBLIC ELEMENTARY AND SECONDARY SCHOOLS: 1970–71 TO 1998–99**

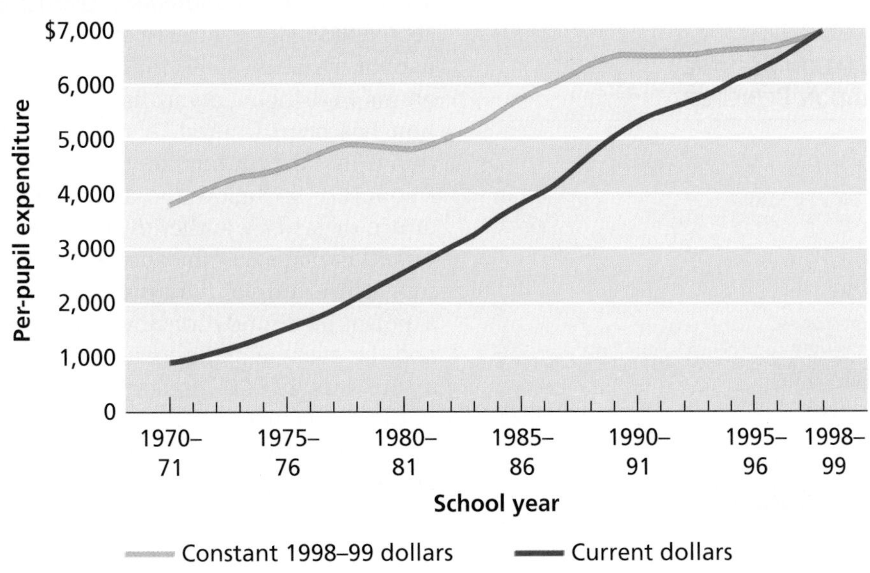

Source: U.S. Department of Education, National Center for Education Statistics. *Statistics of State School Systems: Revenues and Expenditures for Public Elementary and Secondary Education* and Common Core of Data surveys.

driver education, or programs for children with disabilities. Frequently, categorical aid is given to encourage specified education programs; in some states these aid programs are referred to as incentive programs. Categorical aid funds may be granted on a matching basis; thus, for each dollar of local effort, the state contributes a specified amount. Categorical aid has undoubtedly encouraged development of needed educational programs.

GENERAL STATE AID: EQUALITY OF OPPORTUNITY Historically, general aid was based on the idea that each child, regardless of place of residence or the wealth of the local district, should be entitled to receive a basic education. General state aid was established on the principle of equality of opportunity and is usually administered through a foundation program. Creating a *foundation program* involves determining the dollar value of the basic education opportunities desired in a state, referred to as the foundation level, and determining a minimum standard of local effort, considering local wealth. The foundation concept implies equity for taxpayers as well as equality of opportunity for students.

FOUNDATION PROGRAMS: THE WAY THEY WORK Figure 5.9 represents graphically how a foundation program operates. The total length of each bar represents the foundation level of education required per pupil, expressed in dollars. Each school district must put forth the same minimum local effort to finance its schools; this effort could be, for example, a qualifying tax rate that produces the local share of the foundation level. This tax rate will produce more revenue in a wealthy district than it will in a poor district; therefore, the poor district will receive more state aid than the wealthy district. Local school districts do not receive general state aid beyond that amount established as the foundation but are permitted in most instances to exceed foundation levels at their own expense.

EQUALIZATION AND THE FOUNDATION PRINCIPLE

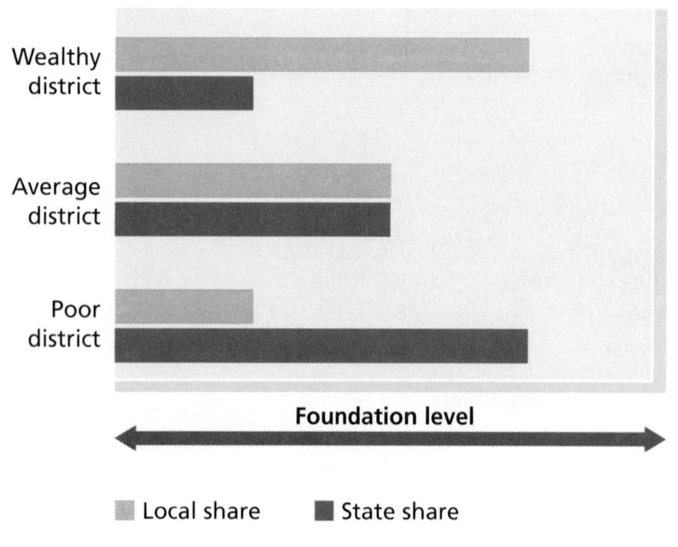

STATE FOUNDATION PROGRAMS: LIMITED EFFECTIVENESS The effectiveness of the use of various state foundation programs in bringing about fiscal equalization has been limited. A major limitation is that the foundation established is frequently far below the actual expenditure or far below the level needed to provide adequate educational opportunity. For example, if a state established a per-pupil foundation level of $1,500 and the average actual per-pupil expenditure was $3,000, equalization would not have occurred.

A second limitation is that most general state aid programs do not provide for different expenditure levels for different pupil needs. Special education and vocational education, for example, both require more money to operate than the usual per-pupil expenditure for the typical elementary or secondary school pupil.

FEDERAL AID The United States has a history of federal aid to education, but it has been categorical and not general aid; it has been related to the needs of the nation at the time. Federal aid actually started before the U.S. Constitution was adopted, with the Northwest Ordinance of 1785, which provided land for public schools in "western territories." Such federal aid has continued in a steady progression to the present. Almost two hundred federal aid-to-education laws have been passed since the Northwest Ordinance.

FEDERAL AID: THE CONTROVERSY Although it is seemingly historically established, federal aid is still controversial. Advocates of federal aid point out that it is a logical answer to the need for providing equality of educational opportunity for all children regardless of wealth or residence. They point out that federal aid to education helps the national defense and general welfare, ultimately, and that these national concerns cannot be adequately pursued at the local or state level. Proponents of federal aid to education also argue that this help does not necessarily mean federal controls, citing the land grant acts and the National Defense Education Act of 1958 as federal aid that was not accompanied by control. They feel that federal aid, through the income tax, is the most equitable way of paying for public education and for providing equal educational opportunity.

Opponents of federal aid point out that education is a state and a local function. They argue that variations in fiscal ability to pay will always exist and that the distribution of federal funds will not guarantee that whatever differences now exist will be reduced appreciably. They point out that the nation is weakened by its dependency on the federal government for funds, that categorical aid means federal control, and that states can use the income tax as effectively as the federal government. Although the debate continues, as is illustrated in Figure 5.10, the amount spent by the federal government for education continues to increase.

PERENNIAL SCHOOL FINANCE ISSUES

The basic challenge in school financing is not likely to be different in the near future from what it has been in the past. That challenge is making an adequate public education system equally available to everyone, along with a system of taxation designed to be equitable—that is, a progressive tax plan, a system in which taxpayers are all called on to support education in proportion to their ability to pay. Both equal opportunity and equitable taxation are difficult to achieve, as was illustrated earlier in this chapter. Some issues from the 1990s have continued into the 2000s. These issues include increasing enrollments, taxpayer revolt, rewards for accountability, and the conditions of schools, all of which are likely to affect the adequacy of school funding and therefore further complicate the basic challenge in school finance—the challenge of providing an adequate education with equality of opportunity through an equitable system of taxation.

ISSUE: INCREASING ENROLLMENTS Enrollment in elementary and secondary schools grew rapidly during the 1950s and 1960s and reached a peak in 1971. From 1971 to 1983 total enrollment decreased rapidly, reflecting the decline in the school-age population over that period. Enrollment reached a low of 44.9 million in 1984. School enrollments have begun increasing again. By 2004 enrollment is projected to reach 55.7 million, an increase of 16 percent from 1992.[16]

FIGURE 5.10 **FEDERAL ON-BUDGET FUNDS FOR EDUCATION, BY LEVEL OR OTHER EDUCATIONAL PURPOSE: 1965–1997, IN CONSTANT FY 1997 DOLLARS**

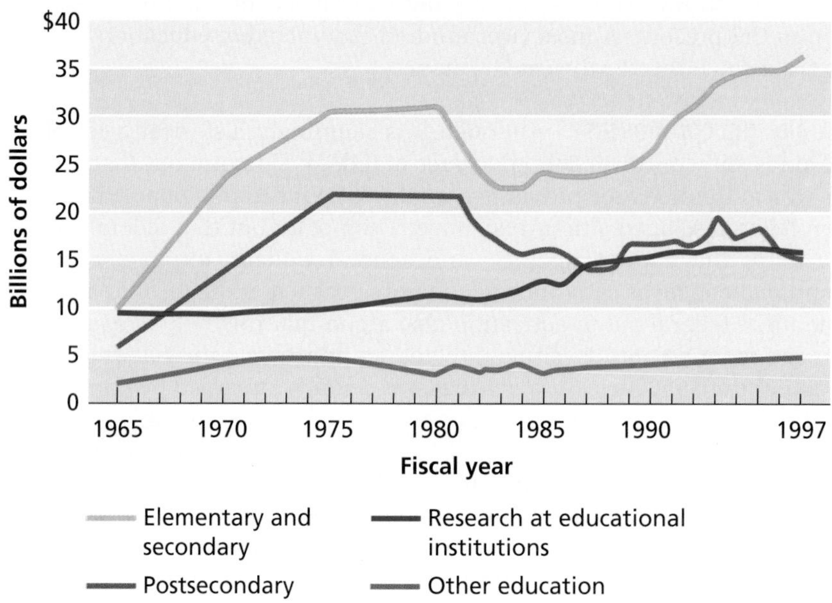

Source: U.S. Office of Management and Budget, *Budget of the U.S. Government,* fiscal years 1967 to 1998: National Science Foundation, *Federal Funds for Research and Development,* fiscal years 1967 to 1997; and unpublished data.

Increased enrollments have effects on the amount of money needed to support education adequately. While the new surge of students will be somewhat gradual, it will undoubtedly increase expenditures, and increased revenue is very likely to be needed to maintain the current level of expenditures per pupil. Furthermore, according to one educator, "the rising public school enrollments will include larger numbers and percentages of minority, limited-English-proficient, poor, and learning disabled students. All these special categories of students will require extra services to meet their needs."[17] Whether additional revenues will be available to provide educational services to the growing student population remains open to speculation.

ISSUE: TAXPAYER REVOLT A most dramatic instance of taxpayer revolt occurred in California in June 1978 with the passage of Proposition 13, which limited by constitutional amendment the property tax as a source of revenue. Subsequent and similar propositions have been added in other states. The trend is toward tax limitation, which has the effect of reducing funds available for education. These efforts, along with a low success rate of local school bond referenda and the closing of school districts for periods of time because of insufficient funds to operate, indicate problems for the funding of public schools.

ISSUE: THE CONDITIONS OF SCHOOLS One of the long-term effects on schools of the taxpayer revolt is now readily observed in states such as California, where 40 per-

Increasing school enrollments throughout the early years of the twenty-first century will create many school finance issues.

cent of the schools have roof and plumbing problems. For more than a decade, a frequent response to tight and reduced funding of schools has been to defer maintenance on buildings. A consequence of this tactic now is that thousands of school buildings across the nation need major repairs. Historically, states paid a large portion of the costs for school building construction; but with increased pressures from other sectors, such as criminal justice and welfare, state legislatures are backing away from supporting school construction and maintenance costs. Table 5.4 illustrates the dramatic differences among states' spending on school facilities.[18]

ACCOUNTABILITY

Accountability in education means holding schools responsible for what students learn. Schools in the coming years will continue to be called on to be accountable, and this trend is directly related to the financing of education. Although there are many definitions of the term *accountability,* in education it means that schools must devise a way of relating the vast expenditure made for education to the educational results. For many years the quality of education was measured by the number of dollars spent or the processes of education used. In other words, a school system that had a relatively high cost per pupil or used educational techniques judged to be effective was considered an excellent system. Seldom was the effectiveness of school systems judged by student outcomes—the educational achievements of students. Now those outcomes and their cost must be clearly accounted for.

Responsibility is the price every man must pay for freedom.

Edith Hamilton

ROOTS OF ACCOUNTABILITY Accountability has its roots in two fundamental modern problems: the continuous escalation of educational costs and (closely related) the loss of faith in educational results. The failure of the U.S. educational system, particularly in the cities and in some remote rural areas, has been accurately documented. The expectations of citizens for their children have not

accountability Schools' obligation to take responsibility for what students learn.

TABLE 5.4 Per-Pupil Spending on School Facilities by States

State	Per-Pupil Facilities Spending	State	Per-Pupil Facilities Spending
Alaska*	$2,254	New Mexico	93
Hawaii*	740	New Hampshire	84
Florida*	290	Wyoming	80
Connecticut	281	Mississippi	72
Delaware	275	New Jersey	61
Maine	203	North Dakota	48
North Carolina*	195	South Carolina†	41
Massachusetts*	193	Ohio†	38
New York	167	Idaho	30
Vermont	163	Utah	21
Indiana	155	Kansas	16
Minnesota*	153	Alabama†	14
Washington	150	Michigan	13
Georgia*	123	Arkansas	11
Rhode Island	117	California	10†
Maryland*	113	Montana	6
Pennsylvania	105	West Virginia†	0‡
Colorado	105	Tennessee	Not provided
Virginia	104	Arizona	Reported as unknown
Kentucky*	104	Wisconsin	Reported as unknown

Note: Illinois, Iowa, Louisiana, Missouri, Nebraska, Nevada, Oklahoma, Oregon, South Dakota, and Texas had no regular, ongoing program to assist districts with construction costs and are not included in the table.

*State has a comprehensive program, including facility-condition data, funding, and technical assistance and compliance review.

†California issues bonds every two years for school construction, but state officials report that sales scheduled in 1994 did not succeed; the amount shown represents the state's deferred-maintenance program, which does not depend on bond sales.

‡West Virginia provides state aid for school construction—$500 million since 1990—but provided none in 1994.

Source: U.S. General Accounting Office.

been met. Although U.S. public schools historically have done the best job of any nation in the world in providing education for *all the children of all the people,* they still have failed for some of their constituents. Educational accountability is necessary.

When the Elementary and Secondary Education Act of 1965 went into effect, the federal government issued its first formal call for accountability; it asked to receive documented results of educational attainment. Since then, many political and educational leaders have called for increased accountability. Many policy initiatives, such as Goals 2000 and Standards-Based Education, have been launched in the name of accountability.

BECOMING ACCOUNTABLE How can school systems become accountable? First, they must specify goals. In other words, if one goal of an elementary school is "to have pupils learn to read," then this goal must be spelled out specifically for each grade or child, whichever makes better sense, and success in meeting the goal must be measured and reported. Only in this way can results be conveyed to the public. Some states are requiring a "school report card" to be submitted to the public annually. The report cards provide information about student achievement by subject, as measured by standardized tests, along with financial and other relevant data about the school district.

EXPENSES AND EDUCATIONAL RESULTS The second aspect of accountability, accounting for expenses related to educational results, is easier to achieve because of modern technology. Financial accounting systems that are designed specifically to record expenditures on each educational program can effectively reveal the costs of educational results. When costs are known, one must measure them against what has been accomplished in performance. Advanced computer technology has increased the sophistication of accountability reporting systems; thus, better-informed educational decisions are possible, and the educational establishment has a way to regain the public's confidence.

THE IMPORTANCE OF TEACHER ACCOUNTABILITY Teachers play an important role in the quest for accountability. They are the primary contact with students, and they are responsible for instruction and student achievement. Therefore, they are expected to do their utmost to motivate students to learn and achieve. Accountability rests on data; therefore, teachers need to keep accurate records with respect to achievement, particularly if standardized tests are not utilized.

REWARDS FOR BEING ACCOUNTABLE The other side of the accountability coin is the question of rewards for success and sanctions for failure. In the 1980s many reward programs consisted of bestowing special designations and plaques on schools. In the 1990s there was a shift to the use of money as a reward or sanction. Now there are several interesting new approaches, with financial implications, that recognize schools and individual teachers or principals.

RECOGNIZING SCHOOLS Several states have established programs and plans to recognize schools that demonstrate increasing student success. For example, Florida, Indiana, South Carolina, and Texas have statewide programs that provide extra money as rewards and "performance incentives" to schools whose students show higher levels of progress. Kentucky has one of the most ambitious and comprehensive approaches to school accountability. As part of the Kentucky Education Reform Act, which was passed by the legislature in 1990 in response to *Rose* v. *The Council for Better Education* (1989), a $26 million reward fund was established. The fund is divided among those schools whose students show a 10 percent improvement on state-established measures of achievement. In 1995 38 percent of the Kentucky schools shared in the reward, which averaged about $2,000 per teacher. The staff in each school decides how the money will be distributed. The Kentucky plan also addresses accountability for those schools whose student success declines. One significant step is to assign a "distinguished educator" to the school for the next year. This highly experienced principal or teacher works with the school to analyze what they have been doing and what they can do to increase student success.

TABLE 5.5 What Numbers Reveal about a School

Increasingly, states and school districts are putting out statistic-laden report cards on schools. Here's how to decode them to get their true meaning.

School size
Lower dropout rates, higher attendance, fewer discipline problems. These are some advantages of small high schools (750 students or fewer) compared with facilities of 2,000 or more. But big isn't necessarily bad. Large schools may have a richer selection of courses and extracurriculars and can fight the ill effects of size by creating smaller groups of students who take most of their classes together.

Spending
Secondary schools spend, on average, $6,812 per student; 82.5 percent goes for staff compensation. You can usually obtain a school district's per-pupil rate but not an individual school's tally. Low-spending districts often can't attract top teachers. A high figure, though, can deceive. It could reflect new books, a big sports budget, or extensive—and costly—special-ed programs.

Safety
A low number of suspensions, expulsions, or arrests—say, five suspensions a month—could mean a quiet school or a principal who doesn't always crack down on offenders. (Ask any student which is the case.) To see how safe the halls are, find out why students are punished—cheating, using drugs, carrying weapons, fighting, abusing faculty. For an unvarnished picture of safety issues, talk to local police or merchants.

Technology
On average: There are 7.8 students per computer in schools; nearly 9 in 10 schools have one or more Internet connections; about 1 in 3 has Web access in classrooms. See if your school measures up. And check to make sure it knows how to use technology, urges Edith McArthur of the National Center for Education Statistics. Do teachers integrate technology into lesson plans? Does the school pay for tech training for teachers?

Class size
Don't use teacher–student ratio as a guide. The "teacher" side often includes counselors and aides. Ask for average class size in specific subjects and average teacher load—the number of students a teacher sees each day. A load of 125 students should be the upper limit for English; teachers need time to grade essays.

Teacher turnover rate
The average is 6.7 percent at public schools. That's *too* high, experts say—unless a new principal is pushing out mediocre staff. Richard Murnane, professor at the Harvard Graduate School of Education, says three years of teaching is a good foundation. But, he warns, "there's no evidence that 10 years is better than three."

Advanced placement numbers
Schools will tell you how many students take AP tests. A preponderance of 5s and 4s—the top grades—is impressive. But ask how many kids in AP courses actually take the test. If a significant percentage don't, the teachers in the school's AP classes might focus on elite kids instead of preparing all the students for the exam.

Test scores
Some schools brag about their SAT numbers, but don't be *that* bowled over. High scores correlate with wealthy parents, says longtime test critic Monty Neill. Instead, ask about criterion-referenced test scores, which show if students have mastered a body of knowledge. And ask for three years of scores for a sense of trends.

College acceptance rate
Would you trust 500 graduating seniors to report accurately their post-high school plans? That's why college acceptance rate isn't always reliable. Ask what percentage of students receive a college-prep education—or what percentage of students take the SAT or ACT college-entrance exam.

Graduation/dropout rate
Most schools base it on senior year alone. For the real attrition, track a four-year class: How many freshmen, how many graduates? (Good luck—*U.S. News* reporters failed to ferret this out from schools.) An equally vital query: How are potential dropouts encouraged to stay in?

Source: "Outstanding Schools: By the Numbers: What They Reveal about Schools." *U.S. News & World Report* (January 18, 1999):86–87.

REWARDING TEACHERS AND PRINCIPALS Other accountability initiatives target teachers and principals directly through focused evaluation and training programs, as well as offering financial rewards. For example, the Texas Successful Schools program includes a Principals' Performance Incentive program that awards up to $5,000 to principals whose campuses meet performance gain criteria. Other states are considering similar programs.

SCHOOL AND SCHOOL DISTRICT REPORT CARDS In the past, report cards were used only to evaluate students. A new element in the accountability movement is the use of new forms of report cards to "grade" schools, school districts, and states. Advocates of report cards argue that parents and voters need to know how well their school or school district is doing in comparison to others. They also point out that evaluating schools is complex; there are many factors that need to be considered. A report card can incorporate many factors and present a clear picture. Opponents express concern that report cards still are overly simplistic representations. They argue that report cards increase competition, which is not supposed to be a part of public education. Proponents argue back that competition will make low-performing schools improve and/or inform parents so that they can make the choice of sending their children to another school.

Clearly, an evaluation of schools needs to take into account a number of factors, some of which may be easy to score while others are more subtle. Class size, the amount of expenditures on technology, and test scores can be quantified. However, there are other factors, such as safety and the feel of the organizational culture, that are not easily counted. This means that these report cards will likely become increasingly complex and less easy to understand. As schools, school districts, states, and the federal government publish more report cards, there will be an increasing need to have a guide for interpreting the information presented. One such guide is presented in Table 5.5.

GLOBAL PERSPECTIVES: International Comparisons in Spending for Schools

Debate continues about the amount of investment the United States makes in public education and how well this amount compares with what other countries invest. International comparisons are difficult to make. Teacher salaries are different, the way in which budgets and educational functions are organized is different, and measuring student success is difficult. Yet the comparisons need to be made.

One way to compare education expenditures is to examine the percentage of a nation's gross domestic product that is spent on education. The results of this analysis for selected countries are presented in Figure 5.11. As with many international comparisons the United States are neither at the top nor at the bottom. Another way to compare would be class size. How does the United States compare to other countries in terms of the number of pupils per teacher? This analysis for selected countries is presented in Table 5.6. Again, there is a great deal of variation, the United States being neither at the top nor at the bottom. Figure 5.11 and Table 5.6 reflect the difficulties and complexities of attempting to draw comparisons. The details of a particular nation's policies and beliefs about public

FIGURE 5.11 PUBLIC EXPENDITURES FOR EDUCATION AS A PERCENTAGE OF THE GROSS DOMESTIC PRODUCT: SELECTED COUNTRIES, 1995

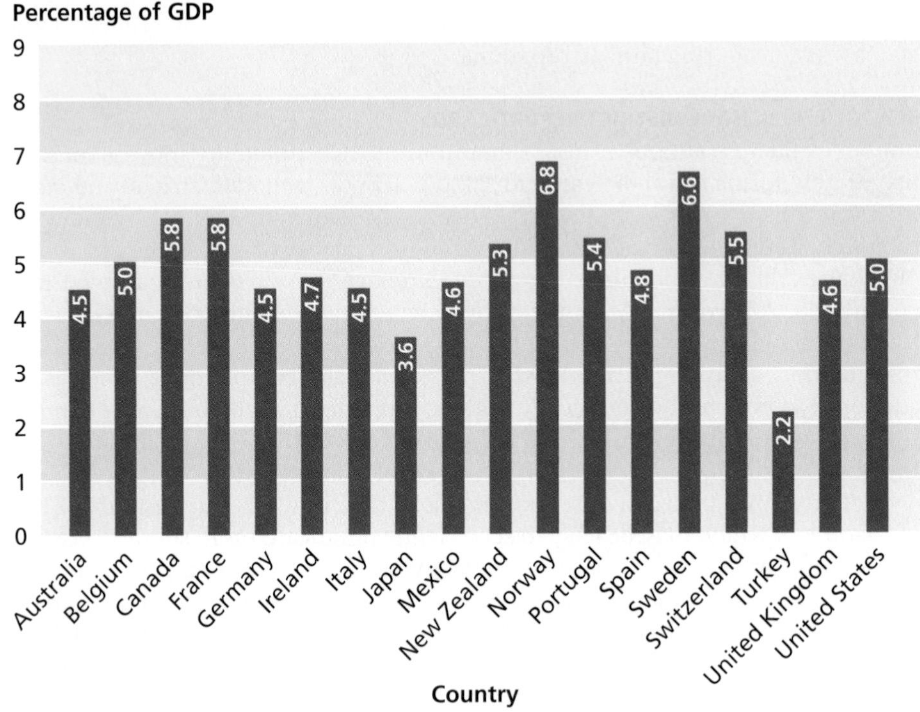

Source: Organization for Economic Cooperation and Development, unpublished data; National Center for Education Statistics. *Digest 99*. Washington, DC: Author, 1999.

education are not unveiled. Only educators at the local site can understand and explain what is important to their school's success and why.

SUMMARY

Two key ways to develop understanding of how the system works is to study how it is organized and the ways that it is financed.

THE STRUCTURE OF THE AMERICAN EDUCATION SYSTEM

Teaching does not take place in a classroom that is an island, disconnected from the rest of the system. All parts are intertwined. What a teacher does in his or her classroom is affected by the rest of the school, the principal, the district, the state, and the federal government. Conversely, what you do in your classroom will affect the rest of the system. Contrary to the stereotype associated with the self-contained classroom, American education is a highly interconnected system.

TABLE 5.6 **PUPILS PER TEACHER IN PUBLIC AND PRIVATE ELEMENTARY AND SECONDARY SCHOOLS, BY LEVEL OF EDUCATION: SELECTED COUNTRIES, 1996**

Country	Elementary	Junior High Schools (Lower Secondary)	Senior High Schools (Upper Secondary)
Australia	18.1	—	—
Austria	12.7	9.2	8.5
Canada	17.0	20.0	19.5
Denmark	11.2	10.1	12.1
France	19.5	—	—
Germany\5\	20.9	16.0	13.1
Ireland	22.6	—	—
Italy	11.2	10.8	9.8
Japan	19.7	16.2	15.6
Netherlands	20.0	—	—
New Zealand	22.0	18.1	14.1
Spain	18.0	17.8	14.2
Sweden	12.7	12.2	15.2
Turkey	—	—	—
United Kingdom	21.3	16.0	15.3
United States	16.9	17.5	14.7

Source: Digest of Education Statistics, 1999. Washington, DC: National Center for Education Statistics, U.S. Department of Education.

There are different levels of the organization of education in the United States. The organization of nearly all schools is by classrooms, with the principal being at the top of the line in authority and responsibility. At the school district level, each school reports to a superintendent, and school district policies are established by the school board. All schools, public and private, are under the authority of the state, including the state board of education and the state legislature. The federal government plays an ever increasing role through its provision of funds for targeted educational needs and, as will be explained in Chapter 6, the establishment of law. For teachers, it is essential that they understand the jobs and know the names of the key individuals in their school, district, and state. Teachers must maintain their line relationships by following through on tasks and assignments and being sure to communicate up the line of authority. A continuing issue of debate and concern is that of local control. As states and the federal government increase their involvement with and oversight of education, those at the local level have reduced opportunities to adjust to local needs.

THE FINANCING OF EDUCATION: SOURCES OF FUNDS AND THE MOVE FROM EQUITY TO ADEQUACY

It is also important to understand the financing of education. The brief overview of issues related to taxation, aid programs, and developing a fair and equitable system for financing education should bring you to an appreciation of the highly complex and difficult challenge of paying for education. There are no simple solutions that will be correct. Increasing sales taxes versus tax limitations, general aid versus categorical aid, and local versus state versus federal support are basic questions.

The existence and operation of schools depend on having continuing sources of money. The primary source of funds for public education is taxes. The property taxes, sales taxes, and state and federal income taxes are the primary sources for tax revenues. The state distributes the funds to school districts using various formulas that are based on the number of students being served and adjusted to accommodate some differences in local needs. Most states have recently experienced lawsuits questioning equity and adequacy in the way that funds are distributed. In these court cases it has been made clear that it is the state that has the responsibility for guaranteeing equal educational opportunity for all of its citizens. As school enrollments have increased and school facilities have aged, another emerging issue is the need to find funds to repair school facilities, build additional schools, and reduce class size.

DISCUSSION QUESTIONS

1. State and federal governments are playing an increasing role in determining what schools can and should do. What do you see as the benefits and problems that this increasing involvement may present to you as a teacher?
2. Have you had any firsthand experiences with school-based management? What do you see as the effects of this feature of school governance?
3. Is local control an issue in your state? What examples have you encountered that illustrate the tension between state and local education interests?
4. When is it appropriate for teachers to engage in politics? How can teachers influence what goes on in their schools? How can they influence decisions at the district and board levels?
5. What are the advantages of using sales and income taxes to fund elementary and secondary education instead of relying on the property tax?
6. What are some of the likely implications of using lotteries and gambling to fund schools?
7. What are three trends that could seriously affect the adequacy of school funding? Why?
8. Explain why the federal government should or should not provide funds for the repair of school buildings.

JOURNAL ENTRIES

1. Teachers need to understand many important aspects of organizations. One aspect has to do with who has responsibility for making final decisions. Develop an organizational chart for a school that you know. Use solid lines to represent line relationships and dotted lines to signify staff relationships. Draw the arrangement of personnel in regard to each of the following decisions: *(a)* determining a child's grade on his or her report card, *(b)* expelling a student (hint—don't forget that the school is part of a school district), *(c)* deciding on the topic for a staff development day, and *(d)* determining whether a particular teaching activity will be used. After considering these different decisions, write a short essay in which you address your thoughts and feelings about the authority and accountability of teachers within the school as an organization.

2. Develop a topic outline of the concerns and issues that came to your mind as you read the school finance sections of this chapter. What topics have implications for you as a teacher? What topics have implications for you as a taxpayer? Then write a journal entry in which you examine your ideas about how schools should be paid for.

PORTFOLIO DEVELOPMENT

1. For a school district where you think you would like to be employed, develop an organizational chart that includes the names, positions, and titles of key administrators and staff. Don't forget to include school board members and perhaps head teachers or department chairs. The more information you have at hand, the better prepared you will be in the future when it is time to apply for a position and to interview in that district.
2. School finance and spending will continue to be hot topics for school districts, state legislatures, and taxpayers. Start a file of newspaper clippings and notes from television news reports that deal with school finance and spending. Review the items in your file. Do certain topics and themes, such as school building construction, continue to be reported? When you are ready to apply for a position, having knowledge about finance and spending issues will make you better informed and prepared.

SCHOOL-BASED EXPERIENCES

1. Visit a school and develop an organization chart for the school. Place the names of people and their roles on the chart. For one or more people in each role group (e.g., teacher, custodian, secretary), find out who supervises and evaluates them. Also, ask them whether there are other people who influence or help them in their work. The purpose here is to determine the line and staff relationships. You quite likely will find that most people have a number of organizational relationships.
2. Seek an opportunity to study a school budget. Determine the different sources of revenue (e.g., local, state, grants, activity fees). What are the biggest line items? Which of these items does the principal have authority over? Are there some monies that are discretionary for teachers? Note that in most schools, especially high schools, there will be a surprising number of activities that generate cash. Inquire about the implications of having cash on hand, and ask how these amounts are secured and what policies guide their uses.

WEBSITES

Key words to use in conducting a web search include "school organizations," "school finance," "education expenditures," and, for each state, the name of the state department of education.

1. <www.ed.gov/pubs/SER/> Reports on "Studies of Education Reform." The full text of twelve recent studies that examined various aspects of education reform, which were funded by the U.S. Department of Education's Office of Educational Research and Improvement (OERI) can be found at this Online Library.
2. <www.ed.gov/NCES/> The National Center for Education Statistics of the U.S. Department of Education has on-line data and reports that describe many characteristics of schools, school finance, and international comparisons.

3. <www.darkwing.uoregon.edu/~ericcem/> The University of Oregon has an ERIC center and national research center on educational management. They provide many reports and publications related to the organization of schools.
4. <www.nasbe.org/> The National Association of State Boards of Education is a good source for information about shared interests and topics that are of concern to state boards of education.
5. <www.ecs.org/ecs/23aa.htm> The Education Commission of the States is a policy study center for and association of the state governors. Many interesting and useful position papers and conference activities for state-level policymakers are sponsored by this commission.
6. <www.edweek.org> *Education Week* is an up-to-date source of information about school finance and innovations in the organization of schools. Each week's issue will have several interesting articles dealing with these topics from local, state, and national perspectives.
7. <www.ncsl.org/public/sitesleg.htm> The National Council of State Legislatures is an association that facilitates the interstate exchange of information about education policy. Use this website to find out about state legislatures and education-related policy initiatives.

NOTES

1. B. Fuller, E. Burr, L. Huerta, S. Puryear, and E. Wexler, *School Choice: Abundant Hopes, Scarce Evidence on Results.* Berkeley, CA: Policy Analysis for California Education, 1999.
2. D. D. Goldhaber, "School Choice: An Examination of the Empirical Evidence on Achievement, Parental Decision Making, and Equity." *Educational Researcher* (December 1999): 16–25.
3. P. Wohlstetter and S. A. Mohrman, *Assessment of School-Based Management.* Los Angeles: Center on Educational Governance, University of Southern California in Los Angeles, 1996.
4. B. Nelson, P. Berman, J. Ericson, N. Kamprath, R. Perry, D. Silverman, and D. Solomon, *The State of Charter Schools 2000.* Washington, DC: Office of Educational Research and Improvement, U.S. Department of Education, 2000.
5. *Private Independent Schools 2000, 53rd Annual Edition.* Wallingford, CT: Bunting and Lyon, 2000.
6. Bobette Reed and William L. Dandridge, *Minority Leaders for Independent Schools.* Boston: National Association of Independent Schools.
7. B. Fuller, "Is School Choice Working?" *Educational Leadership* (1996): 37–40.
8. *Bending without Breaking.* Denver, CO: Education Commission of the States 1996.
9. Richard C. Hunter, "The Mayor versus the School Superintendent." *Education and Urban Society 29* (2) (February 1997): 217–232.
10. D. W. Drury, *Reinventing School-Based Management.* Alexandria, VA: National School Boards Association, 1999.
11. L. M. McDowell, *Early Estimates of Public Elementary and Secondary Education Statistics: School Year 1999–2000.* Washington, DC: National Center for Education Statistics, 2000.
12. Steven Stark, Craig R. Wood, and David S. Honeyman, "The Florida Education Lottery: Its Use as a Substitute for Existing Funds and Its Effects on the Equity of School Funding." *Journal of Education Finance 18* (Winter 1993): 231–242.
13. *Helena Elementary School District* v. *State* (1989).
14. Consumers Union Education Services, *Captive Kids: Commercial Pressures on Kids at School.* Yonkers, NY: Consumers Union, 1996.
15. U.S. Department of Education, National Center for Education Statistics, *Statistics in Brief May 2000.* Washington, DC: Table 5.

16. U.S. Department of Education, National Center for Education Statistics, *Projections of Education Statistics to 2007,* U.S. Department of Education, 1997.

17. Daniel U. Levine, "Educational Spending: International Comparisons." *Theory Into Practice 33*(2) (Spring 1994): 126–131.

18. *School Facilities: States' Financial and Technical Support Varies* (GAO/HEHS-96-27). Washington, DC: General Accounting Office, 1996.

BIBLIOGRAPHY

The Future of Children. Financing schools theme issue (Winter 1997).

Good, T. L., and Braden, J. S. *The Great School Debate: Choice, Vouchers, and Charters.* Mahwah, NJ: Erlbaum Associates, 2000.

Goodman, R. H., and Zimmerman, W. G., Jr. *Thinking Differently: Recommendations for 21st Century School Board/Superintendent Leadership, Governance, and Teamwork for High Student Achievement.* Arlington, VA: Educational Research Service, 2000.

Odden A., and Clune, W. H. "School Finance Systems: Aging Structures in Need of Renovation." *Educational Evaluation and Policy Analysis* 20.3: 157–177.

Sarason, S. *How Schools Might Be Governed and Why.* New York: Teachers College Press, 1997.

Wong, K. K. *Funding Public Schools.* Lawrence, KS: University Press of Kansas, 1999.

*trust ppl & agencies @ other locations - horizontal perspective

*gov't unit empowered by state law to administer the school system of a local comm. - School district

*responsible for ed. - State

*board members chosen - regulatory advisory service

*foundation level - dollar value; equity for the tax payer & equality for students

*In the past, primary source of revenue for schools - local property taxes

CHAPTER

6

Legal Foundations of Education

EDUCATION IN THE NEWS

Prayers Are Heard at Football Games Despite Ruling

By Cathy Lynn Grossman
USA Today, August 28, 2000

ASHEVILLE, N.C.—Advocates of school prayer who say the government should not limit prayer at public events kicked off a season of defiance this weekend in high school stadiums across the South.

Urged by local pastors and Christian broadcasters, parents and students stood in bleachers to shout, recite or whisper a pre-kickoff Lord's Prayer.

Many were moved to action by a mistaken impression that the U.S. Supreme Court prohibited student-led prayer entirely, ending a long-standing pre-game tradition.

The court ruled 6–3 in June that schools may not facilitate prayer, even if led by a student chaplain elected by peers.

In Asheville, seedbed of a national advocacy campaign called We Still Pray, hundreds of voices scattered in stands at A.C. Reynolds High School mixed "Our Father who art in heaven" amid the excited chatter of 4,000 teens and parents at Friday's game.

Mississippi school officials were cautious after actor Tom Lester (Eb on *Green Acres*) and Paul Ott, radio talk-show host, called for fans to join hands and recite the prayer at local games. "We support the law although we don't agree with it," says N. Z. Bryant, deputy director of the Mississippi High School Activities Association. Friday night prayers swept the playing fields in Hattiesburg and other cities but without benefit of public loudspeakers.

At Batesburg-Leesville (S.C.) High School, the student body president led prayers from the press box, in direct opposition to the court ruling. A group called No Pray, No Play is promoting the same idea in Texas schools.

Civil liberties experts are still in the game, though.

They say people may pray, in school—alone or in unison—on the playing fields, in the classrooms or halls just as they always have. But schools must remain neutral and may not compel a captive audience to listen or participate. If they violate these guidelines on religious expression they may face civil lawsuits. Already there are rumbles of a lawsuit in Batesburg-Leesville.

"Schools don't have the luxury of ignoring Supreme Court rulings they don't like," says Steve Benen of Americans United for Separation of Church and State. . . .

LEARNER OUTCOMES

After reading and studying this chapter, you will be able to

1. Explain the relationships between the U.S. Constitution and the role and responsibilities of

(continued)

the states in ensuring the availability of public schools for all children.

2. Describe critical issues about the role of public schools for which the courts are being used to resolve points of debate.
3. Identify and describe court-established guidelines related to the use of public funds for private schools.
4. Identify and describe court-established guidelines related to religious activities in public schools.
5. Outline the role of statutes and court decisions related to civil rights and affirmative action as they relate to schools.
6. Summarize key components of the rights and responsibilities of teachers as determined by key U.S. Supreme Court decisions.
7. Be clear about a teacher's responsibilities and liabilities related to negligence.
8. Distinguish between students' rights and responsibilities as citizens and their rights and responsibilities as students. ■

Aspiring teachers typically will not have given consideration to the fact that there is a legal aspect to teaching. As citizens of the United States, teachers are, of course, subject to the laws of the land. However, in addition, teachers are employees and as such have specified protected rights and responsibilities. Also, teachers are responsible not only for children learning, but also for their safety and protecting their rights. In each of these areas elements of the legal system, its processes, and its rulings come into play. As is illustrated in the *Education Headlines* feature, schools and educators are frequently drawn into areas of debate for society at large. All too frequently, it seems, the courts are turned to for resolution. Hot areas of debate include prayer in schools, racial equality, and teachers' and children's rights as citizens versus their rights in school.

The first big idea that we address in this chapter emphasizes that the legal foundations of education are the U.S. Constitution and the Bill of Rights. All else evolves from interpretations of the Constitution. Another big idea has to do with the separation of church and state, which is addressed in the Establishment Clause of the First Amendment to the Constitution. Another big idea is embedded in the Fourteenth Amendment, the Equal Protection Clause, which guarantees equal opportunity for a public education for all children regardless of their race, gender, ability, or disability. The rights and responsibilities of teachers as employees are addressed by the legal system as well. For example, teachers are protected from termination without cause. A related very important big idea is teacher responsibility, including providing safe and well-supervised educational activities for students. Teachers also need to understand that children retain their rights as citizens while having related rights and responsibilities as students. Another big idea is that policymakers such as Congress, state legislatures, and local school boards also establish laws in the forms of statutes, policies, rules, and procedures. Teachers must know about and understand how these affect classroom practice as well.

To illustrate each of these ideas, this chapter presents an important set of social, political, and educational issues that have been debated within and addressed by the legal system. We will examine topics such as the appropriateness of using public funds to support private education, desegregation, teachers' rights, and students' rights. We will draw on excerpts from the Constitution, state statutes, and court decisions to point out some of the important issues that have been addressed through the legal system. Each of the topics presented in this chapter, as well as the legal processes behind it, applies directly to what you can do and should not do as a teacher and a school employee. The chapter is organized into three major sections. The first section explains the legal basis and framing of the public education system. The second section addresses the legal rights and responsibilities of teachers. The third section examines the rights of students.

FIGURE 6.1 SOURCES OF LEGAL CONTROL IN U.S. EDUCATION AS THEY AFFECT THE CLASSROOM TEACHER

ENABLING AND LEGISLATIVE AGENTS

- People of the state and their rights under the U.S. Constitution
- Constitution of the state
- Statutes of the state legislature
- State school board policies
- Local school board policies

↓

The Classroom Teacher

↑

- Local administrative officers
- State superintendent of public instruction
- Opinions of the attorney general
- Decisions of the state court
- Decisions of the U.S. Supreme Court

INTERPRETIVE AND ADMINISTRATIVE AGENTS

LEGAL ASPECTS OF EDUCATION

The legal foundation of the United States is the U.S. Constitution, and a pivotal part of the Constitution is the Bill of Rights. Within the boundaries of U.S. law, each state is guided by its own constitution. There are several additional sources of laws at the federal, state, and local levels, and there are a number of processes for addressing disputes. As is illustrated in Figure 6.1, in many ways the teacher is the implementer at the intersection of the cross-pressures between those who enact laws and those who interpret them. Some but not all laws are developed out of the legislative process. These are referred to as **enabling laws,** those that provide opportunity or make it possible for educators to do certain things. Also, laws may impose mandates or prohibitions. Once legislation is enacted into law, if a question of interpretation is raised, then the **judicial interpretive** process is engaged. If an administrative interpretation is not accepted, then the judicial process can come into play. The judicial process is also used when it appears that a law has been violated. The interpretations of the state and federal court systems form a body of case, or common, law. The sampling of legal topics presented in this chapter include examples from constitutional law, state and federal statutes, and case law based on court interpretations. All apply directly to schools, teachers, and students.

enabling laws laws make it possible for educators to do certain things.

judicial interpretive the judicial process of drawing conclusions about the intent of the wording in the Constitution and statutes.

LEGAL PROVISIONS FOR EDUCATION: THE U.S. CONSTITUTION

The educational systems of the United States, both public and nonpublic, are governed by law. The U.S. Constitution is the fundamental law for the nation, and a state legislature has no right to change the Constitution. When a state legislature makes laws that apply to education, these laws must be in accordance with both the U.S. Constitution and that state's constitution.

Three of the amendments to the U.S. Constitution are particularly significant to the governance of education, both public and private, in the United States. Interpretations of each of these amendments—the First, Tenth, and Fourteenth—by the courts have had profound impacts on the role and purpose of schools, the

The United States Constitution laid the groundwork for the notion of equal access to education for all.

opportunities of all students to have access to an education, and the responsibilities and rights of teachers, students, and school administrators.

The powers not delegated to the United States by the Constitution, nor prohibited by it to the States, are reserved to the States respectively, or to the people.

Tenth Amendment, U.S. Constitution.

TENTH AMENDMENT The U.S. Constitution does not specifically provide for public education; however, the Tenth Amendment has been interpreted as granting this power to the states. The amendment specifies that "The powers not delegated to the United States by the Constitution, nor prohibited by it to the States, are reserved to the States respectively, or to the people." Therefore, education is legally the responsibility and the function of each of the fifty states. Education in the United States is not nationalized as it is in many other nations of the world.

Each state, reflecting its responsibility for education in its state, has provided for education either in its constitution or in its basic statutory law. For example, Section 1, Article X of the Illinois Constitution reads:

> A fundamental goal of the People of the State is the educational development of all persons to the limits of their capabilities.
>
> The State shall provide for an efficient system of high quality educational institutions and services. Education in public schools through the secondary level shall be free. There may be such other free education as the General Assembly provides by law.
>
> The State has the primary responsibility for financing the system of public education.

The current Michigan Constitution states in Section 2, Article VIII:

> The Legislature shall maintain and support a system of free public elementary and secondary schools as defined by law. Each school district shall provide for the education of its pupils without discrimination as to religion, creed, race, color, or national origin.

The Utah Constitution, Section 1, Article X reads:

> The Legislature shall provide for the establishment and maintenance of a uniform system of public schools, which shall be open to all children of the State, and be free from sectarian control.

Through such statements the people of the various states commit themselves to a responsibility for education. The state legislatures are obliged to fulfill this commitment. While the interpretation of the Tenth Amendment places the responsibility for education on the states, the rights of citizens of the United States are protected by the Constitution and cannot be violated by any state.

FIRST AMENDMENT The First Amendment ensures freedom of speech, of religion, and of the press, as well as the right to petition. It specifies:

> Congress shall make no law respecting an establishment of religion, or prohibiting the free exercise thereof; or abridging the freedom of speech, or of the press; or the right of the people peaceably to assemble, and to petition the Government for redress of grievances.

As is illustrated in the cases presented later in this chapter, two important clauses in the First Amendment have been applied repeatedly to issues confronting public education: (1) the *Establishment Clause,* "Congress shall make no law respecting an establishment of religion," and (2) the *Free Speech Clause,* which has direct implications for teacher and student rights.

FOURTEENTH AMENDMENT The Fourteenth Amendment protects specified privileges of citizens. It reads in part:

> No state shall make or enforce any law which shall abridge the privileges or immunities of citizens of the United States; nor shall any State deprive any person of life, liberty, or property without due process of law; nor deny to any person within its jurisdiction the equal protection of the laws.

The application of the Fourteenth Amendment to public education as considered in this chapter deals primarily with the *Equal Protection Clause:* "nor shall any State . . . deny to any person within its jurisdiction the equal protection of the laws." Equal educational opportunity is protected under the Fourteenth Amendment. In effect, the rights of citizens of the United States are ensured by the Constitution and cannot be violated by state laws or action.

CHURCH AND STATE

Our nation has a strong religious heritage. For example, in colonial times, education was primarily a religious matter; furthermore, much of this education was conducted in private religious schools. Many private schools today are still under religious sponsorship. But debate about the rightful role of religion in public education continues. Should public funds be used to support students in religious schools? Can there be prayer at high school commencement services or in classrooms? Does the teaching of creationism amount to public support for religion, or is it merely the presentation of an alternative scientific view? Agreements have not been reached through the debate process, so proponents of differing viewpoints have turned to the courts.

Court cases concerned with separation of church and state most frequently involve both the First and Fourteenth Amendments of the U.S. Constitution. The First Amendment is interpreted as being applicable to the states by the Fourteenth Amendment. For example, a state law requiring a daily prayer to be read

Religion, morality, and knowledge being necessary to good government and happiness of mankind, schools and the means of education shall forever be encouraged.

Northwest Ordinance, 1787

in classrooms throughout the state could be interpreted as "depriving persons of liberty" (see the Fourteenth Amendment due process clause) and as the state establishing a religion, or at least "prohibiting the free exercise thereof" (see the First Amendment establishment clause). States are not permitted to make laws that abridge the privileges of citizens, and the right to the free practice of religion must be ensured.

Court cases related to the separation of church and state can be classified in three categories: (1) those dealing with the use of public funds to support religious education, (2) those dealing with the practice of religion in public schools, and (3) those dealing with the rights of parents to provide private education for their children. Key cases related to each of these categories are presented next.

PUBLIC FUNDS AND RELIGIOUS EDUCATION The use of public funds to support religious schools has been questioned on many occasions. Typically, state constitutions deny public funds to sectarian institutions or schools. However, public funds have been used to provide transportation for students to church schools and to provide textbooks for students in parochial schools.

Approximately 85 percent of the students who attend nonpublic schools are attending church-related schools. Of this number, some 70 percent are enrolled in parochial (Catholic) schools. In states with relatively large enrollments in parochial schools, there have been continuing efforts to obtain public financial assistance of one form or another for nonpublic school students. These attempts have often been challenged in the courts. We will present a sampling of these cases and issues here to illustrate the reasoning and to assess trends in this difficult area. A summary of cases related to the use of public funds for private education is presented in Table 6.1.

TRANSPORTATION FOR STUDENTS OF CHURCH SCHOOLS The landmark case on the use of public funds to provide transportation for students to church schools was *Everson* v. *Board of Education,* ruled on by the U.S. Supreme Court in 1947. The Court held that in using tax-raised funds to reimburse parents for bus fares expended to transport their children to church schools, a New Jersey school district did not violate the establishment clause of the First Amendment. The majority of the members of the Court viewed the New Jersey statute permitting free bus transportation to parochial school children as "public welfare legislation" to help get the children to and from school safely and expeditiously. Since the *Everson* decision, the highest courts in several states, under provisions in their own constitutions, have struck down enactments authorizing expenditures of public funds to bus children attending denominational schools; others have upheld such enactments.

THE *LEMON* TEST: EXCESSIVE ENTANGLEMENT A useful rubric emerged from the U.S. Supreme Court decision in *Lemon* v. *Kurtzman* (1971). This case dealt with an attempt by the Rhode Island legislature to provide a 15 percent salary supplement to teachers who taught secular subjects in nonpublic schools and a statute in Pennsylvania that provided reimbursement for the cost of teachers' salaries and instructional materials in relation to specified secular subjects in nonpublic schools. The Court concluded that the "cumulative impact of the entire relationship arising under the statutes in each state involves excessive entanglement between government and religion." The Court pointed out another

TABLE 6.1 SELECTED U.S. SUPREME COURT CASES RELATED TO THE USE OF PUBLIC FUNDS FOR PRIVATE EDUCATION

Case	Issue	Decision
Cochran v. *Louisiana Board of Education* (1930)	Loan of public school textbooks to children in private schools	Court ruled that state loans of secular textbooks to nonpublic school children served public purposes and did not violate the federal constitutional ban on spending public funds for private purposes.
Everson v. *Board of Education* (1947)	Use of tax-raised funds to reimburse parents for transportation of students to church schools	Court ruled that reimbursement did not violate the First Amendment.
Board of Education of Central School District No. 1, Town of Greenbush v. *Allen* (1968)	Loan of public school textbooks to children in private schools	Court ruled that the loan of books did not alone demonstrate an unconstitutional degree of support for a religious institution.
Lemon v. *Kurtzman* (1971)	Legislation to provide direct aid for secular services to nonpublic schools, including teacher salaries, textbooks, and instructional materials	Court ruled the legislation unconstitutional because of the excessive entanglement between government and religion.
Wolman v. *Walter* (1977)	Provision of books, standardized testing and scoring, diagnostic services, and therapeutic and remedial services to nonpublic school pupils	Court ruled that providing such materials and services to nonpublic school pupils was constitutional.
	Provision of instructional materials and field trips to nonpublic school pupils	Court ruled that providing such materials and services to nonpublic school pupils was unconstitutional.
Grand Rapids School District v. *Ball* (1985), and *Aguilar* v. *Felton* (1985)	Instruction of nonpublic school students in supplementary education by public school teachers	Court ruled that the action violated the establishment clause in that it promoted religion.
Zobrest v. *Catalina Foothills School District* (1993)	Provision of a school district interpreter for a deaf student attending a Catholic high school	Court ruled that government programs that neutrally provide benefits to a broad class of citizens without reference to religion are not readily subject to an establishment clause challenge.
Board of Education of Kiryas Joel Village School District v. *Grumet* (1994)	Creation and support of a public school district for Hasidic Jews by New York State	Court ruled that the district violated the establishment clause in that it was a form of "religious favoritism."
Agostini v. *Felton* (1997)	School districts' provision of Title I teachers to serve disadvantaged students in religious schools	Court overturned ban provided the district assigns teachers without regard to religious affiliation, all religious symbols are removed from classrooms, teachers have limited contact with religious personnel, and public school supervisors make monthly unannounced inspections.

In Zobrest *v.* Catalina *the Supreme Court ruled that no establishment clause was violated in the case of providing an interpreter for a student who was deaf attending a Catholic high school.*

defect of the Pennsylvania statute: It provided for the aid to be given directly to the school. In the *Everson* case the aid was provided to the student's parents, not to the church-related school. The Court posed three questions that have since become known as the *Lemon* test: (1) Does the act have a secular purpose? (2) Does the primary effect of the act either advance or inhibit religion? (3) Does the act excessively entangle government and religion? Most subsequent cases dealing with the use of public funds in nonpublic school settings have referred to this test.

SPECIAL SITUATIONS The U.S. Supreme Court seems to have wavered from a strict application of the *Lemon* test in two recent cases: *Zobrest* v. *Catalina* and *Kiryas Joel* v. *Grumet.*

In a 1994 case, *Board of Education of Kiryas Joel Village School District* v. *Grumet,* the U.S. Supreme Court ruled that a New York State law that created a public school to serve children with disabilities in a village of Hasidic Jews was a form of "religious favoritism" that violated the First Amendment. Interestingly, in this case, as in some others recently, the justices ignored the *Lemon* test in making the decision. Instead, the focus was on the legislature's creation of a special school district; the justices noted the risk that "the next similarly situated group seeking a school district of its own will receive one." Another implication of this decision was the indication that the court would be willing to revisit *Aquilar* v. *Felton* (1985) and *Grand Rapids* v. *Ball* (1985), which invalidated sending public school teachers to private religious schools to provide supplemental instruction.

Whether a public school district could provide an interpreter for a student who was deaf attending a Catholic high school was the central question in *Zobrest* v. *Catalina Foothills School District.* Under a federal statute, the Individuals with Disabilities Education Act (IDEA), students who are deaf are entitled to have a sign language interpreter in all regular classes. In *Zobrest* v. *Catalina* the Court concluded that no establishment clause violation occurred because the provision of the interpreter was a "private decision of individual parents." In terms of the federal statute, the Court determined that this was a situation in which "government programs that neutrally provide benefits to a broad class of citizens defined without reference to religion are not readily subject to an establishment clause challenge just because sectarian institutions may also receive an attenuated benefit."

CHILD BENEFIT THEORY The use of public funds to provide secular services has led to a concept referred to as child benefit theory. **Child benefit theory** supports the provision of benefits to children in nonpublic schools with no benefits to the schools or to a religion. More recent decisions supporting the use of public funds for transportation and textbooks for students in private schools have generally been based on the child benefit theory; this theory emerged out of commentary about the *Everson* v. *Board of Education* case. The reasoning was that transportation and books provide benefits to the children and not to the school or to a religion. Those opposed to the child benefit theory argue that aid to children receiving sectarian education instruction is effectively aiding the institution providing instruction.

The child benefit theory, as supported by the U.S. Supreme Court, has penetrated federal legislation. For example, the Elementary and Secondary Education Act of 1965 (ESEA) and its subsequent amendments provided for assistance to both public and nonpublic school children. Title I of ESEA, which dealt with assistance for the education of children from low-income families, stated that children from families attending private schools must be provided services in proportion to their numbers.

TITLE I TEACHERS IN RELIGIOUS SCHOOLS In one recent decision, *Agostini* v. *Felton* (1997), the U.S. Supreme Court seemed to be providing increased flexibility and easing the tensions created by *Aguilar* v. *Felton* (1985). In *Aguilar* the Court struck down the use of Title I funds to pay public school teachers who taught in programs to help low-income students in parochial schools. But in *Agostini* the Court decided that under specific safeguards Title I teachers can be sent to serve disadvantaged students in religious schools; refer to Table 6.1 on page 233.

The issue of public aid to church-related schools is still in the process of being settled. Although it is clear that aid for certain secular services (such as transportation, textbooks, and—under prescribed circumstances—testing, diagnostic, therapeutic, and remedial services) can be provided, it is not yet absolutely clear what further aid will be approved. In fact, the whole body of law in this area continues to be somewhat confused and contradictory. Some state legislatures are continuing to try to find new ways to provide aid to religious schools without violating the First Amendment. See Figure 6.2 for a summary of statements related to public funds and religious education.

Another issue related to separation of church and state focuses on religious activities in public schools—the subject of the next section.

RELIGIOUS ACTIVITIES IN PUBLIC SCHOOLS The limits and boundaries of the First Amendment in relation to public schools have been and will continue to be tested in the courts, especially in relation to religion. Several cases have dealt with the teaching of creationism and evolution, the practice of religion, and the religious use of public facilities. Each case has contributed to a gradual process of clarification of what can and what should not be done to ensure the separation of church and state. Table 6.2 on page 237 summarizes U.S. Supreme Court judgments in some of these cases.

child benefit theory
A criterion used by the U.S. Supreme Court to determine whether services provided to nonpublic school students benefit children and not a particular school or religion.

FIGURE 6.2 SUMMARY OF STATEMENTS ON CHURCH AND STATE RELATED TO PUBLIC FUNDS AND RELIGIOUS EDUCATION

Laws and policies that have the effect of establishing religion in the schools will not be upheld by the courts.

Public tax funds to pay for secular textbooks for loan to students and transportation of religious school children have been upheld by the courts.

Public tax funds to pay for salaries of teachers in religious schools have not been upheld by the courts.

Tuition payments for parents of religious school children have not been upheld; in Minnesota, a tax deduction has been upheld for parents of children in public *and* private schools.

Special support services such as speech and hearing teachers may be provided to students in religious schools.

Religious schools may be reimbursed for administrative costs of standardized tests, test scoring, and record keeping required by the state.

Public tax funds may not be used in support of public school teachers offering remedial or enriched instruction in religious schools.

A continuing topic of debate and judicial action is the place of prayer in public schools as determined by the First Amendment.

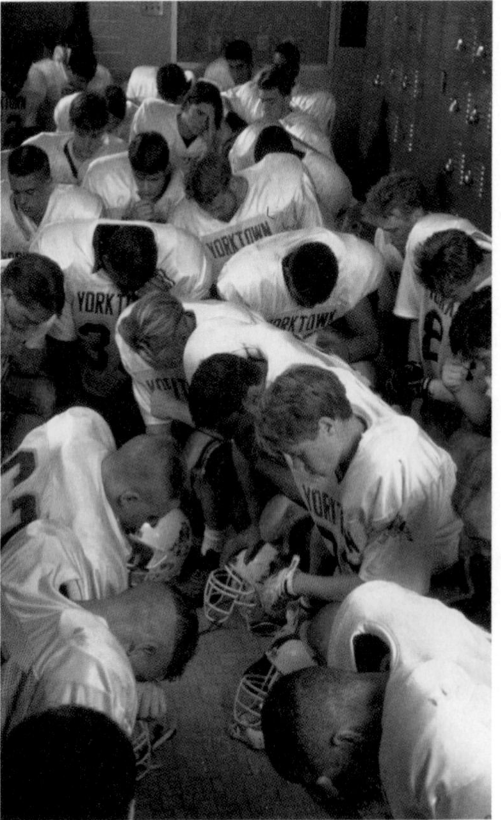

PRAYER IN SCHOOL As was illustrated in the *Education in the News* feature at the beginning of this chapter, a number of attempts have been and continue to be initiated by school districts to incorporate some form of prayer into public school classrooms and activities. One such case began when the school district for Santa Fe High School, in Texas, adopted a series of policies that permitted prayer initiated and led by a student at all home athletic games. In June 2000 the U.S. Supreme Court ruled in *Santa Fe Independent School District, Petitioner* v. *Jane Doe* that the clear intent of the district policies was in violation of the Establishment Clause. The six-to-three majority observed, "The District, nevertheless, asks us to pretend that we do not recognize what every Santa Fe High School student understands clearly—that this

TABLE 6.2 Selected U.S. Supreme Court Cases Related to the Practice of Religion in Public Schools

Case	Issue	Decision
Creationism		
Epperson v. *State of Arkansas* (1968)	Arkansas antievolution statute	Court held that to forbid the teaching of evolution as a theory violated the First Amendment.
Edwards v. *Aguillard* (1987)	Balanced treatment of biblical and scientific explanations of the development of life	A state cannot require that schools teach the biblical version of creation.
Practice of Religion		
Wallace v. *Jaffree* (1985)	Legislation authorizing prayer in public schools, led by teachers, and a period of silence for meditation or voluntary prayer	Court held that state legislation authorizing a minute of silence for prayer led by teachers was unconstitutional.
Mozert v. *Hawkins County Public Schools* (1987)	Request that fundamentalist children not be exposed to basal reading series in the public schools of Tennessee	Rejected by the Sixth Circuit Court of Appeals, which reasoned that the readers did not burden the students' exercise of their religious beliefs.
Board of Education of the Westside Community Schools v. *Mergens* (1990)	The right of a student religious club to hold meetings at a public school	Court ruled that based on Equal Access Act (EAA) of 1984, if only one non-curriculum-related student group meets, then the school may not deny other clubs.
Lee v. *Weisman* (1992)	Inclusion of a religious exercise in a graduation ceremony where young graduates who object are induced to conform	Prayers as an official part of graduation exercises are unconstitutional.
Use of Facilities		
Police Department of the City of Chicago v. *Mosley* (1972)	Government's refusal of use of a public forum to people whose views it finds unacceptable	"There is an equality of status in the field of ideas," and "government must afford all points of view an equal opportunity to be heard."
Lamb's Chapel v. *Center Moriches Union Free School District* (1993)	A church's screening of a family-oriented movie on public school premises after school hours	The district property had been used by a wide variety of audiences, so there was no danger of the district's being perceived as endorsing any given religion.
Santa Fe Independent School District, Petitioner v. *Jane Doe* (2000)	School district policy supporting student-led prayer before football games	"The policy is invalid on its face because it establishes an improper majoritarian election on religion, and unquestionably has the purpose and creates the perception of encouraging the delivery of prayer at a series of important school events."

Our examination of those circumstances above leads to the conclusion that this policy does not provide the District with the constitutional safe harbor it sought.

Santa Fe Independent School District v. Jane Doe

policy is about prayer." Later in the decision the Court noted, "This policy likewise does not survive a facial challenge because it impermissibly imposes upon the student body a majoritarian election on the issue of prayer." In other words, the district would be imposing a particular religious activity of the majority on all, a clear violation of the Establishment Clause. "It further empowers the student body majority with the authority to subject students of minority views to constitutionally improper messages. The award of that power alone, regardless of the students' ultimate use of it, is not acceptable." In concluding, the Court stated, "The policy is invalid on its face because it establishes an improper majoritarian election on religion, and unquestionably has the purpose and creates the perception of encouraging the delivery of prayer at a series of important school events."

In an attempt to clarify what is and is not permissible in relation to prayer and other religious activities in public schools, the U.S. Department of Education has published a set of guidelines for religious expression. Points from these guidelines are summarized in Figure 6.3.

The Louisiana Creationism Act advances a religious doctrine by requiring either the banishment of the theory of evolution from public school classrooms or the presentation of a religious viewpoint that rejects evolution in its entirety. The Act violates the Establishment Clause of the First Amendment because it seeks to employ the symbolic and financial support of government to achieve a religious purpose.

Edwards v. Aguillard

CREATIONISM VERSUS EVOLUTION One of the most famous trials involving religion and a teacher occurred in Tennessee in 1925, when a science teacher, John Scopes, was found guilty of teaching evolution. Although the decision was later reversed on a technicality, the Scopes "monkey trial" has been kept alive in the theater and through the more recent efforts of certain religious groups advocating that creation be taught in place of, or along with, the scientific construct of evolution. Creationists advance an interpretation of the origin of human life that is based in the Bible. In 1968 the Court ruled against states that had attempted to ban the teaching of evolution and then in 1987 ruled in *Edwards* v. *Aguillard* that the Arkansas legislature violated the establishment clause of the First Amendment when it required equal time for the teaching of creationism and evolution. Still, creationists have continued to push their agenda. For example,

FIGURE 6.3 GUIDELINES FOR RELIGIOUS EXPRESSION IN PUBLIC SCHOOLS

- The right to voluntary prayer or religious discussion does not include the right to have a captive audience listen or to compel other students to participate.
- Students may engage in prayer and religious discussion during the school day as long as they are not disruptive.
- Students may pray or discuss their religious views and attempt to persuade others in informal settings such as cafeterias and hallways, subject to the same rules of order as apply to other student activities and speech.
- School officials may not mandate or organize prayer at graduation or baccalaureate ceremonies.
- Schools may teach about religion as part of courses in history, the arts, culture, and society.

Source: Teacher's Guide to Religion in the Public Schools. Washington, DC: Department of U.S. Education, 1999.

in 1999 the Kansas state board of education removed evolution from the science standards. This action then became a major election issue, since in Kansas state board members are elected, and several conservative board members lost. As can readily be seen in Figure 6.4, a clear majority of the public support the teaching of evolution. In fact 83 percent of those surveyed believed that evolution should be taught in school, while fewer than 30 percent wanted creationism taught as science in public schools.

Regardless of past Supreme Court decisions, some topics, such as the posting of the Ten Commandments in classrooms and Bible reading in public schools, continue to be challenged by legislatures, individuals, and various groups. The intensity of the feelings on both sides is reflected in the *Education in the News* story presented at the beginning of this chapter. One of the outcomes of the ongoing challenges is an accumulating series of judicial interpretations that can serve as guidelines about what can and cannot be done. The summary statements presented in Figure 6.5 outline the overall pattern of the many judicial decisions related to religion and the public schools.

FIGURE 6.4 PUBLIC SUPPORT FOR THE TEACHING OF EVOLUTION

QUESTION: "The Kansas state board of education has recently voted to delete evolution from their new state science standards. Do you support or oppose the decision?"

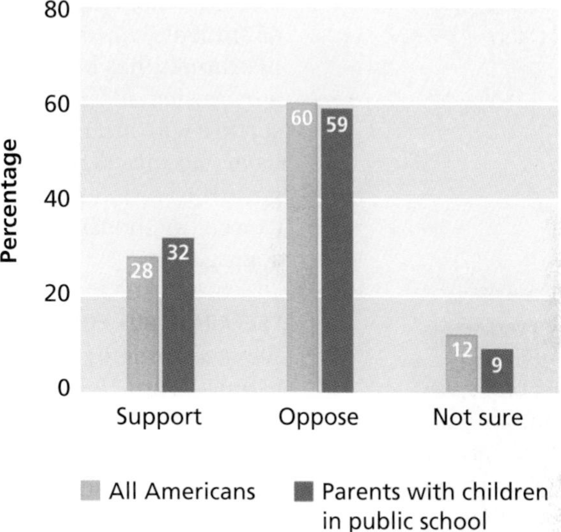

Source: People for the American Way Foundation.

SEGREGATION AND DESEGREGATION

A troublesome problem for American society has been the history of legal and social separation of people based on their race; in other words, **segregation.** Up until the middle of the twentieth century the public school systems in many states contributed to

Multiethnic education requires reform of the total school.

James A. Banks

FIGURE 6.5 SUMMARY STATEMENTS ON CHURCH AND STATE AND THE PRACTICE OF RELIGION IN PUBLIC SCHOOLS

To teach the Bible as a religion course in the public schools is illegal, but to teach about the Bible as part of the history of literature is legal.

To dismiss children from public schools for one hour once a week for religious instruction at religious centers is legal.

Reading of scripture and reciting prayers as religious exercises are in violation of the establishment clause.

Public schools may teach the scientific theory of evolution as a theory; a state may not require that the biblical version of evolution be taught.

If school facilities are made available to one group, then they must be made available to all other groups of the same general type.

segregation
Legal and social separation of people on the basis of their race.

this problem through the operation of two separate sets of schools, one for whites and one for African Americans ("Negroes"). Segregated schools were supported by state laws and by the official actions of state and local government administrators. This kind of segregation, based in legal and official actions, is called **de jure segregation.**

Since 1954 the courts and communities have made intensive efforts to abolish the racial segregation of school students, a process that has been called **desegregation.** A major instrument that the courts have used to accomplish this end has been **integration,** the busing of students to achieve a balanced number of students, in terms of race, in each school within a school district. A second instrument has been the use of magnet schools, which are schools that emphasize particular curriculum areas, disciplines, or themes. The hope is that these schools will attract a diverse set of students. These efforts to integrate the schools have had mixed success, and now there is increasing concern over the **resegregation** of schools based on where people live. Segregation—or resegregation—caused by housing patterns and other nonlegal factors is called **de facto segregation.**

de jure segregation
The segregation of students on the basis of law, school policy, or a practice designed to accomplish such separation.

desegregation
The process of correcting illegal segregation.

integration
The process of mixing students of different races in school.

resegregation
A situation in which formerly integrated schools become segregated again because of changes in neighborhood population patterns.

de facto segregation
The segregation of students resulting from circumstances such as housing patterns rather than law or school policy.

"SEPARATE BUT EQUAL": NO LONGER EQUAL Before 1954 many states had laws either requiring or permitting racial segregation in public schools (de jure segregation). Until 1954 lower courts adhered to the doctrine of "separate but equal" as announced by the Supreme Court in *Plessy* v. *Ferguson* (1896). In *Plessy* v. *Ferguson* the Court upheld a Louisiana law that required railway companies to provide separate but equal accommodations for the African American and white races. The Court's reasoning at that time was that the Fourteenth Amendment implied political, not social, equality.

THE FAILURE OF THE SEPARATE-BUT-EQUAL DOCTRINE This separate-but-equal doctrine appeared to be the rule until May 17, 1954, when the Supreme Court repudiated it in *Brown* v. *Board of Education of Topeka.* The Court said that in education the separate-but-equal doctrine has no place and that separate facilities are inherently unequal. In 1955 the Court rendered the second *Brown* v. *Board of Education of Topeka* decision, requiring that the principles of the first decision be carried out with all deliberate speed.

From 1954, the time of the *Brown* decision, to 1964, little progress was made in eliminating segregated schools. On May 25, 1964, referring to a situation in Prince Edward County, Virginia, the Supreme Court said, "There has been entirely too much deliberation and not enough speed in enforcing the constitutional rights which we held in *Brown* v. *Board of Education.*" The Civil Rights Act of 1964 added legislative power to the 1954 judicial pronouncement. The act not only authorized the federal government to initiate court suits against school districts that were laggard in desegregating schools but also denied federal funds for programs that discriminated by race, color, or national origin.

Subsequently, many types of efforts have been made to meet the expectations of the Court decisions and legislation. The objective of these initiatives has been to promote integration, that is, to achieve a representative mix of students of different races in schools. In the more than forty years since *Brown* there have been many efforts by school districts and communities, and many additional lawsuits. Figure 6.6 summarizes some key Supreme Court decisions on school desegregation and integration.

FIGURE 6.6 SUMMARY STATEMENTS ON SEGREGATION AND DESEGREGATION

The assignment of a child to a school on the basis of race is in violation of the equal protection clause of the Fourteenth Amendment.

Where school boards have indirectly contributed to segregated communities, the school district can be required to desegregate.

Desegregation plans that have the effect of delaying integration of the school have not been upheld by the courts.

Busing may be required for the operation of a desegregated school system.

Once a school district has been fully desegregated, the school board does not need to draw up a new plan if resegregation occurs because of demographic shifts.

The merger of school districts may be required where the involved districts helped create the segregated school systems.

The neighborhood school concept is not in conflict with the Equal Protection Clause.

Once the district has achieved desegregation in all facets of school operations, it can be released from court supervision.

RELEASE FROM COURT ORDERS After forty-plus years of court actions related to desegregation and school district responses, questions were raised about the conditions that must be in place for a school district to be released from federal court supervision. Three cases in the 1990s offered instances of conditions under which the courts would back away. *Board of Education of Oklahoma City Public Schools* v. *Dowell* (1991) is important for at least three reasons: First, the U.S. Supreme Court made it clear that "federal supervision of local school systems was intended as a temporary measure to remedy past discrimination." Second, the Court stated that in relation to desegregation, "the District Court should look not only at student assignments, but to every facet of school operations—faculty, staff, transportation, extracurricular activities and facilities." And third, for the first time, the Court defined what full compliance with a desegregation order would mean:

> In the present case, a finding by the District Court that the Oklahoma City School District was being operated in compliance with the commands of the equal protection clause of the Fourteenth Amendment, and that it was unlikely that the school board would return to its former ways, would be finding that the purposes of the desegregation litigation had been fully achieved.

Two other cases added additional clarity to what the Court expects in order to release a school district from supervision. In *Freeman* v. *Pitts* (1992) the U.S. Supreme Court ruled that districts do not have to remedy racial imbalances caused by demographic changes, but the districts still have the burden of proving that their actions do not contribute to the imbalances. The third case was a return to *Brown.* The Court had ordered the 10th Circuit Court to

Attempts to integrate students of different races by busing them to schools outside their own neighborhoods have proven to be a difficult and emotional issue for communities.

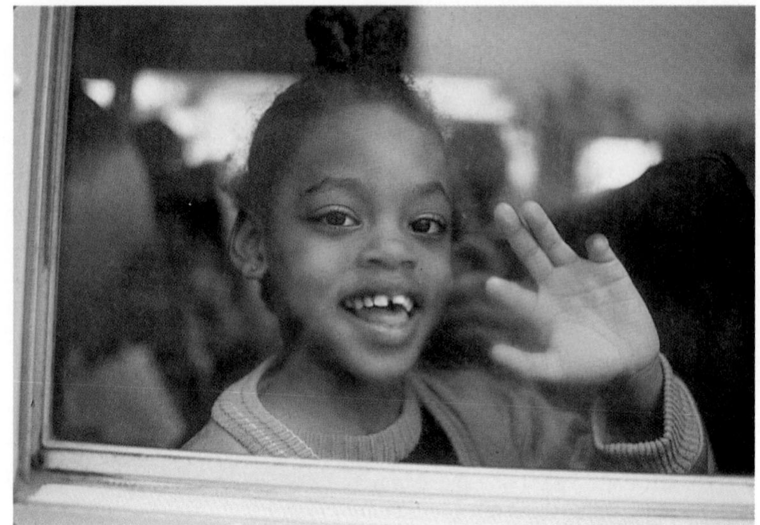

reexamine its 1989 finding that the Topeka district remained segregated. In 1992 the Appellate Court refused to declare Topeka successful. The court concluded that the district had done little to fulfill the duty to desegregate that was first imposed on it in 1954. The judges wrote that to expect the vestiges of segregation to "magically dissolve" with so little effort "is to expect too much."

These three cases in combination made it clear that it is possible for school districts to be released from court order. The decisions also made it clear that school districts have to make concerted efforts across time to address any and all remnants of de jure segregation. Further, it now appears that school districts are not expected to resolve those aspects of de facto segregation that are clearly beyond their control.

A fourth case, which seems to be never ending, is that of Kansas City, Missouri. In 1977 a group of parents sued to force improvements in the city's schools. In 1984 a court ruling stated that the city and state had not done enough to erase the remnants of a segregated school system. Since then, more than $2 billion has been spent on developing state-of-the-art schools that include Olympic-size swimming pools, indoor running tracks, and computers. Teacher salaries were increased, class sizes were reduced, and a wide range of special programs were established. However, there has been little success in either attracting or retaining white students, and student academic success has not improved. In 1995, by a five-to-four vote, the Supreme Court overturned a federal judge's order that the state pay for two costly aspects (tuition and transportation for suburbanites) of Kansas City's massive desegregation program. Up to this point, the state, as well as local taxpayers, had been paying for the desegregation initiative. In November 1999 a U.S. District judge dismissed the case; then in March 2000 the U.S. Court of Appeals for the 8th District reinstated the then twenty-three-year-old desegregation case. In May 2000 the state moved closer to taking over operation of the district or breaking it up by removing the district's accreditation. At that time student test scores had not improved, and the district was 72 percent black, with seven out of ten students from low-income families. This continuing saga illustrates how difficult and problematic the interplay of race, poverty, economics, law, and politics can be when schools are placed at the center of social reform.

INTEGRATION FIFTY YEARS LATER At present there are more than 500 formerly segregated school districts under some federal court jurisdiction. Table 6.3 presents a summary of the legal reasoning behind several key cases. Unfortunately, while de jure segregation has been removed, it has been replaced in many situations with a more virulent form of segregation. The demographics and economic conditions of the country have changed in ways that have not facilitated integration in local schools. Many strategies have been tested, and there are some indicators of success, but the goal is still a dream in many ways.

THE RISK OF RESEGREGATION Currently, there is concern in several regions of the country about apparent trends toward resegregation, which occurs when a recently integrated school population returns to being almost totally a minority school population. The historic progress that has been made toward integration

TABLE 6.3 SELECTED U.S. SUPREME COURT CASES RELATED TO SCHOOL DESEGREGATION AND INTEGRATION

Case	Issue	Decision
Plessy v. *Ferguson* (1896)	Whether a railway company should be required to provide equal accommodations for African American and white races	The Court indicated in its decision that the Fourteenth Amendment implied political, not social, equality. Thus the doctrine of "separate but equal" was established.
Brown v. *Board of Education of Topeka* (1954)	Legality of separate school facilities	The separate-but-equal doctrine has no place in education, and dual school systems (de jure segregation) are inherently unequal.
Griffin v. *County School Board of Prince Edward County* (1964)	Whether a county may close its schools and provide assistance to private schools for whites only	The Court instructed the local district court to require the authorities to levy taxes to reopen and operate a nondiscriminatory public school system.
Board of Education of Oklahoma City Public Schools v. *Dowell* (1991)	The conditions under which a school district may be relieved of court supervision	Court supervision was to continue until segregation was removed from every facet of school operations.
Freeman v. *Pitts* (1992)	Whether court supervision may be withdrawn incrementally, and whether a school district is responsible for segregation based on demographic changes (de facto segregation)	A district court is permitted to withdraw supervision in discrete categories in which the district has achieved compliance; also "the school district is under no duty to remedy imbalance that is caused by demographic factors."

Federal statutes and court cases have ensured equal opportunity for all the students in this class.

of African Americans appears to be slowly eroding because of a combination of demographic, economic, and social factors. In addition, more Hispanic students are attending schools with decreasing proportions of white students. Interpreting these trends is difficult. Still, there is reason to be concerned if this trend toward resegregation continues.

THE SUCCESSES OF THE DESEGREGATION AGENDA Desegregation has had some measurable benefits. For example, African Americans who graduate from integrated schools have higher incomes than those who graduate from segregated schools. They are more likely to graduate from college and to hold good jobs. In addition, the number of middle-class black families is growing. Still, there is a long way to go before the dream of full socioeconomic equality is achieved. It seems certain that schools will continue to be a primary vehicle for advancing this dream from the points of view of the courts.

EQUAL OPPORTUNITY

The Equal Protection Clause of the Fourteenth Amendment has been instrumental in shaping many court cases and federal statutes that are directed toward preventing discrimination in schools. A judgment of **discrimination** can be defined as a determination that an individual or a group of individuals—for example, African Americans, women, or handicapped people—has been denied constitutional rights. In common usage the term applies to various minorities or to individual members of a minority who lack rights typically accorded the majority. The principle that discrimination violates the Equal Protection Clause was reinforced in Titles VI and VII of the Civil Rights Act of 1964 and in Title IX of the Education Amendments Act of 1972. Title VI of the Civil Rights Act states:

> No person in the United States shall, on the ground of race, color, or national origin, be excluded from participation in, be denied the benefits of, or be subjected to discrimination under any program or activity receiving federal financial assistance.

discrimination
Denial of constitutional rights to an individual or a group.

Title VII states:

> It shall be an unlawful employment practice for an employer (1) to fail or refuse to hire or to discharge any individual, or otherwise to discriminate against any individual with respect to his compensation, terms, conditions, or privileges of employment, because of such individual's race, color, religion, sex, or national origin; or (2) to limit, segregate, or classify his employees or applicants for employment in any way which would deprive or tend to deprive any individual of employment opportunities or otherwise adversely affect his status as an employee, because of such individual's race, color, religion, sex, or national origin.

Title IX of the Education Amendments Act of 1972 states:

> No person in the United States shall, on the basis of sex, be excluded from participation in, be denied the benefits of, or be subjected to discrimination under any education program or activity receiving federal financial assistance.

AFFIRMATIVE ACTION In the years since the 1964 Civil Rights Act, numerous statutes and court cases have encouraged steps designed to ensure that underrepresented populations have equal opportunity. These **affirmative action** initiatives have included such actions as formalizing and publicizing nondiscriminatory hiring procedures and setting aside a certain number of slots in hiring or college admission programs. Over time, concern has increased about the possibility of **reverse discrimination**—situations in which a majority or an individual member of a majority is not accorded equal rights because of different or preferential treatment provided to a minority or an individual member of a minority. This concern has resulted in a new set of court cases, such as *University of California* v. *Bakke* (1978), each of which is attempting to redress what is perceived as a new imbalance.

The legal basis for affirmative action is found in Titles VI and VII of the Civil Rights Act of 1964 and in Title IX of the Education Amendments Act of 1972. However, affirmative action procedures and methods continue to be clarified and, in some instances, questioned. For example, in 1996 the citizens of California passed Proposition 209, which bans the state and its local governments from using racial and gender preferences in hiring, contracting, and college admissions. Proposition 209 and other legal initiatives will be examined in the courts.

affirmative action
Policies and procedures designed to compensate for past discrimination against women and members of minority groups; for example, assertive recruiting and admission practices.

reverse discrimination
A situation in which a majority or an individual of a majority is denied certain rights because of preferential treatment provided to a minority or an individual of a minority.

OPPORTUNITIES FOR STUDENTS WITH DISABILITIES The judicial basis for current approaches to the education of students with disabilities also is closely linked to the civil rights and equal opportunity initiatives. In addition, several specifically targeted statutes address the education of people with disabilities. Three statutes that are particularly important are Section 504 of the Rehabilitation Act; Public Law 94-142, the Education for All Handicapped Children Act (EAHCA); and the Individuals with Disabilities Education Act (IDEA)

SECTION 504 OF THE REHABILITATION ACT Under this civil rights act established in 1973, recipients of federal funds are prohibited from discriminating against "otherwise qualified individuals." Note that Section 504 is a federal statute and regulations, not a court decision. Three important themes addressed in Section 504 are Equal Treatment, Appropriate Education, and Handicapped Persons. Equal Treatment, as in other civil rights contexts, must be addressed. However, this does not necessarily mean the same treatment. For example, giving the same assessment procedure to students with disabilities and other students may not be equal treatment. Educational judgments in relation to students with disabilities require a "heightened standard." The measures must fit the students' circumstances, and procedural safeguards must be employed. Appropriate Education means that the school system and related parties must address individual needs of students with disabilities as adequately as do the education approaches for other students. In Section 504, a "handicapped person" is

> Any person who (i) has a physical or mental impairment which substantially limits one or more major life activities, (ii) has a record of such an impairment, or (iii) is regarded as having such an impairment. (34 CFR 104.3)

PUBLIC LAW 94-142 (EAHCA) Passed by Congress in 1975, Public Law 94-142 has been amended several times since. This law assures "a free appropriate public education" to all children with disabilities between the ages of three and twenty-one. Children with exceptional needs cannot be excluded from education because of their needs. The law is very specific in describing the kind and quality of education and in stating that each child with a disability is to have an individually planned education. Details of this plan must be spelled out in a written Individualized Education Plan (IEP), formulated by general and special education teachers, and subject to the parents' approval. Originally, the law provided for substantial increases in funding; in subsequent years, however, the funding authorizations have been lower than the original commitment. Two priorities for funding were identified: (1) the child who currently receives no education and (2) the child who is not receiving all the services he or she needs to succeed. These priorities place the emphasis on need rather than on the specific disability.

THE INDIVIDUALS WITH DISABILITIES EDUCATION ACT (IDEA) This act (1992) developed tighter specifications for the delivery of education services to children with disabilities. At the time more than half of children with disabilities were not receiving appropriate educational services. The purpose of IDEA is to make available to all children with disabilities a free appropriate public education. IDEA establishes at the federal level an Office of Special Education Programs headed by a deputy assistant secretary. Further, the act makes clear that states shall not be immune under the Eleventh Amendment of the Constitution from suit in federal court for a violation of the act. The act encourages the education of individuals with disabilities by making grants to states and local education agencies for children aged three to five, requires the federal government to be responsive to the increasing ethnic diversity of society and those with limited English proficiency, and funds programs to provide education to all children with disabilities.

AIDS AS A DISABILITY The 1990 Americans with Disabilities Act expanded the definition of *disability* in such a way as to include people with AIDS. Also, under IDEA the courts have found that AIDS is a disabling condition. AIDS is an issue charged with emotion, as was desegregation. People do not always approach these difficult situations with calmness or equanimity. The courts, as well as school administrators and teachers, are constantly struggling to determine what

PROFESSIONAL DILEMMA

What Will You Do If a Child in Your Classroom Has AIDS?

The arrival of AIDS has caused widespread concern, major new directions in medical research, and alarm in communities where there has been limited knowledge and understanding. The health threat to all, including teachers and students, is real. Teachers need to become sufficiently informed that they and their students can be protected from the risk of infection and at the same time not be seen as creating unnecessary alarm. Knowing what to do and not to do if an AIDS-infected child or adult is attending your school is very important.

There are several sides to this issue. First of all, as has been pointed out in this chapter, *all* children have a legal right to attend public school (see the U.S. Constitution and your state's constitution). And the school is responsible for providing an appropriate education to all children (see PL 94-142, IDEA, and Section 504).

It is important to learn the truth about the potential for other children, and you, to become infected through casual contact with a child who is HIV-positive or has AIDS. Becoming infected through casual contact with someone who has AIDS is impossible. To contract HIV, the AIDS virus, one must be in contact with blood (such as bleeding from the nose, gums, cuts, or open sores) or other body fluids. Transmission of AIDS through sex and the sharing of needles and razors is well documented. Even when there is contact with contaminated blood on the skin or mucus membranes in the nose or mouth, infection is rare. There are no known cases of the AIDS virus being transmitted through eating utensils or bathroom facilities. However, if an infected child is injured and starts to bleed, then preventive actions are necessary.

The Centers for Disease Control (CDC) recommends that spilled blood *always* be treated as though it contains disease. Always wear latex gloves when wiping up blood. Contaminated surfaces should be cleaned with a solution of 1 part bleach diluted with 10 parts water. If you want more information about AIDS, the CDC operates a 24-hour toll-free hot line seven days a week (800) 342-2437.

- What should you do to familiarize yourself with the steps and resources that your school has in place for responding to any accident that might happen?
- As a teacher, how will you respond to a child in your classroom who has been identified as HIV-positive?
- What will you do to ensure that the other children in your classroom treat the infected child equitably?

is appropriate education for students with AIDS and what are suitable educational environments for children with AIDS-related disabilities. Some exceptional and spiritually strong children, such as Ryan White, have challenged the educational system's capabilities. Ryan White was an Indiana adolescent with AIDS who, because of attitudes within his school, was forced to leave town. Because of Ryan's example, others with disabilities will have the courage to challenge the limits of school systems. In these situations educators, the courts, and policymakers will be further tested—but at the same time will have the opportunity to move the educational system ahead by developing creative approaches and innovative practices. Calm heads will be needed, as will wisdom from all the players, for the education system to succeed for all its students.

TEACHERS' RIGHTS AND RESPONSIBILITIES

Teachers have the same rights as other citizens. The Fourteenth Amendment gives every citizen the right to **due process** of law: both *substantive due process* (protection against the deprivation of constitutional rights such as freedom of expression) and *procedural due process* (procedural protection against unjustified deprivation of substantive rights). Most court cases related to teachers evolve from either liberty or property interests. Liberty interests are created by the Constitution itself; property interests are found in forms of legal entitlement such as tenure or certification.

Teachers also have the same responsibilities as other citizens. They must abide by federal, state, and local laws and by the provisions of contracts. As professionals, they must also assume the heavy responsibility of educating young people. We will discuss specific court cases briefly here to illustrate some of the issues and decisions related to aspects of teacher rights and responsibilities. Note that the cases selected do not necessarily constitute the last word regarding teacher rights but rather provide an overview of some of the issues that have been decided in the courts. Table 6.4 summarizes the issues and decisions in selected cases involving teacher rights and responsibilities. This summary table is not intended to provide a complete understanding of the court decisions cited; please read the text for better comprehension. Note also that most of the court cases were decided in the 1970s and 1980s; more recently, new federal statutes have been the defining force.

CONDITIONS OF EMPLOYMENT

Many conditions must be met for you to be hired as a teacher. These include your successfully completing a professional preparation program, being credentialed or licensed by the state, and receiving a contract from the hiring school district. In each of these instances you have rights established in law and statute, as well as responsibilities.

due process
The legal procedures that must be followed to safeguard individuals from arbitrary, capricious, or unreasonable policies, practices, or actions.

teacher certification and licensure
The process whereby each state determines the requirements for certification and for obtaining a license to teach.

TEACHER CERTIFICATION AND LICENSURE The primary purpose of **teacher certification and licensure** is to make sure there are qualified and competent teachers in the public schools. Certification laws usually require, in addition, that the candidate show evidence of citizenship, good moral character, and good physical health. A minimum age is frequently specified. All states have established requirements for teacher certification and licensure. Carrying out the policies of certification is usually a function of a state professional standards board. The board first has to make certain that applicants meet legal requirements; it then issues the appropriate license/certificates. Certifying agencies may not arbitrarily refuse to issue a certificate to a qualified candidate. The courts have ruled that local boards of education may prescribe additional or higher qualifications beyond the state requirements, provided that such requirements are not irrelevant, unreasonable, or arbitrary. A teaching certificate or license is a privilege that enables a person to practice a profession—It is not a right. But teacher certification is a property interest that cannot be revoked without constitutional due process.

TABLE 6.4 Selected U.S. Supreme Court Decisions Related to Teachers' Rights and Responsibilities

Case	Issue	Decision
Discrimination		
North Haven Board of Education v. *Bell* (1982)	Allegation by former women faculty members of sex discrimination in employment	Court ruled that school employees as well as students are protected under Title IX.
Cleveland Board of Education v. *LeFleur* (1974)	Rights of pregnant teachers	Court struck down the board policy forcing all pregnant teachers to take mandatory maternity leave.
Burkey v. *Marshall County Board of Education* (1981)	Paying female coaches half the salary of male coaches	Court ruled that the policy violated the Equal Pay Act, Title VII of the Civil Rights Act of 1964.
Contract Rights		
Board of Regents of State Colleges v. *Roth* (1972)	Rights of nontenured teachers	Teacher had been hired under a one-year contract. Court concluded that he did not have a property interest that would entitle him to procedural rights under the Fourteenth Amendment.
Perry v. *Sindermann* (1972)	Rights of nontenured teachers	Court ruled that a state employee may acquire the property interest if officially fostered customs, rules, understandings, and practices imply a contract promise to grant continuing contract status and thus establish a de facto tenure system.
Bargaining		
Hortonville Joint School District No. 1 v. *Hortonville Education Association* (1976)	Rights of boards of education to dismiss teachers who are striking illegally	Court said the law gave the board power to employ and dismiss teachers as a part of the municipal labor relations balance.
Lehnert v. *Ferris Faculty Association* (1991)	Obligation of nonunion members to pay union dues	Court ruled that nonunion teachers must pay a "service fee" for their pro rata share of the costs of activities of the state and national affiliates, but not for lobbying or other political activities.
Academic Freedom		
Pickering v. *Board of Education* (1968)	Dismissal of an Illinois teacher for criticizing a school board and superintendent in a letter published by a local newspaper	Court upheld teacher's claim that his First and Fourteenth Amendment rights were denied.

A big moment; signing a contract to teach is a professional commitment by the teacher and a legal one for the school district.

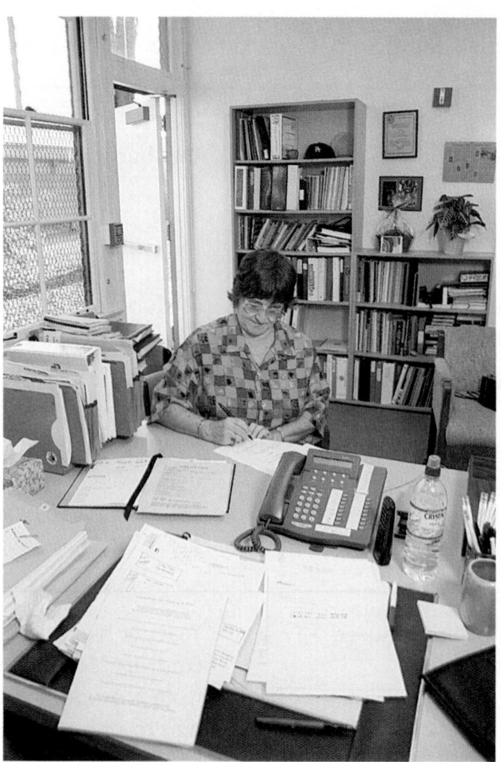

TEACHER EMPLOYMENT CONTRACTS Usually, boards of education have the statutory authority to employ teachers. This authority includes the power to enter into contracts and to fix terms of employment and compensation. In some states, only specific members of the school board may sign teacher contracts. When statutes confer the employing authority to boards of education, the authority cannot be delegated. It is usually the responsibility of the superintendent to screen and nominate candidates to the board. The board, meeting in official session, then acts officially as a group to enter into contractual agreement. Employment procedures vary from state to state, but the process is fundamentally prescribed by the legislature and must be strictly followed by local boards.

A contract usually contains the following elements: the identification of the teacher and the board of education, a statement of the legal capacity of each party to enter into the contract, a definition of the assignment specified, a statement of the salary and how it is to be paid, and a provision for signature by the teacher and by the legally authorized agents of the board. In some states, contract forms are provided by state departments of education, and these forms must be used; in others, each district establishes its own.

Teachers are responsible for making certain that they are legally qualified to enter into contractual agreements. For example, a teacher may not enter into a legal contract without having a valid teaching certificate issued by the state. Furthermore, teachers are responsible for carrying out the terms of the contract and abiding by them. In turn, under the contract they can legally expect proper treatment from an employer.

TEACHER TENURE Teacher tenure legislation exists in most states. In many states, tenure or fair dismissal laws are mandatory and apply to all school districts without exception. In other states they do not. The various laws differ not only in extent of coverage but also in provision for coverage.

tenure
A system of school employment in which educators retain their positions indefinitely unless they are dismissed for legally specified reasons through clearly established procedures.

Tenure laws are intended to provide security for teachers in their positions and to prevent removal of capable teachers by capricious action or political motive. Tenure statutes generally include detailed specifications necessary for granting tenure and for dismissing teachers who have tenure. These statutes have been upheld when attacked on constitutional grounds. The courts reason that because state legislatures create school districts, they have the right to limit their power.

BECOMING TENURED AND TENURE RIGHTS A teacher becomes tenured by serving satisfactorily for a stated time. This period is referred to as the probationary period and typically is three years. The actual process of acquiring tenure after serving the probationary period depends on the applicable statute. In some states the process is automatic at the satisfactory completion of the probationary period; in other states, official action by the school board is necessary. Teachers may be dismissed for any one of numerous reasons, including "nonperformance of duty, incompetency, insubordination, conviction of crimes involving moral turpitude, failure to comply with reasonable orders, violation of contract provisions or local rules or regulations, persistent failure or refusal to maintain orderly discipline of students, and revocation of the teaching certificate."[1]

A school board in Tennessee dismissed Jane Turk from her tenured teaching position after she was arrested for driving under the influence of alcohol (DUI).[2] Turk's appeal was upheld by the lower-court judge because there was no evidence of an adverse effect on her capacity and fitness as a teacher. The school board appealed to the Tennessee Supreme Court, which rejected the board's appeal, finding that the school board "acted in flagrant disregard of the statutory requirement and fundamental fairness in considering matters that should have been specifically charged in writing." Tennessee law requires that before a tenured teacher can be dismissed, "the charges shall be made in writing specifically stating the offenses which are charged." Nevertheless, teacher tenure may be affected by teacher conduct outside school as well as inside. This issue, in a sense, deals with the personal freedom of teachers: freedom to behave as other citizens do, freedom to engage in political activities, and academic freedom in the classroom.

Tenure laws are frequently attacked by those who claim that they protect incompetent teachers. There is undoubtedly some truth in the assertion, but it must be stated clearly and unequivocally that these laws also protect the competent and most able teachers. Teachers who accept the challenge of their profession and dare to use new methods, who inspire curiosity in their students, and who discuss controversial issues in their classrooms need protection from politically motivated or capricious dismissal. Incompetent teachers, whether tenured or not, can be dismissed under the law by capable administrators and careful school boards that allow due process while evaluating teacher performance.

RIGHTS OF NONTENURED TEACHERS Although due process has been applicable for years to tenured teachers, nontenured teachers do not, for the most part, enjoy the same rights. Tenured teachers enjoy two key rights: protection from dismissal except for cause as provided in state statutes, and the right to prescribed procedures, also spelled out in the statutes. Nontenured teachers may also have due process rights, if these are spelled out in state statutes; however, in states that do not provide for due process, nontenured teachers may be nonrenewed without any reasons being given. If a nontenured teacher is dismissed (as distinguished from nonrenewed) before the expiration of the contract, the teacher is entitled to due process. But most states make only perfunctory provisions, such as specified calendar dates for nonrenewal of contracts. Cases in Massachusetts[3] and Wisconsin[4] point to the necessity of following due process in dismissing nontenured teachers. In the Massachusetts case the court said: "The particular circumstances of a dismissal of a public school teacher provide compelling reasons for application of a doctrine of procedural due process."[5] In the Wisconsin case the court said:

> A teacher in a public elementary or secondary school is protected by the due process clause of the Fourteenth Amendment against a nonrenewal decision which is wholly without basis in fact and also against a decision which is wholly unreasoned, as well as a decision which is impermissibly based.

In 1972 the Supreme Court helped to clarify the difference between the rights of tenured and nontenured teachers. In one case (*Board of Regents* v. *Roth,* 1972) it held that nontenured teachers were assured of no rights that were not specified in state statutes. In this instance the only right that probationary teachers had was the one to be notified of nonrenewal by a specified date. In a second case the Court ruled that a nontenured teacher in the Texas system of community colleges was entitled to due process because the language of the institution's policy manual was such that an unofficial tenure system was in effect. Guidelines in the policy manual provided that a faculty member with seven years of employment in the system acquired tenure and could be dismissed only for cause (*Perry* v. *Sindermann,* 1972).

Whether a teacher is tenured or not, that person cannot be dismissed for exercise of a right guaranteed by the U.S. Constitution. A school board cannot dismiss a teacher, for example, for engaging in civil rights activities outside school, speaking on matters of public concern, belonging to a given church, or running for public office. These rights are guaranteed to all citizens, including teachers. However, if a teacher's behavior is disruptive or dishonest, a school board can dismiss the person without violating the right to freedom of speech.

DISCRIMINATION School districts are prohibited from use of discriminatory practices in the hiring, dismissal, promotion, and demotion of school personnel. In addition to court decisions, federal statutes, such as the Civil Rights Acts of 1964 and 1991, have had a defining influence on the legal basis for judgments of discrimination. For example, the 1991 law expanded protection beyond race to include discrimination based on sex, disability, medical conditions, religion, and national origin. Further, employment decisions must be "job-related for the position in question." The 1991 law also places the burden on the defendant (schools) to show that a legitimate nondiscriminatory reason exists for any personnel decision that may be challenged.

RIGHT TO BARGAIN COLLECTIVELY The right of teachers to bargain collectively has been an active issue since the 1960s. In the past, teacher groups met informally with boards of education to discuss salaries and other teacher welfare provisions. Sometimes the superintendent was even the spokesperson for such teacher groups. In more recent years, however, formal collective procedures have evolved. These procedures have been labeled collective bargaining, professional negotiation, cooperative determination, and collective negotiation. Teachers' groups have defined collective bargaining as a way of winning improved goals and not the goal itself. The right of employees to bargain collectively and the obligation of the district to bargain are not constitutionally granted but are typically guaranteed by statute.

A contract arrived at by a teachers' union means that salaries, working conditions, and other matters within the scope of the collective bargaining agreement can no longer be decided unilaterally by the school administration and board of education. Instead, the contract outlines how the teachers' union and its members will participate in formulating the school policies and programs under which they work.

The first teachers' group to bargain collectively with its local board of education was the Maywood, Illinois, Proviso Council of West Suburban Teachers, Union Local 571, in 1938. In 1957 a second local, the East St. Louis, Illinois, Federation of Teachers was successful in negotiating a written contract. The breakthrough, however, came in December 1961, when the United Federation of Teachers, Local 2 of the American Federation of Teachers (AFT), won the right to bargain for New York City's teachers. Since then, collective bargaining agreements between boards of education and teacher groups have grown phenomenally. Both the AFT and the National Education Association (NEA) have been active in promoting collective bargaining. Today, approximately 75 percent of the nation's teachers are covered by collective bargaining agreements.

RIGHT TO STRIKE Judges have generally held that public employees do not have the right to strike. For example, the Supreme Court of Connecticut,[6] and the Supreme Court of New Hampshire[7] ruled that teachers may not strike. The court opinion in Connecticut stated:

> Under our system, the government is established by and run for all of the people, not for the benefit of any person or group. The profit motive, inherent in the principle of free enterprise, is absent. It should be the aim of every employee of the government to do his or her part to make it function as efficiently and economically as possible. The drastic remedy or the organized strike to enforce the demands of unions of government employees is in direct contravention of this principle.

At least eight states—Alaska, Hawaii, Illinois, Minnesota, Ohio, Oregon, Pennsylvania, and Wisconsin—do permit strikes in their collective bargaining statutes. At least twenty states have statutes that prohibit strikes, however. And whether or not there are specific statutes prohibiting strikes, boards of education threatened by strikes can usually get a court injunction forestalling them. Both the NEA and the AFT view the strike as a last-resort technique, although justifiable in some circumstances.

Although the number of collective bargaining agreements between boards of education and teacher groups have grown phenomenally, many states have statutes that prohibit teachers from striking.

In 1976, by a six-to-three vote, the U.S. Supreme Court ruled that boards of education can discharge teachers who are striking illegally. Ramifications of this decision, which involved a Wisconsin public school, are potentially far-reaching. The Court viewed discharge as a policy question rather than an issue for adjudication: "What choice among the alternative responses to the teachers' strike will best serve the interests of the school system, the interests of the parents and children who depend on the system, and the interests of the citizens whose taxes support it?" The Court said the state law in question gave the board the power to employ and dismiss teachers as a part of the balance it had struck in municipal labor relations (*Hortonville Joint School District No. 1* v. *Hortonville Education Association,* 1976).

One can argue that strikes are unlawful when a statute is violated, that the courts in their decisions have questioned the right of public employees to strike, and that some teachers and teacher organizations consider strikes unprofessional. In any given case the question before teachers seems to be whether the strike is a justifiable and responsible means—after all other ways have been exhausted—of declaring abominable educational and working conditions and trying to remedy them.

ACADEMIC FREEDOM

A sensitive and vital concern to the educator is **academic freedom**—freedom to control what one will teach and to teach the truth as one discovers it, without fear of penalty. Academic freedom is thus essentially a principle of pedagogical philosophy that has been applied to a variety of professional activities. A philosophical position, however, is *not necessarily* a legal right.[8] Federal judges have generally recognized certain academic protections in the college classroom while exhibiting reluctance to recognize such rights for elementary and secondary school teachers. For example, the contract of a history teacher at the University of Arkansas–Little Rock was not renewed after he announced that he taught his classes from a Marxist point of view. The court ordered that the teacher be reinstated in light of the university's failure to advance convincing reasons related to the academic freedom issue to warrant his nonrenewal.[9] In another case a university instructor claimed that he was denied tenure because he refused to change a student's grade. He argued that awarding a course grade was the instructor's right of academic freedom. Because the university had given several valid reasons for the nonrenewal of the instructor's contract, however, the court did not order a reinstatement.[10]

ACADEMIC FREEDOM FOR ELEMENTARY AND SECONDARY TEACHERS Although federal courts generally have not recognized academic freedom for elementary and secondary school teachers, the most supportive ruling was made in 1980[11] in a case that involved a high school history teacher whose contract was not renewed after she used a simulation game to introduce her students to the characteristics of rural life during the post–Civil War Reconstruction era. Although the role playing evoked controversy in the school and the community, there was no evidence that the teacher's usefulness had been impaired. Therefore, the school erred in not renewing the teacher's contract, and she was ordered reinstated.

academic freedom
The opportunity for a teacher to teach without coercion, censorship, or other restrictive interference.

In *Pickering* v. *Board of Education* (1968) the U.S. Supreme Court dealt with academic freedom at the public school level. Marvin L. Pickering was a teacher in Illinois who, in a letter published by a local newspaper, criticized the school board and the superintendent for the way they had handled past proposals to raise and use new revenues for the schools. After a full hearing, the board of education terminated Pickering's employment, whereupon he brought suit under the First and Fourteenth Amendments. The Illinois courts rejected his claim. The U.S. Supreme Court, however, upheld Pickering's claim and, in its opinion, stated:

> To the extent that the Illinois Supreme Court's opinion may be read to suggest that teachers may constitutionally be compelled to relinquish the First Amendment rights they would otherwise enjoy as citizens to comment on matters of public interest in connection with the operation of the public schools in which they work, it proceeds on a premise that has been unequivocally rejected in numerous prior decisions of this Court.

When standards are set in place, a successful school is one that provides both excellence and equity—a challenging education for every child. When a school adopts high standards for all, it is telling each of its students clearly, 'We respect you and believe that you can learn.'

Diane Ravitch

It is difficult to define precisely the limits of academic freedom. In general, the courts strongly support it yet recognize that teachers must be professionally responsible when interacting with pupils. In most instances teachers are not free to disregard a school board's decision about which textbook to use, but they are able to participate more when it comes to their choice of supplementary methods. Teachers have usually been supported in their rights to criticize the policies of their local school boards, wear symbols representing stated causes, participate in unpopular movements, and live unconventional lifestyles. But where the exercise of these rights can be shown to have a direct bearing on a teacher's effectiveness, respect, or discipline, these rights may have to be curtailed. For example, a teacher may have the right to wear a gothic costume to class, but if the wearing of the outfit leads to disruption and an inability to manage students, the teacher may be ordered to wear more conventional clothes.

In summary, academic freedom for teachers is more limited than it is for higher-education faculty. First Amendment protection of free speech is increasingly limited to a teacher's actions outside of the classroom and school. Before arguing for academic freedom and free speech in the classroom, a teacher must show that she or he did not defy legitimate state and local curriculum directives, followed accepted professional norms and acted in good faith when there was no precedent or policy.

BOOK BANNING AND CENSORSHIP Ever since the United States has had public schools, there have been people who have taken issue with what has been taught, how it has been taught, and the materials used. The number of people challenging these issues and the intensity of their feeling have escalated since the mid-1970s. Well-organized and well-financed pressure groups have opposed the teaching of numerous topics, including political, economic, scientific, and religious theories; the teaching of values grounded in religion, morality, or ethnicity; and the portrayal of stereotypes based on gender, race, or ethnicity. Some complaints have involved differences of opinion over the central role of the school—whether the school's job is to transmit traditional values, indoctrinate students, or teach students to do their own thinking.

Several court cases since the 1970s have involved the legality of removing books from the school curriculum and school libraries. The courts have given some guidance but have not fully resolved the issue. In 1972 a court of appeals held that a book does not acquire tenure, so a school board was upheld in the removal of *Down These Mean Streets.* The seventh circuit court in 1980 upheld the removal of the book *Values Clarification,* ruling that local boards have considerable authority in selecting materials for schools. Removal of books on the basis of the vulgar language they contain has also been upheld.

The U.S. Supreme Court treated this issue in 1982.[12] The decision disappointed people who had hoped that the justices would issue a definitive ruling on banning of books. Instead, Justice William Brennan ruled that students may sue school boards on the grounds of denial of their rights, including the right to receive information. The Court also indicated that removal of a book because one disagrees with its content cannot be upheld. The net effect of this decision was that the school board decided to return the questionable books to the library.

The latest censorhip battleground has to do with limiting access to the World Wide Web. Many school districts and schools are applying filters that restrict access to particular types of websites. New questions related to defining what is meant by "responsible use" and who decides—teachers, principals, or school districts—are now occupying school boards, legislative bodies, and the courts.

LIABILITY FOR NEGLIGENCE

With about 47 million students enrolled in elementary and secondary schools, it is almost inevitable that some will be injured in educational activities. Each year, some injuries will occasion lawsuits in which plaintiffs seek damages. Such suits are often brought against both the school districts and their employees. Legal actions seeking monetary damages for injuries are referred to as *actions in tort.* Technically, a **tort** is a legal wrong—an act (or the omission of an act) that violates the private rights of an individual. Actions in tort are generally based on alleged negligence; the basis of tort liability or legal responsibility is negligence. Understanding the concept of negligence is essential to understanding liability.

Legally, *negligence* is a failure to exercise or practice due care. It includes a factor of foreseeability of harm. Court cases on record involving negligence are numerous and varied. The negligence of teacher supervision of pupils is an important topic that includes supervision of the regular classroom, departure of the teacher from the classroom, supervision of the playground, and supervision of extracurricular activities. **Liability** is the responsibility for negligence—responsibility for the failure to use reasonable care when such failure results in injury to another.

NEGLIGENT CHEMISTRY TEACHER In a California high school chemistry class, pupils were injured while experimenting in the manufacture of gunpowder.[13] The teacher was in the room and had supplemented the laboratory manual instructions with his own directions. Nevertheless, an explosion occurred, allegedly caused by the failure of pupils to follow directions. A court held the teacher and the board of education liable. Negligence in this case meant the lack of supervision of laboratory work, a potentially dangerous activity requiring a high level of "due care."

tort
An act (or the omission of an act) that violates the private rights of an individual.

liability
Responsibility for the failure to use reasonable care when such failure results in injury to another.

FIELD TRIP NEGLIGENCE In Oregon a child was injured while on a field trip.[14] Children were playing on a large log in a relatively dry area on a beach. A large wave surged up onto the beach, dislodging the log, which began to roll. One of the children fell seaward off the log, and the receding wave pulled the log over the child, injuring him. In the subsequent court action the teacher was declared negligent for not having foreseen the possibility of such an occurrence. The court said:

Although negligence is a vague concept, courts have ruled that teachers were responsible in specific cases of injury to students on school field trips.

> The first proposition asks this court to hold, as a matter of fact, that unusual wave action on the shore of the Pacific Ocean is a hazard so unforeseeable that there is no duty to guard against it. On the contrary, we agree with the trial judge, who observed that it is common knowledge that accidents substantially like the one that occurred in this case have occurred at beaches along the Oregon coast. Foreseeability of such harm is not so remote as to be ruled out as a matter of law.

Although liability for negligence is a vague concept involving due care and foreseeability, it is defined more specifically each time a court decides such a case.

GOVERNMENTAL IMMUNITY FROM LIABILITY Historically, school districts have not been held liable for torts resulting from the negligence of their officers, agents, or employees while the school districts are acting in their governmental capacity. That immunity was based on the doctrine that the state is sovereign and cannot be sued without its consent. A school district, as an arm of state government, would therefore be immune from tort liability. Unlike school districts, however, employees of school districts have not been protected by immunity; teachers may be held liable for their actions. Teachers must act as reasonable and prudent people, foreseeing dangerous situations. The degree of care that is required increases with the immaturity of the pupil. Lack of supervision and foresight forms the basis of negligence charges.

Recent decades have seen a trend away from governmental immunity. As of 1986, more than half of the states had abrogated governmental immunity either judicially, statutorily, or through some form of legal modification. There has also been an increase in the number of lawsuits.

LIABILITY INSURANCE Many states authorize school districts to purchase insurance to protect teachers, school districts, administrators, and school board members against suits. It is important that school districts and their employees and board members be thus protected, either through school district insurance or through their own personal policies. The costs of school district liability insurance have increased so dramatically in recent years that many school districts

FIGURE 6.7 SUMMARY STATEMENTS ON TEACHERS' RIGHTS AND RESPONSIBILITIES

Prospective teachers must fulfill the requirements of laws and policies regarding certification before being employed as teachers.

Boards of education have the authority to employ teachers, including the authority to enter into contracts and to fix terms of employment and compensation.

School districts are prohibited from use of discriminatory practices; discrimination in employment and salary of teachers on the basis of sex is in violation of Title IX of the Education Amendments Act.

Most states have tenure laws that provide teachers with protection against arbitrary dismissal; rights of nontenured teachers are found in state laws.

Teachers may speak out on matters of public concern, even in criticism of their school board, as long as their speech is not disruptive or a lie.

Boards of education may remove books from library shelves under their authority to select materials for schools; however, the removal of a book merely because someone disagrees with its content was not upheld by the U.S. Supreme Court.

Many states provide for school boards and teacher unions to bargain collectively on wages, hours, and terms and conditions of employment.

Teacher strikes are unlawful when a statute is violated; in some states it is legal for teachers to strike.

Teachers are expected to exercise due care in foreseeing possible accidents and in working to prevent their occurrence; teachers may be sued for their negligence that led to pupil injury.

are contemplating the elimination of extracurricular activities. Consequently, state legislatures are being pressured to fix liability insurance rates for school districts; they are also being asked to pass laws to limit maximum liability amounts for school-related cases. For teachers, membership in the state affiliates of the NEA and membership in the AFT include the option of liability insurance programs sponsored by those organizations.

As a summary of the discussion of this section, Figure 6.7 lists brief statements related to the rights and responsibilities of teachers.

STUDENTS' RIGHTS AND RESPONSIBILITIES

The rights of students have been through some dramatic shifts since the late 1960s. Before 1969, school authorities clearly had the final say as long as what they decided was seen as reasonable. A key U.S. Supreme Court decision in 1969 changed the balance by concluding that students do not "shed their constitutional rights to freedom of speech or expression at the schoolhouse gate." Going farther on behalf of student rights, in 1975 the Court decided that the principle of due process applied to students. These decisions led to several successful student challenges of school policies and procedures. In the late 1980s Court decisions moved back toward increasing the authority of public school officials. Along the way student life has become more complex, not only because of such threats as the increased use of drugs and the presence of weapons and gangs, but also because a diverse multicultural and shifting political context has made it more difficult to determine what is and what is not appropriate to be able to do and say within a school environment.

To illustrate some of the issues and decisions related to student rights and responsibilities, we present specific court cases here. Note that the cases do not necessarily constitute the last word regarding student rights, but rather provide an overview of some of the issues that have been decided by the courts. Table 6.5 is a summary of key cases; however, it is not intended to provide a complete understanding of the court decisions. You should read the following subsections and pursue references provided in the Notes and Bibliography to learn more about these and other student rights issues.

STUDENTS' RIGHTS AS CITIZENS

Through a series of court decisions, all children in the United States have been granted the opportunity for a public school education. Further, although school officials have a great deal of authority, children as students maintain many of the constitutional rights that adult citizens enjoy all the time. As obvious as each of these points might seem, each has been the subject of debate and court decision.

STUDENTS' RIGHT TO AN EDUCATION American children have a right to an education; this right is ensured in many state constitutions. It has been further defined by court decisions and is now interpreted to mean that each child shall have an equal opportunity to pursue education.

The right to an education, however, is not without certain prerequisites. Citizenship alone does not guarantee a free education. Statutes that establish public school systems also generally establish how operating costs will be met. Real estate taxes are the usual source of funds, so proof of residence is necessary for school attendance without tuition. *Residence* does not mean that the student, parent, or guardian must pay real estate taxes; it means that the student must live in the school district in which he or she wants to attend school. Residence, then, is a prerequisite to the right of a free public education within a specific school district.

HOMELESS CHILDREN HAVE THE RIGHT TO GO TO SCHOOL There are more than 500,000 homeless children in the United States. Because access to public school usually requires a residence address and a parent or guardian, as well as transportation, in the past homeless children were squeezed out of the system. Congress addressed this growing problem in 1987 with passage of the Stewart B. McKinney Homeless Assistance Act, which requires that "each State educational agency shall assure that each child of a homeless individual and each homeless youth have access to a free, appropriate public education." The law was amended in 1990 to require each school district to provide services to the homeless that are comparable to the services offered other students in the schools. These services include allowing homeless children to finish the school year in the school they were in before they lost their housing, providing transportation to school, tutoring to help

TABLE 6.5 SELECTED U.S. SUPREME COURT DECISIONS RELATED TO STUDENTS' RIGHTS AND RESPONSIBILITIES

Case	Issue	Decision
Plyler v. *Doe* (1982)	Rights to education of illegal aliens	Court struck down Texas law that denied a free public education to children of illegal aliens.
Goss v. *Lopez* (1975)	Suspension of high school students without a hearing	Court ruled that only in an emergency can a student be suspended without a hearing.
Wood v. *Strickland* (1975)	Question of whether school board members can be sued for depriving students of their constitutional rights (through suspension)	Students can seek damages from individual school board members but not from the school district.
Tinker v. *Des Moines Independent Community School District* (1969)	Free speech rights of students to wear black armbands to protest U.S. involvement in Vietnam	Court ruled against school district—recognized to an extent constitutional rights of pupils.
Board of Education, Island Trees Union Free District No. 26 v. *Pico* (1982)	School board's decision to remove books from the school library	Court issued decision that under certain circumstances, children may challenge board's decision to remove books.
Ingraham v. *Wright* (1977)	Power of states to authorize corporal punishment without consent of the student's parent	Court ruled that states may constitutionally authorize corporal punishment.
Bethel School District No. 403 v. *Fraser* (1986)	Power of school officials to restrain student speech	School officials may discipline a student for making lewd and indecent speech in a school assembly attended by other students.
Hazelwood School District v. *Kuhlmeier* (1988)	School district control of student expression in school newspapers, theatrical productions, and other forums	School administrators have broad authority to control student expression in the official student newspaper, which is not a public forum but is seen as part of the curriculum.
Honig v. *Doe* (1988)	Violation of the Education for All Handicapped Children Act (PL 94-142); school indefinitely suspended and attempted to expel two emotionally disturbed students	PL 94-142 authorizes officials to suspend dangerous children for a maximum of ten days. Justice Brennan said, "Congress very much meant to strip schools of unilateral authority to exclude disturbed students."
New Jersey v. *T.L.O.* (1985)	Search and seizure	School officials must have a reasonable cause when engaged in searches.

catch students up, and giving homeless children the opportunity to take part in school programs offered to other children.

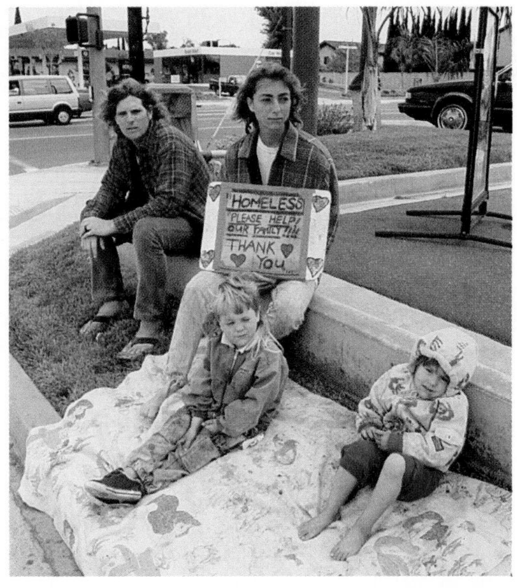

". . . each State educational agency shall assure that each child of a homeless individual and each homeless youth have access to a free, appropriate public education" (1987 Stewart B. McKinney Homeless Assistance Act).

STUDENTS' RIGHT TO SUE The U.S. Supreme Court has affirmed that students may sue school board members who are guilty of intentionally depriving students of their constitutional rights. In *Wood* v. *Strickland* (1975) the Supreme Court held that school officials who discipline students unfairly cannot defend themselves against civil rights suits by claiming ignorance of pupils' basic constitutional rights. As a result of this decision, Judge Paul Williams, a federal judge in Arkansas, ordered that certain students who had been suspended could seek damages from individual school board members—though not from the school district as a corporate body. The judge also ruled that the school records of these pupils must be cleared of the suspension incident. From these decisions it is apparent that the U.S. Supreme Court is taking into account the rights of students.

STUDENTS' RIGHT TO DUE PROCESS Much of the recent involvement of the courts with student rights has concerned due process of law for pupils. Due process is guaranteed by the Fourteenth Amendment. The protection clause states that "nor shall any State . . . deny to any person within its jurisdiction the equal protection of the laws." Due process of law means following those rules and principles that have been established for enforcing and protecting the rights of the accused. As was explained earlier, due process falls under two headings—procedural and substantive. *Procedural* due process has to do with whether or not the procedures used in disciplinary cases are fair; *substantive* due process is concerned with whether or not the school authorities have deprived a student of basic substantive constitutional rights such as personal liberty, property, or privacy.[15]

The application of due process to issues in schools is a recent phenomenon. Historically, schools functioned under the doctrine of **in loco parentis** ("in the place of a parent"). This doctrine meant that schools could exercise almost complete control over students, because they were acting as parent substitutes. Under the doctrine of in loco parentis, the courts have usually upheld the rules and regulations of local boards of education, particularly about pupil conduct. However, the courts have not supported rules that are unconstitutionally "vague" and/or "overboard." The following cases illustrate the difficult balance between protecting students' right to due process and giving schools sufficient authority to pursue their mission.

in loco parentis "in the place of a parent"—a term used to describe the implied power and responsibilities of schools.

PROCEDURAL DUE PROCESS IN CASES OF SUSPENSION AND EXPULSION Procedural due process is frequently scrutinized in cases of suspension and expulsion. These cases most often result from disciplinary action taken by the school, which may

DEBATE

YES

Should Teachers and Support Staff Be Able to Suspend Students?

NO

Celina Mann, a high school Spanish and ESL teacher in San Diego, California, also serves as a mentor teacher, department chair, and professional growth advisor. Mann is an NEA activist at the local, state, and national levels. You can reach her via e-mail at dmann@pacbell.net.

Americans can show that they truly respect teachers by trusting us to take whatever steps are necessary to effectively discipline our students.

That's not an easy task today—not when so many students come to school without adequate rest or nourishment. Not when so many students are familiar with violence, carry the frustration and anger of abandonment, and are burdened with drug and alcohol problems.

These students don't have the coping skills necessary to deal with their problems. They lack the discipline they need at home.

Yet we find ways to teach most of them grammar and math, values and respect. Most, but unfortunately, not all. We don't have the resources or the time to reach all the troubled students in our classes.

So we seek help from administrators. Some of them deal with the problems. Some are supportive. Some send kids to the few available continuation schools for students with behavior problems.

But other administrators allow students with chronic behavior problems to continue disrupting classes without consequences.

Some transfer students from school to school without addressing the cause of their problems. Most don't want a high "number of suspensions per site" on their records.

Where administrators fail in providing a quality learning environment for all students, teachers must be allowed to step in.

In San Diego, we have that right.

Article 11 in the contract negotiated by the San Diego Education Association states:

"A teacher may suspend any pupil for his/her class or class period . . . for the day of suspension and the day fol-

Paula Varner teaches English as a Second Language to Clarkmoor Elementary students in Tacoma, Washington. A 28-year veteran teacher and NEA activist, Varner has taught in California and worked as an adjunct professor in Washington. She can be reached at pjvarner@yahoo.com.

The decision to suspend a student requires thoughtful consideration, research, investigation, and consultation with others. Making that decision is an awesome responsibility that teachers and support staff shouldn't take on.

Here's why:

- No one, including a principal, should be able to suspend a student on a moment's notice. Suspension is serious business. It has long-term consequences for all those involved.
- Teachers and support employees don't have enough time to do everything required to make sure suspension is the right decision.

The events leading up to a suspension are rarely black and white. They require time to sort out, time to get to the truth, and time to find the punishment that both suits the crime and benefits the student. Administrators have the time; teachers don't.

- Classroom educators often don't see all sides of the suspension issue. I know I didn't until I did the coursework and internship required to earn an administrative/principal's certificate.

When substituting for a principal years ago, I suspended a student for a weapons violation in a "no tolerance" district. But I did so after making use of every resource available to me—teachers, parents, district administrative personnel, and the cooperating principal for the building.

Finally, the father and I worked together thoughtfully to fashion a creative and cooperative punishment that we believed would affect the child in a positive way.

As the acting principal, I was able to rearrange a portion of my day to spend the hours necessary to deal with this sit-

lowing. The suspension is to be a last resort after the failure of other forms of discipline."

The contract goes on to stipulate that teachers must notify parents and administrators, teachers can repeat the suspension if the behavior continues, and students will not be returned to a teachers' classroom "without the concurrence of the teacher and principal."

Our contract covers only certificated personnel, but I believe classroom support staff—often entrusted with rule enforcement and behavior management—should also have the right to suspend students.

When all staff have the power to enforce a natural sequence of consequences, students will be more likely to behave appropriately in all settings.

Given our contractual rights, you may think that suspensions are widely used, even abused, here. But that's not the case.

No one wants to suspend students. Still, after all other disciplinary methods have failed, suspension can be a valuable and effective way to deal with habitual behavior problems and extreme circumstances.

Suspensions can help diffuse tensions by giving students and teachers a time out. They allow all involved to start a new day under a new light. And they help restore an orderly and productive learning environment.

All students have the right to be taught. When we have the right to suspend, we can protect the rights of the students who want to learn. And we can do what we want to do—teach.

Source: Should Teachers and Support Staff Be Able to Suspend Students? *NEA Today,* April 1999, p. 43.

uation. As a classroom educator, I would have had to take time away from other students to handle things well.

- Teachers and support employees don't have the legal training they need to handle suspensions. A suspension is, by definition, a denial of the right to a free and appropriate public education. Denial of a basic right requires following due process and specific, detailed procedures.
- The laws governing suspension—in Washington state, at least—are complex, especially in the special education arena. A mistake or omission can lead to significant personal liability and civil rights complaints. Who needs that aggravation?
- Teachers and support staff have other—often better—ways to deal with inappropriate student behavior than suspensions.

As spelled out in a school's discipline policy, teachers can send kids to time-out in or out of the classroom, assign detention, contact parents, have kids write letters of apology, take away recess, take away some other privilege, or find another, appropriate punishment.

If these avenues fail to correct the problem, teachers can take the case to the principal with a recommendation, then leave the matter there.

- Finally, teachers and support employees should make decisions based on their educational value to the students involved.

Suspensions won't do any good if students aren't learning from them. And they won't do any good if they don't, in the long run, contribute to a quality education.

WHAT'S YOUR OPINION?

Should teachers and support staff have the right to suspend students?

Go to **www.ablongman.com/johnson** to cast your vote and see how NEA readers responded.

or may not have violated a pupil's substantive constitutional rights. For example, in *Goss* v. *Lopez* (1975) the U.S. Supreme Court dealt with the suspension of high school students in Columbus, Ohio. In that case the named plaintiffs claimed that they had been suspended from public high school for up to ten days without a hearing. The action alleged deprivation of constitutional rights. Two students who were suspended for a semester brought suit charging that their due process rights were denied—because they were not present at the board meeting when the suspensions were handed out.

Students have procedural due process rights including the opportunity for some kind of hearing.

In ruling that students cannot be suspended without some kind of hearing, the Court said:

> The prospect of imposing elaborate hearing requirements in every suspension case is viewed with great concern, and many school authorities may well prefer the untrammeled power to act unilaterally, unhampered by rules about notice and hearing. But it would be a strange disciplinary system in an educational institution if no communication was sought by the disciplinarian with the student in an effort to inform him of his defalcation and to let him tell his side of the story in order to make sure that an injustice is not done. Fairness can rarely be obtained by secret, one-sided determination of the facts decisive of rights. . . . Secrecy is not congenial to truth-seeking and self-righteousness gives too slender an assurance of rightness. No better instrument has been devised for arriving at truth than to give a person in jeopardy of serious loss notice of the case against him and opportunity to meet it.

Procedural due process cases usually involve alleged violations of the Fourteenth Amendment, which provides for the protection of specified privileges of citizens, including notice to the student, impartiality of the hearing process, and the right of representation. These cases may also involve alleged violations of state constitutions or statutory law that call for specific procedures. For example, many states have procedures for expulsion or suspension. Expulsion usually involves notifying parents or guardians in a specific way, perhaps by registered mail, and giving students the opportunity for a hearing before the board of education or a designated hearing officer. Suspension procedures are usually detailed as well, designating who has the authority to suspend and the length of time for suspension. Teachers and administrators should know due process regulations, including the specific regulations of the state where they are employed.

SUBSTANTIVE DUE PROCESS AND STUDENTS' RIGHTS TO FREE SPEECH Substantive due process frequently addresses questions of students' constitutional rights to free speech versus the schools' authority to maintain order in support of education. The *Tinker* case (*Tinker* v. *Des Moines Independent Community School District,* 1969) was significant. It involved a school board's attempt to keep students from wearing black armbands in a protest against U.S. military activities in Vietnam. In 1969 the U.S. Supreme Court ruled against the Des Moines school board. The majority opinion of the Court was that

> the wearing of armbands in the circumstances of this case was entirely divorced from actually or potentially disruptive conduct by those participating in it. It was closely akin to "pure speech" which, we have repeatedly held, is entitled to comprehensive protection, under the First Amendment. . . .
>
> First Amendment rights, applied in the light of the special characteristics of the school environment, are available to teachers and students. It can hardly be argued that either students or teachers shed their constitutional rights to freedom of speech or expression at the schoolhouse gate.

In the *Tinker* opinion the Court clearly designated that the decision "does not concern aggressive, disruptive action or even group demonstrations." The decision did make it clear that whatever their age, students have constitutional rights; and the decision has had widespread effect on the operation of schools in the United States. Schools have had to pay attention to U.S. law. Educators as well as lawyers have been guided by the principles set forth in the decision regarding the constitutional relationship between public school students and school officials.

A more recent U.S. Supreme Court decision appears to have at least narrowed the breadth of application of the *Tinker* ruling. The case involved Matthew Fraser, a high school senior in a school outside Tacoma, Washington. In the spring of 1983 Fraser was suspended from school for two days after he gave a short speech at a school assembly nominating a friend for a position in student government. School officials argued that Fraser's speech contained sexual innuendos that provoked other students to engage in disruptive behaviors unfavorable to the school setting. The U.S. District Court for the Western District of Washington held that Fraser's punishment violated his rights to free speech under the First Amendment and awarded him damages. The U.S. Court of Appeals for the Ninth Circuit affirmed the decision, holding that Fraser's speech was not disruptive under the standards of *Tinker.*[16] However, the Supreme Court reversed the decision. In the majority opinion in *Bethel School District No. 403* v. *Fraser* (1986), Chief Justice Warren Burger wrote, "The determination of what manner of speech in the classroom or in school assembly is inappropriate properly rests with the school board."

STUDENTS' RIGHTS AND RESPONSIBILITIES IN SCHOOL

The right, or privilege, of children to attend school also depends on their compliance with the rules and regulations of the school. To ensure the day-to-day orderly operation of schools, boards of education have the right to establish reasonable rules and regulations controlling pupils and their conduct. Boards' actions have been challenged in numerous instances, however. Challenges have concerned questions such as corporal punishment, the rights of married students, dress codes, student publications' freedom of expression, and involvement with drugs.

DRESS CODES AND GROOMING Lower-court cases dealing with grooming have been decided in some instances in favor of the board of education—in support of their rules and regulations—and in other instances in favor of the student. A general principle seems to be that if the dress and grooming do not incite or cause disruptive behavior or pose a health or safety problem, the court ruling is likely to

Court cases dealing with student grooming have found in favor of both school boards and students.

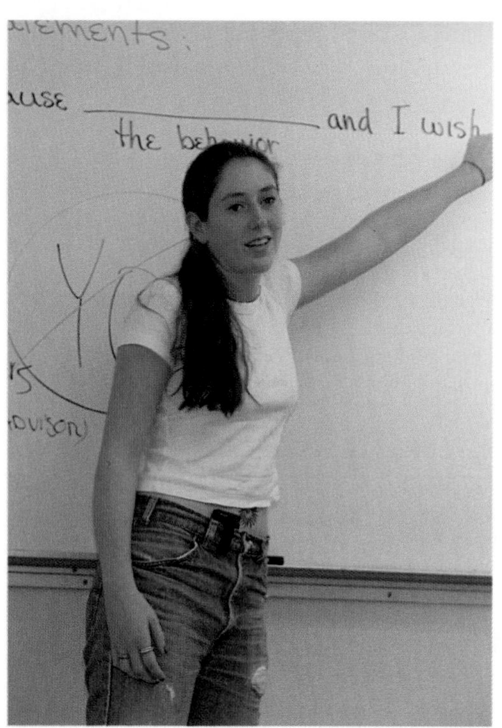

support the student. Dress codes, once very much in vogue, are less evident today. Although the U.S. Supreme Court has yet to consider a so-called long-hair case, federal courts in every circuit have issued rulings in such cases; half of them found regulations on hair length unconstitutional, and half upheld them. In all, over a two-decade period, federal and state courts decided more than 300 cases on this subject. If there is a trend, it is that students have won most of the cases that dealt with hairstyle. The courts have usually refused to uphold dress and hair length regulations for athletic teams or extracurricular groups unless the school proves that the hair or dress interfered with a student's ability to play the sport or perform the extracurricular activity.[17]

In the late 1970s and continuing through the 1980s, courts entertained fewer challenges to grooming regulations. The later decisions, however, continued to be consistent with earlier court rulings. Courts have supported school officials who attempted to regulate student appearance if the regulation could be based on concerns about disruption, health, or safety. Presumably, controversy over the length of students' hair or grooming in general is no longer critical because officials and students have a more common ground of agreement about what is acceptable. However, as the new century begins, new questions could be raised in relation to school efforts to control the clothing and other grooming symbols of gangs.

CORPORAL PUNISHMENT In 1977 the U.S. Supreme Court ruled on and finally resolved many of the issues related to corporal punishment (*Ingraham* v. *Wright*, 1977). The opinion established that states may *constitutionally* authorize corporal punishment without prior hearing or notice and without consent by the student's parents, and may as a matter of policy elect to prohibit or limit the use of corporal punishment. It also held that corporal punishment is not in violation of the Eighth Amendment (which prohibits "cruel and unusual punishments").

In response to the greater sensitivity to student rights, many school districts have adopted administrative rules and regulations to restrict the occasions, nature, and manner of administering corporal punishment. Some school districts specify that corporal punishment may be administered only under the direction of the principal and in the presence of another adult.

SEX DISCRIMINATION Until relatively recently, educational institutions could discriminate against females—whether they were students, staff, or faculty. In 1972 the Ninety-Second Congress enacted Title IX of the Education Amendments Act to remove sex discrimination against students and employees in federally assisted programs. The key provision in Title IX states, "No person in the United States shall, on the basis of sex, be excluded from participation in, be denied the benefits of, or be subjected to discrimination under any education program or activity receiving federal financial assistance." Title IX is enforced by the Department of Education's Office of Civil Rights. An individual or organization can allege that any policy or practice is discriminatory by writing a letter of complaint to the secretary of education. An administrative hearing is the next step in the process. Further steps include suing for money damages under Title IX, which the U.S. Supreme Court affirmed in *Franklin* v. *Guinneth County Schools* (1992).

MARRIAGE AND PREGNANCY In the past it was not unusual for school officials to expel students who married. Some educators reasoned that marriage brought on additional responsibilities, such as the establishment of a household, and therefore that married students could not perform well in school. They also believed that exclusion would help deter other teenagers from marrying. Courts tended to uphold school officials in these positions. Both courts and school officials acted consistently in not rigidly enforcing compulsory attendance statutes for underage students who married.

A recipient (e.g. a school district) shall not apply any rule concerning a student's actual or potential parental, family, or marital status which treats students differently on the basis of sex.

Title IX of the Education Amendments of 1972

School officials today cannot prohibit a student from attending school merely because he or she is married. This position is based on the above-mentioned Title IX, and on the notion that every child has a right to attend school. Public policy today encourages students to acquire as much education as they can. Not only are married students encouraged to remain in school, but they are also entitled to the same rights and privileges as unmarried students. Thus, they have the right to take any course the school offers and to participate in extracurricular activities open to other students. That is, participation in extracurricular activities cannot be denied a student solely on the basis of married status. However, a student's attendance and participation rights may be removed if his or her behavior is deleterious to other students.

Today's schools also enroll more pregnant students than ever before. Title IX prohibits their exclusion from school or from participation in extracurricular activities. Many school systems have reorganized their school programs so that courses can be offered during after-school hours or in the evenings to accommodate married and pregnant students. This arrangement makes it easier for students to work during the day and complete their education at a time that is convenient for them. Such programs often include courses and topics aimed at the specific audience, as well as counseling programs to assist students with their adjustment to marriage and family life.

CHILD ABUSE AND NEGLECT Government bodies in the United States have the right to exercise police power, which means that government is entrusted with the responsibility of looking after the health, safety, and welfare of all its citizens. In effect, each state acts as a guardian over all its people, exercising that role specifically over individuals not able to look after themselves. This guardianship extends to care for children who have been either abused or neglected by their parents. All fifty states have statutes dealing with this issue. These statutes generally protect children under the age of eighteen, but the scope of protection and definitions of abuse and neglect vary considerably among the states. In 1974 Congress passed the Child Abuse Prevention and Treatment Act, which provides financial assistance to states that have developed and implemented programs for identifying, preventing, and treating instances of child abuse and neglect.

The severity of this problem has been highlighted by the requirement of mandatory reporting of suspected abuse and neglect. Formerly, this reporting was limited mainly to physicians, but today educators are also required to report instances of suspected abuse and neglect. Some teachers are reluctant to do so because they fear a breakdown in student–teacher–parent relationships and the possibility of lawsuits alleging invasion of privacy, assault, or slander. Their fear should be diminished, however, by statutes that grant them immunity for acting in good faith.

SCHOOL RECORDS Before November 19, 1974, the effective date of the Buckley Amendment, the law regarding the privacy of student records was extremely unclear. Even today many school administrators—and most parents—do not realize that parents now have the right to view their children's educational records. Many teachers, too, are not yet aware that their written comments, which they submit as part of a student's record, must be shown at a parent's request, or at a student's request if the student is eighteen or older. Students over the age of eighteen have the right to see their school records for themselves.

The law (Public Law 93-380 as amended by Public Law 93-568) requires that schools receiving federal funds must comply with the privacy requirements or face loss of those funds. What must a school district do to comply? According to a 1976 clarification by HEW, the Buckley Amendment requires that the school district

> Allow all parents, even those not having custody of their children, access to each educational record that a school district keeps on their child.
>
> Establish a district policy on how parents can go about seeing specific records.
>
> Inform all parents what rights they have under the Amendment, how they can act on these rights according to school policy, and where they can see a copy of the policy.
>
> Seek parental permission in writing before disclosing any personally identifiable record on a child to individuals other than professional personnel employed in the district (and others who meet certain specific requirements).[18]

The loss of federal funds could present serious problems to some school districts, so the need for procedures to meet the requirements of the Buckley Amendment is self-evident. Many school districts have carefully formulated procedures; others are striving to clarify procedures in order to prevent conflicts.

STUDENT PUBLICATIONS A significant decision relative to "underground" student newspapers was made in Illinois in 1970.[19] Students were expelled for distributing a newspaper named *Grass High,* which the students produced at home and which criticized school officials and used vulgar language. The students were expelled under an Illinois statute that empowered boards of education to expel pupils guilty of gross disobedience or misconduct. A federal court in Illinois supported the board of education, but on appeal the Court of Appeals for the Seventh Circuit reversed the decision. The school board was not able to validate student disruption and interference as required by *Tinker.* The expelled students were entitled to collect damages. An implication is that the rights of students regarding newspapers they print at home are stronger than their rights of free expression in official school publications.

Early in 1988, in a landmark decision (*Hazelwood School District* v. *Kuhlmeier*), the U.S. Supreme Court ruled that administrators have broad authority to control

*School newspapers have been judged by the Supreme Court to not be a public forum, but rather a supervised learning experience for journalism students (*Hazelwood School District *v.* Kuhlmeier, *1988).*

student expression in official school newspapers, theatrical productions, and other forums that are part of the curriculum. In reaching that decision the Court determined that the *Spectrum,* the school newspaper of the Hazelwood District, was not a public forum. A school policy of the Hazelwood District required that the principal review each proposed issue of the *Spectrum.* The principal objected to two articles scheduled to appear in one issue. One of the articles was about girls at the school who had become pregnant; the other discussed the effects of divorce on students. Neither article used real names. The principal deleted two pages of the *Spectrum* rather than delete only the offending articles or require that they be modified. He stated that there was no time to make any changes in the articles and that the newspaper had to be printed immediately or not at all.

Three student journalists sued, contending that their freedom of speech had been violated. The Supreme Court upheld the principal's action. Justice Byron White decided that the *Spectrum* was not a public forum, but rather a supervised learning experience for journalism students. In effect, the censorship of a student press was upheld by the Supreme Court.

In Justice White's words,

> schools must be able to set high standards for the student speech that is disseminated under [their] auspices—standards that may be higher than those demanded by some newspaper publishers and theatrical producers in the "real" world—and may refuse to disseminate student speech that does not meet those standards.
>
> Accordingly, we hold that the standard articulated in *Tinker* for determining when a school may punish student expression need not also be the standard for determining when a school may refuse to lend its name and resources to the dissemination of student expression.

The issue of institutional control over publications has not yet been fully resolved. In response to questions about student publications and their distribution, school boards have endeavored to write rules and regulations that will withstand judicial scrutiny. A prompt review and reasonably fast appeal procedures are vital. Students should also be advised of distribution rules and abide by them.

RIGHTS OF STUDENTS WITH DISABILITIES Before the early 1970s the access to education of students with disabilities was left to the discretion of different levels of government. In the early 1970s court decisions established the position that students with disabilities were entitled to an "appropriate" education and to procedural protections against arbitrary treatment. Congress subsequently specified a broad set of substantive and procedural rights via Section 504 of the Rehabilitation Act and Public Law 94-142, the Education for All Handicapped Children Act (EAHCA). Since that time there has been a continuing series of legislative and legal refinements and extensions of the intents to see that students with special needs have appropriate educational opportunities. The problem has been to define what is meant by "appropriate." This examination and clarification process continues to unfold.

One recent case dealing with student rights dealt with a violation of PL 94-142. That law requires public school officials to keep disruptive or violent students with disabilities in their current classrooms pending hearings on their behavior. In the decision made in *Honig* v. *Doe* (1988), the U.S. Supreme Court upheld lower-court rulings that San Francisco school district officials violated the act in 1980 when they indefinitely suspended and then attempted to expel two students who were emotionally disturbed and who the officials claimed were dangerous.

The act authorizes officials to suspend dangerous children with disabilities for a maximum of ten days. Longer suspensions or expulsions are permissible only if the child's parents consent to the action taken or if the officials can convince a federal district judge that the child poses a danger to himself or herself or to others. The rules under which school officials must operate also are more limiting if the misbehavior is a manifestation of the student's disability.

It is clear that Congress meant to restrain the authority that schools had traditionally used to exclude students with disabilities, particularly students who are emotionally disturbed, from school. But PL 94-142 did not leave school administrators powerless to deal with dangerous students.

STUDENT AND LOCKER SEARCHES Most courts have refused to subject public school searches to strict Fourth Amendment standards. In general, the Fourth Amendment protects individuals from search without a warrant (court order). Many lower courts, however, have decided in favor of a more lenient interpretation of the Fourth Amendment in school searches. The rationale is that school authorities are obligated to maintain discipline and a sound educational environment and that that responsibility, along with their in loco parentis powers, gives them the right to conduct searches and seize contraband on reasonable suspicion without a warrant. First, however, school officials may only search for evidence that a student has violated a school rule or a law. Also, there must be a valid rule or law in place.

School authorities do not need a warrant to search a student's locker or a student vehicle on campus. For searches of a student's person, however, courts apply a higher standard. Where reasonable suspicion exists, a school official will likely be upheld. Reasonable suspicion exists when one has information that a student is in possession of something harmful or dangerous, or when there is evidence of illegal activities such as drug dealing (money, a list of customers, or selling papers). The second consideration is the way in which the search of a student's person is conducted. School officials are advised to have students remove contents from their clothing rather than having a teacher or administrator do it. A further caution is not to force students to remove all their clothing or undress to their underwear. To date, courts have not upheld school officials in strip searches; these cases evoke the greatest judicial sympathy toward student claims for damages on grounds of illegal searches.[20]

Where reasonable suspicion exists, school authorities do not need a warrant to search a student's locker or a student's vehicle on campus.

PEER SEXUAL HARASSMENT Title IX prohibits sex discrimination, and this includes students' harassing other students. Teasing, snapping bra straps, requesting sexual favors, making lewd comments about one's appearance or body parts, telling sexual jokes, engaging in physical abuse, and touching inappropriately are examples of peer sexual harassment. It is important for teachers to make it clear that sexual harassment will not be tolerated. School districts are supposed to have in place a grievance procedure for sex discrimination complaints. Students and/or their parents can file a complaint with the Office of Civil Rights also. All allegations must be investigated promptly, and schools must take immediate action in cases where harassment behaviors have been confirmed. Keep in mind that sexual harassment is not limited to high school students; middle school and in some cases elementary school children are also sexually harassed.

EDUCATIONAL MALPRACTICE Culpable neglect by a teacher in the performance of his or her duties is called **educational malpractice.** The courts of California[21] and New York[22] dismissed suits by former students alleging injury caused by educational malpractice. The plaintiffs claimed that they did not achieve an adequate education and that this was the fault of the school district. In the California case the student, after graduating from high school, could barely read or write. The judge in his opinion stated:

> The science of pedagogy itself is fraught with different and conflicting theories . . . and any layman might—and commonly does—have his own emphatic viewpoints on the subject. . . . The achievement of literacy in the schools, or its failure, is influenced by a host of factors from outside the formal teaching process, and beyond the course of its ministries.

In essence, the judge stated that there was no way to assess the school's negligence. In the New York case the judge said, "The failure to learn does not bespeak a failure to teach." In the twenty-first century, with the continuing push for accountability, there are likely to be more tests of the educational malpractice question.

educational malpractice Culpable neglect by a teacher in the performance of his or her duties as an educator.

As a summary of the topics covered in this section, Figure 6.8 lists brief statements related to the rights and responsibilities of students.

RELEVANT RESEARCH

Zero Tolerance, Zero Sense

STUDY PURPOSE/QUESTIONS: Legal research begins with the analysis of incidents and cases related to a particular statute or interpretation of the U.S. Constitution, in this case zero tolerance. In response to the tragedy at Columbine High School, many state legislatures and school districts have mandated that there be no flexibility when it comes to students making threats or bringing weapons to schools, that is, **zero tolerance.** Most of the established policies mandate that the student be expelled.

STUDY DESIGN: Stories from many individual situations were summarized. For example, one six-year-old made national news when he was expelled for bringing a weapon to kindergarten. The "weapon" was a plastic knife in his lunch sack, which his grandmother had put there so that he could spread peanut butter. Then there was the high school potential valedictorian who was expelled for making a "terrorist threat" on a student government election campaign poster. In this study, state statutes and district policies were examined as well.

STUDY FINDINGS: "Kids whose misbehaviors in the past would have occasioned oral reprimands from a teacher or perhaps a trip to the principal's office are now being labeled a threat to school safety. And, those very same kids-will-be-kids incidents are now prompting punishments ranging from suspension to expulsion to referral to the juvenile court system for behaviors that even the schools agree do not actually compromise safety." Another finding is that parents think of zero tolerance as keeping guns and drugs out of schools. However, zero tolerance, in many settings, has become a catch phrase for schools that are unable or unwilling to prevent school violence. This approach is also making students less inclined to confide in teachers and administrators

IMPLICATIONS: As with many policies, there needs to be a common sense approach to zero tolerance. Teachers and administrators, those closest to the action, need to have flexibility in judging the seriousness of perceived threats and in dispensing consequences. Texas has been innovative in its approach by identifying three levels of severity and three levels of response. At the most serious level, bringing a gun, knife, or drugs to school and aggravated assault result in expulsion. At the middle level, simple assault, use of alcohol, and a few other violations result in temporary removal from school. For the lowest-level offenses, school officials have discretion to determine the severity of the offense and the punishment. Zero tolerance has become a widespread policy approach. To what extent should school officials have flexibility in determining the severity of a threat? Or should there be a universal mandated response? Where should the line be drawn, if there is to be one?

Source: Margaret Graham Tebo, "Zero Tolerance, Zero Sense." *American Bar Association Journal* (April 2000), 119–120.

GLOBAL PERSPECTIVES: Legal Aspects of Education in Other Countries

The legal aspects of school systems in other countries offer some interesting differences in comparison to the U.S. system. For example, other democratic countries do not have the apparently never ending debates about the separation of church and state. As nearby as provinces of Canada and as far away as Belgium and the Netherlands, public dollars fund nondenominational and church-based schools. In the Dutch system there are three separate school systems: public, Catholic, and Protestant. Each is supported with public funds, yet each is governed independently.

zero tolerance
A policy that specifies the consequences for an act that is to be applied to all offenders regardless of circumstances.

Germany incorporates instruction in religion in all schools. In fact, often there is one teacher who is hired specifically to teach religion in regularly sched-

FIGURE 6.8 Summary Statements on Students' Rights and Responsibilities

State constitutions provide that a child has the right to an education; to date, students have been unsuccessful in suing school board members on the ground that they have not learned anything.

The due process clause provides that a child is entitled to notice of charges and the opportunity for a hearing prior to being suspended from school for misbehavior.

Students enjoy freedom of speech at school unless that speech is indecent or leads to disruption; courts are in agreement that school officials can regulate the content of student newspapers. Underground newspapers are not subject to this oversight.

Students may be awarded damages from school board members for a violation of their constitutional rights if they can establish that they were injured by the deprivation and that the school official deliberately violated those rights.

The use of corporal punishment is not prohibited by the U.S. Constitution, but excessive punishment may be barred by the Fourteenth Amendment.

Students may be restricted in their dress when there are problems of disruption, health, or safety.

Assignments of students to activities or classes in general on the basis of sex is not consistent with Title IX. These assignments may be made in such areas as sex education classes or when sports are available for both sexes.

Restricting a student's activities on the basis of marriage or pregnancy is inconsistent with the equal protection clause and Title IX.

Teachers are required to report to proper authorities suspected instances of child abuse and neglect.

Parents have the right to examine their children's educational records. Students age eighteen and older have the right to examine their records.

School officials may search students, lockers, and student property without a search warrant; but they must have reasonable grounds for believing that a student is in possession of evidence of a violation of a law or school rule.

uled classes. Students have to take instruction on religion, and are given a choice of Protestant or Catholic classes. In the higher grades, this instruction shifts toward more emphasis on human values.

Also, in Germany there are no school boards, and there are no publicly elected state boards of education. The school system is run by government bureaucracies. The curriculum and exams are set by the state. However, parents are very actively involved in the education of their children at the school site. For example, when there is a parent evening, *both* parents will attend. At these evenings much of the talk between parents will be about the homework assignments that their children have been doing. The reason is that parents are expected to help their children with homework. In Germany children have three to four hours of homework assignments *every day.* The school day ends at 1:00 P.M. Children return home and work on their homework during the afternoon.

There is a different approach to consideration of special-needs children in Germany. These children either have tutors or are assigned to different schools.

If a child cannot keep up with the others at a school, he or she is told, "You do not belong here." The parents and the child will then either have to work harder at keeping up or move to a different school.

Another legal aspect of the education system in Germany is that teachers as government employees cannot be sued. One consequence is that teachers do not supervise children during nonteaching times. Also, as government employees, teachers are not evaluated after their first year of teaching. As this description of schooling in Germany illustrates, the legal aspects of education and schools can be very different from country to country. Be careful not to assume that schools are the same everywhere.

SUMMARY

LEGAL ASPECTS OF EDUCATION

The legal foundation for education in the United States, including the rights and responsibilities of teachers and students, is the U.S. Constitution. Education is not mentioned directly in the U.S. Constitution, but the Tenth Amendment has been interpreted as assigning responsibility to each state for the education of its citizens. The rights of teachers and students are based in the First and Fourteenth Amendments. The First Amendment ensures freedom of speech, religion, and the press and the right to petition. The Fourteenth Amendment protects specified privileges of citizens Under the Equal Protection Clause. Following from the U.S. Constitution are the many other forms of law, including state constitutions, federal and state statutes, and the policies of school boards.

A sampling of legal issues facing schools include questions about the separation of church and state and which religious activities can be done in public schools; segregation, integration, and resegregation; affirmative action; and equal opportunity for students as well as for adults. Whatever the outcome, of these and other controversies, a continuing responsibility of school administrators and teachers is to ensure that there are no forms of discrimination and that all have an equal opportunity to access and receive an education.

TEACHERS' RIGHTS AND RESPONSIBILITIES

The legal rights and responsibilities of teachers are the same as those of other citizens. For example, the courts have said that a teaching certificate is a license to practice a profession that cannot be revoked without constitutional due process. At the same time the courts have ruled that local boards of education may prescribe requirements beyond the state requirements for licensure. The tenure statutes of individual states usually spell out the grounds and procedures for dismissing teachers. The law regarding academic freedom is unsettled, especially for elementary and secondary teachers; federal judges have been reluctant to recognize academic freedom rights at this level.

Legal controversy over curriculum continues; it is likely that school boards, administrators, and teachers will continue to receive complaints about what has been taught, how it has been taught, and what materials have been used.

The implications of the many forms and sources of law and court actions are highly significant for the teaching profession. From the many court decisions relating to education a general framework has evolved for acceptable conduct of teachers within the school setting. Today's teacher must not imagine that personal ignorance of acceptable standards of conduct will be overlooked by the courts; nor, however, should the teacher be intimidated by the courts. Teachers need to be diligent at all times to avoid liability for negligence. Teachers should be aware that failure to exercise or practice due care constitutes negligence.

STUDENTS' RIGHTS AND RESPONSIBILITIES

All students, including students with disabilities, have the right to a public school education; but they must behave in ways that ensure an orderly and safe school environment. Students have the right to see their school records, to sue, and to receive procedural and substantive due process. Students must not dress in ways that are disruptive or present a risk to health or safety, harass other students, or violate school standards in school publications.

In summary, the legal lens offers a very important view of education, schools, teaching and learning. From the U.S. Constitution through state statues to school board policies, school administrators and teachers are surrounded with protected rights and identified responsibilities. Most of these rights and responsibilities apply to nontenured teachers and to teacher education students. However, it is of the utmost importance that you learn about and keep in mind the legal specifics of the school districts and school where you will be teaching. As in other parts of life, ignorance of the law is not an acceptable defense for teachers.

DISCUSSION QUESTIONS

1. Each year state legislators offer up many bills related to the operation of public schools. What are some current or recent examples in your state or another of proposed bills that the courts would probably find unconstitutional?
2. The appropriate place for prayer in public schools continues to be a source of contention. What will you say and do if a parent wants you to have a moment of prayer in your classroom?
3. How should you as a teacher accommodate the religious interest of children in your class who are of a religion other than Christianity, such as Judaism, Muslim, or Buddhism?
4. Ever since 1954 the courts have ruled that de jure segregation in schools is unconstitutional. Now there is a clear trend in many parts of the country to a de facto resegregation of schools. What do you see as the causes of this trend? What do you see as the trend's most important educational implications?
5. Each fall there are teacher strikes somewhere in the country that delay the opening of school. Have you ever been involved in a strike of any kind? What do you think are the most critical consequences of teacher strikes? If your association/union leaders called for a strike, would you join the picket line or teach your classes?
6. What are your thoughts about the balancing of student rights against school officials' need to maintain an environment conducive to learning? Should school officials have more authority? Should students have greater freedom?
7. AIDS is a legally recognized disability. If, as a teacher, you are to have an HIV-positive student in your classroom, what are that student's rights under the law? What are your responsibilities as a teacher?

JOURNAL ENTRIES

1. Prayer in public schools is the subject of seemingly endless debates. As a teacher, you will probably be asked to offer an opinion or be asked to include

a moment of silence in your classroom. Now is the time for you to prepare your position. Certainly, you have a personal position as to whether prayer should be permitted/encouraged/required in public schools. On one page list the key points in your personal position. Then review the position of the courts as outlined in this chapter. Is your personal position consistent with legal precedent? Annotate your list to indicate which points are supported or refuted by law.

2. Academic freedom is a complex idea with uncertain legal foundation, especially for schoolteachers; most court cases involving academic freedom have dealt only with college faculty. Issues related to academic freedom are more uncertain still for beginning teachers. For the first several years you will be a probationary teacher—in other words, untenured. What are your thoughts about the amount of academic freedom you will have during those first years? Do you plan to select the topics you will teach? What about the lesson designs and specific activities you will use? What are the chances of your slipping into some area of controversy? How will you guard against this happening? Take fifteen minutes or so to prepare a journal entry on this topic.

PORTFOLIO DEVELOPMENT

1. Pick a school district where you think you would like to be employed as a teacher. Obtain a copy of the teacher employment contract from the district human resources/personnel office and study it. What does the contract say about your rights as a district employee and as a teacher? About your responsibilities? There may be references to other legal documents such as an employee handbook and board policies; if so, become familiar with those documents too. Together, these documents set the parameters for what you can, should, and should not do as a teacher. Place these documents and your notes in a folio file folder and save them for later uses.
2. From time to time newspapers and weekly newsmagazines carry reports about disagreements between students and school officials. Collect these reports, paying special attention to the legal interpretations drawn by each side, and consider the implications for you. In all instances keep in mind that both teachers and students have legal responsibilities as well as rights. These clippings and notes may be a useful resource for you someday, when as a teacher you are confronted with a question about student and teacher rights.

SCHOOL-BASED EXPERIENCES

1. Beginning teachers do not have the same rights as tenured teachers, but they do have rights. With a partner, compare and contrast the rights of beginning teachers in two school districts. Some of the items to check are: length of the probationary period, basis for tenure decision, how the tenure decision-making process works, and the rights of probationary teachers.
2. Interview an experienced teacher about students rights. Ask the teacher to provide examples of situations where it was important for the teacher to be aware of student rights. What were the critical points to be considered? What were the related responsibilities of the teacher? What advice would this teacher have for today's beginning teachers?

WEBSITES

Many resources that deal with law and legal aspects of education are available on the web. Potential search words include "U.S. Supreme Court," "school law," "teacher rights," and "student rights." Some especially useful websites are listed below.

1. <www.lcweb.loc.gov/catalog/> The Library of Congress Catalog provides a quick way to access the text of government bills, including those that relate to education.
2. <www.access.digex.net/~edlawinc/> This is a good source of texts on policies, laws, and U.S. Supreme Court decisions that deal with education.
3. <www.janweb.icdi.wvu.edu/kinder> and <www.schoolnet.ca/sne> There are many sources for information on special education topics. The ADA (Americans with Disabilities Act) Document Center and the Special Needs Education Network are two useful sites to check first.
4. <www.abanet.org> The American Bar Association provides access to its journal, analyses of court decisions, and a large database of court decisions.
5. <www.law.cornell.edu> The Cornell Law School website is easy to use and provides access to court decisions, news related to court cases, directories, and current awareness items.

NOTES

1. Michael LaMorte, *School Law: Cases and Concepts.* 6th ed. Boston: Allyn and Bacon, 1999, 167.
2. *Turk* v. *Franklin Special School District* (1982).
3. *Lucia* v. *Duggan* (1969).
4. *Gouge* v. *Joint School District No. 1* (1970).
5. Haskell C. Freedman, "The Legal Rights of Untenured Teachers," *Nolpe School Law Journal 1* (Fall 1970): 100.
6. *Norwalk Teachers Association* v. *Board of Education* (1951).
7. *City of Manchester* v. *Manchester Teachers' Guild* (1957).
8. Frank R. Kemerer, "Classroom Academic Freedom: Is It a Right?" *Kappa Delta Pi Record 19* (Summer 1983): 101.
9. *Cooper* v. *Ross* (1979).
10. *Hillis* v. *Stephen F. Austin University* (1982).
11. *Kingsville Independent School District* v. *Cooper* (1980).
12. *Board of Education, Island Trees Union Free District No. 26* v. *Pico* (1982).
13. *Mastrangelo* v. *West Side Union High School District* (1935).
14. *Morris* v. *Douglas County School District* (1966).
15. Lee O. Garber and Reynolds C. Seitz, *The Yearbook of School Law, 1971.* Danville, IL: Interstate, 1971, 253.
16. Thomas J. Flygare, "De Jure," *Phi Delta Kappan 68* (October 1986): 165–166.
17. *Long* v. *Zopp* (1973).
18. Lucy Knight, "Facts about Mr. Buckley's Amendment," *American Education 13* (June 1977): 7.
19. *Scoville* v. *Board of Education* (1970).
20. William D. Valente, *Law in the Schools.* Columbus, OH: Merrill, 1980, 282.
21. *Peter W.* v. *San Francisco Unified School District* (1976).
22. *Donahue* v. *Copiague Union Free School District* (1978).

BIBLIOGRAPHY

Essex, Nathan L. *School Law and the Public Schools: A Practical Guide for Educational Leaders.* Boston: Allyn and Bacon, 1999.

Fraser, James W. *Between Church and State: Religion and Public Education in a Multicultural America.* New York: St. Martin's Press, 2000.

LaMorte, Michael W. *School Law: Cases and Concepts.* 6th ed. Boston: Allyn and Bacon, 1999.

School Law Yearbook: Reference Guide to Education Law. Frederick, MD: Aspen Publishers, 2000.

Zirkel, Perry A. "Courtside." *Phi Delta Kappan.* (A regular column in the *Phi Delta Kappan* providing timely and pertinent information about legal issues.)

PART 4

CHAPTER 7
Antecedents of American Education

CHAPTER 8
The Important Role of Education in Our Developing Nation

CHAPTER 9
Using Recent History to Improve Student Learning

Historical Foundations of Education

Viewing Education through Historical Lenses

Part Four briefly surveys the history of education. Historians see past events through various lenses. And they interpret history—including the history of American education—according to the particular lens through which they view it.

Celebrationist historians tend to see the brighter side of historical events and may tend, for example, to praise schools for past accomplishments. By contrast, *liberal* historians tend to study educational history through lenses that focus on conflict, stress, and inconsistencies. *Revisionist* historians use yet another lens, seeing celebrationist history as fundamentally flawed and concluding that we often learn more by studying what has been wrong with education than by rehearsing what has been right. *Postmodernist* historians believe that a person sees the history of education through the unique lenses of her or his social class, race, ethnicity, gender, age, and so on.

Some historians provocatively argue that it is really not possible to "know" history; rather, they say, we can only make assumptions and guess about the past. This idea is further discussed in a thought-provoking essay at the beginning of Chapter 9.

Although this part of the book presents many interesting and potentially useful details about the history of education, each of the following three chapters also proposes several "big ideas" about history that we hope will be particularly useful generalizations for you.

In addition, we challenge you to think critically as you read the next three chapters and to formulate your own opinions about the content, major ideas, and relevancy of this historical material, thereby eventually developing your own informed and unique lens through which to view educational history.

The following questions will help you to focus your learning as you read Part Four:

1. Who were some of the most important early educators in the world and what lessons might we learn from them today?
2. What was life probably like for colonial American parents, students, and teachers?
3. What role(s) have American governmental agencies played in education down through history?
4. What major changes have taken place in our educational systems during the past half century?
5. What are the really important big ideas in educational history?
6. How might an understanding of educational history be used to improve student learning today?

CHAPTER

7

Antecedents of American Education

EDUCATION IN THE NEWS

Quintilian Defines "An Ideal Teacher"

ROME, A.D. 85—Well-known orator and philosopher Marcus Fabius Quintilianus, better known as Quintilian, in an appearance today at the Forum, offered some advice to parents and educators alike:

"Let him therefore adopt a parental attitude to his pupils, and regard himself as the representative of those who have committed their children to his charge. Let him be free from vice himself and refuse to tolerate it in others. Let him be strict but not austere, genial but not too familiar; for austerity will make him unpopular, while familiarity breeds contempt. Let his discourse continually turn on what is good and honorable; the more he admonishes, the less he will have to punish. He must control his temper without however shutting his eyes to faults requiring correction: his instruction must be free from affectation, his industry great, his demands on his class continuous, but not extravagant He must be ready to answer questions and to put them unasked to those who sit silent. In praising the recitations of his pupils he must be neither grudging nor overgenerous: the former quality will give them a distaste for work, while the latter will produce a complacent self-satisfaction. In correcting faults he must avoid sarcasm and above all abuse: for teachers whose rebukes seem to imply positive dislike discourage industry."

The Spanish-born teacher, whose reputation as a rhetorician continues to grow throughout the Roman Empire, made his remarks at the dedication of a new Latin grammar school located on the Appian Way.

Quintilian says he plans to publish all his thinking on rhetoric and education in a multivolume work that will emphasize reading as an important part of an orator's training and will contain a comprehensive survey of Greek and Latin writers.

LEARNER OUTCOMES

After reading and studying this chapter, you will be able to

1. Explain Quintilian's concept of an ideal teacher, almost 2000 years ago, and compare it with your own concept of an ideal teacher today.
2. List some of the most important early educators in the world and explain their contributions to education.
3. Explain the early church's influence and role in education.
4. Detail the major educational accomplishments of the early Eastern societies, the ancient Greeks, the ancient Romans, and the Europeans of the Middle Ages, Renaissance, Reformation, and Age of Reason.
5. Analyze how contemporary educators might use knowledge of the antecedents of American education to improve student learning today. ■

In this chapter we will look at some of the antecedents of the U.S. educational system. Chapters 8 and 9 will then deal with the evolution of formal education in the United States. We offer these historical chapters to you because there is much to be learned from past successes and failures in education. Remember, as you read this part of the book that there are various methods of **historical interpretation**—various lenses through which to view the past—and that historians often disagree when attempting to understand history. History is not an exact science by any means; rather, it is open to different interpretations.

Several major historical ideas are presented in this chapter. The first of these big ideas relates to the fact that since the very beginning of time, adults have always informally educated their children to prepare them for adult life. Another major idea presented in this chapter is that as people developed a written language, they created a need for schools as a means of teaching these writing skills and passing on knowledge to succeeding generations. Yet a third major historical idea presented in this chapter relates to the fact that countless early societies throughout the world developed unique educational programs to serve their perceived needs. Finally, this chapter proudly proclaims that progress and advancement in every society has been and still is, in large part, dependent on education.

We challenge you to think creatively and critically about the history presented in these three chapters. Strive to learn the historical facts and then make your own historical interpretations.

THE BEGINNINGS OF EDUCATION (TO A.D. 476)

It is generally believed that human beings have been on earth for several million years. But not until about ten thousand years ago did people start to raise food, domesticate animals, build canoes, and live in some semblance of community life; and not until approximately six thousand years ago was written language developed.

Once there was written language, humans felt the need for formal education. As societies became more complex and the body of knowledge increased, people recognized a need for schools. What they had learned constituted the subject matter; the written language allowed them to record this knowledge and pass it from generation to generation.

It would be unfair, and simply not historically accurate, to overlook the informal education that has been provided for children down through the ages by aboriginal peoples throughout the world. All people, regardless of their time and place in history, have cared for their young and prepared them for life. This surely was true of the very earliest humans, who fed and protected their children and informally taught them—probably by example and admonition—the skills they needed to survive as adults. For instance, Native Americans, who lived and flourished in North America for thousands of years before the first Europeans arrived and established formal schools, educated generations of their children. Many other early societies (in China, Africa, and South America, for example) also successfully provided the education that their children needed to help build their flourishing cultures. Unfortunately, records do not exist that would help us

historical interpretation
Different ways to study and understand history, such as celebrationist, liberal, revisionist, and postmodernist historians' approaches.

The aboriginal ancestors of today's Native Americans, like other aboriginal peoples, probably taught their children by admonition and example.

better understand these earliest informal educational systems. If such records did exist, we would probably be quite impressed with the educational efforts of our aboriginal ancestors.

GLOBAL PERSPECTIVES: Educational Ideas Borrowed from around the World

The educational ideas now used in the United States had their inception a long time ago. Our contemporary schools are a mixture of educational ideas, concepts, and practices borrowed from around the world. Much of whatever credit and accolades our current American educational system receives must be shared with those who long ago conceived of the idea of formal education and who then slowly developed and refined these educational concepts.

This chapter is devoted to a brief review of some of the early educational developments that occurred long before any formal education took place in the United States. These developments became the basis on which our schools were built and are the antecedents of American education.

NON-WESTERN EDUCATION

It is impossible to determine the date that schools first came into existence. However, the discovery of cuneiform mathematics textbooks that have been dated to 2000 B.C. suggests that some form of school probably existed in Sumeria at that time. There is also evidence to suggest that formal schools existed in China during the Hsia and Shang dynasties, perhaps as early as 2000 B.C. Let's briefly explore several examples of the origins of education.

HINDU EDUCATION The ancient Hindu societies were deeply rooted in the caste system, in which family status determined a person's social and vocational position in life. The Hindu religion emphasized nonearthly values; this resulted in little interest in education for anyone but boys from the highest castes. Priests were in charge of what education existed. Clues from the writing of Buddha suggest that education involved a heavy emphasis on morals, writing with a stick in the sand, and frequent punishments with a rod. Further education was reserved for the priestly caste, which, over the ages, gradually cultivated such disciplines as logic, rhetoric, astronomy, and mathematics. Many of our contemporary educational values, including our European languages, are partially derived from those of the early Hindu societies.

HEBREW EDUCATION Perhaps no culture has valued education more than the Hebrew societies. Hebrew education was derived from the Jewish Scriptures, which taught religious faithfulness and strict adherence to Old Testament laws. Discipline was harsh both at home and in school and was justified by many Bible verses such as the proverb "He that spareth his rod, hateth his son." Early Hebrew schools taught boys to read and write, and girls to prepare food, spin, weave, sing, and dance. Teachers were greatly respected; the Talmud dictates, "If your teacher and your father have need of your assistance, help your teacher before helping your father, for the latter has given you only the life of this world, while the former has secured for you the life of the world to come." From Hebrew society we have inherited, at least in part, the value we place on education.

CHINESE EDUCATION It has been said that China has been civilized longer than any other society in the world. The Chinese invented printing, gunpowder, and the mariner's compass, among other things. Chinese education has always been characterized by tradition, formality, and conformity—all designed to help students function in a regular, mechanical, and predictable routine.

In the sixth century B.C., two philosophers/reformers exerted enormous influence on Chinese thinking and education through their writings. The first of these was Lâo-tsze, who wrote,

> Certain bad rulers would have us believe that the heart and the spirit of man should be left empty, but that instead his stomach should be filled; that his bones should be strengthened rather than the power of his will; that we should always desire to have people remain in a state of ignorance, for then their demands would be few. It is difficult, they say, to govern a people that are too wise.
>
> These doctrines are directly opposed to what is due to humanity. Those in authority should come to the aid of the people by means of oral and written instruction; so far from oppressing them and treating them as slaves, they should do them good in every possible way.

The second Chinese reformer, Hkung-tsze (551–478 B.C.), who later became known as Confucius, is the most famous Asian philosopher. Since his time, all Chinese students have been taught Confucius's five cardinal virtues (universal charity, impartial justice, conformity, rectitude of heart and mind, and pure sincerity) as well as many of his famous sayings, such as "There are three thousand crimes . . . of these no one is greater than disobedience to parents." Interestingly, early Chinese education did not include geography, history, science, language, or mathematics—all subjects that are highly valued by early Western societies. Also, unlike many of their Western counterparts, early Chinese educators placed little importance on the individual. From early Chinese educational traditions we have inherited our respect for others and for authority, patience, as well as advances in written language.

AFRICAN EDUCATION In Egypt civilization and intellectual advancement occurred at a very early time. There, as in most early societies, education was provided only for privileged males. The fact that the pyramids were built several thousand years before Christ attests to the skills of this ancient civilization. In addition, several notable Greek philosophers, including Pythagoras, Plato, Lycurgus, and Solon, completed their education in Egypt.

Egyptian society was divided into castes, with priests holding the highest position and receiving instruction in philosophy, astronomy, geometry, medicine, history, and law. The priests also provided education for others who were worthy of that privilege.

Most of the great early Eastern civilizations developed educational systems long before Western civilizations did. Eastern civilizations contributed substantially to the development of knowledge, education, and schools in the world.

WESTERN EDUCATION—THE GREEKS

It was not until about 500 B.C. that a Western society advanced sufficiently to generate an organized concern for formal education. This happened in Greece during the **Age of Pericles,** 455–431 B.C. Greece consisted of many city-states, one of which was Sparta, a militaristic state whose educational system was geared to support military ambitions. Spartan infants were exposed to the elements for a stated period; if they survived the ordeal, they were judged sufficiently strong for soldiering if male or to bear healthy children if female. From the ages of eight to eighteen, boys were wards of the state. During this time they lived in barracks and received physical and moral training. Between the ages of eighteen and twenty, boys underwent rigorous war training, after which they served in the army. All men were required to marry by the age of thirty so that they might raise healthy children to serve the state. The aims of Spartan education centered on developing such ideals as courage, patriotism, obedience, cunning, and physical strength. Plutarch (A.D. 46–120), a writer of later times, said that the education of the Spartans "was calculated to make them subject to command, to endure labor, to fight, and to conquer." There was very little intellectual content in Spartan education.

The very spring and root of honesty and virtue lie in good education.
Plutarch

In sharp contrast to Sparta was Athens, another Greek city-state, which developed an educational program that heavily stressed intellectual and aesthetic objectives. Between the ages of eight and sixteen, some Athenian boys attended a series of public schools. These schools included a kind of grammar school, which taught reading, writing, and counting; a gymnastics school, which taught sports and games; and a music school, which taught history, drama, poetry, speaking, and science as well as music. Because all city-states had to defend themselves against aggressors, Athenian boys received citizenship and military training between the ages of sixteen and twenty. Athenian girls were educated in the home. Athenian education stressed individual development, aesthetics, and culture.

The Western world's first great philosophers came from Athens. Of the many philosophers that Greece produced, three stand out: Socrates (470–399 B.C.), Plato (427–347 B.C.), and Aristotle (384–322 B.C.).

Age of Pericles
A period (455–431 B.C.) of Greek history in which sufficiently great strides were made in human advancement to generate an organized concern for formal education.

Socratic method
A way of teaching that centers on the use of questions by the teacher to lead students to certain conclusions.

SOCRATES Socrates left no writings, but we know much about him from the writings of Xenophon and Plato. In the **Socratic method** of teaching, a teacher asks a series of questions that leads the student to a certain conclusion. This method is still commonly used by teachers today.

Of the many ancient Greek philosophers, Socrates stands out the most.

Socrates traveled around Athens teaching the students who gathered about him. He was dedicated to the search for truth and at times was very critical of the existing government. In fact, Socrates was eventually brought to trial for inciting the people against the government by his ceaseless questioning. He was found guilty and given a choice between ending his teaching or being put to death. Socrates chose death, thereby becoming a martyr for the cause of education. Socrates' fundamental principle, "Knowledge is virtue," has been adopted by countless educators and philosophers throughout the ages. Incidentally, some authorities speculate that Socrates might not really have existed, but rather might have been a mythical character created by other writers.

PLATO Plato was a student and disciple of Socrates. In his *Republic,* Plato set forth his recommendations for the ideal society. He suggested that society should contain three classes of people: artisans, to do the manual work; soldiers, to defend the society; and philosophers, to advance knowledge and to rule the society. Plato's educational aim was to discover and develop each individual's abilities. He believed that each person's abilities should be used to serve society. Plato wrote, "I call education the virtue which is shown by children when the feelings of joy or of sorrow, of love or of hate, which arise in their souls, are made conformable to order." Concerning the goals of education, Plato wrote, "A good education is that which gives to the body and to the soul all the beauty and all the perfection of which they are capable."

History illumines reality, vitalizes memory, provides guidance in daily life . . .

Marcus Cicero in first century B.C.

ARISTOTLE Like Plato, Aristotle believed that a person's most important purpose was to serve and improve humankind. Aristotle's educational method, however, was scientific, practical, and objective, in contrast to the philosophical methods of Socrates and Plato. Aristotle believed that the quality of a society was determined by the quality of education found in that society. His writings, which include *Lyceum, Organon, Politics, Ethics,* and *Metaphysics,* were destined to exert greater influence on humankind throughout the Middle Ages than the writings of any other man.

Insight into some of Aristotle's views concerning education can be obtained from the following passage from *Politics:*

> There can be no doubt that children should be taught those useful things which are really necessary, but not all things; for occupations are divided into liberal and illiberal; and to young children should be imparted only such kinds of knowledge as will be useful to them without vulgarizing them. And any occupation, art, or science, which makes the body or soul or mind of the freeman less fit for the practice or exercise of virtue, is vulgar; wherefore we call those arts vulgar which tend to deform the body, and likewise all paid employments, for they absorb and degrade the mind.[1]

The early Greek philosophers, including Plato and Aristotle, articulated the idea that females and slaves did not possess the intelligence to be leaders and therefore should not be educated. Unfortunately, our world's current struggle with racism and sexism, deeply rooted in Western civilization, is traceable to the ancient world.

WESTERN EDUCATION—THE ROMANS

In 146 B.C. the Romans conquered Greece, and Greek teachers and their educational system were quickly absorbed into the Roman Empire. Many of the educational and philosophical advances made by the Roman Empire after that time were actually inspired by enslaved Greeks.

ROMAN SCHOOLS Before 146 B.C., Roman children were educated primarily in the home, though some children attended schools known as *ludi,* where the rudiments of reading and writing were taught. The Greek influence on Roman education became pronounced between 50 B.C. and A.D. 200, during which time an entire system of schools developed. Some children, after learning to read and write, attended a *grammaticus* school to study Latin, literature, history, mathematics, music, and dialectics. These **Latin grammar schools** were somewhat like twentieth-century secondary schools in function. Students who were preparing for a career of political service received their training in schools of rhetoric, which offered courses in grammar, rhetoric, dialectics, music, arithmetic, geometry, and astronomy.

The Roman Empire contained numerous institutions of higher learning that were continuations of former Greek institutions. A library founded by Vespasian about A.D. 70 later came to be known as the Athenaeum and eventually offered studies in law, medicine, architecture, mathematics, and mechanics.

QUINTILIAN Quintilian (A.D. 35–95) was the most influential Roman educator. In a set of twelve books, *The Institutes of Oratory,* he described current educational practices, recommended the type of educational system needed in Rome, and listed the great books that were in existence at that time.

Quintilian had considerable insight into educational psychology; concerning the punishment of students, he wrote,

> I am by no means in favor of whipping boys, though I know it to be a general practice. In the first place, whipping is unseemly, and if you suppose the boys to be somewhat grown up, it is an affront to the highest degree. In the next place, if a boy's ability is so poor as to be proof against reproach he will, like a worthless slave, become insensible to blows. Lastly, if a teacher is assiduous and careful, there is no need to use force. I shall observe further that while a boy is under the rod he experiences pain and fear. The shame of this experience dejects and

Latin grammar school
An early type of school that emphasized the study of Latin, literature, history, mathematics, music, and dialectics.

discourages many pupils, makes them shun being seen, and may even weary them of their lives.[2]

Regarding the motivation of students, Quintilian stated,

> Let study be made a child's diversion; let him be soothed and caressed into it, and let him sometimes test himself upon his proficiency. Sometimes enter a contest of wits with him, and let him imagine that he comes off the conqueror. Let him even be encouraged by giving him such rewards that are most appropriate to his age.[3]

These comments apply as well today as they did when Quintilian wrote them nearly two thousand years ago. Quintilian's writings were rediscovered in the 1400s and became influential in the humanistic movement in education.

The Romans had a genius for organization and for getting the job done. They made lasting contributions to architecture, and many of their roads, aqueducts, and buildings remain today. This genius for organization enabled Rome to unite much of the ancient world with a common language, a religion, and a political bond—a condition that favored the spread of education and knowledge throughout the ancient world.

RELEVANT RESEARCH

School Violence

STUDY PURPOSE/QUESTIONS: A study of the history of education reveals that school discipline has historically been relatively harsh; in fact, many people would argue that students were often treated too severely in past schools. Student misbehavior that is so severe that it is called "school violence" is a relatively new problem in our schools. The study reported here has attempted to understand the extent of school violence in our public schools.

STUDY DESIGN: The U.S. Department of Education systematically attempts to collect information on different types of school violence by asking public agencies to report such events. The U.S. Department of Education then periodically publishes compilations of these reports.

STUDY FINDINGS: The results of this 1996–97 study revealed more than 400,000 incidences of crime reported in public schools. A breakdown of the types of school crimes was as follows:

Fights with weapons	10,950
Theft and robbery	122,650
Rape, sexual battery	4,170
Fights without weapons	187,890
Vandalism	98,490

IMPLICATIONS: This and other similar studies show that, unfortunately, our public schools have become increasingly violent. Educators, parents, public officials, and the general public need to be aware of this very serious problem and work diligently together to reduce violence in our society and in especially in our schools.

Source: U.S. Department of Education.

EDUCATION IN THE MIDDLE AGES (476–1300)

By A.D. 476 (the fall of the Roman Empire) the Roman Catholic Church was well on the way to becoming the greatest power in government and education. In fact, the rise of the church to a very powerful position is often cited as a main cause of the Western world's plunge into the Dark Ages. As the church stressed the importance of gaining entrance to heaven, life on earth became less important. Many people viewed earthly life as nothing more than a way to a life hereafter. You can see that a society in which this attitude prevailed would be unlikely to make intellectual advances, except perhaps in areas tangential to religion.

This section will briefly review the history of education in the Dark Ages and the revival of learning. We begin by sketching the achievements of two educators who lived during the Dark Ages: Charlemagne and Alcuin.

THE DARK AGES (400–1000)

As the name implies, the Dark Ages was a period in the Western world when human learning and knowledge not only stood still but actually regressed. This regression was due to a variety of conditions, including political and religious oppression of the common people. However, there were some examples of human progress during this time. In fact, some historians believe this historical period was not "dark" at all but was an era of considerable human progress—another example of the differing lenses through which various historians view the past.

CHARLEMAGNE During the Dark Ages, one of the bright periods for education was the reign of Charlemagne (742–814). Charlemagne realized the value of education; and as ruler of a large part of Europe, he was in a position to establish schools and encourage scholarly activity. In 768, when Charlemagne came into power, educational activity was at an extremely low ebb. The church conducted the little educating that was carried on, mainly to induct people into the faith and to train religious leaders. The schools where this religious teaching took place included *catechumenal schools,* which taught church doctrine to new converts; *catechetical schools,* which at first taught the catechism but later became schools for training church leaders; and *cathedral* (or *monastic*) *schools,* which trained clergy.

Astronomy was one of the seven liberal arts taught during the time of Charlemagne and Alcuin. The other eighth-century liberal arts were grammar, rhetoric, logic, arithmetic, geometry, and music.

ALCUIN Charlemagne sought far and wide for a talented educator who could improve education in the kingdom, finally selecting Alcuin (735–804), who had been a teacher in England. While Alcuin served as Charlemagne's chief educational advisor, he became the most famous educator of his day. His main educational writings include *On Grammar, On Orthography, On Rhetoric,* and *On Dialectics.* In addition to trying to improve education generally in the kingdom, Alcuin headed Charlemagne's Palace School in Frankland. Charlemagne himself often sat in the Palace School with the children, trying to further his own meager education.

Roughly during Alcuin's time, the phrase ***seven liberal arts*** came into common usage to describe the curriculum that was then taught in many schools. The seven liberal arts consisted of the trivium (grammar, rhetoric, and logic) and the quadrivium (arithmetic, geometry, music, and astronomy). Each of these seven subjects was defined broadly, so collectively they constituted a more comprehensive study than today's usage of the term suggests. The phrase *liberal arts* has survived time and is commonly used now.

THE REVIVAL OF LEARNING

Despite the efforts of men such as Charlemagne and Alcuin, little educational progress was made during the Dark Ages. However, between 1000 and 1300—a period frequently referred to as the "age of the revival of learning"—humankind slowly regained a thirst for education. Two events supported this revival of interest in learning: the rediscovery of the writings of some of the ancient philosophers (mainly Aristotle) and renewed interest in them and the reconciliation of religion and philosophy. Before this time the church had denounced the study of philosophy as earthly and ungodly.

THOMAS AQUINAS Thomas Aquinas (1225–1274), more than any other person, helped to change the church's views on learning. This change led to the creation of new learning institutions, among them the medieval universities. The harmonization of the doctrines of the church with the doctrines of philosophy and education was rooted in the ideas of Aristotle. Himself a theologian, Aquinas formalized **scholasticism** (the logical and philosophical study of the beliefs of the church). His most important writing was *Summa Theologica,* which became the doctrinal authority of the Roman Catholic Church. The educational and philosophical views of Thomas Aquinas were made formal in the philosophy Thomism—a philosophy that has remained important in Roman Catholic parochial education.

MEDIEVAL UNIVERSITIES The revival of learning brought about a general increase in educational activity and a growth of educational institutions, including the establishment of universities. These medieval universities, the true forerunners of our modern universities, included the University of Bologna (1158), which specialized in law; the University of Paris (1180), which specialized in theology; Oxford University (1214); and the University of Salerno (1224). By 1500, approximately eighty universities existed in Europe.

Although the Middle Ages produced a few educational advances in the Western world, we must remember that much of the Eastern world did not experience the Dark Ages. Mohammed (569–632) led a group of Arabs through northern Africa and into southern Spain. The Eastern learning that the Arabs brought to Spain spread slowly throughout Europe over the next few centuries through the writings of such scholars as Avicenna (980–1037) and Averroes (1126–1198).

seven liberal arts
A medieval curriculum that consisted of the trivium (grammar, rhetoric, logic) and the quadrivium (arithmetic, geometry, music, astronomy).

scholasticism
The logical and philosophical study of the beliefs of the church.

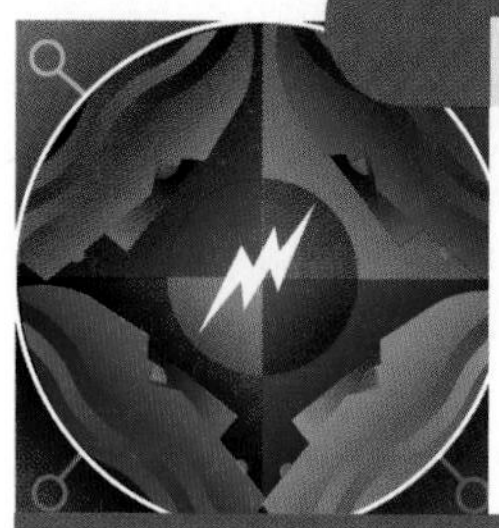

PROFESSIONAL DILEMMA

Can a Knowledge of History Help to Improve Multicultural Education?

When you become a teacher, you will be expected to provide multicultural education for your students, regardless of the age level or subjects you teach. Most teachers today face the dilemma of wanting to provide their students with a high-quality multicultural program, but being frustrated with the lack of time and support for doing so.

As you will learn, racial and ethnic prejudice and injustice have been present throughout U.S. educational history. Unfortunately, there is still considerable racial and ethnic strife in the United States today, and much of this strife has filtered into the halls of education. Debates rage about how schools should meet the educational demands of a complex multicultural society. As a teacher, you will be expected to join in this debate and help search for answers.

James Banks, a leading researcher in multicultural education at the University of Washington, feels past efforts have been too superficial. He asserts that "additive approaches" treat multicultural material as "an appendage to the main story of the development of the nation and to the core curriculum." Instead, multicultural education should integrate multicultural perspectives throughout the curriculum, on an equal footing with white European perspectives.

Despite the lack of time and adequate school district encouragement and support, there are many things that a determined and creative teacher can do to integrate multicultural education throughout the curriculum. Teachers can also encourage the school district to develop and support comprehensive programs for multicultural education and then participate in developing these plans.

- What are the historical antecedents that have contributed to the lack of racial and ethnic understanding in U.S. society?
- Should education programs seek to eliminate cultural differences among individuals or to preserve and perhaps celebrate them?
- What can you do in your classroom to improve multicultural education?
- What additional information would you like about multicultural education, and where might you find such information?

These Eastern contributions to Western knowledge included significant advances in science and mathematics, including the Arabic numbering system.

EDUCATION IN TRANSITION (1300–1700)

Two very important movements took place during the transition period of 1300–1700: the Renaissance and the Reformation. The Renaissance represented the protest of individuals against the dogmatic authority the church exerted over their social and intellectual life. The Renaissance started in Italy (around 1300) when humans reacquired the spirit of free inquiry that had prevailed in ancient Greece. The Renaissance slowly spread through Europe, resulting in a general revival of classical learning called *humanism*.

The second movement, the Reformation, represented a reaction against certain beliefs of the Roman Catholic Church, particularly those that discouraged

Erasmus (1466–1536) was one of the most famous educators of the Renaissance.

learning and that, in consequence, kept lay people in ignorance. This section will survey aspects of both the Renaissance and the Reformation.

THE RENAISSANCE

The common people were generally oppressed by wealthy landowners and royalty during the eleventh and twelfth centuries. In fact, the common people were thought to be unworthy of education and to exist primarily to serve landed gentry and royalty. The Renaissance represented a rebellion on the part of the common people against the suppression they experienced from both the church and the wealthy who controlled their lives. At that time masses of common people developed a spirit of inquiry and demanded a better life.

VITTORINO DA FELTRE One educator from the Renaissance period was a man from the eastern Alps by the name of Vittorino da Feltre (ca. 1278–1446).[4] Vittorino studied at the University of Florence, where he developed an interest in teaching. He also developed a keen interest in classical literature and, along with other educators of that time, began to believe that people could be educated and also be Christians at the same time—a belief that the church generally did not share.

Vittorino established several schools, taught in a variety of others, and generally helped to advance the development of education during his lifetime. He believed that education was an important end in itself and thereby helped to rekindle an interest in the value of human knowledge during the Renaissance.

ERASMUS Erasmus (1466–1536) was one of the most famous humanist educators, and two of his books, *The Right Method of Instruction* and *The Liberal Education of Boys,* formed a humanistic theory of education. Erasmus had a good deal of educational insight. Concerning the aims of education, he wrote:

> The duty of instructing the young includes several elements, the first and also the chief of which is that the tender mind of the child should be instructed in piety; the second, that he love and learn the liberal arts; the third, that he be taught tact in the conduct of social life; and the fourth, that from his earliest age he accustom himself to good behavior, based on moral principles.[5]

THE REFORMATION

It is difficult for people today to imagine the extent to which the Roman Catholic Church dominated the lives of the common people through most of what we think of as Europe during the fifteenth and sixteenth centuries. The Roman Catholic Church and the Pope had an enormous amount of influence over European royalty during this time. In fact, some historians suggest that the Pope and other officials of the Roman Catholic Church were in some ways more powerful than many individual kings and queens. After all, the Roman Catholic Church could and frequently did claim that unless members of royalty abided by its rules, they were destined to spend eternity in hell—an extremely frightening prospect for any human being. Consequently, it is understandable that the church came to be a powerful influence throughout most of Europe.

What can only be taught by the rod and with blows will not lead to much good; they will not remain pious longer than the rod is behind them.

Martin Luther

LUTHER AND MELANCHTHON The Protestant Reformation had its formal beginning in 1517. In that year Martin Luther (1483–1546) published his ninety-five theses, which stated his disagreements with the Roman Catholic Church. One of these disagreements held great implications for the importance of formal education. The church believed that it was not desirable for each person to read and interpret the Bible for himself or herself; rather, the church would pass on the "correct" interpretation to the laity. Luther felt not only that the church had itself misinterpreted the Bible, but also that people were intended to read and interpret the Bible for themselves. If one accepted the church's position on this matter, formal education remained unimportant. If one accepted Luther's position, however, education became necessary for all people so that they might individually read and interpret the Bible. In a sense, education became important as a way of obtaining salvation. It is understandable that Luther and his coworker in education, Melanchthon (1497–1560), soon came to stress universal elementary education. Melanchthon's most important educational writing was *Visitation Articles* (1528), in which he set forth his recommendations for schools. Luther and Melanchthon felt that education should be provided for all, regardless of class, and should be compulsory for both sexes. They also believed that it should be state-controlled; state-supported; and centered on classical languages, grammar, mathematics, science, history, music, and physical education. Luther's argument for increased governmental support for education has a familiar contemporary ring:

Martin Luther (1483–1546) was an early supporter of state-sponsored, state-controlled education for all people.

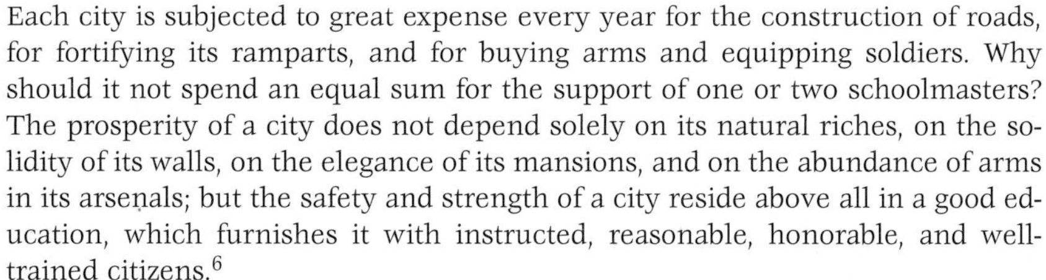

> Each city is subjected to great expense every year for the construction of roads, for fortifying its ramparts, and for buying arms and equipping soldiers. Why should it not spend an equal sum for the support of one or two schoolmasters? The prosperity of a city does not depend solely on its natural riches, on the solidity of its walls, on the elegance of its mansions, and on the abundance of arms in its arsenals; but the safety and strength of a city reside above all in a good education, which furnishes it with instructed, reasonable, honorable, and well-trained citizens.[6]

IGNATIUS OF LOYOLA To combat the Reformation movement, Ignatius of Loyola (1491–1556) organized the Society of Jesus (Jesuits) in 1540. The Jesuits worked to establish schools in which to further the cause of the Roman Catholic Church, and they tried to stem the flow of converts to the Reformation cause. Although the Jesuits' main interest was religious, they soon grew into a great teaching order and were very successful in training their own teachers. The rules by which the Jesuits conducted their schools were stated in the *Ratio Studiorum;* a revised edition still guides Jesuit schools today. The improvement of teacher training was one of the Jesuits' main contribution to education.

Another Catholic teaching order, the Brothers of the Christian Schools, was organized in 1684 by Jean Baptiste de la Salle (1651–1719). Unlike the Jesuits, who were primarily interested in secondary education, de la Salle and his order were interested in elementary schools and in preparing elementary school teachers. De la Salle was one of the first educators to include student teaching in the preparation of teachers.

My whole method aims at changing the school drudgery into play and enjoyment.
Comenius

COMENIUS Among many other outstanding educators during the transition period was Johann Amos Comenius (1592–1670). Comenius is perhaps best remembered for his many textbooks, which were among the first to contain illustrations. The invention and improvement of printing during the 1400s made it possible to produce books, such as those of Comenius, more and more rapidly

The textbooks written by Comenius (1592–1670) were among the first to contain illustrations.

and economically, a development that was essential to the growth of education. Much of the writing of Comenius reflected the increasing interest that was then developing in science.

LOCKE John Locke (1632–1704) was an influential English educator during the late seventeenth century. He wrote many important educational works, including *Some Thoughts on Education* and *Essay Concerning Human Understanding.* He viewed a young child's mind as a blank slate (*tabula rasa*) on which an education could be imprinted. He believed that teachers needed to create a nonthreatening learning environment—a revolutionary idea at that time.

MODERN PERIOD (1700–PRESENT)

As we have suggested, educational progress in the world was slow and took place in only a few places through the seventeenth century. This section will show why many of our current educational ideas can be traced to the early 1700s. We will look at the Age of Reason and the concept of the "emergence of common man."

THE AGE OF REASON

The first movement of the early modern period that influenced education was a revolt of the intellectuals against the superstition and ignorance that dominated people's lives at the time. This movement became the keynote of the period known as the **Age of Reason;** and François Marie Arouet (1745–1827), a Frenchman who wrote under the name Voltaire, was one of its leaders. Those who joined this movement became known as *rationalists* because of the faith they placed in human rational power. The implication for education in the rationalist movement is obvious: If one places greater emphasis on human ability to reason, then education takes on new importance as the way by which humans develop this power.

DESCARTES AND VOLTAIRE The work of Descartes (1596–1650) laid the foundations for rationalism. Cartesian thinking resulted in three axioms that gradually became well accepted by thinking people. These axioms were (1) that reason was supreme, (2) that the laws of nature were invariable, and (3) that truth could be verified empirically—verified by exact methods of testing. These ideas became the basis for disputing some of the traditional teaching of the church and for resisting the bonds that royalty had traditionally placed on the common people. These axioms also influenced the thinking of Voltaire. Voltaire was an articulate writer who was also brilliant, clever, witty, and vain—qualities that helped him to become extremely influential. In fact, many authorities give him considerable credit for both the American and French Revolutions, which took place during his lifetime.

Age of Reason The beginning of the modern period of educational thought: a period in which leading European thinkers emphasized the importance of reason. The writings of Voltaire strongly influenced the rationalist movement.

While Voltaire was not technically an educator, his writings helped to bring about a renewed interest in learning and a conviction that knowledge, and therefore education, was extremely powerful in shaping the lives of people. His views contributed to the development of educational philosophies such as rationalism and empiricism, which helped to elevate the importance of education in the Western world.

Freedom of Speech

FREDERICK THE GREAT One of the influential leaders during the Age of Reason was Frederick the Great (1712–1786). Frederick was a friend of Voltaire and supported the notion that education was of value. He was a liberal thinker for his time and was one of the few leaders who did not attempt to force the common people into a particular form of religion. Frederick also permitted an unusual amount of freedom of speech for his era and generally allowed the common people a degree of liberty that most rulers considered dangerous.

As a consequence, education had an opportunity to develop, if not flourish, during his reign as leader of Prussia. During Frederick's reign Prussia passed laws regarding education and required teachers to obtain special training as well as licenses to teach.

The progress of education during Frederick's reign was meager in comparison to what we know today; nevertheless, for his time, Frederick must be given considerable credit for contributing to the development of schools during the Age of Reason. Concerning education for all children, Frederick stated, "In the open country it is sufficient if they learn to read and write a little; if they know too much they will go to towns and become secretaries and such like." It is likewise true that Frederick did not place much value on education for young children beyond learning to read and write. It is interesting to note, however, that he was particularly interested in better training for teachers.

Philosopher Jean Jacques Rousseau (1712–1778) felt that education should seek to return humans to their natural state.

THE EMERGENCE OF COMMON MAN

The second pivotal trend of the early modern period that affected education was the influential concept sometimes called the "emergence of common man." Whereas the Age of Reason was sparked by a revolt of the learned for intellectual freedom, the thinkers who promoted the **emergence of common man** argued that common people deserved a better life—politically, economically, socially, and educationally.

ROUSSEAU One of the leaders in this movement was Jean Jacques Rousseau (1712–1778), whose *Social Contract* (1762) became an influential book in the French Revolution. Scholars have suggested that *Social Contract* was also the basal doctrine of the American Declaration of Independence.[7] Rousseau was a philosopher, not an educator, but he wrote a good deal on the subject of education. His most important educational work was *Émile* (1762), in which he states his views concerning the ideal education for youth. Rousseau felt that the aim of education should be to return human beings to their "natural state." His view on the subject is well summed up by the opening sentence of *Émile:* "Everything is good as it comes from the hand of the author of nature: but everything degenerates in the hands of man." Rousseau's educational views came to be known as *naturalism.* Concerning the best method of teaching, Rousseau wrote,

> Do not treat the child to discourses which he cannot understand. No descriptions, no eloquence, no figures of speech. Be content to present to him appropriate objects. Let us transform our sensations into ideas. But let us not jump at once from sensible objects to intellectual objects. Let us always proceed slowly from one sensible notion to another. In general, let us never substitute the sign for the

emergence of common man
A concept that coincided with the Age of Reason and emphasized the rights of the common people for a better life, politically, economically, socially, and educationally. Rousseau was a leading thinker promoting these ideas.

DEBATE

Should Kids Read *Goosebumps*?

Down through history, parents and teacher have pondered what children should read. Long ago, the Bible or other religious materials were the commonly available children's books. But over time, as a wider selection of children's books became available, controversy inevitably arose as to what children should be allowed to read, both at home and in the school. Such controversy continues today, as the following debate feature shows.

YES

Suzanne Wargo is a media specialist at William J. Johnston Middle School in Colchester, Connecticut. A member of the Colchester Education Association, Wargo is active on several state-level NEA committees. She's also a reporter for the Norwich Bulletin *and can be reached at* suewargo@aol.com.

Kids love to be scared! From the time babies are aware of their surroundings, we play peek-a-boo with them, hoping to startle them into a giggle. We scare kids at amusement parks, on television, at the movies, and around the campfire—and they love it.

So it's no wonder that R. L. Stine's young adult novels, and particularly his *Goosebumps* book series, are so popular.

From the publication of the first book in 1992, I had a giant waiting list of youngsters eager to check the books out. I couldn't keep the books on the racks, and my daily circulation rate hit new highs.

So when parents ask me if students should be allowed to read *Goosebumps,* I always respond with a resounding "yes." Here's why:

- *Any child who is reading is an improvement over one who is not.* Kids love to read about scary ideas and scary situations. These books reach them where they are.

  Are they great literature? Certainly not. But, given the fast-paced electronic age today's kids are growing up in, *Goosebumps* keeps young people reading—and that's worth a lot.

- *Books in the* Goosebumps *series aren't harmful.* A fan of scary books myself, I've read a few of them. To me, *Goosebumps* books are fun and a bit silly, but they don't make kids feel genuinely afraid for their safety.

- *Students will outgrow books by R. L. Stine and learn to love reading.* Like thousands of other adolescents, my own daughter has read more than 50 of Stine's books. Now 15, she's moved on to Mary Higgins Clark. I was stuck myself on Nancy Drew mysteries, but I've moved on to read bigger and greater things. Your students will, too.

- *With some guidance, parents and teachers can make reading* Goosebumps *an educational experience.* When parents

NO

Alberta Graham, now a reading specialist at Lakeview Elementary School in Neenah, Wisconsin, has taught grades 1, 3, 4, and 5 and worked as a reading teacher. An active member of the Neenah Education Association and the Fox Valley Reading Council, Graham can be reached at agraham@vbe.com.

I confess: I'm jealous. R. L. Stine is a prolific writer, knows his audience, and is the beneficiary of a marvelous marketing scheme for *Goosebumps.*

But he's not an educator, and his books have little educational value.

As a reading specialist, I try to get children to read a variety of genres and authors to increase their reading ability and get a well-rounded education.

I want children to read quality fiction and nonfiction books to learn about each other, their school community, and their world. I want them to develop an understanding of other cultures and be introduced to creative and diverse thinking.

When measured against these criteria, the choice of *Goosebumps* as reading material leaves much to be desired.

Now that's not to say that *Goosebumps* has absolutely no value at all. The books are well-orchestrated to sustain interest and keep the reader turning pages. They keep children interested in science fiction engrossed. And the child who reads *Goosebumps* is, at least, reading something.

But Stine's work aims at such a low level, develops little artistic setting, and has few interesting characters and next to no mind-expanding value.

It's great to get children "hooked on books," but Stine is stuck on the "hook," not the "book."

There are many who attack public education in the media as simplistic, faddish, and not rooted in the basics, let alone the classics. The popularity of Stine's work has only helped to strengthen that premise.

Characters in Stine's books don't have real lives with real families and real communities. They live only for their role in the plot development and then are discarded. There is no carryover to develop the family or community spirit that today's children need so desperately.

YES NO

balk at buying yet the zillionth volume, I urge them to start a conversation with their kids about some of the plots—there are occasional morals worthy of discussion.

When parents express frustration over the quality of the content—or lack of it—in the series, I suggest they introduce their kids to Edgar Allen Poe's *The Tell Tale Heart.* I've heard some terrific audio versions guaranteed to pique the imagination of any 9- or 10-year-old.

In the classroom, teachers can capitalize on students' interest by doing a unit on the horror genre. Students can do *Goosebumps* written reports, create art projects, and write letters to Stine himself. I've seen many a young *Goosebumps* aficionado inspired to write the great American horror novel during a unit like that.

- *Telling kids they can't read something will only increase the attraction.* My mother wouldn't let me watch *The Three Stooges* because she thought it too violent. I grew up with many a young boy my age pretending to poke and slap in imitation of the Stooges' brand of comedy. It only made me more eager to sneak around the rule and find out for myself.

- *Finally, there's nothing wrong with fear as fun—at any age.* With memories of reading Stephen King's *The Shining* during the blizzard of '78, I still love a scary book and giggle when my daughter plots to jump out at me in the dark when I least expect it.

Source: "Should Kids Read *Goosebumps?*" *NEA Today* (October 1997): 43.

Stine would be of great assistance to the slow-developing reader if he were to put more picturesque language in his books so that readers could use their imaginations to develop a "movie in their heads" with vivid detail.

But he doesn't. Stine's books, each with the same basic style and format, don't help students open their minds.

They do stop students—captivated by this one genre—from exposing themselves to the vast array of quality reading material that would widen their horizons, not inhibit their thoughts.

Stine engages his readers on only one plane—horror. The videos loosely based on his books are even gorier. They debilitate, rather than strengthen, children's minds.

Although Stine has done well in the marketing field, his books do not produce the reading enhancement that I look for when I'm choosing books for children.

Needless to say, I'm opposed to any series of books that creates a single-genre rut that children have trouble breaking out of.

Stine's books limit the horizons of children's reading. Instead of helping to raise moral fiber, they lower it. Instead of broadening perspectives, they narrow them.

As a reading specialist, I will not spend my hard-earned money on this type of limiting literature.

WHAT'S YOUR OPINION?

Should kids read *Goosebumps?*

Go to **www.ablongman.com/johnson** to cast your vote and see how NEA readers responded.

> thing, except when it is impossible for us to show the thing. . . . I have no love whatever for explanations and talk. Things! Things! I shall never tire of saying that we ascribe too much importance to words. With our babbling education we make only babblers.[8]

Rousseau's most important contributions to education were his belief that education must be a natural process, not an artificial one, and his compassionate, positive view of the child. Rousseau believed that children were inherently good—a belief that was in opposition to the prevailing religiously inspired belief that children were born full of sin. The contrasting implications for teaching methods suggested by these two views are self-evident, as is the educational desirability of Rousseau's view over that which prevailed at the time. Although

Swiss educator Johann Heinrich Pestalozzi (1746–1827) put Rousseau's theory into practice.

Rousseau never taught a day of school in his life, he likely did more to improve education through his writing than any of his contemporaries.

Rousseau saw children through a different set of lenses than most educators of his day. As a result, his views of children were not quickly accepted. In fact, many of his counterparts belittled his notion that children were born good and became "degenerate" at the hands of society. Eventually, of course, nearly all educators came to believe that Rousseau's views of children were correct. This raises an interesting question for contemporary educators: To what degree should one stand by and defend one's educational convictions—even when others do not accept them?

PESTALOZZI Johann Heinrich Pestalozzi (1746–1827) was a Swiss educator who put Rousseau's theory into practice. Pestalozzi established two schools for boys, one at Burgdorf (1800–1804) and the other at Yverdun (1805–1825). Educators came from all over the world to view Pestalozzi's schools and to study his teaching methods. Pestalozzi enumerated his educational views in a book entitled *Leonard and Gertrude.* Unlike most educators of his time, Pestalozzi believed that a teacher should treat students with love and kindness:

> I was convinced that my heart would change the condition of my children just as promptly as the sun of spring would reanimate the earth benumbed by the winter. . . . It was necessary that my children should observe, from dawn to evening, at every moment of the day, upon my brow and on my lips, that my affections were fixed on them, that their happiness was my happiness, and that their pleasures were my pleasures. . . . I was everything to my children. I was alone with them from morning till night. . . . Their hands were in my hands. Their eyes were fixed on my eyes.[9]

Key concepts in the Pestalozzian method included the expression of love, understanding, and patience for children; compassion for the poor; and the use of objects and sense perception as the basis for acquiring knowledge.

HERBART One of the educators who studied under Pestalozzi and was influenced by him was Johann Friedrich Herbart (1776–1841). While Pestalozzi had successfully put into practice and further developed Rousseau's educational ideas, it remained for Herbart to organize these educational views into a formal psychology of education. Herbart stressed apperception (learning by association). The **Herbartian teaching method** developed into five formal steps:

1. *Preparation:* Preparing the student to receive a new idea
2. *Presentation:* Presenting the student with the new idea
3. *Association:* Assimilating the new idea with the old ideas
4. *Generalization:* The general idea deriving from the combination of the old and new ideas
5. *Application:* Applying the new knowledge

Herbart's educational ideas are contained in his *Science of Education* (1806) and *Outlines of Educational Doctrine* (1835).

Johann Friedrich Herbart (1776–1814) was a German philosopher, educator, and author who expanded the work of Pestalozzi.

FROEBEL Friedrich Froebel (1782–1852) was another European educator who was influenced by Rousseau and Pestalozzi and who made a significant contribution to education. Froebel's contributions included the establishment of the first kindergarten (or *Kleinkinderbeschaftigungsanstalt,* as he called it in 1837), an emphasis on social development, a concern for the cultivation of creativity, and the concept of learning by doing. He originated the idea that women are best suited to teach young children. Froebel wrote his main educational book, *Education of Man,* in 1826.

Two other developments in the late 1800s were also important European antecedents of American education: the maturing of the scientific movement, hastened by the publication of Charles Darwin's *On the Origin of Species* (1859), and the formulation of educational psychology near the end of the century.

The student of educational history must realize that even though many educational advances had been made by 1900, the average European received a pathetically small amount of formal education, even at that late date. Historically, education had been available only to the few who were fortunate enough to be born into the leisure class; the masses of people in the working class had received little or no education up to that time. What little formal education the working person might have received was usually provided for religious purposes by the church.

Friedrich Froebel (1782–1852) was a German educator and author who founded the kindergarten.

USING EARLY HISTORY TO IMPROVE STUDENT LEARNING As in all chapters in this book, you should ask how this chapter on historical antecedents to our educational system might be of practical use to you as a contemporary educator in your efforts to improve student learning. In an attempt to help you begin searching for answers to this critical question, we offer the following for your consideration:

1. If it is true, as many people have suggested, that you cannot really understand something unless you understand its past, then historical information about the antecedents of our educational system should help you better understand today's schools and the education profession.
2. A common characteristic of our very most successful educators is that they are proud of their profession; and an understanding of the essential role and accomplishments of schools and teachers throughout history helps to build appreciation for, and genuine pride in, the teaching profession.

In what other ways, if any, do you think this chapter might help you to improve student learning?

Herbartian teaching method
An organized teaching method based on the principles of Pestalozzi that stresses learning by association and consists of five steps: preparation, presentation, association, generalization, and application.

SUMMARY

A famous Roman educator by the name of Quintilian, who lived nearly 2,000 years ago, opened this chapter by describing his concept of an ideal teacher. Many people would say that his ideas about the qualities of a good teacher remain remarkably appropriate for today. What do you think?

THE BEGINNINGS OF EDUCATION (TO A.D. 476)

Any study of the beginnings of formal education should start with a recognition of the fact that parents have undoubtedly always attempted to provide, one way or another, the informal education their children need to survive in their society. Formal schools very likely did not come into existence until four or five thousand years ago, as humans developed written languages. Schools evolved slowly in various parts of the world, including Chinese, Hindu, Hebrew, and African societies.

Current evidence suggests that one of the first well-organized, educational systems was that evolved by the Greeks during what is commonly called the Age of Pericles. This system produced many philosophers whose ideas and writings have been influential through the ages right down to today. Greek knowledge and schools were eventually blending into Roman schools and libraries. The Romans developed a reputation for good organization, which enabled them to unite a large part of the Western world with a common language, religion, and political system, all of which facilitated the advancement of knowledge, schools, and education.

EDUCATION IN THE MIDDLE AGES (476–1300)

The Roman Catholic Church became a major power in Western governments and in education during the Middle Ages. During this time different types of schools slowly evolved in different parts of the world. Knowledge and schooling progressed in some societies while declining in others, but religion usually played a major role in the control and curriculum of schools during this time. In fact, most of the famous educators, philosophers, and writers of the time were religious leaders. The concept of liberal arts education, which is still prominent today, had its origins in the Middle Ages. One of this period's most notable educators was an Englishman named Alcuin, who served as Emperor Charlemagne's educational advisor and left many educational writings that are still considered relevant.

During the later part of the Middle Ages, there was a revived interest in learning that was due, in large part, to the work of Thomas Aquinas, who developed an education philosophy that is commonly referred to as scholasticism. This philosophy reconciled the religious ideas of the powerful Roman Catholic Church with the more secular educational ideas of early Greeks, which allowed schools to pursue nonreligious subjects. Our modern-day universities also trace their origins to the later part of the Middle Ages.

EDUCATION IN TRANSITION (1300–1700)

This period of educational history is commonly divided into two time periods: the Renaissance and the Reformation. The Renaissance represented a rebellion on the part of the common people against the economic, educational, and religious suppression under which the royalty and landed gentry made them live. These common people gradually demanded a better life and developed a spirit of inquiry, which created an interest in education and schooling.

The Reformation, brought about largely by the work of Martin Luther and his colleague Melanchthon, gave great impetus to the concept of providing education for the common people. Luther believed that all people should be taught to read so they could read the Bible for themselves, in opposition to the then-common belief of the Roman Catholic Church that priests should read and interpret the Bible for the common people. This radical idea of Luther's created great controversy; it also created a need for schools for all the people and thereby gave great impetus to the development of education, school systems, and knowledge. The Reformation also spawned many notable educators and writers, including Ignatus of Loyola, Comenius, and Locke.

MODERN PERIOD (1700–PRESENT)

The last three centuries have seen a sometimes erratic, but nevertheless fairly continuous, progression of educational development and advancement throughout the world. In the Western world, this time period is often divided into the Age of Reason, which emphasized people's rational and scientific abilities, and the emergence of common man, which sought to create a better education and life for all people. Many important educators and philosophers contributed to both of these movements, including Voltaire, Descartes, Rousseau, Pestalozzi, Herbart, Froebel, and others.

This chapter has also suggested that history can be viewed through different lenses, each of which will likely produce slightly different views and opinions of history. We have also proposed several big historical ideas that grow out of the more detailed education history discussed in the chapter. These included the idea that adults in early societies undoubtedly also attempted to provide the informal education that they felt necessary for children to succeed in their society; more formal schools likely came into existence only as people developed written languages; all societies around the world have developed their own forms of education, down through the ages, designed to fulfill their unique needs; and human progress has, in large part depended on education.

DISCUSSION QUESTIONS

1. What were the major factors that first caused humans to create schools, especially in the Eastern world?
2. What were the major differences between the Spartan and Athenian school systems? Why did these differences exist?
3. Discuss the educational achievements of the Roman Empire.
4. What factors contributed to the decline of education during the Dark Ages?
5. What were the major educational advances made during the Reformation period?
6. What were the strengths and weaknesses of Jean Jacques Rousseau's ideas about children and education?

JOURNAL ENTRIES

1. Think about and list some of the more important antecedents of U.S. education. Select your top five items and briefly tell why each was important.

2. Select a person mentioned in this chapter (or another non-U.S. figure from the history of education who is of interest to you) and learn more about that person. Make journal entry notes about what you learn.

PORTFOLIO DEVELOPMENT

1. Write a paper summarizing and criticizing the work and writing of one of the early educators mentioned in this chapter.
2. Make a list of historical educational ideas mentioned in this chapter that are still valid and useful for educators today.

SCHOOL-BASED EXPERIENCES

1. Over two hundred years ago, Jean Jacques Rousseau advocated that children should be taught with love, patience, understanding, and kindness. As you work in the school, experiment with this basic approach to see whether it is effective. You might also wish to observe experienced teachers: To what extent do they teach children with love, patience, understanding, and kindness? We suggest that you experiment with other ideas in this chapter as you observe and participate in the classroom.
2. As you work in schools, observe how they have changed relative to schools of the past. How are schools today similar to those of the past? How much and in what ways are students today similar to their historical counterparts? In what ways are they probably different?

WEBSITES

We recommend you do a web search using key words such as "museums, education"; "history, education"; "schools, world"; "education, Greek"; and so forth. Other useful sites are listed below.

1. <www.cedu.niu.edu/blackwell> The Blackwell History of Education Museum and Research Collection is one of the largest collections of its kind in the world. Much of the collection is listed on this website. The Blackwell Museum has developed a variety of instructional materials (also listed on its site) designed to help you learn more about the antecedents of American education.
2. <www.tandf.co.uk/jnls/hed.htm> History of Education Journal of the History of Education Society. Located in England.
3. <www.qut.edu.au/edu/cpol/anzhes/links.html> The History of Education and Childhood. An international archive of links and source materials about the history of education and the history of childhood. An excellent site.
4. <www.qut.edu.au/edu/cpol/anzhes/links.html> The site for the History of Education Review, the official journal of the Australian and New Zealand History of Education Society.

NOTES

1. Paul Monroe, *Source Book of the History of Education.* New York: Macmillan, 1901, 282.
2. Quintilian, *The Institutes of Oratory,* trans. W. Guthrie. London: Dewick and Clark, 1905, 27.
3. Quintilian, 12.
4. Glenn Smith et al., *Lives in Education.* Ames, IA: Educational Studies Press, 1984, 84–88.

5. Gabriel Compayre, *History of Pedagogy,* trans. W. H. Payne. Boston: Heath, 1888, 12–13, 88–89.
6. Compayre, 115.
7. Paul Monroe, *History of Education.* New York: Macmillan, 1905, 283.
8. Compayre, 299.
9. Compayre, 425.

BIBLIOGRAPHY

Armytage, W. H. G. "William Byngham: A Medieval Protagonist of the Training of Teachers." *History of Education Journal* 2 (1951): 107–110.

Brosterman, Norman. *Inventing Kindergarten*. New York: Harry N. Abrams, 1997.

Butts, R. Freeman. *A Cultural History of Western Education.* New York: McGraw-Hill, 1955.

Chambliss, J. J., ed. *Nobility, Tragedy and Naturalism: Education in Ancient Greece.* Minneapolis: Burgess, 1971.

Cole, Luella. *A History of Education: Socrates to Montessori.* New York: Holt, Rinehart & Winston, 1950.

Compayre, Gabriel. *History of Pedagogy.* Translated by W. H. Payne. Boston: Heath, 1888.

Conger, S. M. *Mary Wollstonecraft and the Language of Sensibility.* Cranbury, NJ: Associated University Presses, 1994.

Forbel, Frederich. *The Education of Man.* Trans. by W. N. Hailman. New York: Appleton, 1896.

Golden, M. *Children and Childhood in Classical Athens.* Baltimore: Johns Hopkins Press, 1990.

Gutek, Gerald L. *Historical and Philosophical Foundations of Education.* Upper Saddle River, NJ: Prentice Hall, 1997, Chapters 1–10.

Hamilton, Edith. *The Greek Way.* New York: W. W. Norton, 1930.

Keating, M. W. *Comenius.* New York: McGraw-Hill, 1931.

Lucas, Christopher J. *Our Western Educational Heritage.* New York: Macmillan, 1972.

Meyer, Adolph E. *An Educational History of the Western World.* New York: McGraw-Hill, 1965.

Pulliam, J. D., and Van Patten, J. *History of Education in America.* 6th ed. Englewood Cliffs, NJ: Prentice-Hall, 1995.

Reagan, T. *Non-Western Educational Traditions: Alternative Approaches to Education Thought and Practice.* Mahwah, NJ: Lawrence Erlbaum, 1996.

CHAPTER 8

The Important Role of Education in Our Developing Nation

EDUCATION IN THE NEWS

Why Study History?

By Diane Ravitch, *American History Illustrated,* March /April 1991

Why study history? The simplest and truest answer is that the study of history makes people more intelligent. History is an investigation of causes; it is a way of finding out how the world came to be as it is. Without history, we are without memory and without explanations. Those who do not know history—their own history and that of their society and other societies—cannot comment intelligently on the causes of events—cannot understand their own lives nor the changes in their society and in the world. The person who knows no history is like an amnesiac, lacking a sense of what happened before and therefore unable to tell the difference between cause and effect.

Unfortunately, many people get the impression from studying history in school with poorly trained teachers and with boring textbooks that history is nothing more than a recitation of dull facts about battles and kings. Sadly, some states certify people to teach social studies who have never studied a single history course in college; and some districts routinely assign coaches with no history education to teach history. And such teachers tend to use the history textbook as a script that students are supposed to memorize and regurgitate.

History ought to be the most exciting course taught in school or college. It ought to be the course that introduces students to great men and women who risked their lives for principle or who committed foul deeds for the sake of power. It ought to be the course that arouses heated discussion about historical controversies, with students contesting different versions of the past or disputing the meaning of events. Just as students need to think about the present, they need to think about the past and to realize that it was just as complicated as the present and not a cut-and-dried affair as the textbooks so often imply.

Pick up the newspaper on any day, and the stories presuppose a basic knowledge of history. They refer to events in Eastern Europe or the Soviet Union or Africa or China, assuming that the reader has some knowledge of World War I, World War II, the Russian Revolution, Stalinism, colonialism, imperialism, the postwar decolonization movement, the Universal Declaration of Human Rights, the Solidarity movement, the Chinese revolution, Maoism, the Chinese Cultural Revolution, and so on.

The person who has studied history can read the newspapers and magazines with a critical eye; can understand new developments because he or she has a historical context in which to place them; can mentally reject erroneous statements; and is resistant to indoctrination and propaganda.

When we teach history, we teach not only what happened in the past, but how to reason, how to weigh evidence, how to analyze continuity and change, and how to

(continued)

assess contending ideas. We need the substance of history, and we need the historical thinking that informs rational judgment. We must teach history in elementary schools, junior high schools, senior high schools, colleges, and universities. But that is not enough. We must teach it on the television and in the movies, in museums and libraries, and around the dinner table.

Why study history? To gain the habits of mind and the intellectual tools that are required to be a free person.

LEARNER OUTCOMES

After reading and studying this chapter, you will be able to

1. Explain the degree to which you believe education students should study the history of education.
2. Analyze what life was like for the colonial schoolteacher, student, and parent.
3. Articulate the roles government (local, state, and national) played in colonial America, soon after winning the war of independence, in the 1800s, and in the early twentieth century.
4. Explain what has characterized the education received by various minorities and women throughout the development of our nation.
5. Analyze how an understanding of early American educational history might be used to improve student learning today. ■

Although this chapter presents a good amount of rather detailed information about the development of education in what is now the United States, it does so around the following major historical ideas.

Native Americans developed an effective system of informal education that served their needs well long before the first Europeans reached North America. Like all educational systems throughout the world, Native American educational traditions passed the peoples' culture on to their children and taught them the skills needed to succeed in their society.

Another major idea presented in this chapter deals with the fact that, as one might expect, the early American colonists brought their educational ideas and practices with them from Europe. In other words, nearly all of the educational practices and educational materials were essentially the same as those found in Europe at that time.

Yet another big historical idea found in this chapter is that the religious motive was extremely strong in colonial America, and it permeated colonial education. Colonists generally thought that children must learn to read so they could read the Bible and thereby gain salvation and eventual admittance to heaven and avoidance of hell. Beyond this desire, there was little demand for mass education in the colonies.

The last big idea presented in this chapter deals with the fact that education has played a critical role in the historical development of the United States. The framers of our Constitution clearly recognized that our new democracy was dependent on an educated citizenry.

PROVIDING EDUCATION IN THE NEW WORLD

The earliest settlers from Europe brought with them a sincere interest in providing at least rudimentary education for their children. Naturally, they brought their European ideas about education with them and, soon after arrival, created educational programs throughout colonial America. This section will briefly examine these early colonial school programs.

COLONIAL EDUCATION

The early settlement of the East Coast was composed of groups of colonies: the Southern Colonies, centered in Virginia; the Middle Colonies, centered in New York; and the Northern Colonies, centered in New England.

SOUTHERN COLONIES The Southern Colonies soon came to be made up of large tobacco plantations. Because of the size of the plantations, people lived far apart, and few towns grew up until later in the colonial period. There was an immediate need for cheap labor to work on the plantations; in 1619, only twelve years after Jamestown was settled, the colony imported the first boatload of slaves from Africa. Other sources of cheap labor for the Southern Colonies included white Europeans from a variety of backgrounds, people who purchased passage to the New World by agreeing to serve a lengthy period of indentured servitude on arrival in the colonies. There soon came to be two very distinct classes of people in the South—a few wealthy landowners and a large mass of laborers, most of whom were slaves. The educational provisions that evolved from this set of conditions were precisely what one would expect. No one was interested in providing education for the slaves, with the exception of a few missionary groups such as the English Society for the Propagation of the Gospel in Foreign Parts. Such missionary groups tried to provide some education for slaves, primarily so that they could read the Bible. The wealthy landowners usually hired tutors to teach their children at home. Distances between homes and slow transportation precluded the establishment of centralized schools. When the upper-class children grew old enough to attend college, they were usually sent to well-established universities in Europe.

MIDDLE COLONIES The people who settled the Middle Colonies came from various national (Dutch, Swedish) and religious (Puritan, Mennonite, Catholic) backgrounds. This is why the Middle Colonies have often been called the melting pot of the nation. This diversity of backgrounds made it impossible for the inhabitants of the Middle Colonies to agree on a common public school system. Consequently, the respective groups established their own religious schools. Many children received their education through an apprenticeship while learning a trade from a master already in that line of work. Some people even learned the art of teaching school through apprenticeship.

NORTHERN COLONIES The Northern Colonies were settled mainly by the Puritans, a religious group from Europe. In 1630 approximately one thousand Puritans settled near Boston. Unlike people in the Southern Colonies, people in New England lived close to one another. Towns sprang up and soon became centers of political and social life. Shipping ports were established, and an industrial economy developed that demanded numerous skilled and semiskilled workers—a condition that eventually created a large middle class.

EARLY SCHOOL LAWS These conditions of common religious views, town life, and a large middle class made it possible for the people to agree on common public schools and led to very early educational activity in the Northern Colonies. In 1642 the General Court of Massachusetts enacted a law that stated:

> This Co^t [Court], taking into consideration the great neglect of many parents & masters in training up their children in learning . . . do hereupon order and decree, that in every towne y chosen men . . . take account from time to time of all parents and masters, and of their children, concerning their . . . ability to read & understand the principles of religion & the capitall lawes of this country.

This law did nothing more than encourage citizens to look after the education of children. Five years later (1647), however, another law was enacted in Massachusetts that required towns to provide education for the youth. This law, which was often referred to as the **Old Deluder Satan Act,** because of its religious motive, stated:

> It being one chiefe proiect of y ould deluder, Satan, to keepe men from the knowledge of y Scriptures. . . . It is therefore orded [ordered], ye evy [every] towneship in this jurisdiction, aft y Lord hath increased y number to 50 household, shall then forthw appoint one w [with] in their towne to teach all such children as shall resort to him to write & reade . . . & it is furth ordered y where any towne shall increase to y numb [number] of 100 families or househould, they shall set up a grammar schoole, y m [aim] thereof being able to instruct youth so farr as they shall be fited for y university [Harvard].

These Massachusetts school laws of 1642 and 1647 served as models for similar laws that were soon created in other colonies.

TYPES OF COLONIAL SCHOOLS Several different kinds of elementary schools sprang up in the colonies, such as the **dame school,** which was conducted by a housewife in her home; the writing school, which taught the child to write; a variety of church schools; and charity, or pauper, schools taught by missionary groups.

To go back a few years, in 1635 the Latin Grammar School was established in Boston—the first permanent school of this type in what is now the United States. This school was established when the people of Boston, which had been settled only five years before, voted "that our brother Philemon Pormont, shal be intreated to become scholemaster, for the teaching and nourtering of children with us." The grammar school was a secondary school, its function was college preparatory, and the idea spread quickly to other towns. Charlestown opened its first grammar school one year later, in 1636, by contracting William Witherell "to keep a school for a twelve month." Within sixteen years after the Massachusetts Bay Colony had been founded, seven or eight towns had Latin grammar schools in operation. Transplanted from Europe, where similar schools had existed for a long time, these schools were traditional and aimed to prepare children for college and "for the service of God, in church and commonwealth."

Harvard, the first colonial college, was established in 1636 for preparing ministers. Other early American colleges included William and Mary (1693), Yale

Old Deluder Satan Act
An early colonial educational law (1647) that required colonial towns of at least fifty households to provide education for youth.

dame school
A low-level primary school in the colonial and other early periods, usually conducted by an untrained woman in her own home.

(1701), Princeton (1746), King's College (1754), College of Philadelphia (1755), Brown (1764), Dartmouth (1769), and Queen's College (1770). The curriculum in these early colleges was traditional, with heavy emphasis on theology and the classics. An example of the extent to which the religious motive dominated colonial colleges can be found in one of the 1642 rules governing Harvard College, which stated: "Let every Student be plainly instructed, and earnestly pressed to consider well, the maine end of his life and studies is, to know God and Jesus Christ."

THE STRUGGLE FOR UNIVERSAL ELEMENTARY EDUCATION

When the colonists arrived in this country, they simply established schools like those they had known in Europe. The objectives of colonial elementary schools were primarily religious.

CHRISTOPHER DOCK A good idea of what a colonial elementary school was like, and the extent to which religion dominated its curriculum, can be gleaned from the following account of a school conducted in 1750 by Christopher Dock, a Mennonite school teacher in Pennsylvania:

> The children arrive as they do because some have a great distance to school, others a short distance, so that the children cannot assemble as punctually as they can in a city. Therefore, when a few children are present, those who can read their Testament sit together on one bench; but the boys and girls occupy separate benches. They are given a chapter which they read at sight consecutively. Meanwhile I write copies for them. Those who have read their passage of Scripture without error take their places at the table and write. Those who fail have to sit at the end of the bench, and each new arrival the same; as each one is thus released in order he takes up his slate. This process continues until they have all assembled. The last one left on the bench is a "lazy pupil."
>
> When all are together, and examined, whether they are washed and combed, they sing a psalm or morning hymn, and I sing and pray with them. As much as they can understand of the Lord's Prayer and the Ten Commandments (according to the gift God has given them), I exhort and admonish them accordingly.[1]

Beyond the power of diffusing old wealth, education has the prerogative of creating new. It is a thousand times more lucrative than fraud; and adds a thousand fold more to a nation's resources than the most successful conquest.

Horace Mann

MONITORIAL SCHOOLS In 1805 New York City established the first monitorial school in the United States. The monitorial school, which originated in England, represented an attempt to provide mass elementary education for large numbers of children. Typically, the teacher would teach hundreds of pupils, using the better students as helpers. By 1840, however, nearly all monitorial schools had been closed; the children had not learned enough to justify continuance of this type of school.

HORACE MANN Between 1820 and 1860 an educational awakening took place in the United States. This movement was strongly influenced by Horace Mann (1796–1859). As secretary of the State Board of Education, Mann helped to establish **common elementary schools** in Massachusetts. These common schools were designed to provide a basic elementary education for all children. Among Mann's many impressive educational achievements was the publication of one of the very early professional journals in this country, *The Common School Journal.* Through this journal, Mann kept educational issues before the public.

common elementary schools
Schools designed to provide a basic elementary education for all children, originated in the mid-nineteenth century.

In 1852 Massachusetts passed a compulsory elementary school attendance law, the first of its kind in the country requiring all children to attend school. By 1900, thirty-two other states had passed similar **compulsory education** laws.

Financing public education has always been a challenge in America. As early as 1795, Connecticut legislators decided to sell public land and create a permanent school fund to help finance public schools. Other states soon also took action to establish school funding plans.

The right beginning of this work of school improvement is in awakening, correcting, and elevating public sentiment in relation to it.
Henry Barnard

HENRY BARNARD The first U.S. Commissioner of Education was a prominent educator named Henry Barnard (1811–1900). He was a longtime supporter of providing common elementary schools for all children and wrote enthusiastically about the value of education in the *Connecticut Common School Journal* and in the *American Journal of Education,* which he founded. He had also served as the Rhode Island commissioner of public schools and as the Chancellor of the University of Wisconsin before holding the prestigious position of Commissioner of Education for the entire United States. Barnard also strongly supported kindergarten programs for very young children as well as high school programs for older students.

Horace Mann (1796–1859) helped to establish common schools designed to provide a basic elementary education for all children in Massachusetts.

GLOBAL PERSPECTIVES: Educational Transplantation from Europe

As indicated in Chapter 7, Pestalozzianism and Herbartianism considerably affected elementary education when they were introduced into the United States in the late 1800s. Pestalozzianism emphasized teaching children with love, patience, and understanding. Furthermore, children should learn from objects and firsthand experiences, not from abstractions and words. Pestalozzian concepts soon spread throughout the country. Herbartianism was imported into the United States at the Bloomington Normal School in Illinois by students who had learned about the ideas of Herbart while studying in Germany. Herbartianism represented an attempt to make a science out of teaching. The more formal system that Herbartianism brought to the often disorganized elementary teacher was badly needed at the time. Unfortunately, Herbartianism eventually contributed to an extreme formalism and rigidity that characterized many American elementary schools in the early 1900s. One school administrator bragged that at a given moment in the school day he knew exactly what was going on in all the classrooms. One can infer from this boast that teachers and students often had a strict, rigid educational program imposed on them.

If we look back at the historical development of U.S. elementary education, we can make the following generalizations:

- Until the late 1800s the motive, curriculum, and administration of elementary education were primarily religious. The point at which elementary education began to be more secular than religious was the point at which states began to pass compulsory school attendance laws.
- Discipline was traditionally harsh and severe in elementary schools. The classical picture of a colonial schoolmaster equipped with a frown, dunce cap, stick, whip, and a variety of abusive phrases is more accurate than one might expect. It is no wonder that children historically viewed school as an unpleasant place. Pestalozzi had much to do with bringing about a gradual

compulsory education
School attendance that is required by law on the theory that it is to the benefit of the state or commonwealth to educate all the people.

change in discipline when he advocated that love, not harsh punishment, should be used to motivate students.

- Elementary education was traditionally formal and impersonal. The ideas of Rousseau, Pestalozzi, Herbart, and Froebel helped to change this condition gradually and to make elementary education more student-centered; this was becoming apparent about 1900.
- Elementary schools were traditionally taught by poorly prepared teachers.
- Although the aims and methodology varied considerably from time to time, the basic content of elementary education was historically reading, writing, and arithmetic.

THE NEED FOR SECONDARY SCHOOLS

Contemporary U.S. high schools have a long and proud tradition. They have evolved from a series of earlier forms of secondary schools that were created to serve the needs of society at various points in the nation's history.

LATIN GRAMMAR SCHOOL The first form of secondary school in the American colonies was the Latin grammar school mentioned previously, first established in Boston in 1635 only five years after colonists settled in the area. The Latin grammar school focused largely on teaching Latin and other classical subjects, such as Greek, and was strictly college preparatory.

Harvard was the only university in existence in the colonies at that time. The entrance requirements to Harvard stated:

> When any Scholar is able to understand Tully, or such like classicall Latine Author extempore, and make and speake true Latine in Verse and Prose, suo ut aiunt marte; and decline perfectly the Paradigms of Nounes and Verbes in the Greek tongue; let him then, and not before, be capable of admission into the college.

Latin Grammar School was designed primarily to prepare students for higher education.

European colleges and later colonial colleges also demanded that students know Latin and Greek before they could be admitted. For instance, in the mid-eighteenth century the requirements for admission to Yale stated:

> None may expect to be admitted into this College unless upon Examination of the President and Tutors, they shall be found able Extempore to Read, Construe, and Parce Tully, Vergil and the Greek Testament; and to write true Latin in Prose and to understand the Rules of Prosodia, and Common Arithmetic, and Shal bring Sufficient Testimony of his Blameless and inoffensive Life.

The excellent become the permanent.
Jane Addams

Because Latin grammar schools were designed to prepare students for college, it is little wonder that the curriculum in these schools was so classical and traditional. Needless to say, a very small percentage of boys attended any Latin grammar school because very few could hope to attend college. Girls did not attend because colleges at that time did not admit them. As late as 1785 there were only two Latin grammar schools in Boston, and the combined enrollment in these two schools was only sixty-four young men.

AMERICAN ACADEMY By the middle of the eighteenth century, there was a need for more and better-trained skilled workers. Benjamin Franklin (1706–1790), recognizing this need, proposed a new kind of secondary school in Pennsylvania. This proposal brought about the establishment, in Philadelphia in 1751, of the first truly American educational institution: the American Academy. Franklin established this school because he thought the existing Latin grammar schools were not providing the practical secondary education that youth needed. The philosophy, curriculum, and methodology of Franklin's academy were all geared to prepare young people for employment. Eventually, similar academies were established throughout America, and these institutions eventually replaced the Latin grammar school as the predominant secondary education institution. They were usually private schools, and many of them admitted girls as well as boys. Later on, some academies even tried to train elementary school teachers.

Comprehensive high school gave millions a shot at careers.
Mortimer B. Zuckerman

HIGH SCHOOL In 1821 an English classical school (which three years later changed its name to English High School) opened in Boston, and another distinctively American educational institution was launched. This first high school, under the direction of George B. Emerson, consisted of a three-year course in English, mathematics, science, and history. The school later added to its curriculum the philosophy of history, chemistry, intellectual philosophy, linear drawing, logic, trigonometry, French, and the U.S. Constitution. The school enrolled about one hundred boys during its first year.

The high school was established because of a belief that the existing grammar schools were inadequate for the day and because most people could not afford to send their children to the private academies. The high school soon replaced both the Latin grammar school and the private academy, and it has been with us ever since.

About 1910 the first junior high schools were established in the United States. A survey in 1916 showed 54 junior high schools existing in thirty-six states. One year later a survey indicated that the number had increased to about 270. More recently, some school systems have abandoned the junior high school in favor of what is called the *middle school,* which usually consists of grades 6, 7, and 8.

AIMS OF AMERICAN EDUCATION

The aims of education in the United States have gradually changed over the years. During colonial times the overriding aim of education at all levels was to enable students to read and understand the Bible, to gain salvation, and to spread the gospel.

After the colonies won independence from England, educational objectives—such as providing U.S. citizens with a common language, attempting to instill a sense of patriotism, developing a national feeling of unity and common purpose, and providing the technical and agricultural training the developing nation needed—became important tasks for the schools.

COMMITTEE OF TEN In 1892 a committee was established by the National Education Association to study the function of the U.S. high school. This committee, known as the **Committee of Ten,** made an effort to set down the purposes of the high school at that time and made the following recommendations:

- High school should consist of grades 7 through 12.
- Courses should be arranged sequentially.
- Students should be given very few electives in high school.
- One unit, called a Carnegie unit, should be awarded for each separate course that a student takes each year, provided that the course meets four or five times each week all year long.

The Committee of Ten also recommended trying to graduate high school students earlier to permit them to attend college sooner. At that time the recommendation implied that high schools had a college preparatory function. These recommendations became powerful influences in the shaping of secondary education.

SEVEN CARDINAL PRINCIPLES Before 1900 teachers had relatively little direction in their work because most educational goals were not precisely stated. This problem was partly overcome in 1918 when the Commission on Reorganization of Secondary Education published the report *Cardinal Principles of Secondary Education,* usually referred to as the Seven Cardinal Principles. In reality the Seven Cardinal Principles constitute only one section of the basic principles discussed in the original text, but it is the part that has become famous. These principles stated that the student should receive an education in the following fields:

Educational opportunity had become a measure of the aspirations and possibilities of American democracy.

Marvin Larerson

1. Health
2. Command of fundamental processes
3. Worthy home membership
4. Vocation
5. Civic education
6. Worthy use of leisure
7. Ethical character

THE EIGHT-YEAR STUDY The following goals of education, or "needs of youth," were listed by the Progressive Education Association in 1938 and grew out of the Eight-Year Study of thirty high schools conducted by the association from 1932 to 1940:

Committee of Ten
A historic National Education Association (NEA) committee that studied secondary education in 1892.

1. Physical and mental health
2. Self-assurance

RELEVANT RESEARCH

Critiquing Historical Sources

STUDY PURPOSE/QUESTIONS: As you prepare for your teaching career, you should have an opportunity to read and think about original historical research sources. Such historical materials constitute the "relevant research" sources for those who strive to understand and learn from the past—something all educators should do.

STUDY DESIGN: The following letter, written in 1712 by Nathaniel Williams, briefly describes the curriculum of the first Latin grammar school established in the colonies—the Boston Latin Grammar School, which was created in 1635, soon after the first colonists settled in the area.

STUDY FINDINGS:

Curriculum of the Boston Latin Grammar School (1712)

The three first years are spent first in Learning by heart & then acc: to their capacities understanding the Accidence and Nomenclator, in construing & parsing acc: to the English rules of Syntax Sententiae Pueriles Cato & Cordcrius & Aesops Fables.

The 4th year, or sooner if their capacities allow it, they are entered upon Erasmus to which they are allou'd no English . . . & upon translating English into Latin out of m^r Garreston's Exercises.

The fifth year they are entred upon Tullies Epistles . . . the Elegancies of which are remarked and improv'd in the afternoon of the day they learn it, by translating an English which contains the phrase somthing altered, and besides recited by heart on the repetition day. . . .

The sixth year they are entred upon Tullies Offices & Luc: Flor: for the forenoon, continuing the use of Ovid's Metam: in the afternoon, & at the end of the Year they read Virgil. . . . Every week these make a Latin Epistle, the last quarter of the Year, when also they begin to learn Greek, & Rhetorick.

The seventh Year they read Tullie's Orations & Justin for the Latin & Greek Testam^t Isocrates Orat: Homer & Hesiod for the Greek in the forenoons & Virgil Horace Juyenal & Persius afternoons . . . Every fortnight they compose a theme. . . .

IMPLICATIONS: Each reader must deliberate and decide the implications of this small bit of original historical documentation of the Boston Latin Grammar School curriculum. What was the apparent function of the Boston Latin Grammar School? For whom was this curriculum apparently intended, and for what purpose? In what ways was this curriculum similar to that of secondary schools throughout the world today? In what ways was it different? What, if anything, can contemporary educators learn from the Boston Latin Grammar School?

Source: "Letter from Nathaniel Williams to Nehemia Hobart," in Robert F. Seybold, *The Public Schools of Colonial Boston.* Cambridge, MA: Harvard University Press, 1935, 69–71.

3. Assurance of growth toward adult status
4. Philosophy of life
5. Wide range of personal interests
6. Esthetic appreciations
7. Intelligent self-direction
8. Progress toward maturity in social relations with age-mates and adults
9. Wise use of goods and services
10. Vocational orientation
11. Vocational competence

"PURPOSES OF EDUCATION IN AMERICAN DEMOCRACY" Also in 1938, the Educational Policies Commission of the National Education Association (NEA) set forth the "Purposes of Education in American Democracy." These objectives stated that students should receive an education in the four broad areas of self-realization, human relations, economic efficiency, and civic responsibility.

"EDUCATION FOR ALL AMERICAN YOUTH" In 1944 this same commission of the NEA published another statement of educational objectives, entitled "Education for All American Youth":

> Schools should be dedicated to the proposition that every youth in these United States—regardless of sex, economic status, geographic location, or race—should experience a broad and balanced education which will
>
> 1. equip him to enter an occupation suited to his abilities and offering reasonable opportunity for personal growth and social usefulness;
> 2. prepare him to assume full responsibilities of American citizenship;
> 3. give him a fair chance to exercise his right to the pursuit of happiness through the attainment and preservation of mental and physical health;
> 4. stimulate intellectual curiosity, engender satisfaction in intellectual achievement, and cultivate the ability to think rationally; and
> 5. help to develop an appreciation of the ethical values which should undergird all life in a democratic society.

"IMPERATIVE NEEDS OF YOUTH" In 1952 the Educational Policies Commission made yet another statement of educational objectives, entitled "Imperative Needs of Youth":

> 1. All youth need to develop salable skills and those understandings and attitudes that make the worker an intelligent productive participant in economic life. To this end most youth need supervised work experience as well as education in the skills and knowledge of their occupations.
> 2. All youth need to develop and maintain good health and physical fitness.
> 3. All youth need to understand the rights and duties of the citizen of a democratic society, and to be diligent and competent in the performance of their obligations as members of the community and citizens of the state and nation.
> 4. All youth need to understand the significance of the family for the individual and society and the conditions conducive to successful family life.
> 5. All youth need to know how to purchase and use goods and services intelligently, understanding both the values received by the consumer and the economic consequences of their acts.
> 6. All youth need to understand the methods of science, the influence of science on human life, and the main scientific facts concerning the nature of the world and of man.
> 7. All youth need opportunities to develop their capacities to appreciate beauty in literature, art, music, and nature.
> 8. All youth need to be able to use their leisure time well and budget it wisely, balancing activities that yield satisfactions to the individual with those that are socially useful.
> 9. All youth need to develop respect for other persons, to grow in their insight into ethical values and principles, and to be able to live and work cooperatively with others.

10. All youth need to grow in their ability to think rationally, to express their thoughts clearly, and to read and listen with understanding.

These various statements concerning educational objectives, made over the last century, sum up fairly well the history of the aims of U.S. public education. These changing aims also show how perspectives on the purposes of education have evolved over time; this is yet another example of viewing education through different lenses.

HISTORY OF FEDERAL INVOLVEMENT

The Past is Prologue.

Engraved on the National Archives in Washington, D.C.

The federal government of the United States has had a long and extensive involvement in educational affairs. In fact, it has historically supported education at all levels in a variety of ways and continues to do so today. The recent role of the federal government in educational affairs is discussed in Chapters 5 and 6. This section will look briefly at some of the early federal efforts to help provide education for U.S. citizens.

U.S. CONSTITUTION The U.S. Constitution does not mention education. Therefore, by virtue of the Tenth Amendment—which states, "The powers not delegated to the United States by the Constitution, nor prohibited by it to the states, are reserved to the states respectively, or to the people"—education is a function of each state. There is some question whether the makers of the Constitution thoughtfully intended to leave education up to each state or whether they merely forgot to mention it. Some historians believe that the founders wisely realized that local control of education would build a better nation. Other historians believe that the framers of the Constitution were so preoccupied with what they believed were more important issues that they never thought to make national provision for education.

NORTHWEST ORDINANCE Even though the Constitution does not refer to education, the federal government has been active in educational affairs from the very beginning. In 1785 and 1787 the Continental Congress passed the Northwest Ordinance Acts. These acts provided for disposing of the Northwest Territory and encouraged the establishment of schools in the territory by stating, "Religion, morality and knowledge being necessary to good government and the happiness of mankind, schools and the means of education shall forever be encouraged." As the various states formed in the Northwest Territory, they were required to set aside the sixteenth section of each township to be used for educational purposes.

MORRILL LAND GRANT In 1862, when it became apparent that existing colleges were not providing the vocational education needed, the federal government passed the Morrill Land Grant Act to provide for schools to serve this purpose. The Hatch Act of 1887 established agricultural experimental stations across the country, and the Smith-Lever Agricultural Extension Act of 1914 carried the services of land grant colleges to the people through extension services. These early federal acts did much to improve agriculture and industry at a time when the rapidly developing nation badly needed such improvement.

SMITH-HUGHES ACT In 1917 the federal government passed the first act providing financial aid to public schools below the college level, the Smith-Hughes Act.

This act provided for high school vocational programs in agriculture, trades and industry, and homemaking. High schools were academically oriented then, and the Smith-Hughes Act stimulated the development of badly needed vocational programs.

The 1930s were Depression days, and the government was trying to solve national economic difficulties. Legislation was enacted during these years to encourage economic development, and this legislation indirectly provided financial aid to education. Five relief agencies related to education during this time included the Civilian Conservation Corps, National Youth Administration, Federal Emergency Relief Administration, Public Works Administration, and Federal Surplus Commodities Corporation.[2]

The more recent involvements of the federal government, from 1940 to the present, are discussed in the next chapter.

PREPARATION OF TEACHERS

Because present-day teachers have at least four—and often five to eight—years of college education, it is difficult to believe that teachers have historically had little or no training. One of the first forms of teacher training grew out of the medieval guild system, in which a young man who wished to enter a certain field of work served a lengthy period of apprenticeship with a master in the field. Some young men became teachers by serving as apprentices to master teachers, sometimes for as long as seven years.

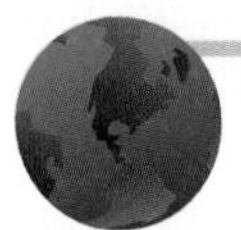

GLOBAL PERSPECTIVES: European Beginnings of Teacher Training

The first formal teacher-training school in the Western world of which we have any record was mentioned in a request to the king of England, written by William Byngham in 1438, requesting that "he may yeve withouten fyn or fee (the) mansion ycalled Goddeshous the which he hath made and edified in your towne of Cambridge for the free herbigage of poure scolers of Gramer."[3]

Byngham was granted his request, and established Goddeshous College as a teacher-training institution on June 13, 1439. Students at this college gave demonstration lectures to fellow students to gain practice teaching. Classes were even conducted during vacations so that country schoolmasters could also attend. Byngham's college still exists today as Christ's College of Cambridge University. At that early date of 1439, Byngham made provision for two features that are still considered very important in teacher education today: scheduling classes so that teachers in service may attend and providing some kind of student teaching experience. Many present-day educators would probably be surprised to learn that these ideas are nearly six hundred years old.

COLONIAL TEACHERS Elementary school teachers in colonial America were very poorly prepared; more often than not, they had received no special training at all. The single qualification of most of them was that they themselves had been students. Most colonial college teachers, private tutors, Latin grammar school teachers, and academy teachers had received some kind of college education, usually at one of the well-established colleges or universities in Europe. A few had received their education at an American colonial college.

Teachers in the various kinds of colonial elementary schools typically had only an elementary education, but a few had attended a Latin grammar school or a private academy. It was commonly believed that to be a teacher required only that the instructor know something about the subject matter to be taught; therefore, no teacher, regardless of the level taught, received training in the methodology of teaching.

Teaching was not considered a prestigious occupation, and the pay was poor. Consequently, many schoolteachers viewed their jobs as only temporary. For young women who taught elementary school, the "something better" was usually marriage. Men frequently left teaching for careers in the ministry or business. Not uncommonly, career teachers in the colonies were undesirable people. Records show that many teachers lost their jobs because they paid more attention to the tavern than to the school or because of stealing, swearing, or conduct unbecoming to a person in such a position.

Since many colonial schools were conducted in connection with a church, the teacher was often considered an assistant to the minister. Besides teaching, other duties of some early colonial teachers were "to act as court messenger, to serve summonses, to conduct certain ceremonial services of the church, to lead the Sunday choir, to ring the bell for public worship, to dig the graves, and to perform other occasional duties."

TEACHERS AS INDENTURED SERVANTS Sometimes the colonies used white indentured servants as teachers; many people who came to the United States bought passage by agreeing to work for some years as indentured servants. The ship's captain would then sell the indentured servant's services, more often than not by placing an ad in a newspaper. Such an ad appeared in a May 1786 edition of the *Maryland Gazette:*

Men and Women Servants

JUST ARRIVED

In the ship *Paca,* Robert Caulfield, Master, in five Weeks from Belfast and Cork, a number of healthy Men and Women SERVANTS.

Among them are several valuable tradesman, viz.

Carpenters, Shoemakers, Coopers, Blacksmiths, Staymakers, Bookbinders, Clothiers, Diers, Butchers, Schoolmasters, Millrights, and Labourers.

Their indentures are to be disposed of by the Subscribers,

Brown, and Maris
William Wilson

Records reveal that there were many indentured servants and convicted felons among early immigrants who were advertised and sold as teachers. In fact, it has been estimated that at least one-half of all the teachers in colonial America may have come from these sources. This is not necessarily a derogatory description of these early teachers when we remember that many poor people bought their passage to the colonies by agreeing to serve as indentured servants for a period of years and that in England at that time, hungry and desperate people could be convicted as felons and deported for stealing a loaf of bread.

TEACHING APPRENTICESHIPS Some colonial teachers learned their trade by serving as apprentices to schoolmasters. Court records reveal numerous such indentures of apprenticeship; the following was recorded in New York City in 1772:

> This Indenture witnesseth that John Campbel Son of Robert Campbel of the City of New York with the Consent of his father and mother hath put himself and by these presents doth Voluntarily put and bind himself Apprentice to George Brownell of the Same City Schoolmaster to learn the Art Trade or Mastery—for and during the term of ten years. . . . And the said George Brownell Doth hereby Covenant and Promise to teach and instruct or Cause the said Apprentice to be taught and instructed in the Art Trade or Calling of a Schoolmaster by the best way or means he or his wife may or can.

TEACHER TRAINING IN ACADEMIES One of Benjamin Franklin's justifications for proposing an academy in Philadelphia was that some of the graduates would make good teachers. Speculating on the need for such graduates, Franklin wrote,

> A number of the poorer sort [of academy graduates] will be hereby qualified to act as Schoolmasters in the Country, to teach children Reading, Writing, Arithmetic, and the Grammar of their Mother Tongue, and being of good morals and known character, may be recommended from the Academy to Country Schools for that purpose; the Country suffering at present very much for want of good Schoolmasters, and obliged frequently to employ in their schools, vicious imported servants, or concealed Papists, who by their bad Examples and Instructions often deprave the Morals and corrupt the Principles of the children under their Care.

The fact that Franklin said some of the "poorer" graduates would make suitable teachers reflects the low regard for teachers typical of the time. The academy that Franklin proposed was established in 1751 in Philadelphia, and many graduates of academies after that time did indeed become teachers.

NORMAL SCHOOLS Many early educators recognized this country's need for better-qualified teachers; however, it was not until 1823 that the first teacher-training institution was established in the United States. This private school, called a **normal school** after its European prototype, which had existed since the late seventeenth century, was established by the Reverend Mr. Samuel Hall in Concord, Vermont. Hall's school did not produce many teachers, but it did signal the beginning of formal teacher training in the United States.

The early normal school program usually consisted of a two-year course. Students typically entered the normal school right after finishing elementary school; most normal schools did not require high school graduation for entrance until about 1900. The nineteenth-century curriculum was much like the curriculum of the high schools of that time. Students reviewed subjects studied in elementary school, studied high school subjects, had a course in teaching (or "pedagogy" as it was then called), and did some student teaching in a model school, usually operated in conjunction with the normal school. The subjects offered by a normal school in Albany, New York, in 1845 included English grammar, English composition, history, geography, reading, writing, orthography,

normal school The first type of American institution devoted exclusively to teacher training.

First State Normal School was adapted from European teacher training schools and is still standing in Lexington, Mass.

arithmetic, algebra, geometry, trigonometry, human physiology, surveying, natural philosophy, chemistry, intellectual philosophy, moral philosophy, government, rhetoric, theory and practice of teaching, drawing, music, astronomy, and practice teaching.

Horace Mann was instrumental in establishing the first state-supported normal school, which opened in 1839 in Lexington, Massachusetts. Other public normal schools, established shortly afterwards, typically offered a two-year teacher-training program. Some of the students came directly from elementary school; others had completed secondary school. Some states did not establish state-supported normal schools until the early 1900s.

STATE TEACHERS' COLLEGES During the early part of the twentieth century, several factors caused a significant change in normal schools. For one thing, as the population of the United States increased, so did the enrollment in elementary schools, thereby creating an ever increasing demand for elementary school teachers. Likewise, as more people attended high school, more high school teachers were needed. To meet this demand, normal schools eventually expanded their curriculum to include secondary teacher education. The growth of high schools also created a need for teachers who were highly specialized in particular academic subjects, so normal schools established subject matter departments and developed more diversified programs. The length of the teacher education program was expanded to two, three, and finally four years; this longer duration fostered development and diversification of the normal school curriculum. The demand for teachers increased from about twenty thousand in 1900 to more than two hundred thousand in 1930.

Another factor contributed to the growth of the normal schools: The United States had advanced technologically to the point where more college-educated citizens were needed. The normal schools assumed a responsibility to help meet this need by establishing many other academic programs in addition to teacher training. As normal schools extended their programs to four years and began granting baccalaureate degrees, they also began to call themselves state teachers' colleges. For most institutions the change in name took place during the 1930s.

FIGURE 8.1 EVOLUTION OF TEACHER PREPARATION INSTITUTIONS

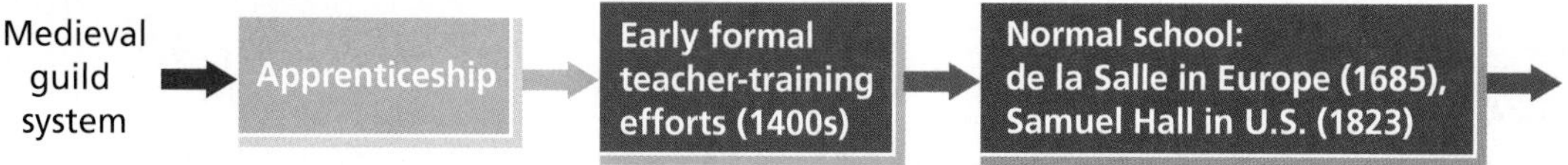

Private colleges and universities enter teacher training on a large scale (1900s)

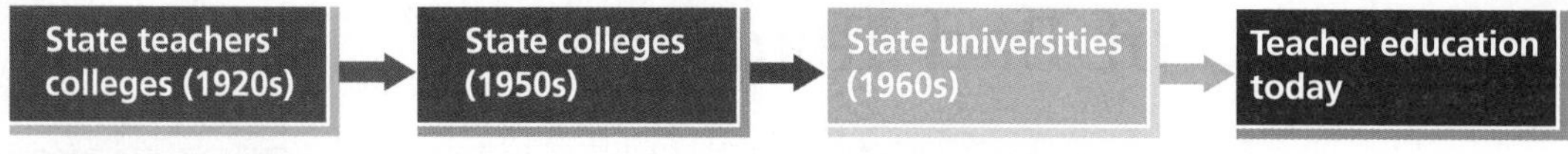

RECENT TEACHER EDUCATION Universities entered the teacher preparation business on a large scale about 1900. Before then some graduates of universities had become high school teachers or college teachers; but not until about 1900 did universities begin to establish departments of education and add teacher education to the curriculum.

Just as the normal schools expanded in size, scope, and function to the point where they became state teachers' colleges, so the state teachers' colleges expanded to become *state colleges.* This change in name and scope took place for most institutions about 1950. The elimination of the word *teacher* really explains the story behind this transition. The new state colleges gradually expanded their programs beyond teacher education and became multipurpose institutions. One of the main reasons for this transition was that a growing number of students coming to the colleges demanded a more varied education. The state teachers' colleges developed diversified programs to try to meet their demands.

Many of these state colleges later became state universities, offering doctoral degrees in a wide range of fields. Some of our largest and most highly regarded universities evolved from normal schools. Figure 8.1 diagrams the evolution of U.S. teacher preparation institutions.

Obviously, establishing the teaching profession was a long and difficult task. Preparation of teachers has greatly improved over the years from colonial times—when anyone could be a teacher—to the present, when not everyone can meet the rigorous requirements for permanent teacher certification.

EVOLUTION OF TEACHING MATERIALS

As we have said, the first schools in colonial America were poorly equipped. In fact, the first elementary schools were usually conducted by housewives right in their homes. The only teaching materials likely to be found then were a Bible and perhaps one or two other religious books, a small amount of scarce paper, a few quill pens, and hornbooks.

THE HORNBOOK The **hornbook** was the most common teaching device in early colonial schools (see Figure 8.2). Hornbooks differed widely but typically consisted of a sheet of paper showing the alphabet, covered with a thin transparent sheet of cow's horn and tacked to a paddle-shaped piece of wood. A leather thong

hornbook
A single printed page containing the alphabet, syllables, a prayer, and other simple words, tacked to a wooden paddle and covered with a thin transparent layer of cow's horn; used in colonial times as the beginner's first book or preprimer.

DEBATE

Should NEA Affiliates Help Get Rid of Bad Teachers?

Linda Lohr, a thirty-year teaching veteran and NEA activist in Columbus, Ohio, now works as a consulting teacher in the Peer Review and Assistance Program there. She's working on a manual designed to guide others launching peer review and assistance programs and can be reached at lohr3@aol.com.

Some people say a union's sole purpose is to protect its members from illegal hirings and firings and ensure safe working conditions. They get nervous about the prospect of an experienced teacher being placed in a peer assistance and review program.

After all, they say, how can a union turn on its own members?

My answer: A union's job is not now, nor has it ever been, to protect incompetence. There's no disloyalty in a union looking out for the best interests of the profession as a whole.

A good peer assistance and review program isn't made up of vigilantes collaborating with administrators to endanger the jobs of fellow teachers. A good program enlists the assistance of sympathetic peers to help restore ailing teachers to productive service.

At one time or another, most of us have been troubled by a teacher down the hall whose classroom struggle has become apparent to all who pass by.

For the past 12 years, the Peer Assistance and Review Program in Columbus has been reaching out to that teacher—entry-level or experienced—and offering confidential advice, assistance, and empathy.

Capable teachers assume the role of mentors, visiting classrooms at least 20 times during the school year. Who better to assist colleagues than veteran teachers who've proven their own success?

As a mentor, I can observe classes without the restrictions of someone who's responsible for the day's agenda. I can watch to see if learning takes place. I can focus on specific issues—like questioning techniques, classroom management, or gender equity.

Throughout the year, my ultimate goal is to improve performance. I want the teachers who are assigned to me to

A seventeen-year high school history teacher in Mattoon, Illinois, Bill Harshbarger is a member of NEA Today's Local Editor Advisory Board. He edits local and regional newsletters, attends NEA and state affiliate assemblies, and has served on several bargaining teams. He can be reached at Harsh8@aol.com.

Let's not delude ourselves into thinking that "getting rid of" a teacher is a painless experience.

Most released teachers won't start a better career for better pay. Some will voice their frustration and anger. Some will fight for their jobs. Some, we may find, are good teachers after all.

When you hand a colleague his walking papers, you may feel some pain, too. You may get a knot in your stomach, lose sleep, and avoid looking at yourself in the mirror.

Anguish aside, there are many good reasons why teachers should stay out of the judging and firing business. Here are just a few.

- *It's unnecessary.* Most states have a system to weed out teachers through university preparation programs, certification tests, probationary periods, periodic evaluations, and due process hearings. Every district has a procedure to fire teachers.

In fact, teachers are being fired or forced to resign all the time. Creating a new layer of bureaucracy to duplicate what's already being done is a misuse of valuable teaching resources.

- *It's a myth—manufactured and sold by NEA's critics—that the Association "saves" bad teachers.* The Association only "saves" the jobs of teachers who are wrongly accused or improperly dismissed.

Critics of tenure protection conveniently ignore the fact that the courts still won't allow vindictive administrators or special interest vigilantes to roam school corridors looking for victims to burn at their particular, twisted, political stakes.

YES NO

succeed. When they fail—which they sometimes do—I feel like I've failed, too.

The worst time in the Peer Assistance and Review Program office comes in the spring when consulting teachers reluctantly acknowledge that someone hasn't shown adequate improvement and isn't going to make it.

But let's face it: Some people are not cut out to be teachers or to sustain a lifetime career in education. When assistance doesn't help, those people need to be counseled away from teaching or given other alternatives.

In every case, the Columbus Education Association stands ready to offer help and assurance that every member will receive due process.

Nearing the end of my career, I have a vested interest in leaving my profession in capable hands. In recent years, the Ohio state legislature has taken more and more control over teacher assessment. School administrators are under pressure to be business managers rather than instructional leaders and facilitators.

I want to keep the evaluation and retention of good teachers in the hands of practitioners for whom classroom performance is the top priority. And I believe our consulting teachers have the time, expertise, and perspective necessary to do the job right.

In Columbus, we're doing our best to ensure productive classrooms for our students and productive careers for our peers. The end result is the top quality teaching and learning we're all striving for.

Source: "Should NEA Affiliates Help Get Rid of Bad Teachers?" *NEA Today* (November 1997): 43.

- *A teacher-driven dismissal system might not be any better than the present dismissal system.* Principals are trained and certified to evaluate. There's no evidence to show that teachers with little evaluation training will do a better job. If they can, then we've wasted tons of money on principal-training programs.

It makes no sense to train teachers as evaluators if they're simply going to do the same thing that principals are already doing. Reformers who argue that the system isn't working should focus on fixing the poor performance of the principals rather than creating new teams of teachers to perpetuate the same mistakes.

Finally, does anyone believe that the teachers who are selected to become judges of their colleagues are going to be any less influenced than principals by bias, pettiness, and political pressures?

- *It's too easy to misjudge teaching.* Principals justify their jobs in part by claiming they have to make the "hard" decisions. They should also take responsibility for their mistakes. A local affiliate gains little by doing this onerous job for them.

- *Peer review will divide Association members and decrease membership.* A local affiliate that bargains for the right to fire its own members may have trouble signing them up.

- *There are better ways for an affiliate to help improve teaching while unifying Association members.* Let's bargain for release time to work and plan together. Let's set up compassionate mentoring programs, reduce class size, and deal effectively with chronically disruptive students. Let's support each other.

But let's be cautious about rushing in where angels—and principals—fear to tread.

WHAT'S YOUR OPINION?

Should NEA Affiliates Help Get Rid of Bad Teachers?

Go to **www.ablongman.com/johnson** to cast your vote and see how NEA readers responded.

was often looped through a hole in the paddle so that students could hang the hornbooks around their necks. Hornbooks provided students with their first reading instructions. Records indicate that hornbooks were used in Europe in the Middle Ages and were common there until the mid-1700s.

As paper became more available, the hornbook evolved into a several-page "book" called a *battledore.* The battledore, printed on heavy paper, often resembled

FIGURE 8.2 HORNBOOK

The hornbook was the most common teaching device in colonial American schools. What made it so popular?

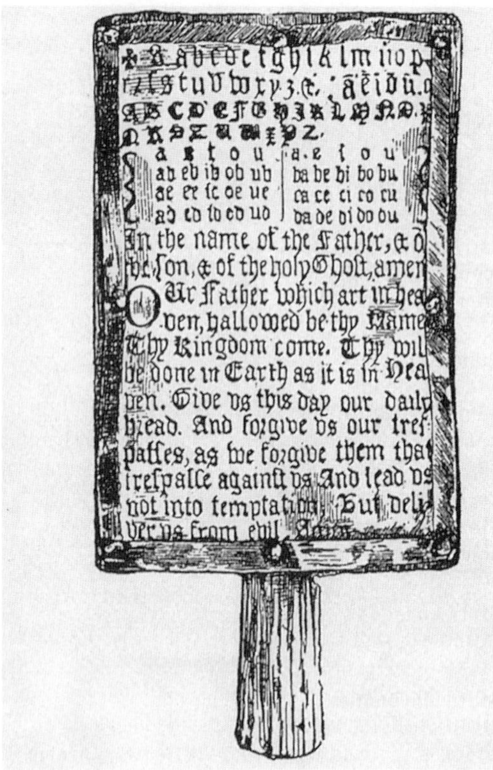

FIGURE 8.3 1690 ADVERTISEMENT

This 1690 advertisement promotes the New England Primer, *the first true textbook to be used in colonial American elementary schools. What were the contents of, and the motivation behind, this primer?*

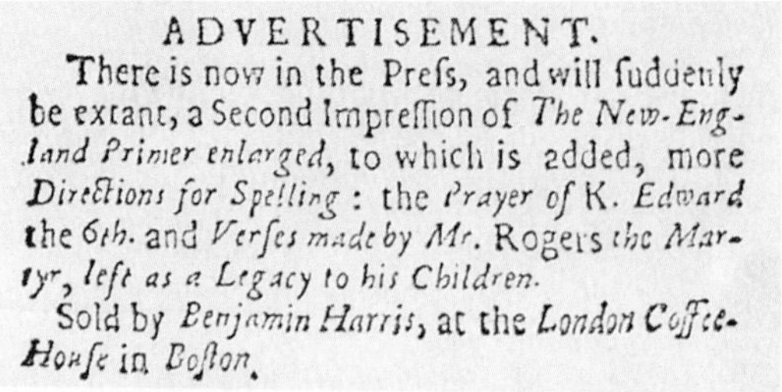

ADVERTISEMENT.

There is now in the Preſs, and will ſuddenly be extant, a Second Impreſſion of *The New-England Primer enlarged*, to which is added, more *Directions for Spelling*: the *Prayer of K. Edward the 6th.* and *Verſes made by Mr.* Rogers *the Martyr, left as a Legacy to his Children.*

Sold by *Benjamin Harris*, at the *London Coffee-Houſe* in *Boſton*.

an envelope. Like the hornbook, it typically contained the alphabet and various religious prayers and/or admonitions.

NEW ENGLAND PRIMER The first real textbook to be used in colonial elementary schools was the *New England Primer.* Records show that the first copies of this book were printed in England in the 1600s. Copies of the *New England Primer* were also printed as early as 1690 in the American colonies. An advertisement for the book appeared in the *News from the Stars Almanac,* published in 1690 in Boston (see Figure 8.3). The oldest extant copy of the *New England Primer* is a 1727 edition, now in the Lenox Collection of the New York Public Library.

The *New England Primer* was a small book, usually about 2½ by 4½ inches, with thin wooden covers covered by paper or leather. It contained fifty to one hundred pages, depending on how many extra sections were added to each edition. The first pages displayed the alphabet, vowels, and capital letters. Next came lists of words arranged from two to six syllables, followed by verses and tiny woodcut pictures for each letter in the alphabet. Figure 8.4 shows a sampling of these pictures and verses. The contents of the *New England Primer* reflect the heavily religious motive in colonial education.

BLUE-BACKED SPELLER The primer was virtually the only reading book used in colonial schools until about 1800, when Noah Webster published *The American Spelling Book.* This book eventually became known as the *Blue-Backed Speller* because of its blue cover. It eventually replaced the *New England Primer* as the most common elementary textbook. In fact, Noah Webster's *American Spelling Book* is the third biggest selling book the world has even known, having sold about 100 million copies, compared to *Quotations from the Works of Mao Tse-tung,* which has sold about 800 million copies, and the Bible, which has sold an estimated 2 billion copies. A later series of school books, *The McGuffey Readers,* authored by William

Holmes McGuffey, sold about 60 million copies. The speller was approximately 4 by 6½ inches; its cover was made of thin sheets of wood covered with light blue paper. The first part of the book contained rules and instructions for using the book; next came the alphabet, syllables, and consonants. The bulk of the book was taken up with lists of words arranged according to syllables and sounds. It also contained rules for reading and speaking, moral advice, and stories of various sorts. Figure 8.5 shows a page from a *Blue-Backed Speller* printed about 1800.

Very few textbooks were available for use in colonial Latin grammar schools, academies, and colleges, although various religious books, including the Bible, were often used. A few books dealing with history, geography, arithmetic, Latin, Greek, and certain classics were available for use in colonial secondary schools and colleges during the eighteenth century. Harvard College had a large library for its day because John Harvard, its benefactor, had bequeathed his entire collection of four hundred volumes to the school.

FIGURE 8.4 **PAGE FROM THE *New England Primer***

How does this page from the New England Primer *reveal the religious motive in colonial American education?*

In Adam's Fall
We finned all.

Thy Life to mend,
This Book attend.

The Cat doth play,
And after flay.

A Dog will bite
A Thief at Night.

An Eagle' flight
Is out of fight.

The idle Fool
Is whipt at SchooL

AN EARLY SCHOOL By 1800 nearly two hundred years after the colonies had been established, school buildings and teaching materials were still very crude and meager. You can understand something of the physical features and equipment of an 1810 New England school by reading the following description written by a teacher of that school:

> The size of the building was 22 × 20 feet. From the floor to the ceiling it was 7 feet. The chimney and entry took up about four feet at one end, leaving the schoolroom itself 18 × 20 feet. Around three sides of the room were connected desks, arranged so that when the pupils were sitting at them their faces were toward the instructor and their backs toward the wall. Attached to the sides of the desks nearest to the instructor were benches for small pupils. The instructor's desk and chair occupied the center. On this desk were stationed a rod, or ferule; sometimes both. These, with books, writings, inkstands, rules, and plummets, with a fire shovel, and a pair of tongs (often broken), were the principal furniture. . . .
>
> The room was warmed by a large and deep fireplace. So large was it, and so efficacious in warming the room otherwise, that I have seen about one-eighth of a cord of good wood burning in it at a time. In severe weather it was estimated that the amount usually consumed was not far from a cord a week. . . .
>
> The school was not infrequently broken up for a day or two for want of wood. The instructor or pupils were sometimes compelled to cut or saw it to prevent the closing of the school. The wood was left in the road near the house, so that it often was buried in the snow, or wet with rain. At the best, it was usually burnt green. The fires were to be kindled about half an hour before the time of beginning the school. Often, the scholar, whose lot it was, neglected to build it. In consequence of this, the house was frequently cold and uncomfortable about half of the forenoon, when, the fire being very large, the excess of heat became equally distressing. Frequently, too, we were annoyed by smoke. The greatest amount of suffering, however, arose from excessive heat, particularly at the close of the day. The

Royalties from the Blue-Backed Speller *supported Noah Webster (1758–1843) while he prepared his famous dictionary of the English language.*

pupils being in a free perspiration when they left were very liable to take cold. . . .

Instructors have usually boarded in the families of the pupils. Their compensation has varied from seven to eleven dollars a month for males; and from sixty-two and a half cents to one dollar a week for females. Within the past ten years, however, the price of instruction has rarely been less than nine dollars in the former case, and seventy-five cents in the latter. In the few instances in which instructors have furnished their own board the compensation has been about the same, it being assumed that they could work at some employment of their own enough to pay their board, especially the females.[4]

FIGURE 8.5 **PAGE FROM THE *BLUE-BACKED SPELLER***

Noah Webster's Blue-Backed Speller *came to replace primers around 1800. In addition to the alphabet, syllables, consonants, lists of words, and rules for reading and speaking, the* Speller *contained stories like the one shown here. What does this example tell you about the motives behind early nineteenth-century elementary education?*

OF PRONUNCIATION.  85

FABLE I. *Of the Boy that ſtole Apples.*

AN old Man found a rude Boy upon one of his trees ſtealing Apples, and deſired him to come down; but the young Sauce-box told him plainly he wou'd not. Won't you? ſaid the old Man, then I will fetch you down; ſo he pulled up ſome tufts of Graſs, and threw at him; but this only made the Youngſter laugh, to think the old Man ſhould pretend to beat him out of the tree with graſs only.

Well, well, ſaid the old Man, if neither words nor graſs, will do, I muſt try what virtue there is in Stones; ſo the old Man pelted him heartily with ſtones; which ſoon made the young Chap haſten down from the tree and beg the old Man's pardon.

M O R A L.

If good words and gentle means will not reclaim the wicked, they muſt be dealt with in a more ſevere manner.

SLATES About 1820 a new instructional device was introduced in American schools: the slate. These school slates were thin, flat pieces of slate stone framed with wood. The pencils used were also made of slate and produced a light but legible line. The wooden frames of some of the slates were covered with cloth so that noise would be minimized as students placed the slates on the desk. There were even double slates made of two single slates hinged together with cord or leather. Students wrote their assignments on the slates, just as today's students write on tablet paper. Later on, large pieces of slate made up the blackboards that were added to classrooms.

By about 1900 pencils and paper had largely replaced the slate and slate pencil as the writing implements of students. The invention of relatively economical mass production of pencils in the late 1800s made them affordable for student use and thereby had a considerable impact on schools.

MCGUFFEY'S *READER* In the same way that Noah Webster's *Blue-Backed Speller* replaced the *New England Primer,* McGuffey's *Reader* eventually replaced the *Blue-Backed Speller.* These readers were carefully geared to each grade and were meant to instill in children a respect for hard work, thrift, self-help, and honesty. McGuffey's *Reader* dominated the elementary school book market until approximately 1900, when it was gradually replaced by newer and improved readers written by David Tower, James Fassett, William Elson, and others.

During the twentieth century, teachers have gradually adopted a variety of tools to assist them in educating young people. This variety has come about partly through the influence of Pestalozzi, John Dewey, and others, who demonstrated that children learn best by firsthand experiences. Likewise, school buildings have become larger, more elaborate, and better designed to encourage learning. Today, many schools are equipped with an impressive array of books, laboratory equipment, movie projectors, filmstrip projectors, tape recorders, television devices, single-concept films, teaching machines, computers, programmed materials, and learning devices of all kinds. Some modern school buildings are not only excellent from an educational standpoint, but magnificent pieces of architecture as well. One cannot help but be awed by the contrast between U.S. education today and its humble beginning centuries ago.

The Reader *by William Holmes McGuffey (1800–1873) gradually replaced the* Blue-Backed Speller *as the dominant elementary schoolbook until 1900.*

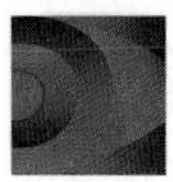

EDUCATION FOR DIVERSE POPULATIONS

This section will summarize briefly the development of education of African Americans and females in the United States. We will also review the extremely important role of private education in America.

EDUCATION OF AFRICAN AMERICANS

It is sad but true that until very recently, few efforts were made in this country to provide an education for African Americans. In the following section we will briefly explore why this was the case and discuss some of the early African American educators who struggled to correct this injustice.

SLAVERY In 1619, only a dozen years after Jamestown was established, the first boatload of enslaved people arrived in the colonies. In that year John Rolfe wrote in his *Journal* that the captain of a Dutch ship "sold us twenty Negroes." These enslaved people were imported as a source of cheap labor for the new colonies.

The number of imported slaves steadily increased; between 1700 and 1750, thousands of Africans were brought to the American colonies each year. By the Revolutionary War there were approximately 700,000 enslaved Africans in the colonies; by 1860 there were about 4.5 million.

CHURCH EFFORTS TO EDUCATE AFRICAN AMERICANS Probably the first organized attempts to educate the African Americans in colonial America were by French and Spanish missionaries.[5] These early missionary efforts set an example that influenced the education of both African Americans and their numerous biracial children. Educating slaves posed an interesting moral problem for the church. The English colonists had to find a way to overcome the idea that converting enslaved people to Christianity might logically lead to their freedom. The problem they faced was how to eliminate an unwritten law that a Christian should not be a slave. The church's governing bodies and the Bishop of London settled the matter by decreeing that conversion to Christianity did not lead to formal emancipation.

The organized church nevertheless provided the setting in which a few African Americans were allowed to develop skills in reading, leadership, and educating their brethren. Often African Americans and whites attended church together. Eventually, some preachers—former slaves—demonstrated exceptional skill in "spreading the gospel." The Baptists in particular, by encouraging a form

African American Children's School. Early efforts to provide formal education for African American children were "few and far between."

of self-government, allowed African Americans to become active in the church. This move fostered the growth of African American congregations; thus, Baptist congregations gave enslaved as well as free African Americans an opportunity for education and development that was not provided by many other denominations.

The efforts of the English to educate enslaved people were carried out largely by the Society for the Propagation of the Gospel in Foreign Parts. The society was created by the Church of England in 1701. In 1705 the Reverend Samuel Thomas of Goose Creek Parish in South Carolina established a school fostered by the society, enrolling sixty African American students. Nine years later the society opened a school in New York City where two hundred African American pupils were enrolled. Despite vigorous opposition from many whites, who believed that educating enslaved people was a "dangerous business," the society went on to establish other schools for African Americans. The degree of success of these early efforts varied greatly. Initially, many people were not generally opposed to educating African Americans; however, education seemed to make enslaved people aware of their plight. In the South, many people attributed the growing unrest concerning slavery to the education of enslaved people. Insurrections, uprisings, and threats to overseers, masters, and their families produced fear among the whites. Consequently, some states even passed legislation that eliminated any form of education for enslaved people.

BENJAMIN BANNEKER Benjamin Banneker, a distinguished African American, was born in Baltimore County, Maryland, in 1731. Baltimore maintained a liberal policy toward educating African Americans, and Banneker learned to read, write, and do arithmetic at a relatively early age. He became extremely well educated. One of his accomplishments was to manufacture the first clock made in the United States in 1770. He then turned his attention specifically to astronomy. Without any instruction but with the help of books borrowed from a supportive white inventor, Banneker soon was able to calculate eclipses of the sun and moon. His accuracy far excelled that of any other American and his astronomical calculations received much acclaim after they were published. George Washington appointed him to help survey what became Washington, DC. The outstanding works of this inventor aroused the curiosity of Thomas Jefferson, who in 1803 invited Banneker to his home, Monticello. The acknowledgment of an African American's achievement by a noted U.S. leader was still another milestone in the education of African Americans.

Frederick Douglass (1817?–1895) was an influential antislavery lecturer, writer, and consultant to President Lincoln.

FREDERICK DOUGLASS Frederick Douglass, born in slavery in Maryland in 1817, ran away and began talking to abolitionist groups about his experiences in slavery. He attributed his fluent speech to listening to his master talk. Douglass firmly believed that if he devoted all his efforts to improving vocational education, he could greatly improve the African Americans' plight. He thought that previous attempts by educators to combine liberal and vocational education had failed, so he emphasized vocational education solely.

One of the first Northern schools established for African Americans appears to have been that of Elias Neau in New York City in 1704. Neau was an agent of the Society for the Propagation of the Gospel in Foreign Parts.

In 1807 several free African Americans, including George Bell, Nicholas Franklin, and Moses Liverpool, built the first schoolhouse for African Americans in the District of Columbia. Not until 1824, however, was there an African American teacher in that district—John Adams. In 1851 Washington citizens attempted to discourage Myrtilla Miner from establishing an academy for African American girls. However, after much turmoil and harassment the white schoolmistress from New York did found her academy; it is still functioning today.

JOHN CHAVIS The African Americans' individual successes in acquiring education, as well as their group efforts to establish schools, were greatly enhanced by sympathetic and humanitarian white friends. One African American who was helped by whites was John Chavis, a free man born in 1763 in Oxford, North Carolina. Chavis became a successful teacher of aristocratic whites, and his white neighbors sent him to Princeton "to see if a Negro would take a college education." His rapid advancement under Dr. Witherspoon soon indicated that the venture was a success. He returned to Virginia and later went to North Carolina, where he preached among his own people. The success of John Chavis, even under experimental conditions, represented another step forward in the education of African Americans.

PRUDENCE CRANDALL Prudence Crandall, a young Quaker, established an early boarding school in Canterbury, Connecticut. The problems she ran into dramatize some of the Northern animosity to educating African Americans. Trouble arose when Sarah Harris, a "colored girl," asked to be admitted to the institution. After much deliberation, Miss Crandall finally consented, but white parents objected to the African American girl's attending the school and withdrew their children. To keep the school open, Miss Crandall recruited African American children. The pupils were threatened with violence, local stores would not trade with her, and the school building was vandalized. The citizens of Canterbury petitioned the state legislature to enact a law that would make it illegal to educate African Americans from out of state. Miss Crandall was jailed and tried before the state supreme court in July 1834. The court never gave a final decision because defects were found in the information prepared by the attorney for the state; the indictment was eventually dropped. Miss Crandall continued to work for the abolition of slavery, for women's rights, and for African American education. Prudence Crandall became well known, and she deserves considerable credit for the advances made by minorities and women in the United States.

Finally, Boston, the seat of Northern liberalism, established a separate school for African American children in 1798. Elisha Sylvester, a white man, was in charge. The school was founded in the home of Primus Hall, a "Negro in good standing." Two years later, sixty-six free African Americans petitioned the school committee for a separate school and were refused. Undaunted, the patrons of Hall's house employed two instructors from Harvard; thirty-five years later, the school was allowed to move to a separate building. The city of Boston opened its first primary school for the education of African American children in 1820—one more milestone in the history of African American education.

EARLY AFRICAN AMERICAN COLLEGES Unfortunately, despite these efforts, African Americans received pathetically little formal education until the Emancipation Proclamation, issued by President Abraham Lincoln on January 1, 1863. At that time the literacy rate among African Americans was estimated at 5 percent. Sunday school represented about the only opportunity most African Americans had to learn to read. In the late 1700s and early 1800s some communities did set up separate schools for African Americans; however, only a very small percentage ever attended the schools. A few colleges such as Oberlin, Bowdoin, Franklin, Rutland, and Harvard admitted African American students; but, again, very few attended college then. There were even a few African American colleges such as Lincoln University in Pennsylvania (1854) and Wilberforce University in Ohio (1856); however, the efforts and opportunities for the education of African Americans were pathetically few relative to the size of the African American population.

Booker T. Washington (1856–1915), an early African American educator, founded Tuskegee Institute in Alabama in 1880 to help African American children acquire the education they needed to compete in society.

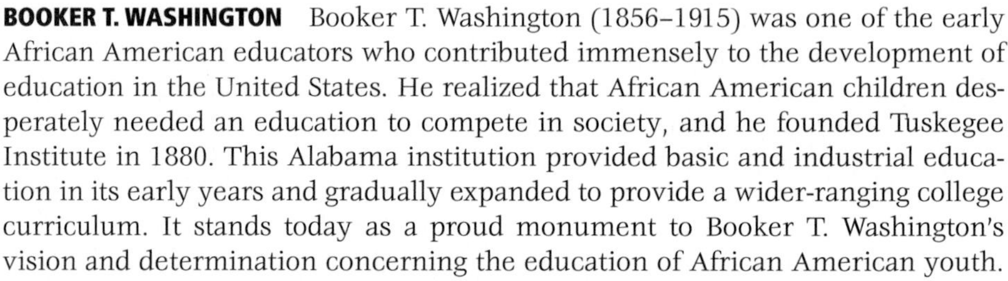

BOOKER T. WASHINGTON Booker T. Washington (1856–1915) was one of the early African American educators who contributed immensely to the development of education in the United States. He realized that African American children desperately needed an education to compete in society, and he founded Tuskegee Institute in 1880. This Alabama institution provided basic and industrial education in its early years and gradually expanded to provide a wider-ranging college curriculum. It stands today as a proud monument to Booker T. Washington's vision and determination concerning the education of African American youth.

Although there was no great rush to educate African Americans, the abolishment of slavery in 1865 signaled the beginning of a slow but steady effort to improve their education. By 1890 African American literacy had risen to 40 percent; by 1910 it was estimated that 70 percent of African Americans had learned to read and write. These statistics showing the rapid increase in African American literacy are impressive; however, they are compromised by a report of the U.S. Commissioner of Education showing that by 1900, fewer than 70 of 1,000 public high schools in the South were provided for African Americans. Ironically, while educational opportunities for African Americans were meager, for other minority groups such as Native Americans and Hispanic Americans they were practically nonexistent.

The most significant developments in the education of African Americans have been in the twentieth century, mostly since 1950. They are discussed more fully in Chapter 9.

EDUCATION OF WOMEN

Emma Willard (1787–1870) was a pioneer in female higher education who established Middlebury Female Seminary, Waterford Female Academy, and Troy Female Seminary.

Historically, women have not been afforded equal educational opportunities in the United States. Furthermore, many authorities claim that U.S. schools have traditionally been sexist institutions. Although there is much evidence to support both these assertions, it is also true that an impressive list of women have made significant contributions to educational progress.

Colonial schools did not provide education for girls in any significant way. In some instances girls were taught to read, but females could not attend Latin grammar schools, academies, or colleges. We will look briefly at a few of the many outstanding female educators who helped to develop our country's educational system, in spite of their own limited educational opportunity.

EMMA WILLARD Emma Willard (1778–1870) was a pioneer and champion of education for females during a time when there were relatively few educational opportunities for them. While well-to-do parents hired private tutors or sent their daughters away to a girl's seminary, girls from poor families were taught only to read and write at home (provided that someone in the family had these skills). Emma Willard opened one of the first female seminaries in 1821 in Troy, New York. Her school offered an educational program equal to that of a boys' school. In a speech designed to raise funds for her school, she proposed the following benefits of seminaries for girls:

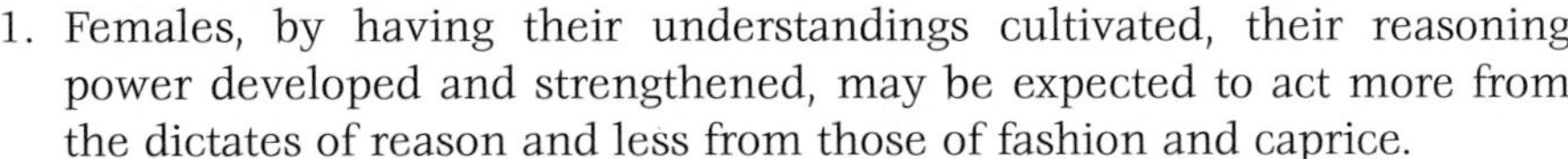

1. Females, by having their understandings cultivated, their reasoning power developed and strengthened, may be expected to act more from the dictates of reason and less from those of fashion and caprice.
2. With minds thus strengthened, they would be taught systems of morality, enforced by the sanctions of religion; and they might be expected to acquire juster and more enlarged views of their duty, and stronger and higher motives to its performance.
3. This plan of education offers all that can be done to preserve female youth from a contempt of useful labor. The pupils would become accustomed to it, in conjunction with the high objects of literature and the elegant pursuits of the fine arts; and it is to be hoped that both from habit and association they might in future life regard it as respectable.
4. The pupils might be expected to acquire a taste for moral and intellectual pleasures which would buoy them above a passion for show and parade, and which would make them seek to gratify the natural love of superiority by endeavoring to excel others in intrinsic merit rather than in the extrinsic frivolities of dress, furniture, and equipage.
5. By being enlightened in moral philosophy, and in that which teaches the operations of the mind, females would be enabled to perceive the nature and extent of that influence which they possess over their children, and the obligation which this lays them under to watch the formation of their characters with unceasing vigilance, to become their instructors, to devise plans for their improvement, to weed out the vices of their minds, and to implant and foster the virtues. And surely there is that in the maternal bosom which, when its pleadings shall be aided by education, will overcome the seductions of wealth and fashion, and will lead the mother to seek her happiness in communing with her children, and promoting their welfare.[6]

The school is an institution in which female status would be nurtured and encouraged.

Catharine Beecher

Many other female institutions were established and became prominent during the mid- and late 1800s, including Mary Lyon's Mount Holyoke Female

Seminary; Jane Ingersoll's seminary in Cortland, New York; and Julia and Elias Mark's Southern Carolina Collegiate Institute at Barhamville, to name just a few. Unfortunately, not until well into the twentieth century were women generally afforded access to higher education.

Even though women eventually could attend college, they were not given equal access to all fields of study. Considerable progress has been made in recent years, but remnants of this problem still exist today.

Maria Montessori (1870–1952) developed a theory and methods for educating young children that are still practiced in the United States.

GLOBAL PERSPECTIVES: Maria Montessori

Maria Montessori (1870–1952), born in Italy, became first a successful physician and later a prominent educational philosopher. She developed her own theory and methods of educating young children. Her methods utilized child-size school furniture and specially designed learning materials. She emphasized independent work by children under the guidance of a trained directress. Private Montessori schools thrive in the United States today.

ELLA FLAGG YOUNG Ella Flagg Young is yet another example of an outstanding early female educator. Overcoming immense obstacles, she earned a doctorate at the age of 50 under John Dewey, was appointed head of the Cook County Normal School in Illinois, and became superintendent of the gigantic Chicago public school system in 1909—all achievements that were unheard of for a female at that time. She was also elected the first female president of the male-dominated National Education Association.

Mary McLeod Bethune (1875–1955) believed that education was the key to helping African American children move into the mainstream of American life.

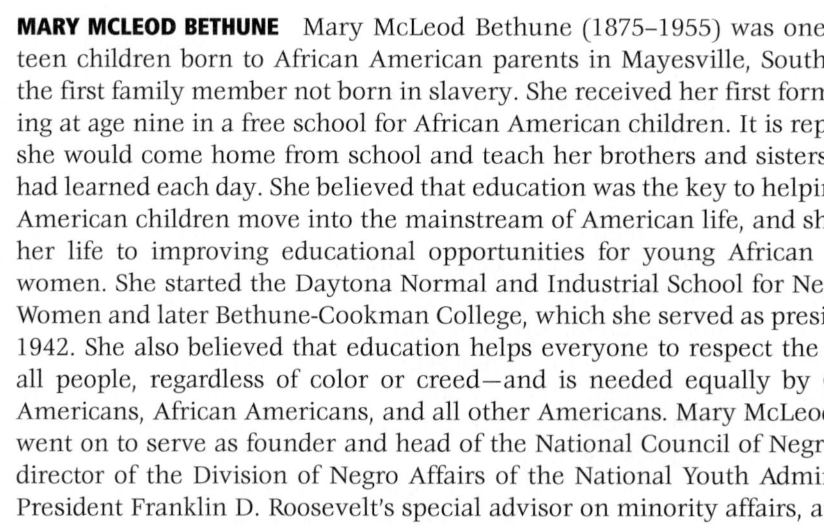

MARY MCLEOD BETHUNE Mary McLeod Bethune (1875–1955) was one of seventeen children born to African American parents in Mayesville, South Carolina, the first family member not born in slavery. She received her first formal schooling at age nine in a free school for African American children. It is reported that she would come home from school and teach her brothers and sisters what she had learned each day. She believed that education was the key to helping African American children move into the mainstream of American life, and she devoted her life to improving educational opportunities for young African American women. She started the Daytona Normal and Industrial School for Negro Young Women and later Bethune-Cookman College, which she served as president until 1942. She also believed that education helps everyone to respect the dignity of all people, regardless of color or creed—and is needed equally by Caucasian Americans, African Americans, and all other Americans. Mary McLeod Bethune went on to serve as founder and head of the National Council of Negro Women, director of the Division of Negro Affairs of the National Youth Administration, President Franklin D. Roosevelt's special advisor on minority affairs, and special consultant for drafting the charter of the United Nations.

Insight into the optimistic outlook that allowed Mary McLeod Bethune to accomplish so much can be gleaned from her diary entry of 7 December 1937:

> Tuesday at five in the afternoon I attended a tea at the executive mansion. This was an annual occasion at which Mrs. Roosevelt entertained the women administrative workers in the government.

One curious but affable woman inquired, "Who are you?"

"My name is Mary McLeod Bethune."

"What do you do?"

"I am the Director of Negro Affairs in the N.Y.A."

"Isn't it nice of Mrs. Roosevelt to have you here?"

"Yes, isn't it nice of Mrs. Roosevelt to have us *all* here!"

While I felt very much at home, I looked about me longingly for other dark faces. In all that great group I felt a sense of being quite alone.

Then I thought how vitally important it was that I be here, to help those others get used to seeing us in high places. And so, while I sipped tea in the brilliance of the White House, my heart reached out to the delta land and bottom land.

I know so well why I must be here and why I must go to tea at the White House—to remind them always that we belong here; we are a part of America.

Mary McLeod Bethune was an effective, energetic human rights activist throughout her life, and also a dedicated and professional career educator.

The fact that women have made significant contributions to our educational progress through the years has been well documented. In addition to the examples just mentioned and those discussed elsewhere in this book, we can add the following: Catharine Beecher (who founded the Hartford Female Seminary), Jane Addams (who proposed an expanded school as part of her new liberal social philosophy), Susan Anthony (who was a teacher in her early professional life), and Margarethe Meyer Schurz (who founded the first kindergarten in this country).

THE NINETEENTH AMENDMENT The first great interest in advancing the cause of females came about in the mid-1800s in the United States. The women's rights convention held at that time passed twelve resolutions that attempted to spur interest in feminism and provide for females more equal participation and rights in U.S. society. The Civil War also furthered interest in the rights of women throughout the country, very likely as a spinoff of the abolition of slavery. It is interesting to note that not all of the people who were in favor of doing away with slavery supported improved rights for women. For instance, not until 1920, when the Nineteenth Amendment passed, did women have the right to vote.

Unfortunately, the right to vote did not necessarily do much to improve the status of women; females continued to be denied equal educational and employment opportunities for a long time. The civil rights movement after World War II served as another impetus to the women's movement and gave rise to an additional round of improvements for females in American society. Some authorities would trace the emergence of the current feminist movement to the 1960s, when a variety of activist groups coalesced to work against discrimination of all kinds in U.S. society.

Many would argue that adequate educational provisions and opportunities for females, minorities, and the handicapped are still lacking in our school systems today at all levels.

PRIVATE EDUCATION IN AMERICA

Private education has been extremely important in the development of the United States, and private schools carried on most of the education in colonial times. The

PROFESSIONAL DILEMMA

Can a Teacher Both Defend and Criticize Past and Present Schools?

When you become a teacher, you will undoubtedly be able to find both good and bad things about your school. You will also eventually face a parent who is critical of your school and who suggests that schools used to be better in the past. You will then be faced with the common professional dilemma of having to decide to what degree you are willing to defend your classroom and/or school.

Are schools in the United States better or worse today than they were in the "good old days"? Those who argue that schools have deteriorated often point out that the one-room school practiced many of the educational "innovations" that one reads about today. For instance, in small one-room schools students received a considerable amount of individual attention. Cooperative learning, which is being touted as a promising educational practice today, was commonplace, with older students helping the younger ones. Those who hark back to the one-room school frequently point out that values and ethics were a part of the school curriculum and that students were taught love of country, respect for law and authority, and often religious values.

On the other side of this debate, those who defend contemporary schools point out that U.S. society has become much more complex and that students must now receive a very different and more elaborate educational experience if they are to be successful. The small, simpler schools of the past could not possibly offer the curricular variety and wealth of experiences that are afforded students today. Defenders of contemporary schools argue that U.S. society could not have advanced to its present state if it had been limited to the education typically provided in the past. They point to the advancements of society as proof that public schools have generally provided an excellent education for most students.

This controversy concerning whether or not our schools have improved or degenerated through history will likely continue. One of the reasons it is important for educators to understand their profession's history is that this understanding will enable them to capitalize on historical successes and to minimize past mistakes. As a future teacher, you should consider educational history and ponder the successes and failures of our ever evolving school system.

- Should schools return to a focus on basic skills?
- How realistic, valid, and representative are memories of the "good old days"? Is it reasonable to consider returning to an earlier state of U.S. educational history? Why or why not?
- To what degree should teachers defend or criticize their school? How and when?

first colonial colleges—Harvard, William and Mary, Yale, and Princeton—were private. Many of the other early colonial schools—which can be thought of as **religious-affiliated schools**—were operated by churches, missionary societies, and private individuals.

religious-affiliated school A private school over which, in most cases, a parent church group exercises some control or to which the church provides some form of subsidy.

THE RIGHT OF PRIVATE SCHOOLS TO EXIST In 1816 the state of New Hampshire attempted to take over Dartmouth College, which was a private institution. A lawsuit growing out of this effort ultimately resulted in the U.S. Supreme Court's first decision involving the legal rights of a private school. The Supreme Court decided that a private school's charter must be viewed as a contract and cannot be broken arbitrarily by a state. In other words, the Court decided that a private school could not be forced against its will to become a public school.

Subsequent court decisions have reconfirmed the rights of private education in a variety of ways. Generally speaking, for instance, courts have reconfirmed that private schools have a right to exist and in some cases even to share public funds, as long as these funds are not used for religious purposes. Examples of such actions include the use of state funds to purchase secular textbooks and to provide transportation for students to and from private schools.

Not until after the Revolution, when there was a strong sense of nationalism, did certain educators advocate a strong public school system for the new nation. However, such recommendations were not acted on for many years. In the meantime some Protestant churches continued to expand their schools during the colonial period. For instance, the Congregational, Quaker, Episcopal, Baptist, Methodist, Presbyterian, and Reformed churches all, at various times and in varying degrees, established and operated schools for their youth. It was the Roman Catholics and Lutherans, however, who eventually developed elaborate **parochial school** systems—systems of schools operated by the denominations.

PAROCHIAL SCHOOLS As early as 1820 there were 240 Lutheran parochial schools in Pennsylvania. Although the number of Lutheran schools in that particular state eventually dwindled, Henry Muhlenberg and other Lutheran leaders continued to establish parochial schools until the public school system became well established. The Missouri Synod Lutheran Church has continued to maintain a well-developed parochial school system. Currently there are approximately 1,700 Lutheran elementary and secondary schools, which enroll about 200,000 pupils, in the United States. Most of these schools are operated by the Missouri Synod Lutheran Church.

The Roman Catholic parochial school system grew rapidly after its beginnings in the 1800s. Enrollment in Catholic schools mushroomed between 1900 and 1960 from about 855,000 to over five million. The Roman Catholic parochial school system in the United States is now the largest private school system in the world.

THE IMPORTANCE OF PRIVATE EDUCATION The concept of public education—that is, education paid for through public government—is a relatively new idea in the history of U.S. education. For many years, if parents or religious groups wanted to provide education for their children, they had to do so with their own resources. In this part of the book there have been many references to private schools and private education; at this juncture we simply wish to reiterate the tremendous importance of private education. In fact, were it not for private education as the predecessor, it is difficult to imagine how we would have evolved a public education system. Private education still plays an enormously important role at all levels of education in the United States.

***"Give me your tired, your poor,
Your huddled masses yearning to breathe free,
The wretched refuse of your teeming shore,
Send these, the homeless, tempest-tossed, to me:
I lift my lamp beside the golden door."***

Emma Lazarus

The major shift from private to public education occurred during the nineteenth century. For instance, in 1800 there was no such thing as a state system of public education anywhere in the United States—no elementary schools, secondary schools, or state colleges or universities. In fact, until the nineteenth century, all forms of education that were available were private in nature—from elementary school through graduate school. By the year 1900, however, nearly all states had developed a public system of education running from elementary school through graduate school.

parochial school An educational institution operated and controlled by a religious denomination.

Many historians suggest that the overriding motive for private education has always been religious in nature. Initially, parents wanted their children to learn to read so that they could study and understand the Bible and thus gain salvation. Even the earliest colleges were designed primarily to prepare ministers.

(Harvard College, for instance, was created in 1636 for the express purpose of training ministers.)

Likewise, Benjamin Franklin created his unique academy as a private institution to provide technical training to young men because there was no public institution yet created to do so. It was not until 1874 that the Michigan State Supreme Court established that it was legal for school districts to tax citizens for general support of public high schools. By that time, private schools had been providing secondary education for our nation's youth for two centuries.

SUMMARY

Sooner or later, most of us question the value of the subjects we study in school, and the subject of educational history also comes under such scrutiny. We opened this chapter with a provocative and insightful essay by Diane Ravitch, a well-respected educational historian, dealing with the question "Why Study History?" You might wish to reread it at this point.

PROVIDING EDUCATION IN THE NEW WORLD

Our earliest colonists brought their educational ideas and expectations with them from Europe and, soon after arriving in the New World, set about creating schools that fulfilled their needs. By today's standards these early efforts to provide education in the colonies were simple and rudimentary, but it is noteworthy that these early settlers, who were faced with very serious basic survival challenges, nevertheless made efforts to educate their children. These efforts varied widely, from private tutorial education for plantation owners' children in the South, to religious schools in the Middle Colonies, to public schools in the North. Most education was driven by religious motives, and much of the formal education beyond that needed to read the Bible was provided only for boys from the more well-to-do families.

The Northern Colonies were the first to pass laws regarding education, and teachers, who were generally poorly trained, ranged from housewives who conducted class in their kitchens to ministers who taught school in the church. It took almost 200 years after the first colonists arrived before a movement slowly started to provide universal education for all children, thanks to the pioneering efforts of people like Horace Mann, who is often called the father of the "Common Schools."

The Latin Grammar School, which was transplanted from Europe like other educational ideas, was the first form of secondary education in colonial America. These few schools taught Latin and other subjects needed to prepare boys for college and, more than likely, the ministry. Benjamin Franklin is credited with creating the American Academy, a later form of vocational secondary school that was uniquely American. The modern-day high school had its beginning in the 1820s, and the first junior high schools came into existence about 1810.

The aims of American schools have been the subject of considerable controversy, and historically important attempts to clarify them have periodically been made through various statements such as the Committee of Ten in 1892, the Seven Cardinal Principals in 1918, the Eight-Year Study in 1932–1940, the

1938 Purposes of Education in American Democracy, Education for all American Youth in 1944, and the 1952 Imperative Needs of Youth.

Our federal government has played an increasing role in education over time, even though our U.S. Constitution does not mention education and therefore supposedly leaves education up to the states—yet another of the many controversial subjects in the field of education.

Teacher education has also evolved during our nation's history, from being scattered and unregulated to our present-day rigorous and highly regulated teacher education programs. Likewise, the tools available for teachers to use have slowly evolved from the simple hornbook and slate to the impressive array of printed and electronic teaching materials available for use in our schools today.

EDUCATION FOR SPECIAL POPULATIONS

Unfortunately, educational opportunities for minorities, women, and people with disabilities were virtually nonexistent in our nation's early history and developed only very slowly until quite recently, in spite of the efforts of people such as Benjamin Banneker, Frederick Douglass, John Chavis, Prudence Crandall, Booker T. Washington, Emma Willard, Ella Flagg Young, Mary McLeod Bethune, and Maria Montessori, to name just a few.

The history of education in the United States is filled with many messages. Some tell of successes, some of failures, others of dedicated teachers, of humble beginnings, of individuals' thirst for knowledge—even of those who have been willing to die for the truth. A chronology of these highlights of the historical development of education is presented in Appendix 9.1.

The historical record has implications for today's educator. Teachers can learn much from educational history if they listen carefully to these messages from the past. In particular, they will come to realize how very important education is to the preservation and progress of U.S. society—perhaps more important than any other human endeavor.

DISCUSSION QUESTIONS

1. How did the development of public education differ in the Northern, Middle, and Southern Colonies?
2. Discuss the evolution of elementary schools.
3. What historical conditions led to that uniquely American institution, the comprehensive high school?
4. How has the concept of the nature of humankind changed in the past three hundred years? What effect has this change had on teacher education?
5. What are the highlights of the history of education of African Americans?
6. What are the highlights of the history of education of women in the United States?
7. Discuss the roles that private schools have played in U.S. education.

JOURNAL ENTRIES

1. Try to learn more about the historical development of education in the particular field you are thinking of entering. Record in your journal any especially pertinent things that you learn.

2. List some of the more important things you learned from this chapter. Which, if any, of the items you listed will likely have practical value for you as a future educator? In what ways?

PORTFOLIO DEVELOPMENT

1. Summarize the evolution of the goals of public schools in colonial America and the United States. Develop a chart that creatively portrays this evolution.
2. Write an essay on the importance of education in the historical development of the United States.

SCHOOL-BASED EXPERIENCES

1. George Santayana said, "Those who cannot remember the past are condemned to repeat it." Keeping that idea in mind as you read through this chapter, try to generate a list of practical suggestions that you can use as you work in the schools. Examples might include the practical idea of Pestalozzi for working effectively with children, some of the famous historical aims of U.S. public education, and some of the moral wisdom espoused in early textbooks such as the *New England Primer* and McGuffey's *Reader.* During your clinical experiences in the schools, think about how some of the historical ideas presented in this chapter apply to today's teachers.
2. While you are in the schools, visit with older teachers and administrators to discuss the ways in which schools have changed over the years. Also ask how students have changed, how teaching methods have changed, and how parents have changed.

WEBSITES

We recommend that you do a web search using key words such as "school history," "American schools," "history of education," "American history," and "museums, school." In addition, several informative sites are listed below.

1. <www.cedu.niu.edu/blackwell> The Blackwell History of Education Museum and Research Collection is one of the largest collections of its kind in the world. Most of the collection is listed on its web page. The Blackwell Museum has also developed instructional materials in a variety of media to help you learn more about the history of education.
2. <www.greatbooks.org> A source of information about literature and great books.
3. <www.cr.nps.gov/nr/twhp/wwwlps/lessons/58iron/58iron.htm> Historical website about Iron Hill School, an African American one-room school in northern Delaware.
4. <www.msc.cornell.edu> and <www.history.cc.ukans.edu> These home pages offer examples of old one-room county schools.
5. <www.gutenberg.net> Project Gutenberg provides on-line texts of public-domain books, including classics of educational history and philosophy such as John Dewey's *Democracy and Education: An Introduction to the Philosophy of Education.*

NOTES

1. Paul Monroe, *Source Book of the History of Education.* New York: Macmillan, 1901.
2. Roe L. Johns and Edgar L. Morphet, *Financing the Public Schools.* Englewood Cliffs, NJ: Prentice-Hall, 1960, 378.
3. W. H. G. Armytage, "William Byngham: A Medieval Protagonist of the Training of Teachers," *History of Education Journal* 2 (Summer 1951): 108.
4. Monroe, 282.
5. Much of the material dealing with the history of African Americans up to the signing of the Emancipation Proclamation (1863) was taken from the doctoral dissertation of Samuel David, *Education, Law, and the Negro.* Urbana: University of Illinois, 1970.
6. Emma Willard, "A Plan for Improving Female Education," in *Women and the Higher Education.* New York: Harper & Brothers, 1893, 12–14.

BIBLIOGRAPHY

Bial, Raymond. *One-Room School.* Boston: Houghton Mifflin, 1999.

Buetow, Harald A. *Of Singular Benefit: The Story of U.S. Catholic Education.* New York: Macmillan, 1970.

Butts, R. Freeman. *Public Education in the United States: From Revolution to Reform.* New York: Holt, Rinehart & Winston, 1978.

Cohen, Sheldon S. *A History of Colonial Education 1607–1776.* New York: Wiley, 1974.

Cremin, Lawrence A. *American Education: The Colonial Experience, 1607–1783.* New York: Harper & Row, 1970.

——. *American Education: The National Experience, 1793–1976.* New York: Harper & Row, 1990.

——. *The Transformation of the School: Progressivism in American Education, 1876–1957.* New York: Knopf, 1961.

Duck, Lloyd. *Understanding American Education: Its Past, Practices, and Promise.* Burke, VA: Chatelaine Press, 1996.

Eldridge, Michael. *Transforming Experience: John Dewey's Cultural Instrumentalism.* Nashville, TN: Vanderbilt University Press, 1998.

Franklin, John Hope. *From Slavery to Freedom: A History of African-Americans.* New York: Knopf, 1994.

Gartner, Lloyd P., ed. *Jewish Education in the United States: A Documentary History.* New York: Teachers College Press, 1970.

Goodsell, W. *Pioneers of Women's Education in the United States.* New York: McGraw-Hill, 1931.

Herbst, Jurgen. *The Once and Future School: Three Hundred and Fifty Years of American Secondary Education.* New York: Routledge, 1996.

Holmes, Madelyn, and Weiss, Beverly J. *Lives of Women Public Schoolteachers: Scenes from American Educational History.* New York: Garland Publishing, 1995.

"Lessons of a Century," *Education Week,* Dec. 15, 1999. The final installment of an excellent yearlong series dealing with the history of education.

Morgan, Harry. *Historical Perspectives on the Education of Black Children.* Westport, CT: Praeger, 1995.

Reese, William J. *The Origins of the American High School.* New Haven, CT: Yale University Press, 1995.

Smith, L. Glenn. *Lives in Education: People and Ideas in the Development of Teaching.* Ames, IA: Educational Studies Press, 1993.

Szasz, Margaret Connell. *Indian Education in the American Colonies 1607–1783.* Albuquerque: University of New Mexico Press, 1988.

CHAPTER 9

Using Recent History to Improve Student Learning

Is History Knowable?

By John P. Diggins, *American History Illustrated,* March/April 1991

A curious irony faces the contemporary world of scholars. As the public becomes more and more interested in history—witness the remarkable response to the television series on the Civil War and the number of nonfiction best-selling books—literary critics, philosophers, and even some historians are coming to doubt the ability of anyone to reconstruct the past. Due to improved narrative writing and documentary cinema technique, history has become more readable and accessible. But theory-struck scholars are asking if it is knowable.

Centuries ago such a question was seldom raised. From classical antiquity to the birth of Christianity and up through the Renaissance and the eighteenth-century Enlightenment, history was regarded as either the voice of memory, the witness to experience, the vision of destiny, or the story of the decline and fall of previous regimes and hence the lessons of corruption that were to be avoided (one of the concerns of the framers of the Constitution).

In the latter half of the nineteenth century, some thinkers began to question the idea of history as the repository of truth. History could no longer be regarded as a scientific study of events that could be written as they actually happened; nor could it be regarded as a moral drama of good and evil with the implication that the ultimate triumph of righteousness confirms the march of progress. Even before the shock of the outbreak of the First World War, some intellectuals doubted whether history could be understood as rational and progressive and whether moral judgments were clear, fixed, absolute, and applicable to all situations. The conclusion drawn by even the famous "progressive historians" Charles Beard, Frederick Jackson Turner, and Vernon L. Parrington held history to be relative and in need of continuous revision in response to new questions and needs deriving from what the philosopher John Dewey called the "problematic situation" of the present.

This progressive perspective prevailed in American educational and political culture for the first half of the twentieth century (and it has echoes in the current demand that history be responsive to the needs of minorities and others who have been excluded or, to use a trendy expression, "marginalized"). Progressive historiography lent credence to the ideology of liberalism, particularly the Jeffersonian conviction that the study of the past must serve the present and that each generation is sovereign unto itself and cannot be bound by the dead hand of precedent and tradition. Yet today, just as different groups are making claims upon American history, history itself, in the minds of some, can no longer make any truth-claims of its own. . . .

(continued)

LEARNER OUTCOMES

After reading and studying this chapter, you will be able to

1. Decide, explain, and defend the degree to which you believe it is possible to know, understand, and profit from the history of education.
2. List and detail several of the most important improvements that have been made in the American educational system over the past half century.
3. Explain important educational contributions that have been made during the last half century by private schools, the federal government, researchers, teacher organizations, teacher educators, and other groups that have helped to improve U.S. schools.
4. List and explain several of the major ideas regarding the history of U.S. education.
5. Explain why a knowledge of the history of education is important to educators and how it might be used to improve student learning today. ■

Many dramatic changes have occurred in education in the United States over the past half century. Examples of these rapid and often controversial changes will be briefly discussed in this chapter. However, the big historical ideas that we present in this chapter surround the ideas that (1) there has been phenomenal growth in both the size and complexity of U.S. educational establishments in the last half century; (2) the current information age has placed tremendous new demands and expectation on our schools and teachers; (3) providing excellent equal educational opportunities to all students continues to be a major, yet unrealized challenge to our society and to our schools; and perhaps most important, (4) an understanding of the history of education is of very practical value in helping contemporary educators to improve student learning.

MORE STUDENTS AND BIGGER SCHOOLS

Since World War II, U.S. education has been characterized by a great deal of growth and change: growth in terms of school enrollment, educational budgets, complexity, and federal influence; change in terms of court decisions, proliferation of school laws, confusion about goals, school financial difficulties, struggles for control, and diversification of curricula.

THE RAPID GROWTH OF THE EDUCATIONAL ENTERPRISE

Perhaps the single most dramatic change that has occurred in education over the past half century is the sheer expansion in size of the educational enterprise, which took place in many ways.

ENROLLMENT GROWTH The total number of public school students in the United States nearly doubled from 1940 to 1990. Although part of this rapid growth in school enrollment was attributable to overall population growth, a good part was

As school enrollments have increased in the past 50 years, communities have needed to build new buildings and find other strategies for coping with classroom shortages.

due to the fact that greater percentages of people were going to school. Furthermore, people were staying in school much longer, as shown by the almost doubled enrollment in higher education.

NEED FOR MORE SCHOOLS As school enrollment dramatically increased, the need for new classrooms and buildings to house these students also increased. This need for new schools was generally concentrated in cities and suburbs. In fact, ironically, because of increased busing, school district consolidation, and shifting population, some smaller rural schools were no longer needed, while more densely populated areas saw a drastic shortage of classrooms. Many schools had to resort to temporary mobile classrooms. Other strategies for coping with classroom shortages included larger classes, split scheduling that started some classes very early and others very late in the day, and classes held in a variety of makeshift places such as gymnasiums, hallways, and storage closets. Many schools also rented additional space in nearby buildings. Fortunately, taxpayers were generally willing eventually to approve the necessary bond referenda to provide the needed additional schools during this period of rapid growth in student enrollment.

NEED FOR MORE TEACHERS Naturally, this surge in student enrollments required many additional teachers, and at times colleges simply could not produce enough. In this situation, states lowered teacher certification requirements, sometimes to the point at which no professional education training was required at all. Over time, however, the nation seemed to meet the demand for more teachers.

A person who wants to learn will always find a teacher.

Persian proverb

As one would expect, the increased numbers of students and teachers cost a great deal more money. More buses had to be purchased, more books and other instructional materials had to be obtained, more school personnel had to be hired—More of everything required to provide education was needed.

SCHOOL DISTRICT CONSOLIDATION

The consolidation of school districts was one notable administrative trend of this period. The number of separate school districts was reduced from 117,000 in 1940 to 16,000 in 1980. There was a corresponding decline in the number of one-teacher schools over this same period.

ONE-ROOM SCHOOLS For many years the **one-room school,** a single classroom taught by a single teacher and encompassing all grades, symbolized traditional education in the United States. Although school consolidation undoubtedly had many educational advantages and saved school dollars in some ways, it did necessitate the busing of more students over greater distances.

Dr. Mark W. DeWalt, at Susquehanna University, completed a study that yielded surprising results: The private one-room school made a modest comeback in the 1980s. This phenomenon is shown in Figure 9.1, which indicates that there was considerable growth in the number of private one-room schools between 1971 and 1987. DeWalt attributes this growth, at least in part, to the U.S. Supreme Court's decision in *Wisconsin* v. *Yoder* (1972), which upheld Amish parents' rights to educate their own children. This decision opened up the opportunity for Amish parents, as well as other parents with similar levels of commitment, to establish their own private elementary schools.

In terms of longer trends, of course, the overall number of one-room schools has diminished greatly. There were approximately 150,000 public one-room schools in existence in 1930, compared to just slightly more than 500 today.

one-room school
A school in which all grade levels are taught by a single teacher in a single room.

GROWTH OF BUSING Both the number and the percentage of students who were bused increased considerably from 1940 to 1980, as did the total cost and per-

FIGURE 9.1 ONE-ROOM SCHOOLS

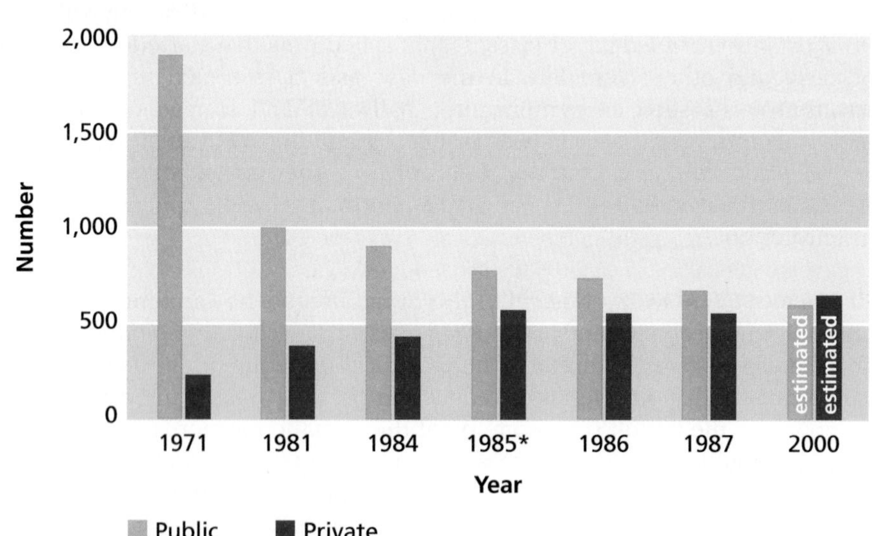

Source: Education Week, February 1, 1989, 3.

One of thousands of one-room country schools established to educate rural children during the westward movement in America.

pupil cost of busing. In addition to the general busing of students necessitated by school district consolidation, integration efforts have often involved busing students out of their neighborhood schools. This controversial practice is discussed elsewhere in this book.

Busing students to school is still a very big operation for the U.S. educational enterprise. It is estimated that about 60 percent of all students are bused to school by about 450,000 school buses.

BIGGER SCHOOL BUDGETS Educational growth has driven the nation's public education costs to record heights. This rapid increase is illustrated by the fact that the approximate material cost of public education was $2 billion in 1940, $5 billion in 1950, $15 billion in 1960, $40 billion in 1970, $97 billion in 1980, and $208 billion in 1990. Even if the figures are corrected for inflation, public education has become considerably more expensive: The percentage of the gross domestic product spent on education rose from 3.5 percent in 1940 to 7 percent in 1980.[1]

GROWTH OF PROGRAMS

As enrollment increased and schools became larger, more diverse curricula and programs developed in U.S. schools.

CURRICULAR GROWTH Curricular growth, like most change, was the result of an accumulation of many smaller events. One such event was the publication in 1942 of the report of the Progressive Education Association's Eight-Year Study (1932–1940) of thirty high schools. The study showed that students attending

DEBATE

Should Seat Belts Be Mandatory on School Buses?

YES

Ozzie Hill, Jr., drives a school bus for the Camp Lejeune Department of Defense Dependent Schools in North Carolina. A former NEA local affiliate president, he's now the Human and Civil Rights Coordinator for the Lejeune Education Support Association. He can be reached at **ozdehill@gibralter.net.**

As a school bus driver, my job is to see to it that children go from home to school and school to home as safely as possible. I can do that job best when I'm driving a well-maintained school bus, equipped with seat belts for every child.

I drive a school bus for preschoolers that's equipped with seat belts and car seats. In North Carolina, three-year-olds riding the bus to preschool sit in a secured car seat. Four- and five-year-olds riding the bus to preschool wear seat belts, too.

I like to think that riding on my bus is one of the most constructive, daily safety lessons that many of these preschoolers will ever have.

I teach my young riders that they must always buckle up while riding in a bus, car, or plane. That's a terrific message to send to so many kids at such an early age.

But I worry that all this great training is for naught.

When these kids reach the age of six, they no longer have to wear their seat belts. In fact, the buses they ride to elementary school don't even have seat belts. Where's the consistency here? What kind of message are we sending?

A school bus is long and deep. A major accident can cause children to be tossed from one end of the bus to the other. So can braking for a stray animal, swerving to avoid an obstacle in the road, or simply stopping short.

We all know that seat belts are intended to keep people in their seats, to prevent the kind of injuries that might result when kids are tossed around like salad. And we know that seat belts keep kids from standing or jumping up and distracting the driver. So what are we waiting for?

Some say it's human nature to wait for tragedy to strike before making unpleasant change. It took a long time to mandate bike helmets, for example. And it can take forever to get a stop light at a busy intersection.

NO

Debbie Moore, a school bus driver for ten years, has served as president, vice-president, and now as secretary of the Gwinnett Bus Drivers Association in Georgia. In 1993, the Georgia Association of Educators named Moore its ESP of the Year. She can be reached at **dm9165@bellsouth.net.**

School buses don't have seat belts for good reasons. They're unnecessary, and worse, they're hazardous.

School buses are designed specifically for safety:

- The body of the bus is made of layers of reinforced steel, forming a protective cage around the passengers.
- The floor of the bus is raised so that, in the event of a collision, most vehicles would strike the bus underneath the actual student seating area.
- The fuel tank is enclosed with a steel cage, and the seats are covered in flame-resistant kevlar.
- Side windows, roof hatches, emergency doors, and pop-out windows offer numerous emergency exits.
- But the best protection for school bus riders is the bus's internal "compartmentalization" design.

Bus seats have high backs and are placed close together at an angle. If there's a sudden stop or impact, students slide forward, and their chests and abdomens hit the seat in front of them. If the students on the bus are wearing lap belts, their foreheads hit the seat in front of them, transferring the force to their spinal columns, and causing more serious injuries.

School buses designed for maximum safety don't need seat belts—and most drivers don't want them. Why? Most drivers think seat belts on buses pose a significant safety hazard.

- First, a seat belt can be a deadly weapon. The buckle can be used to strike another person. The belt itself can be used to choke someone.
- Second, in the event of an accident, seat belts can trap students on board. Fires can engulf buses in flames and smoke

YES | NO

But we don't have forever. We're talking about children and safety. Truth be told, parents, educators, and lawmakers should have insisted years ago that school buses be equipped with seat belts.

Some say the cost of putting seat belts on every single American school bus is just too high. But the cost of maintaining the status quo could be higher.

If one child's life can be saved, if one child can be spared from injury, then it will have been well worth the cost of installation.

I used to be against seat belts. But, as the laws became tougher, I settled down—and buckled up. Now I feel uneasy and unsafe without one wrapped around me.

When I forget to put my seat belt on, my own children remind me. Fastening seat belts is second nature to them now. And that's how it should be.

Kids are learning, but we need to do our part, too. We need to model correct behavior. We need to drive as carefully as we can—and we need to make sure other drivers know how to drive safely when school buses are in their midst.

We need to teach students how to get on and off our buses safely. And we need to do whatever it takes to get seat belts on our buses. I don't want my charges—or yours—to be the ones who could have been saved, if only they'd been wearing their seat belts.

Source: "Should Seat Belts Be Mandatory on School Buses?" *NEA Today* (October 1998): 47.

in roughly three minutes. The delay in unbuckling a jammed seat belt could be the difference between life and death.

Not only could small fingers have problems unbuckling in an emergency, but dangling seat belts could become a danger to exiting students, causing them to trip.

- Third, it would be nearly impossible for bus drivers to make sure that all students are buckled up properly at all times. The special needs students on the bus I drive now wear their seat belts so loosely that, in the event of an accident, the kids would slide out, and the seat belts would wind up around their necks.

Right now, school buses are the safest form of transportation on the road. In 1995–96, there were 16 pupils killed on school buses nationwide—out of 24.5 million students riding the buses every day over a distance of 5 billion miles.

Most bus accidents that year were collisions, which school buses are built to withstand with minimum injury to passengers. And most bus fatalities occur outside of the bus, in loading and unloading zones.

Even one student death is one too many, but seat belts aren't the answer. We can improve school bus safety by strictly enforcing the no-pass law, putting an aide on every bus, improving the training we offer drivers, and getting more support from parents and administrators when there are discipline problems on buses.

But by far the best way we can boost bus safety is to boost bus safety instruction. By teaching students how to behave on and around buses, we can do more to prevent injuries and deaths than seat belts could ever do.

WHAT'S YOUR OPINION?

Should seat belts be mandatory on school buses?

Go to **www.ablongman.com/johnson** to cast your vote and see how NEA readers responded.

"progressive" schools achieved as well as students at traditional schools. This report helped to create a climate that was more hospitable to experimentation with school curricula and teaching methodologies. The publication of a series of statements on the goals of U.S. education (the 1938 "Purposes of Education in American Democracy," the 1944 "Education for All American Youth," and the 1952 "Imperative Needs of Youth") helped to broaden our schools' curricular offerings. (All of these goal statements were discussed more fully in Chapter 8.)

In 1958, shortly after the Soviet Union launched *Sputnik,* the world's first artificial satellite, Congress passed the National Defense Education Act (NDEA). This act provided a massive infusion of federal dollars to improve schools' science,

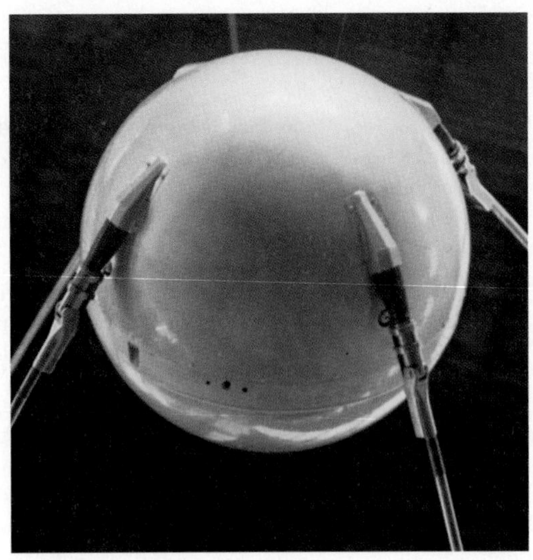

The 1958 Soviet launching of Sputnik resulted in new federal funds to improve science and mathematics school programs.

mathematics, engineering, and foreign language programs. Eventually, innovative curricula such as SMSG mathematics, BSCS biology, and PSCS physics grew out of these programs. Other school programs, such as guidance, were later funded through the NDEA. Note that in this case the federal government called on the schools to help solve what was perceived to be a national defense problem. Regardless of the motive, the NDEA represented another milestone that contributed significantly to the growth of the U.S. educational enterprise.

If one were to compare today's school curriculum with that in any school sixty years ago, one would find impressive changes. The 1940 curriculum was narrow and was designed primarily for college-bound students, whereas today's curriculum is broader and designed for students of all abilities. This growth in the school curriculum has come about through the dedicated work of many people and represents one of the truly significant accomplishments in education in the United States.

GROWTH OF SPECIAL EDUCATION PROGRAMS Perhaps curriculum growth is best illustrated in the area of special education. Public schools historically did not provide special education programs for children with disabilities; rather, they simply accommodated such children as best they could, usually by placing them in regular classrooms. Teachers had little or no training to help them understand and assist the special child. In fact, relatively little was known about common disabilities.

Not until the federal government passed a series of laws during the mid-twentieth century—including Public Law 94-142, the Education for Handicapped Children Act—did schools begin to develop well-designed programs for students with disabilities. These new special education programs required teachers who had been trained to work with students with visual impairments, students who are hearing-impaired, students with behavior disorders, and so forth. States and colleges then developed a wide variety of teacher-training programs for special educators. The percentage of public school students enrolled in various special education programs increased from 1.2 percent in 1940 to 11.4 percent in 1990. In actual numbers of students, this represented a total of about 310,000 special education students in 1940 compared to about 4,641,000 in 1990.

Special education has developed rapidly over a relatively short period of time in our recent history. It continues to evolve rapidly today and will likely do so in the future. And as you can imagine, those who believe we should continue to put a high priority on special education programs view these programs through lenses shaped by their own knowledge, experiences, and historical perspective.

ASIAN AMERICAN EDUCATION The Second World War brought about what many consider to have been unwarranted discrimination against Japanese Americans;

RELEVANT RESEARCH

Student Homework

STUDY PURPOSE/QUESTIONS: Down through the ages, teachers have pondered the value of asking students to do school work at home. For instance, even before formal schools existed, parents would demonstrate the skills they wanted their children to develop and then undoubtedly required the child to practice those skills that they would need as adults in their society—a very early form of homework. Students today are increasingly also asked to practice those skills they begin to learn in school, a contemporary and controversial phenomenon called "homework." The value of homework has been the subject of many research studies, including the one reported here, which focuses on the time devoted to homework versus organized sports versus TV watching by students ages three to eleven.

STUDY DESIGN: This study was conducted by Sandra Hofferth at the Institute of Social Research, located at the University of Michigan, and involved a survey of 3,600 children in about 2,395 schools in an attempt to understand the total minutes spent each week on studying, participating in organized sports, and watching television. The survey was conducted in 1981 and repeated sixteen years later in 1997 in an attempt to discern trends in these areas.

STUDY FINDINGS: The results of this study were as follows:

	Age Group	1981	1997
Minutes spent on **studying** each week	3 to 5	12	36
	6 to 8	44	123
	9 to 11	169	217
Minutes spent on **organized sports** each week	3 to 5	31	176
	6 to 8	180	278
	9 to 11	189	314
Minutes spent on **watching TV** each week	3 to 5	799	808
	6 to 8	767	758
	9 to 11	1100	816

Both in 1981 and in 1997, time spent watching TV was by far the winner, followed by sports; (you probably guessed it) studying homework came in last. Furthermore, students ages nine through eleven, spent considerable less time watching TV in 1997 (816 minutes per week) than they did in 1981 (1,100 minutes per week).

IMPLICATIONS: There is a wide divergence of opinions about the value of homework, among both parents and educators. In the final analysis each school and each teacher must decide on the amount and type of homework, if any, he or she will ask students to do. Unfortunately, history does not shed a great deal of light on the value of homework, other than to remind us that students today have many more diversions (including TV and organized sports) that compete with homework for their time.

Source: Sandra Hofferth, Institute of Social Research, University of Michigan.

the U.S. government placed more than 100,000 Japanese American citizens in internment camps and in some cases confiscated their property. It was not until 1990 that the government officially apologized and paid restitution for having done so. In hindsight, many believe that this treatment of U.S. citizens of Japanese background constituted a form of blatant discrimination.

In the decades following the Korean and Vietnam wars, the number of Asian immigrants to the United States has increased dramatically. Large numbers of

The number of Asian students is increasing rapidly throughout the United States.

Vietnamese, Cambodians, Laotians, and Thais have been included in this recent migration. While many of these Asian immigrants have experienced considerable success, the majority have struggled to learn English, receive an education, and find suitable jobs. Many feel that they have been discriminated against and have not received equal educational and employment opportunities. Yet many of the highest-achieving high school students are Asian Americans, proof of the fact that their families typically place a high value on education.

In the new brain-powered economy, education will be the world's largest, most important industry.

Morton Egol

Of course, the very first Asian immigrants arrived in colonial America at a very early stage—especially Chinese immigrants. Asians came, like most immigrants from around the globe, seeking jobs and a better life. Also like most immigrants, the Asians arrived as poor and relatively uneducated people. Unfortunately, people from the Orient were often discriminated against and were seldom offered equal educational opportunity. In 1882, in fact, the U.S. government passed the Chinese Exclusion Act in an attempt to limit the number of Chinese immigrants. Despite these many obstacles, Asians typically found ways to earn a living and to educate their children; and many became very successful in a variety of businesses.

HISPANIC AMERICAN EDUCATION The number of Hispanic American students in U.S. schools has increased dramatically over the past fifty years—but the historical background of this increase can actually be traced to the very first formal schools in North America. The earliest formal schools on this continent were started and conducted by Spanish missionaries in Mexico and the southwestern part of what is now the United States in the sixteenth century. Some historians even assert that the Spanish had established several "colleges" in North America before Harvard was established in 1636. This assertion is probably true if one defines a mission school as a college. As with the other early schools in the Americas, the missionaries established these early Spanish schools primarily for religious purposes: to help people read the Bible and thus gain salvation. Early mission schools in what is now Mexico and in Florida, Cuba, California, Arizona, New Mexico, and elsewhere were taught by the Catholic priests in the Spanish language. After the United States won its independence and grew to include what we now think of as the Southwest, these early Spanish schools gradually became part of the larger English-speaking U.S. school system.

Many important Hispanic Americans have made significant contributions to the development of education down through the ages. Space allows us to mention only a few such people at this point. Rafael Cordero, a self-taught free black Hispanic, established an early (1810) school in San Germán, Puerto Rico. He realized that black children, who were denied a formal education because of their skin color, would profit greatly from schooling. Cordero's schools and his teaching methods eventually became so highly respected that they attracted rich white parents' children as well.

George Sanchez is another example of a Hispanic American educational pioneer. After graduation from the Albuquerque, New Mexico, high school in 1923, Sanchez began his teaching career at age sixteen. He taught in one-room schools to which he traveled on horseback, continuing to attend college whenever possible. George Sanchez eventually obtained a master's degree and a doctorate, after which he held various professorships and government positions; he then became the minister of education in Venezuela. After returning to the United States, he worked in various capacities to advocate the improvement of education for Hispanic American children. Through the courts and through writing, speaking, and advising, Sanchez eventually was able to bring about significant improvements in Mexican American education.

Unfortunately, Hispanic American education did not develop as quickly or as well as it did for the majority population. This discrepency was due at least in part to the fact that many Hispanic Americans were in the lower income brackets, immigrated to the United States without well-developed English language skills, and in many instances suffered discrimination. Like other minority groups in the United States, Hispanic Americans have not historically been afforded equal educational opportunities. But this pattern must change. Schools in the southern and southwestern parts of the United States now have huge numbers of Hispanic American students, and in many of these schools Hispanic American students are, or will become, the majority in the relatively near future.

The education of immigrants from all over the world remains an important challenge for our educational system today as it has throughout our history. For example, about eighteen million immigrants came to the United States in the three decades between 1890 and 1920, while about twelve million have come in the past two decades of the 1980s and 1990s.

A DEVELOPING PROFESSION

The field of education has taken giant strides toward becoming a profession since World War II. In the following pages we will briefly explore the increasing complexities of educational systems in the United States and look at some of the recent developments that have contributed to the professionalization of the field of education.

THE INCREASING COMPLEXITY OF THE EDUCATIONAL ENTERPRISE

The current U.S. educational system is much more complex than school systems of the past, and this complexity is manifested in many different ways.

INCREASING FEDERAL INVOLVEMENT As we noted earlier, the federal government has played important roles in the development of national educational programs. This federal involvement in education has gradually increased over the years, and it reached a peak during the past half century.

The 1940s saw the nation at war. The Vocational Education for National Defense Act was a crash program to prepare workers needed in industry to produce goods for national defense. The program operated through state educational agencies and trained more than seven million workers. In 1941 the Lanham Act provided funds for building, maintaining, and operating community facilities in areas where local communities had unusual burdens because of defense and war initiatives.

GI BILL The GI Bill of 1944 provided for the education of veterans of World War II. Later, similar bills assisted veterans of the Korean conflict. The federal government recognized a need to help young people whose careers had been interrupted by military service. These bills afforded education to more than ten million veterans at a cost of almost $20 billion. Payments were made directly to veterans and to the colleges and schools the veterans attended. In 1966 another GI Bill was passed for veterans of the war in Vietnam.

World War II veterans returned to college motivated by their war experiences and assisted by the federal GI Bill of Rights.

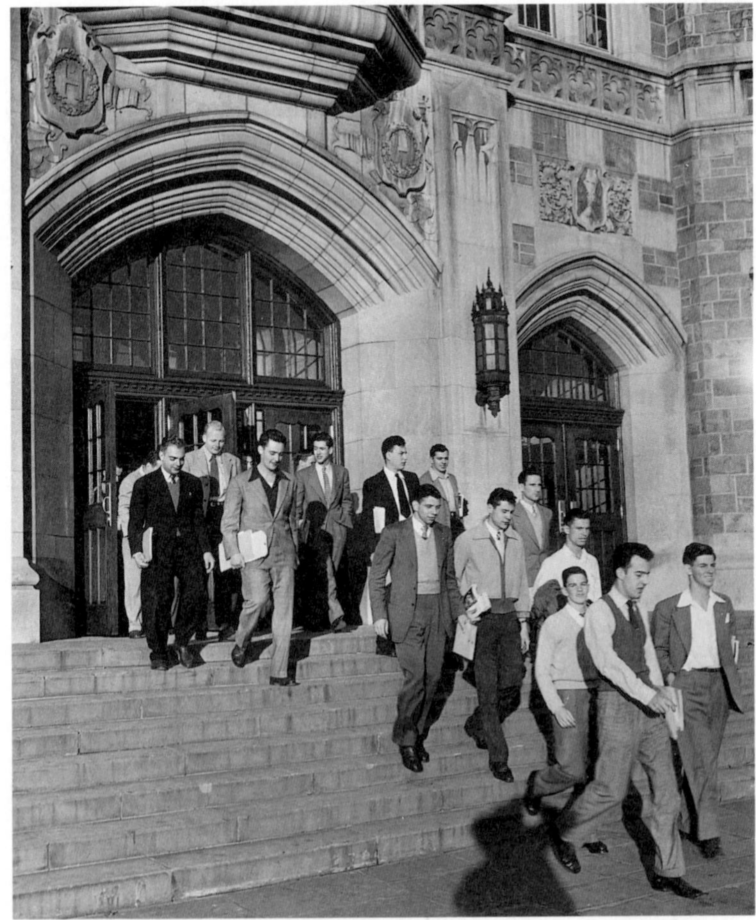

NATIONAL SCIENCE FOUNDATION The National Science Foundation, established in 1950, emphasized the need for continued support of basic scientific research. It was created to "promote the progress of science; to advance the national health, prosperity, and welfare; to secure the national defense; and for other purposes." The Cooperative Research Program of 1954 authorized the U.S. commissioner of education to enter into contracts with universities, colleges, and state education agencies to carry on educational research.

The schools have often attracted the zealous attention of those who wish to influence the future, as well as those who wish to change the way we view the past.

Diane Ravitch

CATEGORICAL FEDERAL AID Beginning in 1957, when the first Soviet space vehicle was launched, the federal government further increased its participation in education. The National Defense Education Act of 1958, the Vocational Education Act of 1963, the Manpower Development and Training Act of 1963, the Elementary and Secondary Education Act of 1965, and the International Education Act of 1966 are examples of increased federal participation in educational affairs. Federally supported educational programs such as Project Head Start, the National Teacher Corp, and Upward Bound are further indications of such participation.

All these acts and programs have involved categorical federal aid to education—that is, aid for specific uses. Some people believe that federal influence on education has recently been greater than either state or local influence. There can be no denying that through federal legislation, U.S. Supreme Court decisions, and federal administrative influence, the total federal effect on education is indeed great. Indications are that this effect will be even more pronounced in the future. It will remain for historians to determine whether this trend in U.S. education is a beneficial one.

THE STRUGGLE FOR EQUAL EDUCATIONAL OPPORTUNITY The past half century has also been characterized by an increasing struggle for **equal educational opportunity** for all children, regardless of race, creed, religion, or sex. This struggle was initiated by the African American activism movement, given additional momentum by the women's rights movement, and eventually joined by many other groups such as Hispanic Americans, Native Americans, and Asian Americans. Other chapters of this book discuss the details of this relatively recent quest for equal educational opportunity. We mention it briefly at this point simply to emphasize that the struggle for equal educational opportunity represents an important but underrecognized recent historical movement in education. Today, many observers are pointing out that with the accelerated growth of minority subcultures within this nation, our economic and political survival depends to a great degree on educational opportunities and achievements for all segments of U.S. society.

THE PROFESSIONALIZATION OF TEACHING As we pointed out in Chapter 8, formal teacher training is a relatively recent phenomenon. Teacher training programs were developed during the first half of the twentieth century. By the midpoint of the century, each state had established teacher certification requirements. Since then, teacher training and certification have been characterized by a "refinement" or "professionalization" movement. Teacher salaries have also improved considerably over this period.

equal educational opportunity
Access to a similar education for all students, regardless of their cultural background or family circumstances.

In addition to teacher education, this professionalization movement touched just about all facets of education: curriculum, teaching methodology, training of school service personnel (administrators, counselors, librarians, media and other specialists), in-service teacher training, teacher organizations, and even school

We should begin improving our schools by appreciating how well they have, in most places and at most times, done so far.

Gerald W. Bracey

building construction. To understand clearly this professionalization movement, one need only compare pictures of an old one-room country school with a modern school building, read both a 1940 and a 1998 publication of the AFT or NEA, contrast a mid-twentieth-century high school curriculum with one from today, or compile a list of the teaching materials found in a 1940 school and a similar list for a typical contemporary school.

CONTINUED IMPORTANCE OF PRIVATE SCHOOLS Chapter 8 explained that religion was the main purpose of education in colonial America. Children were taught to read primarily so that they could study the Bible, and most early colleges were established primarily to train ministers.

As the public school system developed, however, the religious nature of education gradually diminished to the point where relatively few American children attended religious schools. There have always been certain religious groups, however, that have struggled to create and maintain their own private schools so that religious instruction could permeate all areas of the curriculum. The most notable of these religious groups has long been the Roman Catholic Church. Over the past twenty-five years, though, enrollment in non-Catholic religious schools has grown dramatically while Catholic school enrollment has declined.

Despite this recent trend, some Roman Catholic dioceses operate extremely large school systems, sometimes larger than the public school system in the same geographical area. The Chicago Diocese operates the largest Roman Catholic school system, enrolling approximately 150,000 students.

With rare exceptions, private and parochial schools struggle to raise the funds they need to exist. They typically must charge a tuition fee, rely on private contributions, and conduct various fund-raising activities. In recent years some school districts have made tuition vouchers available to parents who choose not to send their children to the public school. The highly controversial subject of tuition waivers is discussed more fully elsewhere in this book.

Chapter 5 gives more details on contemporary private school systems. Here, we wish simply to emphasize that private religious and nonreligious schools pro-

As the public school system developed, the religious nature of education gradually diminished. However, some religious groups maintain their own private schools so that their religious beliefs can be taught throughout the curriculum.

Home schooling is a rapidly growing phenomenon in modern times.

vide elementary and secondary education for a very large number of young people in the United States. Teacher education students should become familiar with these private school systems so that they can decide whether they might be interested in pursuing teaching positions in such schools.

HOME SCHOOLING Many years ago, about the only parents who taught their children at home were those who lived so far from a school that it was impossible for their children to attend. In the past several decades, however, a growing number of parents have been choosing to educate their children at home—at least through the elementary grades and sometimes even through high school. The motivation for **home schooling** varies, but often it stems from a concern that children in the public schools may be exposed to problems such as drugs, alcohol, smoking, or gangs. Other parents have religious motives, wanting their children to be taught in a particular religious context. Still other parents, who may have had bad experiences with public schools, simply feel they can provide a better education for their children at home. Recent laws and court cases have generally upheld the right, within certain parameters, of parents to educate their children if they choose to do so. The number of parents providing home schooling has grown an estimated 15 percent per year in the last decade. The Home Legal Defense Association estimates that over 1.5 million children are now schooled at home. As one would expect, the value of home schooling is widely debated in our society.

CONTINUING/ADULT EDUCATION There have been many forms of education for adults for at least two centuries in this country. Shortly after the United States became a nation, a need to help new immigrants learn English caused schools, churches, and various groups to offer English language instruction; factories found a need to offer job and safety training; churches taught adult religious instruction; and so forth. The New York public schools developed large English language programs as well as adult vocational programs for the unemployed. Adult

home schooling
Teaching children at home rather than in formal schools.

education took a great variety of forms and quickly grew into a vast network of programs dealing with nearly all aspects of life in the United States.

An example of a large early adult education development can be found in the Chautauqua movement at Lake Chautauqua, New York. Started in 1874 by the Methodist Sunday school, this adult education effort expanded to include correspondence courses, lecture classes, music education, and literary study on a wide variety of subjects throughout the eastern part of the nation.

Public schools increasingly offered adult education classes during the nineteenth century. Some of the larger public school systems, such as that in Gary, Indiana, developed adult educational programs with an emphasis on vocational and technical training. Gradually, too, nearly all schools serving rural areas developed adult agricultural programs to improve farming methods.

In 1964 the Economic Opportunity Act provided Adult Basic Education funding to help adults learn to read and write. Since that time there has been a proliferation of continuing/adult education programs of all types throughout the United States. These programs serve an increasingly important purpose in our rapidly changing society. They help new immigrants learn the English language, provide job training for the unemployed, update job skills, teach parenting skills, enable people to move to higher-level employment, help people explore new hobbies, provide enrichment programs for retired folks, and generally make the world of education available to nearly all citizens regardless of age. The exploding popularity of the Elderhostel programs and other activities now offered for senior citizens and the crowded evening parking lots at high schools and colleges throughout the country attest to the popularity and success of continuing/adult education programs. In the future, as the world becomes increasingly complex and as more people remain active and healthy in old age, we predict that such adult/continuing education programs will continue to grow.

Through public education we can in this century hope in no small measure to regain that great gift to each succeeding generation, opportunity, a gift that once was the promise of our frontier.

James Conant

EVOLUTION OF EDUCATIONAL ASSESSMENT Educators have undoubtedly attempted to measure and assess student learning from the very beginning of formal education. However, it is only in the last half century that educational assessment has take on vastly more importance, to the point in contemporary education that assessment has become the tail that wags the educational dog. Let's briefly review this recent evolution of educational assessment. (See Chapter 15 for a more through discussion of this topic.)

Many historians suggest that the increased attention given to educational assessment in the past fifty years was sparked by James Conant, who had become president of Harvard University in 1933. Conant and his colleagues were influenced by the developments in mental testing done by Alfred Binet in France and by Lewis Terman in the United States, which were used extensively by the U.S. Army to test recruits.

Conant seized on a relatively new test called the Scholastic Aptitude Test (SAT), developed by Carl Bright at Princeton University, as a way to assess a student's potential for success at Harvard. He also helped to create a new organization, called the Educational Testing Service (ETS), which became—and remains—the major power in the educational assessment area. By the 1960s over a million high school students were taking the SAT test, which most colleges used as one criterion for admission.

Many so-called standardized tests have been developed over the past half century in an attempt to measure different kinds of aptitude, learning, motivation, and virtually every aspect of education. These standardized tests have come

Adult education programs have been common in the United States since the seventeenth century, but burgeoned during the late twentieth and early twenty-first centuries. Many such programs are offered through public schools.

under much criticism by many educators, parents, and others, who question their fairness and accuracy. Even so, as we will point out in Chapter 15, they continue to be heavily used today.

Educators have faced increasing pressure in recent years to develop improved ways to assess student learning. Much of this pressure has come from taxpayers, government, and the industrial world, often in a demand for greater accountability. Most states have implemented a required system of achievement testing. The results of these achievement tests are commonly used to evaluate and compare schools—a controversial and unfair practice, according to many educators.

In fact, while agreeing that accurate educational assessment is absolutely essential to the educational enterprise, a growing number of educators are questioning many aspects of the increasing emphasis on educational assessment. This topic is discussed much more fully in Chapter 15. Suffice it to point out here that educational assessment has grown rapidly and taken on increasing importance, for better or worse, in the past fifty years.

RECENT TRENDS IN EDUCATION[2]

Education experienced a major change following World War II when John Dewey, George Counts, William Bagley, W. W. Charters, Lewis Terman, and other intellectuals who had held sway during the first half of the twentieth century yielded to a somewhat less philosophically oriented breed of researchers represented by Abraham Maslow, Robert Havighurst, Benjamin Bloom, J. P. Guilford, Lee Cronbach, Jerome Bruner, Marshall McLuhan, Noam Chomsky, and Jean Piaget. The Progressive Education Association closed its doors, and a series of White House conferences on children, youth, and education were inaugurated in an attempt to improve education.

Each generation must define afresh the nature, direction, and aims of education to assure such freedom and rationality as can be attained for a future generation.

Jerome S. Bruner

No school system on earth has been scrutinized, analyzed, and dissected as profoundly and as mercilessly as that in the United States. From the late 1940s to the middle 1950s, educational institutions at all levels were not only flooded with unprecedented numbers of students but also censored and flailed unmercifully by self-ordained critics (Hyman Rickover, Arthur Bestor, and Rudolph Flesch). In retrospect this frantic rush to simultaneously patronize and criticize the institution seems a curious contradiction. The public schools were characterized as "godless, soft, undisciplined, uncultured, wasteful, and disorganized." Critics who remembered the high failure rates on tests given to World War II draftees were determined to raise the public's levels of physical fitness and literacy; others who detected a weakening of moral and spiritual values were eager to initiate citizenship and character-education programs. The enrollments in nonpublic schools doubled, correspondence schools of all kinds sprang into existence, and the popular press carried articles and programs designed to help parents augment the basic skills taught within the school program. In 1955 there were an estimated 450 correspondence schools serving 700,000 students throughout the country.

NEW EMPHASES IN EDUCATION

Education is a painful, continual and difficult work to be done by kindness, by watching, by warning, by precept, and by praise, but above all—by love.
John Ruskin

Fortunately, although some people were highly critical of the schools, not everybody panicked. There were physical fitness programs, character education projects, a general tightening of educational standards, and much more. J. P. Guilford, E. Paul Torrence, Jacob Getzels, and others explored the boundaries of creativity; Alfred Barr and D. G. Ryans carried out exhaustive studies of teacher characteristics; and just about everybody experimented with new patterns of organization. There were primary block programs; inter-age groupings; plans devised by and named for George Stoddard and J. Lloyd Trump; core programs; and a host of other patterns or combinations of plans structured around subject areas, broad groupings of subjects, or pupil characteristics. There were programs for the gifted and the not-so-gifted, and there was a new concern for foreign language instruction as well as the functional use of English. There was also a limited resurgence of Montessori schools and several one-of-a-kind experimental schools such as Amidon and Summerhill. While all this was taking place within the schools, the school systems themselves were consolidating; by 1960 there were only about one-third as many school districts as had existed twenty years earlier.

Automation was highly regarded during the 1950s, but the tools that gave education its biggest boost were more diverse. Social psychologists provided more advanced sociometric tools, which offered new insights into the functioning of groups; reading specialists and psychologists developed highly refined diagnostic instruments for use in studying learning disabilities; and statisticians devised new formulas and designs for controlling and analyzing data with the help of modern computers. New research tools such as regression formulas and factoral analysis yielded data that had been unobtainable earlier. On a somewhat less sophisticated level, more interesting and more flexible teaching tools were developed—audiovisual devices, learning games, more beautifully illustrated books, instructional television, machines for programmed instruction, and computers. Additional personnel such as teacher aides, counselors, social workers, and school psychologists became part of the school scene as well.

analysis of teaching
Procedures used to enable teachers to critique their own performance in the classroom.

ANALYSIS OF TEACHING Another emphasis found expression in the **analysis of teaching.** For half a century, researchers had been attempting to identify the characteristics and teaching styles that were most closely associated with effective instruction. Hundreds of studies had been initiated, and correlations had been done among them. During the 1950s the focus began changing from identification of what ought to occur in teaching to scrutiny of what actually does

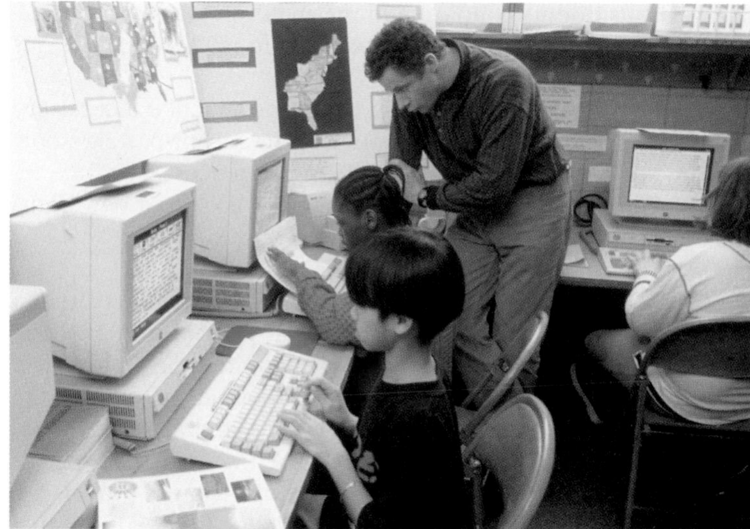

Personal computers are among the teaching and learning tools that developed in the late twentieth century.

occur. Ned Flanders and other researchers developed observational scales for assessing verbal communications between and among teachers and students. The scales permitted observers to categorize and summarize specific actions on the part of teachers and students. These analyses were followed by studies of nonverbal classroom behaviors.

Another series of investigations involving the wider range of instructional protocols was patterned after the time-and-motion studies used earlier for industrial processes. Dwight Allen and several other educators attempted to analyze teacher behaviors, delineate the components of effective teaching, and introduce teacher candidates to the elements judged most important to good teaching. The change in focus from studies of teacher characteristics to analyses of what actually occurs in classrooms has offered educators highly fruitful insights into teaching and learning and has provided usable instruments for further investigations of classroom behavior. It is now possible to assess the logical, verbal, nonverbal, affective, and several attitudinal dimensions of instruction as well as the intricate aspects of cognition and concept development.

TEACHER EFFECTIVENESS Recent research has focused even more closely on the instructional patterns of effective teachers. A review by Marjorie Powell and Joseph Beard, *Teacher Effectiveness: An Annotated Bibliography,* catalogs more than three thousand investigations into instructional competencies. The **effective teaching** movement based on this research offers today's teachers important skills. In common with the schoolteachers of sixty years ago, today's teachers learn to be strong leaders who direct classroom activities, maximize the use of instructional time, and teach in a clear, businesslike manner.

Effective teachers now employ structured, carefully delineated lessons. They break larger topics into smaller, more easily grasped components; and they focus on one thought, point, or direction at a time. They check prerequisite skills before introducing new skills or concepts. They accompany step-by-step presentations with a large number of probing questions. Teachers offer detailed explanations of difficult points and test students on one point before moving on to the next. They provide corrective feedback where needed and stay with

effective teaching
A movement to improve teaching performance based on the outcomes of educational research.

Jean Piaget (1896–1980) was a Swiss developmental psychologist who researched children's stages of learning.

the topic under study until students comprehend the major points or issues. Effective teachers use prompts and cues to assist students through the initial stages of acquisition.

This new emphasis on demonstration, prompting, and practice is a far cry from the relatively unstructured classroom activities of the recent past. We now emphasize carefully created learning goals and lesson sequences. It will be interesting to see whether the educational pendulum swings back to a new focus on student concerns and initiatives at some time in the future.

SOCIOLOGICAL STUDIES A major breakthrough in education has resulted from a series of sociological studies relating to social class, social perceptions, and academic achievement. James Coleman was among the first to demonstrate that it is not teaching equipment as much as children's social relationships that make the difference. Students' parents and peer groups at home and at school mold their perceptions and regulate their performances. These findings and those of Alan Rosenthall and Christopher Jencks have given new direction to schools' efforts. Educators' concerns have changed, at least partially, from educational hardware to studies of pupil populations.

STUDY OF THE LEARNING PROCESS Several leading educational researchers in the United States and Europe have sought to analyze and describe how children learn. All of these investigators have stressed the importance of successful early learning patterns and the problems associated with serious learning deficits. They also believe that important elements within the environment may be changed or modified to promote learning.

Maria Montessori, an Italian physician, believed that children should be encouraged to teach themselves through the use of manipulative materials. She developed a wide range of educational resources, many of which could be matched or sequenced according to specific attributes (size, color, pitch, etc.). Montessori did much to promote the concept of pupil discovery and the use of tactile learning materials.

GLOBAL PERSPECTIVES: Jean Piaget

Jean Piaget (1896–1980), a Swiss psychologist, was educated at the University of Paris. Through his work with Alfred Binet, who developed one of the first intelligence tests, Piaget became very interested in how children learn. He spent long hours observing children of different ages and eventually created a theory of mental or **cognitive development.** Piaget believed that children learn facts, concepts, and principles in four major stages. Up until about age two, he suggested, a child is at the *sensorimotor stage* and learns mainly through the hands, mouth, and eyes. From about two to seven years of age, a child is at the *preoperational stage* and learns primarily through language and concepts. Between ages seven and eleven, a child's learning is characterized by *concrete operations,* which involve the use of more complex concepts such as numbers. The final learning stage identified by Piaget is called the *formal operations* phase. This stage typically begins between ages eleven and fifteen and continues throughout adulthood. During this final stage the learner employs the most sophisticated and abstract learning processes. While children do not all fit neatly into these categories, Piaget's work has contributed much to educators' understanding of the

cognitive development
A learner's acquisition of facts, concepts, and principles through mental activity.

learning process and has helped teachers to develop more appropriate teaching strategies for students at different developmental stages.

Psychologist B. F. Skinner (1904–1990) developed a behavioral theory that suggested students could be trained, or conditioned, to learn just about anything a teacher desired.

Robert Havighurst, a University of Chicago professor, has identified specific developmental tasks that he believes children must master if they are to develop normally. He even suggests that there may be periods during which certain tasks must be mastered if they are to become an integral part of children's repertoire of responses. There may also be "teachable moments" (periods of peak efficiency for the acquisition of specific concepts/skills) during which receptivity is particularly high. Havighurst, like Piaget, has caused educators to look carefully at the motivations and needs of children.

A contemporary of Havighurst, Jerome Bruner of Harvard, has also postulated a series of developmental steps or stages that he believes children encounter as they mature. These involve action, imagery, and symbolism. Bruner's cognitive views have stressed student inquiry and the breaking down of larger tasks into components.

Benjamin Bloom, author of Bloom's Taxonomy of Educational Objectives and distinguished service professor at the University of Chicago, has attempted to identify and weigh the factors that control learning. He believes that one can predict learning outcomes by assessing three factors: (1) the cognitive entry behaviors of a student (the extent to which the pupil has mastered prerequisite skills), (2) the affective entry characteristics (the student's interest in learning the material), and (3) the quality of instruction (the degree to which the instruction offered is appropriate for the learner). Bloom's research is reflected in models of direct instruction, particularly mastery learning, in which teachers carefully explain, illustrate, and demonstrate skills and provide practice, reinforcement, corrective feedback, and remediation.

B. F. SKINNER Burrhus Frederic (B. F.) Skinner (1904–1990) became one of the foremost early educational psychologists in U.S. education. He developed a **behavioral theory**—a theory focusing on outward behavior—that suggested students could be successfully trained or conditioned to learn just about anything a teacher desired. This required the teacher to break down the learning into small sequential steps. Skinner even experimented with teaching machines that presented the learner with small sequential bits of information—an idea that has been revived today in computer-assisted instruction. Skinner published many works including *The Technology of Teaching, Beyond Freedom and Dignity,* and *Walden Two.* He contributed much to present-day understanding of human learning and helped to advance the technology of teaching.

EDUCATIONAL CRITICS Another development in education was triggered by a phalanx of critics, including Edgar Friedenberg (*Coming of Age in America*); Charles Silberman (*Crisis in the Classroom*); Jonathan Kozol (*Death at an Early Age*); Ivan Illich (*Deschooling Society*); John Holt (*How Children Fail*); and a government report, *A Nation At Risk* (1983), which focused on low educational standards. Some critics, such as Silberman, urge schools to refurbish what they already have; others, including Illich, want to abandon the schools altogether. These critics have not gone unnoticed. Friedenberg's call for alternatives to traditional education, Silberman's endorsement of open education, and Kozol's plea

behavioral theory
A theory that considers the outward behavior of students to be the main target for change.

PROFESSIONAL DILEMMA

How Can the Busy Teacher Keep Up with Historical and Contemporary Research?

Ask any teacher what her or his major problems are and "not having enough time" will likely be near the top of the list. So it is perhaps not surprising that many teachers find it difficult to keep up with current research that may help educators do a better job. And yet one of the important hallmarks of a professional is finding, evaluating, and implementing the results of valid and reliable research results. For instance, when a person goes to a medical doctor, he or she expects that physician to be using knowledge based on the most recent medical research. By the same token, parents have a right to expect, when they send their children to school, that teachers will be using the most recent educational research in their educational practice. Thus, the professional dilemma is: How do busy teachers locate, read, evaluate, and implement the best research results into their teaching? This task is made even more difficult by the fact that although a great volume of education research is constantly being conducted, a fair amount of it is not necessarily valid or reliable.

Teachers who are determined to put good research results into practice must first be able to read, understand, and evaluate educational research. To learn how to do this, you will probably need to take some basic research courses at a nearby college or university. You will also need to read research reports found in a variety of professional journals in your specialty fields. This may mean subscribing to such journals or getting your school to make them available. Probably you will also wish to attend a variety of professional meetings where research is presented and discussed. And after you locate good research findings, you will need to do careful planning when you implement these research results in your classroom.

Unfortunately, there is no simple solution to this professional dilemma. We know that, because we, too, struggle with this problem. However, we are convinced that the first step to solving this dilemma is becoming determined to offer your clients (your students and their parents) the very best education possible. We also are convinced that to do so requires a knowledge of the best and most recent educational research.

- What are your feelings about this professional dilemma at this point in your career development?
- What might you be able to do at this time to help you prepare to deal with this dilemma?
- To what degree do you feel your current teachers are keeping up with, and using, research in their teaching?

for equal opportunity are all reflected to some degree in innovative programs from coast to coast.

LITIGATION'S INFLUENCE ON EDUCATION In the years since 1970 an astonishingly large segment of school patrons and students have resorted to courts of law in confrontations with school officials and teachers. Chapter 6 discusses many of these law cases. Suits have been filed challenging pupil placements, grades, the failure of the school to teach properly, disciplinary actions, dress codes, and numerous other previously accepted educational practices. The Buckley Amendment of 1974, which gives students and their parents the right to view official school records, added immeasurably to the demands of those seeking redress of grievances. In addition, courts have extended the rights of due process to include students at all levels in an effort to protect their constitutional rights. Due process requires that rules and regulations facilitate the educational goals of the

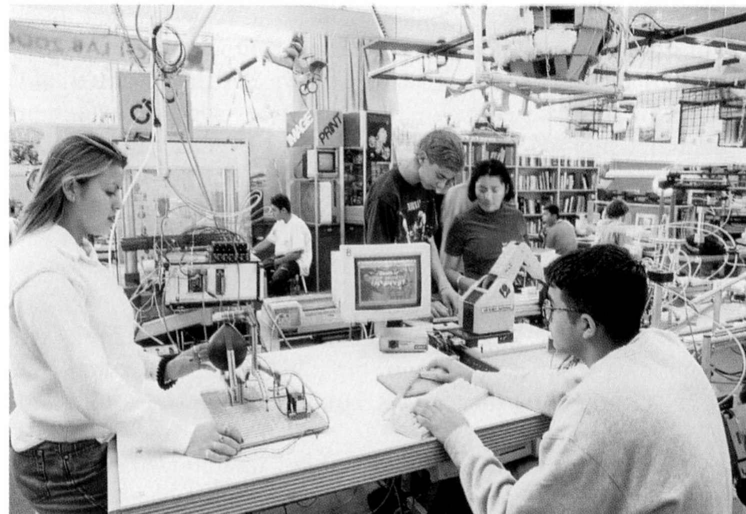

The last decades have witnessed rapid school changes and reform through local, state wide, and national efforts.

school and be clearly publicized. There must also be provision for a fair hearing when regulations are violated.

It is unfortunate that legal recourse has become a major modus operandi, for legal maneuvering is generally a substitute for good faith and mutual respect. However, individual abuses have probably diminished in the face of threatened legal sanctions.

SCHOOL REFORM Schools have constantly evolved, changed, and been reformed down through the ages, usually slowly, but sometimes rather quickly. The last several decades have witnessed relatively rapid school changes and reform in the United States. Some advocates of school reform would probably claim that there has been more talk about school reform than action. There is certainly some truth in this assertion, in large part because of talk on the part of politicians at all levels of government. Unfortunately, these same politicians have not always been willing to provide sufficient funding to improve our schools. In fact, political talk about school reform is often motivated by a desire to cut taxes.

Nevertheless, countless efforts to reform U.S. education have gone forward over the past half century. These have included small local efforts; many statewide mandated efforts; and even many national efforts, usually advocated by the federal government and/or the courts. Many of these more recent reform efforts are reported throughout this book. The past fifty years may well eventually be called "the school reform era" by future educational historians.

GLOBAL PERSPECTIVES: Educators' Worldwide Responsibility

These last three chapters, which have briefly reviewed the history of education, point out that many, perhaps even most, present-day educational concepts and practices were first developed long ago and in various parts of the world. Contemporary teachers in the United States owe a great debt of gratitude to their historical counterparts around the globe who pioneered and developed the profession.

History has shown that educators throughout the world have learned much from one another and that education has improved and profited greatly from this sharing of educational ideas. The benefit of sharing is even greater today than it has been in the past and will increase as societies become ever more dependent on one another. Educators such as you will have to work even harder to share educational ideas in the future.

EDUCATION 2000 GOALS PROGRESS Much publicity was generated in 1990 when then President George Bush and U.S. governors adopted an ambitious ten-year plan to improve our nation's schools using eight broadly bases goals. A ten-year evaluation of the success in meeting these goals, conducted by the National Education Goals Panel, is shown in Table 9.1.

As Table 9.1 shows, these ambitious goals were largely unachieved. Still, they remain very desirable, even if probably a bit unrealistic, national educational goals in the minds of most people.

SCHOOL PUBLIC OPINION OVER THE PAST HALF CENTURY A public opinion survey, first conducted in 1950 and repeated in 1999, revealed the following interesting

TABLE 9.1 STATES' PROGRESS TOWARD MEETING EDUCATION GOALS: 1989 TO 1999

	Number of States and District of Columbia*		
Progress from 1989 to 1999	Better	No change	Worse
Goal 1: Students start school ready to learn			
Percent of 2-year-olds immunized	6	45	0
Goal 2: School completion			
High school completion rates	4	42	5
Goal 3: Student achievement			
Reading achievement, 4th grade	8	36	0
Math achievement, 4th grade	7	32	0
Goal 4: Teacher education/professional development			
Teaching certificates	1	41	9
Goal 5: International math and science achievement	insufficient data		
Goal 6: Adult literacy	insufficient data		
Goal 7: Safe, disciplined, alcohol/drug-free schools			
Student marijuana use	0	11	16
Student alcohol use	0	27	1
Student safety	1	22	1
Goal 8: Parental participation			
Parental involvement from teachers' perspective	0	45	6

*The number of states does not always total 51 because of rounding, ties, and insufficient data.

Source: National Education Goals Panel.

shifts over this fifty-year span of time: In 1950, 24 percent of those surveyed thought that teachers should be asked their political beliefs, whereas in 1999 only 9 percent thought so; in 1950, 39 percent said that religion should be taught in the public schools, whereas in 1999 the number had increased to 50 percent; in 1950, 44 percent said that teachers were underpaid, whereas in 1999, 61 percent said so; and in 1950, 67 percent of those polled thought that students were being taught more worthwhile and useful things in school than were children twenty years before, but in 1999 only 26 percent thought so. These shifts in public opinion about public schools provide food for thought for contemporary educators.

MAJOR EDUCATIONAL EVENTS OF THE PAST CENTURY As we recently moved into the twenty-first century, many people have reflected on educational accomplishments in the United States over the past hundred years. As would be expected, opinions differ considerably on this subject. Ben Brodinsky, an education journalist, has suggested that the GI Bill of Rights should perhaps be thought of as the single most important educational event of the past century. He lists the desegregation of schools as the second most important and the federal Education for All Handicapped Children Act as the third most important educational event of the past one hundred years.

There is no doubt that there were many very important educational events and accomplishments during the past one hundred years—The list could go on and on. One example of significant progress made by the U.S. educational system in the past half century is reflected in the increase in the percentage of students completing high school: from 50.8 percent in 1940 to 72.4 percent in 1990. What would you put on your list of the most important educational events and/or accomplishments of the last century?

USING HISTORY TO IMPROVE STUDENT LEARNING As is true in all areas of human learning, some people question the value of history. As you would conclude from the past three chapters dealing with the history of U.S. education, we authors strongly believe that an understanding of the history of education indeed has much value and can help a teacher to improve student learning.

One rather obvious way in which historical knowledge can be useful to an educator is to help her or him capitalize on historical educational successes and avoid past educational failures. If a school district is contemplating moving to a new student grouping system, for instance, teachers would greatly profit from knowing the experiences of other schools that have used those student grouping systems in the past.

Many people have attempted to point out how a knowledge of history can have practical uses, and in the case of this book, might help improve student learning. Sam Wineburg claims that a knowledge of history has the potential of helping to humanize people. Building on this idea, Carl Degler suggests that a knowledge of history might help a person better understand what it means to be human. Paul Gagnon asserts that developing some understand of history helps a person to mature, helps to hearten a person, and helps to set people free. David McCullough suggests that history has the potential value to enlarge and intensify life and reminds us that history is by far the greatest part of human experiences. William McNeill points out that history tells us who we are and how to behave and that a knowledge of past successes and failures has the potential to help us make correct choices more easily.

We hope that these ideas about the value of historical knowledge will help to convince you that all educators can profit from a better understanding of the history of education and that such knowledge can help you improve student learning.

SUMMARY

There are reputable historians who seriously question the extent to which it is possible for us to really know and understand the past. This interesting question is explored by John P. Diggins in this chapter's opening essay, "Is History Knowable?" It behooves each of us to ponder this question as we critically study the history of our profession.

MORE STUDENTS AND BIGGER SCHOOLS

Over the past fifty years, the U.S. education system has experienced unprecedented growth in both size and complexity. The great increase in numbers of students over this half century has created a challenging need for more school buildings and many more teachers. Population increases and shifts from rural settings to cities require bigger schools and large, elaborate school busing systems. There has also been an amazing expansion of educational curriculums and program diversification for different types of students at all levels over the past fifty years. All of this growth in size and programs have resulted in a tremendous increase in school budgets—from about $2 billion in 1940 to about $208 billion in 1990 for our public schools alone over this fifty-year period. More detailed information on current school costs can be found in Part Three of this book.

Programs for students with special needs have increased tremendously in recent history. This impressive growth is shown by the fact that in 1939–40 about 310,000 children were served in the various special education programs, whereas fifty years later, in 1989–90, this number had increased to about 4,641,000 students—a fifteenfold increase. There has also been notable growth in other educational programs designed to better serve the needs of the increasingly diverse student population now found in our schools.

A DEVELOPING PROFESSION

Our U.S. educational systems have also grown in complexity over the last half century, especially in funding and control. Our federal government has increased its involvement in public education through legislation such as the GI Bill, the National Science Foundation, the National Defense Education Act, the Elementary and Secondary Act, Project Head Start, Upward Bound, and the National Teacher Corp, to name just a few. And each of these federal acts, while providing funds for specific school programs, have also placed new demands and regulations on our schools.

The various states have also made our schools more complex by passing many more laws that place new demands on our teachers and schools. Examples of such state laws include those dealing with school funding requirements, curriculum demands, program approval systems, testing programs, and teacher certification requirements.

Likewise, our court systems at all levels have made countless rulings over the last half century that have greatly affected our school systems. Notable among these court decisions have been those dealing with school racial integration, equal educational opportunity, parents' and students' rights, teachers' rights, the legal rights of various special populations, and the constitutionality of some laws. A more complete and current discussion of administrative, financial, and legal aspects of our educational systems is presented in Part Three of this book.

Many other recent trends in education were also discussed in this chapter. These included professional advancements such as analysis of the teaching act, teacher effectiveness research, sociological studies, the development of new learning theories, and other research efforts designed to help us better understand and improve student learning. There has been an increasing number of widely read critics of our schools over the past half century; examples include Friedenberg, Silberman, Kozol, Illich, and Holt. Various governmental agencies at the state and national levels have also been critical of our schools in recent years, resulting in many reports and calls for school reforms.

This chapter ends with suggestions of how a knowledge of recent educational history might be used to improve student learning, which of course, is the main purpose and goal of all chapters in this book. Finally, Appendix 9.1 presents a brief history of education chronology.

It is difficult to draw meaningful inferences from recent events that have not yet stood the test of time. Implications of recent educational events will eventually be found in the answers to questions such as these:

- What should be the role of the federal government in education?
- How can equal educational opportunity be achieved in the United States?
- How professionalized should the school system be?
- To what degree should educational policy and practice be influenced by litigation?
- How will school reform movements change the practice of education?

The answer to these questions, and other questions you may have in mind, will be colored by the lenses through which people view the world, children, and schools. We believe that viewing all educational questions through well-informed historical lenses yields more valid answers.

DISCUSSION QUESTIONS

1. Other than those mentioned in this chapter, what additional recent educational developments seem particularly important to you? Why are they important?
2. Has the increased federal involvement in education been good or bad for schools?
3. In your opinion, how much progress has the United States really made in providing equal educational opportunity? Defend your answer.
4. In what respect, if any, has education become professionalized, in your opinion?
5. What is happening in education at this very moment that is likely to be written about in future history of education books?

JOURNAL ENTRIES

1. Interview a retired teacher about the educational changes she or he has observed over the past fifty years. Ask what advice this retired educator has for beginning teachers today, and record the answers.

2. Describe and evaluate a learning experience you remember from your own elementary school days. What made the experience memorable, and what role did the teacher play in the learning process?

PORTFOLIO DEVELOPMENT

1. Prepare a creative educational history project (using a poster, videotape, audio recording, slide presentation, or some other creative medium) dealing with a topic, person, or idea that is of interest to you. Design your project so that it can be used as part of your job placement credentials.
2. Create a list of the most useful outcomes of U.S. education over the past fifty years. What can you as a beginning teacher learn, if anything, from your list?

SCHOOL-BASED EXPERIENCES

1. Most of the developments discussed in this chapter are so recent that they continue to influence contemporary classrooms. As you work in the schools, look to see how the continuing struggle for equal educational opportunity is progressing. Also, analyze what you observe in order to determine the degree to which teaching has been professionalized—a movement that has gained impetus during the last fifty years. Finally, as you participate in classrooms, look for evidence that the work of educational pioneers discussed in this chapter (such as Bloom, Montessori, Skinner, and Piaget) has made an impact in U.S. classrooms.
2. Discuss with experienced educators the changes they have observed during their careers. Visit with older educational administrators to discuss changes they have seen in their work over the years. Ask older people about their school experiences.

WEBSITES

We recommend that you do a web search using key words such as "history, education"; "museums, education"; and "school museums." Some useful websites are listed below.

1. <www.cedu.niu.edu/blackwell> The Blackwell History of Education Museum and Research Collection, located at Northern Illinois University, is one of the largest collections of its kind in the world. Most of the Blackwell holdings are listed on its web page. The Blackwell Museum has developed a wide variety of instructional materials (also listed on its web page) to help you learn more about the history of education.
2. <www.scholastic.com/Instructor> Contains a variety of educational materials such as articles, contests, free materials for teachers, and chats with other educators on any subject, including the history of education.
3. <www.si.edu> Provides links to each museum of the Smithsonian Institution in Washington, D.C.
4. <www.blackhistory.eb.com> Encyclopedia Britannica has initiated a black history site that contains much information about African American history.
5. <www.laca.org/Johnstown/FCSlinks.html> Links to sites that deal with one-room schools.
6. <www.cdickens.com/articles/dickjane.htm> Information about the Dick and Jane readers.

NOTES

1. U.S. Department of Commerce, Bureau of the Census, *Digest of Education Statistics 1982.* Washington, DC: U.S. Government Printing Office, 1982, 23.
2. We thank Dr. Donald Barnes for many of the ideas presented in this section.

BIBLIOGRAPHY

Campbell, John Martin. *The Prairie Schoolhouse.* Albuquerque, NM: University of New Mexico Press, 1996.

Capella, Gladys; Geismar, Kathryn; and Nicoleau, Guitele, eds. *Shifting Histories: Transforming Schools for Social Change.* Cambridge, MA: Harvard Educational Publishing Group, 1995.

Cremin, Lawrence A. *American Education: The Metropolitan Experience 1876–1980.* New York: Harper & Row, 1988.

——. *The Transformation of the School: Progressivism in American Education 1876–1957.* New York: Knopf, 1961.

Gutek, Gerald L. *Education in the United States: An Historical Perspective.* Englewood Cliffs, NJ: Prentice Hall, 1986.

——. *Historical and Philosophical Foundations of Education.* Upper Saddle River, NJ: Prentice Hall, 1997.

Katznelson, Ira, and Weir, Margaret. *Schooling for All: Class, Race, and the Decline of the American Ideal.* New York: Basic Books, 1985.

Krug, Edward. *The Shaping of the American High School.* New York: Harper & Row, 1964.

"The Negro and American Education." *Changing Education* (a journal of the American Federation of Teachers) (Fall 1966).

Perkinson, Henry J., ed. *Two Hundred Years of American Educational Thought.* New York: David McKay, 1976.

Ravitch, Diane. *The Troubled Crusade: American Education 1945–1980.* New York: Basic Books, 1983.

Spring, Joel. *The American School 1642–1990.* White Plains, NY: Longman, 1994.

"The Struggle for Integration." *Education Week,* March 24, 1999. Part 3 of an excellent year-long series dealing with the history of education.

Wilson, Anna Victoria, and Segall, William E. "African American Teachers during the Civil Rights Movement." *Journal of Midwest History of Education Society 23* (1996): 61–64.

Youniss, James, and McLellan, Jeffery A. "Catholic Schools in Perspective." *Phi Delta Kappan* (October 1999): 105–113.

APPENDIX 9.1

IMPORTANT DATES IN THE HISTORY OF WESTERN EDUCATION

ca. 4000 B.C.	Written language developed
ca. 2000	First known schools
1200	Trojan War
479–338	Period of Greek brilliance
469–399	Socrates
445–431	Greek Age of Pericles
427–346	Plato
404	Fall of Athens
384–322	Aristotle
336–323	Ascendancy of Alexander the Great
303	A few private Greek teachers set up schools in Rome
167	First Greek library in Rome
146	Fall of Corinth: Greece falls to Rome
A.D. 31–476	Empire of Rome
35–95	Quintilian
40–120	Plutarch
70	Destruction of Jerusalem
476	Fall of Rome in the West
734–804	Alcuin
800	Charlemagne crowned Emperor
980–1037	Avicenna
1100–1300	Crusades
1126–1198	Averroes
ca. 1150	Universities of Paris and Bologna
1209	Cambridge founded
1225–1274	St. Thomas Aquinas
1295	Voyage of Marco Polo
1384	Order of Brethren of the Common Life founded
ca. 1400	Thirty-eight universities; 108 by 1600
ca. 1423	Printing invented
ca. 1456	First book printed
1460–1536	Erasmus
1483–1546	Martin Luther
1487	Vasco da Gama discovered African route to India
1491–1556	Ignatius of Loyola
1492	Columbus landed in America
ca. 1492	Colonists began exploiting Native Americans
ca. 1500	250 Latin grammar schools in England
1517	Luther nailed theses to cathedral door; beginning of Reformation
1519–1521	Magellan first circumnavigated the globe
1534	Founding of Jesuits
1536	Sturm established his Gymnasium in Germany, the first classical secondary school
1568	Indian school established in Cuba by the Society of Jesus
1592–1670	Johann Comenius

1601	English Poor Law established principle of tax-supported schools
1618	Holland had compulsory school law
1620	Plymouth Colony, Massachusetts, settled
1635	Boston Latin Grammar School founded
1636	Harvard founded
1642	Massachusetts law of 1642 encouraged education
1632–1704	John Locke
1647	Massachusetts law of 1647 compelled establishment of schools
ca. 1600s	Hornbooks evolved
1661	First newspaper in England
1672	First teacher-training class, Father Demia, France
1684	Brothers of the Christian Schools founded
1685	First normal school, de la Salle, Rheims, France
1697	First teacher training in Germany, Francke's Seminary, Halle
1700–1790	Benjamin Franklin
1712–1778	Jean Rousseau
1723	Indian student house opened by College of William and Mary
1746–1827	Johann Pestalozzi
1751	Benjamin Franklin established first academy in the United States
1758–1843	Noah Webster
1762	Rousseau's *Émile* published
1775–1783	Revolution, United States
1776–1841	Johann Herbart
1782–1852	Friedrich Froebel
1778–1870	Emma Willard
1789	Adoption of Constitution, United States
1796–1859	Horace Mann
1798	Joseph Lancaster developed monitorial plan of education
1799–1815	Ascendancy of Napoleon, Waterloo
1804	Pestalozzi's Institute at Yverdon established
1806	First Lancastrian School in New York
1811–1900	Henry Barnard
1819	Dartmouth College Decision
1821	First American high school
1821	Troy Seminary for Women, Emma Willard; first higher education for women in United States
1823	First private normal school in United States, founded by Rev. Hall in Concord, Vermont
1825	Labor unions come on the scene
1826	Froebel's *The Education of Man* published
1827	Massachusetts law compelled high schools
1837	Massachusetts had first state board, Horace Mann first secretary
1839	First public normal school in United States, Lexington, Massachusetts
1855	First kindergarten in United States, based on German model, founded by Margarethe Meyer Schurz
1856–1915	Booker T. Washington
1857–1952	John Dewey
1861–1865	Civil War
1861	Oswego (New York) Normal School, Edward Sheldon
1862	Morrill Land Grant Act: college of engineering, military science, agriculture in each state
1868	Herbartian Society founded
1870–1952	Maria Montessori
1872	Kalamazoo Decision made high schools legal
1875–1955	Mary Bethune
1888	Teachers College, Columbia University, founded
1892	Committee of Ten established
1896–1980	Jean Piaget
1904–1990	B. F. Skinner
1909–1910	First junior high schools established at Berkeley, California, and Columbus, Ohio
ca. 1910	First junior colleges established at Fresno, California, and Joliet, Illinois
1917	The Smith-Hughes Act encouraged agriculture, industry, and home economics education in the United States
1932–1940	The Eight-Year Study of thirty high schools completed by the Progressive Education Association

1941 Japanese bombed Pearl Harbor
1941 Lanham Act
1942 Progressive Education Association published the findings of the Eight-Year Study; reported favorably on the modern school
1944–1946 Legislation by 78th U.S. Congress provided subsistence allowance, tuition fees, and supplies for the education of veterans of World War II, the GI Bill
1945 The United Nations Educational, Scientific, and Cultural Organization (UNESCO) initiated efforts to improve educational standards throughout the world
ca. 1946–1947 Beginning of U.S. "baby boom"; eventually caused huge increase in school enrollments
1948 *McCollum* v. *Board of Education;* U.S. Supreme Court ruled it illegal to release children for religious classes in public school buildings
1948 Fulbright programs began; by 1966 involved 82,500 scholars in 136 nations
1950 National Science Foundation founded
1952 GI Bill's educational benefits extended to Korean War veterans
1954 U.S. Supreme Court decision required eventual racial integration of public schools
1954 Cooperative Research Program
1957 Soviet Union launched *Sputnik*
1958 Federal Congress passed the National Defense Education Act
1959 James B. Conant wrote *The American High School Today*
1961 Federal court ruled *de facto* racial segregation illegal
1961 Peace Corps established
1961 Approximately four million college students in the United States
1962 In *Engle* v. *Vitale,* U.S. Supreme Court ruled compulsory prayer in public school illegal
1963 Vocational Education Act
1963 Manpower Development and Training Act
1964 Economic Opportunity Act provided federal funds for such programs as Head Start
1964 Civil Rights Act
1965 Elementary and Secondary Education Act allowed more federal funds for public schools
1965 Higher Education Act
1966 GI Bill's educational benefits extended to Vietnam war veterans
1966 One million Americans travel abroad
1966 U.S. International Education Act
1966 Coleman Report suggested that racially balanced schools did not necessarily provide a better education
1967 Education Professions Development Act
1972 Indian Education Act, designed to help Native Americans help themselves
1972 Title IX Education Amendment outlawing discrimination on the basis of sex
1973 In *Rodriguez* v. *San Antonio Independent School,* U.S. Supreme Court ruled that a state's system for financing schools did not violate the Constitution although there were large disparities in per-pupil expenditure.
1975 Indochina Migration and Refugee Assistance Act (Public Law 94-23)
1975 Public Law 94-142, requiring local districts to provide education for children with special needs
1979 Department of Education Act
1980 U.S. Secretary of Education position became a cabinet post
1983 *High School: A Report on Secondary Education in America* by the Carnegie Foundation
1983 *A Nation at Risk: The Imperative for Educational Reform,* report by the National Commission on Excellence in Education
1983 Task Force on Education for Economic Growth, Action for Excellence, Education Commission of the States Report

1983	Task Force on Federal Elementary and Secondary Education Policy, Making the Grade, the Twentieth Century Fund Report
ca. 1980–1984	Fundamentalist religious movement advocating prayer in the schools and teaching of Biblical creation story
1984	Public Law 98-377 added new science and mathematics programs, magnet schools, and equal access to public schools
1984	Perkins Vocational Education Act to upgrade vocational programs in schools
1984	Public Law 98-558 created new teacher education scholarships and continued Head Start and Follow Through programs
1985	NCATE Redesign Standards published
1986	Holmes Group report published
1986	Carnegie Report of the Task Force on Teaching As a Profession
1989	Presidential Education Summit with governors
1990	U.S. Supreme Court decision to allow Bible clubs in schools
1992	U.S. Supreme Court decision finds officially sanctioned prayers or invocations unconstitutional
1994	National Educational Goals: 2000 adopted by federal government
ca. 1990s	Development of school voucher plans and charter schools
2001	President Bush promises to push school reform

PART 5

CHAPTER 10
Philosophy: The Passion to Understand

CHAPTER 11
Educational Theory in American Schools: Philosophy in Action

CHAPTER 12
Building an Educational Philosophy

Philosophical Foundations of Education

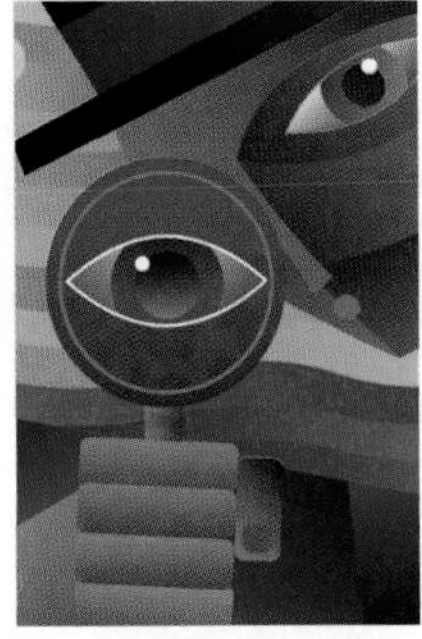

Viewing Education through Philosophical Lenses

The lens of philosophy provides a way to examine and interpret the world—to ask basic questions about human nature, beauty, principles of right and wrong, and how knowledge and reality are defined. Philosophical thinking helps to uncover the essentials—the basic principles that undergird teaching and learning.

The philosophical lens is especially important because our personal philosophy of life is seldom explicit. Rather, philosophy lives in peoples' minds and hearts and is seldom expressed in words or explicit ideas. Our personal philosophy becomes evident in the manner in which we respond to everyday problems and questions. For example, we all conform to authority at least sometimes; some of us resist authority and tradition, and a few of us even seek out challenges to innovate or to defend our social order. But rarely do we examine our lives to find out what kinds of answers are evidenced by our actions, our hesitations, and our indifferences. The lens of philosophy helps us to focus on the underlying issues and assumptions and beliefs that are not always evident to us in the hectic pace of contemporary life.

Because philosophy deals with underlying values and beliefs, it naturally pervades all aspects of education. The lens of philosophy presents opposing views about human nature, knowledge, and about the world in which we live. By examining these different, often opposing views you will be able to identify your own philosophical position and state it in clearer language and concepts.

The following questions will help you to focus your learning as you read:

1. What is knowledge? Is it merely the mastery of facts or is it the ability to solve problems?
2. Is knowledge the understanding of big ideas or is it the mastery of large quantities of information?
3. What are the implications of different views of knowledge for the teaching methods and assessment procedures that you choose to use?
4. Are children innately good, needing only gentle encouragement and guidance, or are children self-centered individuals who need to be disciplined and socialized?
5. What knowledge, skills, and attitudes are of most worth and should be part of every school curriculum?
6. Do teachers have a responsibility to question societal values and actively bring about social change or should they represent and articulate the current views of society to their students?

CHAPTER

10

Philosophy: The Passion to Understand

EDUCATION IN THE NEWS

The Cheating Game

By Mary Lord, *U.S. News & World Report*, November 22, 1999

Umpteen pages to plow through for honors English, Anatomy, and U.S. History . . . Geometry problems galore . . . It was a typical weeknight for high school sophomore Leah Solowsky. Before tackling her first assignment—a Spanish essay on healthy eating—the honor roll student logged onto her computer to chat with pals. Suddenly, it hit her . . . perhaps she could download some of her workload.

Solowsky cruised to the Alta Vista search engine, clicked on "Spanish' " and typed in "*la dieta*." Fifteen minutes later, she had everything she needed to know about fruits, vegetables and grains—all in flawless *español.* She quickly retyped the information and handed in her paper the next day. "I had a ton of homework, I wasn't doing that well in the class, and I felt, Hey, this is one way to boost my grade," explains Solowsky, now a junior with a B plus average at highly competitive Guilliver Preparatory School in Miami. "I didn't think it was cheating because I didn't even stop to think about it."

Everyday across America, millions of students from middle school to medical school face similar ethical quandaries—research indicates that most choose to cheat. In a recent survey conducted by Who's Who Among American High School Students, eight percent of high-achieving high schoolers admitted to having cheated at least once; half said they did not believe that cheating was necessarily wrong—and 95% of cheaters said they have never been caught.

Academic fraud has never been easier. Students can tamper electronically with grade records, transmit quiz answers via pager or cell phone, and lift term papers from hundreds of web sites. At the same time, an overload of homework combined with intense pressure to excel in school, from hard-driving peers and parents makes cheating easy to justify—and hard to resist. Valedictorians are as likely to cheat as laggards, and girls have closed the gap with the boys. In fact, the only thing that makes Leah Solowsky's case unusual is that she got caught, earning a zero on her Spanish paper and getting barred from the national honor society.

Most cheaters don't get caught. In fact, perhaps the major reason students cheat is that they get away with it time and time again. Numerous studies say that students almost never squeal on a classmate who cheats. And most instructors just don't want to play cop. "I'm not here to prevent students from cheating," says Robert Corless, an applied mathematics professor at the University of Western Ontario, who eliminated take home exams a few years ago after he caught students collaborating on them. "I'm here to help the genuine learners catch fire." He'll close off the easy routes, but that's about it. "Spending my time listening to appeals or accusations of cheating is not my idea of spending it well."

(continued)

Do the cheaters actually mend their ways? Leah Solowsky isn't glad she was caught plagiarizing last year, but she acknowledges that the experience did teach her a thing or two. "I learned that teachers aren't as stupid as some people think they are," she says with just a hint of humor. Pausing to think for a moment, she adds: "I mean cheating should affect your conscience because you are doing something wrong."

LEARNER OUTCOMES

After reading and studying this chapter, you will be able to

1. Define philosophy and describe methods of inquiry used by philosophers.
2. List major philosophical questions associated with the three major branches of philosophy: metaphysics, epistemology, and axiology.
3. Elaborate on the major tenets of idealism, realism, pragmatism, and existentialism.
4. Compare writers from different schools of philosophy: Plato, Kant, Martin, Aristotle, Locke, Whitehead, Peirce, Dewey, Sartre, Kierkegaard, and Greene.
5. Describe the characteristics of Eastern and Native North American ways of knowing.

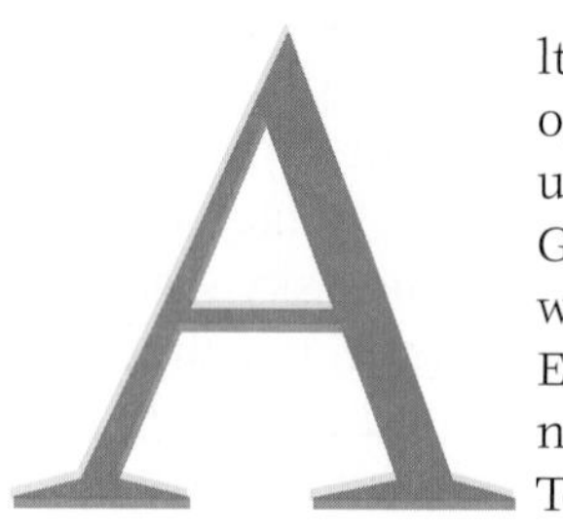

Although there are many different ways of defining philosophy, it is best thought of as a passion to understand the underlying meaning of everything. Derived from the Greek *philos,* which means love, and *sophos,* which means wisdom, the word *philosophy* means "love of wisdom." Early philosophers were fond of pointing out that they did not claim to be wise—they were merely lovers of wisdom. To many philosophers, conveying information is not as important as helping others in their own search for wisdom.

Searching for wisdom is closely related to the essence of multiculturalism. Philosophy demands a habit of mind that is always searching to understand and incorporate different points of view, different voices. Philosophy compels us to consider the beauty and cohesion of seemingly diverse worlds of thought and existence.

In this chapter you will explore different ways of looking at the world in which you live. Such big ideas as human nature, ways of knowing, analytic and prophetic thinking will offer very different perspectives about yourself and your place in the larger world. This chapter presents a unique way of thinking about societal issues and education. You will see how the art of asking larger questions about the nature of things can either clarify or challenge your personal beliefs about teaching and learning, about values and societal norms, about discipline and motivation.

STRUCTURE AND METHODOLOGY OF PHILOSOPHY

Education is inextricably intertwined with a passion to understand. Both philosophy and education are vitally concerned with a search for truth. By its very name education calls teachers "to lead from ignorance." Philosophy compels teachers to lead students in a direction that is meaningful and of most worth. Philosophy reminds teachers to continue the search for truth and not to be satisfied with pat answers, even answers that are provided by so-called experts. To a philosopher, an expert is not one who professes truth or beauty; an expert is one who searches and questions.

Education presupposes ideas about human nature, the nature of reality, and the nature of knowledge. These questions are ultimately of a philosophical character. Teachers must constantly confront the underlying assumptions that guide conduct, determine values, and influence the direction of all existence. Hence, the study of philosophy is at the heart of the study of education.

THE BRANCHES OF PHILOSOPHY

Philosophy is not a collection of sterile, objective facts. Rather, it is like an internal desire; it drives persons to search for better answers and better understandings. At its deepest level, philosophy consists of sets of profound and basic questions that remain constant because the basic dilemmas posed by these questions are yet to be answered adequately. At this basic level, philosophy does not provide answers; rather, it offers a range of possibilities or arguments that can be examined and used to guide decisions.

Because the questions of philosophy are so important, the study of philosophy is structured around them. Philosophy includes branches that investigate large and difficult questions—questions about reality or being, about knowledge, about goodness and beauty and living a good life. Throughout the centuries, entire branches of philosophy have evolved that specialize in and center on major questions. For example, questions about the nature of reality or existence are examined in metaphysics, questions about knowledge and truth are considered in epistemology, and questions about values and goodness are central to axiology.

METAPHYSICS **Metaphysics** is an area of philosophy that is concerned with questions about the nature of reality. Literally *metaphysics* means "beyond the physical." It deals with such questions as "What is reality?" "What is existence?" "Is the universe rationally designed or ultimately meaningless?" Metaphysics is a search for order and wholeness—a search applied not to particular items or experiences, but to all reality and to all existence.

In brief, metaphysics is the attempt to find coherence in the whole realm of thought and experience. Concerning the world, metaphysics includes the question of what causes events in the universe to happen, including the theories of creation and evolution. Metaphysics also involves questions concerning the nature of humans. Is human nature physical or spiritual (the mind–body problem)? Does a person make free choices, or do events and conditions force one into determined decisions?

The questions in metaphysics, especially those about humanity and the universe, are extremely relevant to teachers and students of education. Theories about how the universe came to be and about what causes events in the universe are crucial if scholars are to interpret the physical sciences properly. George F. Kneller writes about the power of metaphysics in generating questions that lack scientific answers.

metaphysics
An area of philosophy that deals with questions about the nature of ultimate reality.

> Teachers often say, "If Johnnie kept his mind on his work, he would have no trouble in school." But what does the teacher mean here by "mind"? Is the mind

> different from the body? How are the two related? Is the mind the actual source of thoughts? Perhaps what we call "mind" is not an entity at all. Physiological and psychological studies of the brain have given us factual information and cyberneticians have compared the mind (or brain) to a computer. But such comparisons are crude; they do not satisfy our concern about the ultimate nature of the mind. Here again, knowing metaphysics and being able to think metaphysically helps the teacher when considering questions of ultimate meaning.[1]

Many important decisions we make have ethical dimensions: What should we teach? How should we treat students, parents, teachers, and administrators? In order to address such matters, we must conceive of moral bases on which to make these decisions and try to forecast the potential ramifications of them for individuals and society.

Gail McCutcheon

A teacher's classroom approach will be linked to the teacher's metaphysical beliefs. If, for example, the teacher believes that very specific basic knowledge is crucial to the child's intellectual development, it is likely that this teacher will focus on the subject matter. If, on the other hand, the teacher holds that the child is more important than any specific subject matter, it is likely that this teacher will focus on the child and allow the child to provide clues as to how he or she should be instructed.

EPISTEMOLOGY Epistemology is a branch of philosophy that examines questions about how and what we know. What knowledge is true, and how does knowledge take place? The epistemologist attempts to discover what is involved in the process of knowing. Is knowing a special sort of mental act? Is there a difference between knowledge and belief? Can people know anything beyond the objects with which their senses acquaint them? Does knowing make any difference to the object that is known?

Because epistemological questions deal with the essence of knowledge, they are central to education. Teachers must be able to assess what is knowledge to determine whether a particular piece of information should be included in the curriculum. How people know is of paramount importance to teachers because their beliefs about learning influence their classroom methods. Should teachers train students in the scientific methods, deductive reasoning, or both? Should students study logic and fallacies or follow intuition? Teachers' knowledge of how students learn influences how they will teach.

AXIOLOGY **Axiology** is an area of philosophy that deals with the nature of values. It includes such questions as "What is good?" and "What is value?" Questions about what should be or what values we hold are highlighted in axiology. This study of values is divided into ethics (moral values and conduct) and aesthetics (values in the realm of beauty and art). Ethics deals with such questions as "What is the good life, and how ought we to behave?" One major question to be examined is "When does the end justify any means of achieving?" Aesthetics deals with the theory of beauty and examines such questions as "Is art public and representative, or is it the product of private creative imagination?"[2] Good citizenship, honesty, and correct human relations are all learned in schools. Sometimes these concepts are taught explicitly; but often, students learn ethics from *who* the teacher is as well as from *what* the teacher says.

Both ethics and aesthetics are important issues in education. Should a system of ethics be taught in the public school? If so, which system of ethics should be taught? Aesthetics questions in education involve deciding which artistic works should or should not be included in the curriculum and what kind of subject matter should be allowed or encouraged in a writing, drawing, or painting class. Should teachers compromise their own attitudes toward a piece of artwork if their opinion differs from that of a parent or a school board?

axiology
An area of philosophy that deals with the nature of values. It includes questions such as "What is good?" and "What is value?"

THINKING AS A PHILOSOPHER

Philosophy provides the tools people need to think clearly. As with any discipline, philosophy has a style of thinking as well as a set of terms and methodologies that distinguish it from other disciplines. Philosophers spend much of their energy developing symbols or terms that are both abstract (apply to many individual cases) and precise (distinguish clearly). Developing ideas that embrace more and more instances (abstraction) while at the same time maintaining a clear and accurate meaning (precision) is difficult, but this tension is at the heart of the philosopher's task. The entire process is what is meant by understanding: uncovering the underlying, the foundational, and the essential principles of reality.

Being a philosopher, I have a problem for every solution.
Robert Zend

In the physical sciences, experimenters try to do the same thing when they devise a theory. The major difference between the scientist who empirically examines the material world and the philosopher who examines all reality is that the physical scientist mainly targets particular events or things in the material world and then tries to explain these events by some theory. The philosopher, on the other hand, strives to clarify the underlying principles for all events, material or immaterial, that are logically related. Philosophers tend to search for concepts that are larger than what the physical scientist is researching, and they also examine not only what seems to be, but what ought to be.

There is great variety in the ways philosophers think. Hence it is difficult to set forth a simple set of rules or thinking steps that can accurately be labeled philosophical thinking. To give you a sense of philosophical thinking, it is easier (and more accurate) to describe two different thinking styles that philosophers use interchangeably as they wrestle with large, unstructured questions. The first way of thinking can be labeled **analytic thinking.** Philosophers employ this style when they attempt to examine questions of the "what seems to be" type. A second philosophical style of thinking is called **prophetic thinking.** It focuses on questions of the "what ought to be" type.

analytic thinking
A thinking strategy that focuses on questions of the "what seems to be" type; includes abstractions, imagination, generalization, and logic.

ANALYTIC WAYS OF THINKING IN PHILOSOPHY When philosophers encounter a contemporary problem, they often spend time analyzing it: attempting to clarify or find the "real" problem, not just the surface issues. To do so philosophers use abstraction, imagination, generalization, and logic. These analytic thinking processes help focus the problem clearly and precisely.

prophetic thinking
A thinking strategy that focuses on questions of the "what ought to be" type; includes discernment, connection, tracking hypocrisy, and hope.

ABSTRACTION The notion of **abstraction** covers a multitude of meanings. The word *abstract* is derived from the Latin verb *abstrahere,* meaning to "draw away." Abstraction, then, involves drawing away from a concrete level of experience to a conceptual plane of principles or ideas. The process of abstraction can be thought of as a three-step process that moves thinking from singular concrete instances to more general, universal ideas. The three steps involve (1) focusing attention on some feature within one's experience, (2) examining the precise characteristics of the feature, and (3) remembering the feature and its characteristics later so as to apply them to other instances or combine them with other ideas.

abstraction
A thought process that involves drawing away from experiences to a conceptual plane

In general, philosophers distinguish between two basic types of abstraction: (1) parts, or abstractions of characteristics that could also be physically removed (features such as tabletops, legs, drawers, and the like), and (2) attributes, or abstractions of characteristics that cannot be physically removed, such as shape, structure, or form. This second type of abstract thinking is the stuff of philosophers; they seek to understand the essential aspects of both material and immaterial things. These underlying, substantial aspects are sometimes referred to as qualities, relations, and functions.

When teachers are asked to examine a new textbook series, for example, they will often be presented with promotional material about the important subject matter and learning tools that the series contains. The process of abstraction helps teachers to pull away from the "bells and whistles" or the concrete examples in the text. Abstraction enables teachers to consider the underlying themes that are implicit and that provide a cohesive structure to the entire text series. Abstraction helps teachers to uncover hidden messages.

IMAGINATION AND GENERALIZATION According to Herbert Alexander,[3] the second step of analytic thinking is the use of imagination. Imagination can be thought of as the altering of abstractions. In philosophy the use of imagination assists the process of abstraction by filling in the details of an idea, selecting details, and relating ideas to one another.

Imaginative explorations occur in many different ways. Usually, they occur when a person first focuses on some abstraction or idea. Ideas come when one makes observations, reflects about past experiences, reads, views a dramatic work or piece of art, or converses with others. Once ideas are selected, imaginative explorations can be made about them. Basic assumptions about things can be examined, arguments can be justified or clarified, and ideas can be distinguished from or related to other ideas. Experiential evidence, logical consistency, and a host of other criteria can be employed. The outcome of the whole imaginative process is the development of a system of ideas that has greater clarity and more interrelationships to other ideas or sets of propositions. This last step of the imaginative exploration process is sometimes referred to as *generalization,* because it ultimately results in the development of a comprehensive set of ideas.

Generalization sets ranges and limits to the abstractions that have been altered by imagination. As one's imagination relates more and more ideas to one another, the process of generalization determines which relationships should be emphasized or de-emphasized.

As an example of the analytical thinking process, consider a simple chair that is located in a kitchen. First, the philosopher would abstract from the chair some idea on which to focus; for instance, the idea of support. Support is an underlying substantial characteristic of all chairs. Second, the philosopher might imagine how many physical parts of a chair could be removed without loss of the chair's ability to provide support. Are four legs always necessary for support? What must be supported for an object to be a chair? As the philosopher ponders these questions (which are spurred by the imagination), precise generalizations can be made about basic aspects of the concept of support. New questions or hypotheses can be developed. For example, how does the support provided by chairs relate to the support that a teacher should provide to students? What does teaching support really mean?

When teachers consider new ways to support student motivation, they can use the same analytic thinking processes. For example, teachers often imagine different types of mathematics contests or science Olympiads that might spur students' interests. As they imaginatively apply these contests to the classroom setting, teachers may abstract the competitiveness component as a necessary aspect of contests and Olympiads. Teachers may then wonder about the hidden messages of winning at the expense of others' losses. Teachers may generalize that the competitive approach could bring about knowledge wars; knowledge contests might make students less willing to share what they know with others. To complete this inquiry, teachers need to utilize logic.

LOGIC Philosophy deals with the nature of reasoning and has designated a set of principles called *logic*. Logic examines the principles that allow us to move from one argument to the next. There are many types of logic, but the two most commonly studied are deductive and inductive logic. Deduction is a type of reasoning that moves from a general statement to a specific conclusion. Induction is a type of reasoning that moves in the opposite direction, from the particular instance to a general conclusion.

Philosophy provides the tools people need in order to think clearly. It is important for educators to have a philosophy, both as a means of developing their ability to think clearly about what they do on a day-to-day basis and as a means of seeing how their workaday principles and values extend beyond the classroom to the whole of humanity and society. Studying philosophy enables you to recognize the underlying assumptions and principles of things so you can determine what is significant.

PROPHETIC WAYS OF THINKING IN PHILOSOPHY In contrast to the search for underlying universal principles that is the focus of an analytic way of thinking, *prophetic thinking* seeks to uncover multiple, even divergent realities or principles. Prophetic thinking has emerged as a counterpoint to the highly successful but rigid analytic thinking style. According to Cornel West, a prophetic thinker is one who goes beyond abstraction. A prophetic thinker lives in multiple realities, feeling and touching these realities to such a degree that understanding is ultimately achieved. And a prophetic thinker understands multiple realities so well that bridges can be built between and among the multiple worlds. In his book *Prophetic Thought in Postmodern Times,* West identifies four basic components of prophetic thinking: discernment, connection, tracking hypocrisy, and hope.[4]

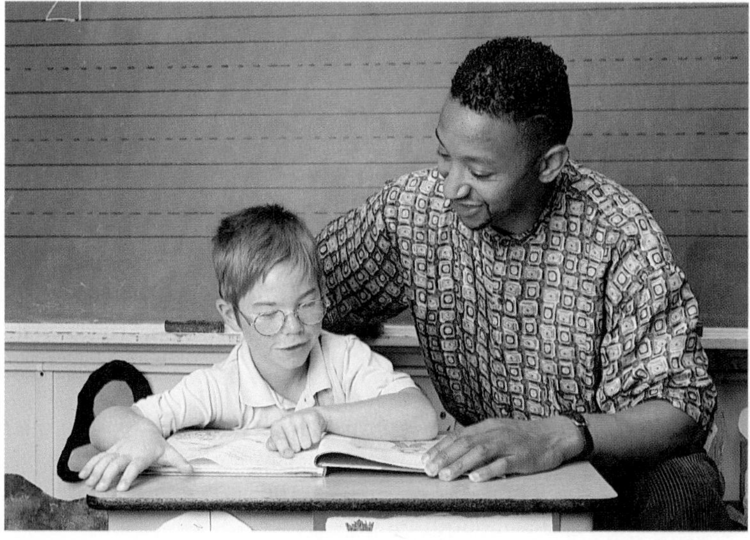

Teachers not only teach content but also find ways to help students seek connections to the world around them and apply ideas to their daily lives.

PROFESSIONAL DILEMMA

Should Ethics Be Taught in Public Schools?

Should a teacher instruct students about matters of right and wrong? You may feel that this question demands an obvious affirmative answer. A problem arises, however, when you are asked to clarify the specific ethics that should be taught. How do you, as a teacher in a multicultural school setting, determine what moral values should be the focus of instruction?

One school of thought, influenced largely by the work of Lawrence Kohlberg, endorses direct instruction in ethics. The educational theorists who endorse this position contend that there exists a body of ethics that spans all cultures. This body of ethics can be articulated at any point in time and should be taught directly to students in public schools. People—especially parents—may also feel that children are faced with an increasingly complex and dangerous society and cannot be expected simply to absorb the proper morals and values from the world around them. Because of this, the schools should step in.

In contrast to this point of view, those influenced by the educational theories proposed by Syd Simon in his text *Values Clarification* reject the direct instruction of ethics on the grounds that democracy demands that its citizens be free to clarify their own sets of values. This school of thought calls for public schools to refrain from the direct instruction of ethics and asks teachers to help students define their own sets of individually selected values. The approach requires teachers to remain neutral in their presentations of opposing value systems. The teacher's role is simply to assist students in the clarification of the consequences of selecting any one set of ethics or values.

This difficult problem of teaching ethics is especially problematic for a democracy.

- Who shall select the set of ethics to be taught?
- If the majority is given this right, then what becomes of the individual rights of minorities?
- Yet is it possible to teach a value-free curriculum?
- Does the very act of instruction imply a certain value system expressed and upheld by the individual teacher?

DISCERNMENT Discernment is the capacity to develop a vision of what should be out of a sophisticated understanding of what has been and is. This first component of prophetic thought is quite different from the abstract approach of the analytic thinker. The prophetic thinker is more concerned with the concrete, specific aspects of reality. To discern a situation is to take the entire situation into account to get beyond abstract principles. A discerning teacher is one who sees beyond mere test scores, beyond simple classroom rules. A discerning teacher examines the total content of a child's life and makes decisions based on this context. An outsider could criticize a discerning teacher for bending rules or being inconsistent. Yet a prophetic thinker would applaud the teacher for being wise. The prophetic thinker is a bit of a historian, building the future upon the best of the past and present.

CONNECTION A prophetic thinker must relate to or connect with others. Rather than considering humankind in the abstract, prophetic thinkers value and have empathy for other human beings. They show empathy, the capacity to get in contact with the anxieties and frustrations of others.

Many teachers really do care and work hard to help students. However, they are often unable to make the connection that would complete caring relations with their students. Teachers' willingness to empathize with students is often thwarted by society's desire to establish teaching on a firm scientific footing. But to students, the failure to connect means that teachers sometimes look as though they simply do not care. According to Nel Noddings,[5] both teachers and students have become victims in the search for the one best method of instruction.

TRACKING HYPOCRISY While the relationship between empathy and teaching is important, it is equally important for the prophetic teacher to identify and make known "the gap between principles and practice, between promise and performance, between rhetoric and reality."[6] West cautions that tracking hypocrisy ought to be done in a self-critical rather than in a self-righteous manner. It takes boldness as well as courage to point out inconsistencies between school policies and practices, but when doing so a prophetic teacher remains open to others' points of view. New evidence may reveal that one's position is no longer valid, or it may enhance one's original thinking.

Hypocrisy—Prejudice with a halo.

Ambrose Bierce

The important aspect of tracking hypocrisy is not being right or wrong but helping others and oneself examine the relationship between what is said and what is practiced. Recently, for example, the hypocrisy of standardized norm-referenced testing has been tracked by many prophetic educators. Although to date no clear alternatives have been uncovered, there is increased interest in and experimentation with new forms of testing, thanks to the courage of critical educators.

HOPE The fourth and perhaps most important component of prophetic thought is simply hope. West admits that given the numerous and horrific examples of people's inhumanity to one another, it is hard to take hope seriously. Still, without it, all thought is meaningless. West says:

> To talk about human hope is to engage in an audacious attempt to galvanize and energize, to inspire and to invigorate world-weary people. Because that is what we are. We are world-weary; we are tired. For some of us there are misanthropic skeletons hanging in our closet. And by misanthropic I mean the notion that we have given up on the capacity to do anything right; the capacity of human communities to solve any problem.[7]

West challenges educators to see "skeletons" as challenges, not as conclusions. Even when confronted with educators' failures at creating a better community of scholars, the prophetic teacher must remember that the world is unfinished, that the future is open-ended, and that what teachers think and do can make a difference.

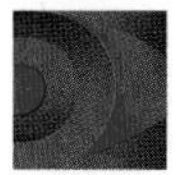

SCHOOLS OF PHILOSOPHY AND THEIR INFLUENCE ON EDUCATION

As philosophers attempt to answer questions, they develop answers that are clustered into different schools of thought. These schools of philosophical thought are somewhat contrived; they are merely labels developed by others who have attempted to show the similarities and differences among the many answers philosophers develop. Throughout the centuries these schools of philosophic thought have been used as organizing frameworks for the diversity of responses from so many thinkers. As you examine the schools of thought described in this section, keep in mind that the philosophers who represent these schools are individual thinkers, like yourself, who do not limit their thinking to the characteristics of any one label or school of thought. Four well-known schools of thought are idealism, realism, pragmatism, and existentialism. In addition to these, we will touch upon Eastern thought and Native North American thought. Technically, these two final clusters of thought are not termed *schools* because they encompass greater diversity and often extend beyond the limits of philosophy into beliefs, customs, and group values.

IDEALISM

The roots of idealism lie in the thinking of the Greek philosopher Plato. Generally, idealists believe that ideas are the only true reality. It is not that idealists reject the material world; rather, they hold that the material world is characterized by constant change and uncertainty, whereas ideas endure throughout time. Hence, **idealism** is a school of philosophy that holds that ideas or concepts are the essence of all that is worth knowing. The physical world we know through our senses is only a manifestation of the spiritual world (metaphysics). Idealists believe in the power of reasoning and de-emphasize the scientific method and sense perception, which they hold suspect (epistemology). They search for universal or absolute truths that will remain constant throughout the centuries (axiology).

Idealists—Foolish enough to throw caution to the winds . . . have advanced mankind and have enriched the world.
Emma Goldman

EDUCATIONAL IMPLICATIONS OF IDEALISM The educational philosophy of the idealist is idea-centered rather than subject-centered or child-centered because the ideal, or the idea, is the foundation of all things. Knowledge is directed toward self-consciousness and self-direction and is centered in the growth of rational processes about the big ideas. Some idealists note that the individual, who is created in God's image, has free will and that it is this free will that makes learning possible. The idealist believes that learning comes from within the individual rather than from without. Hence, real mental and spiritual growth do not occur until they are self-initiated.

Ideals are like stars: you will not succeed in touching them with your hands, but like the seafaring man on the desert of waters, you choose them as your guides, and following them you reach your destiny.
Carl Schurz

Idealists' educational beliefs include an emphasis on the study of great leaders as examples for us to imitate. For idealists the teacher is the ideal model or example for the student. Teachers pass on the cultural heritage and the unchanging content of education, such as knowledge about great figures of the past, the humanities, and a rigorous curriculum. Idealists emphasize the methods of lecture, discussion, and imitation. Finally, they believe in the importance of the doctrine of ideas.

No one philosopher is an idealist. Rather, philosophers answer questions, and some of their answers are similar. These similarities are what make up the different schools of philosophy. To describe adequately any one school of philosophy, such as idealism, one needs to go beyond these general similarities and examine the subtle differences posed by individual thinkers. Plato and Socrates, Immanuel Kant, and Jane Roland Martin represent different aspects of the idealist tradition.

idealism
A school of philosophy that considers ideas to be the only true reality.

PLATO AND SOCRATES According to Plato (427?–347? B.C.), truth is the central reality. Truth is perfect; and it cannot, therefore, be found in the world of matter

RELEVANT RESEARCH

Teaching for Critical Thinking

STUDY PURPOSE/QUESTIONS: Teaching critical thinking is an important component of education, and research studies about critical thinking abound. Many schools have adopted critical thinking as a specific district outcome. But there is a great deal of controversy concerning the precise meaning of critical thinking, and this confusion makes instruction difficult.

A variety of thinking models have emerged, and schools have had to carefully reflect and select which critical thinking model to adopt. This selection is not simple, for cognitive scientists do not agree about the proper way to conceptualize critical thinking. For many years, however, two researchers have investigated how schools can effectively develop students' critical thinking skills.

STUDY DESIGN: Robert Ennis, from the University of Illinois, has concentrated his research on students' attainment of a set of skills. Meanwhile, Richard Paul, from Sonoma State University, has focused on students' attainment of a set of critical thinking dispositions or attitudes.

STUDY FINDINGS: Ennis has concluded that teachers who clarify a precise set of steps in the critical thinking process can more effectively teach students to be critical thinkers. Paul has concluded that critical thinking emerges when students are encouraged and in fact taught to think from another's perspective. He calls this the dialog/dialectic thinking process.

IMPLICATIONS: As a prospective teacher you will need to consider whether critical thinking is a set of steps or an underlying disposition or attitude. Research points to the efficacy of both approaches. Your philosophy of education can guide you in determining which one is most appropriate.

Sources: Robert Ennis and S. Norris, *Evaluating Critical Thinking.* Pacific Grove, CA: Midwest Publications, 1989.

Richard Paul. *Critical Thinking: What Every Person Needs to Survive in a Rapidly Changing World.* Rohnert Park, CA: Center for Critical Thinking and Moral Critique, 1990.

because the material world is both imperfect and constantly changing. Plato did not think that people create knowledge; rather, they discover it. In one of his dialogues, he conjectures that humanity once had true knowledge but lost it by being placed in a material body that distorts and corrupts that knowledge. Thus, humans have the arduous task of trying to remember what they once knew.

The modern world knows the philosophy of Socrates only through Plato, who wrote about him in a series of texts called "dialogues." Socrates spoke of himself as a midwife who found humans pregnant with knowledge, but knowledge that had not been born or realized. This Socratic "Doctrine of Reminiscence" speaks directly to the role of the educator. Teachers need to question students in such a way as to help them remember what they have forgotten. In the dialogue *Meno,* Plato describes Socrates' meeting a slave boy and through skillful questions leading the boy to realize that he knows the Pythagorean theorem, even though he does not know that he knows it. This emphasis on bringing forth knowledge from students through artful questioning is sometimes called the Socratic method.

Socrates' and Plato's ideas have stimulated a great deal of thinking about the meaning and purpose of humankind, society, and education. Their ideas have influenced almost all philosophers who came after them, whether others

Although the Socratic method dates back to 400 B.C., the art of asking probing questions and using dialog to enhance learning is still widely used today.

supported or rejected their basic ideas. Alfred North Whitehead even stated that modern philosophy is but a series of footnotes to Plato.

Writing in the *Republic,* Plato depicts his central ideas about knowledge in an allegory about human beings living in a cave. He says:

> If I am right, certain professors of education must be wrong when they say that they can put knowledge into the soul which was not there before, like sight into a blind eye. . . . Whereas, our argument shows that the power and capacity of learning exists in the soul already; and that just as the eye was unable to turn from darkness to light without the whole body, so too the instrument of knowledge can only by the movement of the whole soul be turned from the world of becoming into that of being, and learn by degrees to endure the sight of being, and of the brightest and best of being, or in other words, of the good.[8]

German philosopher Immanuel Kant (1724–1804) believed in freedom, the immortality of the soul, and the existence of God.

IMMANUEL KANT The German philosopher Immanuel Kant (1724–1804), in the *Metaphysics of Morals* and the *Critique of Practical Reason,* spelled out his idealistic philosophy. Kant believed in freedom, the immortality of the soul, and the existence of God. He wrote extensively on human reason and noted that the only way humankind can know things is through the process of reason. Hence, reality is not a thing unto itself but the interaction of reason and external sensations. Reason fits perceived objects into classes or categories according to similarities and differences. It is only through reason that we acquire knowledge of the world. Once again, it is the idea or the way that the mind works that precedes the understanding of reality.

In *The Critique of Pure Reason,* Kant clarifies the relationship between a priori and a posteriori knowledge. He writes:

> But, though all our knowledge begins with experience, it by no means follows that all arises out of experience. For, on the contrary, it is quite possible that

our empirical knowledge is a compound of that which we receive through impressions, and that which the faculty of cognition supplies for itself (sensuous impressions given merely the *occasions*), an addition which we cannot distinguish from the original element given by sense, till long practice has made us attentive to, and skillful in separating it. It is, therefore, a question which requires close investigation, and is not to be answered at first sight—whether there exists a knowledge all together independent of experience, and even of all sensuous impressions? Knowledge of this kind is called *a priori,* in contradistinction to empirical knowledge, which has as its sources *a posteriori,* that is, in experience.[9]

JANE ROLAND MARTIN Often labeled a feminist scholar, Jane Roland Martin (b. 1929) is a contemporary disciple of Plato's dialogues. In "Reclaiming a Conversation"[10] Martin describes how women have historically been excluded from the "conversation" that constitutes Western educational thought. Martin advocates a return to Plato's approach. Dialogues such as the *Apology,* the *Crito,* and the *Phaedo* illustrate educated persons—well-meaning people of good faith, people who trust and like each other, people who might even be called friends—getting together and trying to talk ideas through to a reasonable conclusion. They engage in conversation, learning something from one another and from the conversation itself.

For Martin, to be educated is to engage in a conversation that stretches back in time. Education is not simply something that occurs in a specific building at a specific time. Nor is it simply training or preparation for the next stage in life. Education is the development of the intellectual and moral habits, through the give-and-take of the conversation, that ultimately give "place and character to every human activity and utterance." Education—the conversation—is the place where one comes to learn what it is to be a person.

The direction in which education starts a man will determine his future life.

Plato

Cast in this light, Martin's charge about the historical exclusion of women from the conversation is serious. To exclude any group is to deny members of that group the right to become persons. In addition, the educational conversation requires a multiplicity of perspectives and a diversity of voices. Without such diversity people will all look and sound and think alike, and eventually the conversation will wind down.

The following excerpt illustrates Jane Roland Martin's ideas about the predominance of a masculine voice in the world of education:

Education is also gender-related. Our definition of the function of education makes it so. For if education is viewed as preparation for carrying on the processes historically associated with males, it will inculcate traits the culture considers masculine. If the concept of education is tied by definition to the productive process of society, our ideal of the educated person will coincide with the cultural stereotype of a male human being, and our definitions of excellence in education will embody "masculine" traits.[11]

REALISM

Realism's roots lie in the thinking of Aristotle (384–322 B.C.). **Realism** is a school of philosophy that holds that reality, knowledge, and value exist independent of the human mind (metaphysics). In other words, realism rejects the idealist notion that only ideas are the ultimate reality. Refer to Figure 10.1, which illustrates the dualistic position of idealism and realism.

realism
A school of philosophy that holds that reality, knowledge, and value exist independent of the human mind. In contrast to the idealist, the realist contends that physical entities exist in their own right.

FIGURE 10.1 DUALISTIC POSITION OF IDEALISM AND REALISM

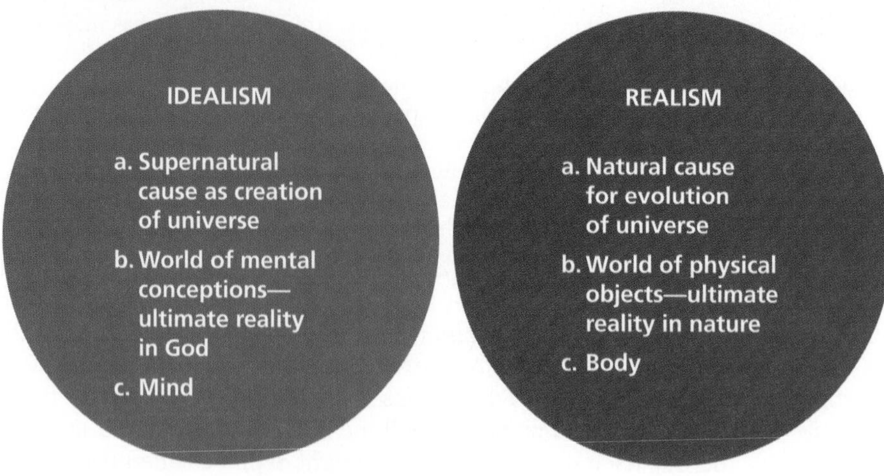

IDEALISM
a. Supernatural cause as creation of universe
b. World of mental conceptions—ultimate reality in God
c. Mind
REALISM
a. Natural cause for evolution of universe
b. World of physical objects—ultimate reality in nature
c. Body

EDUCATIONAL IMPLICATIONS OF REALISM Realists place considerable importance on the role of the teacher in the educational process. The teacher should be a person who presents content in a systematic and organized way and should promote the idea that there are clearly defined criteria one can use in making judgments (axiology). Contemporary realists emphasize the importance of scientific research and development. Curriculum has reflected the impact of these realist thinkers through the appearance of standardized tests, serialized textbooks, and a specialized curriculum in which the disciplines are seen as separate areas of investigation.

Realists contend that the ultimate goal of education is advancement of human rationality. Schools can promote rationality by requiring students to study organized bodies of knowledge, by teaching methods of arriving at this knowledge, and by assisting students to reason critically through observation and experimentation (epistemology). Teachers must have specific knowledge about a subject so that they can order it in such a way as to teach it rationally. They must also have a broad background to show relationships that exist among all fields of knowledge.

Ancient Greek philosopher Aristotle (384–322 bc) believed that one could acquire knowledge of ideas or forms through an investigation of matter.

The realist curriculum would be a subject-centered curriculum and would include natural science, social science, humanities, and instrumental subjects such as logic and inductive reasoning. Realists employ experimental and observational techniques. In the school setting, they would promote testing and logical, clear content. To understand the complexity of the realist philosophy, we must once again turn to the ideas of individual thinkers: Aristotle, Locke, and Whitehead.

ARISTOTLE Aristotle thought that ideas (forms) are found through the study of the world of matter. He believed that one could acquire knowledge of ideas or forms by investigating matter. To understand an object, one must understand its absolute form, which is unchanging. To the realist, the trees of the forest exist whether or not there is a human mind to perceive them. This is an example of an independent reality. Although the ideas of a flower can exist without matter, matter cannot exist without form. Hence, each tulip shares universal properties with every other tulip and every other flower. However, the particular properties of a tulip differentiate it from all other flowers.

Aristotle's writings are known for their analytic approach. In contrast to Plato, whose writings are written in the form of a conversation, Aristotle took great care to write with precision. In *Nicomachean Ethics,* Aristotle discusses the nature of moral responsibility:

John Locke (1632–1704) believed that a person's mind is like a blank tablet at birth and that a person's sensory experiences make impressions on this tablet.

> It is sometimes difficult to determine what ought to be chosen or endured in order to obtain or avoid a certain result. But it is still more difficult to abide by our decisions; for it generally happens that the consequences we expect are painful or the act we are forced to do is shameful; therefore we receive blame or praise according as we yield or do not yield to the constraint.
>
> What class of acts then may rightly be called compulsory? Acts may be called absolutely compulsory whenever the cause is external to the doer and he contributes nothing. But when an act, though involuntary in itself, is chosen at a particular time or for a particular end, and when its cause is in the doer himself, then, though the act is involuntary in itself, it is voluntary at that time and for that end.[12]

JOHN LOCKE John Locke (1632–1704) believed in the tabula rasa (blank tablet) view of the mind. Locke stated that the mind of a person is blank at birth and that the person's sensory experiences make impressions on this blank tablet. Locke distinguished between sense data and the objects they represent. The objects, or things people know, are independent of the mind or the knower insofar as thought refers to them and not merely to sense data. Ideas (round, square, tall) represent objects. Locke claimed that primary qualities (such as shapes) represent the world, while secondary qualities (such as colors) have a basis in the world but do not represent it.

> The little or almost insensible, impressions on our tender infancies, have very important and lasting consequences: and there it is, as in the fountains of some rivers, where a gentle application of the hand turns the flexible waters into channels, that make them at first, in the source, they receive different tendencies, and arrive at last at very remote and distant places.
>
> I imagine the minds of children as easily turned, this or that way, as water itself; and though this be the principal part and our main care should be about the inside yet the clay cottage is not to be neglected. I shall therefore begin with the case and consider first the health of the body.[13]

Philosopher and mathematician Alfred North Whitehead (1861–1947) attempted to reconcile idealism and realism.

ALFRED NORTH WHITEHEAD Alfred North Whitehead (1861–1947), a philosopher and mathematician, attempted to reconcile some aspects of idealism and realism. He proposed "process" to be the central aspect of realism. Unlike Locke, Whitehead did not see objective reality and subjective mind as separate. He saw them as an organic unity that operates by its own principles. The universe is characterized by patterns, and these patterns can be verified and analyzed through mathematics.

> Culture is activity of thought and receptiveness to beauty and humane feelings. Scraps of information have nothing to do with it. . . . In training a child to activity of thought, above all things we must beware of what I will call "inert ideas"—that is to say, ideas that are merely received into the mind without being used, or tested, or thrown into fresh combinations.

> In the history of education, the most striking phenomenon is the schools of learning, which at one epoch are alive with a ferment of genius, in a succeeding generation exhibit merely pedantry and routine. The reason is that they are overladen with inert ideas. Education with inert ideas is not only useless: it is, above all things, harmful—*Corruptio optimi, pessima.* Except at rare intervals of intellectual ferment, education in the past has been radically infected with inert ideas. . . . Every intellectual revolution which has ever stirred humanity into greatness has been a passionate protest against inert ideas.[14]

PRAGMATISM

Pragmatism is a late nineteenth-century American philosophy that affected educational and social thought. It differs from most forms of idealism and realism by a belief in an open universe that is dynamic, evolving, and in a state of becoming (metaphysics). It is a process philosophy, which stresses becoming rather than being. Wedded as they are to change and adaptation, pragmatists do not believe in absolute and unchanging truth. For pragmatists truth is what works. Truth is relative because what works for one person might not work for another, just as what works at one time or in one place or in one society may not work in another (axiology).

EDUCATIONAL IMPLICATIONS OF PRAGMATISM Like the realist, the pragmatist believes that we learn best through experience; but pragmatists are more willing to put that belief into practice. While realists are concerned with passing organized bodies of knowledge from one generation to the next, pragmatists stress applying knowledge—using ideas as instruments for problem solving (epistemology). Realists and idealists call for a curriculum centered on academic disciplines, but pragmatists prefer a curriculum that draws the disciplines together to solve problems—an interdisciplinary approach. Refer to Figure 10.2, which illustrates the relationships among realism, idealism, and pragmatism.

FIGURE 10.2 RELATIONSHIP OF REALISM, IDEALISM, AND PRAGMATISM

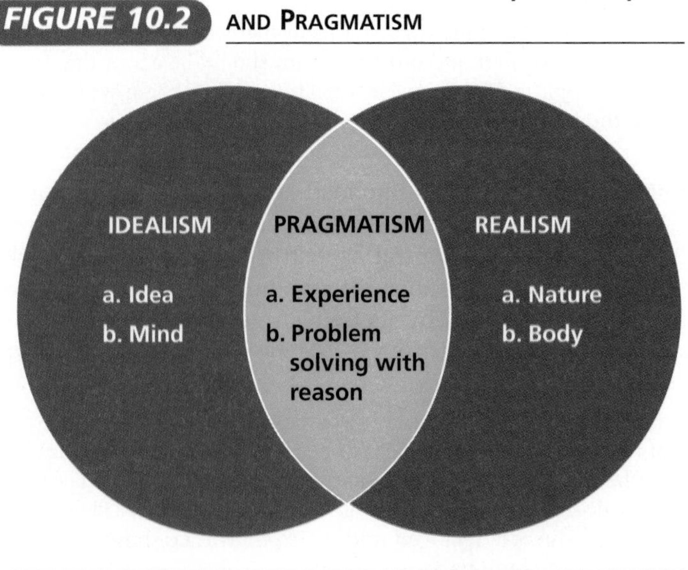

pragmatism
A late nineteenth-century American school of philosophy that stresses becoming rather than being.

CHARLES SANDERS PEIRCE Charles Sanders Peirce (1839–1914) is considered the founder of pragmatism. He introduced the principle that belief is a habit of action undertaken to overcome indecisiveness. He believed that the purpose of thought is to produce action and that the meaning of a thought is the collection of results of actions. For example, to say that steel is "hard" is to mean that when the operation of scratch testing is performed on steel, it will not be scratched by most substances. The aim of Peirce's pragmatic method is to supply a procedure for constructing and clarifying meanings and to facilitate communication.

Charles Sanders Peirce (1839–1914) believed that the purpose of thought is to produce action.

JOHN DEWEY Early in his philosophical development, John Dewey (1859– 1952) related pragmatism to evolution by explaining that human beings are creatures who have to adapt to one another and to their environments. Dewey viewed life as a series of overlapping and interpenetrating experiences and situations, each of which has its own complete identity. The primary unit of life is the individual experience.

Dewey wrote the following passage early in his career. In it he shows his zeal for education as a social force in human affairs.

> I believe that all education proceeds by the participation of the individual in the social consciousness of the race. This process begins unconsciously almost at birth, and is continually shaping the individual's powers, saturating his consciousness, forming his habits, training his ideas, and arousing his feelings and emotions. Through this unconscious education the individual gradually comes to share in the intellectual and moral resources which humanity has succeeded in getting together. . . .
>
> In sum, I believe that the individual is a social individual and that society is an organic union of individuals. If we eliminate the social factor from the child we are left only with an abstraction; if we eliminate the individual factor from society, we are left only with an inert and lifeless mass.[15]

EXISTENTIALISM

In **existentialism,** reality is lived existence, and the final reality resides within the individual (metaphysics). Existentialists believe that we live an alien, meaningless existence on a small planet in an unimportant galaxy in an indifferent universe. There is no ultimate meaning. Whereas some people might be paralyzed by this view, existentialists find the definition of their lives in the quest for meaning (epistemology). The very meaninglessness of life compels them to instill life with meaning.

The only certainty for the existentialist is that we are free. However, this freedom is wrapped up in a search for meaning. We define ourselves; that is, we make meaning in our world by the choices we make. In effect we are what we choose (axiology).

EDUCATIONAL IMPLICATIONS OF EXISTENTIALISM The existentialist believes that most schools, like other corporate symbols, de-emphasize the individual and the relationship between the teacher and the student. Existentialists claim that when educators attempt to predict the behavior of students, they turn individuals into objects to be measured, quantified, and processed. Existentialists tend to feel that tracking, measurement, and standardization militate against the creation of opportunities for self-direction and personal choice. According to the existentialist,

existentialism
A school of philosophy that focuses on the importance of the individual rather than on external standards.

DEBATE

Should Schools Sell Cola Companies Exclusive Rights?

Dee McNosky, a special education resource teacher at Bedford Junior High School in Texas, has been teaching for fourteen years. She's the past president of NEA's affiliate in the Hurst-Euless-Bedford district outside of Fort Worth. That district recently signed a five-year, $1.5 million deal with Pepsi-Cola.

President Kennedy said that a rising tide lifts all boats. That statement, in reference to a growing economy, probably holds true most of the time.

But when it comes time to fund public education, that rising tide is nowhere to be found.

Regardless of the strength of the economy, it's never a good year for local school boards to raise taxes, for states to contribute more aid for public education, or for the federal government to increase the financing of its entitlement programs for our public schools.

Too often, that leaves educators with the task of finding other ways to raise money. To help fund quality public schools here, my district has chosen to sign a five-year, $1.5 million contract with Pepsi.

Check your knee-jerk reactions at the door. This isn't commercialism—it's sponsorship.

Corporate sponsorship exists in almost every facet of our lives. In America today, corporations sponsor everything from symphonies to museum exhibits, bowl games to race cars, Olympic athletes to the Public Broad-casting System.

Why shouldn't corporations become sponsors of public education, too?

Pepsi's sponsorship in my district goes way beyond the promotion of soft drinks. In fact, the Pepsi machines in our elementary schools aren't even available for student use. Instead, elementary students have access to machines that sell only bottled water and fruit juices.

What is available to our students, courtesy of Pepsi, is money for quite a few things that might not otherwise be funded. These include:

- Career-oriented software for our junior and senior high schools.

Judy Gump has been teaching in Madison, Wisconsin, for three years. She serves as adviser to Memorial High School's Gay/Straight Alliance and has advised the school newspaper there. Gump's school district was the first in the nation to sign an exclusive $1.5 million deal with Coca-Cola.

On July 21, 1997, the Madison Metropolitan School District became the first school district in the nation to approve an exclusive marketing deal—worth a potential $1.5 million—with Coca-Cola.

Not only does the contract promote a high-sugar, caffeinated beverage that has virtually no nutritional value to children who are then supposed to sit still in a classroom and learn, it also develops a "partnership," between Coke and the Madison public schools.

This "partnership" hinges on promotions designed to bring the Coke logo into our schools and breed a new generation of brand loyal consumers.

As a high school teacher, I don't want that kind of "partner." The idea that our battle-fatigued and under-funded public schools can be any sort of equal "partner" with a multinational corporation would be laughable, if it weren't so insidious.

In Wisconsin, budget caps are responsible for keeping school budgets so tight that our English department can barely afford to replace books, not to mention buy new ones, and contract negotiations are always a drawn out and humiliating affair.

Other districts are even worse off than ours. Who can forget the school in Georgia that, desperate to win a few bucks in prize money, organized "Coke in Education Day," then suspended a student who unveiled his Pepsi T-shirt during the big photo?

It's tempting to think that a district can take the money and run, but the structure of the contract prevents this. This is not just a contract for "pouring rights"—this is a complex vending/marketing agreement, with the kids as the targeted consumers.

YES NO

- A software program for college-bound students that leads them to sources for tuition assistance.
- Discretionary funds that each school's site-based improvement teams will use to achieve the goals they set for their students.
- Money for a local educational foundation that provides grants to fund special projects developed, implemented, and evaluated by educators in the district. In fact, Pepsi's contributing enough money to make the foundation a permanent fixture in our community.

Relationships between corporations and school districts are not a new phenomenon. Many districts purchased Apple computers because of the relationship Apple developed with public schools, or were "adopted" by local businesses that wanted to help out.

Our contract with Pepsi is no different.

Our strong economy has buoyed corporations, but public education has not been lifted by the swell. Since the state of public education affects every segment of society, it's only fitting that corporations use some of their profits to support public schools.

It's important to remember that public schools don't exist *only* for the people who have children in them. They exist for society as a whole—and society as a whole should help maintain their upkeep.

After all, individually and collectively, each of us is a stakeholder in the future of public education. That means corporate America, too.

Source: "Should Schools Sell Cola Companies Exclusive Rights?" *NEA Today* (September 1998): 59.

In our district, some of the many promotions that were so "generously" offered include software that flashes the Fruitopia logo as often as nine times in 10 minutes, Coke interns who can earn $5 an hour organizing events that promote Coke in the schools, and the ever-popular Coke Teacher of the Year.

These promotions are at the heart of these exclusive marketing agreements. Beverage companies aren't interested in helping our children by funding their schools. They're interested in buying brand loyalty.

Sure, school districts are facing a paralyzing budget crunch. But attempts to fill the budget gaps with short-term, short-sighted, stopgap measures like these exclusive vending contracts only divert attention from the real issue—lack of public funding and lack of political commitment to quality public schools.

Children have the right to a quality education, one that allows them to make choices about their futures. When corporations worm their way into the schools, they make the choices, they set the agenda.

Trust me, I know. In Madison, our school board was unable to resist the lure of this "easy money." Next year, Coke Dollars will be handed out, each high school will have two Coke interns, and several new programs will have been created so Coke can contribute a few dollars and, more importantly, promote themselves in our public schools.

Frankly, I don't want to see the day when my high school's "Fine Arts Day" is replaced by a "Coke in Education Day" because we need a few new desks.

WHAT'S YOUR OPINION?

Should schools sell cola companies exclusive rights?

Go to **www.ablongman.com/johnson** to cast your vote and see how NEA readers responded.

education ought to be a process of developing a free, self-actualizing person—a process centered on the feelings of the student. Therefore, proper education does not start with the nature of the world and with humankind, but with the human individual or self.

The existentialist educator would be a free personality engaged in projects that treat students as free personalities. The highest educational goal is to search for oneself. Teachers and students experience existential crises; each such crisis involves an examination of oneself and one's life purposes. Education helps to fill in the gaps with understanding that the student needs in order to fulfill those purposes; it is not a mold to which the student must be fitted. Students define themselves by their choices.

The existentialist student would have a questioning attitude and would be involved in a continuing search for self and for the reasons for existence. The existentialist teacher would help students become what they themselves want to become, not what outside forces such as society, other teachers, or parents want them to become.

Existentialist thinkers are as varied as the notions of individual thought and self-defined meaning would suggest. There are atheistic existentialists as represented by Jean-Paul Sartre, theistic existentialists as exemplified by Sören Kierkegaard, and humanistic existentialists such as Maxine Greene.

JEAN-PAUL SARTRE Modern existentialism was born amidst the pain and disillusionment of World War II. Jean-Paul Sartre (1905–1980) broke with previous philosophers and asserted that existence (being) comes before essence (meaning).

Sartre saw no difference between being free and being human. This view opens great possibilities; yet it also creates feelings of dread and nausea as one recognizes the reality of nonbeing and death as well as the great responsibilities that accompany such radical freedom to shape oneself out of one's choices. The process of answering the question "Who are we?" begins at a very crucial event in the lives of young people called the existential moment—that point somewhere toward the end of youth when individuals realize for the first time that they exist as independent agents.

In the following selection, Jean-Paul Sartre offers a defense of existentialism:

> What do we mean by saying that existence precedes essence? We mean that man first of all exists, encounters himself, surges up in the world—and defines himself afterwards. If man as the existentialist sees him is not definable, it is because to begin with he is nothing. He will not be anything until later, and then he will be what he makes of himself. Thus, there is no human nature, because there is no God to have a conception of it. Man simply is.[16]

Philosopher Maxine Greene (b. 1917) contends that living is philosophy and that freedom means overcoming obstacles that obstruct our attempts to find ourselves and fulfill our potential.

SÖREN KIERKEGAARD Sören Kierkegaard (1813–1855), a Danish theologian and philosopher, criticized science, contending that its objectivity was an attempt to drive society away from the Christian faith. He described three stages to life: the aesthetic stage, in which humans live in sensuous enjoyment and emotions dominate; the ethical stage, in which humans achieve an understanding of their place and the function of life; and the religious stage—for Kierkegaard the highest stage—in which humans stand alone before God. It is only through faith that individuals can bridge the gap between humans and God. Kierkegaard believed that individuals must come to understand their souls, that they deny the reality of God through education. He also maintained that individuals must accept responsibility for their choices, which they alone can make.

MAXINE GREENE A theme that permeates most of Maxine Greene's work is her unyielding faith in human beings' willingness to build and transcend their lived worlds. To Greene (b. 1917) philosophy is a deeply personal and aesthetic experience. Her writing blurs the distinction between philosophy and literature. This is appropriate because Greene contends that living is philosophy. Greene contends that schools must be places that offer "an authentic public space where diverse human beings can appear before one another as best they know to be."[17]

Freedom means the overcoming of obstacles or barriers that impede or obstruct people's struggle to define themselves and fulfill their potential. Greene contends that the "obstacles" or "walls" individuals encounter are human constructs subject to removal. From this perspective the educator has the formidable task of promoting freedom in each individual. But because embracing freedom is a matter of choice, it cannot be taught, only encouraged.

Through education individuals

> can be provoked to reach beyond themselves in this intersubjective space. It is through and by means of education that they may be empowered to think about what they are doing, to become mindful, to share meanings, to conceptualize, to make varied sense of their lived worlds.[18]

EASTERN WAYS OF KNOWING

Most studies of Western philosophy typically begin with the Greek philosophers. Yet there is evidence that Platonic philosophy owed much of its development to Indian philosophy, which emphasizes the illusory quality of matter from Hinduism and Buddhism. Although there are many different philosophical writings among the Far Eastern, Middle Eastern, and Near Eastern philosophers, **Eastern ways of knowing** as a group stress inner peace, tranquillity, attitudinal development, and mysticism. Western philosophy has tended to emphasize logic and materialism; whereas Eastern ways of knowing, in general, stress the inner rather than the outer world, intuition rather than sense, and mysticism rather than scientific discoveries. This has differed from school to school, but overall Eastern ways of knowing begin with the inner world and then reach to the outer world of phenomena. Eastern ways of knowing emphasize order, regularity, and patience that is proportional to and in harmony with the law of nature.

Eastern philosophers have always concerned themselves with education, which they view as a way of achieving wisdom, maintaining family structure, establishing law, and providing for social and economic concerns. Instruction includes the things that one must do to achieve the good life, and education is viewed as necessary not only for this life but for achievement of the good life hereafter.

Eastern ways of knowing have not been as singular as has Western thought. One needs to study Eastern thinking system by system, culture by culture, and philosopher by philosopher. One good reason to study Eastern ways of knowing is that they offer vantage points from which to examine Western thought. Eastern ideas encourage one to question seriously the Western world's most basic commitments to science, materialism, and reason.

When a man has pity on all living creatures, then only is he noble.

Buddha

INDIAN THOUGHT Far Eastern Indian thought has a long, complex history and is permeated by opposites. To Western philosophers, opposites need to be reconciled; but to the Eastern mind this need for consistency is unimportant. For example, great emphasis is placed on a search for wisdom, but this does not mean a rejection of worldly pleasures. Though speculation is emphasized, it has a very practical character. Far Eastern Indian thinkers insist that knowledge be used to improve both social and communal life and that people should live according to their ideals. In Far Eastern Indian philosophy there is a prevailing sense of

Eastern ways of knowing
A varied set of ideas, beliefs, and values from the Far, Middle, and Near East that stress inner peace, tranquility, attitudinal development, and mysticism.

Ancient Chinese philosopher Confucius (551–479 B.C.) believed that people need standards for all of life and so he developed rules for a wide range of activities.

universal moral justice, according to which individuals are responsible for what they are and what they become.

Hinduism, Buddhism, and Jainism are three religions that provide different contexts for these Indian philosophical principles. Hinduism does not generally encourage asceticism or a renunciation of the world, but teaches that one should be able to control and regulate oneself. Fundamental truths include the concept that there is an ultimate reality that is all-pervading and is the final cause of the universe. This reality is uncreated and eternal. Meditation on this ultimate reality leads to a life of virtue and righteousness. Buddhism stresses nonattachment to material things and concern for humanity; it emphasizes a sense of harmony with the universe where one is under no constraint to change forces within or without. Jainism is a religion that rejects systems as absolutes and affirms them only as partial truths or "maybes." Jains believe that the universe has existed from all eternity, undergoing an infinite number of revolutions produced by the powers of nature. Adherents of Jainism have great respect for all life and take vows to avoid injury to any form of life.[19]

CHINESE THOUGHT The emphasis of Far Eastern Chinese philosophy is on harmony: Correct thinking should help one achieve harmony with life. This harmony of government, business, and family should then lead toward a higher synthesis. Confucianism and Taoism provide two major contexts for Chinese thought.

For more than two thousand years, Confucian thought has influenced education, government, and culture in China. Confucius (551–479 B.C.) believed that people need standards for all of life, so rules were developed for a wide range of activities. Confucian thought gives education a high place but stresses building moral character more than merely teaching skills or imparting information. This moral approach has a practical component. Children should obey and defer to parents and respect the wisdom adults have gained in their journey through life. Following these principles enables children to become *chun-tzu,* persons distinguished by faithfulness, diligence, and modesty.

The central concept of Taoism is that of the "Tao," the Way or Path. The Tao is the way the universe moves, the way of perfection and harmony. It is conformity with nature. Perhaps the most significant aspect of the Tao is letting things alone, not forcing personal desires onto the natural course of events. It is a noncompetitive approach to life. Taoists believe that conflict and war represent basic failures in society, for they bring ruin to states and a disrespect for life.

JAPANESE THOUGHT Japanese thought is rooted in Shinto, a way of thinking that recognizes the significance of the natural world. This respect for all nature permeates Japanese thought and life. Shinto accepts the phenomenal world (the world people apprehend through their senses) as absolute; this acceptance leads to a disposition to lay greater emphasis upon intuitive, sensible, concrete events rather than upon universal ideas. On the social level, Japanese express this focus on the natural world through many artifacts, including the patterns of traditional kimonos. Within the house, flowers are arranged in vases and dwarf trees placed in alcoves, flowers and birds are engraved on lintels, and nature scenes are painted on sliding screens. Seventeen-syllable poems, called haikus, cannot be disassociated from nature.

The Japanese perspective is one of acceptance, enjoyment of life, and kinship with nature. Intuition is often prized over intellectualism, and there is a strong feeling for loyalty, purity, and naturalness. Japanese philosophy has successfully fused Confucian, Buddhist, and Taoist beliefs and practices and has permeated them with a distinct Japanese perspective. One example of this is the development of Zen Buddhism. Zen emphasizes a dependence on oneself rather than on an outside source for answers and wisdom; it depends more on intuition than on intellectual discovery.

MIDDLE EASTERN THOUGHT Many philosophies and religions (including Judaism, Christianity, and Islam) owe their origin to the Middle East. Historically, the Middle East has been a meeting ground between civilizations of the East and the West; partly because of this fact, Middle Eastern thought is more disjointed than that of the Far East. Judaism traces its origins to the call of Abraham (around 1750 B.C.). Abraham believed in a God who had a special interest in humanity. Throughout the centuries Judaic thought has included a belief in one God who created the world and who cares for the world and all its creatures. In earlier conceptions of Judaism, God was viewed as possessing human qualities, but later became more idealized and incorporeal; "I am who I am."

Christianity began as a Jewish sect centered in Jerusalem. This sect proclaimed Jesus of Nazareth as the Messiah. The words and deeds of Jesus formed the basis of the New Testament, which early Christians saw as the fulfillment of Judaism. Christianity incorporates many of the Judaic beliefs, but it places greater emphasis on concepts such as grace and redemption.

Islam is the most prominent religion in the contemporary Middle East. Mohammed (A.D. 571–632) was born in Mecca. Through a revelation, Mohammed was called on to bring all people to worship Allah, the one true God. His mission was to restore to the Arabs the pure faith of their father, Abraham, and to free them from bondage and idolatry. Mohammed taught that Allah is a purposeful God who created things to reach certain desired goals. Those who follow the will of Allah will be eternally rewarded in paradise, an oasis of flowing waters. For those who do not follow the will of Allah, there is eternal suffering.

EDUCATIONAL IMPLICATIONS OF EASTERN WAYS OF KNOWING Eastern educational thought places great emphasis on the teacher–student relationship. Change springs from this relationship; that is, the student is changed as a result of contact with the guru, master, or prophet. Eastern educational thought emphasizes transformation: The individual must be transformed to face life. Attitude shaping is important because the attitude a person holds toward life will determine the individual's levels of goodness and wisdom.

A recurring educational aim in Eastern ways of knowing is to put humanity in tune with nature. There is great emphasis on observing nature and learning through wanderings and pilgrimages. The importance of achieving wisdom, satori, enlightenment, or nirvana is supreme. All paths must lead to this, and from this wisdom spring virtue, right living, and correct behavior.

GLOBAL PERSPECTIVES: The Fabric of Eastern Ways of Knowing

As you can see, Eastern thought is like a rich fabric of diverse ideas. It emphasizes sets of views that are quite different from the neat categorizations of Western thought. Eastern thought suggests that cohesive views can be achieved without the necessity of neat, hierarchically distinct categories. Although they are quite difficult to summarize, the philosophy and thought of the Far, Near, and Middle East suggest new ways of looking at long-accepted meanings and assumptions. As such, the study of Eastern thought is an important part of all future educators' preparation in an increasingly multicultural society.

NATIVE NORTH AMERICAN WAYS OF KNOWING

Just as the rich past and diverse cultures make it difficult to summarize Eastern thought, Native North American ways of knowing are equally difficult to synthesize. **Native North American ways of knowing** include a varied set of beliefs, positions, and customs that span different tribes in North America. These beliefs, positions, and customs center on the relationship of humans to all of nature, including the earth, the sun, the sky, and beyond. Because Native North American ways of knowing center on the relationship of humans to all of nature, it is sometimes difficult to separate knowing from a way of life. In fact, to understand is to live and to develop an ever closer, more profound human-to-nature relationship. The types of relationships and the symbols that inform these human-to-nature relationships differ widely among tribes.

Traditionally, Native Americans view time as a flow of events with no beginning or end.

Lee Little Soldier, Native American educator

Although Native North American ways of knowing are as different as the four hundred–plus tribes in North America, these ways of knowing do have similar elements. They all include traditional stories and beliefs that dictate a way of knowing and living. All include a reverence for nature and a sense of humans' responsibility to nature. And all groups make reference to a supreme being—although the names are different, the relationships vary, and the expectations of some supreme beings are interpreted through natural elements. Thus, the Black Hills are sacred to the Lakota, the turtle is revered as Mother Earth by the Ojibwa, and so on. Native North American ways of knowing are orally developed rather than written. Hence, they change slightly from age to age. Additionally, the ways of knowing are subject to interpretation by the shaman, or holy one.

NAVAJO THOUGHT The Navajo nation is the largest tribe in the United States. The Navajos' early history was nomadic, and their thoughts and customs are known for their unique ability to assimilate with and adapt to the thought and customs of other tribes. As with most Native North American cultures, the Navajo universe is an all-inclusive unity viewed as an orderly system of interrelated elements. At the basis of Navajo teachings and traditions is the value of a life lived in harmony with the natural world. Such a view enables one to "walk in beauty." To understand the Navajo world view, one must note the teachings of the "inner forms" of things. These inner forms were set in place by First Man and First Woman. The concept of "inner form" is similar to the concept of a "spirit" or "soul"; without it, the Navajos say, the outer forms would be dead.[20]

native North American ways of knowing
A varied set of beliefs, philosophical positions, and customs that span different tribes in North America.

LAKOTA THOUGHT The Native American culture of the Great Plains, of which the Lakota form part, is based on mystical participation with the environment. All aspects of this ecosystem, including earth, sky, night, day, sun, and moon, are elements of the oneness within which life was undertaken. The Lakota celebrate the "sacred hoop of life" and observe seven sacred rites toward the goal of ultimate communion with Wakan-Tanka, the great Spirit.[21]

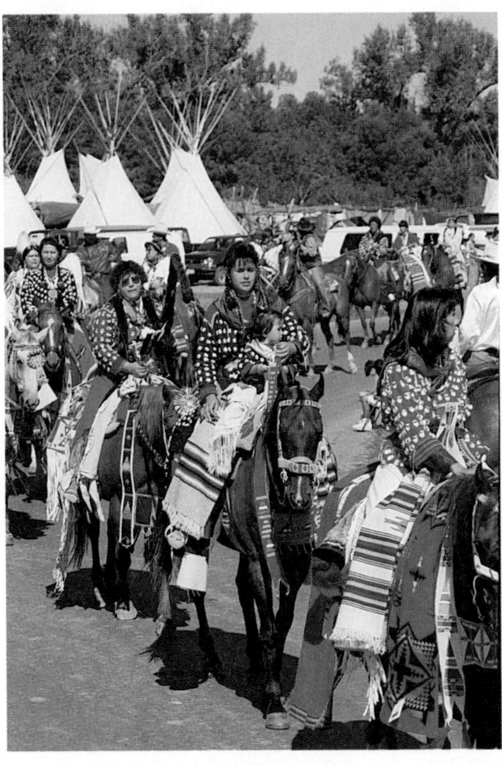

Native North American ways of knowing provide a perspective that connects knowledge to the earth that surrounds us and of which we are a part.

HOPI THOUGHT The Hopi follow the path of peace, which they believe is a pure and perfect pattern of humankind's evolutionary journey. The Road of Life of the Hopi is represented as a journey through seven universes created at the beginning. At death the conduct of a person in accordance with the Creator's plan determines when and where the next step on the road will be taken. Each of the Hopi clans has a unique role to play, and each role is an essential part of the whole. Hopis must live in harmony with one another, with nature, and with the plan. Out of this complex interplay, then, the plan is both created and allowed to unfold.

> We feel that the world is good. We are grateful to be alive. We are conscious that all men are brothers. We sense that we are related to other creatures. Life is to be valued and preserved. If you see a grain of corn on the ground, pick it up and take care of it, because it has life inside. When you go out of your house in the morning and see the sun rising pause a moment to think about it. When you take water from a spring, be aware that it is a gift of nature. (Albert Yava, Big Falling Snow, Hopi)[22]

EDUCATIONAL IMPLICATIONS OF NATIVE NORTH AMERICAN WAYS OF KNOWING Native North American educational thought emphasizes the importance of nature. The pursuit of knowledge and happiness must be subordinate to a respect for the whole universe. To know is to understand one's place in the natural order of things. To be is to celebrate through ritual and stories the spirit that informs all reality. These principles encourage educators to study the physical and social world by examining the natural relationships that exist among things, animals, and humans. Studying ideas in the abstract or as independent entities is not as important as understanding the relationships among ideas and the physical reality. Hands-on learning, making connections, holding discussions, and celebrating the moment are essential components of an educational experience.

SUMMARY

STRUCTURE AND METHODOLOGY OF PHILOSOPHY

The study of philosophy permeates every aspect of the teacher's role and provides the underpinning for every decision. This chapter described how philosophy is related to daily teaching decisions and actions, and it clarified some of the major ideas that different philosophers have developed in their private quest for wisdom.

Philosophy revolves around three major types of questions: those that deal with the nature of reality (metaphysics), those that deal with knowledge and truth (epistemology), and those that deal with values (axiology). We encourage prospective teachers to identify the personal philosophical positions that inform their own learning and teaching. We do not advocate any one philosophical position. Rather, the most successful teachers are those who are dedicated to and thoroughly understand their preferred beliefs. Decisions about the nature of the subject matter emphasized in the curriculum are metaphysical commitments to reality—What is real? Questions related to what is true and how we know are epistemological. Classroom methods are practices that aim to assist learners in acquiring knowledge and truth in the subject area. Classroom activities that deal with ethics (what is right or wrong), beauty, and character are in the realm of axiology (values). The task of the teacher is to identify a preferred style, understand that style as thoroughly as possible, and utilize that style with each unique group of learners.

This chapter also described two approaches to philosophical thinking: analytic and prophetic. Analytic thinking provides clarity and precision, while prophetic thinking fosters breadth and sensitivity. Both thinking approaches are valuable and help educators to understand the essential and critical features of situations or problems.

SCHOOLS OF PHILOSOPHY AND THEIR INFLUENCE ON EDUCATION

We have surveyed four classical Western schools of philosophical ideas: realism, idealism, pragmatism, and existentialism. For each school we introduced representative philosophers and their ideas so as to give prospective teachers a sense of how they might develop their own educational philosophy.

The chapter concluded with overviews of Eastern and Native North American ways of knowing. The Eastern and Native North American ways of knowing are varied and diverse. Despite such diversity, many of these ways of knowing share an underlying sensitivity to nature and an emphasis on wisdom, virtue, spirituality, and harmony within the larger universe. The educational implications of these ways of knowing include the importance of teaching respect for the earth and awareness of the interrelationships among all things.

DISCUSSION QUESTIONS

1. How would you describe philosophy to a young child?
2. In your opinion, which is the most important aspect of a given philosophy (for the teacher): the metaphysical component, the epistemological component, or the axiological component? State the rationale for your choice.
3. Early Greek philosophers suggest that all knowledge is based on experience. Discuss the implications of this statement for teaching methodology.
4. Describe the ways that Eastern and Native North American ways of knowing might influence what and how you teach.

JOURNAL ENTRIES

1. Classroom activities that deal with what is good or bad are in the realm of axiology (values). Prepare lists of the goods and the evils of the U.S. educational system. Then propose solutions to counteract as many of the evils as possible.
2. Consider the four components of prophetic thinking: discernment, empathy, tracking hypocrisy, and hope. Select one of these components and apply it to the educational controversy over school prayer. Record your thoughts, feelings, and observations.

PORTFOLIO DEVELOPMENT

1. According to idealistic philosophy, character education may be enhanced through study and imitation of exemplars/heroes in the historical record. Identify an exemplary educator from history and describe how you could teach character through that person's example. Place your essay in your folio as an example of your teaching methodology.
2. Assist a student as a mentor or tutor. Before beginning, gather samples of the student's thinking and schoolwork. Try to think like the student and by so doing uncover areas in which the student needs help. Develop a diagnosis that details what changes will be beneficial. Place these ideas in your folio as an example of your diagnostic and metacognitive skills.

SCHOOL-BASED EXPERIENCES

1. In reflecting on your classroom experiences, you may feel that you need more knowledge about philosophical concepts and views to enable you to develop your own personal educational philosophy. Some of your colleagues may have similar feelings. Consider establishing a study group to discuss philosophical views. The group could develop questions to ask your supervisor. Invite the supervisor to respond to your questions in one of your study group sessions.
2. As you visit schools and classrooms, be alert for indications of philosophical concepts and different philosophical views. You might wish to talk with teachers about their educational ideas. Many schools have written statements describing their philosophy of education. You could ask several schools to send you a copy of their philosophy of education. When you receive them, look for similarities and differences among the philosophical statements.

WEBSITES

We recommend that you do a web search using key words focused on philosophical schools such as "idealism," "realism," "pragmatism," and "existentialism"; also use key words focused on individual thinkers such as "Aristotle," "Peirce," "Kierkegaard," and so on. Some interesting sites are described below:

1. <www.philosophy.about.com/homework/philosophy/mbody.htm> This site contains articles written by philosophers throughout the ages. It also offers information about the lives of different philosophers and provides a quotation index. The site also provides links to philosophical journals and even has a discussion room. It is an excellent general information site about philosophy and its influence on education.
2. <www.philosophy.about.com/homework/philosophy/library/bleastern_web.htm> This site is maintained by About.com, Inc. This site emphasizes Eastern philosophy and provides text and resources related to Jainism, Taoism, Buddhism, Hinduism, and many other Eastern ways of knowing.
3. <www.educacao.pro.br/journal.htm> This site is the Journal of The Encyclopedia of Philosophy of Education. It is an international site of philosophers from Brazil, Australia and the United States. The site contains articles, short tests, and news and reviews about the philosophy of education.
4. <www.marsists.org/reference/subject/philosophy/front_pg.htm> This site contains a miniature library of philosophy. It is filled with readings from classical philosophers from Galileo to contemporary existentialists. The site is dedicated to tracing the development of ideas on the relation between consciousness and matter.

NOTES

1. George F. Kneller, "The Relevance of Philosophy," in *Introduction to the Philosophy of Education.* Berrien Springs, MI: Andrews University Press, 1982, 7–8.
2. Kneller, 31.
3. Herbert G. Alexander, *The Language and Logic of Philosophy.* Lanham, MD: University Press of America, 107–108, 1987.
4. Cornel West, *Prophetic Thought in Postmodern Times.* Monroe, ME: Common Courage Press, 1993.
5. Nel Noddings, *The Challenge to Core in Schools.* New York: Teachers College Press, 1993, 2.
6. West, 5.
7. West, 6.
8. Plato, *The Republic,* trans. B. Jowett. New York: Dolphin Books, 1960, 208.
9. Immanuel Kant, *Critique of Pure Reason.* Trans. J. M. D. Meiklejohn. New York: Wiley, 1855. Originally published 1781, Introduction, Part I.10.
10. Jane Roland Martin, "Reclaiming a Conversation," in *The Ideal of the Educated Woman.* New Haven, CT: Yale University Press, 1985, 1–7.
11. Martin, 178.
12. Aristotle, *Nicomachean Ethics.* Trans. James E. C. Weldon. New York: Macmillan, 1897, Chapter 1.
13. John Locke, "Some Thoughts Concerning Education," in *The Works of John Locke,* Volume X. London: Printed for W. Otridge and Son et al., 1812, 6–7.
14. Alfred North Whitehead, *The Aims of Education.* New York: The Free Press, 1929, 1957, 1–2.
15. John Dewey, "My Pedagogic Creed," *The School Journal 54* (3) (16 January 1989): 77–80. Reprinted with the permission of the Center for Dewey Studies, Southern Illinois University at Carbondale.

16. Jean-Paul Sartre, *Existentialism and Human Emotions.* New York: Philosophical Library, 1957, 17.
17. Maxine Greene, *The Dialectic of Freedom.* New York: Teachers College Press, 1988.
18. Greene, 12.
19. Howard A. Osman and Samuel M. Craven, *Philosophical Foundations of Education.* Columbus, OH: Merrill Publishing, 1986, 66–85.
20. Terry P. Wilson, *Navajo: Walking in Beauty.* San Francisco: Chronicle Books, 1994.
21. Terry P. Wilson, *Lakota: Seeking the Great Spirit.* San Francisco: Chronicle Books, 1994.
22. Terry P. Wilson, *Hopi: Following the Path of Peace.* San Francisco: Chronicle Books, 1994.

BIBLIOGRAPHY

Abel, Donald C. *Theories of Human Nature.* New York: McGraw-Hill, 1992.

Adler, Mortimer. "A Revolution in Education." *American Educator 6* (4) (Winter 1982): 20–24.

——. *Ten Philosophical Mistakes: Basic Errors in Modern Thought.* New York: Macmillan, 1985.

Bahm, Archie J. *Comparative Philosophy: Western, Indian, and Chinese Philosophies Compared.* Rev. ed. Albuquerque, NM: World Book, 1995.

Bellanca, James. *Values and the Search for Self.* Washington, DC: National Education Association, 1975.

Coleman, James S. "International Comparisons of Cognitive Achievement." *Phi Delta Kappan* (February 1985): 403–406.

Dewey, John. *Democracy and Education.* New York: Macmillan, 1916.

Ennis, Robert, and Norris, S. *Evaluating Critical Thinking.* Pacific Grove, CA: Midwest Publications, 1989.

Grant, Carl A. "Challenging the Myths about Multicultural Education." *Multicultural Education* (Winter 1994).

Knight, George P. *Issues and Alternatives in Educational Philosophy.* Berrien Springs, MI: Andrews University Press, 1982.

Ladson-Billings, Gloria. "What We Learn from Multicultural Education Research." *Educational Leadership* (May 1994).

Littleton, Scott C. *Eastern Wisdom.* New York: Henry Holt and Company, 1996.

Nakamura, Hajime. *Ways of Thinking of Eastern Peoples.* Honolulu: University of Hawaii Press, 1968.

Nerburn, Kent, and Mengelkoch, Louise. *Native American Wisdom.* Novato, CA: The Classic Wisdom Collection, 1991.

Paul, Richard. *Critical Thinking: What Every Person Needs to Survive in a Rapidly Changing World.* Rohnert Park California Center for Critical Thinking and Moral Critique, 1990.

Scheffler, Israel. *Conditions of Knowledge: An Introduction to Epistemology and Education.* Chicago: University of Chicago Press, 1978.

Searle, John R. (1993). "Rationality and Realism: What Is at Stake?" *Daedalus 122* (4) (Fall 1993): 55–83.

Soltis, Jonas F. *An Introduction to the Analysis of Educational Concepts.* 2nd rev. ed. Reading, MA: Addison-Wesley, 1978.

Taylor, A. E. *Elements of Metaphysics.* 12th ed. London: Methuen, 1946.

Thatcher, Margaret. "Moral Foundations of Society: A Contrast between West and East." *USA Today Magazine* (Society for the Advancement of Education) (July 1996).

Whitehead, Alfred North. *The Aims of Education.* New York: The Free Press, 1929, 1957, 1–2.

Wilson, Terry P. *Navajo: Walking in Beauty.* San Francisco: Chronicle Books, 1994.

_____. *Lakota: Seeking the Great Spirit.* San Francisco: Chronicle Books, 1994.

_____. *Hopi: Following the Path of Peace.* San Francisco: Chronicle Books, 1994.

CHAPTER

11

Educational Theory in American Schools: Philosophy in Action

A Wake-Up Call

By Megan Rutherford, *Time*, November 15, 1999

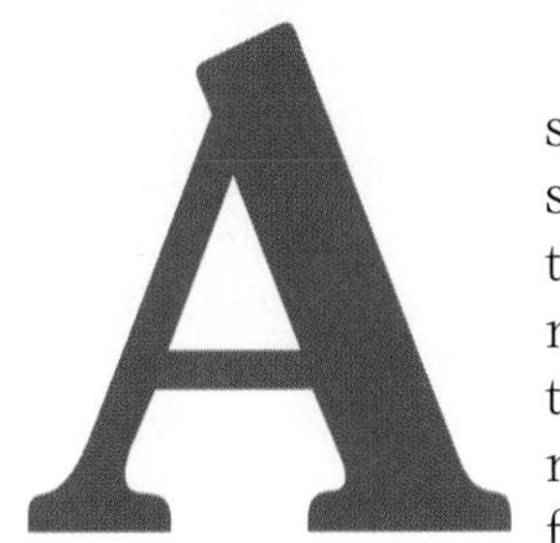

As kids enter high school, parents worry that mediocre grades may shut them out of top colleges, which may prevent them from getting fulfilling jobs that pay well. Those are legitimate fears, says Francis Schoonmaker, an associate professor at Teachers College in New York City, "But so far in this country, we still have doors people can take advantage of, even if they don't have high grades." Families struggling with less than stellar report cards may take comfort in the knowledge that straight A's are often looked upon as potentially problematic. A flawless record can be a sign that classes are not challenging or that adults are putting excessive pressure on a child to perform well. "You should be able to make mistakes," says Nancy Devlin, a New Jersey psychologist. "The student who's getting all A's is following the rules, doing what he's told, filling in the blanks." Sometimes the C student who asks the crazy questions is the one who's truly gifted and talented." And while grades below C seldom make children or their parents proud, they can serve as a call to action. Says Doris Dillon, a teacher and consultant in San Jose, California, "The only punishment for poor grades should be a reward—more quality time working together as a parent-child team. With encouragement from teachers and parents, falling a few times is not harmful and can be the jolt that awakens greater interest and responsibility."

LEARNER OUTCOMES

After reading and studying this chapter, you will be able to

1. Identify the major tenets of the authoritarian educational theories of perennialism, essentialism, behaviorism, and positivism.
2. Identify the major tenets of the nonauthoritarian educational theories of progressivism, reconstructivism, humanism, and constructivism.
3. Compare authoritarian and nonauthoritarian educational theories.
4. Relate educational theories to learning and curriculum development.
5. State the relationship of progressivism to democracy and society.
6. Relate the tenets of critical pedagogy to societal change. ■

This chapter introduces a number of significant educational theories that are based on various philosophies and ways of knowing. It offers a number of big ideas or key concepts that will help you identify the underlying views about knowledge and learning that are implicit in the way classrooms are organized and subject matter is presented. Some of these big ideas include authoritarian and nonauthoritarian approaches to education, mastery learning versus individual development, and convergent versus divergent thinking.

The four classical schools of philosophy that we presented in the previous chapter take different approaches to questions about ultimate reality (metaphysics), knowledge (epistemology), and values (axiology). Although philosophical ideas are of little importance if they remain abstract, they can be powerful forces when they are brought into action in educational theory. One can think of educational theory as the application of philosophy to the classroom. The way curriculum is organized, the manner in which instruction is delivered, the character of school environments, and the processes used in testing and grading are informed by the philosophical views held by educators, parents, and legislators. Such views vary greatly from school district to school district and from state to state. Educational theorists attempt to clarify how these different approaches to curriculum, instruction, and assessment work or do not work together. Table 11.1 describes the relationships between the four schools of philosophy—idealism, realism, pragmatism, and existentialism—and education.

The four schools of philosophy give rise to different, sometimes competing learning foci, curricular goals, teaching methods, and approaches to character and aesthetic development. Educational theorists attempt to develop cohesive ideas about teaching and learning by drawing on one or more compatible philosophies. For example, a behaviorist educational theorist could focus on the mind, the physical world, or the social world. It would not be appropriate for the behaviorist to focus on personal choice, however, because behaviorism essentially aims to control human behavior through reinforcement.

This chapter describes eight educational theories that draw on different philosophies. We will group the educational theories according to the degree to which each theory relies on external versus internal authority. This distinction between an authoritarian (external) versus a nonauthoritarian (internal) locus of control can also be used to group the schools of philosophy outlined in the previous chapter. That is, as indicated in Table 11.1, the ideas and principles that surround idealism and realism imply that external authority is important to the attainment of truth and goodness, whereas pragmatism and existentialism focus more on the innate worth of the individual.

If liberty and equality, as is thought by some, are chiefly to be found in democracy, they will be best attained when all persons alike share in the government to the utmost.

Aristotle

Many teachers hold the view that the purpose of education is to train pupils' minds so that they can deal better with the intellectual concepts of life; these teachers emphasize, in addition, the mastery of facts and information. The general notion of this authoritarian point of view—the idea that any child can learn any subject at any level if the subject matter is properly presented—remains a strong challenge to teachers to arouse motivation for subject mastery among pupils. The concept of *mastery learning* suggests that, except for the few children who have mental, emotional, or physical impairments, every child can master the entire curriculum of the school when adequate time and resources are provided. Continued attention to test scores, grade-level achievement, and other measures of subject matter competency reflect the importance that is still at-

TABLE 11.1 Educational Implications of Philosophy

Educational Aspect	Authoritarian Focus		Nonauthoritarian Focus	
	Idealism	Realism	Pragmatism	Existentialism
Learning focus	Subject matter of the mind: literature, intellectual history, philosophy, religion	Subject matter of the physical world: mathematics, science	Subject matter of social experience	Subject matter of personal choice
Curriculum goal	The same education for all	Mastery of laws of universe	Creation of a new social order	Personal freedom and development
Preferred teaching method	Teaching for the handling of ideas: lecture, discussion	Teaching for mastery of information and skills: demonstration, recitation	Problem solving: project method, product development	Individual exploration: discovery method, authentic pedagogy
Character development	Imitation of exemplars, heroes	Training in rules of conduct	Group decision making in light of consequences	Development of individual responsibility for decisions and preferences
Aesthetic development	Study of the masterworks; values of the past heritage	Study of design in nature	Participation in art projects based on cross-cultural and universal values	Development of a personal view of the world; self-initiated activities

Source: Adapted from Morris, Van Cleve, and Young Pai, *Philosophy and the American School,* Second Edition. Copyright 1976 by Houghton Mifflin. Used with permission.

tached to the authoritarian view of education. School boards, parents, and the general public increasingly demand that teachers provide concrete evidence that their pupils have made progress in mastering subject matter. Teachers who identify with these authoritarian views are considered to be more traditional regarding teaching strategies.

In contrast, many teachers uphold John Dewey's view that the mind is not just a muscle to be developed. They accept the notion that human beings are problem solvers who profit from experience. These educators also give credence to the nonauthoritarian existential position, which emphasizes the importance of the individual and of personal awareness. In light of the fact that Dewey's philosophical views have prevailed in U.S. teachers' colleges for the past half century, it is not surprising that schools in the United States reflect this nonauthoritarian view more than do other schools throughout the world. When teaching techniques are focused on student interactions, teachers may find that some students appear to be aimless with regard to subject matter. In such instances the teacher is challenged to arouse student interest through inquiry leading to subject content, whereas the more traditional teacher is challenged to arouse student interest in subject matter directly.

Educational theorists explain how the authoritarian and nonauthoritarian sets of teaching and learning principles differ from each other. They clarify how each set forms a cohesive whole and describe the benefits and shortcomings of adhering to either set. Eight educational theories considered here are perennialism, essentialism, behaviorism, positivism, progressivism, reconstructionism, humanism, and constructivism. To varying degrees, each of these educational views is used by classroom teachers and applied to the way teachers organize their classroom, their instruction, and their assessments. As you study these different educational theories, you will find that one or more of them clearly meshes with your own views. Understanding your own position in terms of known theory will be an invaluable asset as you develop your personal philosophy of education.

AUTHORITARIAN EDUCATIONAL THEORIES

Perennialism, essentialism, behaviorism, and positivism are educational theories that espouse an authoritarian approach to subject matter, classroom organization, teaching methods, and assessment. Although each theory forms a distinct cohesive whole, all four are rooted in an authoritarian principle—that is, that truth and goodness are entities that are best understood by the person with expertise who is in authority. The students' role is, then, to attempt to master and follow the directions of those in power who have experience and authority.

This chapter will present each educational theory's ideas on curriculum, teaching, and learning. In addition, for each theory we will describe a representative program along with an illustrative class activity.

PERENNIALISM

The things taught in schools and colleges are not an education but the means of education.

Ralph Waldo Emerson

perennialism
An educational theory that focuses on enduring principles of knowledge; nature, human nature, and the underlying principles of existence are considered constant, undergoing little change.

The basic educational view of **perennialism** is that the principles of knowledge are enduring. The term *perennial* may be defined as "everlasting," and the perennialist seeks everlasting truths. Although there are superficial differences from century to century, the perennialist views nature, human nature, and the underlying principles of existence as constant, undergoing little change. Because of its emphasis on ageless truth, perennialism is closely associated with idealism.

Perennialists stress the importance of time-honored ideas, the great works of past and present thinkers, and the ability to reason. To know reality, perennialists maintain, one must examine individual things and concepts so as to find their essence. To find the essence, one must discard the particulars and search for the unchanging underlying essentials. The essence of human beings lies in what they have in common: the ability to reason.

For the perennialist the intellect does not develop merely by contact with relevant experiences. The intellect must be nourished by contact with ideas because truth ultimately resides in the nature of the things rather than in the sensory aspects of things. Perennialists contend that instead of focusing on current events or student interests, educators should teach disciplined knowledge, with particular emphasis on students' mastery of established facts about the great

Perennialists focus learning on subject matter of a disciplinary and spiritual nature, like mathematics, language, logic, great books, and doctrines.

ideas and works found in literature, the humanities, mathematics, science, and the arts. (See the Perennialist Class Activity box.)

PERENNIALIST FOCUS OF LEARNING The focus of learning in perennialism lies in activities designed to discipline the mind. Subject matter of a disciplinary and spiritual nature, such as mathematics, language, logic, great books, and doctrines, must be studied. The learner is assumed to be a rational and spiritual person. Difficult mental calisthenics such as reading, writing, drill, rote memory,

PERENNIALIST CLASS ACTIVITY

Ms. Rosemont's literature class had been studying the works of Henry David Thoreau. In the classroom session on "Reading" from *Walden,* discussion focused on the following questions:

- Do the classics embody truth? Why or why not?
- Have all our emotions and problems been written about by great authors?
- Are none of our experiences unique? Why or why not?
- What makes a book great?
- Does popular literature ever serve a noble purpose? Why or why not?
- With whom can one talk about the best book?
- Can only great poets read the works of great poets? Why or why not?
- Does dealing with truth help us become immortal? Why or why not?
- How can we get the most benefit from our reading?

This lesson followed the Great Books procedure for questioning and could, therefore, be considered a perennialist investigation of human nature.[1]

In this perennialist class activity the nature of the learner is *active,* the nature of the subject matter is *structured,* the use of the subject matter is *cognitive,* and the thinking approach is *convergent.*

and computations are important in training the intellect. Perennialism holds that learning to reason is also very important—an ability attained by additional mental exercises in grammar, logic, and rhetoric, as well as through use of discussion methodologies. Reasoning about human matters and about moral principles that permeate the universe links perennialism to idealism. As the individual mind develops, the learner becomes more like a spiritual being. The learner is closer to ultimate knowledge when he or she gradually assumes the mind qualities of God. Idealism also harmonizes with some findings on the psychology of learning—findings suggesting that the mind can combine pieces of learning into whole concepts that have meaning.

PERENNIALIST CURRICULUM Perennialists believe that early schooling is best directed toward preparing children for maturity, and they emphasize the three Rs in the elementary schools. In this view, perennialism and essentialism (described below) share some thoughts. Some lay and ecclesiastical perennialists consider character training, enhanced through Bible study, to be as important as the three Rs at the elementary level. A perennialist program for the secondary level is directed more toward educating the intellectually elite. Perennialism favors trade and skill training for students who are not engaged in the rigors of the general education program. Perennialists agree that the curriculum at the secondary level should provide a general educational program for the intellectually gifted and vocational training for the less gifted. However, not all perennialists agree on a curriculum design for general education.

THE GREAT BOOKS: A PERENNIALIST PROGRAM The Great Books program, associated with Robert M. Hutchins and Mortimer Adler, has brought attention to perennialism. Proponents of the Great Books program maintain that studying the works of the leading scholars of history is the best way to a general education. Perennialists debate the use of contemporary sources. Some contend that students can draw upon modern sources to obtain knowledge and that the Great Books program should be flexible enough to include newer works of literature, science, and so forth.

ESSENTIALISM

Essentialism holds that there is a common core of information and skills that an educated person in a given culture must have. Schools should be organized to transmit this core of essential material as effectively as possible. There are three basic principles of essentialism: a core of information, hard work and mental discipline, and teacher-centered instruction. Essentialism seeks to educate by providing training in the fundamentals, developing sound habits of mind, and teaching respect for authority. The back-to-the-basics movement is a truncated form of essentialism because it focuses primarily on the three Rs and discipline.

essentialism
An educational theory that holds that there is a common core of information and skills that an educated person must have; schools should be organized to transmit this core of essential material.

Although essentialism shares many of the same principles as perennialism, there are several important differences. Essentialism draws equally from both idealism and realism. Essentialists are not so intent on transmitting underlying, basic truths; rather, they advocate the teaching of a basic core of information that will help a person live a productive life today. Hence, this core of information can and will change. This is an important difference in emphasis from the notions of everlasting truth that characterize the perennialist. In addition, essentialism

DEBATE

Should Today's Education Be Relevant to Tomorrow's Job Market?

YES

Norish Adams, coordinator of curriculum and research at the Florida A&M University Developmental Research School, has been a pioneer in the school-to-work movement in her area. A veteran teacher, preservice instructor, and NEA activist, Adams can be reached at nadams2@famu.edu.

Over the course of my 30-year career, I've found no approach to teaching—and I've tried dozens—that has been as successful as one that ties subject knowledge to career development.

When students explore the future job market as an authentic component of learning, concepts take on more meaning than when introduced as abstract rules, definitions, and manipulations.

Here's what I've seen:

- *Linking school and work enriches curriculum.* The beauty, creativity, and challenges of mathematics, for example, are richly revealed when viewed from the perspective of a doctor, master carpenter, quilter, astronaut, political analyst, or artist.

- *Linking school and work motivates students.* Some of my students participate in a five-day career shadowing program at a nearby corporation. They learn firsthand about becoming a computer scientist, engineer, human resource director, and support employee with the space flight program.

Back in class, they write about their experiences and file their work in "course/career portfolios" that focus their thinking on school, work, and the connections between the two.

As one of my most reluctant students said, "The best part of keeping the portfolio is that it helps me see how all this required stuff fits into my life and helps to make it better."

- *Linking school and work keeps options open for all students, without "tracks."* At the public high school in Tallahassee where I work, we don't have separate vocational and academic paths for students, relegating application to one and theory to the other.

Students in academic classes need not ask, "When will I ever really use this?" Teachers will never have to say, "You'll understand next year when you go to college."

NO

Janette Gerdes teaches English and literature at Signal Hill School in Illinois. She was nominated for a Golden Apple Award in 1997 and recognized in Who's Who Among American Teachers in 1998. A member of the Belleville Education Association, Gerdes can be reached at jgerdes@stclair.k12.il.us.

Teachers should never allow the near-sacred mission of learning to be polluted by letting the public schools become the minor leagues for corporate America.

The goal of public schools should not be to train children to be worker drones. The goal should be to educate them so that they may enjoy full, happy, and productive lives.

If we educate kids to be thinkers, questioners, and problem-solvers, they'll do fine in the ever-changing, rarely predictable job market.

When I started teaching 10 years ago, the Internet was still used almost exclusively by scientists and government, a much smaller percentage of families owned home computers, and no one had even heard of anything called the World Wide Web.

Since then, we've seen huge changes in technology and the media, the Cold War has ended, and HMOs have overtaken American health care. What could we have taught the class of 1988 that would be relevant to today's job market anyway?

What we need to teach our students is how to read, write, think, question, and learn. Let the employers handle the specifics of job training.

Of course it's wholly appropriate to use technology to shape young minds. We should use whatever tools are available to turn kids on to learning, and kids love computers.

But a student with a well-rounded education—rather than one targeted for a job market that's likely to be obsolete by the time she's ready to enter it—has the advantage in the job market and, more importantly, will be better prepared to lead a full, satisfying life.

NEA Today ran a cover story on the school-to-work movement last spring, which included anecdotes of students who

YES | NO

Instead, we're in the process of creating six career academies in the areas of business, health sciences, architecture and design, engineering, public policy, and education. These areas were selected based on job predictions in Florida and the nation, as well as surveyed student interests.

Our goal: to give all students a rigorous education in the basics, plus the skills they'll need in problem-solving, technology, business, and public policy to thrive in today's job market—and tomorrow's.

- *Linking school and work helps students find their way with a minimum of struggle and cost.* Ninety percent of our students go on to postsecondary education. Many must work to help pay college costs, and they can't afford the luxury of taking six or seven years to graduate.

Our schoolwide career development program ensures that our graduates don't enter college unprepared to make wise, informed choices about their major, and that they don't flounder or drop out during the first year or two of college.

- *Linking school and work is the best way to prepare students for whatever lies ahead.* Young people who understand the world they will work in will take the classes, engage in the activities, do the reading, join the organizations, and enter the competitions that will prepare them for the jobs of the 21st century—whatever they may be.

Source: "Should Today's Education Be Relevant to Tomorrow's Job Market?" *NEA Today* (January 1999): 43.

became more motivated by participating in career-based learning.

But I suspect there are also kids who were turned off. And, worse, students focusing on math classes as a prelude to careers as pilots still might not see the point of studying literature or history.

This type of schooling sends such a terrible message to students—that learning is meaningful only when connected to a future job.

We have to be better than that, better than our money-obsessed culture. We have to show kids that there is more to life than a job, even a rewarding one.

There is the beauty of the natural world. There is freedom and the history of the struggle to achieve it. There is the tapestry of diverse cultures. There are great writers who speak to us from across the decades and centuries. And, yes, boys and girls, there is the immense pleasure of learning for its own sake.

I understand that people must have jobs to survive. But I will always teach my junior high English and literature students that life is about more than survival. . . .

WHAT'S YOUR OPINION

Should today's education be relevant to tomorrow's job market?

Go to **www.ablongman.com/johnson** to cast your vote and see how NEA readers responded.

stresses the disciplined development of basic skills rather than the perennialist goals of uncovering essences or underlying principles. (See the Essentialist Class Activity box.)

ESSENTIALIST FOCUS OF LEARNING Essentialism's goals are to transmit the cultural heritage and develop good citizens. It seeks to do this by emphasizing a core of fundamental knowledge and skills, developing sound habits of mental discipline, and demanding a respect for authority in a structured learning situation. The role of the student is that of a learner. School is a place where children come to

Essentialist teaching methods require formal discipline through emphasis on required reading, lectures, memorization, repetition, and examinations.

learn what they need to know, and the teacher is the person who can best instruct students in essential matters.

ESSENTIALIST CURRICULUM The essentialist curriculum focuses on subject matter that includes literature, history, foreign languages, and religion. Teaching methods require formal discipline and feature required reading, lectures, memorization, repetition, and examinations. Essentialists differ in their views on curriculum, but they generally agree about teaching the laws of nature and the accompanying universal truths of the physical world. Mathematics and the natural sciences are examples of subjects that contribute to the learners' knowledge of natural law. Activities that require mastering facts and information about the physical world are significant aspects of essentialist methodology. With truth defined as observable fact, instruction often includes field trips, laboratories, audiovisual materials, and nature study. Habits of intellectual discipline are considered ends in themselves.

The business of education is not to make the young perfect in any one of the sciences, but so to open and dispose their minds as may best make them capable of any, when they shall apply themselves to it.

John Locke

Essentialism envisions subject matter as the core of education. Severe criticism has been leveled at U.S. education by essentialists who advocate an emphasis on basic education. Essentialism assigns to the schools the task of conserving

ESSENTIALIST CLASS ACTIVITY

Ms. Wright's second graders had just learned to count money. She decided to let them play several games of "musical envelopes." There was one envelope per student, each containing a different amount of paper "nickels," "dimes," "quarters," and "pennies." When the music stopped, students had to count the money in their envelopes. The one with the most money for each game got a special prize.[2]

In this essentialist class activity the nature of the learner is *passive,* the nature of the subject matter is *structured,* the use of the subject matter is *cognitive,* and the thinking approach is *convergent.*

the heritage and transmitting knowledge of the physical world. In a sense the school is a curator of knowledge.

With the burgeoning of new knowledge in contemporary society, essentialism may be contributing to the slowness of educational change. In this context, essentialism has been criticized as obsolete in its authoritarian tendencies. Such criticism implies that essentialism does not satisfy the twentieth-century needs of U.S. youth. Essentialist educators deny this criticism and claim to have incorporated modern influences in the system while maintaining academic standards.

Education makes a people easy to lead, but difficult to drive, easy to govern, but impossible to enslave.

Franklin Delano Roosevelt

ESSENTIAL SCHOOLS MOVEMENT The Essential Schools movement is a contemporary school reform effort developed by Dr. Theodore Sizer. Sizer contends that students need to master a common core of information and skills, and he encourages schools to strip away the nonessentials and focus on having students "use their minds well." The Essential Schools movement does not specify what specific content is essential in a given culture at a given time. Rather, "essential schools" are required to analyze clearly what this core of information should be and to change the curriculum to emphasize this core.

BEHAVIORISM

B. F. Skinner (1904–1990), the Harvard experimental psychologist and philosopher, is the recognized leader of the movement known as **behaviorism.** Skinner verified Pavlov's stimulus-response theory with animals and, from his research, suggested that human behavior could also be explained as responses to external stimuli. (See the Behaviorist Class Activity box.) Because of its focus on the careful examination of environment, behaviors, and responses, behaviorism is closely linked to realism. Other behaviorists' research expanded on Skinner's work in illustrating the effect of the environment, particularly the interpersonal environment, in shaping individual behavior. In the words of Charles Wolfgang and Carl Glickman,

> Behaviorists share a common belief that a student's misbehavior can be changed and reshaped in a socially acceptable manner by directly changing the student's environment. The Behaviorist accepts the premise that students are motivated by the factor that all people will attempt to avoid experiences and stimuli that are not pleasing and will seek experiences that are pleasing and rewarding.[3]

BEHAVIORIST CLASS ACTIVITY

Students in Mr. Drucker's civics class were given merit tokens for coming into the room quietly, sitting at their desks, preparing notebooks and pencils for the day's lesson, and being ready to begin answering comprehension questions in their workbooks. On Fridays students were allowed to use their tokens at an auction to buy items that Mr. Drucker knew they wanted. Sometimes, however, students had to save tokens for more than two weeks to buy what they liked best.

In this behaviorist class activity the nature of the learner is *passive,* the nature of the subject matter is *amorphous* (unstructured), the use of the subject matter is *affective* (having to do with feelings) or *cognitive,* and the thinking approach is *convergent.*

behaviorism
A psychological theory that asserts that behaviors represent the essence of a person and that all behaviors can be explained as responses to stimuli.

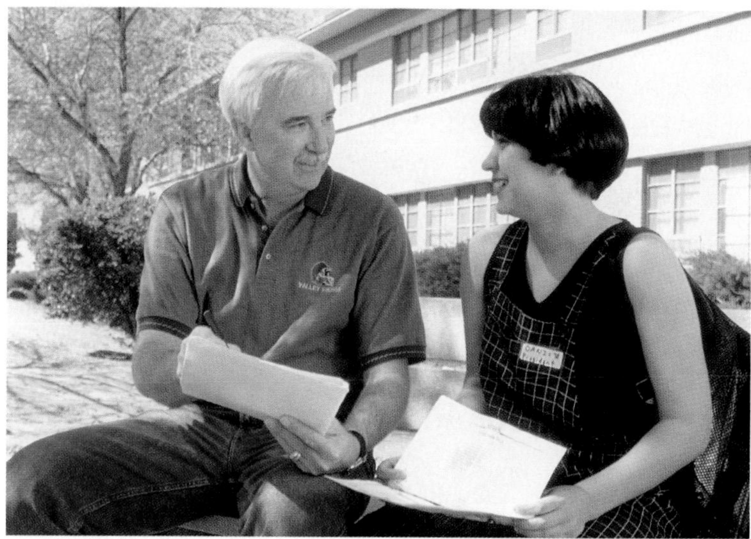

Behaviorists contend that learning takes place when approved behavior is observed and then positively reinforced.

BEHAVIORIST FOCUS OF LEARNING Behaviorism is a psychological and educational theory that holds that one's behavior is determined by environment, not heredity. This suggests that education can contribute significantly to the shaping of the individual, because the teacher can control the stimuli in a classroom and thereby influence student behavior. Behaviorists believe that the school environment must be highly organized and the curriculum based on behavioral objectives, and they hold that knowledge is best described as behaviors that are observable. They contend that empirical evidence is essential if students are to learn and that students must employ the scientific method to arrive at knowledge. The task of education is to develop learning environments that lead to desired behaviors in students.

A teacher affects eternity; he can never tell where his influence stops.
Henry Adams

REINFORCEMENT: A BEHAVIORIST PRACTICE The concept of reinforcement is critical to teacher practices in behaviorism. The behaviorist teacher endeavors to foster desired behaviors by using both positive reinforcers (things students like, such as praise, privileges, and good grades) and negative reinforcers (things students wish to avoid, such as reprimands, extra homework, and lower grades). The theory is that behavior that is not reinforced (whether positively or negatively) will eventually be "extinguished"—will cease to occur. In general, behaviorists contend that learning takes place when approved behavior is observed and then positively reinforced.

A teacher may provide nonverbal positive reinforcement (smiling, nodding approval) or negative reinforcement (frowning, shaking the head in disapproval). Similarly, nondirective statements, questions, and directive statements may be positive or negative. Both children and adults respond to the models other people (peers, adults, heroes) represent to them by imitating the model behavior. Behaviorists contend that students tend to emulate behaviors that are rewarded.

The behaviorists have supplied a wealth of empirical research that bears on the problems of attaining self-control, resisting temptation, and showing concern for others. Behaviorists do not attempt to learn about the causes of students' earlier problems. Rather, the teacher must ascertain what is happening in the classroom environment to perpetuate or extinguish students' behavior.

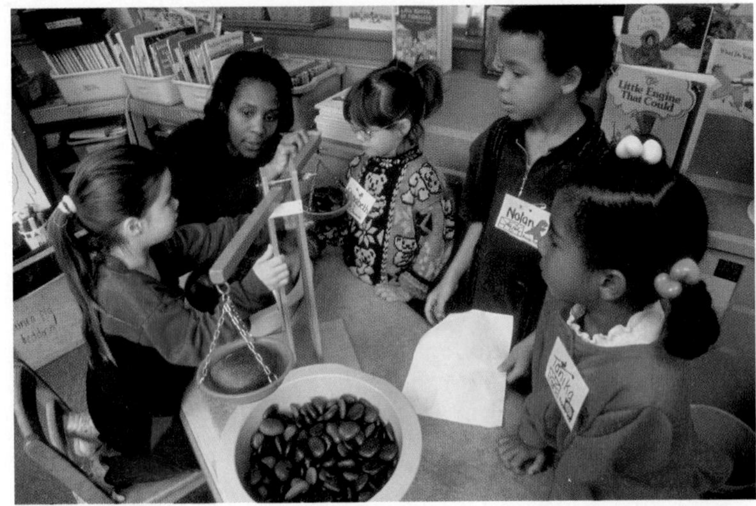

Positivism focuses learning on acquisition of facts based on careful empirical observation and measurement of the world.

POSITIVISM

The educational theory of positivism stems from what the social scientist Auguste Comte (1798–1857) described as "positive knowledge." Comte divided the thinking of humankind into three historical periods, each of which was characterized by a distinct way of thinking. The first was the theological era, in which people explained things by reference to spirits and gods. The second was the metaphysical era, in which people explained phenomena in terms of causes, essences, and inner principles. The third was the positive period, in which thinkers did not attempt to go beyond observable, measurable fact.

The positivist position rejects essences, intuition, and inner causes that cannot be measured. Empirical verification is central to all proper thinking. This theory rejects beliefs about mind, spirit, and consciousness and holds that all reality can be explained by laws of matter and motion. In sum, **positivism** limits knowledge to statements of observable fact based on sense perceptions and the investigation of objective reality. Positivism became a rallying point for a group of scholars in Vienna. Because the group consisted largely of scientists, mathematicians, and symbolic logicians, positivism became known as logical positivism.

POSITIVIST FOCUS OF LEARNING Practiced as an educational theory, positivism focuses learning on the acquisition of facts based on careful empirical observation and measurement of the world. Positivism requires schools to develop content standards that represent the best understandings of experts who have already uncovered important ideas based on their own observation and measurement. Students are encouraged both to master these expert understandings and to develop their own skills of observation, classification, and logical analysis.

positivism
A social theory that limits truth and knowledge to what is observable and measurable.

OBJECTIVE TESTING: A POSITIVIST REQUIREMENT Testing students' acquisition of content standards is a valued activity for the positivist educator. Creating objective tests that are free from bias is critical to education. Because empirical knowledge is proven by years of careful analysis, there is a set of truths that students should master and understand according to a clear set of criteria. The only way to ensure that such knowledge has been attained and understood is to test

POSITIVIST CLASS ACTIVITY

Humberto Diaz introduced the meaning of surface tension to his junior high science students. During class he then distributed eyedroppers, water, and pennies to the students. He directed the students to determine how many drops of water could fit on the surface of the penny before spilling over. Students were to collect data and develop a data table and corresponding charts. At the end of the class, Mr. Diaz asked the students to discuss their findings and draw a conclusion.

In this positivist class activity the nature of the learner is *active,* the nature of the subject matter is *structured,* the use of the subject matter is *cognitive,* and the thinking approach is *convergent.*

all students according to the same objective set of criteria. (See the Positivist Class Activity box.)

What we have to learn to do, we learn by doing.
Aristotle

NONAUTHORITARIAN EDUCATIONAL THEORIES

Progressivism, reconstructionism, humanism, and constructivism espouse a nonauthoritarian approach to subject matter, classroom organization, teaching methods, and assessment. Although each theory forms a distinct cohesive whole, all four are rooted in a nonauthoritarian principle; that is, the belief that truth and goodness belong to all persons no matter what their station. Teachers are learners and learners are teachers, and education is the process in which individuals help one another to clarify personal meaning.

Once again, we will present each nonauthoritarian theory's ideas on curriculum, teaching, and learning. In addition, for each theory we will describe a representative program along with an illustrative class activity.

PROGRESSIVISM

In the late 1800s, with the rise of democracy, the expansion of modern science and technology, and the need for people to be able to adjust to change, people in Western societies had to have a new and different approach to getting knowledge to solve problems. A U.S. philosopher, Charles S. Peirce (1839–1914), founded the philosophical system called *pragmatism.* This philosophy held that the meaning and value of ideas could be found only in the ideas' practical results. Later, William James (1842–1910) extended Peirce's theory of meaning into a theory of truth. James asserted that the satisfactory working of an idea constitutes its whole truth. Pragmatism was carried much farther by John Dewey (1859–1952), who was a widely known and influential philosopher and educator. Dewey insisted that ideas must always be tested by experiment. His emphasis on experiment carried over into his educational philosophy, which became the basis for what was usually described as progressive education. **Progressivism** is an educational theory that emphasizes that ideas should be tested by experimentation and that learning is rooted in questions developed by learners.[4]

progressivism
An educational theory that emphasizes that ideas should be tested by experimentation and that learning is rooted in questions developed by the learner.

Progressivism, the educational theory developed by philosopher John Dewey (1859–1952), emphasizes that ideas should be tested by experimentation and that learning is rooted in questions developed by the learners.

The one real object of education is to have a man in the condition of continually asking questions.

Bishop Mandell Creighton

From its establishment in the mid-1920s through the mid-1950s, progressivism was the most influential educational view in the United States. Progressivists basically oppose authoritarianism and favor human experience as a basis for knowledge. Progressivism favors the scientific method of teaching and learning, allows for the beliefs of individuals, and stresses programs of student involvement that help students learn how to think. Progressivists believe that the school should actively prepare its students for change. Progressive schools emphasize learning *how* to think rather than *what* to think. Flexibility is important in the curriculum design, and the emphasis is on *experimentation,* with no single body of content stressed more than any other. This approach encourages *divergent thinking*—moving beyond conventional ideas to come up with novel interpretations or solutions. And because life experience determines curriculum content, all types of content must be permitted. Certain subjects regarded as traditional are recognized as desirable for study as well. Progressivist educators would organize scientific method-oriented learning activities around the traditional subjects. Such a curriculum is called experience-centered or student-centered; the essentialist and perennialist curricula are considered subject-centered. Experience-centered curricula stress the *process* of learning rather than the result.

Progressivism as a contemporary teaching style emphasizes the process of education in the classroom. It is more compatible with a core of problem areas across all academic disciplines than with a subject-centered approach to problem solving. It would be naive to suggest that memorization and rote practice should be ruled out. In progressive teaching, however, they are not stressed as primary learning techniques. The assertion is that interest in an intellectual activity will generate all the practice needed for learning. (See the Progressivist Class Activity box.)

PROGRESSIVISM AND DEMOCRACY A tenet of progressivism is that the school, to become an important social institution, must take on the task of improving the U.S. way of life. To this end, progressivism is deemed a working model of democracy. Freedom is explicit in a democracy, so it must be explicit in schools. But freedom, rather than being a haphazard expression of free will, must be organized to have meaning. Organized freedom permits each member of the school society to take part in decisions, and all must share their experiences to ensure that the decisions are meaningful. Pupil–teacher planning is the key to democracy in classrooms and is the process that gives some freedom to students, as well

PROGRESSIVIST CLASS ACTIVITY

Ms. Long's second graders read "Recipe for a Hippopotamus Sandwich" from *Where the Sidewalk Ends: Poems and Drawings of Shel Silverstein* (New York: Harper & Row, 1974). Ms. Long asked each student to draw a picture of the hippopotamus sandwich. For homework she instructed the children to read the poem to someone, show the picture, and then tell about the person's reaction on the following day.[5]

In this progressivist class activity the nature of the learner is *active,* the nature of the subject matter is *structured,* the use of the subject matter is *cognitive,* and the thinking approach is *divergent.*

as teachers, in decisions about what is studied. For example, the teacher might ask students to watch a film about an issue of interest and have them list questions about the issue that were not answered by the film but that they would like to investigate. Students and the teacher can then analyze the questions and refine them for research. Such questions can become the basis for an inquiry and problem-solving unit of study. However, even if pupil–teacher planning is not highlighted as a specific activity, any progressivist lesson allows students to give some of their own input in ways that influence the direction of the lesson. In that sense, progressivist lessons always involve pupil–teacher planning. For instance, asking students to make statements about life in 1908, using copies of pages from 1908 Sears and Roebuck catalogs as their information source, allows students to focus on any items from the catalogs *they* choose, not items determined by the teacher.

Progressivism sees the learner as an experiencing, thinking, exploring individual. Its goal is to expose the learner to the subject matter of social experiences, social studies, projects, problems, and experiments that, when studied by the scientific method, will result in functional knowledge from all subjects. Progressivists regard books as tools to be used in learning rather than as sources of indisputable knowledge.

PROGRESSIVISM AND SOCIALIZATION Many people believe that the socialization aspect of progressivism—the fact that it represents the leading edge of U.S. culture and helps students learn how to manage change—is its most valuable aspect. However, progressivism is criticized for placing so much stress on the processes of education that the ends are neglected. Its severest critics contend that progressive educators have little personal commitment to anything, producing many graduates who are uncommitted and who are content to drift through life. Progressivists counter by stating that their educational view is relatively young and that therefore they expect criticism; after all, trial-and-error methods are a part of the scientific method. The advent of progressivism as a counterview to the more traditional educational views provided exciting discussions that continue among thinkers in education.

RECONSTRUCTIONISM

Reconstructionism emerged in the 1930s under the leadership of George S. Counts, Harold Rugg, and Theodore Brameld. Reconstructionism recognized that progressivism had made advances beyond essentialism in teacher–pupil relations and teaching methodology. However, progressivism fixated too heavily on the needs of the child and failed to develop long-range goals for society. Spurred by the Great Depression of the 1930s, reconstructionism called for a new social order that would fulfill basic democratic ideals. Advocates believe that people should control institutions and resources and that this could happen if there were an international democratic world government. Reconstructionism draws on both pragmatism (like progressivism) and existentialism.

reconstructionism
An educational theory that calls on schools to teach people to control institutions and to be organized according to basic democratic ideals.

CRITICAL PEDAGOGY: A RECONSTRUCTIONIST CURRICULUM An education for a reconstructed society would require that students be taught to analyze world events, explore controversial issues, and develop a vision for a new and better world. Teachers would critically examine cultural heritages, explore controversial issues, provide a vision for a new and better world, and enlist students' efforts to

Reconstructionists teach students to analyze critically world events, explore controversial issues, and develop a vision for a new and better world.

promote programs of cultural renewal. Although teachers would attempt to convince students of the validity of such democratic goals, they would employ democratic procedures in doing so. (See the Reconstructionist Class Activity box.)

A contemporary version of reconstructionism is rooted in the work of Henry Giroux, who views schools as vehicles for social change. He calls teachers to be transformative intellectuals and wants them to participate in creating a new society. Schools should practice "critical pedagogy," which unites theory and practice as it provides students with the critical thinking tools to be change agents.[6]

RECONSTRUCTIONIST CLASS ACTIVITY

Mr. Ragland asked his second graders to look at a cartoon that pictured a well-dressed man and woman in an automobile pulled by a team of two horses. The highway they were traveling along passed through rolling farmland with uncrowded meadows, trees, and clear skies in the background. He led a discussion based on the following questions:

1. What is happening in this picture?
2. Do you like what is happening in the picture? Why or why not?
3. What does it say about the way you may be living when you grow up?
4. Are you happy or unhappy about what you have described for your life as an adult?
5. How can we get people to use less gasoline now?
6. What if we could keep companies from making and selling cars that could not travel at least forty miles on one gallon of gasoline? How could we work to get a law passed to do this?

In this reconstructionist class activity the nature of the learner is *active,* the nature of the subject matter is *structured,* the use of the subject matter is *affective,* and the thinking approach is *divergent.*

RECONSTRUCTIONISM AND WORLD REFORMATION A persistent theme of reconstructionism is that public education should be the direct instrument of world reformation. Reconstructionism accepts the concept that the essence of learning is the actual experience of learning. Reconstructionism espouses a theory of social welfare designed to prepare learners to deal with great crises: war, inflation, rapid technological changes, depression. Based on the experiences of World War I, the Great Depression, and World War II, reconstructionist educators believe that the total educational effort must be seen within a social context.

As we indicated earlier, John Dewey had an immense influence on progressivism. Dewey also made major contributions to reconstructionist philosophy with his efforts to define the individual as an entity within a social context. Reconstructionists go farther in urging that individuals, as entities within a social context, engage in specific reform activity. Reconstructionist classroom teachers tend to use affective (emotion-related) emphases and moral dilemmas in directing students' attention toward social reform.

Paulo Freire (1922–1997) was a contemporary social reconstructionist who dedicated his life to freeing society from an educational system that he saw as devised by the dominant class "for the purpose of keeping the masses submerged and contained in a culture of silence."[7] Having experienced hunger and poverty firsthand in the 1930s, Freire worked among the poor to assist them in improving their lot in life. He proposed a problem-posing approach to education, to replace what he called the "banking" method—in which one privileged class knows the truth and deposits it in the appropriate amounts into the empty and limited minds of the unwashed or dispossessed. Freire advocated an education that expands every human being's ability to understand and transform the world.

HUMANISM

Humanism is an educational approach that is rooted both in the writings of Jean Jacques Rousseau and in the ideas of existentialism. Rousseau (1712–1778), the father of Romanticism, believed that the child entered the world not as a blank slate but with certain innate qualities and tendencies. In the opening sentence of *Émile,* Rousseau's famous treatise on education, he states that "God makes all things good; man meddles with them and they become evil."[8] Thus, Rousseau believed in basic goodness at birth. He also believed that humans are born free but become enslaved by institutions. Humanistic education mingles some of these ideas from Rousseau with the basic ideas of existentialism.

Humanistic educational theory is concerned with enhancing the innate goodness of the individual. It rejects a group-oriented educational system and seeks ways to enhance the individual development of the student. (See the Humanist Class Activity box.)

Humanists believe that most schools de-emphasize the individual and the relationship between the teacher and the student. Humanists claim that as educators attempt to predict behavior of students, they turn individuals into objects to be measured. According to the humanist, education should be a process of developing a free, self-actualizing person—a process that is centered on the student's feelings. Therefore, education should not start with great ideas, the world, or humankind, but with the individual self.

humanism
An educational theory that contends that humans are innately good—that they are born free but become enslaved by institutions.

HUMANISTIC CURRICULUM Because the goal of humanism is a completely autonomous person, education should be without coercion or prescription. Students

Humanists believe that education should be without coercion or prescription and that students should be active learners and make their own choices.

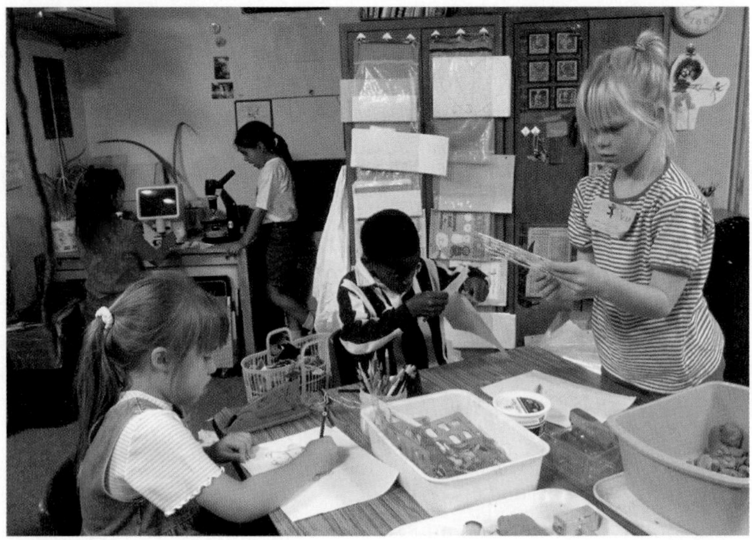

should be active and should be encouraged to make their own choices. The teacher who follows humanistic theory emphasizes instruction and assessment based on student interests, abilities, and needs. Students determine the rules that will govern classroom life, and they make choices about the books to read or exercises to complete.

Humanists honor divergent thinking so completely that they delay giving their own personal opinions and do not attempt to persuade students to particular points of view. Even though they emphasize the affective and thereby may make students feel a certain urgency about issues, it is always left to the individual student to decide when to take a stand; what kind of stand to take; whether a cause merits action; and, if so, what kind of action to engage in.

HUMANIST CLASS ACTIVITY

Ms. Fenway wanted her ninth graders to think about the effectiveness of television and radio advertising. She asked students to write down any five slogans or jingles they could remember and the products advertised. Ms. Fenway selected from their items at random and tested the class. For each slogan, class members had to identify the product advertised. The test was corrected in class by the students, who were very surprised that the grading scale was reversed. Those who had all correct answers received Fs, and those who had only one correct answer received As. When asked why she had reversed the grades, Ms. Fenway responded, "Why do you think advertising is so effective?" She asked whether students resented some companies' selling tactics. Then she told students to help her make a list of questions to ask themselves in order to avoid spending money in ways they might later regret. She also asked for specific examples of spending money for items they later wished they had not bought.[9]

In this humanist class activity the nature of the learner is *active,* the nature of the subject matter is *structured,* the use of the subject matter is *affective,* and the thinking approach is *divergent.*

HUMANISTIC SCHOOL ENVIRONMENTS Martin Buber's writings describe the heart of humanistic school environments. In *I and Thou,* Buber portrays two different ways in which individuals relate to the outside world. In the I–It relationship, one views something outside oneself in a purely objective manner, as a thing to be used and manipulated for selfish ends. In contrast, I–Thou relationships are characterized by viewing other people as sacred entities who deserve profound respect. Such relationships focus on the importance of understanding and respecting diverse, subjective, personal meanings. Buber was deeply concerned that people were treated as objects (Its) rather than as Thous, especially in business, science, government, and education.[10]

Many students today believe that educators treat them as Social Security Numbers stored in a computer. In college classes of 100 or more, it is difficult for teachers to remember students' names, let alone get to know them as individuals. Often teachers assign material, mark papers, and give grades without ever really conversing with students. When the semester ends, students leave class and are replaced by other, equally anonymous students. Buber did not believe that schools had to be this way. He contended that in a proper relationship between teacher and student, there is a mutual sensibility of feeling. There is empathy, not a subject–object relationship.

A humanistic school environment is one in which people (both teacher and student) share their thoughts, feelings, beliefs, fears, and aspirations with each other. Nel Noddings labels this *an environment of caring.* According to humanists, this kind of caring relationship should pervade the educational process at all levels as well as society at large.

In his book *Summerhill,* A. S. Neill provides a radical picture of a school environment that focuses on the development of caring, I–Thou relationships. Neill describes schools that treat teachers and students as individuals, allow students to create their own rules, make class attendance optional, and stress caring relationships over academic achievement. A number of schools in England and Canada were modeled after *Summerhill,* and some are still in existence.[11]

Inspired by humanism, many educators attempt to personalize education in less radical ways. Examples include individualizing instruction, open-access curriculum, nongraded instruction, and multiage grouping. Each of these approaches attends to the uniqueness of the learner. Block scheduling permits flexibility for students to arrange classes of their choice. Free schools, storefront schools, schools without walls, and area vocational centers provide humanistic alternatives to traditional school environments.

Educational programs that address the needs of the individual are usually more costly per pupil than traditional group-centered programs. Consequently, as taxpayer demands for accountability mount, humanistic individualized programs are often brought under unit-cost scrutiny. Nonetheless, growing numbers of educators are willing to defend increased expenditures to meet the needs of the individual learner within the instructional programs of the schools.

CONSTRUCTIVISM

constructivism
An educational theory that emphasizes hands-on, activity-based teaching and learning during which students develop their own frames of thought.

Constructivism is an educational theory that emphasizes hands-on, activity-based teaching and learning. Constructivism is closely associated with existentialism. The American Psychological Association (APA) has encouraged teachers to reconsider the manner in which they view teaching. The APA contends that students are active learners who should be given opportunities to construct their

PROFESSIONAL DILEMMA

Should I Use Homogeneous or Heterogeneous Ability Grouping?

The issue of how to group students for instruction can be very controversial. Some propose homogeneous grouping and others argue for heterogeneous grouping. Homogeneous ability grouping is a practice that seems to have merit. Permitting students who require the same level of instruction to be clustered in a single setting makes planning and resource allocation much easier. Such grouping patterns permit students to receive instruction that is tied to their specific needs, because they are with others who need the same information or skill development.

Those who oppose homogeneous ability grouping contend that labeling students and placing them in similar ability groups based on their academic skill sets up structures that often inhibit future growth and development. Both teachers and parents begin to view students according to these labels; and, once tracked by ability, students seldom break out of the initial labels assigned at an early age. These critics call for multiability or heterogeneous grouping. They believe that having students from a variety of backgrounds and ability levels work together is more in keeping with a democratic society. Furthermore, such multiability grouping permits students to help one another, fostering cooperativeness and caring among those from different backgrounds. Indeed, opponents of tracking programs have pointed to the disproportionate number of minority and low-income students who seem to make up the lower-level groups.

- List other pros and cons of homogeneous ability grouping that you can think of. List other pros and cons of heterogeneous ability grouping.
- Should one type of grouping be used in all instructional settings or circumstances, or should the types of grouping be varied according to task and context?

own frames of thought. Teaching techniques should include a variety of different learning activities during which students are free to infer and discover their own answers to important questions. Teachers need to spend time creating these learning situations rather than lecturing. Constructivist educators consider true learning to be the active framing of personal meaning (by the learner) rather than the framing of someone else's meaning (the teacher's).

Few high school students look upon the language which they speak and write as an art, not merely a tool, yet it ought to be, the noblest of all arts, looked upon with respect, even with reverence, and used always with care, courtesy, and deepest respect.

Mary Ellen Chase

Such a view of teaching and learning has profound ramifications for the school curriculum. If students are to be encouraged to answer their own questions and develop their own thinking frame, the curriculum needs to be reconceptualized. Constructivist theorists encourage the development of critical thinking and the understanding of big ideas rather than the mastery of factual information. They contend that students who have a sound understanding of important principles that were developed through their own critical thinking will be better prepared for the complex, technological world.

CONSTRUCTIVIST CURRICULUM Constructivist ideas about curriculum stand in sharp contrast to the authoritarian approaches we described earlier. Traditionally, learning has been thought of as a mimic activity, a process that involves students repeating newly presented information. Constructivism, on the other hand, focuses on the personalized way a learner internalizes, shapes, or trans-

RELEVANT RESEARCH

Developing Authentic Assessments

STUDY PURPOSE/QUESTIONS: E. E. Zehr studied more than two hundred Iowa K–12 teachers who were actively involved with innovative methods of teaching science. These teachers used an interdisciplinary approach, relating science to current technology and societal issues. Zehr found that although teachers were willing to assess students in multiple domains, they used traditional test items to determine grades—typical recall questions that focused on definitions, ideas, and skills taught directly in the classroom. Therefore, in 1995–1996, Elizabeth Hammerman and Diann Musial initiated a study focused on helping thirty teachers translate interdisciplinary teaching approaches to interdisciplinary, active performance assessments.

STUDY DESIGN: Hammerman and Musial employed a pre/post research design to determine the effectiveness of a set of in-service experiences designed to give teachers time to reflect on a new conception of science. The researchers contended that if teachers were able to observe scientists in the real world, not only their ability to teach science more authentically but also their ability to design authentic assessments would be enhanced. Pre/post tests were employed to assess changes in teachers' self-efficacy in the teaching of science along with pre/post tests of teachers' understanding of performance assessment. Finally, the researchers challenged the teachers to design performance assessments in science and evaluated these assessments according to the degree that they mirrored the characteristics of science in the real world.

STUDY FINDINGS: Hammerman and Musial reported positive results. After watching videos of real-world scientists and meeting scientists from the local community, teachers were asked to list the important dimensions and characteristics of contemporary science. They were then asked to evaluate one of their instructional science units and to change it so that the teaching materials and approaches would better reflect science in the real world. Teachers were also challenged to assess the important dimensions of science that they had noticed in the real-world scientists' behaviors and words. At the end of these activities, teachers demonstrated greater self-efficacy in teaching science; and they developed assessments that included hands-on inquiry, data analysis, conceptual understanding, and writing prompts. These assessments went far beyond traditional multiple-choice tests.

IMPLICATIONS: This study suggests that teachers need to reevaluate their own understanding of science. It suggests that teachers still focus on the acquisition of content and that this is reflected in the manner in which they assess students. If teachers reexamine the real meaning of science, social science, mathematics, and language arts, they will begin to see that these disciplines involve much more than traditional content mastery; they generally include a hands-on, inquiry approach toward attaining knowledge. This realization by teachers will ultimately translate into their assessment practices.

Source: Elizabeth Hammerman and Diann Musial, *Classroom 2061: Activity-Based Assessment in Science Integrated with Mathematics and Language Arts.* Arlington Heights, IL: IRI/Skylight Training and Publishing, 1995.

forms information. Learning occurs through the construction of new, personalized understanding that results from the emergence of new cognitive structures. Teachers and parents can invite such transformed understandings, but neither can mandate them.

Accepting this simple proposition—that students learn by shaping their own understandings about their world—makes the present structure of the school difficult. According to constructivist principles, educators should invite students to

Constructivist educators invite students to experience the world's richness and empower them to ask their own questions and seek their own answers. Problem-based learning is an example of constructivist pedagogy.

experience the world's richness and empower them to ask their own questions and seek their own answers. The constructivist teacher proposes situations that encourage students to think. Rather than leading students toward a particular answer, the constructivist teacher allows students to develop their own ideas and chart their own pathways. But schools infrequently operate in such a constructivist way. Typically, schools determine what students will learn and when they will learn it.

Schooling doesn't have to be this way, however. Schools can better reflect the constructivist point of view by allowing students to search for their own understanding. Nel Noddings writes:

> Having accepted the basic constructivist premise, there is no point in looking for foundations or using the language of absolute truth. The constructivist position is really post-epistemological and that is why it can be so powerful in inducing new methods of research and teaching. It recognizes the power of the environment to press for adaptation, the temporality of knowledge, the existence of multiple selves behaving in consonance with the rules of various subcultures.[12]

PROBLEM-BASED LEARNING: A CONSTRUCTIVIST PEDAGOGY Problem-based learning has recently emerged as a student-centered teaching and learning approach that is in keeping with constructivist tenets. Based on Dewey's concept of teaching through student-centered problems, this educational methodology centers student activities on tackling authentic contemporary problems. Problem-based learning is a radical approach in that it challenges educators to focus curriculum on student interests and concerns rather than on content coverage. (See the Constructivist Class Activity box.)

In a problem-based experience, students are presented with a "hook." The hook might be a letter from a civic group, a request from an environmental agency, or any other motivating beginning. The hook describes a contemporary dilemma and requests students to take on some real-life role to solve the problem. Problem-based learning usually requires students to spend time finding the core problem, clarifying the problem, assessing what is and is not known about

CONSTRUCTIVIST CLASS ACTIVITY

Reiko Nishioka's sophomore biology class had just completed reading Michael Crichton's novel *Jurassic Park* when a letter from movie producer Steven Spielberg arrived addressed to each student in the class. The letter requested each student's assistance in Spielberg's effort to determine what aspects of the novel were or were not scientifically accurate with regard to dinosaurs. The letter asked students to prepare a written summary and to send the summary, along with proper documentation, to Spielberg's production company. Because time was limited, Spielberg requested that the summaries be completed within three weeks. Reiko provided time for her students to think about the letter and then asked them to determine what they would do next.

In this constructivist class activity the nature of the learner is *active,* the nature of the subject matter is *unstructured,* the use of the subject matter is *authentic* to real life, and the thinking approach is *divergent.*

the problem, gathering needed data to complement what has been uncovered, and finally presenting a position statement and/or suggesting a solution. Throughout the process, teachers act as guides or coaches and give great latitude to student interest. Students learn content and skills within the problem context. Teachers spend time selecting problems that are compatible with student maturity levels and curricular needs.

GLOBAL PERSPECTIVES: Looking beyond the Boundaries

Throughout this chapter, educational theories have been presented as consistent sets of ideas linked logically together. This kind of categorization is strongly related to the types of writings that were part and parcel of the work of European thinkers in the eighteenth and nineteenth centuries. It is no surprise that current educational theories in the United States tend to display such clear sets of distinctions; in large part, immigrants to this country during those centuries came from Germany, Poland, Ireland, Scandinavia, England, France, Italy, and Switzerland. The last half of the twentieth century has expanded this European focus. Faster and better communication, the opening of once-closed societies, and increased interdependence have permitted differing thinking schemes to intermesh and at times conflict with one another.

Such clashes, although uncomfortable, help educators to break or at least readjust the limitations of categorical boundaries. The comfort of categories can cause stagnation or can even imprison. Neat sets of proven ideas provide sets of solutions, but these solutions are limited by the original thinking schemes that generated them. Calling into question these categories of thought is hard to do without the infusion of other types of thinking. The influx of Asian, African, and other types of thinking is especially helpful in breaking down the rigidity of thought boundaries, because many of the thinking schemes from these cultures do not require such rigid boundary sets. These flexible thinking schemes provide a type of cohesion different from that of strict logical distinctions.

SUMMARY

AUTHORITARIAN EDUCATIONAL THEORIES

This chapter provided an overview of eight leading educational views that are held in part or entirely by teachers in American schools. The authoritarian-based educational theories include perennialism, essentialism, behaviorism, and positivism. Each of these theories emphasizes the importance of controlling the subject matter content, thinking processes, and discipline procedures within the classroom setting. Teachers are held responsible for controlling these areas of the school environment.

NONAUTHORITARIAN EDUCATIONAL THEORIES

The nonauthoritarian educational theories include progressivism, reconstructionism, humanism, and constructivism. Each of these educational theories places less emphasis on the external control of the teacher and more emphasis on student control. Progressivism promotes individual student inquiry, whereas reconstructionism encourages critical thinking and promotes social activism. Humanism stresses student freedom, and constructivism emphasizes the importance of supporting personal meaning.

Although your ultimate teaching style might not be completely committed to perennialism, essentialism, behaviorism, positivism, progressivism, reconstructionism, humanism, or constructivism, the basic description of these views should help you to identify several preferences. An individual's preferences are compatible with, if not formulated by, her or his philosophy. The extent to which one's teaching practices fits one's philosophy, and vice versa, is related to effective teaching.

Some classroom teachers continue to be skeptical about educational theory as a basis for teaching practice. Yet new theories about educating children continue to proliferate, while older beliefs remain strong in today's schools. This chapter illustrates the relationship of current educational views to the classical philosophies but describes the educational views in terms of the learner, subject matter orientation, and authoritarian and nonauthoritarian tendencies.

DISCUSSION QUESTIONS

1. What were the characteristics and behaviors of one of your favorite teachers who was authoritarian toward students? Of a favorite teacher who was nonauthoritarian toward the students?
2. When might a teacher focus on personalized situations involving such things as death or injustice to stimulate student learning? How would such a strategy relate to the back-to-basics expectations of many U.S. schools?
3. The concept of reinforcement is very influential on the teacher practices of behaviorists. How would you use positive reinforcers and negative reinforcers while teaching your subject area?
4. Experienced teachers often advise a beginning teacher: "Be firm with the students and let them know at the beginning how you intend to teach your classes." Is this advice good or bad? Discuss the pros and cons of such a procedure.

5. Constructivism rules out some of the conventional notions about educating youth. It emphasizes students' construction of personalized understandings of the world rather than an established curriculum. What implications does constructivism have for grouping students?

JOURNAL ENTRIES

1. Schools are being challenged to develop students who can achieve in a complex business world. Interview business executives from two different companies in order to determine the importance of ethics in the operations of the businesses. Determine the extent to which the executives' ethical values were influenced by teachers. In your journal, list recommendations for teachers made by the executives. Describe a teaching approach that responds to these recommendations.
2. Describe the teaching method and classroom environment that you believe has been most effective for you as a learner. Identify the educational theory or theories that would encourage the teaching method and environment you have selected. Create a graphic that visually represents your own theory of teaching and learning.

PORTFOLIO DEVELOPMENT

1. Develop a hands-on, activity-based lesson in a subject that you enjoy. Type up the entire lesson, with teacher and student directions and activity pages. Then write an introductory rationale that describes which educational theories are supported by the way you designed the lesson. Include this lesson in your folio as an example of your ability to analyze lessons in terms of theories.
2. Select one major concept from one of the national standards documents (available at your college library). Describe what teaching methods you would use to help students attain an understanding of that particular concept. Then annotate the teaching methods, explaining their theoretical foundations. Include this in your portfolio to illustrate your ability to apply theory to practice.

SCHOOL-BASED EXPERIENCES

1. This chapter contains special boxes that give examples of classroom activities typically associated with various educational theories. As you work in the schools, take this book (or copies of the class activity features) with you and see whether you can determine which theory various teachers that you observe seem to be reflecting. Having done so, decide which educational theory you subscribe to and determine whether your own classroom activity is consistent with that typically associated with your personal educational philosophy.
2. Set up several interviews with teachers who organize their classrooms and teaching materials differently. Using probing questions, try to uncover the educational theory or theories that account for the differing teaching approaches.

WEBSITES

We recommend that you do a web search using key words focused on educational theories such as "perennialism," "essentialism," "progressivism," and "constructivism";

also use key words focused on individual educators such as "Dewey," "Neill," "Freire," "Sizer," and so on. Several helpful sites are listed below.

1. <www.x.ed.uicu.edu/EPS/Educational-Theory> *Educational Theory* is a periodical that was founded by the John Dewey Society and the Philosophy of Education Society. This website offers articles from the journal that deal with educational theory and the philosophy of education.
2. <www.webs.csu.edu/~big0ama/mpes/mpes.html> The Midwest Philosophy of Education Society site offers on-line texts of philosophy of education presentations drawn from the society's annual conferences. In addition, this site provides a list of Internet sites for over fifty professional journals in the area of philosophy and education.
3. <www.bgsu.edu/offices/phildoc/thinking.html> This site offers resources related to the teaching of philosophy to children. *Thinking: The Journal of Philosophy for Children* features transcripts of children discussing philosophical ideas, research reports, news from overseas centers, and programs devoted to philosophy for children.

NOTES

1. Lloyd Duck, *Instructor's Manual for Teaching with Charisma.* Boston: Allyn and Bacon, 1981, Item 4, 53–54.
2. Duck, Item A, 40.
3. Charles H. Wolfgang and Carl D. Glickman, *Solving Discipline Problems: Strategies for Classroom Teachers.* Boston: Allyn and Bacon, 1980, 121.
4. John Dewey, *Democracy and Education.* New York: Macmillan, 1916, 1–9.
5. Duck, Item D, 41.
6. Henry A. Giroux, "Teachers As Transformative Intellectuals," *Social Education 49* (1985): 376–379.
7. Paulo Freire, *Pedagogy of the Oppressed.* New York: Continuum Press, 1989.
8. Jean Jacques Rousseau, *Émile.* Trans. Alan Bloom. New York: Basic Books, 1979.
9. Duck, Item C, 50–51.
10. Martin Buber, *I and Thou.* Trans. Ronald G. Smith. New York: Charles Scribner, 1958.
11. A. S. Neill, *Summerhill.* New York: Hart, 1960.
12. Nel Noddings, "Constructivism in Mathematics Education," *Journal for Research in Mathematics Education 4.* Reston, VA: National Council for the Teaching of Mathematics.

BIBLIOGRAPHY

Bagley, William C. "An Essentialist's Platform for the Advancement of American Education." *Educational Administration and Supervision 24* (April 1938): 241–256.

Brameld, Theodore. *Patterns of Educational Philosophy.* New York: Holt, Rinehart & Winston, 1971.

Brasio, Richard A. "Capitalism's Emerging World Order: The Continuing Need for Theory and Brave Action by Citizen-Educators." *Educational Theory 43* (4) (Fall 1993): 467–482.

Bricker, David C. *Classroom Life As Civic Education.* New York: Teachers College Press, 1989.

Brown, Lyn Mikel. "Educating the Resistance." *The High School Journal* (February/March 1996).

Casey, M. B., and Tucker, E. C. "Problem-Centered Classrooms: Creating Lifelong Learners." *Phi Delta Kappan 76* (2) (1995): 139–143.

Castle, K. "Constructing Knowledge of Constructivism." *Journal of Early Childhood Teacher Education 18* (1) (1997): 55–67.

Duck, Lloyd. "The Creation v. Evolution Debate: What Do Social Studies Teachers Need to Know?" *Religion and Public Education 21* (1994).

Greene, Maxine. "A Constructivist Perspective on Teaching and Learning in the Arts," in Catherine Twomey Fosnot, ed., *Constructivism, Theory, Perspectives, and Practice.* New York: Teachers College Press, 1996.

Jervis, Kathe, and McDonald, Joseph. "Standards: The Philosophical Monster in the Classroom." *Phi Delta Kappan* (April 1996).

Joyce, B. R., Weil, M., and Calhoun, E. *Models of Teaching.* 6th ed. Needham Heights, MA: Allyn & Bacon, 2000.

Kohn, Afie. *Punished by Rewards: The Trouble with Gold Stars, Incentive Plans, A's, Praise, and Other Bribes.* Boston: Houghton Mifflin, 1993.

Lauderdale, William B. *Progressive Education: Lessons from Three Schools.* Phi Delta Kappa Fastback No. 166. Bloomington, IN: Phi Delta Kappa, 1981.

"The Moral Child." *U.S. News and World Report* (June 3, 1996).

Morris, Van Cleve, and Pai, Young. *Philosophy and the American School.* 2nd ed. Boston: Houghton Mifflin, 1976.

Raines, Peggy, and Shadiav, Linda. "Reflection and Teaching: The Challenge of Thinking beyond the Doing." *The Clearing House* (May/June 1995).

Sizer, Theodore R. *Horace's Compromise: The Dilemma of the American High School.* Boston: Houghton Mifflin, 1985.

Skinner, B. F. "Programmed Instruction Revisited." *Phi Delta Kappan* (October 1986): 103–110.

Stanley, William B. *Curriculum for Utopia: Social Reconstructivism and Critical Pedagogy in the Postmodern Era.* Albany, NY: State University of New York Press, 1992.

Stepien, W. S.; Gallagher, S.; and Workman, D. *Problem-Based Learning for Traditional and Interdisciplinary Classrooms.* Aurora, IL: Illinois Mathematics and Science Academy, 1992.

Strike, Kenneth A., and Soltis, Jonas F. *The Ethics of Teaching.* New York: Teachers College Press, 1985.

Wolfgang, Charles H., and Glickman, Carl D. *Solving Discipline Problems: Strategies for Classroom Teachers.* Boston: Allyn and Bacon, 1980.

CHAPTER 12

Building an Educational Philosophy

EDUCATION IN THE NEWS

Authors Add Character to Curriculum

By Stephaan Harris, *USA Today,* August 25, 1999

For years parents have heard child-care experts, clergy, and others deliver a similar message: Kids learn to live their lives by the example you set as much as by what you tell them.

Educators Theodore and Nancy Sizer argue that the same applies to the way that schools impart lessons in character education. If schools want children to have traits of good character—fairness, consideration, and empathy among them—then faculty members have to show those traits in the way they treat others.

The Sizers assert that the way a school operates teaches values in and of itself and will determine whether students develop a sense of morality. The Sizers pinpoint such common bad practices as "bluffing" in which students and teachers aren't honest with each other. They give a scenario of a teacher with 118 students and a family occupying much of her home life. She plans a discussion for the next day on a book she hasn't had time to review. Meanwhile, one of her students has homework in all classes and attempts to read just enough to get by. The Sizers use this example to illustrate how students and teachers should be direct with each other and not cut corners.

The Sizers argue that often things not related to academics play a role in behavior, which leads to how students and teachers perceive themselves and each other. For example, the authors believe that the tendencies of high school teachers to have heavy class loads, often 150 to 180 students, interferes with building character. As students shuffle from class to class, it becomes unlikely teachers will tear themselves away from busy routines to get to know students well. The anonymity and detachment afford students freedom from adult scrutiny.

The Sizers also write that a dilapidated, neglected school building has a huge impact. It can lead students to believe that they aren't worthy of adequate facilities. Meanwhile, fed up teachers concentrate on transferring to better run schools instead of focusing on how their students learn. "We all learn from the institutions in which we work and the places we live. If they're run down and shabby, we get the message that no one gives a damn," Ted says.

The Sizers use discussions as a springboard for teaching values in their 300 student charter high school, located on a former army base in Devens, Mass., serving rural and suburban students. Ted says the school forsakes most electives, with the exception of foreign language, to give more attention and class time to core subjects. Classes are also kept small, so teachers spend more time on students. He says that during one history lesson, the students discussed ethnic cleansing after watching *Schindler's List*.

(continued)

He uses that example to explain how many high school teachers give homework without using class time to encourage analysis of issues. He says students missed the opportunity to learn principles in the process.

The [Sizer's] book arrives as character education lessons are gaining steam across the USA. Ted cautions, though, that schools cannot depend on temporary programs to instill long-lasting values. He says officials should see whether their actions contradict behavior expected from students.

"Schools have to make changes because kids will see through a program," he says. Teenagers have sharp antennae for hypocrisy.

LEARNER OUTCOMES

After reading and studying this chapter, you will be able to

1. Describe the influence of classroom practices on motivation.
2. Analyze underlying differences among discipline practices.
3. List the characteristics of teachers as change agents.
4. Provide examples of teacher leadership behaviors.
5. State the components of their personal philosophy of education. ■

This chapter helps you to clarify your role as a teacher in society and identify effective classroom practices. It offers a number of big ideas or key concepts that will challenge your image of what constitutes a good teacher: Ideas such as classroom environment or climate, voice, control, and community of learners are presented to help you clarify your own approach to education. Classroom organization and discipline strategies create an environment that is authoritarian or nonauthoritarian. Which type of environment is best for today's students? How much teacher control is needed? Classroom climate is described as the interaction of voice and space. Whose voices are predominant and whose voices are muted in today's classrooms? What meanings are considered acceptable and what meanings are considered strange or aberrant? These questions are examined and shown to be important to the development of a classroom climate that is either open and authentic or directed and didactic. The possibility of developing a community of learners in a world of standards-based education is also explored in this chapter. Should teachers be change agents, should they attempt to bring about a better society through their role as teacher, or should they help to emphasize the positive aspects of society and encourage students to be law-abiding citizens? What types of leadership qualities are implicit in today's teacher profession? Should teachers share a personal vision of their own, or should they clarify the vision of the local community? What traits should teachers model, and is there an ideal set of qualities that teachers should possess? These questions strike at the very heart of what it means to be a teacher, and this chapter helps you to wrestle with them and assess your personal philosophy of education.

Extensive surveys of modern views of learning—as expressed in philosophy, psychology, and education journals and studies—reveal a seemingly endless and divergent range of views. Therefore, today's classroom teachers must identify their own beliefs about educating young people. Although labeling the classroom practice of any one teacher is not easy, we recommend that you, as a prospective teacher, carefully identify a personal set of operational principles with regard to classroom techniques. Whether your operational principles are drawn from the brief descriptions in this book or elsewhere, you should strive for consistent teaching behavior within the framework of sound principles—that is, behavior based on your personal philosophy of education. The previous two chapters introduced you to educational philosophies and modern educational theories. This chapter will help you to identify your role as a teacher in society and to clarify effective practices for your classroom.

Educational trends such as the back-to-basics movement are related to certain philosophies of education. The back-to-basics movement centers on subject matter and is clearly in the realms of essentialism and perennialism, whereas the concepts of free schools and open education are experience-based and focus on student activity as identified in progressivism and constructivism. Figure 12.1 illustrates the association of these primary educational theories with

FIGURE 12.1 AUTHORITARIAN VERSUS NONAUTHORITARIAN VIEWS OF THE CLASSROOM

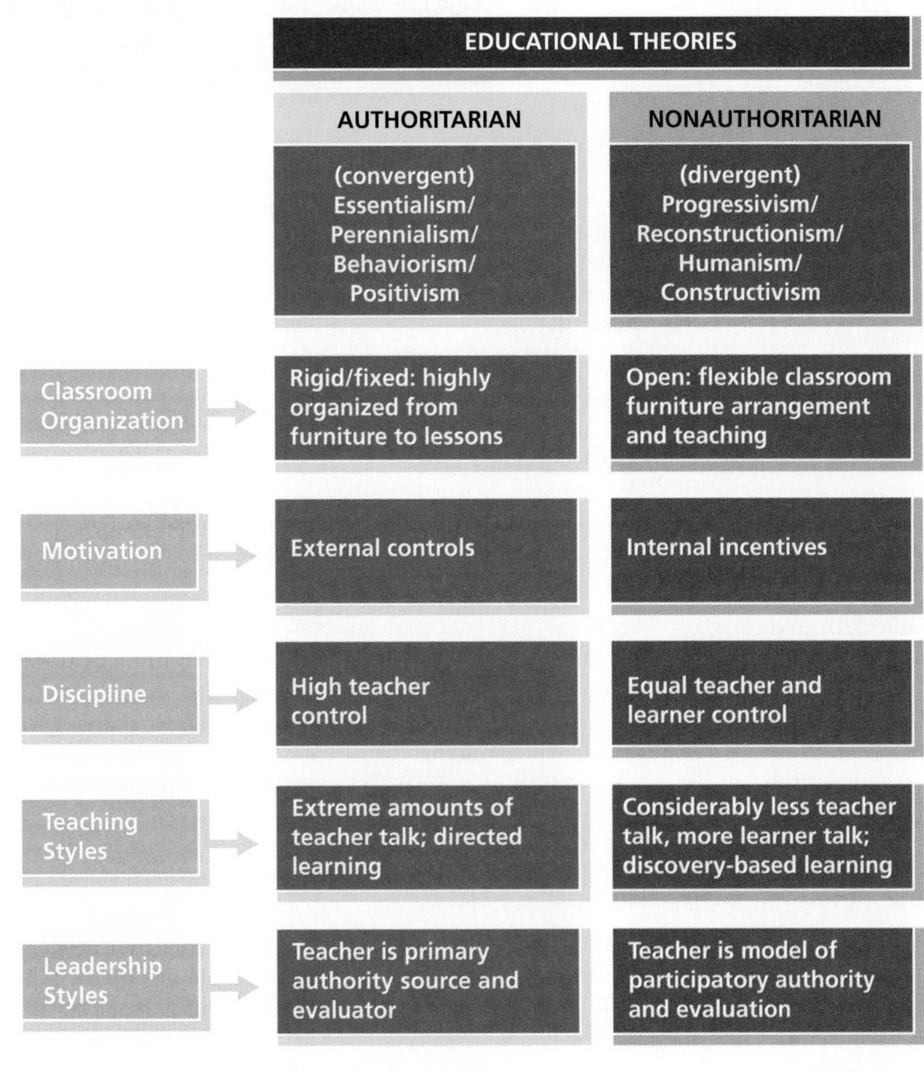

EDUCATIONAL THEORIES
AUTHORITARIAN
NONAUTHORITARIAN
(convergent) Essentialism/ Perennialism/ Behaviorism/ Positivism
(divergent) Progressivism/ Reconstructionism/ Humanism/ Constructivism
Classroom Organization
Rigid/fixed: highly organized from furniture to lessons
Open: flexible classroom furniture arrangement and teaching
Motivation
External controls
Internal incentives
Discipline
High teacher control
Equal teacher and learner control
Teaching Styles
Extreme amounts of teacher talk; directed learning
Considerably less teacher talk, more learner talk; discovery-based learning
Leadership Styles
Teacher is primary authority source and evaluator
Teacher is model of participatory authority and evaluation

A teacher's practices in the classroom reflect his or her personal philosophy.

the authoritarian view, which stresses convergent thinking, and the nonauthoritarian view, which stresses divergent thinking. Note that the terms *authoritarian* and *nonauthoritarian* are meant to denote overall philosophical stances or perspectives with regard to the student and subject matter, not to imply strict or permissive classroom management.

USING PHILOSOPHY IN THE CLASSROOM

Philosophy is not a set of written words. It is a platform on which decisions are made and life is led. A teacher's practices in the classroom reflect his or her personal philosophy. The best goal for beginning educators is to become comfortable with a variety of classroom practices that address the needs of learners. It is not a matter of selecting one methodology over another but rather of understanding these different approaches and using them responsibly. We believe that a sound preparation for teaching addresses the need to develop a workable classroom philosophy—one that incorporates the larger role of teaching in a complex society as well as the microrole of the teacher working with students in the classroom setting.

CLASSROOM ORGANIZATION

All teachers must be able to organize the classroom in such a way that it is conducive to teaching and learning. In fact many school principals are quick to assert that the easiest way to predict the success of a beginning teacher is to evaluate his or her ability to organize the classroom. A common misconception

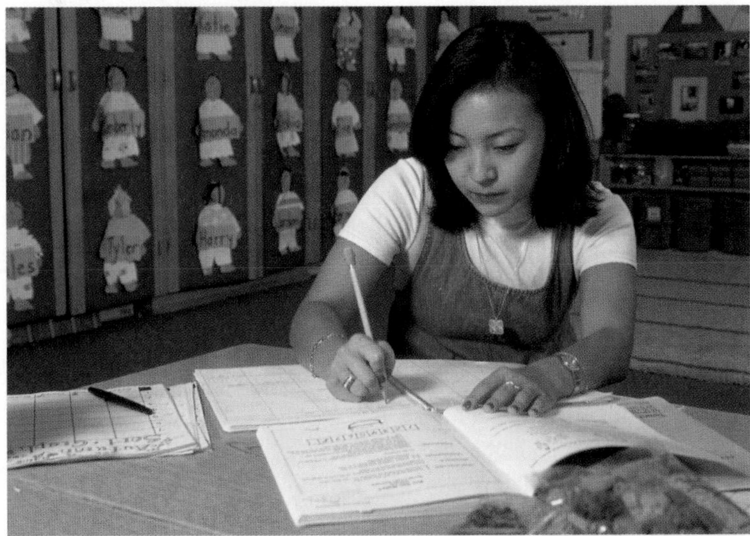

Teachers need to build sound lessons from a basic set of general objectives that correspond to the overall goals of the school district.

is that good classroom organization means maintaining a controlled atmosphere and refusing to allow any behavior that even looks ungoverned or unplanned. Actually, **classroom organization** is a multifaceted dimension of teaching that includes the content, methods, and values that infuse the classroom environment. It is a dimension of teaching that requires analysis and selection similar to that used in the identification of a preferred teaching philosophy. Figure 12.1 shows how closely one's teaching philosophy affects the different components of classroom organization.

LESSON PLANNING Careful lesson planning is mandatory if effective teaching and learning are to follow. If the learners are considered to be passive, the lesson plan may emphasize students' absorption of the factual content of the subject matter. Adherents of teaching styles that consider the learners to be active participants (nonauthoritarian) would tend to emphasize processes and skills to be mastered and view the factual content of the subject matter as important but variable.

Regardless of the expectation for the learner, active or passive, the teacher needs to plan sound lessons. Every lesson should be built from a basic set of general objectives that correspond to the overall goals of the school district. This is not to suggest that every third-grade classroom in a school district should have the same daily learning objectives for the students. Daily lesson objectives can vary from classroom to classroom depending on the particular needs of the students being served. However, if those daily teaching objectives are closely related to the overall objectives of the school district, then cross-district learning will reflect the school district's overall goals.

Lessons should be tied to some form of teaching units. These units should be planned in detail to include suggestions for teaching the lessons, types of materials to be used, and specific plans for evaluation. Initially, these are all philosophical questions for the classroom teacher. The way the teacher approaches these questions says a lot about his or her classroom philosophy.

classroom organization
A multifaceted dimension of teaching that includes the content, method, and values that infuse the classroom environment, planning, and discipline practices.

THE PHYSICAL SETTING The mere arrangement of classroom furniture and the use of classroom materials may be predicated on the teacher's perception of the

DEBATE

Is Environmental Education Scaring Our Kids to Death?

Don Hungerford has taught for twenty-eight years in the Great Falls, Montana, school district. He currently teaches biology at C. M. Russell High School and is a member of the Great Falls Education Association. During the summers, Hungerford works for the Forest Service in civil engineering.

For too long, environmental politics have been a better predictor of what's happening in science class than environmental facts.

While this unfortunate trend in the curriculum may not literally be "scaring our kids to death," it is instilling in them unfounded fears about the state of the world they will someday inherit.

Perhaps more damaging, the environmental curriculum is, in some cases, replacing the teaching of scientific methods with practical instructions on how to become an effective political lobbyist.

Some may call this a form of "teaching science across the curriculum." I call it dangerous. It guts what's most important in any science class—teaching students to bring a scientific approach to the study of everything around them.

I teach second-year biology to 130 juniors and seniors. It's been interesting and not a little disheartening to see students come into the classroom with strongly held, preconceived notions about environmental issues.

Based on the one-sided presentations they've received, many of my students see man as a villain in nature, and industry as the speed racer driving us to extinction.

In a recent discussion about a ballot issue involving mining wastes and water quality, I encouraged my students to look at both sides.

One 18-year-old, voting for the first time, said, "All mining should be stopped. That would eliminate the problem."

"What about the people who make a living at the mine?" asked another student. "One of them could be your father."

"If he worked in such a business," the first student replied, "he would deserve to lose his job." Sadly, I find this attitude quite typical.

I'm not alone in my concern about the current state of affairs. Michael Sanera and Jane Shaw have written a new, well-balanced book about environmental education.

Barbara Lewis teaches grades 4–6 at Jackson Elementary in Salt Lake City, Utah. She's also a consultant and author of several books, including The Kid's Guide to Social Action, The Kid's Guide to Service Projects, and What Do You Stand For: The Kid's Guide to Building Character (800/735-READ).

Some say that "children need to be preserved just as much as the environment." They imply that kids who study the environment will turn into worry warts who will lose their appetites, cease to enjoy watching clouds, and stop making garlands out of flowers.

Not true. Just ask the kids.

In 1994, the National Environmental Education and Training Foundation commissioned a survey of more than 2,000 students nationwide to find out their attitudes about the environment.

Less than half of those surveyed even listed the environment as something to worry about. The rest said they worry more about AIDS, guns, and kidnapping.

Reports from the Wisconsin Center for Environmental Education and Washington State University found that students aren't overwhelmed with tales of pollution and toxic waste. They think environmental problems can be solved—and that they can help.

In fact, the students who took action to protect the environment had higher feelings of self-esteem and control over their lives.

In my own class, I've seen at-risk children grow in self-esteem, self-discipline, critical thinking, and leadership skills by cleaning up hazardous waste and planting trees.

Plus, they learn to care. When several of the trees my students planted died, they went back on their own to replant new trees. As Aaron told me, "I've named my trees Dan and Little Ann, and I'm going to bring my own kids back to meet them."

So why the backlash against environmental education? Some say teachers sometimes distort facts and give unbalanced information about environmental issues. But that can be true in any area of the curriculum. It's hardly an indication that environmental education should be stopped or that it's frightening children.

Facts Not Fear examines environmental curriculum and offers well-referenced research and comprehensive textbook reviews.

The graphs and charts are easy to read and understand and are a good supplement to the text. (For an online excerpt, go to www.perc.org.)

Sanera and Shaw encourage sound decision making based on facts from many different sources—and teachers should approach environmental education in the classroom in the same way.

While there's certainly a place in school for encouraging responsible involvement in the political and policy issues of the day—including environmental ones—this should not replace our attention to the rigorous methods of science.

In a field as politically charged and yet as important as the protection of the environment, we must approach the facts scientifically. A fear-driven approach to environmental issues works as poorly in the classroom as it would in the actual management of our natural environment.

We must guard against allowing fear of environmental problems to grow unchecked in our students. Instead, we must help our students develop the hard-won confidence inspired by a command of the facts. True solutions grow from this confidence.

And such is the progress of science.

Source: "Is Environmental Education Scaring Our Kids to Death?" *NEA Today* (September 1997): 43.

Sure, there are some bad materials out there on environmental education. But instead of dumping on the topic, qualified scientists and educators should evaluate existing material—and weed out the ones that are giving environmental education a black eye.

Subject matter standards would help, too—and they're on the way. The North American Association for Environmental Education is working with the EPA to create new standards for teaching about ecological issues.

The most dangerous aspect of the backlash against environmental education is the accompanying attack on advocacy rights—rights guaranteed by the Constitution.

When second graders in Tucson wrote letters protesting development near their school, they launched a controversy that eliminated environmental education in the state. Further west in Washington State, a principal of an environmental magnet school issued a strict no-advocacy policy to keep controversy down.

We need to encourage advocacy skills—not squash them. When students advocate, they look for solutions, express their opinions, and develop critical thinking skills.

The nation needs youth with problem-solving abilities in environmental issues. If this ability is squelched until they're 18, most young people will be apathetic or intimidated by then, and the ripe fruit of citizen involvement will be largely lost.

WHAT'S YOUR OPINION?

Is environmental education scaring our kids to death?

Go to **www.ablongman.com/johnson** to cast your vote and see how NEA readers responded.

learners as passive or active. Traditionally, the classroom has tended to be arranged in rows and columns at the elementary and secondary levels of schooling. This type of classroom arrangement has often been thought to be the best for classroom control and supervision. Often, however, the elementary teacher will rearrange the classroom into a series of small circles for special groupings in reading, mathematics, and other specific subjects.

Nonauthoritarian theoretical views tend to support more open classrooms. The teacher intends learning for the students to be divergent in nature, and the student is expected to be more active in the learning process. This is not to suggest that one type of classroom arrangement is better than another or that one theory is superior to another; but we do suggest that the teacher in training examine classroom theory as it relates to the physical environment for learning.

The physical setting of the classroom tends to reflect whether the teacher follows a directive or nondirective theory of education.

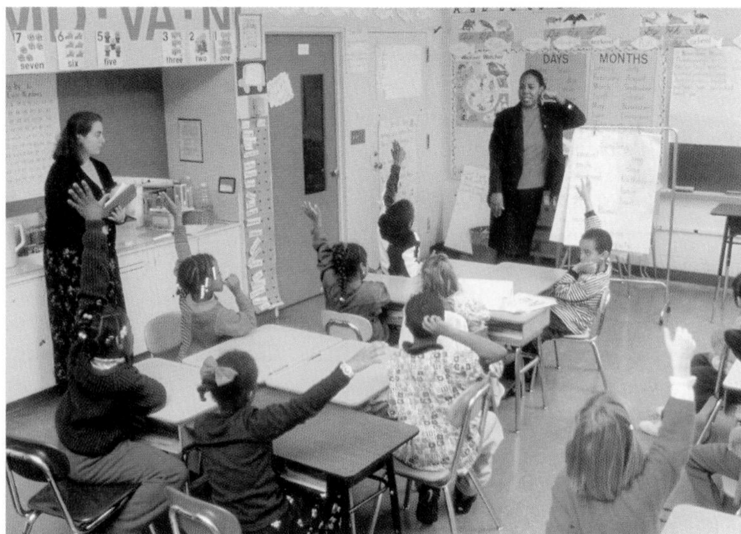

We not only want students to achieve, we want them to value the process of learning and the improvement of their skills, we want them to willingly put forth the necessary effort to develop and apply their skills and knowledge, and we want them to develop a long-term commitment to their learning.

Carole A. Ames

STUDENT ASSESSMENT AND EVALUATION In assessing student progress and assigning grades, most teachers use a variety of techniques including examinations, term papers, project reports, group discussions, performance assessments, and various other tools. If the subject matter is treated as a bundle of information, teacher-made tests will tend to seek certain facts and concepts as "right" answers, suggesting emphasis on convergent thinking. However, if the subject matter is treated as big ideas that are applicable to problem solving, and if students are expected to engage in processes and develop skills to arrive at several "right" answers, teacher-made tests will tend to allow for divergent thinking.

How you develop your classroom philosophy will also dictate the emphasis you place on a student's academic performance. You must decide whether a student is to be compared with his or her peers or with a set of expectations based on individual needs and differences. Generally, teachers who tend to be nonauthoritarian and look for divergence in learning will tend to place less emphasis on group norms. Teachers who favor an authoritarian role for the classroom with a stress on convergence in learning will be more apt to favor student evaluation strategies that are based on group norms.

MOTIVATION

The concept of **motivation** is derived from the word *motive,* which means an emotion, desire, or impulse acting as an incitement to action. This definition of motive has two parts: First, the definition implies that motivation is internal because it relates to emotions, desires, or other internal drives; second, it implies that there is an accompanying external focus on action or behavior. Organizing a learning environment so that it relates to student needs and desires (internal) and also permits active participation in the learning process (external) is important to student motivation.

motivation
Internal emotion, desire, or impulse acting as an incitement to action.

Teachers want students to be motivated to do many things: complete homework, be responsible, be lifelong learners, be on time, have fun, care about others, become independent. However, it is not always clear how one sets up a classroom environment that ultimately promotes these desired outcomes. For ex-

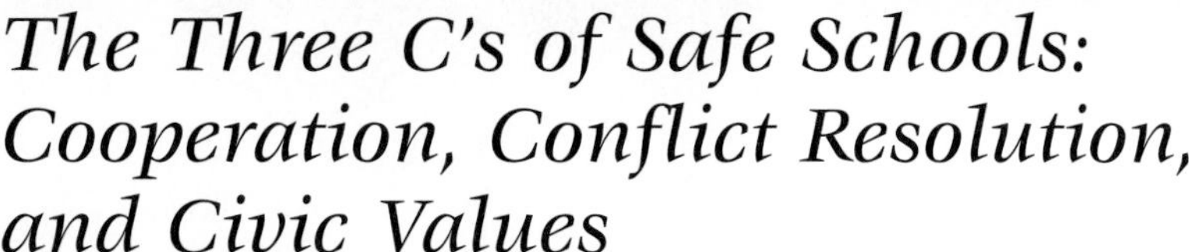

RELEVANT RESEARCH

The Three C's of Safe Schools: Cooperation, Conflict Resolution, and Civic Values

STUDY PURPOSE/QUESTIONS: Whether the school is urban, suburban, or rural, students report frequent problems involving physical aggression (being punched and kicked and seeing teachers being slapped or hit by students), property damage, and incivility (profanity, vulgarity, etc.). Highlands Elementary in Edina, Minnesota, chose to combat these problems by instituting a three-pronged program based on the three C's: cooperative community service, conflict resolution, and civic values. During the 1996–1997 academic year, David and Roger Johnson, Laurie Stevahn, and Peter Hodne conducted a study to determine the impact of the three C's program on Highlands Elementary.

STUDY DESIGN: The study focused on the program's impact on students, faculty, and community. The researchers employed three data collection methods: on-site observation of classrooms, analysis of instructional materials, and a review of journals and records related to the three C's program.

STUDY FINDINGS: The researchers reported positive findings. Almost 100 percent of students' parents were involved in establishing mutual goals, participating in a division of labor, and sharing resources. The school developed a strong sense of community in which members actively seek to resolve conflicts and solve problems together. All students learn to engage in problem-solving negotiations and how to mediate schoolmates' conflicts. Caring, respect, and responsibility values are posted in every classroom; and faculty and staff report that these values guide decision making about curriculum, instruction, and resources.

IMPLICATIONS: The positive results of this study imply that schools may need to incorporate cooperation, conflict resolution, and civic values into the regular instructional program. This notion challenges the extreme versions of realist philosophy and essentialist educational theory—for example, the argument that schools should focus solely on academic growth. To what degree schools should become involved in the direct instruction of values and attitudes is a difficult question. But research results such as these support this type of instruction.

Source: David W. Johnson, Roger T. Johnson, Laurie Stevahn, and Peter Hodne, "The Three C's of Safe Schools," *Educational Leadership 55* (2) (October 1997): 8–13.

ample, in a teacher-dominant orientation, control is primarily in the hands of the teacher. In such an authoritarian setting, motivation tends to come in the form of rules and regulations. Students are given clear directions concerning their responsibilities; and they are expected to follow these directions because the teacher is in charge. For some students this clarity of expectations and rules is comfortable. Students achieve because they must; in such a setting, the second half of motivation (external action) is achieved, but not the first (internal desire). The reason students' internal motivation may suffer is that they recognize that both the task of teaching and the responsibility for their learning belong primarily to the teacher.

In a learner-dominant setting, the responsibility for learning is primarily borne by the students. The teacher attempts to produce a climate of warmth and mutual respect. Students are encouraged to achieve specific outcomes, but ultimately, they are free to select those that most interest them. In this type of

Motivation of learners consists of two aspects: internal desire and action.

setting, the first aspect of motivation (internal desire) is achieved, in that students select the learning outcomes and processes that interest them; however, the second aspect of motivation (external action) is not as clearly achieved, in that students act according to their personal desires and these desires do not always match those of the teacher.

In every real man a child is hidden that wants to play.
Friedrich Nietzsche

As a teacher you should arrange the classroom environment so that it matches your personal philosophy. Your task here is to consider carefully the "sources of power" that best reflect your philosophy of education. Figure 12.2 illustrates as many as five different power sources that relate to five different levels of motivation.[1] Power can be coercive where the motivation is "to obey." Power can take the form of rewards where the motivation is "to get." Power can be seen as legitimate where motivation is "to respect." Power can be in the form of charisma where the motivation is "to cooperate." Finally, power can be knowl-

FIGURE 12.2 SOURCES OF POWER AND TYPES OF MOTIVATION RESPONSES

MOTIVATION RESPONSES

To obey	To get	To respect	To cooperate	To understand
Coercion	Rewards	Legitimacy	Charisma	Knowledge

SOURCES OF POWER

Authoritarian ⟷ Nonauthoritarian

edge where the motivation is "to understand." Your philosophy of teaching could include all of these sources of power. All of them may be necessary at one time or another. On the other hand, it is important to assess how you set up your classroom rules and environment and make certain that they match your personal understanding of where power should lie in the teaching and learning process.

DISCIPLINE

The attention given by the national media to disruptive behavior in the classroom has rekindled conflicting views regarding discipline. Polls of parents and teachers alike list discipline among the top issues confronting the schools. The main source of dissatisfaction for nearly two-thirds of today's teachers is their inability to manage students effectively. Teachers also are concerned about the effect disruptive behavior has on learning. The discipline dilemma—how to achieve *more* teacher control in the classroom while adhering to a more open philosophy that advocates *less* teacher control—precludes the development of a school discipline policy that would satisfy both views. Depending on the school district's expectations, the teacher may be caught between conflicting demands. Whatever the personal philosophy of the teacher, he or she must address the wishes of the district when establishing classroom management schemes. The division of views on classroom discipline has inspired numerous books to assist teachers with discipline problems, and many special courses and workshops have been developed to deal with classroom discipline strategies. But because very few beginning teachers are given extensive exposure to discipline strategies in teacher preparation programs, the vast range of alternatives makes the choice of strategies difficult for teachers who have yet to develop their own styles.

Carl Glickman and Charles Wolfgang have identified three schools of thought along a teacher–student control continuum (Figure 12.3).[2] Noninterventionists hold the view that teachers should not impose their own rules; students are inherently capable of solving their own problems. Interactionists suggest that students must learn that the solution to misbehavior is a reciprocal relation between student and teacher. Interventionists believe that teachers must set classroom standards for conduct and give little attention to input from the students.

FIGURE 12.3 TEACHER–STUDENT CONTROL CONTINUUM

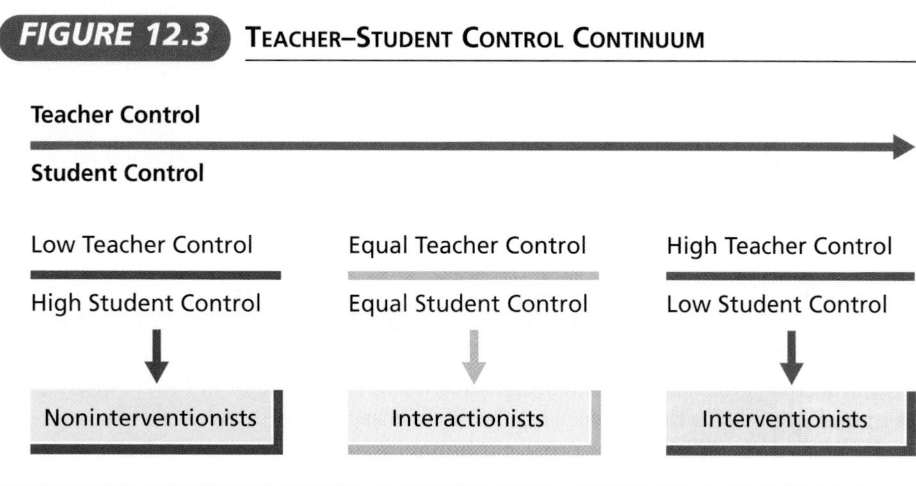

FIGURE 12.4 TEACHER BEHAVIOR CONTINUUM

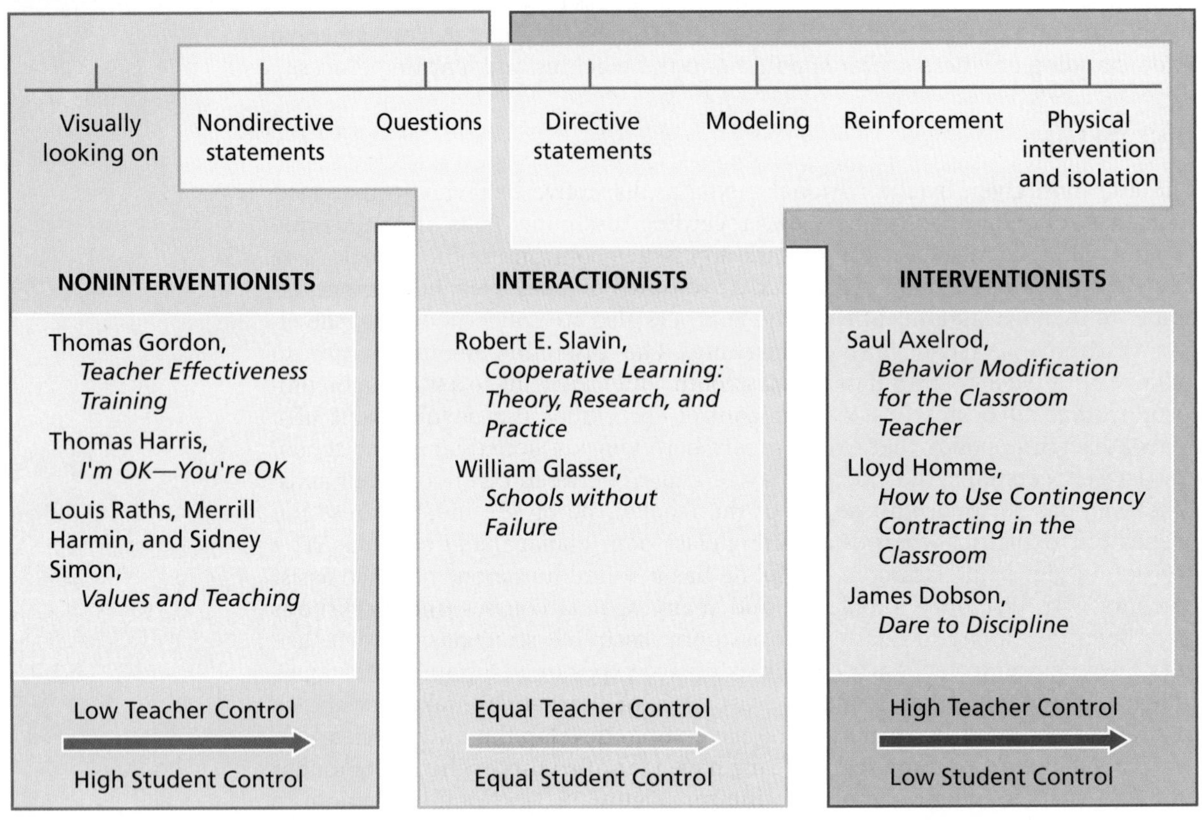

As you prepare to be a teacher, you need to identify your own beliefs regarding discipline in the classroom. The goal is to keep disruptive behavior at a minimum, thus enhancing the students' potential for learning as well as your own job satisfaction. Where maintenance of discipline is the primary concern, one might choose from among the entire range of possibilities along the Glickman–Wolfgang continuum regardless of one's own teaching style preference. Figure 12.4 illustrates how the major theories and behaviors of classroom management relate in terms of control issues along the teacher–student control continuum. It is the professional responsibility of each classroom teacher to understand how each behavior may be used to support his or her preferred teaching philosophy.

control theory
A theory of discipline that contends that people choose most of their behaviors to gain control of other people or of themselves.

CONTROL THEORY The notion of an understanding of **control theory** as a requisite for classroom discipline practices has been advanced by William Glasser. He suggests that a person's total behavior is composed of feelings, physiology, actions, and thoughts. How a person manages these aspects of behavior makes up an operational definition of control theory. Glasser asserts, "Control theory contends that we choose most of our total behaviors to try to gain control of people or ourselves."[3]

As a beginning teacher thinking about classroom discipline, you should recall that it is somewhat natural and human for students not to take responsibility for disrupting class or deviating from classroom norms. As a matter of fact, even teachers often find it difficult to take responsibility for some of their own behavior that deviates from the norm. It is usually being upset that causes inappropriate actions and/or disruption by students or teachers. If you wish to be successful in meeting discipline challenges, you need to accept the totality of control theory. Accepting this means recognizing the elements of feelings, physiology, actions, and thoughts that make up the theory and working with students, counselors, and principals to attempt to adjust classroom behavior.

The mediocre teacher tells. The good teacher explains. The superior teacher demonstrates. The great teacher inspires.
William Arthur Ward

DISCIPLINE WITH DIGNITY Richard Curwin and Allen Mendler suggest that it is not enough to simply "control" students. Educators on all levels must help students learn to become decision makers and critical thinkers about their own actions. Their approach, a program called Discipline with Dignity, provides a method to teach students to take responsibility for their own behavior. The approach offers essential skills and strategies for dealing with angry, disruptive behavior while positively affecting the lives of students. The students learn to manage themselves

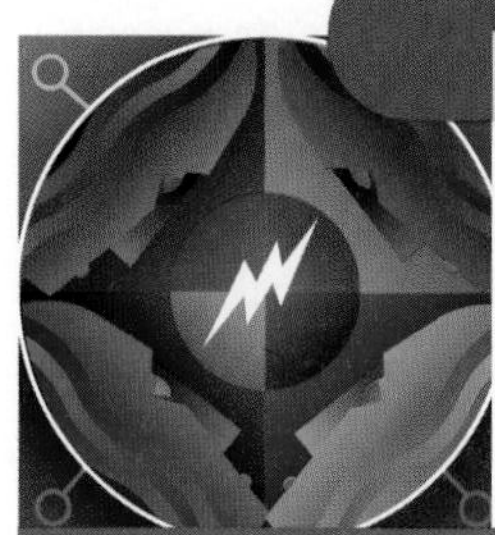

PROFESSIONAL DILEMMA

Should You Use Authentic Assessments to Grade Students?

There is a growing awareness that students should be assessed by means of a variety of methods that go beyond multiple-choice and essay examinations. Teachers are being asked to use student journals, cooperative learning projects, interviews, portfolios, and other methods for assessing what a student can and cannot do. However, debate continues concerning the appropriateness of using these more "authentic ways of assessing" for grading. The term *assess* comes from a Latin verb that means to "sit beside someone." When teachers grade a child, they are not only sitting beside the child; they are also making a value judgment. Is such a value judgment consistent with the notion of assessing strengths and weaknesses?

Some educators respond positively to the question of grading on the basis of authentic assessments. They believe that society values some qualities more than others. Hence, it is appropriate to grade a student's portfolio. Other educators endorse authentic assessments as such but contend that *grading* them limits a child's creativity; it makes the assessments less authentic, because there is an implicit standard that belongs to the teacher. Hence, teachers really are asking students to provide a certain type of portfolio; this makes the portfolio nothing more than a large essay-type test with portfolio entries as the correct answers.

Still other educators do not feel that teachers should use authentic assessments at all. They contend that such assessments are subject to the whims of local community values and that students should not be subject to such limited standards. Students should be assessed more objectively, by means of tried-and-true, universally accepted standards. Clearly defined answers to clearly stated questions, these educators believe, are more important than the open-ended approaches that authentic assessments require.

You will need to determine your own answer to this complex dilemma. Should you rely on authentic assessments? Should you merely use them as indicators of what a child knows or can do? Or should you omit them altogether?

as stress and pressures mount. The program emphasizes prevention by fostering a positive classroom environment and sensitive communication. Students are viewed as partners in the process of ensuring positive, productive classroom environments.

CONFLICT RESOLUTION Another approach to discipline, conflict resolution focuses on the process of teaching students how to recognize problems and then solve them constructively. Students are taught to be conflict managers and are trained to deal with difficulties on the playground, in the hallways, and in the classroom. The student "managers" learn specific skills that enable them, for example, to guide a discussion about a problem between two people who are fighting. There are a variety of ways to train the students, but the underlying benefit is that the students solve their own problems with minimal assistance of adults. Advocates of conflict resolution contend that permitting students to share in the structure and even the enforcement of discipline policies helps them learn to contribute to the school and to the society as a whole.

PEER MEDIATION Peer mediation programs are closely associated with conflict resolution approaches. The focus of peer mediation is not so much the resolution of conflict but rather the proactive cultivation of a climate of peace. In these programs students receive training in empathy development, social skills, and bias awareness. The overall goal of peer mediation training is to help students develop a social perspective wherein joint benefit is considered over personal gain.

RULES FOR DISCIPLINE There is no cookbook formula for classroom discipline rules and procedures. There are, however, some general guidelines that will help the beginning teacher to establish some operating rules that will be accepted and practiced by students. These guidelines are as follows:

1. Students and teachers need to learn the importance of considerate behavior and communication.
2. Students need to be treated with respect. Students who are treated with respect develop strong self-esteem.
3. Teachers need to apply critical thinking skills when creating disciplinary rules or analyzing needed disciplinary action.
4. Teachers need to examine how their actions of a social or instructional nature may have helped trigger misbehavior.

The way the teacher introduces and uses these general principles for establishing rules for discipline will set the tone for classroom interactions, creating an environment that is conducive to learning and that minimizes classroom interruptions.

Classroom discipline strongly reflects the teacher's operating classroom philosophy. As you examine the educational philosophy that wins your interest and support, search for its applications to discipline in your classroom.

classroom climate
A holistic concept that involves a set of underlying relationships and a tone or sense of being and feeling in the classroom.

CLASSROOM CLIMATE

John Goodlad, in his observation of more than one thousand classrooms, found that differences in the quality of schools have little to do with teaching practices. Differences come from what Goodlad called an overall **classroom climate.**[4]

Classroom climate is not a simple set of rules or ways of acting; it is a holistic concept, one that involves a set of underlying relationships and an underlying tone or sense of being and feeling.

Different types of classroom climate have been found to be successful. Goodlad's research showed that successful schools are ones with favorable conditions for learning, parent interest in and knowledge of the schools, and positive relationships between principals and teachers and teachers and students. S. M. Johnson identified school climate as one of the most important components contributing to effective learning and high levels of student motivation.[5] In *The Schools We Deserve,* Diane Ravitch defined a positive school climate as relaxed and tension-free. Teachers and students alike know that they are in a good school, and this sense of being special contributes to high morale.[6]

Vito Perrone set out to uncover the underlying characteristics of a classroom climate that could be linked to increased student achievement. After examining hundreds of studies, Perrone determined that a successful learning climate was one in which (1) students have time to wonder and find a direction that interests them; (2) topics have an "intriguing" quality, something common seen in a new way; (3) teachers permit—even encourage—different forms of expression and respect students' views; (4) teachers are passionate about their work; (5) students create original or personal products; (6) students do something—they participate in activities that matter; and (7) students sense that the results of their work are not predetermined.[7]

The problem with establishing a certain type of school climate is that climate is not something that can be developed artificially. Climate arises from the interactions of all the things that teachers do in the classroom. There are two concepts, however, that can help you examine climate a little more closely: voice and space.

VOICE *Voice* is a term brought to education by Henry Giroux.[8] Giroux's concept of **voice** refers to the multifaceted and interlocking set of meanings through which students and teachers actively engage in dialogue with one another. Each individual voice is shaped by its owner's particular cultural history and prior experience. Voice, then, is the means that students have at their disposal to make themselves "heard" and to define themselves as active participants in the world. Voice is an important pedagogical concept because it alerts teachers to the fact that all learning is situated historically and mediated culturally and derives part of its meaning in interaction with others.

You can teach a student a lesson for a day; but if you can teach him to learn by creating curiosity, he will continue the learning process as long as he lives.

Clay P. Bedford

Teacher voice reflects the values, ideologies, and structuring principles teachers use to understand and mediate the histories, cultures, and subjectivities of their students. For instance, teachers often use the voice of common sense to frame their classroom instruction. It is often through the mediation of teacher voice that the very nature of the schooling process is either sustained or challenged. The power of teacher voice to shape schooling is inextricably related not only to a high degree of teacher self-understanding, but also to the possibility for teachers to join together in a collective voice for social betterment. Thus, teacher voice is significant in terms of its own values as well as in relation to the ways it functions to shape and mediate school and student voices.

Teachers need to be aware of the voices of their students as well as their own voice. Too often, the teacher's voice is the only voice that counts in a classroom. Teachers must analyze the interests that different voices represent less as oppositional components and more as a medley that shapes the individual meanings of all participants in the learning process.

voice
The multifaceted interlocking set of meanings through which students and teachers actively engage with one another.

Each individual voice is shaped by its owner's particular cultural history and prior experience. Voice is the means students have to make themselves "heard" and to define themselves as participants in the world.

SPACE "Authentic public space" is a concept developed by Maxine Greene.[9] She contends that a climate consists of spaces between and among people. The manner in which this space is maintained and the type of space that is created determine the climate. Space that permits students to explore, take risks, make mistakes, and take corrective action is an authentic space—one in which people do not have to engage in pretense. Space that requires perfection, does not tolerate divergent responses, and is limited is a space that restricts freedom.

As Greene sees it, educators must attempt to climb into the consciousness of the learner and see the world as it is presented to and experienced by the learner. By trying to understand the world through learners' eyes, teachers are enabled to intuit the kinds of experiences and explanations that will help the students in their current developmental stage. Ultimately such an approach creates authentic public space in which students "may be empowered to think about what they are doing, to become mindful, to share meanings, to conceptualize, to make varied sense of their lived worlds."[10]

Another way of creating space is by developing a "community of inquiry." This phrase, coined by Charles Sanders Peirce, has come to mean an environment in which students listen to one another with respect, build on one another's ideas, challenge one another to supply reasons for their opinions, assist one another in drawing inferences, and seek to identify one another's assumptions.[11] Teachers ask questions and students answer them without either party's feeling the least twinge of embarrassment, because the process of such thinking and rethinking is natural. An ongoing dialogue ensues and a community of inquiry forms.

Ultimately, classroom climate arises from the beliefs and values held by teachers and students. Your understanding of your own views and beliefs is critical to the climate that will ultimately emerge in your classroom. Your clarity about your most deeply held views on the nature of knowledge, the nature of reality, and the importance of teacher-led versus student-led actions will ensure that your classroom climate authentically represents you.

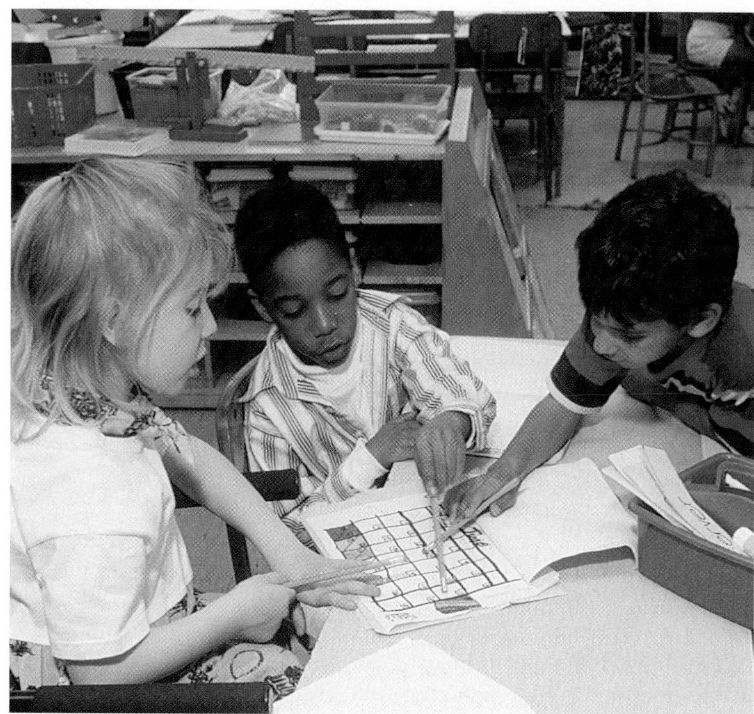

By creating an environment in which students listen to each other with respect and build on one another's ideas, a teacher helps students build a community of inquiry.

USING PHILOSOPHY BEYOND THE CLASSROOM

The way you manage your classroom and the content, teaching methods, and values you stress will be based on your personal view of the proper role of the teacher in society. A classroom philosophy must incorporate this larger societal view into other views that relate to student learning and behavior in the classroom.

Schools play a role within the larger society. This role is determined by a number of factors: the expectations of society's leaders, economic conditions, the ideologies of powerful lobbying groups, and the philosophies of teachers. It is especially important for educators to examine the role of the school in terms of the larger society—because if such reflection does not occur, schools will merely reflect the status quo or the needs and desires of a single powerful group.

change agent
A person who actively endeavors to mobilize change in a group, institution, or society.

adaptation
In the context of social change, an educational approach that favors the promotion of a stable climate in schools to enable students to obtain an unbiased picture of changes that are occurring in society and thus to adapt to those changes.

TEACHERS AS CHANGE AGENTS

An age-old question about the role of schools in society concerns the proper role of the school and the teacher in relation to change. Should teachers be **change agents,** actively working for changes in the existing scheme of things? Or should they reemphasize eternal truths and cultural positions? This question of change versus transmission of ongoing values has been articulated in a variety or ways.

CHANGE AS ADAPTATION Isaac L. Kandel (1881–1965) was a leader in the essentialist movement who advocated change as a process of **adaptation.** The adaptation approach emphasized the importance of promoting stability in schools and

Teachers make their decisions about student outcomes, discipline procedures, instructional methodologies, and assessment methods based on how they view themselves as change agents in the school.

enabling the individual to adapt to the larger environment. The school should provide students with an unbiased picture of the changes that occur in society. But schools cannot educate for a new social order, nor should teachers use the classroom to promote doctrine. Change occurs first in society. Schools follow the lead.[12]

CHANGE AS RATIONAL PROCESS John Dewey believed that schools have a part in social change. He contended that change continually occurs, often without a clearly defined direction. Schools need to assume a leadership role in this change, because educators have the time to study newer scientific and cultural forces, estimate the direction and outcome, and determine which changes may or may not be beneficial. Schools need to provide an environment in which students can learn these analytic skills and participate in helping society determine the direction that is of most worth.[13]

CHANGE AS RECONSTRUCTION The reconstructionist Theodore Brameld contended that every educational system should help diagnose the causes of world problems. Schools need to do more than assess scientific and technological change; they should be places where teachers and students alike can reconsider the very purpose of schooling and study new ways of formulating goals and organizing subject matter. Schools and society alike need to be reconstructed according to a set of human goals based on cross-cultural, universal values.[14]

dialectic
A conflict between opposing forces or ideas; in change theory this conflict is the one between individual needs and the needs of society.

CHANGE AS DIALECTIC Samuel Bowles and Herbert Gintis[15] call for a dialectical humanism through which teachers can help students explore the tension between the individual and society. They identify a conflict, or **dialectic,** between the reproductive needs of society and the self-actualizing needs of the individual. Bowles and Gintis claim that entities such as schools, churches, peer groups, and town meetings attempt to mediate this tension between individual freedom and responsibility for the community. The problem schools face is that they are often unaware that they are mediating this underlying tension, and teachers are often caught in the middle of the dilemma. Teachers are asked to respond to the unique needs of the individual while simultaneously answering to the conflicting needs of society. Bowles and Gintis call upon teachers to develop a participatory democracy in which all interested parties learn both to pursue their interests and to resolve conflicts rationally. Educators must develop a dialectical educational philosophy that seeks a new synthesis between the individual and the community.

As a teacher, you will become part of the educational system. As part of this system, you will be asked to make decisions about student outcomes, discipline procedures, instructional methodologies, and assessment methods. Your decisions regarding these educational issues will be greatly influenced by how you perceive teachers as change agents. You will make different decisions depending on whether you determine that teachers need to help schools adapt, rationally change the social order, reconstruct, or participate in a dialectic. Your task is to consider carefully each of these change paradigms and select the one that matches your personal system of beliefs.

A good teacher is first of all a good human being—someone who in personality, character, and attitude exercises a wholesome and inspiring influence on young people.

Norman Cousins

TEACHERS AS LEADERS

Teachers serve as leaders for their students. Evidence of this can be found in the testimonials that are offered by former students when they have become adults. Most students, whether they have achieved graduate degrees or have followed vocational pursuits immediately after high school, report remembering teachers who had a personal impact on their lives. These students will usually discuss the leadership and modeling behaviors of the teachers they remember.

The idea of teachers as leaders suggests that the new teacher should be aware of the need to develop a beginning repertoire of leadership qualities to which students may look for guidance during their developmental years. These leadership qualities—and the practice of them—are highly dependent on the classroom philosophy that the new teacher puts into practice. Some beginning concepts for teacher leadership are vision, modeling behaviors, and use of power.

VISION Classroom leadership behaviors begin when a teacher possesses both a vision and the intent to actualize that vision for the students. How a teacher actually puts his or her vision into practice depends wholly on the teacher's philosophical convictions. A **vision** is a mental construct that synthesizes and clarifies what you value or consider to be of highest worth. The clearer the vision or mental picture, the easier it is for a leader to make decisions or persuade or influence others. Formulating a vision requires reflection concerning what you believe about truth, beauty, justice, and equality. It is important to consider these issues and formulate a vision about how schools and classrooms should be organized and what ideas should be implemented.

Linda Sheive and Marian Schoenbeit offer five steps to help leaders put their visions into action:[16]

1. Value your vision.
2. Be reflective and plan a course of action.
3. Articulate the vision to colleagues.
4. Develop a planning stage and an action stage.
5. Have students become partners in the vision.

If teachers reflect on their vision, they can plan the course of action they need to use with their learners. Articulation provides teachers with an opportunity to share their vision with colleagues. In-service or staff development

vision
A mental construction that synthesizes and clarifies what a person values or considers to be of highest worth.

Teaching can be looked at in a wide variety of ways ranging from helping students create their own meaning to taking a deliberate stand and arguing for social change.

sessions are excellent times to articulate a classroom vision. Visions require a planning stage and an action stage if they are to become reality. Planning and action stages should involve the students who are intended to be the receivers of this vision. For example, if a teacher wishes students to be reflective in their learning environment, then the teacher needs to help the students understand the benefits of reflectiveness and become partners in the planning. The teacher may engage the students in free and open discussions of the vision and its importance to the learning environment in the classroom.

MODELING If teachers hold certain expectations of learner behaviors in the classroom, it is imperative that they model those behaviors with the students. If the classroom teacher is rigid and fixed in his or her classroom practices and creates an authoritarian atmosphere, then the students will probably respond accordingly. On the other hand, if the teacher provides a more democratic classroom, the students will respond similarly in their classroom encounters. We would caution that a laissez-faire environment will probably produce a classroom where learners have little or no direction. Teachers should consider the modeling effect on the classroom environment and exhibit behaviors consistent with their philosophy of education.

EMPOWERMENT The concept of power in the classroom should not be considered good or bad; power in itself has no value structure. The use of power, however, gives it a good, poor, or bad image. All leaders have power that is associated with their position, but the successful leader is judicious in its use. The nature of the teaching position entrusts a teacher with power both within and outside the classroom. How a teacher uses power in the classroom or in the school building is wholly determined by the classroom philosophy the teacher wants to project.

Teachers' use of power can be classified into two different styles: teacher-dominant and learner-supportive. Past and present practices in schools tend to lean heavily on the teacher-dominant style. Therefore, although many teachers in training study both categories of teaching styles, they tend to see only one major type in practice when they visit schools. We suggest that you continually study both major styles so that you can apply either one as needed on the basis of your classroom objectives for students and your classroom philosophy.

A teacher-dominant power style is based on an authoritarian construct for the classroom. Learners are not expected to be active verbally in the learning process but are generally expected to be receivers and practicing users of teacher-given information. Learning is very convergent. It is selected and given to the learner in the particular way in which the teacher wishes the student to acquire it.

A learner-supportive power style views the learner as someone who is verbally active and who seeks divergence in learning. Learner-supportive power styles encourage the active participation of the learner in exploring learning and helping to determine the extent to which he or she will engage in alternative approaches. Learning is very divergent. These power styles tend to recognize differences in learning, individual interests, and higher-order learning.

Teachers' use of power extends beyond the classroom. Teachers, by their very occupation, are empowered with both rights and responsibilities. They have a unique obligation to advocate the needs of children, to remind society of its obligations to coming generations, to look beyond material wealth, and to consider the spiritual wealth of knowledge. Teachers, by virtue of their occupation, are given certain rights to speak and be heard. The greater society looks to teachers for guidance concerning the future health of the world.

GLOBAL PERSPECTIVES: The World as Classroom

Throughout this chapter we have encouraged you to examine your beliefs and assumptions in an effort to develop a personal philosophy of education. It is also important, however, to consider the limitations that such a philosophy can impose. For example, to what degree does your philosophy incorporate the larger world of thinkers? Does your philosophy affirm or disaffirm varied thinking schemes, varied beliefs, and varied ways of arriving at answers? Relating to global neighbors is no longer a matter of respecting differences. If educators are truly to relate and work collaboratively, their thinking schemes need to intermingle as well. Yet a personal philosophy implies the development of a cohesive set of views about knowledge and the nature of the world. Teachers must balance this need to intermix against the importance of clarifying an individual point of view; this is the challenge the world classroom presents to every teacher.

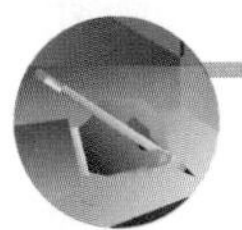

SUMMARY

USING PHILOSOPHY IN THE CLASSROOM

Although your classroom philosophy might not be completely committed to perennialism, essentialism, behaviorism, positivism, progressivism, reconstructionism, humanism, or constructivism, you should be able to apply the characteristics of classroom philosophy discussed in this chapter to help you become comfortable with your own preferences for teaching. Prospective teachers, whether or not they have had educational philosophy coursework in their preparation programs, should find this practical classroom philosophy treatment a useful way to study teaching behaviors and to identify trends and preferences related to a teaching style or philosophy. Perennialist, essentialist, behaviorist, and positivist teachers encourage students to view the subject matter only as experts in that field view the subject matter. Such teacher behaviors exemplify an authoritarian curriculum trend encouraging convergent thinking. Progressivists, reconstructionists, humanists, and constructivists encourage students to explore the subject matter as a means of determining more than one answer to the question at hand. This behavior can be viewed as a nonauthoritarian curriculum trend encouraging divergent thinking.

Remember that there are no perfect teaching styles or teaching methodologies. For this reason, we encourage an eclectic approach—an approach that draws on many different sets of ideas. As a new teacher, you need to know how to minimize the negative effects and weaknesses associated with any particular teaching style. The styles that emphasize convergent thinking, for example, tend to reward students for giving an answer that is the exact phrase the teacher wants. Teachers using such methods must be very careful with their responses, or students will not risk participating in discussion unless they are absolutely certain that they have the exact answer. The divergent types of teaching styles may, in contrast, require students to participate in interesting activities but not make them fully aware of why they are participating or what they are learning. If students are not required to justify the generalizations they make and are not made to see that they are learning many facts and skills, they may end up feeling that all answers are so relative that problem-solving processes are not worthwhile. Teachers who know enough about themselves and their teaching styles to show students how to succeed with both convergent thinking and divergent thinking are well on their way to reaching the ideal of being healthy eclectics.

USING PHILOSOPHY BEYOND THE CLASSROOM

In teaching it is the method and not the content that is the message . . . The drawing out, not the pumping in.

Ashley Montagu

The implications of Part V are straightforward. Teachers who enter classrooms not understanding or knowing much about their educational philosophies or their intended teaching styles, as well as not knowing which classroom organization strategies best serve their philosophies, cannot be successful. We hope that from the material we have presented that you will be able to begin to formulate your own classroom philosophy based on reality, knowledge, and value. Also, you should be able to see how philosophical concepts carry over into and influence the educational views that are extant in our schools. These tasks are the theoretical, rational part of developing a personal philosophy of education.

Finally, to perceive a philosophy is one thing; to teach according to the philosophy is another. In teaching, one may exhibit behavior that is compatible with an eclectic educational philosophy. As long as this eclecticism serves the pedagogical purposes of the teacher and is a basis for consistent behavior by the teacher in the classroom, learning will take place. However, if eclecticism causes the teacher to change behavior frequently and with no apparent purpose, thus distracting pupils from learning, the teacher should reexamine her or his philosophy.

DISCUSSION QUESTIONS

1. What is your vision of democracy in the classroom? To what degree should students be permitted to decide what they will study, when they will study, and how they will study? Why?
2. What characteristics or practices can you identify in a former teacher whom you would label your favorite?
3. Teachers must be able to manage the classroom in such a way that the environment created is conducive to teaching and learning. How do you plan to organize your classroom to set up such an environment?
4. Identify some significant beginning classroom practices that a new teacher should try to develop if he or she wants to be judged a successful teacher.

JOURNAL ENTRIES

1. Think about the different student seating arrangements in various classrooms. Sketch each seating arrangement and describe the types of student interaction and the types of learning that each seating arrangement supports. Draw the seating arrangement that you prefer, and describe the types of student interaction and learning that it encourages.
2. Choose and write down a metaphor for each of the educational theories that you have studied; for example, "constructivism is a shared voyage into new and uncharted territory." Then design a metaphor for your personal educational theory and clarify how it compares to the other educational theory metaphors.

PORTFOLIO DEVELOPMENT

1. Prepare a synopsis of your overall philosophical perspective. Include your views about classroom organization, motivation, discipline, and climate. Try to develop a graphic that clearly shows how all these components connect and are consistent to your overall perspective.
2. Develop a statement that depicts how you intend to function as a teacher/leader within the larger society. Describe one position you support related to a political action.

SCHOOL-BASED EXPERIENCES

1. While you are visiting different classrooms as part of your practicum experiences, catalog the various classroom planning and disciplinary activities that you observe. Following these observations and your recording of practices in real classrooms, classify the various styles that you have observed and identify the classroom philosophy that you feel the teachers were employing. Seek out opportunities to discuss these findings with each teacher you observe.
2. Select a teacher who has a classroom organization approach that matches your own. Set up an interview with the teacher and use probing questions to clarify the underlying reasons why the teacher set up the classroom as he or she did.

WEBSITES

We recommend that you do a web search using key words focused on educational issues such as "discipline," "classroom management," "motivation," and so forth. Three particularly informative sites are listed below.

1. <www.criticalthinking.org/university/default.html> The Foundation for Critical Thinking is dedicated to providing educators, students, and the general public with access to information about critical thinking, theory and practice, concepts, techniques for learning and teaching, and classroom exercises.
2. <www.theteachersguide.com/classmanagement.htm> TheTeachersGuide.Com is a web-based company that provides information, professional articles, resources, books, virtual field trips, and educational software related to classroom management, educational psychology, special education, and the like.
3. <www.aft.org/lessons/two/elements.html> The American Federation of Teachers offers an overview of classroom management with details about discipline codes and practices. The site also discusses the importance of parental involvement.

NOTES

1. R. Schmuck and P. A. Schmuck, *Group Processes in the Classrooms.* Dubuque, IA: Wm. C. Brown, 1983.
2. Carl D. Glickman and Charles H. Wolfgang, "Conflict in the Classroom: An Eclectic Model of Teacher–Child Interaction," *Elementary School Guidance and Counseling 13* (December 1978): 82–87.
3. William Glasser, *Control Theory in the Classroom.* New York: Harper & Row, 1986, 47.
4. John Goodlad, *A Place Called School: Prospects for the Future.* New York: McGraw-Hill, 1984.
5. S. M. Johnson, *Teachers at Work: Achieving Success in Our Schools.* New York: Basic Books, 1990, xvii–xix.
6. Diane Ravitch, *The Schools We Deserve: Reflections on the Educational Crisis of Our Times.* New York: Basic Books, 1985, 303.
7. Vito Perrone, ed., *Expanded Student Assessment for Supervision and Curriculum Development.* Alexandria, VA: Association for Supervision and Curriculum Development, 1991.
8. Henry Giroux, *Ideology, Culture and the Process of Schooling.* Philadelphia: Temple University Press, 1981.
9. Maxine Greene, *The Dialectic of Freedom.* New York: Teachers College Press, 1988.
10. Maxine Greene, "Curriculum and Consciousness," in William Pinar, ed., *Curriculum Theorizing: The Reconceptualists.* Berkeley, CA: McCutchan Publishing, 1975, 12.
11. C. S. Pierre, "The Fixation of Belief," in Justus Buchler, ed., *Philosophical Writings of Peirce.* New York: Dover, 1955, 5–22.
12. Isaac L. Kandel, *Conflicting Theories of Education.* New York: Macmillan, 1938, 77–88.
13. John Dewey, "Education and Social Change," *The School Frontier III* (1937): 235–238.
14. Theodore Brameld, "Imperatives for a Reconstructed Philosophy of Education," *School and Society 87* (1959): 18–20.
15. Samuel Bowles and Herbert Gintis, *Schooling in Capitalistic America.* New York: Basic Books, 1975, 18–20.
16. Linda Tinelli Sheive and Marian Beauchamp Schoenbeit, "Vision and the Worklife of Educational Leaders," in *Leadership: Examining the Elusive.* Alexandria, VA: Association for Supervision and Curriculum Development, 1987, 99.

BIBLIOGRAPHY

Bloom, Benjamin. "The Search for Methods of Group Instruction." *Educational Leadership 42* (9) (1984): 5.

Campbell, D. M.; Cignetti, P. B.; Melenyzer, B. J.; Nettles, D. H.; and Wyman, R. M., Jr. *How to Develop a Professional Portfolio: A Manual for Teachers.* Boston: Allyn and Bacon, 1997.

Canter, L., and Canter, M. *Succeeding with Difficult Students.* Santa Monica, CA: Canter and Associates, 1993.

Curwin, Richard L., and Mendler, Allen N. *Discipline with Dignity.* Alexandria, VA: Association for Supervision and Curriculum Development, 1988.

Finders, M., and Lewis, C. "Why Some Parents Don't Come to School." *Educational Leadership 51* (8) (1994): 50–54.

Gerzon, M. "Teaching Democracy by Doing It!" *Educational Leadership 54* (5) (1997): 6–11.

Glasser, William. *Control Theory in the Classroom.* New York: Harper & Row, 1986.

Howe, Kenneth R. "A Conceptual Basis for Ethics in Teacher Education." *Journal of Teacher Education* (May–June 1986): 5–11.

Kohn, A. "Only for My Kid: How Privileged Parents Undermine School Reform." *Phi Delta Kappan* (1998): 569–577.

Ladson-Billings, G. *The Dreamkeepers: Successful Teachers of African American Children.* San Francisco: Jossey-Bass, 1994.

Lambert, L. "Toward a theory of constructivist leadership," In L. Lambert, D. Walker, D. P. Zimmerman, J. E. Cooper, M. D. Lambert, M. E. Gardner, and P. J. Slack, eds., *The Constructivist Leader.* New York: Teachers College Press, 1995, 28–51.

Martin, Jane Roland. "A Philosophy of Education for the Year 2000." *Phi Delta Kappan* (January 1995): 21–27.

Schmuck, R., and Schmuck, P. A. *Group Processes in the Classroom.* Dubuque, IA: Wm. C. Brown, 1983.

Slavin, Robert E. "When Does Cooperative Learning Increase Student Achievement?" *Psychological Bulletin 94* (1983): 429–445.

——. *Cooperative Learning: Theory, Research and Practice.* Englewood Cliffs, NJ: Prentice-Hall, 1990.

——. (1996). *Education for All.* Exton, PA: Swets & Zeitlinger, 1996.

Stike, Kenneth A. "Professional Ethics and the Education of Professionals." *Educational Horizons* (Fall 1995).

Wallis, Stephen. "Discipline and Civility Must Be Restored to America's Public Schools." *USA Today Magazine* (November 1995): 18–19.

Young, Dan. "Understanding Ethical Dilemmas in Education." *Educational Horizons* (Fall 1995): 31–34.

Zepeda, Sally J., and Ponticell, Judith A. "Classroom Climate and First-Year Teachers." *Kappa Delta Pi Record* (Spring 1996): 43–47.

Zirkel, Perry A., and Gluckman, Ivan B. "Is Corporal Punishment Child Abuse?" *Principal* (January 1996): 12–16.

PART 6

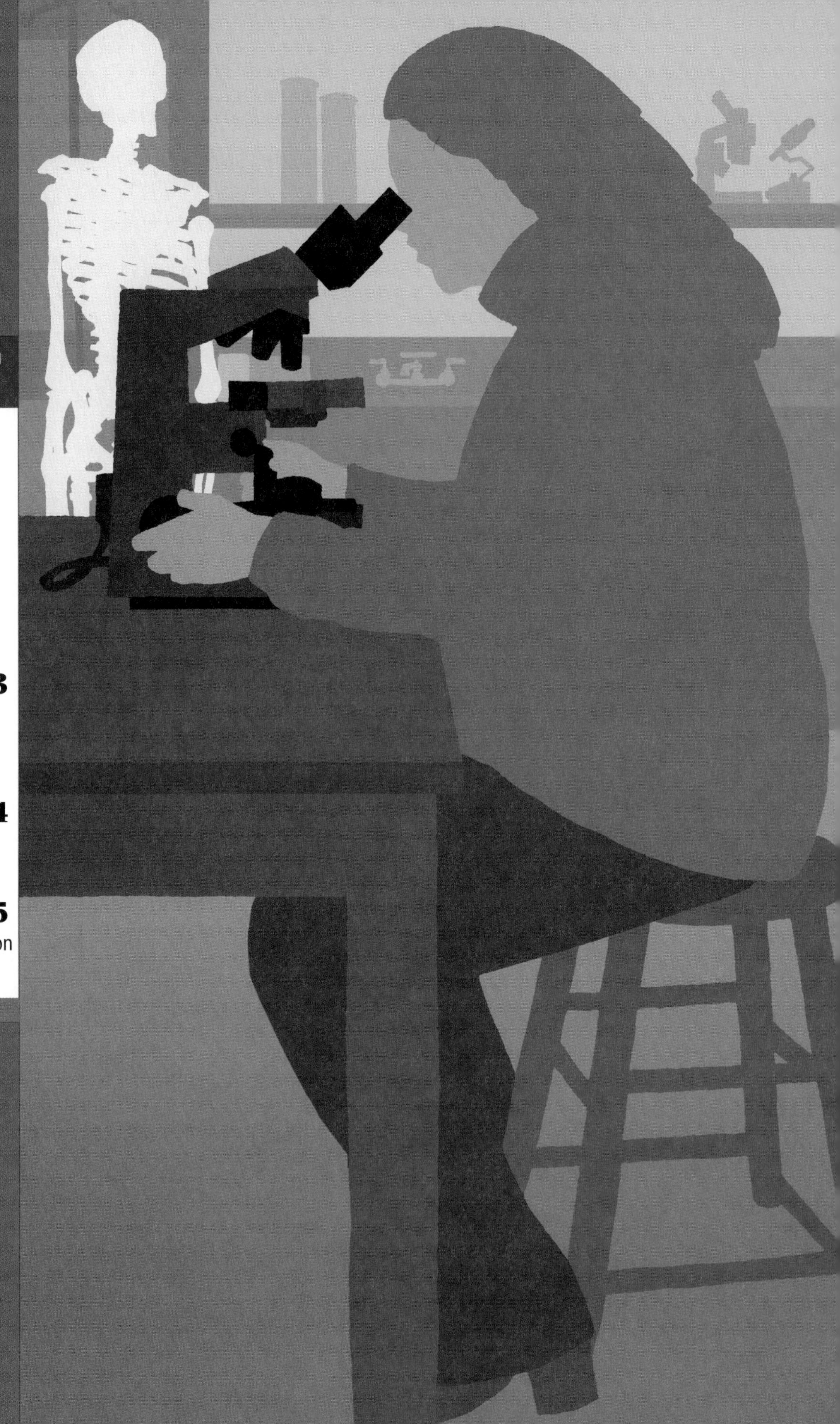

CHAPTER 13
Designing Programs for Learners

CHAPTER 14
Providing Instruction

CHAPTER 15
Standards-Based Education and Assessment

Student Programs, Teacher Practices, and Standards-Based Education and Assessment

Viewing Education through Program Development Lenses

Part Six uses the zoom lens metaphor to examine the big ideas associated with programs, practices, and assessment. Chapter 13 looks at the whole issue of reforming and transforming the educational program for learners.

The big ideas of Chapter 14 relate to instructional organizations and practices that the school provides for the learners.

The concluding chapter of the text, Chapter 15, examines the big ideas associated with the use of standards-based directions for schools and their accompanying educational practices and the myriad of school and classroom assessment practices in the schools.

The following questions will help you to focus your learning as you read:

1. What should be the purpose of general education in the curriculum?
2. How do program alternatives, effective schools, charter schools, and home-based schooling, for example, put pressure on the regular school and its program?
3. How does the beginning teacher assess the magnitude of change on the school program?
4. Why is it important for a teacher to be able to use a variety of teaching techniques?
5. In what way can the Internet be a valuable learning tool for the student?
6. How are program standards related to accountability?
7. How does a teacher use authentic measurement to assess standards?
8. How does a teacher identify and set core competencies to meet standards expectations?

CHAPTER

13

Designing Programs for Learners

EDUCATION IN THE NEWS

Charter Schools Working Together

By Kelly Pearce, *The Arizona Republic,* February 25, 2000

Arizona's charter schools are becoming more savvy, grouping to tackle regional issues. "It's quite a phenomenon because these are competitors vying for the same students," said Vicki Jo Anderson, assistant director of the American Heritage Academy in Clarksdale and a member of the Verde Valley Charter School Association. "It would be like Ford, Chevrolet and Chrysler sitting down and having monthly meetings. We're encouraging it so they can strengthen each other."

The new groups are a sign that the industry is maturing, said Mary Gifford of the Goldwater Institute who is vice-president of the state Board for Charter Schools. Arizona has 360 charter schools with 45,000 students, accounting for about 21 percent of all schools in the country. The Arizona Charter School Association held its fifth annual conference last weekend. The regional groups are an offshoot of the larger organization.

The first started a year ago in Tucson. Others followed in the Verde Valley, where talk has centered around whether schools could share busing, and in Prescott, where schools are producing a brochure to promote themselves to new residents.

Robert Maranto, a charter school researcher based in Virginia, said that the schools discovered it makes sense to unite, especially when it comes to legislation that attempts to hamstring their freedom.

"They realize they could be reregulated," he said.

LEARNER OUTCOMES

After reading and studying this chapter, you will be able to:

1. Compare and contrast the major types of curriculum designs.
2. Identify the different profiles of the types of students the schools must provide for.
3. Explain the differences between junior high schools and middle schools.
4. Analyze the differences between charter schools and regular public schools
5. Discuss the pros and cons of school vouchers, magnet schools, Comer schools, and home-based education.
6. Present either a case for or a case against the restructuring of public schools. ■

Curriculum is the substance of schooling—the primary reason why people attend school.

M. Francis Klein

he school program, formal and informal, is what curriculum is all about. As indicated in the Part VI opener, this chapter looks at curriculum and **change,** the myriad of curriculum **alternatives,** and **continuity** in the curriculum offerings of the school. The curriculum of the school—the printed document that describes the learning experiences for students—serves as the means to attain objectives of the school. Unfortunately, most teachers, when designing a curriculum for learners, begin by introducing their favored or elected textbooks, pet lessons, or units and activities that have served them well over time. This might be labeled the forward approach, first described by Ralph Tyler over fifty years ago.[1] What we propose here, however, is to design a curriculum using a backward approach. By "backward" we mean the following: Rather than beginning with a textbook and used lesson plans, the teacher should begin with the target goals or expected outcomes. Using these ends helps the teacher to identify expected learner performances, the learning experiences needed to produce those performances, and finally the necessary content materials and learning activities. This backward approach provides for an additional curriculum experience: the identification of assessment plans. Assessment procedures should be part of the backward planning process, not held in abeyance until something has been taught. The elements of assessment are derived from the same beginning objectives as the elements of teaching, and they help the teacher design the instruction.

Keep in mind when designing curriculum that although national and content area standards have much in common, each state and region of the nation has particular differences and goals that have to be addressed in the planning process. In this chapter we examine the elements associated with curriculum design—the *what* of curriculum for program development. In particular, we work with the big ideas of change, alternatives, and continuity. Chapter 14 discusses the delivery of this curriculum.

TYPES OF CURRICULUM DESIGN

School systems use a variety of designs to develop curriculum. These types can be illustrated by a continuum that ranges from subject-centered to learner-centered curricula. Figure 13.1 shows that a subject-centered curriculum has separate courses for each of the academic disciplines and the learner-centered curriculum combines disciplines, fusing them around topics and activities. Between the two ends of the continuum are variations of structure that grow out of the school's educational philosophy.

change
Providing permanent alteration of programs.

alternative
Giving variety in programs.

continuity
Having programs relate to one another from grades one to twelve.

As is shown on the continuum, the degree of emphasis on subject and learner in the curriculum leads to different instructional designs: separate courses, fused courses, core courses, and activity courses.

SEPARATE COURSES DESIGN

The separate courses curriculum is the oldest design and continues to be used by most K–12 schools. In this design, all subjects for instruction are separated

FIGURE 13.1 A CURRICULUM CONTINUUM

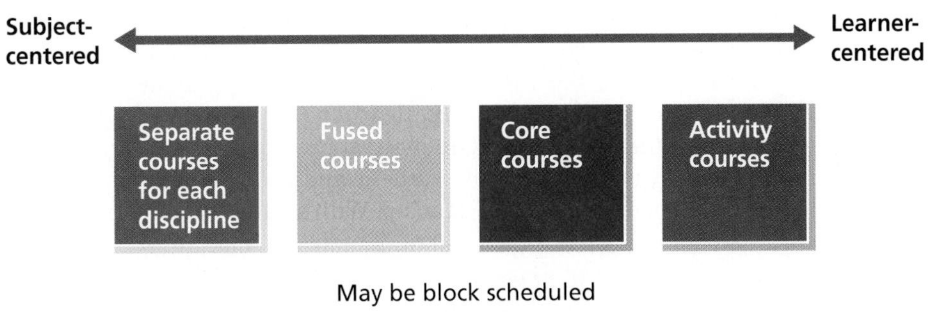

Subject-centered ⟵			⟶ Learner-centered
Separate courses for each discipline	Fused courses	Core courses	Activity courses

May be block scheduled

and generally are offered in isolation from each other. Some attention is given to new ideas and knowledge, but it is seldom ample because the intent of this design is to teach students to set classifications and recognizable arrangements of facts and ideas. An important criterion in selecting knowledge and concepts for study is to choose those that have proved beneficial for solving problems and answering questions. These facts and concepts are the ones that have lasted over time. This curriculum uses the forward approach.

The separate-courses design calls for extensive explanation and oral discourse. It puts the learner into an extensive receiving role and gives no opportunities to explore, experience, and experiment with alternatives. This design uses a formal step-by-step study of ideas and facts, and teachers rely heavily on extensive verbal activities—lectures, some discussion, question and answer—and writing exercises with preplanned teacher topics. Divergent learning needs of the student receive little attention.

FUSED COURSES DESIGN

This design takes the beginning steps to decrease the number of separate courses offered to the learner, fusing them into broader discipline courses that present relationships in wholes to the student rather than in bits and pieces. In place of separate classes in reading, writing, spelling, grammar, speech, and literature, for example, the fused design combines those areas into subjects called English or language arts. The various disciplines of the social sciences, history, economics, and geography are fused into an offering called social studies. Many separate areas of the sciences, including biology, chemistry, and physics, are fused into courses labeled general science.

Despite the fused courses design, most of the teaching practices remain the same as in the single subject design. These offerings are highly verbal and dominated by teacher discourse. Lecture, some discussion, question and answers, and a priori written exercises are commonplace. Although this design does offer greater alternatives by giving teachers and students more latitude within the fused subject area, actual practice suggests that teachers use little latitude in implementing this design. The fused curriculum design is used most often in elementary schools with some modest attempts to use it in the secondary school.

CORE COURSES DESIGN

The core course emphasis permits considerable change and alternatives in program design. It also begins to use the backward approach to design and provides increased attention to divergent thinking and learning for the student. The core curriculum moves beyond the fused curriculum by giving greater attention to the social and psychological needs of the learner (see Table 13.1). It also emphasizes **intrinsic** rather than **extrinsic** motivation. Intrinsic motivation is that which is generated from within by the student and extrinsic motivation is that which is directed to the learner by the teacher. With society becoming more complex and with shrinking geographical barriers between and among people, core curriculum designers attempt to use the learners' multiple talents, skills, and interests to help them learn about this complex world. To balance a growing emphasis on science and technology, the core curriculum design offers greater attention to social values and social vision. The complexity of society comes into greater play with this design.

The core curriculum may have different degrees of organization and may cross broader subject matter lines, but it also places greater stress on the need to integrate subject matter than does the fused design. Sometimes, curriculum theorists refer to core organization as formal or informal.[2] Formal core courses usually have contentlike names such as "An Examination of Scarcity during the Civil War," while informal core courses drop content-type designations and have names such as Core I or Core II. Emphasis in all core designs is on social values, the culture, and its moral content. Students learn problem-solving methods and study facts, descriptive principles, socioeconomic conditions, moral rules of conduct and behavior, and caring for one another.[3] Students acquire not only a body of knowledge, but also personal learning strategies for using that knowledge.

ACTIVITY COURSES DESIGN

At the extreme end of the curriculum continuum is the *activity curriculum.* In its purest form, this curriculum treats the child as the sole center of learning. Because education, like life, is ever changing, the activity curriculum expects to change continually. Students' needs and interests are assessed, and the curriculum is built on that assessment. The psychology of this approach is based on the emotional involvement of the learner: If a child develops an interest in something and becomes emotionally involved with it, learning is enhanced.

The activity curriculum encompasses all subject matter. Completely flexible, the activity curriculum for the early learner may center on topics such as play, pets, toys, boats, letter carriers, or police officers. The emphasis is on observation, play, stories, and handiwork. This curriculum has several characteristics that make it distinctive. First, the interests and purposes of children determine the educational program. Second, common learning (general education) comes about as a result of individual interests. Third, this curriculum is not planned in advance, although guidelines are established to help students choose alternatives intelligently as they progress through the program. Students and teachers plan activities cooperatively, and what they plan and pursue may or may not have any deliberate social direction. In the pursuit of planned goals, problem solving becomes the principal teaching method. Little or no need for extracurricular activities develops, because the regular program accommodates all interests (see Table 13.1).

intrinsic
That which is motivated from within.

extrinsic
Motivation that the student accepts from without.

TABLE 13.1 Contrasts between Subject-Centered and Learner-Centered Curriculum Structures

Subject-Centered Curriculum	Learner-Centered Curriculum
Focus on subjects within the academic disciplines	Focus on learners and their diagnosed needs
Emphasis on subject matter to be learned	Emphasis on promoting all-around growth of learners
Subject matter selected and organized before it is taught	Subject matter selected and organized cooperatively by learners and teachers during the learning period
Learning controlled by the teacher or someone representing authority external to the learning situation	Learning controlled and directed cooperatively by participants in the learning situation (pupils, teachers, parents, supervisors, principals, and others)
Emphasis on facts, information, knowledge for its own sake or for possible future use	Emphasis on learning things to improve living and to solve day-to-day problems
Emphasis on specific habits and skills as separate aspects of learning	Emphasis on habits and skills as integral parts of larger experiences
Emphasis on teachers' improving methods of conveying specific subject matter	Emphasis on students' understanding and improving through the process of learning
Emphasis on uniformity of exposure to learning and uniformity of learning results	Emphasis on variability in exposure to learning and in results expected
Education conforming to set patterns	Education aiding each child to build a socially creative individuality
Education considered schooling	Education considered a continuous, intelligent process of growth

STUDENTS SERVED BY THE CURRICULUM

Teachers working in curriculum design must recognize at least five broad categories of students who attend the school. The number and kind of each category will vary from school district to school district, but every district has some mix of these categories of students. Although the categories as described below are distinctly different, a given student might fall into more than one category. Additionally, culturally different students come in all categories.

TERMINAL STUDENTS

students at risk Students who generally are expected to drop out without intervention.

Terminal students, also called **students at risk,** are those that are going to drop out along the way. Currently, the national dropout rate hovers at 6 percent, with

Technological demands of the society require competent vocational training for students.

minority groups having considerably higher rates. As the numbers of minority students grow in the schools and curriculum change fails to occur, the dropout numbers in the future are likely to grow considerably.

COLLEGE-BOUND STUDENTS

College-bound students are preparing for some form of post–high school education. Nationally, approximately 50 percent of high school graduates begin study beyond high school. These students may attend two-year institutions such as community colleges for associate degrees or four-year institutions for baccalaureate degrees.

VOCATIONAL–TECHNICAL STUDENTS

Vocational–technical students are preparing for entrance into the workforce after high school or post–high school vocational schooling. Although the number of students who fall into this category varies according to the identification criteria used, they are in need of a program different from that for college-bound students. A shortage of qualified applicants is greatest in the technical fields, a fact that has implications for high school programs.

DESTINATION UNKNOWN

Destination unknown students have varying degrees of learning ability but have not "found themselves" yet. They drift through school as **late bloomers** and then may fall into any of the other categories. Those who eventually choose to pursue post–high school programs usually find themselves in need of learning what they missed while in high school.

late bloomers
Students who are late in deciding what they want to do for their life career.

NONTRADITIONAL STUDENTS

Nontraditional students have a large variety of different needs. They may be students with special needs or talents who enjoy a certain measure of federal protection under P.L. 94-142 and its various amendments as discussed in Chapter 6. They need to be provided with the least restrictive learning environments through inclusion programs, mainstream programs, or pull-out programs. Other nontraditional students are English language students whose first language is not English. In some urban and suburban areas there may be as many as twenty-five different native languages and dialects as children's primary or only language.

Currently, the vast majority of curriculum design and attention are given to the college-bound students. Because the numbers of minority students and students with special needs will continue to increase, and if the dropout rate is to be reduced in the future, then curriculum development should proceed with a desire to provide programs for all of the various students to be served.

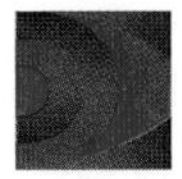

PURPOSES OF CURRICULUM

Every school program, with whatever curriculum design the school adopts, offers a **collage** of learning experiences from the beginning of elementary school to the end of high school. These experiences are variously called *course offerings, plans of study, intended school outcomes,* or *school programs of study.* Whatever title the school uses, however, every curriculum has three major purposes to accomplish: general education, exploratory education, and education for career. The emphasis that each of these purposes receives, regardless of school organization and design, is about the same from school district to school district across the nation. To a large part, this is determined by the state and national standards set for the schools. However, the manner in which these purposes are fulfilled for the learner may vary considerably. This variance is accounted for in the differences in the design components of the curriculum. In all instances, though, the Carnegie unit requirement, a traditional standard for all secondary schools, mandates time and intensity requirements for the course offerings. One Carnegie unit is defined as two hundred minutes of instruction per week for thirty-six weeks. Then set credit requirements become basic minimums for high school graduation.

No nation can remain free which does not recognize the importance of education. Our public schools are the backbone of American life and character.

Samuel M. Lindsay

GENERAL EDUCATION

The general education part of the curriculum addresses the common learning requirements for all learners. These are the basics in the school program and include learning experiences for citizenship participation, good mental health, and development in reading, composition, speaking, listening, computing, the humanities and arts, music, and the social and natural sciences. General education stresses learning the skills of knowledge application and inquiry. The other elements of the curriculum—exploratory education and education for career (see Figure 13.2)—also stress learning these skills but in their particular applications to specific course offerings.

In the past, and to a large extent in the present, most of the school program has been devoted to general education. In particular, the elementary school program is primarily general education. Although some school systems have enriched their elementary programs with the introduction of foreign language

collage
A collection of items that form a type of picture.

FIGURE 13.2 EDUCATIONAL EMPHASIS IN THE N–12 PROGRAM

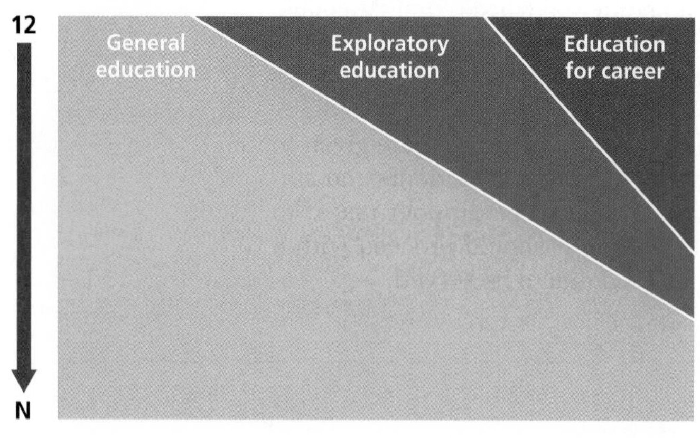

offerings, such as Foreign Language in the Elementary School, every student gets the same exposure to the same basic curriculum. Differences are found in the intensity of the program for individual students, which is usually provided through grouping practices with young children and through career goal preparation for secondary learners.

Early childhood education (ECE) programs that provide general education for the pre-elementary school student may be labeled traditional in nature. They provide the basics of readiness activities to prepare the young learner to enter the elementary school. Unfortunately, many of these programs develop only academic readiness programs for the first grade. Other ECE programs take a developmental approach to readiness, use an activity-type of program, and assist the learner in developing those social skills that will be needed for successful entry into the formal structured elementary school.

At the secondary school level, grades seven to twelve, identification of different student abilities has led to different intensities in programs. For example, all twelfth graders take English, but some take English for the college bound while others may take general English or vocational English. The same is true of the other discipline offerings in the secondary school. How these offerings have been presented has led to many students being uninterested in acquiring or unable to acquire those basic skills and therefore dropping out or **tuning out.** Society's need for people with special skills helped to reduce the major emphasis on general education during the past thirty years, with added emphasis on exploratory and career education. As is typical in education in the United States, the pendulum has swung again during the turn to the twenty-first century, and state and national standards stress the importance of general education. The public now calls for increased attention to the general education component of the curriculum, including greater accountability in school performance in the basics of reading, writing, mathematics, and science.

The societal demands for general education increase as more content is added to this component, such as career and life skills, foreign languages, computer literacy, chemical and sex education, and vocational education. There is little doubt that these are important parts of a general education offering, but adding them leads to tremendous compression of the curriculum, notably in the elementary school, where many of these "new" basics are being introduced. The school day and the school year have not increased in length, and the traditional basics appear to be suffering. Students in the United States on the whole have been soundly criticized for their weaknesses in reading, writing, and computing. In recent years, however, these areas have received restored attention, and national assessments suggest that there have been positive gains for U.S. students. Because of the expanded common learning component for younger students, educators must reassess the general education program and redefine the whole concept of common learnings and the basics.

tuning out
The decision, because of a lack of interest and/or ability, not to pay any attention to the school program the student is in.

Music and appreciation of it are a significant part of the education of young children.

EXPLORATORY EDUCATION

The junior high school, middle school, or intermediate school is a school organization that is unique to the United States. Whereas the elementary and secondary school organizations have been borrowed from European programs, these middle schools provide exploratory education for a particular group of young learners. These schools continue providing general education but also introduce students to a variety of specialized subjects on a limited basis. This variety is of an introductory and exploratory nature and is intended to help students in making educational and career decisions that they will pursue in the senior high school and beyond.

JUNIOR HIGH SCHOOL Providing for exploratory education is the unique function of the junior high school. It is considered a secondary school and is subject to Carnegie standards for course offerings. Five cogent reasons for having the junior high school are as follows:

- The junior high school provides a transitional period, easing students' transfer from the elementary school to the high school. These students, usually in grades six, seven, and eight, or seven, eight, and nine, are early adolescents, and their special physical, emotional, and social needs can be addressed in addition to exploratory learning.
- The junior high school allows students to explore interest, aptitudes, and abilities, thus aiding them in vocational and educational planning.
- The junior high school introduces students to an elaborate program of guidance and counseling that continues through the senior high school.
- The variety of offerings in the junior high school helps to lower the dropout rate. The special interests and abilities of youth are given added attention.
- As a school in the middle, between elementary and senior high school, the junior high school provides greater articulation in programs between elementary and secondary education.

MIDDLE SCHOOL *Middle school* is a newer label for schools with goals of the original junior high school. The new label and renewed emphasis came about

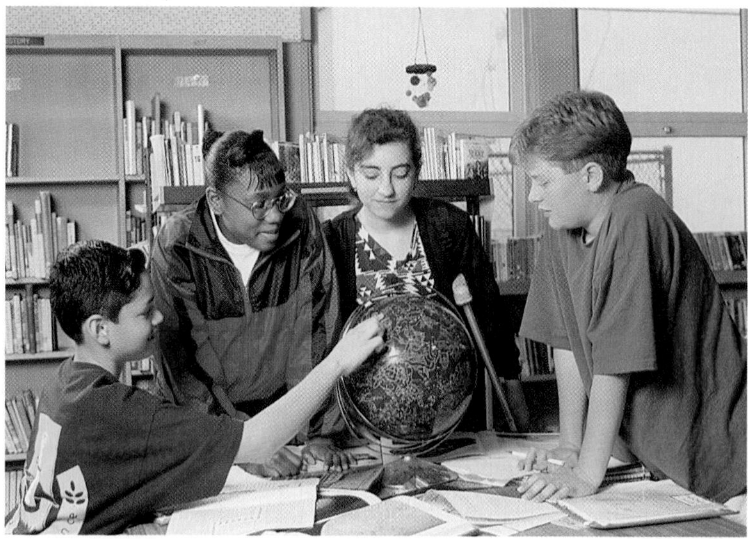

Middle school learners learn well in group learning activities.

because the original intent of the junior high school has seldom, if ever, been achieved. In fact, most junior high schools in the United States are "senior high schools in short pants." The philosophy of the middle school is basically the same, but it usually does not house the ninth grade. It may be one of the combinations of grades five through eight, six through eight, or seven through eight. This grade arrangement first became popular in the 1960s: today, there are over 15,000 such schools nationally.[4]

Somewhat different from the junior high school, the middle school stresses the use of interdisciplinary teaching teams, greater attention to advisory programs, and increased exploratory exposure to unified arts programs.

EDUCATION FOR CAREER

The senior high school assumes the special task of uniting the foundations of general education and the introductions to exploratory education to produce education for career; it offers a balanced education that helps prepare a student to function successfully in the world. For many students the senior high school provides terminal formal education. Others will move on to some form of postsecondary education. Most of the high school course requirements, an expanded provision for general education, are called *constants* of the high school program. In most states these constants are four units in English, four units in social science, three units in mathematics, and three units in science. It is expected that the science units will have accompanying laboratory experiences. Elective courses, called *variables,* give the student an opportunity to pursue in depth a particular avenue of learning that may have begun in an exploratory nature in the junior high/middle school.

To address the growing criticism of secondary education, during the 1990s, state departments of education increased the required general credits for all students in the high school. The requirements are too new for us to have seen any positive effect on students' overall preparation. They have, however, cut back on the number of electives that are available to students. Thus, the high school is somewhat responsible for students' delay in making career decisions because

Many colleges and universities still require the SAT as a prerequisite for admission.

they haven't had opportunities to develop those experiences in depth. This is particularly true of the non-college-bound student.

One way to meet the special needs of the non-college-bound student is to provide a vocational–technical program. This may be provided at the home high school or in a separate facility that the student attends on a half-day basis or to which the student rotates on a semester or shorter basis. Within some of the larger school districts of the country, the vocational school is a complete four-year experience where the student gets his or her general education as well as the vocational career education. Whatever program is provided, the school district has the added responsibility to attend to the student's special social and emotional needs.

Replacing the typical "vo-tech" programs described above are the new emerging **tech-prep** programs. With these programs there is no separate vocational school. The student remains in the regular high school and is prepared to enter the work field of his or her choice during the last two years of the high school program. This requires close working arrangements with local business and industry as they become part of the school district's effort to provide vocational training. What businesses require before taking on these learners in a type of apprentice program is that the school be able to provide them with students who can read and write well, have mathematical skills through algebra or above, and have appropriate science preparation equivalent to technical biology or physics.

tech-prep
A vocational education program in which business and industry provide working programs during the school day as part of the school program.

Many students get into the college prep program and have no intention of going on to a four-year college program. Unless they are honors students, they become frustrated, but they don't wish to be in the **general program** because that program has social stigmas for the learner. The **school-to-work** program has proposed that the secondary school offer four kinds of curricula for the secondary student. In addition to the honors and nonhonors college prep programs, the school offers a prebaccalaureate/tech-prep to prepare students for a two-year postsecondary school and a regular program that prepares them for work-based formal training such as the tech-prep programs.[5] The first two years of such programs would be the same for all four strands of this effort.

general program
The school curriculum that meets minimum state requirements and usually provides for potential dropouts and/or late bloomers.

school-to-work program
A program provided by a business as an alternative program.

ALTERNATIVE CURRICULUM PROGRAMS

Power does not always welcome a challenge. There have always been and will always be entrenched systems, institutions and structures that resist change, that punish dissent and innovation. Whenever there is a challenge to the patriarchal status quo, the old dogs in positions of power start howling, trying vainly to hold onto their comfortable living.

Sister Monica Weiss

A wide range of alternative school programs is available. Many could be labeled innovative, but they may simply serve as different choices for students, teachers, and parents. Some of these are extensions of the regular program beyond the twelfth grade or before the first grade. Most if not all of these alternatives could be termed *school reform.* Evaluate the appropriateness and applicability of these alternatives, and think creatively as you prepare yourself for the schools of this new century.

CHARTER SCHOOLS

In 1989 Minnesota was one of the first states to pass legislation allowing parents to choose which type of public school their children will attend. Since that time, twenty-five states, the District of Columbia, and Puerto Rico have passed charter school legislation. Many other states have charter school legislation pending. The charter school movement affords the following:

- Choice among public schools for families and their children
- Entrepreneurial opportunities for educators and parents to create the kinds of schools and programs they believe make the most sense
- Explicit responsibility for improved achievement, as demonstrated by standardized tests and other measures
- Carefully designed competition in public education

Charter schools receive **waivers** that exempt them from many of the state restrictions and rules that shape traditional schools, but they are held accountable for achieving positive educational results. Financed by local school boards and/or state agencies, the charter school can design school curricula for the needs and interests of specific students.

There is no set definition of charter schools. Guidelines vary by state as to how they are governed, what waivers they have, how many there can be, and other requirements. Currently, more than 1,000,000 students attend nearly 1,000 charter schools in sixteen states and the District of Columbia. Using financial incentives, President Bill Clinton encouraged the creation of 3,000 charter schools for the nation.[6] Arizona leads the nation with 360 schools currently in operation,

Teacher team meetings are a regular part of the teacher's agenda when discussing school alternatives.

waivers
Special regulations of state departments of education that allow schools to deviate from the regular state requirements.

DEBATE

Are Charter Schools Eroding Support for Public Schools?

Linda Vitiellio is in her fifth year as president of the Somerville Teachers Association in Massachusetts. The twenty-year Association activist has taught at Somerville's Carr, Forster, and Winter Hill Schools in grades six, four, and three.

Yes, charter schools erode support for public education. Our experience in the Commonwealth of Massachusetts—especially in my home town of Somerville—is that charter schools siphon off much needed financial support, skim the most able students, and are totally unaccountable to the communities they serve.

Charter schools in my state have been labled "successful" though they are still in their infancy. That notion of success is based on a number of myths.

Myth 1: Charter schools foster innovation and non-charter schools do not.

Reality: Public schools have long offered innovative programs not yet available in many charter schools. Among these programs: ESL/bilingual education, special needs programs, HIV/AIDS education, dropout prevention programs, career education, conflict resolution, and much more.

The Massachusetts charter school law, its supporters say, will improve all schools, because charter schools will share their programs with non-charter public schools.

But the Somerville charter school, run by the for-profit company, SABIS International, uses a copyrighted curriculum that SABIS refuses to share with the public schools unless it is purchased from SABIS. Haven't the taxpayers already paid for it?

Myth 2: Charter schools provide much needed competition.

Reality: In Massachusetts, charter schools receive funds based on the average cost per student, rather than the per-pupil cost specific to the grade level and program of the student.

Special, bilingual, and vocational education programs are factored in the average, along with the less expensive

Linda Page is a lead teacher at the CIVA Charter High School in Colorado Springs, Colorado. A twenty-year public school teacher, Page was a member of the Colorado Springs Education Association charter school development team.

Blaming charter schools for the erosion of support for public education is like blaming yesterday's rain for the carving of the Grand Canyon. It has taken a number of years for public confidence in our public schools to be where it is today. Charter schools, in their relatively short history, can hardly be blamed for the erosion. But they can reasonably be viewed as one response to already eroded support for public education.

As a public school teacher for over 20 years, I believe in public education. My involvement in our NEA local affiliate's charter school effort came about because I wanted to take an active part in improving public schools.

The cry for reform in public education has been growing for a number of years. Whether the outcry is deserved or not is another debate. But if not charter schools, then something else would have come along to respond to public dissatisfaction.

Charter schools, at their best, provide a response to criticism and, in an era of choice, a viable alternative to existing schools.

Charter schools don't take away from public schools. Rather, they are a forum that strengthens our reform efforts. I admit that not all charter schools are performing this function well, but I believe that we professional educators should take the lead in applauding and encouraging this kind of reform movement.

What do we have to fear about an effort that, even at its worst, should challenge us to examine ourselves and what we are doing to improve education?

Our public teachers as a whole are doing an outstanding job. It's too bad that years of criticism have driven some of us to a defensive posture and discouraged leadership and risk-taking.

YES NO

regular education costs. As a result, the student "average" is quite high.

The bottom line: A regular education third grade charter school student in Somerville costs the taxpayer $2,000 more than the third grade student enrolled in the Somerville public schools.

Myth 3: Charter schools fill a need, are accountable, and provide parents with a choice.

Reality: The Massachusetts law allows no local approval of Commonwealth Charter Schools. The decision on whether to grant a charter and where the school will be located is made entirely by the State Board of Education.

The law only requires notice and a public hearing, which doesn't even have to take place in the community where the charter school will be located.

In Somerville, the mayor, Board of Aldermen, School Committee, Parent Teachers Association, and the Somerville Teachers Association all went on record opposed to the granting of a for-profit charter school.

Despite this community sentiment, the charter was granted, though fewer than 20 parents applied for the charter.

The only thing "public" about the Massachusetts Commonwealth charter schools is that they use public money.

In my opinion, charter schools are not just eroding support for public schools, they are destroying them.

Source: "Are Charter Schools Eroding Support for Public Schools?," *NEA Today* (November 1999): 11.

The only way that charter schools can erode public school support is if we as public educators foster the notion that the two kinds of schools cannot exist together. Then students and parents will have to choose one over the other for the wrong reasons.

In my district, the public and charter schools are supporting each other. The public school actually refers students to the charter school if that school seems to be a better match, and vice versa. We now see each other as partners.

We may be doing things differently, but, together, we believe we can provide the best possible education for all students. We know enough about each other to be able to speak honestly about each other's programs—without feeling threatened.

Public education is the backbone of our American society, and I certainly do not want to jeopardize its future.

But if we deny or turn away from the need for systemwide reform—by continuing to do what we've always done—we would be doing just what we want to avoid. We would be jeopardizing the future of our public schools.

Closing our classroom doors—and hoping that the rest of the world will leave us alone—amounts to burying our heads in a sand dune that will indeed erode.

WHAT'S YOUR OPINION?

Are charter schools eroding support for public schools?

Go to **www.ablongman.com/johnson** to cast your vote and see how NEA readers responded.

and this accounts for 21 percent of all such schools in the nation.[7] Because of major questions associated with financial soundness, the charter schools of Arizona are experiencing stricter state controls on their programs. However, these schools have a unique opportunity to develop and implement innovative curriculum strategies. Charter school programs differ greatly across the country. Some are highly organized with technology; others assume a type of magnet school specialty approach; and others almost mirror the school districts where they are chartered. However, whatever these unique programs offer, the achievement performances of the students are held to a national standard that the local school district was not meeting.

EFFECTIVE SCHOOLS

The numerous national school studies that have focused on the characteristics of excellence in education have spawned effective schools research studies; and these studies in turn have identified the characteristics and practices that hallmark an effective school. The researchers have examined data from school districts that show high student achievement and are marked by certain characteristics that contribute to this achievement.

PROGRAM CHARACTERISTICS The program characteristics that have been shown to be typical of an effective school are as follows:

- The instructional program is goal oriented. Students know exactly what is expected of them as they pursue learning.
- There is constant and consistent assessment and monitoring of student progress. There is immediate feedback on student performance.
- Instruction is appropriate to the learner. Individual differences receive close attention.
- The program gives emphasis to basic skills, including both academic and life skills.
- There is continuity of instruction across the grades. The staff works together to provide common types of learning experiences in all parts of the curriculum.
- There is effective grouping for instruction. Where grouping practices are used, they are flexible and correspond to the task at hand and the individual students' differences by task.

ENVIRONMENT CHARACTERISTICS The environment characteristics of an effective school are as follows:

- There is democratic administrative leadership. Fairness in leadership and fairness in decision making create a healthy environment that promotes sound emotional health among teachers and learners.
- There is an orderly, safe environment. The social and academic environment feels secure; both learners and teachers are free from fear for their safety.
- There is clear, firm, and consistent discipline. Learners know what is expected of them and respect those expectations.
- There is a cooperative, familylike atmosphere. Students are encouraged to become part of an interactive family.
- There are few classroom interruptions. School announcements, visitors, and the like do not disturb the learning environment.
- There is parental involvement; parents are encouraged and expected to be partners in their children's learning.
- The school exhibits positive community relations. The school invites community members to participate in the regular program and uses community resources.
- There are adequate facilities and learning materials. School district budgets provide teachers and learners with the types of materials and amount of equipment needed for each school's objectives.
- The school plant is well kept. Plant facilities are attractive and kept at a high degree of maintenance.

SCHOOL VOUCHERS

School **vouchers** have loomed on the horizon for almost three decades, but not until the 1990s did states begin to provide public funds for this type of private education. The administrative and financial implications of the use of vouchers for parents are discussed in Chapter 6. With the rapid growth of the charter schools during the last decade of the past century, the voucher movement has never gained significant acceptance in the legislatures of the nation. Because about four-fifths of all private schools have religious ties, the states have generally been reluctant to provide public money to religious schools through vouchers.

However, in 1999, Florida passed a voucher bill that would allow parents to use the vouchers with private schools of their choice, including religious schools. Where other states have followed this procedure (Wisconsin, Ohio, Maine, and Vermont), the procedure has been continuously challenged in court as a violation of the principle of separation of church and state.[8] As the continuing demands for better schooling for youth continue and the public schools suffer in their ability to meet those demands, the proposed use of educational vouchers will be examined by the various states for use with learners.

As a curriculum alternative, vouchers do provide the possibility for students to experience school programs that are not available in their home schools. These differences may be in science, mathematics, and language programs. Vouchers also allow students to attend schools that have made a significant commitment to the use of technology in education when their home school has not made, or cannot make, the financial commitment to technology.

OUTCOMES-BASED EDUCATION

The philosophy of outcomes-based education is usually associated with William Spady. Outcomes-based education differs from performance-type programs in that it is intended to address meaningful culminating experiences. Demonstrations of outcomes must occur in some contest or performance setting; they must be of high quality; and they are expected to occur at culminating periods, such as at the fifth-, eighth-, and twelfth-grade levels. The demonstrations of competence need to take place in an aura of what Spady calls the "Demonstration Mountain." This mountain contains the traditional zone, which is structured task performances with discrete content skills; the transitional zone, which is complex unstructured task performances with higher-order competencies (competencies in reasoning, analysis, and imagination, for example); and the transformational zone, which is life-role functioning with complex role performance.

Outcomes-based education expects students to be implementers and performers, problem finders and solvers, planners and designers, creators and producers, learners and thinkers, listeners and communicators, teachers and mentors, supporters and contributors, team members and partners, and listeners and organizers. These roles are represented by a pyramid (Figure 13.3). These roles were developed by the Eagle, Colorado, high school and serve as their outcomes-based education restructuring program. Spady goes a step further and avers that the word *school* should be eliminated from people's concepts about education. Instead of focusing on schools, we should be focusing on the creation of learning systems that promote lifelong learning.

vouchers
A type of payment certificate issued by the state to parents to help them pay tuition for their child to attend another school, often for special programming.

FIGURE 13.3 THE OUTCOMES-BASED EDUCATION PYRAMID

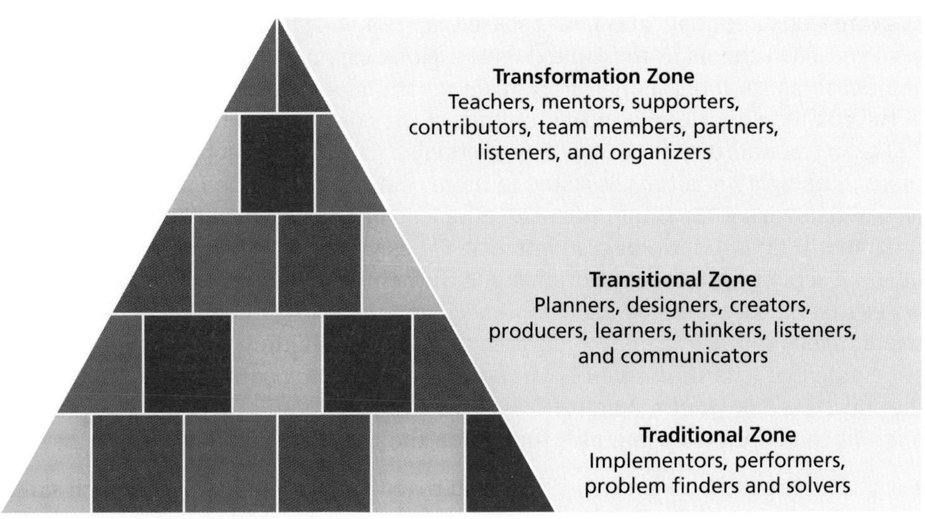

PRIVATE INDUSTRY

Business and industry have a high stake in the educational system of the United States. It is the schools that produce the future workers and captains of industry. For a considerable time now, since the end of World War II, the business and industrial world has been highly critical of the American public for not producing the caliber of worker needed by the industrial world. The entry of business into the educational field began in the late 1950s and continues with greater intensity today. Much of the initial business activity was directed toward vocational programs, and industry began providing some obsolete equipment to the schools in the hopes that these resources would spur schools to improve their programs. However, obsolete equipment for the schools had little positive effect on the effort to improve the programs for the students who would be entering the work force on completion of high school. Before the end of the twentieth century, business and industry made two significant shifts in their participation in education.

The first major shift was to become more directly involved with the schools by providing up-to-date equipment and opening their own business doors for work-study programs. This commitment to education has become more than lip service with such corporate giants as Xerox, IBM, and U.S. West. Their corporate CEOs now take a more active part in helping to support the development of viable programs in the tech-prep and school-to-work programs. The second shift involves private business moving into communities and setting up and operating their own private schools in competition with the public schools. These are known as *schools for profit,* and they are moving rapidly toward providing 10 percent of the total cost for education used in their own schools. These schools are another form of private education and provide an alternative source of curriculum offering. Some of the participants in this venture are Chase Capital, U.S. Trust, and J.P. Morgan Investment Company.[9] Located primarily in urban areas, these schools for profit number over 200 and are found in twenty or more states.

ESSENTIAL SCHOOLS

The Coalition of Essential Schools, founded by Theodore Sizer, former dean of the Harvard College of Education, was started in 1984 with five schools and has grown to over 1,000 schools in the United States. However, only about fifty schools have been at this task long enough to provide meaningful data about the effectiveness of the coalition idea. Some of the findings of the coalition are that small schools of 500 or so students do better than larger schools, high school teachers shouldn't have more than eighty students assigned to them, the content of the curriculum should be pared down so that students can acquire learning in depth, outcomes-based type programs with authentic assessment techniques yield richer learning, and students in small schools do not get shortchanged in their preparation for college. Sizer believes that the key to successful coalition schools is having the local community actively involved in determining just what it wants its children to learn.

By design, coalition schools are not the same. The coalition was founded on the ideal that as students are different all over, so should the schools be different. Yet the common principles that guide the coalition are as follows:

- Teachers design assignments that require students to hone their research skills.
- Assignments are built around assessment, creation, and collaboration.
- Teachers guide, inform, criticize, and evaluate, but the students are responsible for their own learning.
- Mastery projects, research papers, and presentations are used to present evidence of real learning.

The coalition's membership includes public and independent schools, large and small schools, conservative and liberal schools, and parochial and nonsectarian schools.

MAGNET SCHOOLS

During the late 1980s, Buffalo, New York, established *magnet schools* to meet federal court requirements for desegregation. One of the particular aims of the desegregation order in Buffalo was to provide for the growing Native American population. It had been found that the regular school program was not providing for the special needs of Native American and African American students.

Magnet schools, as the name implies, attract particular types of students who have special educational needs. In the case of the Native American students in Buffalo, it was determined that the schools could best meet these students' needs for cultural preservation by concentrating them in impact programs. Even though Native Americans live in concentrated neighborhoods in Buffalo, the regular schools do not attend to their cultural needs, because instruction is geared to the mainstream. Magnet schools attend to diversity through their programs.

Currently, there are magnet schools for African American, Native American, Greek American, and Hispanic American students in Buffalo. No one school is exclusively Native American or Hispanic American; the Buffalo plan calls for a maximum of 50 percent of a school's students to be members of any one minority. If the minority students do not live in the area of the designated magnet school, they are given free bus transportation. The remainder of the student body comes from the regular attendance unit of the school.

Minneapolis and St. Paul, Minnesota, have also established magnet elementary schools, patterned after the program for the schools in Buffalo. The magnet

RELEVANT RESEARCH

Do Magnet Schools Boost Achievement?

STUDY PURPOSE/QUESTIONS: This study by Adam Gamoren sought to answer the major question, "Do urban magnet schools offer better academic opportunities to urban youth?" Other related questions dealt with nonacademic areas of community, parents, students, and the social networks that provide direction to the lives of students.

STUDY DESIGN: For this descriptive survey, Gamoren used existing achievement and questionnaire data gathered by the National Educational Longitudinal Study (NELS) from 1988 to 1992. In particular he used the data from 48 stand-alone public magnet schools in urban areas. He compared these data to similar data NELS had obtained from 213 comprehensive high schools, 57 Catholic schools, and 39 secular private schools at the same time they got the data for the magnet schools. Altogether, there were 3,000 students in the study. The researcher examined data for four areas: mathematics, science, reading, and social studies. He also obtained data on gender; race; family situation (one parent or two); socioeconomic status; and the schools' social, ethnic, and economic composition.

STUDY FINDINGS: Magnet school students had higher achievement gains in all four academic subject areas than did other public or private schools. The gains were significant in science, reading, and social studies. From additional questionnaire data it could be determined that the gains were related to stronger social relationships pursued by the magnet schools with students, teachers, and community.

IMPLICATIONS:

- Not all the magnet schools studied were alike, so it is difficult to generalize with certainty from the findings of the study.
- The study may not be supportive of the advocates of private school choice.
- A question suggested by the study is: Should urban schools place greater emphasis on social relationships among students, teachers, and community?

Source: Adam Gamoren, "Do Magnet Schools Boost Achievement?" *Educational Leadership 54* (2) (October 1996): 42–46.

idea is not new. Many urban areas have had magnet-type schools at the secondary level for many years. Two such schools in New York City have been in operation for quite some time; one was highlighted in the movie *Fame.* Chicago has provided special high schools for technical, pre-engineering, and vocational training for many years. However, these schools have not been sensitive to minority differences and sometimes have become ghetto centers of education or centers of elite programs serving mostly white students. The magnet school concept, as it is currently being used, addresses social and academic needs for special programs for all kinds of students. Magnet schools are now found across the country.

HOME-BASED SCHOOLS

An increasing number of families in the United States have become disenchanted with the public schools because of the seeming lack of strong learner achievement, discipline problems, and lack of strong moral education. Because of this a small but growing number of U.S. families are educating their children

Increasing numbers of parents are resorting to home schooling for their children.

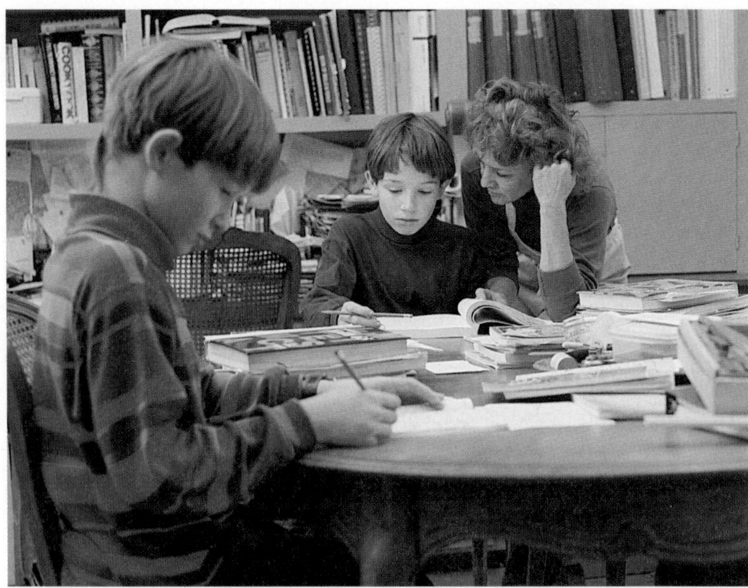

at home. States require that home educators be properly trained and capable of their task. However, the monitoring of these efforts varies considerably from state to state, as it does in the whole area of private education. Home schooling efforts are as different, as there are numbers of schools. They range from complete isolation from the public school to partial use of the public school in areas in which the parents are not qualified to teach. There is increasing home dependence on the electronic world for materials and networking. Local libraries receive more use in areas where there is more home schooling. Although this approach provides an alternative, families have not been quick to choose it. Nationally, about 1 percent of the children are being educated at home.

THE COMER MODEL

James Comer began his pioneering efforts in the late 1960s. It has taken over thirty years for the model to be considered for elementary schools. Basically, the model holds that the relationship between the school and the family is the key to the child's success in school. Success requires collaboration between home and school. Recognizing poor communication between teachers and staff and within the community, plus the ever-present need for staff development, a Comer school adopts strategies that create an inviting school climate. Parents and school become one in the effort to provide a program for the children. Figure 13.4 shows a Comer school development program.

The main features of a Comer School are as follows:

- Three teams: the school planning and management team, the student and student support team, and the parent team
- Three operations: comprehensive school plan, staff development plan, and monitoring and assessment
- Three guiding principles: no fault, consensus, and collaboration

Since 1990 fifty-three District of Columbia schools have adopted the Comer model. Across the nation, there were 389 Comer schools reported in action as of

FIGURE 13.4 COMER SCHOOL DEVELOPMENT PROGRAM

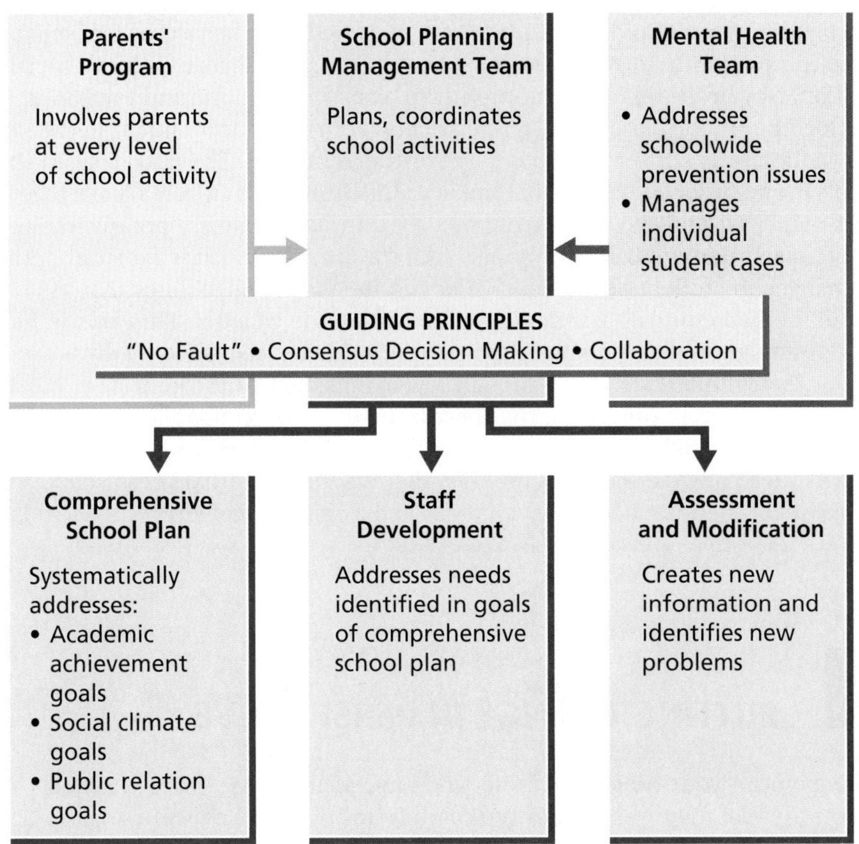
Parents' Program
Involves parents at every level of school activity
School Planning Management Team
Plans, coordinates school activities
Mental Health Team
• Addresses schoolwide prevention issues
• Manages individual student cases
GUIDING PRINCIPLES
"No Fault" • Consensus Decision Making • Collaboration
Comprehensive School Plan
Systematically addresses:
• Academic achievement goals
• Social climate goals
• Public relation goals
Staff Development
Addresses needs identified in goals of comprehensive school plan
Assessment and Modification
Creates new information and identifies new problems

Source: Yale Child Study Center (1991), cited in Gretchen D. Lofland, "Where Children Come First," *Educational Leadership 52* (5) (February 1995): 17. Reprinted with permission of the Association for Supervision and Curriculum Development.

February 2000.[10] As a working target, the Washington, D.C., school district sponsors and supports meaningful activities that engage students, parents, and community in overcoming the environment of drugs, violence, and crime that plagues the District's inner-city schools. The District of Columbia's effort is focused on the elementary school program.

GLOBAL PERSPECTIVES: Schools of Reconciliation in Northern Ireland

Ireland and Northern Ireland have been divided and have shed blood over issues of religion and nationalism since the time of Elizabeth I. The Catholic part of Northern Ireland identifies itself as Irish and Nationalist. The Protestants there identify themselves as British and unionists. Catholics are in a minority but do make up almost 45 percent of the population. Since the Good Friday agreement of April 1998, a strong possibility of reconciliation between the two groups has emerged. The institution that has been chosen to bring this reconciliation about is the school.

The vast majority of Irish students are educated in either a Catholic school or a state-run predominantly Protestant school. Like U.S. efforts to achieve racial integration, Northern Ireland is attempting to bring the Catholic and Protestant cultures together in the classroom. There are now more than forty integrated schools of all grade levels scattered throughout Northern Ireland. The emphasis in these schools is one of social reconstruction. Students from both cultures learn together about their past and the history of bloodshed in it. Teachers who are trained in conflict resolution are called on to use that training daily. All is far from perfect, but changes in student attitudes have begun to take shape. Things that are common to the two cultures are given great stress in the schools. This aids in building common ground among the affected youth. These Irish school efforts are not without their opponents. Even though fewer than half of those in both cultures support these school programs, the schools are growing in popularity. Young parents are placing their children on reconciliation school lists as soon as they are born. As these new generations emerge, there is the hope that these schools will help to effect the intended social changes and a final peace will come to Ireland.

PUTTING CHANGE IN PERSPECTIVE

At this point in your professional life, you have spent many years in schools, and chances are that they were rather typical in terms of how they were organized and how you were taught. Basically, you have passed through a sit-and-listen experience with a teacher using a telling style. You have had one teacher in each single classroom, and you and your classmates sat in chairs at desks that were neatly arranged in rows facing the front of the room. It almost sounds like the old one-room schoolhouse, but it really lacked what was found in the old one-room school. In that school, there was a wide range of ages and abilities. Students were involved in teaching other students; the daily schedule was flexible; the community was an integral part of the school; and the teacher was a respected leader in the community.

If you think seriously about this picture, you begin to wonder what happened. As one-room schools became multiroomed schools, all those practices began to fade. The larger schools adopted the industrial model of the twentieth century. Schooling had become an assembly line, and the products were the students. Teachers became the workers, and the principals took on the role of management. As we close this chapter, keep in mind the positive features of the one-room school and how those practices fit into the notions of restructuring and transforming the schools of the twenty-first century.

Providing opportunities for students to generate their own curriculum requires risks and courage. Teachers must understand the classical view of learning and the official view of learning.

Marsha Grace

ASSESSING THE MAGNITUDE OF CHANGE

Changes come in various forms and sizes. Change in school programs can be vast and sweeping or small and localized. Some of the alternatives that we discussed earlier could be considered vast and sweeping if a majority of school districts were to adopt them. Some elements of them could be considered small and localized if found in only a few districts or in parts of a district—for example, all primary

PROFESSIONAL DILEMMA

"I've Been There, Seen That, and Done That Before"

As American schools interact with the twenty-first century, they have continued to be under increasing national, state, and local pressures to improve their curriculum. The common concern is one of meeting performance standards that most states have adopted. Parents have become avid consumers of the visual and print media, which continuously paint a dire picture of what our youth cannot do. That picture suggests that by the time students reach the eighth grade, they have fallen behind their international counterparts in reading and mathematics. This lapse in learners' performance has led to a rallying cry for school improvement by the professional associations with their standards for performance and federal government's national goals expectations.

Newly trained teachers, prepared to become active change agents, move to their first new teaching positions and encounter veteran teachers who stand back and lament, "Here we go again—I've been there, seen all of that, and done that before!" With each new societal crisis in the latter half of the twentieth century, schools and teachers were led through curriculum revision efforts that were supposed to cure the current ills of schools at that time. Apparently, all of these curriculum revision efforts have been for naught, because society has not seen fit to give credit to schools for their efforts while recognizing that curriculum revision is a continuous effort and the schools need to be supported in that process. However, a close analysis of the revision efforts shows that, though very good in many ways, the revision was really a tinkering effort. It consisted of a twist here and a tweak there with little continuity and balance in the effort. Now the real dilemma for teaching staff is whether to abandon this type of tinkering process in curriculum revision in favor of a massive major overhaul in the school program.

In this live change arena, the big question is "What massively needs to be overhauled and what is the new direction for the school program?" This dilemma goes to the very heart of transforming schools, and many of society's concerns about schools are real. In particular, the new teacher and veteran teachers need to work together on the following issues:

- How can newly trained teachers work with veteran teachers in a nonthreatening way in providing meaningful change in the schools?
- How do schools determine what innovative practices they need to incorporate if they are going to reverse the current lag in student performance? Should they move toward magnet schools, a Comer model, an essential school, or what?
- To what degree should all teachers encourage and enlist parents to be involved in this curriculum decision making?

grades of a district. Additionally, the intensity of change and the strength of its adoption are related to the degree of staff and community support for change as it is being implemented and assessed for its value. Many of the so-called innovations start up but have little staying power and soon pass into oblivion.

Critics of schools, as well as many educators, are asking for transforming types of changes—ones that would dramatically influence the shape, structure, and operations of schools and classrooms. These types of changes are ones that last, with continuing constituencies that support them. An example is the kindergarten. Introduced in the 1800s, the kindergarten had become a mainstay by the 1960s. One of the major difficulties in assessing the magnitude of change is associated with the school itself. The school does not operate in a vacuum, able to do whatever it pleases. It is an instrument of society and therefore must respond to the demands of society. Thus, it finds itself being pulled from all sides on many educational issues and practices.

FIGURE 13.5 STAGES IN THE BACKWARD DESIGN PROCESS

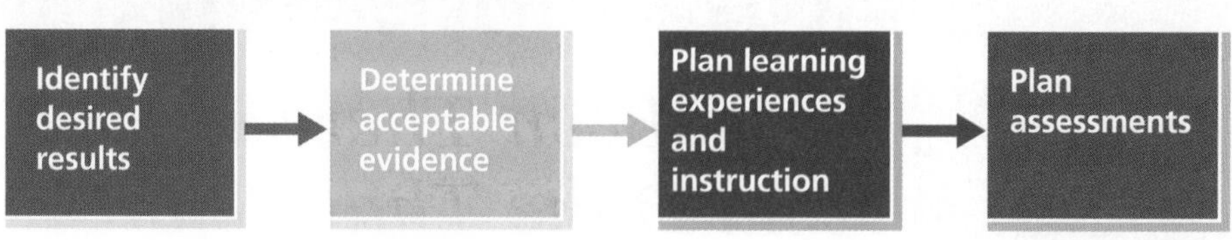

RESTRUCTURING SCHOOLS

The current movement for bringing about major change in the schools is called **restructuring.** Restructuring is an umbrella label that encompasses a variety of innovations and themes. Some of these efforts have been directed at student learning, others at the teaching–learning process. Restructuring involves changing curriculum materials and introducing different teaching strategies. (Chapter 13 has looked at the curriculum, and Chapter 14 will look at instruction.) Restructuring efforts require the adoption of curriculum design and materials that have been built on a solid research base. Earlier, we proposed that curriculum development use the backward design process. Wiggins and McTighe propose stages in that process (See Figure 13.5).[11] We add the plan assessment stage to their figure.

The restructuring movement has two major implications. The most significant one involves the principal. She or he can no longer be the authoritarian figure as the directive leader, but must now work in a more collegial and collaborative manner with the total staff of the school. The second implication is associated with the design of the curriculum. With additional academic courses being added to the graduation requirements list, curriculum offerings and materials must be created for all of the students. This requires continuous design activities for the staff.

TRANSFORMING SCHOOLS

Elementary schools are more receptive than secondary schools to major, transforming change in their programs. Transforming leads to widespread reform. According to Hargreaves and Fink, educational reform must have depth and improve the important aspects of student learning.[12] It must have length and be sustainable over long periods of time. It must have breadth and be capable of extending beyond a few schools to networks of schools. The major stumbling block to this occurring in the secondary school is that school is more focused on subject matter than on students. Secondary schools are more subject oriented, and elementary schools are more learner oriented.

restructuring Making a complete change in the way in which schools are structured, organized, and operated and in which they offer programs and teaching for students.

Secondary schools can assume a reform posture if they begin to see themselves making changes that are beneficial to student learning and growth. The current pressures of Carnegie units and rigid time modules (for example, fifty-minute classes), can be adjusted to accommodate any reform action. The new expectations for learning standards (see Chapter 15) go across the continuum of elementary and secondary education. Therefore, what is needed in the reform efforts is meaningful program articulation between the elementary and secondary programs. This will produce richer learner environments throughout the school program. The alternative programs that we discussed earlier are workable reforms that can be used to transform the program.

SUMMARY

TYPES OF CURRICULUM DESIGN

In this chapter we looked at the big ideas in designing school programs for learners. Those ideas expanded on the concepts of change, alternatives, and continuity in the offerings of the school program. These concepts were introduced with the presentation of different types of curriculum design emphasizing subject-centered or learner-centered programs. Teachers working in program development must keep current with the issues that bear on the types of program that are developed for a school.

STUDENTS SERVED BY THE CURRICULUM

Whatever program emphasis is stressed, the teacher must be aware of and address learners' individual differences. As state standards for expected performances of students increase, increased stress is placed on those students who have difficulty in meeting traditional academic standards. Good curriculum designs attend to these student differences so that all learners have the opportunity to meet expected standard performances and not become dropouts along the way.

PURPOSES OF CURRICULUM

All programs must provide for attention to general and exploratory education and education for career. Society has placed increased importance on general education, and all students must participate in increased requirements in mathematics, science, and English. These increased requirements have to be planned and offered with a variety of alternatives if the different types of learners are to be successful in their pursuit of learning.

ALTERNATIVE CURRICULUM PROGRAMS

When parents experience difficulty in having their schools provide alternative offerings for learners, they can turn to a variety of school programs to get the types of programs they want for their children. As we indicated in this chapter, these programs may be presented in the form of alternative schools, vouchers, home schooling, and the like. These alternative offerings often place subtle pressures on the regular school to begin to make provisions for such programs in the regular school offerings.

PUTTING CHANGE IN PERSPECTIVE

As we have showed in this chapter, changes in education are leading toward a total restructuring of schools in this century. These changes have two major implications for the schools. First, the principal—the school leader—must cease to be an authoritarian type and become a collegial member of the total school staff. Second, the school's curriculum design must provide a wide focus on the many different needs of students. This shift will produce richer learner environments in the school.

DISCUSSION QUESTIONS

1. What are some curriculum design problems associated with increased attention to basic literacy and survival skills?
2. What are some of your choices to be accommodated in whatever curriculum design you propose?
3. How does your teaching field provide for the general education needs of your students?
4. In your opinion, what curriculum alternatives are most appropriate for your content teaching field? Why?
5. Do you support the notion that until significant curriculum reform takes place with a lasting influence, schools will tend to just slide along in the mainstream of society? Why or why not?

JOURNAL ENTRIES

1. Add to your journal a discussion paper on how you can add a more learner-oriented program to your content teaching field.
2. In a journal entry, compare and contrast the potential strengths and weaknesses of charter schools as they are being used in the United States.
3. Interview a fellow student and record his or her responses, pro or con, to the use of vouchers in U.S. education.

PORTFOLIO DEVELOPMENT

1. Select two of your written assignments for this chapter and, after revising them, add them to your portfolio for examination by a potential hiring school district.
2. For eventual inclusion in your portfolio, develop a chart that compares the various program alternatives presented in this chapter.

SCHOOL-BASED EXPERIENCES

1. When making a visit to a school as part of your practicum experience, plan to secure a copy of that school's curriculum guide. Analyze the guide to see whether it best fits the description of a subject-centered or learner-centered curriculum design. Afterward, observe a few of that school's teachers to determine whether they demonstrate the type of design analysis you made.
2. Meet with three or four teachers in the same school district and have them discuss for your data gathering how their program addresses the general education needs of their students.

WEBSITES

We recommend that you practice exploring the web to help you gain deeper insights into the alternative innovative programs offered in this chapter. You should practice developing some of your own key search words for this use. You might begin by using key terms from this chapter such as "tech prep," "charters," "middle school," and "vouchers." Some informative sites are the following:

1. <www.ascd.org> Website of the Association for Supervision and Curriculum Development, exploring new ideas for professional development.

2. <www.pdkintl.org> The Phi Delta Kappa International website offers research information, student activities, and more.
3. <www.drtomkelly.com> Systematic assessment for quality schools.

NOTES

1. Ralph W. Tyler, *Basic Principles of Curriculum and Instruction.* Chicago: University of Chicago Press, 1949, 1, 45.
2. Dennis B. Travis, Dawn Prichard, and Debbra Lang, "Promoting Staff Collaboration and Curriculum Integration: An Evolving District Model," *SPECTRUM 17* (1) (Winter 1999): 34–35.
3. Jonatha W. Vare, and Kathryn S. Miller, "Integrating Caring across the Curriculum," *SPECTRUM 18* (1) (Winter 2000): 27–35.
4. "This We Believe: Developmentally Responsive Middle Schools." ERS Bulletin, Arlington, VA: Educational Research Service, January, 1996, 3.
5. Kenneth C. Gray and Edwin L. Herr, *Other Ways to Win.* Thousand Oaks, CA: Corwin Press, 1995, 146.
6. *San Francisco Chronicle,* "Chronicle Sections" (September 8, 1999): A10.
7. Kelly Pearce, "Charter Schools Working Together," *The Arizona Republic* (February 25, 2000): B1.
8. Martha M. McCarthy, "What Is the Verdict on School Vouchers?," *Phi Delta Kappan 81* (5) (January 2000): 371–378.
9. "For-Profit Schools," *Business Week* (February 7, 2000): 64–72.
10. Yale Child Study Center, *School Development Program.* New Haven, CT: Author, 2000.
11. Grant Wiggins and Jay McTighe, *Understanding by Design.* Alexandria, VA: 1997 ASCD, 9.
12. Andy Hargreaves and Dean Fink, "The Three Dimensions of Reform," *Educational Leadership 57* (7) (April 2000): 30.

BIBLIOGRAPHY

Archilles, Charles. *Let's Put Kids First: Finally Getting Class Size Right.* Thousand Oaks, CA: Corwin Press, 1998.

Bartel, James. *Teaching for Thoughtfulness.* White Plains, NY: Longman, 1995.

Brandt, Ronald S., ed. *Education in a New Era.* Alexandria, VA: Association for Supervision and Curriculum Development, 2000.

Brown, John L., and Moffett, Cherylle A. *The Hero's Journey: How Educators Can Transform Schools and Improve Learning.* Alexandria, VA: Association for Supervision and Curriculum Development, 1999.

Freiberg, H. Jerome, ed. *Beyond Behaviorism: Changing the Classroom Management Paradigm.* Boston: Allyn & Bacon, 1999.

Glasser, William. *Choice Theory: A New Psychology of Human Freedom.* New York: HarperPerennial, 1998.

Hess, Frederick M. *Spinning Wheels: The Politics of Urban School Reform.* Washington, D.C.: Brookings Institution, 1999.

Kessler, Rachael. *The Soul of Education.* Alexandria, VA: Association for Supervision and Curriculum Development, 2000.

Mathews, Jay. *Class Struggle: What's Wrong (and Right) with America's Best Public High School.* New York: Times Books, 1998.

Newman, Joseph W. *America's Teachers: An Introduction to Education.* 3rd ed. New York: Longman, 1998.

Parkay, Forrest W., and Stanford, Beverly Hardcastle. *Becoming a Teacher.* 4th ed. Boston: Allyn & Bacon, 1998.

Sarason, Seymour B. *Charter Schools: Another Flawed Educational Reform.* New York: Teachers College Press, 1998.

Tomlinson, Carol Ann. *The Differentiated Classroom.* Alexandria, VA: Association for Supervision and Curriculum Development, 1999.

CHAPTER 14

Providing Instruction

EDUCATION IN THE NEWS

Program Recognizes Teachers' Extra Efforts

By Abby Goodnough, *New York Times,* August 16, 2000

John Caffrey had been teaching English for 31 years when he heard about a new way to gain recognition for his skills, one available to teachers nationwide. . . . The hitch: applicants had to pass a rigorous, time-consuming assessment that included videos of their teaching, samples of their students' work and essays analyzing their classroom techniques. . . . Mr. Caffrey, who was teaching middle school in Williamsburg, Brooklyn, was not the type to mind the extra work. . . .

"I simply wanted to be recognized as an expert in my field," Mr. Caffery said. "I wanted the confidence that affirmation like that could bring. . . ." So in 1995, Mr. Caffery became one of the first New York City teachers to earn advanced certification from the National Board for Professional Teaching Standards, an independent panel that sets standards for experienced teachers. . . .

National board certification does not replace state certification, which remains an entry level requirement for all teachers. Instead, it helps teachers with at least three years of experience measure their skills using benchmarks set by the panel, which is mostly made up of teachers, but also includes school administrators, union officials, lawmakers, and business leaders. . . . "It recognizes people who go beyond what is expected," said Karen Zumwalt, a professor at Columbia Teachers College. . . .

"When I go into classrooms now I have a sense of accomplishment," said Mr. Caffrey. . . . "I always felt teaching was a noble profession and I worked so hard every day, and it just didn't seem to me that people in the management system recognized that. Now, I have some recognition."

LEARNER OUTCOMES

After reading and studying this chapter, you will be able to:

1. Compare and contrast graded and nongraded schools.
2. Explain the differences between exploratory education and general education.
3. Discuss the pros and cons of ability grouping.
4. Associate learning styles with different teaching models.
5. Discuss the role of technology in education.
6. Analyze the different uses of computers for the classroom. ■

Learning is a treasure that follows its owners everywhere.

Chinese proverb

To the average citizen, all schools are alike. In a sense, this is a true statement because all schools exist for the sole purpose of providing a meaningful educational experience for learners. Although this is the main purpose for schools, the fact remains that schools are as different as their students and communities are. The differences are found in the way in which schools are organized internally for teachers and learners, the materials that are used in instruction, the grouping and learning patterns for students, the instructional practices of the teachers, and the particular resources of each school community. As identified in the introduction to Part VI, one of the big ideas in instruction is **balance.** Balance in instruction suggests that generally, all students will experience similar teacher behaviors in the classroom. Instructional practices will be geared toward an improved climate for student learning. Teachers should provide **variety** in their practices so that individual differences in learners will be met. It is the degree of intensity in balance and variety in instruction that make schools different. In addition to these differences, the application of instructional systems, and technology, with all of their differences and delivery capabilities, provides a unique array of presentations and assessments that can be used by the teacher in the classroom.

It is interesting to note that groups of people visiting the same school will, more often than not, describe what they saw in such a way that one would think they had visited different schools. Their views are governed by their own biases and other interests. Yet we can easily see that there are common practices, materials, and environments in which teachers teach and learners learn. We examine all of these factors in this chapter.

balance
A term used to describe the provision of a complete program of school offerings that meet the needs of all students.

variety
A term used to describe a program that addresses the needs of all types of learners that the school meets.

baby boomlet
The surge in births during the 1980s and 1990s of children who are increasing school enrollments.

ORGANIZING TEACHERS TO PROVIDE INSTRUCTION

As a new professional, you will want to take an active role in helping to determine how the school organizes its staff for the instructional process. You will always be partially restricted by the way in which the school building is constructed. The more conventionally constructed buildings—halls with separate classrooms on either side—do not lend themselves to much flexibility in staffing arrangements. By contrast, open-spaced buildings provide more latitude in the instructional arrangements of staff. Unfortunately, few schools have created an instructional program and then designed buildings to fit the specific program. Most have built the buildings first and then attempted to fit some type of organizational arrangement into the constructed space. As we enter the twenty-first century, increasing numbers of school districts are focusing on the renovation of old school plants and construction of new school plants in order to accommodate the **baby boomlet** that is entering the schools. The need is particularly acute in large urban areas because of an increased school population and many extremely old school buildings. All of these efforts are affected by the ability of each school district to finance new school construction.

SCHOOL ORGANIZATION

It has become commonplace in education in the United States for school districts to be organized around three different age levels of students: elementary (five- to eleven-year-olds), intermediate (eleven- to thirteen-year-olds), and senior high schools (fourteen- to eighteen-year-olds). It is generally thought that students can learn best when they are organized into groupings related to physical, mental, social, and emotional readiness levels. Yet schools are not all organized alike. Other variables come into play when schools are initially organized or examined for organization. Those variables could be district wealth, geographical size with its limitations on transportation, economic factors associated with space utilization, and personal dictates of the community. There is variety in American school organization.

ELEMENTARY Elementary schools may include grades K–4, K–5, K–6, or K–8 (see Figure 14.1). The variety is associated with types of building space available and the planned program. The curriculum in this school is learner centered.

INTERMEDIATE Intermediate grades may be 5–8, 6–8, 7–8, or 7–9. The variance here is usually associated with the school district's choice of a middle school or a junior high school. As we discussed in Chapter 13, middle schools tend to be learner centered, and junior high schools tend to be subject centered.

SECONDARY Secondary schools may include grades 7–12, 9–10, 9–12, 10–12, or 11–12. Usually, the 7–12 pattern is found in rural areas where the junior and senior high school are housed in the same school plant. Senior high school programs are generally subject centered.

FIGURE 14.1 COMMON SCHOOL ORGANIZATIONAL PATTERNS

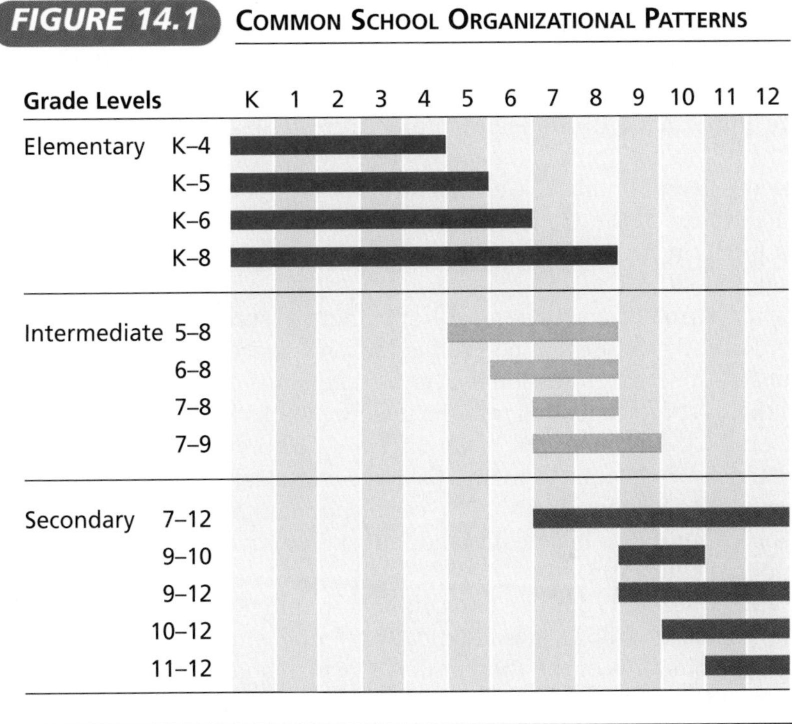

GLOBAL PERSPECTIVES: German Education

Education programs in the United States always suffer in comparisons with other schools of the world, particularly those in Europe. A recent comparison of German and American schools, however, gives a more accurate analysis of the two systems and what they produce. Before comparing the two systems, the analysis places the systems on the same playing field. For example, U.S. schools, in addition to the major charges of teaching the three Rs, must provide social education, including understanding and appreciating differences in ethnicities, races, creeds, and cultures; recreation; avocational education; vocational education; art; music; and theater—and the list goes on. German schools have a much narrower mission. Their focus is on the three Rs, special education, and socialization. Extracurricular activities, from music to sports, are the responsibility of the communities, churches, and amateur athletic associations. Vocational education is the primary responsibility of business and industry. Health and safety are the responsibility of health maintenance organizations (HMOs), government, churches, private institutions, and the home.

After the sixth grade, German students elect, by choice and examination, the main school, *Hauptschule* (about a third of the students), the *Realschule* (about one-fourth of the students, or the *Gymnasium* (about one-third of the students). Whereas the *Hauptschule* and *Realschule* prepare students for vocational education and apprenticeship programs, the *Gymnasium* is the academic school for the development of the mind and college attendance for professional-type careers. Special education students, about 10 percent of the student body, attend well-supported special schools called *Sonderschule.* Although a comprehensive-type high school, *Gesamtschule,* which is patterned after the American comprehensive high school, has been started, fewer than 10 percent of the students attend it.

There is little or no heterogeneous grouping in German schools, and teachers are firmly supportive of ability grouping. In the college preparatory schools, students may shift programs on the basis of interest and societal need, but the longer they wait to do that, the longer it takes them to complete their education because they must make up deficient prerequisites. Classes are spread over twelve months of the year and meet six days per week. However, with time allowed for vacations and holidays, German schools are open about 180 days per year, much like those in the United States. College-bound high school students experience a program that is closer to that of the American college than of the American high school.

Teachers in Germany are better paid and more respected than their U.S. counterparts. Recently, a German poll ranked teachers second behind judges in the list of most respected professionals. As a profession, teaching maintains a type of guild that is somewhat similar to the teaching ranks in U.S. colleges. Most master teachers in the *Gymnasium* have earned a doctorate along the way up their career ladder. The state, Germany, pays teacher salaries, but the communities are responsible for the construction, care, and maintenance of the various schools in their community. Businesses and industries provide the financial support for vocational education.

To compare the students of these two countries requires that similar students be compared. The best of the U.S. academically talented students compare most favorably with the students of the *Gymnasium.* German students who are not in that school are not used for comparison purposes with American students, but all American students of the U.S. comprehensive high schools become data for comparison with foreign students. Therefore, most comparisons are not apples to apples, but rather apples to sauerkraut.

GRADED AND NONGRADED SCHOOLS

Two major types of school organization that are in common use today are graded and nongraded schools. The available school building influences which type of organization is used. However, the district can plan new buildings based on the type of school organization it prefers to use. Keep in mind that humans do not like overcrowding; nor do they like their personal space violated. It is important to address these psychological factors when looking at space and staffing.

Most school buildings have been constructed along conventional lines with large corridors and self-contained classrooms on both sides of the corridors. Library, physical education, and other resource rooms are conveniently located for easy access to students. Use of *fixed space* in this way usually supports a grade-level type of school organization. Flexible space for instruction is often lacking, and there is often little or no cooperation among teachers regarding space utilization.

Open-space facilities tend to be larger instructional areas with movable walls and flexible learning environments. This type of space does not automatically guarantee an instructional program that is developed around the philosophy of open education. It does, however, provide the capacity for nongraded organization. Instead of having corridors faced by small classrooms, with about thirty students per room, an open-space plant has large instructional spaces that can be kept completely open for some varieties of instruction or can be reduced to smaller areas through the use of movable walls and furniture. A school that is configured like this tends to be more conducive to diversified instructional and grouping patterns. Although its popularity increased rapidly in the 1980s and 1990s, the open-space facility is still found primarily at the elementary and middle school levels.

One of the biggest problems associated with the use of open-space facilities is the lack of adequate preparation of teachers. When school districts contemplate the use of open-space facilities, they should plan for adequate in-service staff development. If teachers learn how to be more comfortable in open space, they are more likely to use it as it was intended.

GRADED SCHOOLS The graded school is a borrowed European concept for organizing pupils in some orderly fashion by chronological age. Historically, children in the United States have usually begun formal schooling at the age of five or six. That practice continues today in almost every state of the nation. A few states mandate the age of seven as the starting age for compulsory education, but most use the age of five or six. It became only natural that children starting their first year of formal schooling should be called "first graders." When they returned for a second year of schooling, they were called "second graders." Gradually, requirements and standards were established for each of the formal years of schooling, and the twelve-year graded school emerged. Because of the graded requirements, however, not all students spend twelve years in graded schools. Students who fail to meet some of the graded requirements along the way must repeat a grade or several grades, and they may spend more than twelve years in

open space
Schools that do not have classroom walls separating learning areas.

In non-graded programs, a typical classroom practice is for older students to work with younger students.

school if they wish to receive a secondary school diploma. The diploma, however, typically indicates the equivalent of a minimum of twelve years of successful formal education.

Some of the problems with this type of school organization are the following:

1. Graded schools do not account for learners' differences in academic readiness or in social, mental, or physical maturity. For example, it does not necessarily follow that thirteen-year-old girls and boys, who are vastly different physically, mentally, and emotionally, should be grouped together as seventh or eighth graders in an intermediate school. Girls are typically more mature at this age than are boys, yet they are grouped with boys for learning. Nor are all five- or six-year-olds similar in maturity.
2. Graded schools do not account positively for what a child actually has learned when the school decides that grade-level requirements have not been met and forces the child to repeat the whole grade the following year. As a result, early failure rates among young learners help to contribute to school dropout rates later in the graded school. Individual differences in learning rates and achievement are seldom attended to in these types of schools. Although many elementary schools attempt to address this problem, few secondary schools do anything about it.
3. Because most graded schools tend to use group rather than individual expectations for test performance, and because few of the tests that are used meet accepted criteria for good test making, learners who do not meet standards for grade levels may be unfairly penalized by these tests.

continuous progress education
A term used to describe programs that do not provide for grading for learners by ages.

NONGRADED SCHOOLS The *nongraded school,* as now defined, involves a school organization that allows each child to progress through the system at an individual rate of development. The nongraded school discards the lockstep grade-level concept, with its set curriculum for each grade, in favor of an individual, flexible, and continuous educational program. Sometimes referred to as **continuous progress education,** this plan guides students through a series of stages of development geared to readiness for learning. Students are grouped flexibly according to age, ability, maturity, achievement, and other developmental factors.

Within this grouping, the school encourages students to move ahead through each subject at their own speed; their groupings vary with the progress they make.

When an elementary school becomes nongraded, the kindergarten and early grades are often simply designated as the primary school. The upper elementary school—grades 5, 6, 7, and 8—becomes a new unit of organization labeled the intermediate or middle school; and the high school discards its strict traditional approach and graded pattern in favor of phases of learning and sequential development.

The nongraded school tries to minimize the shortcomings of the graded system. With grade-level designations gone, able students can theoretically advance at a rate commensurate with ability. Whereas in the graded system it takes five years to teach the formal learning skills expected for grades K–4, children in nongraded schools may complete this learning in three, four, or five years. In addition, in the nongraded school, less able students may not have to experience fear of failure or suffer the minimal learning associated with being **"held back."** They may take five or more years to master the necessary skills. This type of organization more easily meets the needs of diverse students—both gifted students and less able youngsters.

Most nongraded instruction has been implemented at the elementary level, although some high schools have attempted it. If nongrading were applied to all formal education, the curriculum could be divided into four parts: primary education, intermediate education, secondary education, and higher education. Each part could be nongraded and could provide a continuous education organized around the individual progress of pupils.

ARRANGEMENTS FOR STAFF

The way a school organizes its staff for instruction is directly related to the school's goals for the program. Staff may be organized according to line and staff notions—or according to more flexible arrangements that let the teachers work together cooperatively.

FIXED ASSIGNMENTS Most school districts are organized around a line and staff concept. Teachers report to department heads or grade-level chairs, who in turn report to the head administrator (principal). All teachers are certified strongly in their teaching areas and tend to put stress on the academic subjects. It is not unusual for the different teaching areas to have little communication across disciplines, and thus there tends to be little **vertical and/or horizontal articulation** (coordination) in the program. It is not that this type of staffing arrangement doesn't support articulation efforts; it is just that articulation doesn't seem to occur. The needs of the students usually become secondary to the importance of the teaching discipline.

DIFFERENTIATED ASSIGNMENTS The needs of students are most apt to be met when the students are exposed to varied learning experiences. In team teaching, learning can be most successful when large-group instruction (100 to 150 students), small-group instruction (8 to 10 students), and independent study are combined. A teaching team, organized by subject or by a combination of subjects, can provide these three kinds of experiences. The distribution of time among large groups, small groups, and independent study will vary according to the

held back
A term used to describe a child who has failed a grade and must repeat it the following year.

vertical articulation
School offerings that relate to each other from grades one through twelve, such as language arts offerings.

horizontal articulation
School offerings that are related to each other across a grade level. These may be a single discipline, such as English, in which there are multiple sections at one grade, or they may cross disciplines at one grade level.

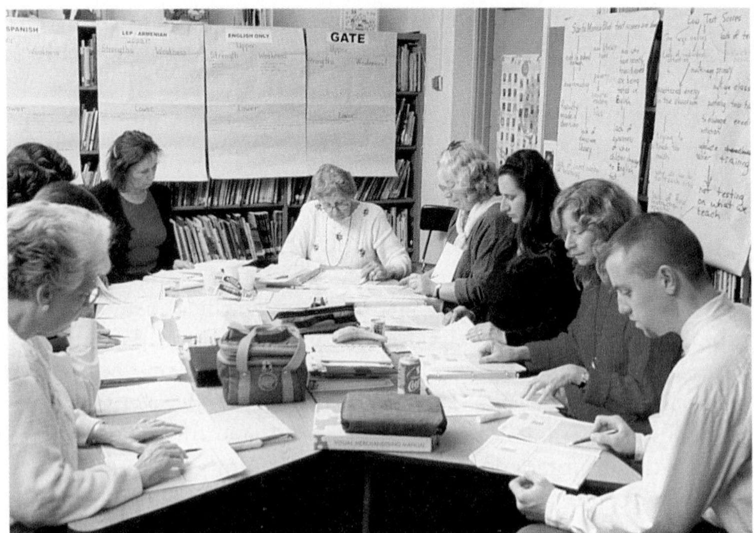

Teachers spend considerable time meeting and planning programs.

hierarchical
Term used to describe teaching teams in which there is a type staff arrangement with different levels of team members.

collegial
Term used to describe teaching teams in which all members of the team are equal partners in the team effort.

differentiated staffing
Term used with hierarchical teams in which the staff arrangement and assignments are more formal and responsibilities are different.

modular scheduling
Scheduling different time periods for instruction.

modules for learning
Time periods used to describe class periods.

flexible scheduling
Scheduling time periods for instruction vary by subject and intended learning outcomes.

subject studied. Advocates of team teaching have suggested that, on the average, students should spend 40 percent of their time in large-group instruction, 30 percent in small-group discussion, and 30 percent in independent study.

The teaching team can be organized in two general ways. The first, a formal approach, is referred to as a **hierarchical** team organization. This approach is a line–staff organization in which a leader heads a team composed of regular teachers and teachers' aides. The second type of organization is referred to as a **collegial,** or equalitarian, team. There is no formal structure to this organization; leadership is shared or exchanged voluntarily, and all teachers receive the same pay and have equal responsibility and similar duties. Collegial team organization is binding, however, in that although teachers enjoy a more informal organization, they must work together at a common task.

Differentiated staffing has added a new dimension to the pattern for team teaching. However, it is merely a refinement of hierarchical teaching. Specifically, it establishes a career ladder that links the paraprofessional job with the superintendent's office. Different levels of instructional personnel are created, and each level requires certain kinds of training and experience. The director of curriculum and instruction becomes the school district program team leader. Each instructional and research staff assignment carries specific instructional responsibilities.

INSTRUCTIONAL SCHEDULING

The terms *modular* and *flexible* refer to two different concepts in instructional scheduling. **Modular scheduling** has existed for some time in both elementary and secondary schools. At the elementary level it has usually been associated with thirty-minute time blocks (**modules for learning**) and at the secondary level, with forty- to sixty-minute time blocks. The secondary school time blocks are tied to the instructional time allocation of the Carnegie unit. A modular schedule is just as rigid as the six- to eight-period schedule used for so many years in the secondary schools. In contrast, **flexible scheduling** uses smaller time blocks (mods), but the schedule changes regularly during the school year

RELEVANT RESEARCH

Block Scheduling Can Enhance the School Climate

STUDY PURPOSE/QUESTIONS: This study by Shortt and Thayer sought to answer the question "Does changing to a school schedule that permits large blocks of time for learning activities have an impact on student achievement?" Other related questions in this study concerned the effects that block scheduling has on school climate and the classroom behaviors of students and teachers.

STUDY DESIGN: Data were collected by the Virginia Department of Education and consisted of principals' perceptions of the impact of block scheduling on school climate and student achievement. The study was conducted in 1997. The principals who responded to the study (164 principals) represented 77 percent of the 168 schools that were using block scheduling at that time. This represented 63 percent of the public high schools in Virginia using block scheduling. There was a typical mix of urban, suburban, and rural schools (17 percent urban, 43 percent suburban, and 40 percent rural). The achievement data collected were aggregated from reports **of norm-referenced tests** given in the eleventh grade and the Iowa Test of Basic Skills. Reading and mathematics were the two content areas examined. Data were analyzed for the spring 1996 and 1997. Schools were classified by using the Metropolitan Statistical Areas as defined by the federal government for statistical activities.

STUDY FINDINGS: In all areas students in block-scheduled programs outperformed student in single-period schools. Reading and mathematics gains were higher for all block schedules. These findings held for the rural suburban and urban classifications of schools in the study. In all areas of the study, school classroom climate was more positive, with students and teachers using block schedules than was the climate in schools that were not using block scheduling. It appears that the key to this finding was the way in which the block scheduled time was used. As time was used productively, the climate was rated more favorably.

IMPLICATIONS: Since this was a singular study, the researchers suggested that

- Additional studies be conducted in other states to determine whether the same findings could be ascertained.
- A hidden variable of added staff development activities may have given more positive results to this study.
- Tighter controls in the design of studies of this kind need to be planned when examining the effects of scheduling on school climate and student achievement.

Because of the staff development activities, the **Hawthorne effect** may have been operating (because of the novelty of the approach, positive findings could be expected to occur).

Source: Thomas L. Shortt and Yvonne V. Thayer. "Block Scheduling Can Enhance School Climate," *Educational Leadership 56*(4) (Dec./Jan. 1999): 76–81.

as students' needs and teaching objectives are altered for particular periods and types of instruction. Combining these two organizational concepts—modular and flexible scheduling—implies that the traditional organization for instruction can be changed to meet changing needs and concepts of learning as students pass through the school.

The regime of the six- or eight-period day of the typical high school does not allow enough flexibility for the best use of teacher and student resources and abilities. Classes tend to be the same size for everything, and the concern is maintaining an average teacher load. An increasing number of educators also question the wisdom of devoting the same amount of time to each subject. Some subjects can be taught best in shorter blocks of time and/or in fewer periods a week; others can best be taught in longer blocks. Some classes may be intentionally kept small; others may exceed the regular thirty-pupil classrooms. The size of the class is best determined by the intended objectives.

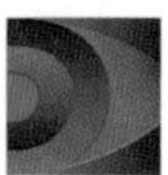

ORGANIZING STUDENTS

Since the 1960s a vast collection of research has accumulated that consistently suggests that children do not all learn at the same rate or in the same way. Schools, however, have tended to ignore that research and group children in manageable-sized clusters of twenty-five to thirty students per teacher, without regard to learning progress. This practice is based on tradition. As a beginning teacher, you will want to address the individual differences among your students. As we discussed in Part II of this text, the diversity of the student body with which you will interact will be increasing. Your concern for that diversity will be reflected in the steps you take to recognize and attend to individual differences.

CLASS SIZE FOR MANAGEMENT AND GROUPING

Determining the optimal class size for elementary and secondary schools continues to be an uncertain exercise. There is little doubt that if all classes could have a one-to-one teacher–student ratio, learning and teaching conditions would approach an ideal setting. However, there are valid arguments for learning environments that take something other than a tutorial approach. Significant numbers of studies on class size have concluded little more than that students can learn in a variety of class sizes. A good case can be made for group learning activities in which the student is expected and encouraged to interact with his or her peers. In addition, for some learning objectives the student is expected to receive significant amounts of information, and this can best be delivered in large groups. The problems associated with the inclusion of learners with special needs have created a new area of instructional research.

GROUPING PHILOSOPHY

Grouping refers to the way in which student groups are created for instruction. Generally, ability grouping has been defended as a way in which the teacher can provide more adequately for individual differences. Elementary schools have tended to group pupils by subject area within the self-contained classroom, and secondary schools have tended to group students by subject, as learners develop and pursue special interests. The usual effects of grouping have caused separate classes to be established for academically talented students, slow learners, and average learners.

The position that school systems take on ability grouping depends largely on their conception of the individual child and of the general purpose of education. If the philosophical position of the school is focused on a predetermined curriculum, the school is more likely to support **homogeneous** ability grouping. In homogeneous grouping, the school uses some set of criteria (such as intelligence scores or achievement tests) to group like students. If, in contrast, the school is concerned about the personal and social development of students and believes

homogeneous
A grouping term that is used to describe a group of learners who are alike in their learning habits, attitudes, and performances.

A common practice in elementary schools is to have small groups of children together for reading instruction with the teacher.

in diversity as a technique of stimulating education, it is more likely to favor **heterogeneous** grouping. In heterogeneous grouping, the school intentionally puts students with a variety of abilities and interests together.

Despite the usual defense for ability grouping—that is, provision for individual differences—school programs still tend to be group-oriented, and individual differences do not receive sufficient attention. Although ability grouping has been defended as a way to help increase learners' achievement levels, this defense is only weakly substantiated by research findings. Many studies report positive achievement results for more able students, but other studies report negative findings for less able students. One type of research finding consistently suggests more positive affective learning in heterogeneous grouping.

One of the chief difficulties in establishing truly homogeneous groups is that the measurement instruments that are used to establish groups are imprecise. Another constraint is the lack of flexible class and teaching assignments: It is almost impossible to select a completely homogeneous class when every class must have thirty students and when scheduling conflicts and student interests cause potentially valid diagnostic testing data to be discarded. If the student population of a school district is a sample of the total population and if that sample is a mirror of some normal curve distribution, then class sizes cannot all be the same and still be classified as homogeneous for learning purposes.

GROUPING PROBLEMS The potential for problems generated by rigid ability grouping far outweighs the scant benefits to be gained. Some of the serious problems associated with rigid homogeneous grouping are the following:

1. Teachers tend to prefer teaching average or above-average groups rather than groups of low ability. Low-ability groups, however, are not always filled with low-ability students. These groups also become dumping grounds for learners with discipline problems, some of whom are not of low academic ability.
2. Students who are given labels of low ability usually perform poorly at least partly because of the teacher's low expectation of them.
3. Problems associated with social class and minority group differences are usually increased by ability grouping.

heterogeneous
A grouping term that is used to describe a group of learners who are not alike in their learning and attitude characteristics.

4. Ability grouping tends to reinforce unfavorable self-concepts among children placed in low-ability groups.
5. Negative self-concepts are more severe among minority group learners who are assigned to low-ability groups.
6. For the learners, ability grouping does not enhance the value and acceptance given to differences in society.
7. Although academically talented students achieve better in high-ability groups, low-ability students tend to perform more poorly in low-ability groups.

Despite the many negative aspects of ability grouping, the advantage of using some limited and flexible grouping pattern is that it can contribute to teaching effectiveness. There is little doubt that the task of instruction—and the general intent to provide individualized programs—is made easier if the breadth of the range of abilities and interests is reduced through grouping. If grouping remains flexible and is based on abilities, needs, interests, and social practices, and if stu-

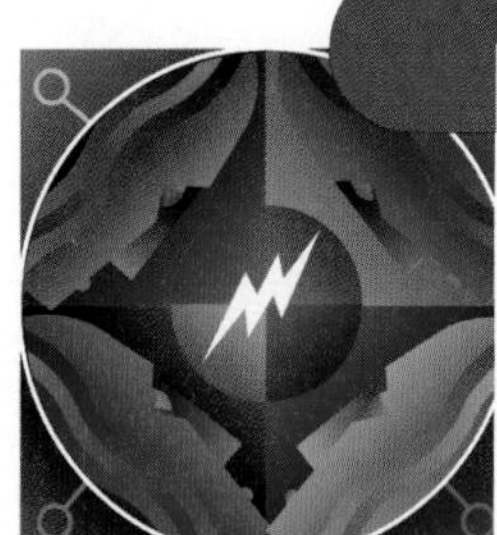

PROFESSIONAL DILEMMA

Adjusting the Attitude of Learners

Teachers in today's schools meet face-to-face with increasing attitude problems of learners. These problems are manifested in a lack of respect for teachers, visual boredom in learning, and a lack of work ethic for career. The lack of respect comes from the societal image of teachers, who experience criticisms such as "Those who can't, teach!" Additionally, whatever is wrong in society tends to be blamed on the teacher and the school program. Teacher authority is usurped by parents and the society, which challenge the teacher's right to discipline students, even the unruly ones. Students call into question the worthiness of professional teachers, who are considered to have lower status when compared with other professions. The fact that teachers tend to be grossly underpaid for the type of workload they face does not offer a positive image for teaching as a career.

Students exhibit boredom and are not motivated to learn because they do not see the relevance of what they are studying. To them, much of what they study seems to be important only for the tests they take and has no relevance to their lives. They yearn for assurance that teachers not only are competent, but also care. The lack of a work ethic may be attributable to an environment that provides everything material that they need and want. This student problem is probably related to the "good life" quality of a society that tends to have everything it needs. Most students have economically secure homes, are provided with an overabundance of goods and services, and are not held accountable for responsible activities in the family.

This dilemma does not paint a glowing picture of what is waiting for the teacher when she or he enters the classroom. If this picture is accurate and is to be altered, then the teacher needs to actively pursue the following:

- Develop with the students a common ground for the establishment of respect for each other. How can the teacher show respect for the students and have the students show respect for the teacher?
- How does the teacher prepare a learning environment that has meaning to the everyday life of the learner?
- How does the teacher work with the home and community in providing a learning atmosphere in which students develop a sense of work ethic and recognize its value?

dents are not locked into fixed groups, the teacher can arrange instruction to achieve a set of appropriate objectives for a particular group.

TRACKING **Tracking** provides rigid, specified programs built on a system of prerequisite courses. A student who is identified with a particular high school program (such as college prep or business) stays "on the track" to complete the program and does not benefit from the flexibility associated with a constants–variables program. Rigid grouping practices are added, and the track becomes more specific. Although tracking programs were once thought to provide for individual differences, they have introduced a rigid program of constants, with little elective participation by the student.

For instance, one of the common tracks, the college preparatory program, has become a rigorous intellectual curriculum designed to prepare the student for more advanced learning. In so doing, it has tended to limit students' development in aesthetics and the appreciation of art and music. The typical college preparatory program requires the student to satisfy requirements of four units in English, three in social studies, three to four in science, three to four in mathematics, three in a foreign language, and at least two in physical education and health. These requirements total eighteen to twenty Carnegie units; therefore, very little time is available for courses in art, music, drama, or practical skills such as computer science or driver education. The broader aspects of basic life-coping skills, aesthetic appreciation, the understanding of others, and any sense of the necessity for economic productivity are simply ignored in a rigid college preparatory track. As state and local curriculum requirements continue to reflect tighter college-type programs for all learners, the nonacademic survival and appreciation skills may be placed in serious jeopardy.

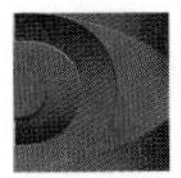

INSTRUCTIONAL PRACTICES

The most significant aspect of the total school program is instruction: the ways in which the intended curriculum experiences are delivered to the learner. There can be no intended student growth if instructional strategies are unrelated to the types of learner behaviors that are expected. For example, if the instructional intent is to have learners acquire the skills of discussion techniques, it is inappropriate to use a lecture format with them. The more appropriate instructional format would be one that involves the students in active discussion. The key to the delivery of successful instruction is the demonstrated assortment of practices of the teachers' instructional skills. These practices should be closely related to planned clusters of learner objectives within each of the academic disciplines. A curriculum that is standards based identifies the content to be taught and the instructional strategies to be used to deliver those standards as presented by the objectives.

tracking
A term used to describe the program of a student that is pointing to a particular outcome, for example, a college prep program. The program has a particular track or required sequence of courses.

GOALS FOR LEARNING

The broad aims and standards that the many national committees and commissions have developed are valuable only if they are related to specific learner outcomes planned for the school. As we indicated in Chapter 13, this relationship should follow the *backward approach* to curriculum development. Teachers who are preparing to plan the curriculum, teach the subjects, and evaluate the intended outcomes should understand how planned objectives for learning are reached. Instructional strategists always hope for a one-to-one relationship between objectives and instructional strategies. Expected types of learning change as the world adjusts to change. Planning for different types of learning is never finished. The instructional planning activity is an active process.

TAXONOMIES Among several attempts to clarify and develop educational objectives, the comprehensive approach of Benjamin Bloom and others—the **taxonomy,** or classification of educational objectives—stands out. These educators classify objectives in three groups, or domains, according to the kind of learning to be produced: cognitive, affective, and psychomotor.

- Cognitive objectives are concerned with memory, recognition of knowledge, and development of intellectual abilities and skills.[1]
- Affective objectives are concerned with interest, attitudes, opinions, appreciations, values, and emotional sets.[2]
- Psychomotor objectives are concerned with the development of muscular and motor skills that relate to the learning process.[3]

These three domains, with all their parts, are presented in Appendix 14.1.

Children engaged in daily physical education show superior motor fitness, academic performance, and attitude toward school as compared to their counterparts who do not participate in daily physical education.

James Pollalschele and Frank Hagen

CONVERGENT LEARNING Teachers work with learners to develop at least two types of learning practice and behavior: *convergent* and *divergent.* The sole objective of convergent learning is that the learner experience the discovery and manipulation of new (for the learner) knowledge but then arrive at closure and acceptance of a single "right" solution or generalization before moving on to new learning. This type of learning is anticipated when the teacher's intent is to work with the learner at the lower levels of each domain in the cognitive taxonomy.

DIVERGENT LEARNING Divergent learning encourages the learner to explore, develop hypotheses, gather information to test those hypotheses, and arrive at a defensible conclusion. The student does not have to search for the one "right" conclusion, because there is none. This type of learning practice prepares students to search for and accept answers that are different from one another. Objectives that focus on divergent learning are characteristic of the higher (more advanced) levels of the cognitive taxonomy.

MODELS OF LEARNING

Students are different. They learn at different rates; they have differing abilities; some are more able and some are less able; some learn more easily through some mediums of instruction while others learn more easily through different mediums of instruction. Teachers need to prepare themselves to offer instructional strategies that attempt to balance learner differences with teacher instructional models to afford the best chance for learning. Joyce, Weil, and Showers offer a thorough presentation of teaching models that teachers can adopt and/or adapt for specific learner objectives with workable teaching strategies.[4] We present some of the more common learning and instruction models that are easily adaptable to a set of objectives for learners.

taxonomy
A classification system.

MASTERY MODEL

The *mastery learning* model attempts to address the problems of differences in learning rates and abilities of students. This model is one of the most well-researched instructional models of the twentieth century.[5] Although students of differing abilities and learning rates may work with the same or similar objectives, they are all still expected to acquire mastery or satisfactory achievement of the objective. Some students may be given more time than others, and some may be provided with opportunities at different levels of mastery to achieve the expectations. One of the keys to the success of a mastery learning model is the teacher's diagnostic and prescriptive work. Teachers must be realistic in their expectations for learners and be reasonably confident that the outcomes they desire are achievable by the students with whom they interact. If mastery learning is planned to be sequential, then the student success rate is particularly important. Students need to experience success in learning.

Mastery learning models are difficult to employ if the school curriculum is rigidly fixed by grade level and all students are expected to master certain objectives every year. Mastery learning programs are most effective in nongraded school programs in which annual units of time are not as crucial. These programs are more flexible, and differences in learning rates can be attended to with fewer problems. Teachers still use specific objectives for learners, however, and clusters of students or individual students work with those objectives.

INDIVIDUALIZED MODELS

Audiotutorial and *individually prescribed instruction (IPI)* models provide for individual pacing of learning activities. Direct student–teacher contact is at a minimum except when the teacher provides remedial, developmental, or enrichment services to the learner as a result of some diagnosis. One of the chief characteristics of IPI strategies is test–teach–test. From predetermined instructional objectives, curricular modules for individualized instruction are developed. For each module a diagnostic test is developed to measure, before instruction starts, how well the learner can reach the module objectives. After diagnosis the learner proceeds through the instructional package and is retested at completion. If learners reach the expected criterion for the learning package, they go ahead at their own rate. The learning packages become individual tutors for the students. The task of the teacher is to monitor learner progress through diagnostic activities and testing.

The term *audiotutorial* refers to audiotape recorders for the instructional delivery system, whereas IPI may use a whole host of instructional delivery systems ranging from paper materials to computers. Teachers using IPI generally follow these steps:

- Step 1: Administer a diagnostic test for the learning module, and establish entering behavior.
- Step 2: Have the learner experience the elements of the learning module indicated by an entry-level test.
- Step 3: Test the learner when he or she completes the module.
- Step 4: If the expected criterion for the module has been attained, move the student to the next pretest and module.

Individually guided education (IGE) was developed by the Kettering Foundation's Institute for the Development of Educational Activities (IDEA) and the

Independent and group learning activities are common practice in the elementary school.

Sears Roebuck Foundation. The current activities of IGE are disseminated through two major national groups. One is the IGE Teacher Education Project at the University of Wisconsin, and the other is the national IGE Project operating out of IDEA in Dayton, Ohio. Whereas IPI takes all learners through the same preplanned program with identical objectives, IGE promotes different specific objectives for individual learners and is heavily process-oriented. Objectives are planned by the teacher and student. IGE strongly emphasizes both individualized and group learning.

These various individualized models can be classified according to the initiator of objectives and instruction. On the one hand, if the teacher initiates the instruction and objectives, the classification is one of IPI. If the learner initiates the instruction and objectives, the individualized model is one of independent study. Figure 14.2 shows this matrix schema of individualized models.

FIGURE 14.2 INDIVIDUALIZED MODELS IDENTIFIED BY SOURCES OF INSTRUCTION AND SOURCES OF OBJECTIVES

Source: Instructional Model	Source: Instructional Objectives — Teacher	Source: Instructional Objectives — Learner
Teacher	A IPI Mastery Learning	B IGE
Learner	C Self-Directed Instruction Thinking Skills Instruction	D Independent Study 4 Mat

THINKING SKILLS MODEL

A *thinking skills* model is yet another learning model for instruction. Developed by Antoinette Worsham, the model presents an eight-step approach for teachers to use if they wish to develop students' thinking skills while delivering the instructional program.[6] As Figure 14.3 shows, the model has two phases, a planning phase and an implementation phase. As the teacher works with the students, he or she uses an **inductive process** to work on skills. That is, the teacher instructs the students in how to ask the questions that are appropriate to skill development and content acquisition. Interestingly enough, this type of learning model holds great promise for transfer from one academic class to another. The model can be used with the cognitive domain levels to help students move from lower-level learning (such as memorization) to higher-level learning (such as independent analysis). If the teacher has objectives for learning related to this hierarchy of learning, then the thinking skills model can be used to promote

FIGURE 14.3 THINKING SKILLS MODEL

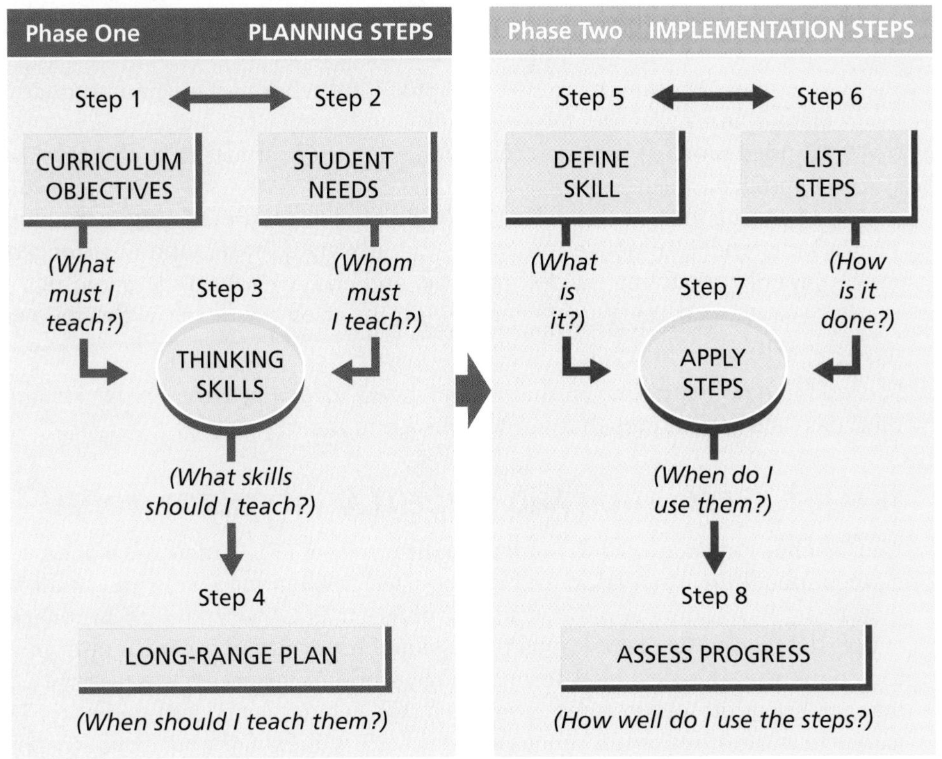

Source: Antoinette Worsham, "A 'Grow As You Go' Thinking Skills Model," *Educational Leadership* (April 1988): 56–57. Reprinted with permission of the Association for Supervision and Curriculum Development. Copyright © 1988 by ASCD. All rights reserved.

attainment of those objectives. Students are encouraged to be reflective in their learning and to keep logs of what they learned and how they learned it. The greatest strength of this model is that the students, if they have acquired the requisite skills, see its applicability to all of their learning encounters and the relationships in learning among the many disciplines they study.

Teachers who brainstorm possible product outcomes with students increase the chance that students will take ownership in their learning.

Kathleen Montgomery

HUNTER MODEL

Madeline Hunter's developmental model has been widely used as a mastery-type model for organizing instruction.[7] Her approach to lesson design has been used in staff development efforts across the nation. Her research suggests that effective teachers use a particular methodology whenever they plan and execute a lesson. In particular, she has posited that a properly taught lesson has eight elements that enhance and maximize learning. Many teacher training programs employ the Hunter Model, often referred to as clinical teaching, in their methods experiences.

The eight steps to the lesson design are as follows:

1. Anticipatory set, which is a type of prompt prior to the beginning of a lesson. It may be a handout, for example.

inductive process
A learning style in which learning begins with pieces of knowledge and these are used to create the whole principle, axiom, concept, or great idea.

2. Purpose or objective of the lesson: why the students need to learn it, what they will be able to do as a result of the lesson, and how they will demonstrate that they have learned the objective.
3. Input or what the students need to know to be successful, that is, vocabulary, skills, and concepts.
4. Modeling or showing in some graphic form what the finished product will look like.
5. Guided practice in which the teacher leads the students in a hear–see–do approach.
6. Checking for understanding through a series of questioning techniques.
7. Independent practice, in which students are released and encouraged to practice modeling, guided practice, and checking for understanding.
8. Closure as a review or wrap-up. Can be used for entry to the following lesson.

Successful demonstrators of this model need to acquire the many subskills, methods, and techniques that are wrapped into the eight steps.

TEACHER EXPECTATION AND STUDENT ACHIEVEMENT MODEL

The Teacher Expectation and Student Achievement (TESA) model is a behavioral change model for instruction and can be used at all grade levels and in all subject areas. Based on the early research of Thomas Good and Jere Brophy and supported by the Phi Delta Kappa professional fraternity, it includes multiple interactions that are designed to encourage students to orally interact with the teacher. The philosophy underlying this model is one of expectation theory. That is, teachers often make inferences about students' behavior and/or ability based on what they know or observe about students. Because this knowledge is often lacking, owing to poor interaction with students, the teacher's inferences are not equitable and can have potentially damaging effect on students. It often leads to the self-fulfilling prophecy that what you expect from a student is usually what the student gives you.[8]

The TESA Model, through staff development activities, does the following:

- Sensitizes teachers to their expectations for students
- Shows how expectations affect student learning
- Involves teachers in the practice of reflection and careful, attentive practice of new instructional behaviors
- Encourages teachers to ask more questions of students who usually are quiet in class and don't participate in class discussions
- Helps teachers to develop a desire to converse more with low achievers both in the classroom and throughout the school

Results of classroom research indicate that improved TESA interactions improve academic performance, gender and diversity awareness, attendance, and classroom climate and reduce student discipline problems.[9]

4MAT MODEL

Developed by Bernice McCarthy,[10] the 4Mat program continues to be a popular staff development program in use as a learning model for teachers. The system provides learning activities and an instructional sequence that accommodate four of the major learning styles identified in research literature:

Small group discussions, led by the teacher, take place in team teaching situations.

- Type 1: Innovative learners are interested primarily in personal meaning. As such, they need to have personal reasons for learning. Instructional modes used with this type of learner are cooperative learning, brainstorming, and an integration of content areas as discussed in Chapter 13 with student-centered curricula.
- Type 2: Analytic learners are interested primarily in acquiring facts to deepen their understanding of concepts and processes. Instructional modes are lecture, independent research, analysis of data, and interacting with experts however they may be used.
- Type 3: Common sense learners are "try-it" learners. They are interested in how things work. Concrete instructional modes work best with them: manipulatives, hands-on tasks, and kinesthetic experiences.
- Type 4: Dynamic learners are those interested in self-directed discovery. Relying on their own intuition, they teach themselves and others. Instructional modes for them are independent study, simulations, role playing and games.

This instructional model is designed to reach all learning styles and thus is intended to help the learner find comfort in a personal learning style. Still, students are expected to experience other types of learning modes and to become comfortable with a broader repertoire of learning.

INSTRUCTIONAL TECHNOLOGY

The last two decades of the twentieth century witnessed an explosion in the creation and use of instructional technology. In a very real sense, technology use in instruction began with the use of pencils, slate boards, and such in the old one-room schoolhouses. From that time to the present, a whole host of technological aids for instruction has evolved. Although not completely inclusive, a list of those aids includes the radio, phonograph, various sound and nonsound projectors, television, videodisc players, dial-access telephone systems, cable and satellite connections, camcorders, videocassette recorders, computers with CD-ROM and

Internet capabilities, telephone and cable-ready modems, digital communication links, Geocast receivers, and others yet to come. The applicability to instruction of this explosion in technology is limited only by one's imagination.

The newest technology, however, has been slow in gaining widespread use in the schools because of its cost and the lack of teacher training in using it. But in continuing to seek uses for modern technology, the schools must always remember the need to direct the use of technology toward a provision of information-rich environments for learning. Teachers must adjust their methods to more coaching than telling and spend increased time working with individual students and small groups of students. Modern technology makes all of this possible as teachers can now quickly create a variety of learning materials that can lead to improved communication strategies and storage and retrieval systems for active learners.

CLASSROOM LEARNING CENTERS

The classroom has always been a center for learning for students. But in reality, the teacher has been the center because of the way in which she or he interacts with the students. Traditionally, that interaction was predominantly teacher directed with students, and all students were engaged in the same learning material at the same time. The teacher used the school library to augment classroom activities, but here too the student was guided by the teacher. Gradually, teachers began to develop and use an additional learning area (learning resource center and/or instructional materials center) as an adjunct to the classroom and the library. These centers have gained significant importance in the schooling process. Using a variety of **hardware** and **software,** the centers were developed and used initially at the elementary level. Over the past two decades these centers have found increased use in the junior and senior high schools.

These centers are not intended to replace the library but are intended to supplement the verbal material support of the library. They may be located in a central part of the school or be a part of every classroom. The centers are usually equipped, for example, with a variety of printed materials, books, programmed materials, closed-circuit television, audiotapes, videotapes, and computers. Students use these centers as assigned by the teacher on an individual and/or group basis or are free to use the center to pursue learning on an individual basis for independent learning activities. With increased use of a variety of instructional models and student-centered curricula, centers have become the support adjunct classrooms for teachers. The only limitation to a center is the teacher's imagination as he or she develops objectives for learning experiences for children.

Carol Ann Tomlinson[11] describes what centers should do:

- Give focus to the goals of a particular program.
- Provide materials that assist students in their learning growth.
- Be sensitive to the differences in learning abilities, reading achievement, and the special interests of learners.
- Provide a wide range of activities that vary from simple to complex.
- Be self-instructional with good directions for students.
- Offer solutions for student help when needed and provide directions for completed student work.
- Have an assessment system for student work and a record-keeping system for the student and the teacher. Student **portfolios** are most appropriate here.

These attributes can be used as the criteria or checklist to evaluate the effectiveness of a center.

hardware
Mechanical equipment used in learning, such as a projector, screen, or computer.

software
Electronic instructions that tell hardware what to do.

portfolios
An account of a student's performance and works; may contain test results, interviews, examples of writing, videos of performances and other examples of a student's work.

EDUCATIONAL TELEVISION

The use of different learning stations helps the teacher provide for individual needs of students.

During the twentieth century humans and technology produced television. Hailed as a boon to education, television was to make the classroom teacher obsolete. Students could now be taken to parts of the world they had never seen and never could see without television. They could also be introduced to multiple complex learning environments. Such was the claim of television proponents for the use of this medium in the schools. Parenthetically, such was the claim for the radio in the 1930s. Although the radio never fully achieved its potential in the formal learning environment, television has become a significant contributor to the learning environment. However, it has not rendered the teacher obsolete.

Television has become an accepted medium for both formal and informal learning. Most homes now have multiple television sets, as do schools. Extensive TV watching by young people provides more observation-type learning than do the eighteen years of formal education. Now equipped with cable and satellite dishes, home viewing has provided a distorted and violent image of the world and its people, whether it be in sports, news, or documentaries.

The overuse of television has been blamed for increasing prejudice and aggressive behavior in young people. Added to the regular programming and its negative impacts on young people is the influence of advertising to which young people are exposed. But despite all of the criticisms mentioned here, television has had and will continue to have a positive contribution to the formal educative process.

Instructional television can be used as an open or closed medium to aid instruction. Closed-circuit systems can be used within a single building or across a school district as it creates its own program offerings using its best teachers for all of the students of a district. Open-circuit use can be employed with the special programs that come via the Communication Satellite System (COMSAT) or selected offerings from the cable networks, for example, the History Channel. The Children's Television Workshop offers programs such as *Sesame Street, The Electric Company,* and *Mister Rogers' Neighborhood.*

With the use of videodiscs and videotapes, prerecorded materials, screened by a teacher, afford flexibility in choosing specific episodes for use at appropriate times. Videotapes can be used to copy particular network and cable offerings for classroom use at any given time. They can also be used in creating **simulation** activities that can be useful in individualizing instruction and the promotion of societal values in the classroom.

simulation
A presentation of an instructional game type of performance in which the particular activity is to be as close to reality as is possible.

Despite all control efforts with young learners as to the appropriateness of what they watch on television, these learners will continue to experience a broad array of offerings, good and bad. Teachers and parents need to be concerned about students' exposure to print and visual media. Reading and evaluation of reading and visual material are important aspects of a child's learning. Students need to be taught how to become critical consumers of television. Teachers can provide the critical analytical skills young people need for evaluating television content for its message and bias. Additionally, students need to become evaluators of the many technical aspects of TV. Technical aspects include the media use of louder commercials, rapid-fire flash sessions to tease the senses, uses of repetition for emphasis, and glorified imagery of TV commercial performers. If the student is to be an intelligent consumer of television rather than a gullible receiver, then he

FIGURE 14.4 Ratio of Students to Computers, 1992–1998

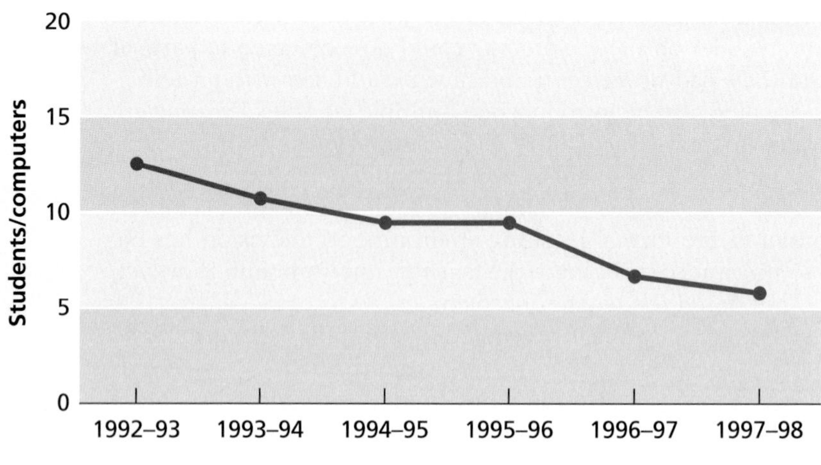

or she needs to know how the technical production and presentation affects the viewer's reception of the message content.

COMPUTER TECHNOLOGY IN EDUCATION

Much of what has been said about movies, radio, teaching machines, and television has been, and continues to be said of the computer. This latest technological advance has been shown to be both a boon and a hazard for education: a boon because of the seemingly unlimited possibilities for improvement of instruction and a hazard because of the potential tendency to assume that the teacher is no longer needed with students but should become the creator of the programs and materials used with students. The purchase and use of computers in schools have increased rapidly during the past decade. Figures 14.4 and 14.5 show the growth of computer use in the schools in the 1990s.[12]

FIGURE 14.5 Ratio of Students to Computers by School Level, 1997–1998

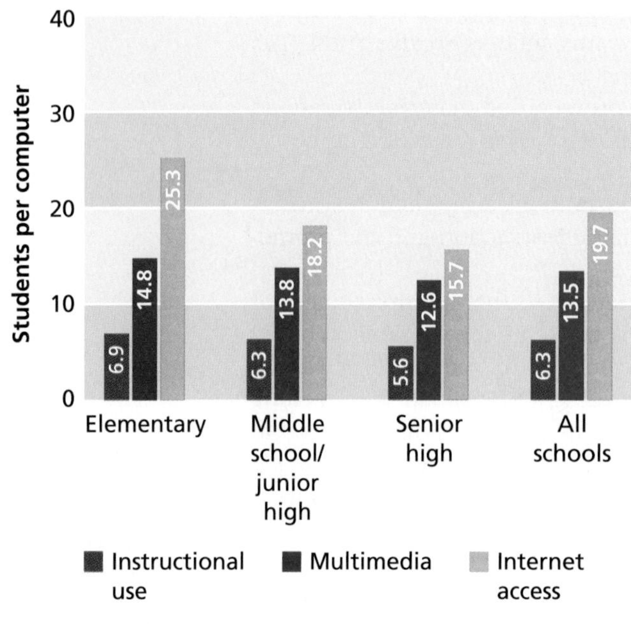

Computer technology in education began with the use of large mainframes computers for instruction. These machines were very limited, however, because of the cost and the proximity of location to the instructional areas of the school. To be used for the early drill and practice routines, student learning stations had to be close to the mainframe and could not always be shared among the many buildings of the school district. It was not until the advent of the microcomputer that computer use for instruction became more economical and flexible. However, use of many of the large mainframe computers has continued, but with different purposes: record keeping and management.

RECORD KEEPING Many school districts either use their own small mainframe or rent mainframe computer time from local businesses and industry to manage their district record keeping. These mainframes maintain records of student performance in the district, district reports to community and state agencies, scheduling of school program, budgeting, and districtwide records of computer-managed instruction. Most states now have direct computer communication with all school districts and intermediate school organizations such as countywide administrative units and/or regional areas. These types of data collection and dissemination are used across the country between states and the federal government.

MANAGEMENT Management data are collected for budgeting, enrollments, school district pupil progress, attendance data, school financial support formulas, building maintenance records, and pupil transportation data. Most of these data, in addition to providing the district with a continuing picture of the state of the school district, are sent into state department of education. Thus, on any given day, the state can generate a picture of the condition of education in the state. Teaching supplies, books, and the like can be ordered for the district on an "at lot," basis and the district realizes savings in quantity purchases. All of this requires ongoing cooperation of the total teaching staff and district support personnel. The mainframe computers have a marvelous capacity for handling these types of administrative chores.

PERSONAL COMPUTERS

Now within reach of the majority of school budgets, the personal computer (PC) has become the instructional support service of most teachers. With costs continually coming down and the capabilities of the PC improving, schools have added vast numbers of PCs to classrooms and special laboratories. Additionally, increasing numbers of homes now have PCs, and many children are starting school being somewhat computer literate. That is, these young learners can engage themselves with the computer, play games on the computer, surf the web if their home computers have Internet access, and receive and send e-mail easily. All of these computer readiness skills of young learners have compelled teachers to make the effort to become computer literate themselves so that they can keep up with their students. Teachers can no longer ignore the computer and hope it will go away. They must meet the computer head on if they are to conquer the technophobia that so many of them have. **Technophobia** expresses itself in the form of frightened teachers who look on mechanical things—technology—as foreign and difficult to understand. In the home, computers have become as important to daily living as the telephone and television. At first these machines seemed complex and unfriendly, but now, in addition to being more powerful, they have become user friendly. Added to these facts is the knowledge that computer software companies have developed a vast storehouse of academic software on disk and CD-ROM for use with the PC.

Four significant problems with the expanded use of PCs remain. The first of these is the use of PCs for instruction. The technology is expanding so rapidly that the market is flooded with new, more sophisticated hardware. Even though

technophobia
A term that is used to describe a fearful attitude that some teachers have toward the use of some technology, usually computers.

Students can work in groups or alone on the computer to meet whatever objectives are being pursued by the students.

costs have been reduced significantly, schools cannot replace PCs every year. So although a major question to be answered when buying new computers is not only the original cost, but also the life cycle of the purchased computer. Apple Computer, IBM, and the many IBM-clone companies have made their newer models more compatible with older versions of the current computer in the school, but this is not always possible with the software.

A second problem is the software itself. Too much software is developed for a particular computer and its current model and is not always compatible with other types of computers. For example, software designed for the Apple Macintosh might not work on a PC. In recent years, the software has begun to be compatible with different computers; It may be made to be used with several types of computers or have conversion programs for multiple uses. Third, many computer activities rely on the Internet. Use of this feature is costly not only for initial installation, but also for day-to-day use. Telephone line costs are enormous. Fourth, and perhaps most important, instructional staff members are not trained to program computers and therefore must rely on the software market for materials they wish to use in instruction. Software companies have developed voluminous numbers of computer programs to be used in the classroom in all content areas. However, teachers must be trained to evaluate this material before investing school funds in it. There remains a significant amount of inferior software on the market, and teachers have to become skilled in culling the junk from the gems.

USING COMPUTERS IN THE CLASSROOM The only limitations for use of computers in the classroom are the skills of the teacher and the teacher's imagination. The continuum of use ranges from the mundane use of drill and practice to acquire basic skills to the creative exploration and creation of simulated laboratory work and visitation to events and places around the world. Some of those creative uses include voice-activated programs for language instruction. Currently, for example, the Pierre Indian Learning Center in Pierre, South Dakota, is using computer programs to teach seven Native American languages to the students of that school. These students come from fifteen reservations in North and South Dakota and Nebraska where these seven languages are found. With the aid of

DEBATE

YES

Should School Computer Labs Be Phased Out?

NO

Barbara Barr is a K–1 teacher at Brookside Elementary School in Nicholasville, Kentucky. This twenty-four year teaching veteran teaches nearly all lessons using classroom computers. In the fall, Barr will work in her district's technology office training teachers how to integrate computers into the curriculum.

Computers belong in all classrooms, not held captive in the computer lab and taught as a specialized subject area at a scheduled time.

All staff and students need to learn how to effectively use this instrument. This can most realistically happen when computers are conveniently accessible in a classroom.

Computer labs have a number of drawbacks. In a lab setting, the computer is learned apart from other subjects and activities. It is much more difficult to integrate technology into other areas of the curriculum within the lab setting. The computer becomes a separate course or activity, rather than a tool used to enhance learning in other areas.

Time limits are another disadvantage to computer labs. Most educators have an assigned time to use the lab. This restricted access limits activities a teacher can conduct with students.

The time limits affect students, too. For example, a student doing a research project on World War II using computers in the classroom has instant access to major databases and can use the Internet to get resources. Research can be performed instantly and on an ongoing basis.

Scheduled time to conduct research in a lab a few times a week doesn't allow ample time to work on projects like this.

Even the physical location of computer labs causes problems in many schools. It is just too inconvenient to have educators take away from their classroom time to shuttle students down the hall or to another part of the school building. Once they get to the lab, there is no access to regular classroom materials.

Having computers located within an educator's classroom setting has a number of advantages. With just one computer in the classroom, we can:

Ferdi Serim taught computer lab at John Witherspoon Middle School in Princeton, New Jersey, until his recent move to New Mexico. Serim is coauthor of the book NetLearning: Why Teachers Use the Internet *and editor of* MultiMedia Schools Magazine.

I call this the "right shoe vs. left shoe" debate. You need both kinds of shoes to get anywhere. In an ideal world, computers belong on every student's lap. But rather than focusing on where we put them, we need to focus on how the computers will be used. Once we know that, we can make better decisions about how they'll be deployed.

For the past ten years, I've worked as an educator in computer labs, in two different districts. I've seen labs used well, and I've seen them used in ways that make me cringe. There is indeed a push by some to get rid of labs. Computer labs should not be phased out. Rather, they should be used in ways that make educational sense.

There is great value in having spaces where entire classes can use technology at the same time, whether it's a computer lab or a library/media center.

Computer labs are effective places to give all students adequate access to technology to perform meaningful work.

A good example of this is when Shannon Dahl, an eighth grade language arts teacher at my school, had her kids create books using the computer. Students gathered autobiographical information, pictures, and relics. They used a range of desktop publishing technologies to print, bind, and produce these one-of-a-kind heirlooms. The project ended in an "author's breakfast" for 125 kids, their families, and the community.

It took Shannon Dahl three weeks to complete the project using the computer lab. If she had only two computers in her room the project would take all year. Having six machines would have allowed her to complete it in 15 weeks. That doesn't make educational sense.

Before getting rid of labs and putting more computers in classrooms, educators should consider these additional benefits of computer labs:

YES — NO

- Create a spread sheet of students' names and have each student enter data for daily attendance, lunch count, and records of monies received.
- Use a scrolling marquee screen saver for spelling words, new vocabulary, announcements, or information.
- Replace messy chalk boards or overheads with PowerPoint presentations or a simple text program using enlarged fonts.
- Instantly access encyclopedia programs, museums, libraries, and universities.

Not only are computers convenient, they are the only teaching instrument that can handle all subjects on every developmental level and still keep up with the latest information. When the student is ready to learn, the classroom computer is there!

Teachers must become comfortable with computers in order to use them effectively. This will happen when computers are available in the classroom on a consistent daily basis.

In my 24 years teaching, I've seen programs come and go with varying degrees of success. Never have I found one simple item that added so much to instruction, while instilling a passion for knowledge in students. Why limit this tremendous tool to scheduled sessions in a room at the other end of the building?

Source: "Should School Computer Labs Be Phased Out?" *NEA Today* (September 1999): 11.

- Most classroom computers are not networked to other school computers. Computer labs allow teachers and students to make projects and information available for collaboration via the school network.
- Classroom computers don't often allow for projection devices to support group activity.

When teachers used my lab, I'd make "housecalls" to other computers with my laptop and an LCD panel for wider viewing by groups of students. The teachers I worked with would rather have a machine that let "everybody" observe a demonstration than five or six machines that only served a fraction of their class.

I will say that simply having a computer lab within a school is not enough. The spectre of the empty, locked lab is responsible for much of the impulse to do away with labs and put the machines back into the classroom.

The lab must be viewed as a shared resource for both the classroom teacher and the computer lab teacher. Computer labs will only work when there are people who know how to use them, and who are empowered to make them serve educators' needs.

WHAT'S YOUR OPINION?

Should school computer labs be phased out?

Go to **www.ablongman.com/johnson** to cast your vote and see how NEA readers responded.

network
A term used to describe a system of small or large set of computers that can operate in unison or harmony for regular and Internet use.

Native speakers and lexicographers, these languages have been restored for instruction. Other computer uses are offered in science classes, where simulated dissections and experiments can be produced for learners to experience.

What follows, in no specific order of importance, are the many routine uses of the computer for both the student and the teacher, assuming that the school has been wired for maximum use. Wiring schools for computer use means that some form of major equipment has been installed so that all computers in the school, or the school district, are interconnected. This is sometimes referred to as a type of **network** installation. Additionally, the computers must have Internet capability, which currently requires telephone lines that can be extremely costly. It wasn't until the late 1990s that almost 80 percent of the schools were somewhat on-line and connected to the Internet. The "somewhat on-line" interpretation relates to the fact that although these schools were connected to the Internet, the connection was a general connection for the school and did not include the classrooms. This figure was reported by the National Center for Education Statistics in 1997.

WORD PROCESSING Word processing is used by both the teacher and student. In its simplest definition, word processing is the use of the computer keyboard as a type of typewriter. However, word processing is instantly seen on the computer monitor, can easily be revised as you go or at the end of the process, and is stored in the computer on a hard drive or a floppy disk. Teachers use word processing for producing instructional materials and creating course outlines student handouts, classroom tests, portfolio assignment, written evaluations of student performance, communications with parents, and letters and other communications with colleagues in school and at other schools. All work is usually stored on a floppy disk so that it can be saved, retrieved, and revised at a later date as the teacher has need for its use.

Students use word processing skills in reporting required assignments, writing essays and reports for learning modules, and preparing their own materials for compilation to their portfolios and for participation in learning programs presented by the teacher via the computer. One of the biggest educational benefits to be gained by the student is his or her ability to compose, correct, and revise their own prose. Their prose creations assist them in meeting the teacher's intentions for learning with writing across the curriculum.

JOURNAL WRITING At some time, teachers and students are engaged in journal writing. Teachers are being required increasingly to track their professional growth activities, and this is usually done in the form of a personal journal. This journal can become part of their own portfolio as a self-evaluating activity that is shared with their supervisors for tenure and assignment activities. With increased accountability practices, even tenured teachers experience career conferencing with supervisors to help them improve professionally.

In schools where teachers use authentic procedures for measurement and evaluation of students, students are expected to use evaluative observations of their performance, commit those observations to a journal writing activity, and retain it in their portfolio. Collections of these journals, over a semester or school year, are used to help arrive at final evaluations of student performance. These types of evaluative activities are discussed in Chapter 15.

SPREADSHEETS Teachers are record keepers. In the past, teachers' grade books contained enormous amounts of data on each student; the PC now affords the teacher the luxury of compiling this information on a floppy disk using standardized spreadsheet software. These data provide the basis for school district reports, reports of student progress to parents, and a running account of student progress used for making evaluations. Students use spreadsheets in various learning activities in mathematics, social studies, and science.

CD-ROMS For databases the CD-ROM (compact disc–read only memory) currently provides more breadth and depth than floppy disks. These CDs contain reading material, pictures, sound, encyclopedia information, and some standalone instructional lessons. Parts or all of what is on a CD-ROM may be stored on the hard drive of a microcomputer so the student can instantly retrieve the material as necessary for whatever lesson he or she is studying. This use of the CD-ROM does not require one disc for every student because the computer can transfer information from the CD-ROM to the hard drive. This, of course, keeps costs to a minimum. Copyright protections for CD-ROM creators allow a school to pay for a site license; in that way the school can offer one ROM on a file server to many students on their individual desktop computers. The technology grants of the federal government have aided immensely in the networking of computers in the schools, and this type of networking has increased the potential for CD-ROM use. The DVD-ROM, with even higher capacity than the CD-ROM, is also gaining in use.

Technorealists believe that Web users must convert information into knowledge and knowledge into wisdom.

Reid Goldsborough

THE INTERNET The Internet is a name given to the worldwide connection of computers linked together and capable of containing endless amounts of information on endless topics. It is like a never-ending encyclopedia. The server computers on the Internet distribute information as it is called for to download computers, which display the information to the user. A portion of the Internet known as the World Wide Web and accessed through a browser offers user-friendly graphics and other multimedia. Whenever you see an Internet address that begins with "www" or "http://," you have identified a particular location on the World Wide Web. Commercial Internet service providers (ISPs) provide connections to the Internet, usually for a monthly or annual fee.

Electronic mail, e-mail, is one of the most popular uses of the Internet. People can communicate by e-mail as quickly as by telephone but without any long-distance charges. The e-Mail, using the modem of the computer, goes through the local ISP and gets transferred from one service area to another. This allows teachers and students to communicate with other teachers and students from all over the world. Teachers can have students improve their writing skills through penpal activities within the classroom or the school district or outside the school district to the nation and the world. E-mail can be used to study other cultures by having direct contact with people all over the world. The use of e-mail accounts gives the user an e-mail identification, which is like a postal address. If, for example, John Doe had such an account with AOL, his e-mail address might be johnd@aol.com.

The Internet provides billboards and discussion-type round tables. Participation in on-line discussions can be done live and allows for ongoing exploration of issues and programs.

The big question to be answered in any discussion of computer technology is "Is Computer technology and all of its costs and uses worth the effort?" Most of the studies that have been done so far do not suggest that the huge costs for use of this technology have been matched by significant gains in student achievement when measured by standardized tests. However, the glitter of computer technology keeps support for this technology strong among parents, school board members, and businesses. With this in mind, one may advocate increased use of the computer as we look to reforming education during the twenty-first century. It certainly has not crippled educational efforts, and with continued efforts, with its use, we may yet see it delivering the student achievement gains looked for in our schools.

SUMMARY

ORGANIZING TEACHERS TO PROVIDE INSTRUCTION

In this chapter we looked at the big ideas of balance, variety, and systems in instructional practices. These concepts were introduced with a discussion of the ways in which teachers can be organized to provide instruction. As was seen, there is variety in the way in which elementary, intermediate, and secondary schools are organized. Additionally, schools can be graded or nongraded. Instructional scheduling can be varied around modular and or flexible organizations.

ORGANIZING STUDENTS

The organization of students affords a variety of alternatives. Grouping may be heterogeneous or homogeneous. We discuss the pros and cons of these grouping arrangements. Additionally, the provisions of tracking programs are discussed with their lack of flexibility in balance of program.

INSTRUCTIONAL PRACTICES

Instructional practices relate to the types of aims and objectives of the program. These goals are tied to the three taxonomies in the cognitive, affective, and psychomotor domains. Within all of these, learning may be either convergent or divergent, and this also depends on the intended objectives. Planning for instruction—instructional strategies—should seek a one-to-one relationship with the instructional objectives.

MODELS OF LEARNING

Several instructional models were presented for discussion, including the mastery models, the individualized models, the thinking skills model, and the popular Hunter, TESA, and 4Mat models. Learners should experience the variety in these models to expand on their repertoire of learning. By experiencing a variety in learning models, the learner may come to find comfort in a personal learning style.

INSTRUCTIONAL TECHNOLOGY

Although education has witnessed an explosion in technology, significant use of that technology has been relatively slow because of cost and a lack of teacher training. As we enter the new century, however, both of those lacks have begun to be altered. Hardware has become more affordable for schools, and the learning gap for the teachers has begun to be closed. Between staff development programs and revised teacher training programs, teachers are much more comfortable with their use of technology. The personal computer has become the mainstay of the school. Now, with its connection to the Internet, the whole world has been opened up as a learning resource for the student.

A knowledge of school instructional practices is important for the teacher to acquire. The learning atmosphere, governed by instructional practices, reflects the attention that schools give to a high-quality learning environment. In addition, how the teacher uses the variety of available technology will determine the successful performance of the learners.

DISCUSSION QUESTIONS

1. Should learning be more divergent or convergent?
2. How do different staffing arrangements affect the program for the learner?
3. Support the notion that the ungraded school is the best type of organization for learners.
4. Why do you believe that computers will receive greater use in the schools of the future?
5. How can technology help to do away with the use of ability grouping?

JOURNAL ENTRIES

1. Reflect in writing about your thoughts on some of the more promising instructional models.
2. Prepare an analysis of an interview with a teacher on his or her use of a PC.
3. Contrast in writing the differences in learning between convergent and divergent emphases.

PORTFOLIO DEVELOPMENT

1. For your portfolio, revisit your reflections on ability grouping with fellow students and record their support or lack of support for your position.
2. Establish a personal five-year staff development plan on your use and development of Internet activities for use in your classroom.

SCHOOL-BASED EXPERIENCES

1. Visit an elementary school and a secondary school and compare the different approaches to space in the two schools.
2. Prepare a checklist on the potential uses of the World Wide Web. Use your checklist when visiting at least three schools and identify the most common and least common uses of the web.

WEBSITES

Practice exploring the web to help you gain deeper insights into the models of learning, instructional practices, and instructional technology as discussed in this chapter. Use some of the key terms identified for you in this chapter as a starting point. Develop some of your own terms. Other informative sites are the following:

1. <www.unicefusa.org/infoactiv/educat.html> UNICEF publications, curriculum guides, and a video catalog.
2. <www.ascd.org> The Association for Supervision and Curriculum site has reading materials, ASCD research reports, and articles from *Educational Leadership*.
3. <www.tc.columbia.edu/~academic/psel/overview.html> Teachers College, Columbia, shares information on educational problems that interfere with healthy learning.
4. <www.worldcampus.psu.edu> An educational technology integration program available on-line for help in bring technology into the classroom.

NOTES

1. Benjamin S. Bloom, ed., *Taxonomy of Educational Objectives.* New York: Longman, Green, 1956, 6–8.
2. David R. Krathwohl, Benjamin S. Bloom, and Bertram B. Masia, *Taxonomy of Educational Objectives.* New York: McKay, 1964, 176–193.
3. Anita J. Harrow, *Taxonomy of the Psychomotor Domain.* New York: McKay, 1972, 1–2.
4. Bruce Joyce, Marsha Weil, and Beverly Showers. *Models of Teaching,* 4th ed. Boston: Allyn & Bacon, 1992.
5. Robert J. Marzano. *A Theory-Based Meta-analysis of Research on Instruction* (Technical Report). Aurora, CO: Mid-Continent Regional Educational Laboratory, 1998.
6. Antoinette Worsham. "A 'Grow as you Go' Thinking Skills Model," *Educational Leadership 45* (7) (April 1988): 56–58.
7. Robert J. Marzano, "20th Century Advances in Instruction." In R. Brandt, (ed.), *Education in a New Era.* Alexandria, VA: Association for Supervision and Curriculum Development, 2000, 78.
8. Chandra Hawley, *Teacher Talk,* Vol. 2; Bloomington, IN: Indiana University, Center for Adolescent Studies, June 29, 1997.
9. Los Angeles County Office of Education, *Teacher Expectations and Student Achievement.* Downey, CA: Los Angeles County Office, June 29, 1999.
10. Bernice McCarthy, *4Mat in Action: Creative Lesson Plans for Teaching to Learning Styles.* Barrington, IL: Excel Excel. 1983.
11. Carol Ann Tomlinson, *The Differentiated Classroom.* Alexandria, VA: Association for Supervision and Curriculum Development, 1999, 76.
12. Market Data Retrieval, *Technology in Education 1998: A Comprehensive Report on the State of Technology in the K–12 Market.* Shelton, CT: Market Data Retrieval, 1988.

BIBLIOGRAPHY

Anderson, Lorin W., and Krathwohl, David R. (Eds.) *A Taxomony for Learning, Teaching, and Assessing.* New York: Addison Wesly Longman, Inc., 2001.

Campbell, Jack. *Individualizing Instruction for the Educationally Handicapped: Teaching Strategies in Remedial and Special Education.* Springfield, IL: Charles Thomas Publisher, 1998.

Dede, Chris, ed. *Learning with Technology.* Alexandria, VA: Association for Supervision and Curriculum Development, 1998.

Fullan, Michael. *Change Forces: The Sequel.* London: Falmer Press, 1999.

Kaplan, Leonard, and Edelfelt, Roy, eds. *Teachers for the New Millennium.* Thousand Oaks, CA: Corwin Press, 1996.

Lambert, Linda. *Building Leadership Capacity in Schools.* Alexandria, VA: Association for Supervision and Curriculum Development, 1998.

Lybbert, Blair. *Transforming Learning with Block Scheduling.* Thousand Oaks, CA: Corwin Press, 1999.

Marsh, David D. *Preparing Our Schools for the 21st Century: 1999 ASCD Yearbook.* Alexandria, VA: Association for Supervision and Curriculum Development, 1999.

Market Data Retrieval. *Technology in Education 1998: A Comprehensive Report on the State of Technology in the K–12 Market.* Shelton, CT: Market Data Retrieval, 1998.

Noack, Ernest G. "Comparing U.S. and German Education—Like Apples and Sauerkraut." *Phi Delta Kappan. 80* (10): (June 1999): 773–776.

Sadker, Myra Pollack, and Sadker, David Miller. *Teachers, School, and Society.* Boston: McGraw-Hill, 2000.

Sergiovanni, Thomas. *The Principalship: A Reflective Practice Perspective.* Boston: Allyn and Bacon, 1995.

——. *The Lifeworld of Leadership.* San Francisco: Jossey-Bass, 1999.

Slavin, Robert E. *Cooperative Learning.* Boston: Allyn & Bacon, 1995.

Tyack, Donald, and Cuban, Larry. *Tinkering toward Utopia: A Century of Public School Reform.* Cambridge, MA: Harvard University Press, 1995.

APPENDIX 14.1

DOMAINS OF LEARNING

The levels of cognitive learning are numerically ordered from the most superficial to the most advanced to establish a hierarchical arrangement for evaluating depth of learning.

COGNITIVE

1.00 Knowledge
1.10 Knowledge of specifics
1.20 Knowledge of ways and means of dealing with specifics
1.30 Knowledge of the universals and abstractions in a field
2.00 Comprehension
2.10 Translation
2.20 Interpolation
2.30 Extrapolation
3.00 Application
4.00 Analysis
4.10 Analysis of elements
4.20 Analysis of relationships
4.30 Analysis of organizational principles
5.00 Synthesis
5.10 Production of a unique communication
5.20 Production of a plan or proposed set of operations
5.30 Derivation of a set of abstract relations
6.00 Evaluation
6.10 Judgments in terms of internal evidence
6.20 Judgments in terms of external criteria

Source: Benjamin S. Bloom, ed., *Taxonomy of Educational Objectives.* New York: Longmans, Green, 1956, 6–8.

AFFECTIVE

1.00 Receiving (attending)
1.10 Awareness
1.20 Willingness to receive
1.30 Controlled or selected attention
2.00 Responding
2.10 Acquiescence in responding
2.20 Willingness to respond
2.30 Satisfaction in response
3.00 Valuing
3.10 Acceptance of a value
3.20 Preference for a value
3.30 Commitment
4.00 Organization
4.10 Conceptualization of a value
4.20 Organization of a value system

5.00 Characterization by a value or value complex
5.10 Generalized set
5.20 Characterization

Source: David R. Krathwohl, Benjamin S. Bloom, and Bertram B. Masia, *Taxonomy of Educational Objectives.* New York: McKay, 1964, 176–193.

PSYCHOMOTOR

1.00 Reflex movements
1.10 Segmental reflexes
1.20 Intersegmental reflexes
1.30 Suprasegmental reflexes
2.00 Basic-fundamental movements
2.10 Locomotor movements
2.20 Nonlocomotor movements
2.30 Manipulative movements
3.00 Perceptual abilities
3.10 Kinesthetic discrimination
3.20 Visual discrimination
3.30 Auditory discrimination
3.40 Tactile discrimination
3.50 Coordinated abilities
4.00 Physical abilities
4.10 Endurance
4.20 Strength
4.30 Flexibility
4.40 Agility
5.00 Skilled movements
5.10 Simple adaptive skills
5.20 Compound adaptive skills
5.30 Complex adaptive skills
6.00 Nondiscursive communication
6.10 Expressive movement
6.20 Interpretive movement

Source: Anita J. Harrow, *Taxonomy of the Psychomotor Domain.* New York: McKay, 1972, 1–2.

CHAPTER

15

Standards-Based Education and Assessment

EDUCATION IN THE NEWS

High-Stakes Testing: They're Here and They're Not Going Away

By Karen Gutloff, *NEA Today,* March 1999

Virginia educators are still reeling from the news that 97 percent of the state's schools posted failing grades in January on the new Standards of Learning (SOL).

The test, given to students in grades 3, 5, 8 and high school, measures knowledge of the state's new academic standards.

Since the SOL tests were first administered in 1998, scores of Virginia teachers have complained of pressure from administrators to dump their curriculum and drill students in SOL test material.

Many are doing just that.

But in other areas, educators are working with administrators to find new ways to prepare students to do well.

Third grade teacher Pam Heath and three colleagues, for example, are helping the Franklin County school district rewrite the math and English curriculum to reflect new standards.

"We call it unpacking the SOLs," says Heath.

"We're identifying the specific skills a child needs in order to master the new standards," says Heath, a member of the Franklin County Education Association. "The next step is to incorporate those skills into the curriculum."

Heath says certification by the National Board for Professional Teaching Standards helped her take a broader view of how students learn best.

"You can't just teach to the test and have student memorize a bunch of isolated facts," she says. "You have to teach for understanding so students can apply concepts to any test question."

This school year, Heath has been traveling to area schools, coaching teachers in how to rework lesson plans to meet the standards.

For example, Heath encourages elementary teachers to forget the toga parties when teaching about ancient civilization, a big part of the SOL test.

"I encourage them to think of the big picture. What is the larger idea about democracy? If students have a bigger understanding of democracy, they can think their way through the questions." . . .

Says Heath: "There's a lot of anxiety and confusion out there about SOL. But I think educators are rising to meet the challenge."

LEARNER OUTCOMES

After reading and studying this chapter, you will be able to:

1. Analyze the different conceptions of standards and identify the consequences that these conceptions have for teaching and learning.
2. Understand the way in which standards influence accountability in the teaching and learning process.

(continued)

3. Compare the different sources for standards and specify the conflicts that result from the varied interests of these sources.
4. Articulate the interrelationships among educational goals, standards, benchmarks, and assessments.
5. Compare the different purposes for assessments and identify what methods of assessment are appropriate for different situations.
6. Analyze the different problems that surround standards-based assessment practices, including high-stakes testing, pressures to cheat, teaching for the test, and the threat of a national examination.
7. Analyze how standards-based education and assessment influence the teaching and learning process.
8. Describe how one school district has addressed implementation of standards-based education and performance assessments to address classroom instructional uses and system accountability. ■

The use of standards is a popular topic of debate in both the business and education worlds. Policymakers at the state and federal levels continually talk about standards. So do school administrators, teachers, curriculum developers, and education reformers. Interestingly, even though people are using the term *standards,* their definitions of the term can be quite different. Some educators view standards as synonymous with rigor and the setting of high expectations for schools, teachers, and students. Others are talking about the specification of learner outcomes. Another use of the term is in relation to a particular approach to instruction.

Three big ideas surround and inform the standards movement. First, there is increased demand from policymakers and the public for accountability. A second big idea is the shared emphasis on the importance of authentically assessing what students have learned. Third, standards require a major change in the way teachers and students think and work in classrooms. In total this movement toward standards-based education represents a major shift in thinking about accountability, teaching, and learning.

The accountability theme is heard in the repeated calls for schools to have rigorous educational standards and that students be tested. In many states, testing has become high stakes, with results being used to determine who is permitted to graduate and receive a diploma or to be admitted to higher education. In other states, accountability has taken the form of legislation that establishes statewide standards and assessments, with test results being used to rank schools. State report cards are being published that describe the rankings based on how well students perform on these state tests. New forms of assessments are emerging, which include an emphasis on core competencies and capstone performances.

The second and third big ideas center on the use of standards in the classroom to guide teaching and learning. Within the classroom there are three related big ideas: The use of standards to determine curriculum, placing heavy emphasis on assessment of student learning, and development of a new model, or paradigm, of teaching and learning called *standards-based education.*

A number of important challenges and critical issues have emerged around the standards movement. Some of the important issues and questions are the following:

- What type of standards are appropriate for today's schools?
- Who determines the content of these standards?
- Is a common set of standards fair to a diverse population?
- Should assessments be made authentic to the context of the world of work?
- Should assessments be tailored to individual development or should they be standardized?
- What is the role of the teacher in a standards environment?
- What is the role of the student in a standards environment?

This chapter addresses each of these big ideas and related themes in the standards movement. The different dimensions that make up a standards-based school program as well as the implications for assessment practices are described. The chapter also tackles issues and questions that surround standards-based education and assessment. At every turn, the emphasis is placed on what teachers need to know and understand about this important education movement. To help in seeing how all of the ideas about standards and assessment can work, the last section of this chapter is the story of how one school district developed its standards and assessments and has addressed the changes in teaching and learning that teachers and their students need to make in the classroom.

STANDARDS-BASED EDUCATION

Standards-based education is a systemic approach to the entire teaching and learning process. Systemic implies that the entire school system (including the instructional methods and resources, assessments, and inservice) is driven and linked by a set of standards that the community of teachers, parents and learners endorse. Achievement of the standards is paramount and rewards (such as diplomas, promotion and sometimes even teacher salaries) are linked to student achievement of the standards. However, what is meant by standards can be quite different. Therefore the first topic is an examination of different conceptions of standards and exploration of various sources of standards.

DIFFERING CONCEPTIONS OF STANDARDS

The term *standards* can have quite different meanings for different people. For some, a standard is a worthy goal or a noteworthy accomplishment by a great performer. Such **world-class standards** are rigorous and generally out of reach for most individuals. For others, a standard is the norm; it is a statement of what most people should be able to achieve. As such this type of standard can be considered the bottom line, one that is reachable by most. Others describe standards in terms of desired student learning in a discipline or content area.

standards-based education
An instructional approach that places students' learning, rather than teachers' teaching, at the center.

WORLD-CLASS STANDARDS Some educators and policymakers think of standards as world-class goals based on the performances of outstanding individuals, such as successful mathematicians, scientists, authors, and athletes. Such world-class standards cannot be met in an elementary and secondary school setting. Rather, these standards are statements of accomplishment to be used for admiration and as models of excellence. Standards in this context are meant to inspire students to do better over time; they are not intended to be met within a single school

world-class standards
Statements of very high levels of student learning intended to ensure that the United States is competitive in a global economy.

World-class standards describe ideal expectations and high levels of performance that represent what is believed to be necessary to be competitive at national and international levels.

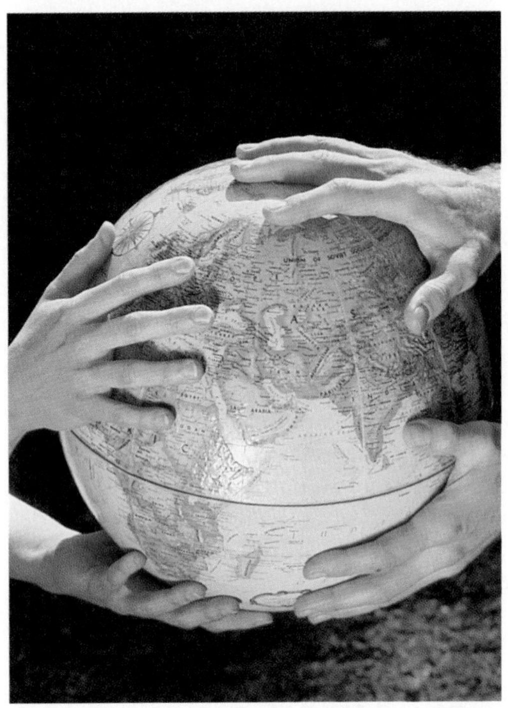

year. Educators who adopt world-class standards tend to look at their curriculum as a developmental process. The purpose of each year in school is to show individual student improvement toward the high standard. A larger view is maintained: Common sets of specific competencies (that all students are expected to master) are not seen to be as important as showing improvement in multiple and diverse ways over time. One important example of world-class standards was Goals 2000, which are presented in Figure 15.1. This set of aspirations emerged out of the 1989 National Education Summit and was supported throughout the 1990s by the nation's governors, President Clinton, and the Congress.

REAL-WORLD STANDARDS Another group of educators believe that standards should be real-world goals. This conception of standards places primary emphasis on the necessary knowledge and skills that will make students employable and enable them to live independent lives. In contrast to world-class standards, real-world standards are seen as being achievable in schools. Real-world standards would set the expectation that teachers will enable students in learning

FIGURE 15.1 THE NATIONAL EDUCATION GOALS 2000

1. All children will start school ready to learn.
2. The high school graduation rate will increase to at least 90 percent.
3. All students will be prepared for responsible citizenship, further learning, and productive employment in a global economy.
4. Teachers will acquire knowledge and skills necessary to prepare students for the next century.
5. U.S. students will be first in the world in math and science achievement.
6. Every adult will be literate and ready for lifelong learning.
7. Every school will be free of drugs, violence, and unauthorized firearms and alcohol.
8. Every school will promote parental involvement in the social, economic, and academic growth of children.

how to balance checkbooks, prepare for a job interview, and manage their daily lives.

DISCIPLINE-BASED STANDARDS Other educators and national associations think of standards as discipline-based. These subject matter acquisition standards are statements about what teachers and students should know and be able to do in various subject areas: science, mathematics, history, geography, social studies, physical education, and the arts. Usually, these discipline-based standards emphasize content acquisition; teachers are encouraged to cover subject matter and make certain that students master specific knowledge and skills.

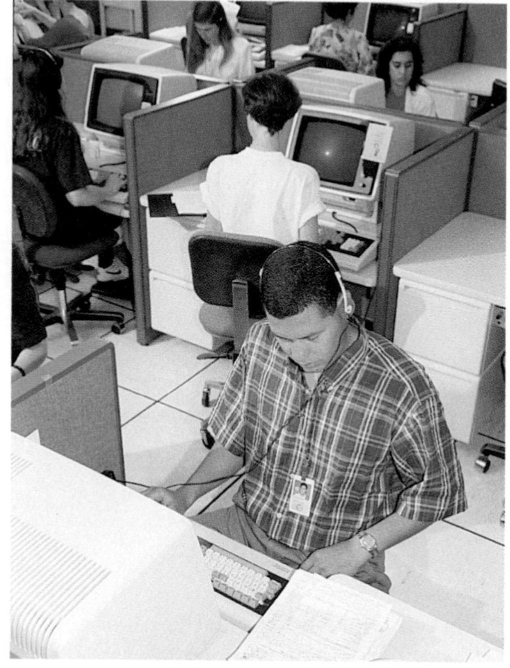

World-class standards are based on aspirations for the future rather than relying on what worked in the past.

WHY STANDARDS DIFFER These diverse conceptions of standards stem from differing expectations that people have for education. Business leaders tend to want high school graduates who are ready for work by being able to read, write, and compute. They expect schools to prepare a supply of future workers. Businesses are willing to provide specific job training, but they do not want to teach what they consider basic skills that all students should have before entering the world of work.

Policymakers are thinking about the larger, long-term needs of society. They tend to want more rigorous academic standards so as to maintain world-class status for the United States. They want students to know more science, history, mathematics, literature, and geography than students in other countries. They expect schools to graduate students who have high-level discipline-specific achievement and can demonstrate world-class performances.

Parents tend to choose standards based on their own personal goals and family histories. Some parents want their children to go to prestigious colleges; others want their children to obtain a high-paying job immediately after high school; still others want their students to achieve a certain professional career such as a medical doctor, lawyer, or engineer. These expectations influence the type of standards that individual parents would support.

Figure 15.2 is a summary of the different dimensions and tensions that

FIGURE 15.2 DIFFERING EXPECTATIONS FOR STANDARDS

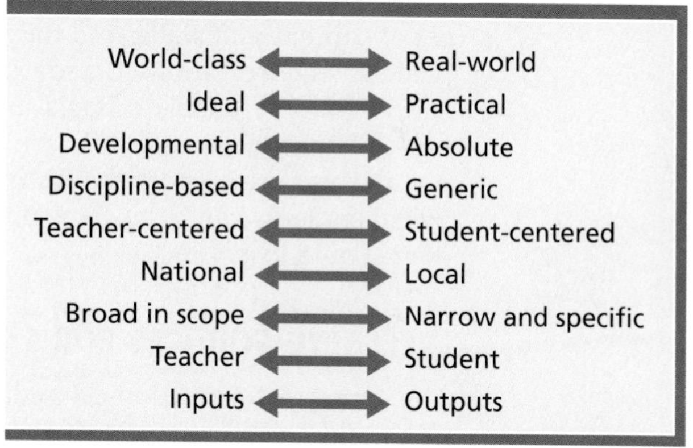

World-class ⟷ Real-world
Ideal ⟷ Practical
Developmental ⟷ Absolute
Discipline-based ⟷ Generic
Teacher-centered ⟷ Student-centered
National ⟷ Local
Broad in scope ⟷ Narrow and specific
Teacher ⟷ Student
Inputs ⟷ Outputs

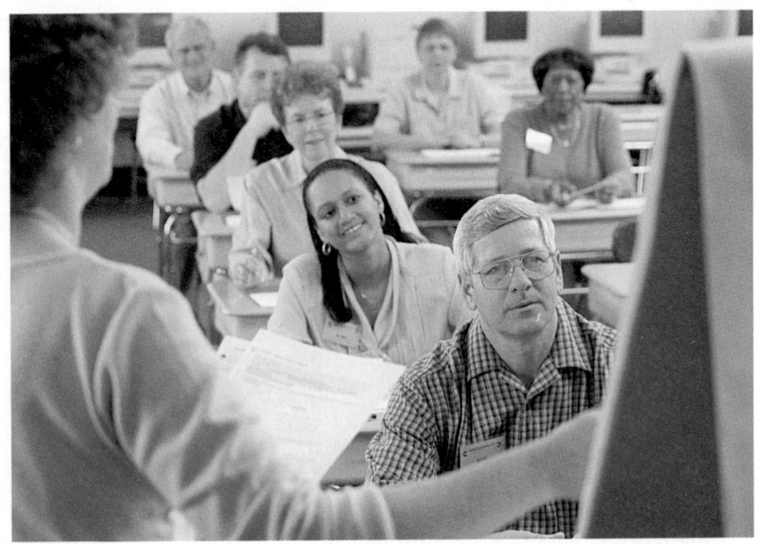

The setting of standards requires understanding different expectations, learning new things, and extensive discussion.

those who develop standards must consider. School districts must wrestle with these differing expectations for schools when they adopt a set of learning standards. It is not easy to have a clearly articulated, coordinated set of standards that meet the expectations of all members of a community. The process of setting standards is not a simple one, and those who write standards often experience criticism from various dissatisfied community members. Despite these difficulties, the development of clear standards enables different constituencies within the school community to clarify their needs and their aspirations. The process of selecting standards also provides a forum for all to conduct dialogs and negotiate what schools should do and for what schools, teachers, and students should be held accountable.

DIFFERING USES OF STANDARDS

Just as standards differ conceptually, they can also be used for different purposes. For example, standards can be used to make school curricula across a district, or state, more alike. They can provide a set of uniform expectations by grade level that must be met by all students before they can progress to the next grade. When standards are used in this way, all teachers are focused on the same set of content and skills, and they are aware of how their work feeds into other grade-level expectations. Standards of this sort are quite specific and attainable. They generally enable schools to show that all students have attained specific types of knowledge and skill development. On the other hand, such standards do not always clearly meet the diverse needs of students. The uniqueness of individual students can be neglected in the push to make clear what the typical student should learn.

DIFFERING SOURCES FOR STANDARDS

The sources of educational standards seem as plentiful as stars in a clear night sky. In fact, within the past decade more and more groups have set standards for students and educators alike. The first group to shine in the development of standards was the National Council of Teachers of Mathematics (NCTM), which researched, developed, sought feedback, and refined a set of standards over a ten-year period. The mathematics standards were first released in 1989 and became the benchmark for other standard-setting projects. During the 1990s the U.S. Department of Education funded subject-area groups and coalitions to prepare standards similar to the mathematics standards in disciplines such as science, history, civics, language arts, geography, the fine arts, and foreign language. Standards continue to be developed and published by many different groups. For example, the National Council for the Social Studies, the Association for the Advancement of Science, and the National Association for Health and Physical Education have all published sets of standards that represent what they believe students should know and be able to do throughout primary, elementary, middle, and secondary school. These national subject-area standards have been used by many states and translated into different sets of state educational standards. Individual school districts have also developed district learning standards based on their unique interpretation of state standards.

In addition to the work of discipline-specific groups that have developed standards for student achievement, professional educator organizations have developed standards for teachers, information specialists, school counselors, and others. These professional standards articulate what educators should know and be able to do within their own profession. There is no single set of teaching standards; rather different professional agencies have adopted their own set. Some examples of these professional standards include mathematics teaching standards from the NCTM and the science teaching standards from the National Research Council, general teaching standards from the National Board for Professional Teaching Standards. There also are the various sets of standards for teacher credentialing that were described in Chapter 1. Although all of these professional teaching standards are worth examining, it is not easy for individual teachers to determine which set is best suited for their individual contexts, philosophies, and teaching styles. The challenge for teachers is to have a clear understanding of each group's rationale for developing a set of standards and a clear set of professional reasons for endorsing one set of standards or another.

THREE TYPES OF STANDARDS

Three types of standards have emerged that are based on the different conceptions and uses of standards: content standards that focus on student achievement of subject matter and school curricula, performance standards that focus on teacher and student accomplishments, and delivery standards that focus on resources and support for schools. Each of these types of standards ultimately focuses on developing student achievement. For example, if teachers attain a certain level of professional expertise (performance standards) and schools meet stringent delivery standards by providing resources that relate to student achievement, all students will ultimately benefit from such a concerted effort on content standards.

CONTENT STANDARDS **Content standards** establish what should be learned in various subject areas. Content standards generally include three different aspects: knowledge, skills, and dispositions. Knowledge content standards describe what students should know. These knowledge content standards are often linked

content standards
Standards that specify learning outcomes in a subject or discipline.

to big ideas, themes, or conceptual strands that should be nurtured throughout a student's education. For example, in the national science standards the big ideas of force and motion, matter and energy, systems, and the nature of science are explicitly described, along with specific grade-level benchmark statements that are linked to these bigger ideas. Benchmark statements are more specific, developmentally appropriate pieces of information that feed into the development of a bigger idea over time. The same is true in the social science national standards; the big ideas of community, scarcity of resources, and democracy and specific statements concerning what students should know in primary, elementary, middle, and secondary school are specified.

In addition to knowledge acquisition statements, the national content standards also specify what thinking and process skills and strategies students and/or teachers should acquire throughout their schooling. These skills and strategies include making a plan, developing a hypothesis, interpreting, extrapolating, drawing conclusions, and communicating results. National standards also include statements about the types of habits or dispositions that should be nurtured in students. These habits or dispositions include curiosity, perseverance, tenacity, ability to ask questions, and open-mindedness. The example below is taken from the standards of the NCTM:

> Number and Operations
>
> Instructional programs from prekindergarten through grade 12 should enable students to
>
> - *understand numbers,* ways of representing numbers, relationships among numbers, and number systems;
> - *understand meanings* of operations and how they relate one to another;
> - *compute fluently* and make reasonable estimates.[1]

An example of a national curriculum standard that combines subject matter and dispositions that specifies what teachers should know and be able to do is the following, taken from the standards of the National Council for the Social Studies:

> Production, Distribution, and Consumption
>
> Social studies teachers should posses the knowledge, capabilities, and dispositions to organize and provide instruction at the *appropriate school* level for the study of how people organize for the Production, Distribution, and Consumption of Goods and Services.[2]

PERFORMANCE STANDARDS **Performance standards** are broad statements about what a student or a teacher should be able to do at a certain level. These statements of performance are usually not a list of discrete facts or skills; rather, they encompass combinations of knowledge and skills. Performance standards are the next logical step after determining a content standard. For example, once we know that we want students to understand the events that surrounded the Revolutionary War, the next logical questions are "How well should students understand? Against what models or specifications?" This is where performance standards come into play. Performance-based standards are used in specifying both student learning and teacher development as described in the discussion of teacher credentialing in Chapter 1.

performance standards
Standards that describe what a student should be able to do with certain combinations of knowledge and skills.

Performance standards seek to answer the question "How good is good enough?" These standards differ from district to district, even though there are many lists of performance standards that have been developed by state and national groups. Some educators contend that one set of uniform performance standards should be developed across the nation to guarantee a minimum level of achievement.

Opportunity-to-learn standards have been proposed by some as a way of ensuring that all students have the necessary resources and conditions to learn.

DELIVERY OR OPPORTUNITY-TO-LEARN STANDARDS Teachers' and students' awareness of content and performance standards will do little to assure achievement unless supports and resources are provided by the district and the community. Hence, some experts have advocated for another type of standards: **delivery or opportunity-to-learn standards.** This type of standard addresses the need for the provision of proper instructional resources, assessments, and system structures to create the proper conditions for students to achieve the content and performance standards. Examples of exemplary delivery standards include guaranteeing that students have sufficient opportunities to relearn when a standard is not achieved, ensuring that sufficient time is offered to students so that they can achieve various standards at their own pace, offering alternative ways to achieve a standard based on individual needs, specifying the types of technology to be available in schools and classrooms, and regularly providing staff inservice that helps teachers to fine-tune instructional techniques that lead to student achievement of specific standards.

AN EXAMPLE OF NATIONAL PERFORMANCE STANDARDS

To date, the New Standards is the only project that has developed and disseminated a national set of student performance standards. New Standards is a collaboration of the Learning Research and Development Center of the University of Pittsburgh and the National Center on Education and the Economy in partnership with state boards of education. Performance standards were derived from the various national discipline standards. The performance standards consist of two parts:

> **Performance descriptions:** Descriptions of what students should know and the ways they should demonstrate the knowledge and skills they have acquired in the four areas assessed by New Standards—English language arts, mathematics, science, and applied learning—at the elementary, middle and high school levels.

delivery or opportunity-to-learn standards Standards that specify the conditions and resources that are available to support students in learning.

Work samples and commentaries: Samples of student work that illustrate standard-setting performances, each accompanied by commentary that shows how the performance descriptions are reflected in the work sample.

One example from the New Standards Performance Description for Reading is as follows:

> Students read at least twenty-five books or book equivalents each year. The materials should include traditional and contemporary literature as well as magazines, newspapers, textbooks, and on-line materials. Examples of activities through which student might produce evidence of reading include:
>
> - Maintain an annotated list of works read.
> - Generate a reading log or journal.
> - Participate in formal and informal book talks.[3]

Another example drawn from the New Standards Performance Description for Reading is

> Students read aloud, accurately (in the range of 85–90%) familiar material in a way that makes meaning clear to listeners by:
>
> - self correcting when subsequent reading indicates an earlier miscue;
> - using a range of cueing systems, e.g. phonics and context clues to determine pronunciation and meanings;
> - reading with rhythm, flow, and meter that sounds like everyday speech.[4]

An example of a performance task in elementary mathematics requires students to show how many different ways you can put nine fish into two bowls. Students are required to show all their work and at the end explain why they made the decisions they did as they solved the problem.[5] Another performance task in elementary science requires students to complete a laboratory activity in which they adjust the mass and/or the volume of an object so that the object does not float on top of water or sink. This task calls for students to explore the range of available floating and sinking objects. To accomplish the task, it is necessary to combine floating and sinking objects to construct one of the correct density.[6]

These examples of performance standards provide a set of benchmarks against which teachers and students can determine how well they are doing in moving toward the full achievement of a standard. Performance standards can be thought of as markers indicating how well one is doing toward full achievement.

STANDARDS FRAMEWORKS

Standards do not stand alone. To be effective, they must be supported by focused instruction, ongoing teacher inservice, and assessments that relate to the standards. To clarify the intention of standards, many states and districts have developed a framework that clarifies how the instruction and assessments might look if they are linked to standards.

One example, taken from the state of Illinois, is typical of many other standards frameworks. In Illinois a set of learning goals is written for each subject area. Then, standards are presented for each goal. In addition to these standards and goals, benchmarks are listed.

In topological surveys a benchmark is a mark on a permanent object that indicates an elevation level. In educational standards a benchmark is a level of development toward the achievement of a standard. Benchmarks usually take the form of statements (rather than marks) describing how the standard might look at a certain level of development. Because standards are meant to permeate school curriculum, it is helpful to describe how each standard might look from a primary perspective, an elementary perspective, a middle school perspective, and a high school perspective. Figure 15.3 is an example of a goal, related standards, and benchmarks drawn from the Illinois standards.

THE DEBATE OVER SETTING STANDARDS

There is conflict among professional groups in setting standards. For example, the National Council for Teachers of English, the International Reading Association, and the Center for the Study of Reading at the University of Illinois received funding from the Department of Education (DOE) to draft curriculum standards in English. However, the DOE rejected the standards that this group proposed and terminated its funding. One reason that the DOE rejected the standards was the excessive emphasis on process rather than on products.

Conflict surrounded the first set of proposed American History standards. Critics flailed at the absence of certain American heroes in the secondary curriculum, and in January 1995 these standards were the focus of a full-scale debate in the U.S. Congress. Some members objected to the absence of Robert E. Lee and the Wright Brothers; others noted that Senator Joseph McCarthy was mentioned nineteen times but Albert Einstein was not mentioned at all. Such criticism led to a Senate resolution condemning the standards as they were proposed. The vote was 99 to 1.

A third type of conflict over standards happens when two groups attempt to develop standards for the same area, as occurred for science between the National Science Standards developed through federal funds by the National Research Council and Benchmarks for Science Literacy developed by the Association for the Advancement of Science. These two sets of national standards exist as independent sources for science teaching. Some argue that having different sets of national standards is positive and provides a necessary dialectic for selecting standards. Such healthy conflict allows for change and guards against developing a rigid, inflexible set of standards. Others note that in the absence of a single set of national standards, schools are left in the precarious position of having to choose their own unique sets of standards, and once again there is little guarantee of what all students will know and be able to do at the end of their public schooling experience.

THE ONGOING DEBATE OVER THE VALUE OF STANDARDS

Many questions color the debate on standards. How will school organization, use of time, graduation requirements, and power relationships change because of the standards movement? Can the same standards really be put in place everywhere without also bringing opportunity-to-learn standards to front and center? How can the plethora of standards be managed by teachers and still be integrated with the move toward thematic or interdisciplinary instruction? If the standards

FIGURE 15.3 Framework for a Statewide Standard

STATE GOAL 6: Demonstrate and apply a knowledge and sense of numbers, including numeration and operations (addition, subtraction, multiplication, division), patterns, ratios and proportions.

As a result of their schooling, students will be able to:

LEARNING STANDARD	EARLY ELEMENTARY	LATE ELEMENTARY
A. Demonstrate knowledge and use of numbers and their representations in a broad range of theoretical and practical settings.	**6.A.1a** Identify whole numbers and compare them using the symbols <, >, or = and the words "less than," "greater than," or "equal to," applying counting, grouping and place value concepts. **6.A.1b** Identify and model fractions using concrete materials and pictorial representations.	6.A.2 Compare and order whole numbers, fractions and decimals using concrete materials, drawings and mathematical symbols.
B. Investigate, represent and solve problems using number facts, operations (addition, subtraction, multiplication, division) and their properties, algorithms and relationships.	**6.B.1** Solve one- and two-step problems with whole numbers using addition, subtraction, multiplication and division.	**6.B.2** Solve one- and two-step problems involving whole numbers, fractions and decimals using addition, subtraction, multiplication and division.
C. Compute and estimate using mental mathematics, paper-and-pencil methods, calculators and computers.	**6.C.1a** Select and perform computational procedures to solve problems with whole numbers. **6.C.1b** Show evidence that whole number computational results are correct and/or that estimates are reasonable.	**6.C.2a** Select and perform computational procedures to solve problems with whole numbers, fractions and decimals. **6.C.2b** Show evidence that computational results using whole numbers, fractions and decimals are correct and/or that estimates are reasonable.
D. Solve problems using comparison of quantities, ratios, proportions and percents.	**6.D.1** Compare the numbers of objects in groups.	**6.D.2** Describe the relationship between two sets of data using ratios and appropriate notations (e.g., a/b, a to b, a:b).

The Illinois Learning Standards for Mathematics *were developed by Illinois teachers for Illinois schools. These goals, standards and benchmarks are an outgrowth of the 1985 Illinois State Goals for Learning influenced by the latest thinking in school mathematics. This includes the National Council of Teachers of Mathematics;* Curriculum and Evaluation Standards for School Mathematics; *ideas underlying recent local and national curriculum projects; results of state, national, and international assessment findings; and the work and experiences of Illinois school districts and teachers.*

Source: Illinois Academic Standards. State Goal 6, Mathematics, Illinois State Board of Education, July 25, 1997.

movement is to be worth the upheaval that it has already begun to generate, such questions must be answered by thoughtful, knowledgeable participants who are engaged in the process of changing what students learn and how they learn. This requires having data about the outcomes from the use of standards, especially evidence about student learning. Therefore, one of the early efforts in the standards movement was significantly increased attention on methods to assess student learning.

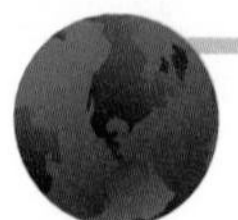

GLOBAL PERSPECTIVES: Australia Is Exploring a New Approach to Education Reform

Innovative projects for organizing curriculum and clarifying what students should learn are underway in other countries. For example, in Queensland, Australia, the New Basics project is being implemented as one way of addressing the question "How do we teach children all they need to know for the global information age without keeping schools open 24 hours a day, 365 days a year?" The approach is a new way of looking at reform by supporting teachers to determine how to teach and by distilling the learning outcomes into four "new basics":

- Life pathways and social futures: Who am I and where am I going?
- Multi-literacies and communications media: How do I make sense of, and communicate with, the world?
- Active citizenship: What are my rights and responsibilities in communities, cultures and economies?
- Environments and technologies: How do I describe, analyze and shape the world around me?[7]

These four basics are similar to the big ideas in the American form of the standards movement. In the Queensland New Basics project, teaching and learning are organized around intellectually demanding, practically oriented projects that they call "rich tasks." In contrast to the American approach, how schools and teachers are organized and teach to these outcomes is up to the schools. There are some design specifications for teaching, however; for example, rich tasks must be "problem-based and relevant to new worlds of work and everyday life and must be seen to be so by parents and the community."[8]

I believe that we should get away altogether from tests and correlations among tests, and look instead at more naturalistic sources of information about how people around the world develop skills important to their way of life.

Howard Gardner, 1987

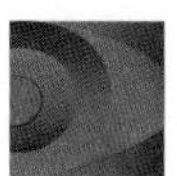

THE CHANGING FACE OF ASSESSMENT

Standards are not an end unto themselves. Simply listing standards in a school brochure will make little difference in the way students learn and achieve. If standards are to have any real effect on schools and on student achievement, they need to be supported by other elements in a school's structure: an articulated curriculum, inservice sessions focused on improving student achievement of standards, and a well-thought-out array of assessments that match the standards.

An important approach to assessment of student learning is interviewing students about what they are learning and asking them to describe how they constructed their solutions.

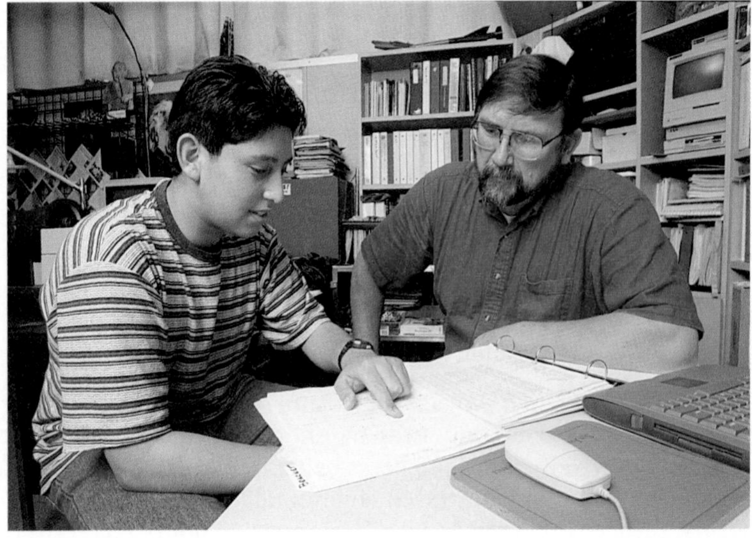

If assessments are linked to standards, changes will need to occur in the types of assessments that are used, the kinds of data that are collected, and the ways in which assessment results are used to enhance students achievement. These changes in the assessment process can be quite dramatic, since assessment in the past has often meant little more than producing grades or doing well on paper-and-pencil achievement tests. When assessments are interwoven into standards-based frameworks, they become much more varied and meaningful to teachers and students alike. The following section examines the changing face of assessment and the ways in which this new face enhances the teaching and learning process.

WHAT IS ASSESSMENT?

Assessment in education implies many things: evaluation, grades, tests, performances, criteria, rubrics, and more. To adequately encompass its many dimensions, it is helpful to examine assessment in a broader sense by analyzing its root meanings. The term *assessment* is derived from the Latin word *assessio,* which means "to sit beside." This image provides an excellent metaphor. Ultimately, assessment can be thought of as the act of sitting beside oneself and analyzing what one observes. In a sense, all assessment is based on this image: the examination of oneself through the perception of an examiner who sits beside and provides feedback. Some theorists contend that all true assessment is ultimately self-assessment. Assessors can provide information, but in the end it is the person being assessed who ultimately accepts the information or rejects it, using the information to further his or her development or setting aside the information as unimportant.

assessment
The examination of oneself based on the perception of an examiner who sits beside and provides feedback.

The image of an assessor sitting beside a learner also implies the use of tools or measuring devices that enable the assessor to gather different types of information. Paper-and-pencil tests, performance assessments, developing portfolios, keeping journals, using observation checklists are examples of different assessment measures. Often these tools are labeled assessments, but in fact they are merely measures that assessors use to provide feedback. Keep in mind that assessment is really the larger process of gathering information, interpreting the information, providing feedback, and ultimately using or rejecting the feedback.

PURPOSES FOR ASSESSMENT

As we noted above, for teachers the ultimate reason for assessment is improving student learning. However, the specific purpose and focus of a particular assessment effort can be more narrowly defined. It is important to clarify these different purposes before attempting to interpret assessment results. Put simply, for teachers and students, assessing is done for two purposes. The first is for providing feedback to the learner and the teacher so that both can understand where to next focus their energies. The second purpose is to make a final judgment about whether or not a certain level of accomplishment has been attained, such as passing a course.

COMPETENCY-BASED ASSESSMENT Assessment can be used to demonstrate a specific competence. A good example of this is the standard road test employed in most states as a prerequisite to receive a driver's license. The critical characteristic of such an assessment is that the assessment is closely related to something that the learner must be able to do. Hence, in the road test, a person drives a car in situations that the driver will typically experience: turning left or right, backing up, parking, and so forth. The person is usually scored through an observation checklist that the assessor uses. Assessments of specific competence in schools include many teacher-made assessments that focus on the specific things that a learner has studied. For example, if learners have been taught a specific method for using a piece of science equipment, such as a gram-balance, a competency-based assessment would include having the learner weigh several objects on a balance. The teacher would typically observe the learner to see whether all the specific techniques in accurately weighing a sample were met.

DIAGNOSTIC ASSESSMENT Assessments can also be used to diagnose and determine what a child knows and does not know in a certain area of interest. These types of assessments provide an array of questions and tasks for a student to perform in a specific area such as reading, writing, or mathematics. In such assessments the questions and tasks are ordered from less difficult to more difficult. As the child performs each task successfully, she or he is given another more difficult question. Eventually, the child will be unable to answer or perform any tasks successfully.

This approach can be used only when the subject area is developmental, that is, when one type of understanding is linked to another in some ordered fashion. For example, in mathematics one cannot be expected to multiply without knowing the principles of addition.

NORM-REFERENCED ASSESSMENT Sometimes assessments are used to demonstrate who is best in some area. In this type of assessment the individual's performance is compared with that of a norm group of similar individuals. When these types of assessments are developed, they are carefully revised on a regular basis to ensure that the tests yield varied test scores from low to high. In other words, when a norm-referenced assessment begins to yield higher and higher test scores, the test developers change the test and make it more difficult so as to maintain a range of scores from low to high. These types of assessment do not reveal all that an individual child knows or is able to do. Rather, they reveal how well a child does in comparison to a representative group of his or her peers. In some ways norm-referenced assessments are like a contest, and it is expected that some students will do well and others less well.

One of the biggest misuses of assessments is in the area of norm-referenced assessments. School districts often use norm-referenced assessments to determine how all of the students are doing in comparison to other students in other districts. Although this is a proper way to use the assessment, teachers must be cautious in concluding that individual students who score low are not doing well. Norm-referenced tests typically sample only a portion of what students in a particular class would be expected to know and do. Therefore, the student might not be performing well in those areas assessed by the tests but doing better in other areas that were not tested. Norm-referenced tests are not intended to be used to interpret how well individual students are or are not doing with respect to what they are being taught. Diagnostic or competency tests should be used to make this determination.

Sometimes state authorities penalize a school district or school that performs below the fiftieth percentile on a norm-referenced test. This is a foolish practice, since norm-referenced tests are designed such that 50 percent will score below the fiftieth percentile. In fact, when schools begin to score regularly above this percentile, the test is made more difficult.

CRITERION-REFERENCED ASSESSMENT Instead of comparing a student's performance with that of a group of students, criterion-referenced assessment compares a student's performance with a specific type of accomplishment or criterion. For instance, one can assess whether students can add two-digit numbers without regrouping. To measure this skill, a student could be asked to answer ten different questions, each of which has only two digits added to two digits and none of which yields an answer greater than nine. If a child successfully answers all ten, or nine or even eight of the ten questions, a teacher can state with some degree of confidence that the child knows how to add two-digit numbers without regrouping. This type of assessment is similar to a competency-based assessment; the only difference is that the criterion may be a very narrow competency such as adding two-digit numbers, in contrast to a competency such as driving a car. Most classroom tests should measure students knowledge in a criterion-referenced manner; that is, a student should be asked to answer questions a number of times that measure the same learning. Then, instead of scoring the test by using some sort of A through F range, the teacher sets an acceptable score that determines that the student can really answer like questions acceptably. For example, a criterion might be answering correctly four of five questions that measure two-digit addition without regrouping.

CAPSTONE/SUMMATIVE ASSESSMENT Assessments can be developed to celebrate a milestone accomplishment or to demonstrate how well a person has mastered something. These types of assessments are used near the end of some major accomplishment. Examples of capstone assessments are recitals and other performances. For example, after completing many courses in education, a student can be asked to manage a classroom of students and demonstrate all the things that he or she has mastered. Hence, student teaching can be a capstone-type assessment. This capstone assessment is evaluated by a master teacher who notes all the accomplishments that are shown by the student teacher throughout the performance. In such an assessment, deficiencies can also be identified, but the major focus is to uncover what a student has mastered throughout a program of study.

On a smaller level, a capstone assessment can be used at the end of a school year. Students can be asked to apply all that they have learned in science by completing a science project or in language by writing a short story or a poem.

PROGRAM ASSESSMENT Assessments can be used to determine whether school programs are effective. One way of assessing the success of a school program is through norm-referenced assessments. But as we noted above, these assessments are quite limited. They measure only how well a group of students do on a standardized paper-and-pencil task in comparison to other groups of students across the country. To determine how well a program is doing, it is important to use multiple assessments. For example, one additional way to assess a school program would be to regularly gather information about how graduates are performing in the real world. Information about how many students successfully graduate without being retained could be another useful indicator. Having a broad array of assessment data can enable school districts to take stock and redirect effort such as changing the types of instruction that are being used and what types of learning are being emphasized.

SERVING STUDENT DIVERSITY A continuing point of criticism about traditional tests is that they do not address or accommodate the diversity of students in today's classrooms. Each student brings a unique set of background experiences, prior knowledge, and cultural perspectives to learning. Asking all students to show what they know on a narrow standardized test is a very real problem. The issues become even more glaring for students who have limited use of English and those with special needs and learning disabilities. Often, simply changing the way in which learning is assessed can provide significant new opportunities to demonstrate that they have learned.

AUTHENTIC CONTEXTUALIZED ASSESSMENT

The notion of assessment is changing. For decades educators have called for better testing, and the response to this request was the proliferation of a number of different kinds of tests with different emphases. Tests of achievement, basic skills, criterion-referenced tests related to specific objectives, tests of cognitive ability, tests of flexibility, and tests of critical thinking were developed. Despite these worthy attempts, assessments still did not ring true. Educators in the classroom viewed these paper-and-pencil instruments as an intrusion and not directly related to what was really happening in the classroom.

Teachers began to realize that when they called for better assessments, they wanted something different than conventional paper-and-pencil, multiple-choice or essay tests. Such assessments lacked a proper context in which students could show what they know and could do. Consider the context of a history examination. Students are generally asked to sit in silence, read questions, and answer them within a specific time period. How motivating is such a context? Aside from generating fear of failure, there is little excitement in such a setting. What teachers were asking for were methods that were not necessarily limited to multiple-choice or essay-type paper-and-pencil instruments. They wanted assessment methods that reflected more directly on the goals and outcomes of classroom instruction. The term ***authentic assessment*** is a response to this growing demand by teachers. Consider the following as a counterexample to the noncontextualized, boring history examination. It illustrates how a contextualized, performance task could be used to assess students' understanding of the Civil War.

> You are a reporter for the Washington Herald during the time of Lincoln's assassination. You have been called into a press conference during which the White House staff has announced the assassination of Abraham Lincoln. You need to write an appropriate eulogy for your newspaper, one that clarifies what President Lincoln has contributed to the country and one that also examines the potential reasons for his assassination. Your eulogy must fit within one column which involves not more than 1,000 words.

This example describes an assessment that is considered *authentic,* one that clearly examines student performance on a learned task. Generally, this is accomplished by using a context or situation that directly relates to what the student has learned. Conventional paper-and-pencil assessments, by contrast, rely on indirect, or proxy, items (for example, multiple-choice questions) from which we attempt to make valid inferences. In contrast to this indirect approach, authentic assessment is based on the premise that students and teachers measure learning with tools or instruments or performances that directly match what and how they have learned. The what and the how must both be taken into consideration. For example, if a student learned that force is a "push or a pull" by using inclined hands-on experiences to determine the meaning of force, then students should not be measured by using a paper-and-pencil multiple-choice test that asks them to define force. To be authentic, the students need to be assessed by using a performance that matches more directly the outcome of instruction. Because the teacher really aimed to have students experience force and label different events as forces, then the assessment should be a performance in which students explore another similar phenomenon and must independently clarify how this phenomenon represents the concept of force.

In other words, authentic assessment activities more closely resemble actual real-life tasks. Sitting in a room with other students and silently answering questions that have one correct answer, with an artificial time limitation, is not a typical life task. It is artificial because in real life, one seldom solves problems in this fashion. Although such controlled paper-and-pencil testing might have a worthy function to fulfill, it does not lend itself to authentic assessment procedures.

Grant Wiggins provides four basic characteristics of authentic assessment:

1. It is designed to represent a real-life performance in the field.
2. The criteria for attaining stated objectives are given more attention during the teaching and learning process than the attention given to criteria in traditional assessment approaches.
3. Student self-assessment plays an integral role.
4. Students are expected to describe and defend their own work.[9]

authentic assessment
A multifaceted performance task that is based in the context of the learner and allows the learner to construct a response that demonstrates what he or she has learned.

Often authentic assessments provide opportunities for students to show what they know and are able to do within and across a number of different disciplines. Some examples of authentic assessments include an audiotape of a student reading to a peer; a log of books read, with critiques; a debate on a current issue; an article written for the school paper; a design for a room or bulletin board; a performance in a play; an original recipe; an original investigation and report; drawing a map of the community; or creating an advertising campaign for a political candidate.

METHODS OF AUTHENTIC ASSESSMENT

To provide opportunities for students to show what they know and do not know, what they can and cannot yet do, multiple assessment methods must be used to sufficiently explore the students learning. At the basis of these tools or methods is the notion of a performance. Thinking of assessments as performances in which the student is given the opportunities to display some sort of learning task is critical to the design of an authentic assessment method.

With this notion of performance, teachers can employ a variety of methods to permit the student to reflect what they have learned. Some of these tools include learning logs, portfolios, peer interviews, teacher–student interviews, observations made by teachers and pupils alike, problem situations that are solved both individually and as a group, independent oral and written reports, group reports, the creation of products, and the development of video. To be authentic, the educators are being asked to employ a wide variety of assessment opportunities to make valid and reliable evaluations of student success.

LEARNING JOURNALS AND LOGS Learning logs are notebooks that contain written descriptions, drawings, reminders, data, charts, conclusions, inferences, generalizations, and any number of other notes that were developed by the student during the learning process. The teachers' role in the development of these learning logs is to generate questions for the student to ponder and respond to during the learning task. The more varied the questions, the better the assessment. For example, during a learning task, students can be asked to relate what they are studying to real life. They can be asked to make a generalization based on what they are doing or to communicate through a mind map drawing how what they are learning relates to something else. The most important element of using a learning logs is the development of a rich bank of questions so that the student practices and records different modes of learning.

FOLIOS/PORTFOLIOS Learning logs can be used to develop a portfolio as well. Samples of student work can be organized and stored in a folio. A folio is like a file cabinet drawer in which all sorts of examples are kept for later use. Having students keep samples of their work (storing them in a folio) may show growth over time. Samples can be self-selected by students or with assistance from others. Students can be asked to annotate their work samples by describing what characteristics make their work noteworthy. This activity relates to Wiggins's third and fourth characteristics of authentic assessment: self-assessment and students defending and describing their work.

A portfolio is a compilation of students' best work based on a selected set of criteria. For example, students can be asked to examine their folio and select their best science and social science diagrams; students can also be asked to write down what characteristics make each example a good diagram. Teachers can also have students select their most accurate drawing or their best graph. In all cases the student must articulate why they chose the items they did. Including elements of a student's log permits the student to display learning in yet another way. Portfolios don't have to be in the more traditional hard-copy format. Portfolios can be electronic, including voice, video, and an archive of written documents.

The important point is that a collection of work is not an assessment unless the student and/or teacher does something with it. Portfolios can have several goals: to show growth over time, to show the breadth of achievements, and to showcase the student's best work. Students and their teacher should formulate a shared goal, the student should select entries from their folio that reflect learning related to the goal, the student (and possibly the teacher) should include written self-assessment about the student's progress, and both should discuss the portfolio, possibly in relation to a rubric that they developed for evaluating the portfolio.

INTERVIEWS Students can also indicate what they have learned by being interviewed either by another student or by the teacher. Face-to-face discussion, using probing questions, is another way in which teachers and students can determine whether something has been learned. Once again, interview questions need to be varied to allow a full range of responses from the student.

OBSERVATION AND ANECDOTAL RECORDS Classroom observation has been a tool that has been used for many years. Within the realm of authentic assessment, observation means using day-to-day classroom activities to determine whether some behavior is being exhibited. To accomplish this properly, teachers need to keep observation notes or checklists, regularly writing down what they see and what type of learning it indicates. These daily observations can be a powerful means of assessing learning.

In addition to formal observations, keeping anecdotal records is an excellent assessment technique. Teachers who keep a diary and jot down any relevant information about the child's learning progress, accomplishments, and other relevant information will find that their understanding of the whole child is increased. One very important caution in using anecdotal records is to be careful in distinguishing between what has been observed (the objective facts) and interpretations of the meaning (judgments).

Observing students at work is a very useful form of assessment.

RELEVANT RESEARCH

A Case Study of Alternative Assessment: Student, Teacher, and Observer Perceptions in a Ninth Grade Biology Classroom

STUDY PURPOSE/QUESTIONS: This single-site phenomenological case study at a suburban high school examined the perceptions of one teacher (Len) as well as his students, colleagues, and principal about alternative assessment strategies and associated phenomena in Len's ninth grade biology classroom. Researcher perceptions are also included. The primary focus of the research was to understand and make sense of the world in which Len existed and where he viewed what he considered more meaningful assessment activities as alternative assessments. The study's intent was to contribute to the understanding of alternative assessment by providing detailed, in-depth analysis of how Len, a thirty-year biology teacher, implemented and perceived assessment.

STUDY DESIGN: This study was a qualitative descriptive case study using a phenomenological perspective that describes the world experienced by the participants in their own terms. Questions guiding the study were: (1) What happened in Len's biology classroom as he used alternative assessment? (2) What were Len's perceptions of alternative assessments? (3) How did students view Len's assessment strategies? (4) What did students think were the primary determinants of their grades?

STUDY FINDINGS: Data were reduced from interview transcripts, observations, and documents into thematic perception generalizations of Len and the other participants toward alternative assessment. The resulting generalizations were as follows:

- Len's early and ongoing informal assessments of students' abilities and attitudes played a key role in his perceptions of individual students' work ethic.
- Len's involvement with professional development experiences had a direct impact on what assessments were used in his classroom.
- Arriving early to school, staying late after school, working weekends, and expending large amounts of physical energy facilitated Len's use of alternative assessments within his standard fifty-minute class period.
- Len felt that he was a "Lone Ranger" in his use of alternative assessments.
- Students worked toward learning goals only if an extrinsic reward existed in the form of either points or grades.
- Students felt that they did best when they worked in cooperative groups, took fewer tests, did projects, were active in class, and experienced less teacher talk.
- Students were more comfortable when the teacher evaluated them than when they evaluated themselves or each other.
- Len's colleagues perceived alternative assessments as requiring too much time for the number of students they taught.
- Len's principal had only limited knowledge about alternative science assessment but thought that her science teachers were "moving in the right direction."

IMPLICATIONS: This study uncovered several problems inherent in alternative assessment. Len discovered that using interviews, observations, and projects as assessment tools required a great deal of extra time and energy. His colleagues remained skeptical about the value of alternative assessments; they were concerned about the time needed to implement and interpret them. Len also found that students did not appreciate the value of self-assessment techniques, which are at the heart of alternative assessment approaches.

The study also clarified positive elements in alternative assessments. Students noted that the collaboration activities that Len used throughout the assessment projects developed their personal understandings of the content. Len felt that he had a clearer, more detailed understanding of individual students' achievement; he also noted that alternative assessment techniques provided insight into students' dispositions and work ethic (aspects that national learning standards emphasize).

This study elucidates questions about the feasibility and use of alternative assessments. Given the heavy investment of time both during the school period and outside of school, is alternative assessment worth the cost? How do teachers who want to use alternative assessments deal with student resistance to self-assessment. Because alternative assessment is focused on clarifying what precisely students know and do not know, how can this descriptive information be translated into letter grades?

Source: Peter D. Veronesi, "A Case Study of Alternative Assessment: Student, Teacher, and Observer Perception in a Ninth Grade Biology Classroom." Paper presented at the Association of Educators of Teachers in Science, January 2–4, p. 2000.

STUDENT PRODUCTS AND PROJECTS Teachers can have students develop closure for their learning by completing a project. Sometimes this project can take the form of a specific product. Products include writing a eulogy for a famous person, developing a room layout, designing a complex machine composed of simple machines, creating a proposal for a new park facility, organizing a senior trip, writing a proposal for improving school safety on the playground, or writing a morning radio news report for the school. Displaying these products and using them to note the content and the skill acquisition that is implicit within each product is another excellent assessment device.

VIDEOTAPES/AUDIOTAPES Teachers can use audiotapes and videotapes to record a student's abilities in areas hard to document any other way. Teachers can also use video to record the process that students used as they develop individual products. These tapes provide excellent assessment tools that teachers can show to students and parents alike to exhibit what students know and can do. The tapes can also show what students still need to learn.

RUBRICS In its simplest and most basic sense, a rubric is a scoring guide. **Rubrics** are often associated with performance assessments because, in evaluating a performance, it is important to clarify what aspects of the performance are noteworthy. Rubrics enable assessors to focus on the important components of a performance. They also provide guidance to ensure that different assessors score in the same manner.

Rubrics can be analytic or holistic measures. *Analytic* means looking at each dimension of the performance and scoring each. *Holistic* refers to considering all criteria simultaneously and making one overall evaluation. You might sum all the analytic scores for a total score, or you might wish to have one holistic dimension within an analytic rubric to provide an overall impression score. By doing this, assessors can access the benefits of both analytic and holistic scoring procedures. Analytic scoring, of course, provides the most specific data for use as a diagnostic assessment; it also limits flexibility because the dimensions are prescribed ahead of time. Holistic scoring does not require specific dimensions to be assessed; as such, it provides more flexibility and allows an assessor to give credit for unexpected dimensions that may contribute to the overall success of a performance. However, holistic scoring provides less direction for students than analytic scoring does. Figures 15.4 and 15.5 are examples of analytic and holistic scoring rubrics.

DESIGNING AUTHENTIC PERFORMANCE ASSESSMENTS

There are three major areas to consider in developing authentic assessments for standards. First, a rich context needs to be designed, one that permits inquiry to occur. Second it is important to fill the context with a wide variety of questions so that different types of thinking can occur. Finally, the critical indicators for learning need to be identified.

rubrics
Scoring guides that describe composite levels of learning typically ranging from novice to expert.

SELECTING A PROPER CONTEXT FOR THE PERFORMANCE The first and most important step in developing authentic assessments is to structure some task that is *complex* enough to permit students to show important learning, that is *motivating* enough to encourage students to think and *rich* enough with multiple opportunities to show how and what students have shaped into an understanding. Some writers call the structure of such a task the *context*. By context they mean the

FIGURE 15.4 ANALYTIC TRAIT RUBRICS FOR FIFTH GRADE SCIENCE EXPERIMENTS

Experiment Design	Scientific Results
4 Design shows student has analyzed the problem and has independently designed and conducted a thoughtful experiment.	4 Pamphlet explained with convincing clarity the solution to the problem. Information from other sources or other experiments was used in explaining.
3 Design shows student grasps the basic idea of the scientific process by conducting experiment that controlled obvious variables.	3 Pamphlet showed that student understands the results and knows how to explain them.
2 Design shows student grasps basic idea of scientific process but needs some help in controlling obvious variables.	2 Pamphlet showed results of experiment. Conclusions reached were incomplete or were explained only after questioning.
1 Design shows student can conduct an experiment when given considerable help by the teacher.	1 Pamphlet showed results of the experiment. Conclusions drawn were lacking, incomplete, or confused.
Data Collection	**Verbal Expression**
4 Data were collected and recorded in an orderly manner that accurately reflects the results of the experiment.	4 Speech presented a clearly defined point of view that can be supported by research. Audience interest was considered, as were gestures, voice, and eye contact.
3 Data were recorded in a manner that probably represents the results of the experiment.	3 Speech was prepared with some adult help but uses experiment's result. Speech was logical and used gestures, voice, and eye contact to clarify meaning.
2 Data were recorded in a disorganized manner or only with teacher assistance.	2 Speech was given after active instruction from an adult. Some consideration was given to gestures, voice, and eye contact.
1 Data were recorded in an incomplete, haphazard manner or only after considerable teacher assistance.	1 Speech was given only after active instruction from an adult.

Source: G. Wiggins, *Educative Assessment.* San Francisco: Jossey Bass, 1998, p. 167.

various activities, hands-on experiences, and questions that encourage learners to think and show what they know.

Selecting the context for a performance of worth begins by considering the learning goals, standards and outcomes of current and past instruction. It is critical that students be assessed on the intended goals and outcomes of their instruction and that the assessments are authentic—that is, that they match the instruction. Too often teachers assess one way but teach in another. Assessing by using paper-and-pencil, single-answer questions when instruction has been

FIGURE 15.5 HOLISTIC ORAL PRESENTATION RUBRIC

5—Excellent	The student clearly describes the question studied and provides strong reasons for its importance. Specific information is given to support the conclusions that are drawn and described. The delivery is engaging and sentence structure is consistently correct. Eye contact is made and sustained throughout the presentation. There is strong evidence of preparation, organization, and enthusiasm for the topic. The visual aid is used to make the presentation more effective. Questions from the audience are clearly answered with specific and appropriate information.
4—Very Good	The student describes the question studied and provides reasons for its importance. An adequate amount of information is given to support the conclusions that are drawn and described. The delivery and sentence structure are generally correct. There is evidence of preparation, organization, and enthusiasm for the topic. The visual aid is mentioned and used. Questions from the audience are answered clearly.
3—Good	The student describes the question studied and conclusions are stated, but supporting information is not as strong as a 4 or 5. The delivery and sentence structure are generally correct. There is some indication of preparation and organization. The visual aid is mentioned. Questions from the audience are answered.
2—Limited	The student states the question studied but fails to describe it fully. No conclusions are given to answer the question. The delivery and sentence structure are understandable, but with some errors. Evidence of preparation and organization is lacking. The visual aid may or may not be mentioned. Questions from the audience are answered with only the most basic response.
1—Poor	The student makes a presentation without stating the question or its importance. The topic is unclear, and no adequate conclusions are stated. The delivery is difficult to follow. There is no indication of preparation or organization. Questions from the audience receive only the most basic or no response.
0	No oral presentation is attempted.

Source: From G. Wiggins, *Educative Assessment.* San Francisco: Jossey Bass, 1998, p. 166.

emphasizing inquiry is inappropriate. The reverse is also true. Assessing students in a hands-on inquiry mode when all instruction was lecture and reading/writing is equally improper.

In addition, the teacher needs to consider how the learning goals and standards relate to the lives and actions of scientists, writers, historians, and mathematicians. Consider what professionals do and how they use their different ways of knowing. Together, these considerations will often trigger ideas for the performance context.

To illustrate this way of determining a context, consider a curriculum that is filled with learning experiences focused on food chains, prey and predator relationships, and the balance of nature. How does this translate into a real-world

Performance assessments should take into account the context in which professionals, such as scientists, work as well as providing opportunities for students to demonstrate their developing knowledge and skill.

context? Having students dissect owl pellets and analyze findings in light of the above concepts provides one such context that is closely tied to the real world and to environmental issues. Like practicing scientists, students could be asked to investigate a set of owl pellets that have been collected from a specific area of the country. Students can apply what they know and use skills and thinking processes throughout the investigation. The assessment should provide students with opportunities to make measurements, make observations, and record observations about the owl pellet. Students can be asked to create data tables that summarize the types of prey that were consumed, make inferences and draw conclusions about food availability, and finally even answer direct questions about food chains.

STUFFING THE CONTEXT WITH MULTIPLE OPPORTUNITIES TO SHOW LEARNING Once a context has been selected, it needs to be structured and filled with opportunities to show how and what students have learned. Asking students to display their cognitive abilities in as many ways as possible enhances the teacher's understanding of students' unique ways of knowing. This is where assessment tools are helpful. Observing students in action and recording these observations in a variety of ways are critical.

ASKING DIFFERENT TYPES OF QUESTIONS TO SHOW LEARNING Teachers have long been aware that questioning is an important way to cue students to display their understanding. Research indicates that the types of questions students are asked determines the academic culture of a classroom. Questions that focus on a single aspect of knowing (knowledge or skills) limit the opportunities for showing understanding (the interactions of knowledge, skills, and habits of mind). Having a clearer picture of the multidimensionality of understanding (ways of knowing) directs teachers to ask a wide variety of different types of questions. This is especially true during an assessment experience. Students should be asked many different types of questions within a rich, hands-on context. Figure 15.6 presents examples of the variety of question types that allow students multiple opportunities to show their various ways of knowing.

FIGURE 15.6 EXAMPLES OF THE TYPES OF QUESTIONS THAT ENCOURAGE STUDENTS SHOWING DIFFERENT WAYS OF KNOWING

Analysis Questions: What are the key parts? Which parts are essential and why?

Comparison Questions: How are these alike? What specific characteristics are similar? How are these different? In what way are they different?

Classification Questions: Into what groups could you organize these things? What are the rules for membership in each group? What are the defining characteristics of each group?

Connections Clarification Questions: What does this remind you of in another context? To what is this connected?

Constructing Support Questions: What data can you cite that supports this conclusion? What is an argument that would support this claim?

Deduction Questions: On the basis of this rule, what would you deduce? What are the conditions that make this inevitable?

Inferring and Concluding Questions: On the basis of these data, what would you conclude? How likely is it that this will occur?

Abstracting Questions: What pattern underlies all these situations? What are the essential characteristics of this thing?

Error Analysis: How is this conclusion misleading? What does not match?

ASSESSING THE IMPORTANT ELEMENTS Once students are engaged in a motivating inquiry, they will be better able to exhibit learning development. It is important that teachers focus on all aspects of learning when they examine student performance and not simply focus on those aspects that are easy to assess. If a context is truly authentic, there should be ample opportunities for students to display what they know and can do across a variety of different standards:

- Knowledge and comprehension of concepts, application of concepts, and connection of concept to real-world context
- Ability to problem solve and exercise thinking skills
- Ability to perform and apply process skills
- Ability to structure their thinking
- Collaboration and other habits of mind
- Communication and ability to modify ideas on the basis of new evidence

A rich assessment context allows students to display many of these components of understanding and skill. The art of assessing well includes identifying indicators—things that can be observed that relate to different aspects of some important standard. Identifying indicators in a performance task is much like acting as an X-ray; teachers need to notice what behaviors count and how successful ways of doing and knowing look. To do this, teachers need to step back from the performance, much like a physician, and identify those actions that are meaningful and more importantly what learning do the actions indicate. Once teachers develop lists of indicators, they can easily assess what a child knows and does not know. These lists can form the basis for assigning grades, discussing student progress, and making decisions about student needs.

Authentic assessment is both an art and a science. Assessment can be thought of as the art of writing a play or a context in which students are placed; once in this context, students cannot help but display the knowledge, thinking, and habits of mind that they have developed. On the other hand, authentic assessment is also like a science in that the educator needs to meticulously identify and examine the important questions and other types of learning indicators that are important to the task.

As can be seen, authentic assessment is an attempt to make testing both in and out of the classroom more closely grounded in the context of student learning and less narrowly focused on a few aspects of what has been learned. By its very name it implies trying to better determine what children have really learned.

PROFESSIONAL ASPECTS OF GOOD ASSESSMENTS

Thus far, we have examined the purposes and described a variety of the methods being applied to performance assessment. However, assessing student learning has more to it than the mechanics of constructing authentic tasks. Assessing student learning is an activity that influences and affects many people. Therefore there are professional and ethical considerations. There also are a number of very technical issues related to whether or not each assessment task is fair and really assesses what was intended. Examples of these professional aspects of assessment are highlighted next.

PRINCIPLES FOR HAVING HIGH-QUALITY ASSESSMENTS Like other professionals who have knowledge that their clients do not have and whose actions and judgments affect their clients, classroom teachers are responsible for conducting themselves in an ethical manner. This responsibility is particularly important in education because, unlike other professions, students have no choice about whether they will or will not attend school.

The National Forum on Assessment, a coalition of education and civil rights organizations, views high-quality assessment as essential to high-quality education. The forum asserts that powerful assessment methods used by skilled educators are necessary for educating all children to high standards.[10] The following principles have been identified as keys to having powerful and responsible assessments:

- **Improve and support student learning.** Assessment practices and methods would be consistent with teacher and district learning goals, instructional practices, and current knowledge about how students learn. In-class assessment is the primary means of assessment, and results should always focus on student growth rather than on sorting and classifying groups.
- **Assess and evaluate performance fairly.** Assessments should ensure that all students receive fair treatment so as not to limit students' present and future opportunities. Assessments allow for multiple methods to assess student progress and are created or adapted appropriately to meet the specific needs of particular populations, such as English as a Second Language learners and students with disabilities.
- **Draw on professional collaboration and development.** Effective assessment systems depend on teachers and other educators who understand the full range of assessment purposes, use a variety of suitable methods, work

collaboratively, and participate in ongoing professional development to improve their capability as assessors.

- **Encourage community participation and communication.** Parents, students, and members of the community should join a variety of experts, teachers, and other educators in shaping the assessment system. Discussion of assessment purposes and methods should involve a wide range of people interested in education. Educators, schools, districts, and states should clearly and regularly discuss assessment system practices and student and program progress with students, families, and the community. Examples of assessments and student work should be made available to parents and the community.
- **Allow for regular reviews**. Assessment systems should be regularly reviewed and improved to ensure that they are beneficial to all students. Reviewers should include stakeholders in the education system and independent experts.

RELIABILITY AND VALIDITY OF ASSESSMENT TASKS Two absolutely critical aspects of any effort to assess student learning, whether the assessment items have been developed by an individual teacher or a national testing company, are reliability and validity. Each of these terms is regularly used in professional discussions; however, their meaning and implications might not be appreciated. The only way in which any assessment of student learning can be counted on and be fair is if each and every item is both valid and reliable.

Validity refers to whether the assessment item measures what it is intended to measure. All too frequently, test items do not measure what the test maker had in mind. For example, a history teacher could have a learning objective related to students being able to describe key social, economic, and political causes of the Civil War. If the teacher then uses a test item that asks students to describe the results of key battles during the Civil War, the test item would not be valid. It did not ask students to demonstrate what they had learned in relation to the stated learning objective. This is a very simple and obvious example of an assessment item that is not valid. Problems related to validity are many and can be extremely complex. Still, it is essential that teachers make every effort in the construction of assessment items to make sure that what students are being asked to do is closely aligned with the statement of standards and learning objectives.

Reliability is an equally important technical aspect of having high-quality assessments. Reliability has to do with the consistency of information about student learning that results from repeated use of each assessment item or task. If two students who have learned the same amount complete the same assessment, do they receive identical scores? If they do, then the item has high reliability. If two students with the same level of learning receive discrepant scores, then the item is not consistent or reliable. Test makers often check for reliability of their items in another way, called test–retest. In this approach to checking reliability the same student would respond to the same test item after a carefully selected time interval, typically a week or two. Here too the reliability question is "How consistent are the results from both administrations of the assessment?" If both assessments have similar results, then the assessment is considered to be reliable.

validity
Addresses the degree to which an assessment measures what it is intended to.

reliability
Addresses the degree to which an assessment is consistent when it is used repeatedly.

THE UPS AND DOWNS OF TESTING

The nationwide movement toward standards, performance, and using a variety of assessment strategies is a good one, especially for teachers and their students. The goals of teaching and learning are made clear, which then makes it easier for teachers to know what to teach and how. Having standards certainly aids students in understanding what is most important to learn. And having standards helps teachers, schools, school districts, and states in determining the learning outcomes that should be assessed. Still, as with any education initiative, the standards movement has had a number of unintended consequences that need to be considered. Several of the more important of these consequences that have direct impact on teachers and students in classrooms are discussed below.

I'm not opposed to testing in general. . . . On the other hand, there is something pathological about the way the standards agenda is being imposed on underfunded, overcrowded, segregated schools. We ought to be honest about the whole agenda—whether you call it standards, proficiencies, competencies, those are the buzzwords. . . . There's something wrong with imposing universal standards on a state or nation until, prior to that time, we have given the children genuinely equal resources. The way it is being done today is invidious, punitive, and humiliating.

Jonathan Kozol

HIGH-STAKES TESTING As the focus on student performance has intensified, policymakers, especially at the state level, have mandated that students be tested regularly. In many states, all students in specific grades—such as third, seventh, and eleventh—are now required to take a state-designed test in certain subject areas such as writing, reading, and mathematics. The reason that testing of this type is called *high-stakes* is that there will be consequences for someone once the test results are known. At a minimum the student test results will be compiled by school and reported to the public. Schools will be named and ranked in the newspaper, and sharp questions will be asked about those that are "low performing." Another way in which testing can be high-stakes is related to the assignment of rewards and sanctions. In a few states, "high-performing" schools receive additional funds. In some districts teachers and/or principals receive salary bonuses if the test scores improve. For example in Maryland, schools that improve share \$2.75 million each year. Much more frequent than rewards is requiring some sort of sanctioning of the low-performing schools. For example, in Kentucky schools that are "in crisis" are assigned an experienced master teacher or principal who is responsible for helping the school improve. Principals can be reassigned and entire school staffs replaced. In other states, such as New Jersey, an entire school district that is designated low performing can be taken over by the state. Tests can be high-stakes for students as well. Twenty-eight states now use standardized exams to determine graduation from high school, and nineteen states use tests to decide student promotions. As is reflected in Figure 15.7, most voters are critical of high-stakes testing.

FIGURE 15.7 NATIONAL POLL RESULTS: MOST VOTERS CRITICAL OF HIGH-STAKES TESTING

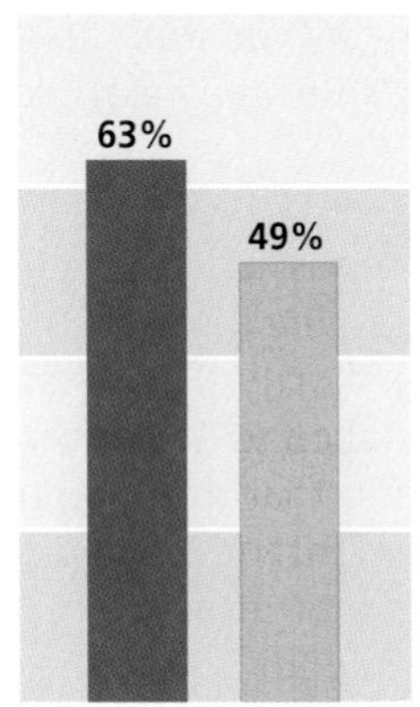

- 63% do not agree that a student's progress for one school year can be accurately summarized by a single test.
- 49% disagree with the idea that students should be kept back a grade if they fail to achieve a passing score on a statewide standardized test.

Source: From "Executive Director Statement," Arlington, VA: American Association of School Administrators, June 19, 2000.

high-stakes testing
Assessments for which the results have major consequences for certain groups or organizations.

PRESSURES TO CHEAT In high-stakes conditions we can expect that teachers and principals will invest concerted effort to have their students do well on the tests. In nearly every school and classroom, teachers will stop their regular instruction for a week or more to help students prepare for the test. These preparations can be as practical as practicing answering multiple choice questions and reviewing what has been taught during the year. The problem comes when teachers—and in some cases principals—help their students to cheat. Cheating ranges from telling students how to answer specific test items to teachers, principals, and school district administrators actually changing students' responses on individual tests. In other instances schools have encouraged certain students, such as those with learning disabilities, to stay at home on the day of testing.

TEACHING TO THE TEST A related issue has to do with balancing the time teachers spend on topics that are likely to be on the test versus instructional time spent on the rest of the curriculum. Any single test is bound to sample a very limited part of what students learn. Also, state tests might have little overlap with what is specified in the various sets of content standards and what is emphasized in the district curriculum materials. Time spent on preparing for high-stakes test reduces the time available to teach related material and other subjects, such as the performing arts, which are not being tested or where the stakes are not as high. In fact, in one recent study of ten states, the overlap in one subject between what state assessments tested and what teachers taught was found to be just 5 percent. Teachers have to be very careful about spending too much time in teaching for the test. If the whole of the district curriculum is aligned with state standards, then those students who have instruction that covers more of the standards should do the best on the tests.

ONE-SIZE-FITS-ALL Another critical issue related to the heavy focus on testing is the assumption that the same test is appropriate for all students, schools, and states. Historically, in the American system of education heavy emphasis has been placed on the importance of attending to individual differences and emphasizing that all students do not develop at the same rate. Now policymakers are mandating that one test be given to all students at a certain grade level at a specified time—in other words, one-size-fits-all. No matter what the uniqueness of individuals may be, all are to take the same relatively narrow test, and major decisions about individual students and/or schools will be based on the test results. Academically able students take the same test as poor urban students do. This practice undermines the credibility of the test and its results and clearly disadvantages certain students and schools.

THE THREAT OF A NATIONAL EXAM A growing concern of some is that the movement toward national curriculum standards and many states using the same tests is just one step away from a national exam, which will lead shortly thereafter to a national curriculum. This is the one-size-fits-all nightmare taken to the extreme. Others believe that there already is a national curriculum and that this is appropriate. A key target of this perspective is the National Assessment for Educational Progress (NAEP), which is administered each year to students in a sample of schools in each state. One of its purposes is to make it possible for policymakers and educators to view nationally how well students are doing. Comparisons can then be made with student achievement in other countries, and most assuredly, comparisons are made from state to state in this country. NAEP is designed to make inferences about student achievement within states. It is not designed to

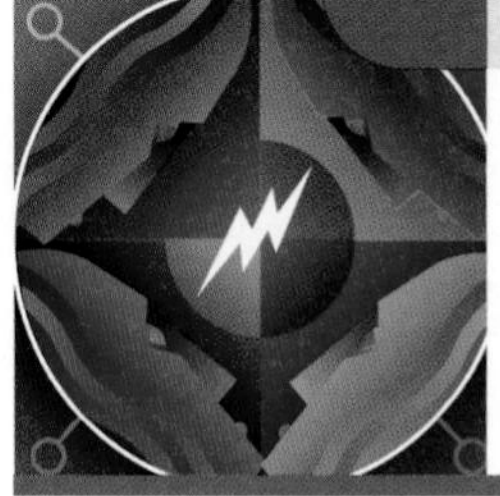

PROFESSIONAL DILEMMA

What Is the Proper Way to Prepare for High-Stakes, State-Mandated Tests?

Schools across the country are now required to administer state assessments linked to learning standards. The assessments tend to be paper-and-pencil, multiple-choice examinations of reading, mathematics, science, social studies, and writing. The assessments are usually given to students in grades 3–4, 7–8, and 10 and 12. Teachers within these targeted grade levels are required to interrupt their regular school instruction and administer these state examinations.

The state-mandated assessments are comprehensive in nature; that is, they cover a wide variety of topics that relate to the state standards. This often poses a dilemma for teachers who instruct at one of the targeted grade levels. Students in their classrooms might show that they have not had proper instruction in one or more aspects of the state content. This can and does occur because the district curriculum might not fully represent state standards, because individual students do not develop at the same pace, or because students transfer from school districts that have diverse curricula.

What can or should a teacher at a targeted grade level do to assist students on these state examinations? Some teachers attempt to teach for the test. That is, they try to get sample test items, and they clarify what was on the prior year's examination. These teachers may even develop teacher-made test questions that mimic the state examination and require students to practice taking these preparation tests. In some states, practice tests can be purchased from private publishing companies. Teachers who teach for the test in this way are sometimes criticized because they take time out of the regular school curriculum. They are also criticized because some educators consider teaching for the test to be improper.

Other teachers do not try to teach for the test, but they do have students practice test-taking techniques. They teach students strategies that could assist them in taking any standardized multiple-choice examination. They too take time out of the normal curriculum, but these teachers contend that the acquisition of such test-taking skills assists in all areas of learning.

A third group of educators refuse to do any test preparation other than to teach the required curriculum for their grade level. These educators believe that state tests should not affect the normal instructional process. If students do not perform well, then the curriculum should be officially changed.

What will you do if you are teaching in one of these target grade levels? Should you teach for the test? Should you teach test-taking techniques? Should you ignore the test and simply follow the normal curriculum? What approach can you defend as the proper one?

make judgments about individual students or schools. Unfortunately, although NAEP has existed for several decades and its findings are very useful, school districts and schools are increasingly unwilling to participate owing to the mounting pressure and time demands of the many other required tests.

INCREASED TEACHER BURDEN As exciting and important as the new approaches to assessment are, one of the downsides is the potential for increased work for teachers. Developing more authentic tasks takes more time than does constructing multiple-choice and true/false test items. Deriving scoring devises for authentic tasks is added work too. Holistic scoring entails first developing a scoring rubric and then examining each student's response in sufficient detail to be able to determine a total score. The load on teachers becomes even heavier in secondary schools, since each teacher has contact with more students. One of

DEBATE

Should States Determine the Specifics of Education Standards?

YES

Beverly LaHaye, founder and chair of Concerned Women for America, turns the argument by advocating that when states include alternative beliefs in education standards, they open the opportunity to learn.

When Kansas' Board of Education set new state science standards, disgruntled liberals painted it as a religious-right attack on evolution. In reality, it was a return to freedom, federalism and fairness in Kansas' public schools.

The idea of "tolerance" that liberals embrace when they advance their agenda was quickly swept under the rug when the possibility of state-mandated teaching of evolution arose. The fact that the movement failed is a victory for all of us.

Instead of allowing the state bureaucracy to dictate that every schoolchild be taught one narrow theory of the Earth's origins, the state board of education established standards that allow children to explore various theories in the science classroom.

Critics argue that Kansas students who have not been spoon-fed an evolution-only science diet may be ill-prepared for college entrance exams. But what could be better preparation for university life than exercises in freethinking and critical analysis, as students compare different theories?

Critics fear this move will "force teachers to raise questions" about the validity of evolution. In a free society, raising questions and exploring a theory's validity should be an innate part of the educational process. Historically, it has been the totalitarian societies that suppressed such activities in schools.

Moreover, one wonders how much confidence advocates of evolution have in the theory if they are afraid of a little scrutiny from schoolchildren.

Many of the controversial issues tearing at our nation today come down to this tyranny of the elite: government leaders, educational experts and Hollywood moguls with nothing but contempt for America's parents.

NO

The editors of USA Today *maintain that when states manipulate standards to impose a particular agenda, they undermine the educational purpose of those standards.*

Over the past decade, nearly every state has established standards of learning. And little by little, teachers, parents and even reluctant students have bought into the common-sense idea that each educational subject should include clearly defined lessons for students to master.

Yet just as some states are crediting standards for their first measurable academic gains in years, the reform has hit a roadblock: resistance from groups that see neutral, professionally developed standards as a threat.

The latest blowup came last week when the Kansas Board of Education decided that the theory of evolution shouldn't be part of the state's science-education standards.

By caving in to pressure from critics who believe evolution threatens their concept of God, the Kansas board commits three educational sins: It cheats Kansas students of fundamental knowledge about science. It imposes one group's religious beliefs on others in public schools. And more broadly, it threatens the standards movement by suggesting that legitimate course content can be manipulated.

Evolution is the process of how living things, from single cells to plants to animals, change over time in response to the conditions they confront. It is the central organizing principle biologists use to understand the living world and its origins. And understanding evolution is the key to understanding such vital processes as how bacteria resist antibiotics.

But as a result of the Kansas board's actions, evolution won't be included on the science-assessment tests Kansas students take—at least until the board is replaced, as the governor has suggested. Nor will it be part of the state's science curriculum that Kansas teachers use.

The teaching of evolution is a popular target in many states, but certainly not the only one. In 1995, a national group writing history–education guidelines tried so hard to

The problem is that the liberals just don't trust parents and local school boards to make responsible decisions for their children's education. And that's as condescending as it is offensive.

Kansas has not forbidden the teaching of evolution; it simply has recognized—in a spirit of federalism—that decisions of what theories are taught belong at the local level, and that parents, not overbearing bureaucracies, know what's best for their kids.

make sure teachers included those overlooked in the past—notably women and minorities—that it left out many traditional "heroes."

And last November, a survey by the American Federation of Teachers found that New Jersey's social-studies standards are impossibly vague. The problem? Committees that wrote them were so anxious to avoid favoring one constituency over another that they left out important chunks of history.

Each attempt to manipulate educational standards undermines the credibility of this valuable reform tool.

Because evolution deals with the origin of life, teaching it always will be controversial. But it can be presented in a way that respects religious diversity. The National Academy of Sciences provides educators with a useful guidebook on how to do so.

Political pressure in such circumstances is, of course, inevitable.

The goal of educational authorities is to ensure that the boards charged with developing standards are insulated from the pressures—not corrupted by them.

WHAT'S YOUR OPINION?

Should states determine specific education standards?

Go to **www.ablongman.com/johnson** to cast your vote.

the important solutions to the risk of increased burden is for teachers within a school or school district to collaborate in the development of assessment tasks. There also is national sharing of assessment items through discipline-based professional associations and various chat rooms on the web. A related key for individual teachers is to keep in mind that many of the traditional activities that teachers have been doing to assess student learning, such as noting their performance in laboratories and in the field, have been more legitimate with the move to authentic assessment. All that is needed is for the teacher to keep a record of observations about student performance.

BRINGING STANDARDS TO THE CLASSROOM: A TRUE STORY

Up to this point, standards have been presented as sets of overarching ideas that national curriculum groups and states are using to guide curriculum. Policymakers also are using standards to assess student learning and to evaluate the performance of schools. In this section the way in which standards are being used in one

Communicating with all constituencies, including taxpayers, parents, and students, is an essential part of developing standards and having shared understanding about assessment methods and the meaning of results.

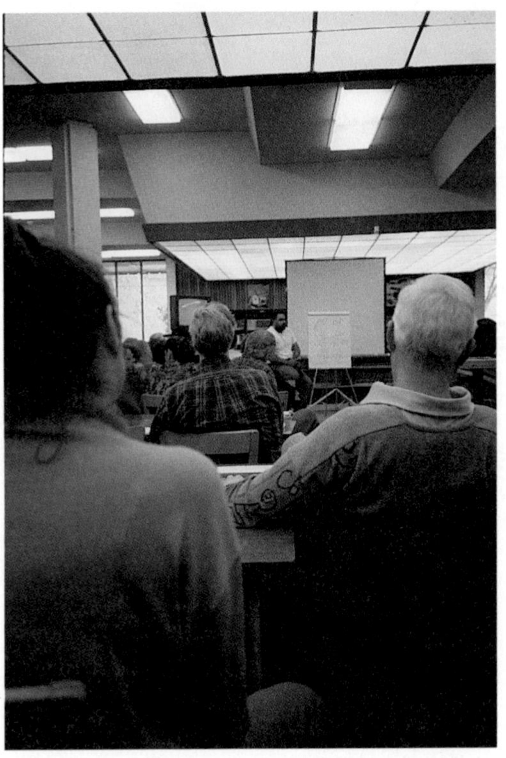

school district and its schools and classrooms is described. Standards are not abstract statements of ideals that teachers can simply ignore. Standards now are driving what teachers teach and, in many districts, how schools—and in some cases teachers—are evaluated. To illustrate how important and useful standards can be, their use in one school district is described herein.

The Douglas County School District, a rapidly growing district south of Denver, Colorado, was among the first to engage in the movement to standards, authentic assessments, and standards-based education. The district's approach, examples of standards, their perspective on standards-based education, and some of what they have learned along the way provide a very informative background for teacher education students. There is no escaping standards, so having firsthand knowledge about how this approach can be used to improve schools, curriculum, teaching, and student learning will be instructive and useful. Understanding how standards-based education can be a positive force in teaching and learning will be extremely helpful in participating in field and clinical experiences, in student teaching, and ultimately in interviewing for a teaching position.

A SCHOOL DISTRICT MOVES TO STANDARDS-BASED EDUCATION

A significant understanding that the Douglas County School District school board and executive leadership team kept in mind as it moved from traditional to standards-based education was that bringing about this very large change would take time, the involvement of all constituencies, and plenty of communication. A particularly important component in their process was to involve community members on committees along with teachers and principals. As standards were being developed, parents and community members were at the table. In addition, the superintendent and the school board respected and used the products that their committees developed.

COMMUNICATING WITH ALL CONSTITUENCIES To aid communication, the school district produced and distributed a newspaper that kept all constituencies informed about progress and what was intended. They identified four reasons to take an interest in academic standards:

> If you're a taxpayer, you have an important stake in what's happening in Douglas County schools. Whether you have children in school or not, your tax dollars support classroom instruction. Standards will provide you with increased knowl-

edge and accountability regarding what students are expected to know and learn. High quality schools also enhance communities, which can positively influence property values.

If you're a parent, you have a very precious interest in the academic expectations of your child. Standards provide a total picture of what is being taught from the time a student enters school until the time he or she graduates. Academic standards will provide you with a road map to help guide your child through school from start to finish.

If you're a student, academic standards will let you know what is expected at each grade level and help you move through Douglas County schools to reach your full potential. The standards will serve as goals for you to plan for and accomplish during the course of your school career, as well as provide a foundation for future educational opportunities.

If you're a school employee, you will be equipped with knowing what the priorities are for learning in Douglas County. Academic standards will provide teachers, administrators, and support personnel with direction that is consistent throughout the school district. Individual schools will know what is expected of them as they develop annual plans for school improvement and set goals for student achievement.[11]

DEFINING CURRICULUM STANDARDS Because there are multiple definitions and meaning of the term *standards,* this school district defined and explained what it means to them: "Content standards are statements describing what a student should know, and be able to do, in specific subject areas. Standards provide increased knowledge and accountability to all interested parties, including taxpayers, parents, students and staff. In total, they provide a road map to the successful completion of each student's high school education."[12]

The school district also focused more closely on what standards would mean for students. After all, students and their learning are at the core of standards-based education. Four distinct benefits of standards for students were identified:

Standards will:

- Provide additional challenges for those students already performing successfully under the current system.
- Clarify expectations of achievement for students who are struggling and "falling through the cracks."
- Help ensure that students will not "slide by" with minimal effort.
- Provide a higher level of accountability to students, parents and the community.[13]

Through multiple means, including the newspapers cited here, the school district worked to communicate about the meaning and progress steps toward having standard-based education in place. At the same time committees were at work developing content standards for each subject area and articulating a developmental sequence of steps in student learning from kindergarten to high school graduation.

CONTENT STANDARDS AND CHECKPOINTS: AN EXAMPLE Content standards were developed for each of the core academic areas first. Then committees worked on standards for art, civics, economics, music, foreign language, and other areas. The district's standards in each area were developed so that they included the related state curriculum standards and those developed by national professional association. For example, in mathematics the state standards and those articulated by the National Council for the Teaching of Mathematics (NCTM) were studied and incorporated in the district's standards. The resultant district's mathematics standards are presented as Figure 15.8.

Because content standards represent the major learning from twelve years of schooling and incorporate the big ideas, they are too complex for a teacher and students at any one grade level to address and master all that is expected. So part of the work of each standards committee was to develop a set of checkpoints that describe subparts of learning within each standard that would be addressed during a particular range of grade levels. These checkpoints are associated with a three- or four-year range of grades, since it is not expected that all children will master each check point at the same time.

ASSESSING STUDENT LEARNING IN STANDARDS-BASED EDUCATION

The core focus in standards-based education (SBE) is not on the writing of standards, but rather on what they mean for student learning. After all, standards and checkpoints are carefully constructed descriptions of key learning that students are expected to accomplish. Stating the learning outcomes is only the first variable in the SBE equation, the second part is assessing what students are learning. Assessments must be done so that students will know what they know and don't know, reports to parents should be based on student performance, and teachers need systematic

FIGURE 15.8 MATHEMATICS STANDARDS (K–12), DOUGLAS COUNTY SCHOOL DISTRICT, COLORADO

1. The student effectively uses a variety of strategies within the problem-solving process.
2. The student demonstrates an understanding of number sense and uses numbers and number relationships to solve meaningful problems and communicates the reasoning used in solving these problems.
3. The student demonstrates an understanding of computational skills and techniques including estimation, mental mathematics, paper and pencil, calculators, and computers and uses these to solve problems.
4. The student demonstrates an understanding of measurement and uses a variety of tools and techniques to solve problems.
5. The student demonstrates an understanding of the properties of geometry and uses these to solve problems.
6. The student demonstrates an understanding of the properties of data collection and analysis, statistics, and probability and uses these to solve problems, and communicates the reasoning and processes used.
7. The student demonstrates an understanding of algebraic methods used to explore, model, and describe patterns and functions.

Source: Douglas County School District R.E. 1, *Setting Standards for Improved Student Achievement.* Castle Rock, Colorado, 1997.

data about learning to use in designing subsequent instruction for each student. Information about how well students are doing is also important to the principal and school district leaders. After all, if students are learning, everyone needs to know and share in their successes; and if students are not successful with a particular standard or are not passing a checkpoint, than corrective action is signaled.

CHECKPOINTS, EXPECTATIONS, AND REPORT CARDS In the Douglas County School District serious consideration has been given to how to assess student learning and how best to report the findings to students, parents, and others. To do this effectively, they developed a set of *expectations* that accompany each checkpoint. These expectations are linked to particular grade levels.

In the traditional approach to reporting, each student received a letter grade, typically ranging from A to F. This single grade represented all that parents or the student would know about what the student had learned. In recent years some school districts have asked teachers to add a narrative paragraph describing what the teacher thought the student had learned. In a standards-based approach, greater attention is placed on directly assessing what students have learned and providing more direct description and assessment of what each student has learned, or not learned yet. To address this need, the Douglas County School District developed a special *Content Standards Report* form. Figure 15.9 is a sample of the reporting form that has been developed. Notice that in this form of reporting, the standard and checkpoints are presented along with the expectation. The expectation describes in operational ways what students are able to do when they have learned what is described in the checkpoint. The reporting form provides a mark by each checkpoint to signify whether or not the student has demonstrated sufficient examples of the expectation to be considered proficient. Space is provided for the teacher to add commentary as needed.

USING CHECKPOINTS TO VIEW THE DEVELOPMENTAL PROGRESSION WITHIN A STANDARD In the Douglas County Schools the same format of reporting is used for all grade levels. The form looks exactly the same for the primary grades as for high school. The standards stay the same. What changes are the list of checkpoints and the description of expectations. The complete list of checkpoints for the mathematics standard that we have been describing here is presented in Figure 15.10. This example is characteristic of what the standards, checkpoints, and expectations are like for all academic areas.

SUPPORTING TEACHERS AND STUDENTS IN IMPLEMENTING STANDARDS-BASED EDUCATION

Standards-based education is a very complex and sophisticated approach to teaching and learning. It is a professional challenge for beginning teachers, as well as experienced teachers, to learn to teach this way. SBE places heavier responsibility and accountability on the student to learn. The teacher's role shifts from conveyor of knowledge and dispenser of grades to coach and facilitator of students as they engage in learning. The expectations and checkpoints are stated and known by the teacher and students before instruction begins. In SBE students not only know what is to be learned beforehand, they also know what the assessment tasks will be like, that is, the types of performances described in the expectations.

MAPPING THE IMPLEMENTATION OF STANDARDS-BASED EDUCATION Recent research on the change process has resulted in an approach to assessing implementation

FIGURE 15.9 INTERMEDIATE MATHEMATICS CONTENT STANDARDS REPORT FOR COMPUTATION

Student Name:

School:

Explanation of Marking System
P = Progressing Appropriately
NP = Not Progressing Appropriately
*** * = See Alternate Form**

Grade:

Year: 1999–2000

Teacher:

Mathematics Standard #3 (Computation): **The student demonstrates an understanding of computational skills and techniques and uses these to solve a variety of problems.**

Checkpoints		Expectations
Intermediate Math (Computation) 1: Mentally multiplies and divides basic combinations of whole numbers.	+	Given multiple opportunities, the student consistently and independently uses multiplication and division facts 0–12, multiplies multiples of 10 by each other, and divides multiples of 10 with up to 3-digits by 1- and 2-digit divisors without remainders.
Intermediate Math (Computation) 2: Uses paper and pencil to add, subtract, multiply, and divide whole numbers, common fractions and mixed numbers, and decimals through hundredths.	+	Given multiple opportunities, the student consistently and independently solves addition, subtraction, multiplication, and division problems involving whole numbers, common fractions and mixed numbers, and decimals.
Intermediate Math (Computation) 3: Uses oral/written language to communicate an understanding of operations (i.e., addition, subtraction, multiplication, division) when used with whole numbers, fractions, mixed numbers, and decimals and the reasoning used to solve problems.	+	Given multiple opportunities, the student consistently and independently uses oral/written language to communicate his/her understanding of how and why an operation (e.g., addition, subtraction, multiplication, division) was used to solve a problem.

Comments:

Source: Douglas County School District R.E. 1, *Setting Standards for Improved Student Achievement.* Castle Rock, Colorado, 1997.

FIGURE 15.10 MATHEMATICS STANDARD #3 AND CHECKPOINTS

The student demonstrates an understanding of computational skills and techniques and uses these to solve a variety of problems.

Primary Checkpoints (K–3)

1. Mentally adds and subtracts basic combinations of whole numbers with sums to 20.
2. Uses paper and pencil to add and subtract whole numbers.
3. Uses oral/written language to communicate an understanding of computational techniques (e.g., regrouping for addition and subtraction) and to communicate the reasoning used to solve problems.

Intermediate Checkpoints (4–6)

1. Mentally multiplies and divides basic combinations of whole numbers.
2. Uses paper and pencil to add, subtract, multiply, and divide whole numbers, common fractions and mixed numbers, and decimals through hundredths.
3. Uses oral/written language to communicate an understanding of operations (i.e., addition, subtraction, multiplication, division) when used with whole numbers, fractions, mixed numbers, and decimals and to communicate the reasoning used to solve problems.

Middle School Checkpoints (7–8)

1. Mentally adds, subtracts, multiplies, and divides fractions, decimals, and integers.
2. Uses paper and pencil to add, subtract, multiply, and divide fractions, decimals, and integers.
3. Uses common ratios, proportions, and percents to solve real-world problems.
4. Understands and uses order of operations with integers.
5. Uses oral/written language to communicate an understanding of computational skills and techniques when used with fractions, decimals, and integers and to communicate the reasoning used to solve problems.

High School Checkpoints (9–12)

1. Mentally adds, subtracts, multiplies, and divides real numbers.
2. Uses paper and pencil to add, subtract, multiply, and divide real numbers.
3. Uses ratios, proportions, and percents involving real numbers to solve real-world problems.
4. Understands and uses order of operations with real numbers.
5. Uses oral/written language to communicate an understanding of computational skills and techniques when used with real numbers and to communicate the reasoning used to solve problems.

Source: Douglas County School District R.E. 1, *Setting Standards for Improved Student Achievement.* Castle Rock, Colorado, 1997.

FIGURE 15.11 STANDARDS-BASED EDUCATION—CONFIGURATION MAP

***Component #4*—Role of Assessment:** (function of assessment for teacher and students, timing of assessment development, use in the process of instruction)

(II)	(III)	(IV)
Assessment of standards or checkpoints occurs **after instruction has occurred** in order to **evaluate student progress** toward meeting standards or checkpoints.	Assessment of standards or checkpoints occurs **as instruction proceeds.** Assessments serve to **clarify a teacher's understanding of the standards or checkpoints and are used for instructional planning** and as summative evaluations.	Assessments are developed **prior to instruction.** Results of assessment of standards or checkpoints are the **basis for instructional planning** and are used to **evaluate overall student progress** toward meeting standards or checkpoints.

(I)
Classroom assessments are used to only to generate student grades.

Examples:

(II)		
"A score of _____ on the final exam indicates you have met the checkpoints."	"Now that I have finished the rubric for this project I am more clear about what I want the kids to know. I will need to change my lesson plans, so they are more focused on those specific skills."	"The assessments for this standard are two projects, several multiple choice tests, and a writing piece. On the last project most kids did well on _____, so I will organize next week's lessons around _____."

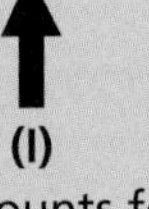

(I)
"This test counts for 40% of your grade."

Source: Douglas County School District R.E. 1, *Setting Standards for Improved Student Achievement.* Castle Rock, Colorado, 1997.

similar to what Douglas County is using to assess student learning. This approach in the change process research is called Innovation Configuration Mapping.[14] As might be expected, not all teachers will do the same things under the name of standards-based education. For example, a teacher might prefer not to tell students before instruction how their learning will be assessed. Or a teacher might get tired of asking students what they have learned during a lesson and want to tell them the right answer. In other words, classroom practices of teachers and students can be quite different when a complex innovation such as SBE is being implemented. What is needed is an implementation rubric, some way to assess how well teachers and students are doing in making the change from their old

(V)	(VI)
Assessments are developed **prior to instruction.** Results of assessment of standards or checkpoints are the **basis for instructional planning, and** are used **to build a shared understanding with students** of what they are supposed to know and be able to do before instruction begins and to **evaluate overall student progress** toward meeting standards or checkpoints.	Assessments are developed **prior to instruction.** Results of assessment of standards or checkpoints are the **basis for instruction** and are used **to build a shared understanding with students** of what they are supposed to know and be able to do before instruction begins. Assessments are **integrated into instruction** and are used as **instructional tools** and as **regular feedback mechanisms for students** and for **summative evaluation.**
"Before we start this unit, let me show you what you have to do to be proficient on this standard. You will need to get a '3' on this rubric in order to meet the standard. Let's take a look at the rubric and the exemplar and see if you can tell why this paper received a high rating."	"Today we will be reviewing your work from last week. Using the rubric, describe what you would do to improve your work. Remember, you will be using this paper along with your other work to demonstrate proficiency at the end of the course."

ways of teaching and learning to the new ways. The change researchers' technique of developing a map of teacher and student ways of working can do this.

The Douglas County School District leadership understood the importance of supporting teachers in making this major change. After all, SBE is still fuzzy in ways. All of the above description of standards, checkpoints, expectations, and new ways of reporting do not tell teachers what to do. Therefore, the school district decided to develop an **innovation configuration (IC) map** for SBE. One of the components that addresses the teacher's role is presented in Figure 15.11. This component describes different ways in which teachers can think about the purpose and use of assessments of learning. The continuum ranges from the

innovation configuration map
A rubric of implementation that describes in word pictures different levels of expertise in using a new approach, such as SBE.

FIGURE 15.12 Standards-Based Education—Configuration Map

***Component #5*—Student Ownership and Understanding of Learning:** (understanding of standards or checkpoints, understanding of progress in relation to standards or checkpoints, understanding of what is needed to improve performance in order to achieve standards or checkpoints)

(I)	(II)	(III)
Students' focus is on the **current activity.**	Students' focus is on **the requirements of the class** and the **grade** they receive.	Students can use the **"language" of standards.** They **can state the standards and checkpoints** that they are expected to learn, but are **unclear about where they are** in meeting the standards or checkpoints or **what they need to do** to achieve them.
Examples:		
"We are reading *The Diary of Anne Frank,* and I will be writing some kind of report when we are finished."	"We are studying how to use primary source materials. I need to get at least a B on the final report."	"I know that we are studying how to select and evaluate primary source materials as related to the Holocaust. I'm not sure exactly what I'll need to know about primary sources, or if I am any good at using them."

Source: Douglas County School District R.E. 1, *Setting Standards for Improved Student Achievement.* Castle Rock, Colorado, 1997.

teacher thinking about assessment after the fact (Variation I) to seeing and using assessment as integrated component of instruction (Variation VI). Beneath each of the variations are examples of what you might hear a teacher say that would be reflective of how the teacher thinks about the purpose of assessment in an SBE classroom.

Once developed, this IC map for SBE was given to teachers and has become a guide for teachers in assessing how well they are doing in making the change from traditional teaching to an SBE approach. The IC map for SBE also has become a guide for developing staff development courses for teachers. For example, key IC map components have become the topics for teacher inservice sessions.

The second IC map component (Figure 15.12) is a student component that addresses the role of the student in learning in the SBE classroom. This component is a critical one. For SBE to be successful, students have to assume more responsibility for their own learning. This component is one that Douglas County

(IV)

Students **understand** what they are **expected to know and be able to do** and can **articulate in specific terms** what it means to reach the standards or checkpoints. They can **describe where they are** in regard to the standards or checkpoints but are **unclear what they need to do** to achieve them.

"I know that we are studying primary source materials as related to the Holocaust, and that's why we are reading *The Diary of Anne Frank.* I know that we will be evaluating and interpreting sources for their usefulness in understanding the Holocaust. I can find sources, but I am not sure how to evaluate their relevance and quality. I am not sure what I'll need to do to become proficient in evaluating these sources."

(V)

Students **understand** what they are **expected to know and be able to do** and can **articulate in specific terms** what it means to reach the standards or checkpoints. They can **describe where they are** in regard to the standard and know what they **need to improve** to achieve it.

"I know that we are studying primary source materials as they relate to the Holocaust and that's why we are reading *The Diary of Anne Frank,* I know that we will be evaluating and interpreting sources for their usefulness in understanding the Holocaust. I am pretty good at locating primary sources, but I have trouble knowing whether they are really quality sources. My teacher has shown some interesting ways to judge the quality of a source, but I need some more practice with them."

School District personnel consider to be at the center of their efforts to change from a traditional instructional program to one that is standards-based.

STANDARDS-BASED EDUCATION AS A PARADIGM CHANGE

Elliott Asp, the Assistant Superintendent for Assessment in Douglas County, has been instrumental in the district's effort to develop standards and to support schools as they implement their approach to standards-based education. Throughout this process, he has been reflecting on what is important and how the thinking changes as one moves from one type of approach to education to a standards-based approach. His picture for describing this paradigm shift is presented as Figure 15.13.

As is illustrated in Figure 15.13, depending on one's way of thinking about standards the questions asked are different, as is the locus of accountability.

FIGURE 15.13 STAGES IN IMPLEMENTING SBE: PROMOTING HIGH ACHIEVING STUDENTS

STANDARDS CENTERED	STANDARDS REFERENCED	STANDARDS BASED
Are we teaching to the standards?	Are students meeting the standards?	How do we modify the system so that all students meet or exceed
*instructional program aligned with the standards.	*student progress in meeting the standards is systematically assessed at the school and district level.	*curriculum, assessment and instruction is routinely modified at the classroom, school and district based on student progress meeting the standards.
*classroom/school accountability	*system accountability	*student/system accountability
LA and Math 1996–97	LA #4 and Math #2 1997–98	LA #4 and Math #2 1999–2000
Sci and SS 1997–98	Sci #1 and SS #3 and #6 1998–99 (secondary only)	
	LA #3 and Math #3 1999–2000	

Source: Douglas County School District R.E. 1, *Setting Standards for Improved Student Achievement.* Castle Rock, Colorado, 1997.

When there is a standards-centered perspective or paradigm, the key questions have to do with whether teachers are teaching the standards. The focus of accountability is on the classroom and that the standards are at the center of the teacher's lessons. In the standards-referenced paradigm the questions shift to examination of the extent to which the students are meeting the standards through school- and district-level assessments. The focus is on how well the education system is doing through examination of assessments such as test scores. This, the standards-referenced perspective, is how most states are viewing SBE. The focus is on holding school districts and schools accountable, not students or teachers. This perspective is high stakes for schools and school districts. It is from this perspective that states name schools and school districts as being "low performing."

Asp's third perspective, or paradigm, is the standards-based one. In this perspective a different set of questions is asked, and there is a different focus for accountability. In this perspective the student, as well as the education system, has a role in accountability. The student is responsible for engaging in learning the standards, one checkpoint at a time, and the education system is responsible for articulation of the standards and assessments. The system also is responsible for using the results of student assessments on each and every checkpoint to continually strive to make the educational opportunities (opportunity to learn type of standards) available to all students and more effective.

In summary, SBE represents a major shift in thinking about teaching and learning. Educators and community representatives have a responsibility to articulate the standards and checkpoints. Student learning can then be based and paced on their progress, as is reflected in the expectations. This is a complex and interrelated set of perspectives, roles, and responsibilities. When a concerted effort is made across a number of years, such as the Douglas County School District has done, teachers are able to improve their approaches to teaching by focusing on what their students are learning, rather than on their presentation of lessons. In SBE, students assume greater responsibility and accountability for their learning. In addition, there are no surprises. The standards, checkpoints, and expectations are known to all.

SUMMARY

STANDARDS-BASED EDUCATION

Standards, assessments, and standards-based education are core components of the standards movement and are affecting everyone who has a stake in public education. This chapter describes the different dimensions that make up a standards-based school program as well as the implications for assessment practices. The chapter also presents conflicts and dilemmas posed by a standards-based approach to education. Some of the conflicts include the differing conceptions of standards endorsed by different groups. World-class standards, real-world standards, and discipline-based standards are compared. These diverse conceptions of standards are related to the differing exceptions that groups have for education. Business leaders, government leaders, parents, and academic professionals have worthy but sometimes conflicting expectations about what schools need to accomplish. These differences influence the kinds of standards that are promoted. Contemporary schools districts wrestle with these differing expectations for students.

Just as standards differ conceptually, they can be used for different purposes. Standards can be used to make school curricula more alike. They can provide a set of uniform expectations by grade level that all students must meet before progressing to the next grade. However, such standards do not always clearly meet the diverse needs of students. In contrast to using standards to make the curriculum more uniform, standards can be used as opportunity-to-learn goals. Opportunity-to-learn standards clarify how students will be enabled to achieve high standards through multiple and diverse events within their schooling. Such opportunity-to-learn standards may be used to customize rather than standardize learning.

The chapter also describes multiple sources of educational standards. In addition to the work of discipline-specific groups that have developed standards for student achievement, professional educator organizations have developed standards for teachers, information specialists, school counselors, and the like. There is no single set of teaching standards; rather, different professional agencies have adopted their own sets. Some examples include mathematics teaching standards from the National Council for Teachers of Mathematics, science teaching standards from the National Research Council, and master teacher standards from the National Board for Professional Teaching Standards. Although all of these professional teaching standards are worth examining, it is not easy for school districts or individual teachers to determine which set is best suited for their context and philosophy.

Three types of standards have emerged based on the different conceptions and uses of standards: content standards, which focus on student achievement of subject matter and school curricula; performance standards, which focus on teacher and student accomplishments; and delivery or opportunity-to-learn standards, which focus on resources and support for schools. Each of these types of standards ultimately focuses on developing student achievement.

THE CHANGING FACE OF ASSESSMENT

Standards are not an end unto themselves. Simply listing standards in a school brochure will make little difference in the way students learn and achieve. Standards should influence both instructional and assessment practices. When assessments are interwoven into a standards-based framework, they become much more varied and meaningful to teachers and students alike.

Assessments that are integrated into a standards-based program need to be multiple and varied. Competency-based assessments are used to demonstrate a specific competence. Diagnostic assessments are used to diagnose and determine what a child knows and does not know in a certain area of interest. Norm-referenced assessments are used to demonstrate who is best in some area. Criterion-referenced assessments are used to determine what individual students know about a very specific topic. Capstone assessments are developed to celebrate a milestone accomplishment or to demonstrate how well a person has mastered something. Program assessments are used to determine whether school programs are effective. Authentic contextualized assessments provide opportunities for students to show what they know and are able to do within and across a number of different disciplines.

BRINGING STANDARDS TO THE CLASSROOM: A TRUE STORY

This chapter concludes with a contemporary example of a districtwide approach to standards-based education. The Douglas County, Colorado, School District is portrayed as a community that has examined the standards that are important to all constituencies, a community that supports a curriculum that directly links to the standards and also supports assessments that match the standards. The central target in this approach is student learning. The standards descriptions, the various forms of assessing, and the activity of teachers and students in the classroom are centered on student learning. In the end, this is what the whole of the standards movement is about: improving the learning performance of all students.

DISCUSSION QUESTIONS

1. What type of standards do you think are most appropriate for today's public schools?
2. What benefits and problems are inherent in developing a common set of standards for all students across the country?
3. Why should we permit students to develop their own portfolios to show what they have learned? What problems would such assessments cause?
4. Is it fair to demand that all students, no matter what their ability or socioeconomic status, are to master a common set of learning standards before obtaining a diploma?
5. Take a moment to study the set of checkpoints and expectations presented in Figure 15.10. Where would you place yourself? Now how do you feel about standards? Do you see how easy it is to visualize the learning that is desired and how, in combination, the developmental progression of checkpoints makes clear the larger meaning of the standard and all that a student is to learn between the time they enter kindergarten and when they graduate from high school?

6. What do you see as being the most critical components of the teacher's role in a standards-based education classroom?

JOURNAL ENTRIES

1. Consider the types of assessments that have been used throughout your college studies. Select one assessment experience that you have found to be especially helpful in displaying what you believe you really know and can do. Describe the assessment, and then list what characteristics of the assessment enabled you to express your understanding.
2. Obtain a copy of your state's learning standards for one discipline. Examine the framework in which the standards are described. Do they have related goals, benchmarks, or other dimensions? Focus on one standard and identify all of the components that relate to that learning standard. In your journal draw a diagram or create a mind map or concept map that shows the interrelationships of all the supporting pieces that surround the standard.
3. Standards-based education and new approaches to assessing learning are being applied in higher education, especially in teacher education programs. The same ideas apply in both settings. To illustrate how similar the approaches to teaching and learning can be, consider the innovation configuration map component presented in Figure 15.11. Think about the teaching of one of your teacher education instructors. Which variation of that component does he or she display most of the time? In other words, would you assess your instructor to be an "a," a "c," or what? Now consider the student component, Figure 15.12, and your approach to learning in that course. How would you rate yourself: "I," "II," or what? For the reflective part of this journal entry, what are implications of this analysis for you as a learner and you as a teacher?

PORTFOLIO DEVELOPMENT

1. Authentic assessments attempt to provide students with an opportunity to show what they know and can do within a real-world setting. Within your major subject area, develop an authentic assessment that would enable students to show what they have learned in relation to one of the national standards.
2. Use the library, the web, or a faculty member to search out information about the activities in one school district relative to their use of standards and assessing learning related to their standards. Look closely at the standards and assessments for your planned teaching area. Develop a page of notes about what you would say in a job interview related to their use of SBE. Also note three or four questions for which you would need to find additional information or develop better understanding before you went to the interview.

SCHOOL-BASED EXPERIENCES

1. Interview several students after they have taken a high-stakes assessment. Ask them to describe their feelings about the assessment experience. Ask the students whether they believe that the assessment was fair. After completing the interviews, develop a summary and a set of conclusions about the strengths and weaknesses of such high-stakes tests.
2. Interview several teachers who are required to administer state assessments linked to standards. Ask the teachers to identify what they do to help students

prepare for the assessments. Ask them whether they believe such assessments are fair. Record the results of your interview, and then write your own stance (from an educator's perspective) with regard to value of statewide and high-stakes assessment.

WEBSITES

We recommend that you do a web search using keywords drawn from learning standards and assessment practices, such as "Project 2061," "NCTM standards," "authentic assessment," "benchmarks," "portfolios," "indicators of learning," "holistic rubrics," "performance assessments," and "state standards." Also use keywords focused on individual thinkers such as: Grant Wiggins, Richard J. Stiggins, Bena Kallick, Lauren Resnick, and Jay McTigue. You can also search specific school district websites to see what they are doing with SBE.

1. <www.project2061.org> The Home page for the American Association for the Advancement of Science's Project 2061, a national initiative to improve K–12 science, mathematics, and technology education.
2. <128.8.182.4/db/edo/ED388889.htm> This website is part of the ERIC database and features Richard Stiggins's article on the characteristics of a sound performance assessment.
3. <www.nagb.org> The home page for the National Assessment of Educational Progress. There are several links, including an overview of plans for improvement and pilot programs.
4. <www.standard.nctm.org> Information about the National Council for the Teaching of Mathematics and its standards can be found at this website.
5. <www.project2061.org/newsinfo/press/rl990923.htm> A joint statement from the National Research Council, the American Association for the Advancement of Science, and the National Science Teachers Association about the Kansas Science Education Standards.
6. <www.relearning.org> The home page for Relearning by Design, this site provides information on standards and authentic assessment.
7. <www.ncss.org> The home page for the National Council for the Social Studies includes the council's standards, background papers, and description of its many other professional activities.
8. <www.dpi.state.wi.us/dpi/oea> The State of Wisconsin Department of Pubic Instruction's OEA resource page. This site has been divided into three categories: Standards, Assessment, and Accountability.
9. <putwest.boces.org/Standards.html> Standards by state and the Goals 2000 Educate America Act.
10. <www.maa.org/features/robson.html> Standards-based education and its implications for mathematics.

NOTES

1. Commission on Standards for School Mathematics, *Curriculum and Evaluation Standards of School Mathematics.* Reston, Virginia: National Council of Teachers of Mathematics, 1989, Revised 2000.
2. National Standards for Social Studies Teachers Task Force, Expectations of Excellence: Curriculum Standards for Social Studies. Washington D.C.: National Council for Social Studies, April, 1994.
3. Standards Development Staff, *New Standards Performance Standards Volume 2.* Pittsburgh: National Center on Education and the Economy, 1997, p. 22.

4. *Ibid.*
5. Standards Development Staff, p. 88.
6. Standards Development Staff, pp. 136–137.
7. The New Basics Project, "Learning Fit for the Real World," *The Australian.* March 4, 2000.
8. *Ibid.*
9. Grant Wiggins, Educative Assessment. San Francisco, CA: Jossey Bass, 1998.
10. National Center for Fair and Open Testing, Principles for Responsible Assessment. New York: National Center for Fair and Open Testing, 1995.
11. Douglas County School District R.E. 1, *Progress Report for Setting Standards for Improved Student Achievement.* Castle Rock, Colorado, 1996, p. 3B.
12. Douglas County School District R.E. 1, *Setting Standards for Improved Student Achievement.* Castle Rock, Colorado, 1997, p. 4.
13. Douglas County School District, 1997, p. 1.

BIBLIOGRAPHY

American Federation of Teachers, National Council on Measurement in Education, and National Education Association. *Standards for Teacher Competence in Educational Assessment of Students.* Washington, DC: Authors, 1990.

American Psychological Association. *Standards for Educational and Psychological Testing.* Washington, DC: Author, 1985.

Arter, J., and Spandel, V. "Using Portfolios of Student Work in Instruction and Assessment." *Educational Measurement Issues and Practice 11* (1) (1992): 36–44.

Asp, E. "The Relationship Between Large-Scale and Classroom Assessment: Compatibility or Conflict?" *Assessing Student Learning: New Rules, New Realities.* Arlington, VA: Educational Research Service, 1998.

Bond, L., and Rober, E. *State Student Assessment Program Database, 1992–1993.* Oakbrook, IL: North Central Regional Educational Laboratory, and Washington, DC: Council of Chief State School Officers, 1993.

Hall, G. E., and Hord, S. M. *Implementing Change: Patterns, Principles and Potholes.* Boston, MA: Allyn and Bacon, 2001.

Hammerman, E., and Musial, D. *Classroom 2061: Activity-Based Assessments in Science Integrated with Mathematics and Language Arts.* Palatine, IL: IRI/Skylight Publishing, 1995.

Lane, S. "The Conceptual Framework for the Development of a Mathematics Performance Assessment Instrument." *Educational Measurement: Issues and Practice 11* (2) (1993): 23–27.

Mabry, L. "Writing to the Rubric." *Phi Delta Kappan 80* (9) (May 1999): 673–682.

Marzano, R., and Kendall, J. *A Comprehensive Guide to Designing Standards-Based Districts, Schools, and Classrooms.* Alexandria, VA: Association for Supervision and Curriculum Development, 1996.

——, Pickering, D., and McTighe, J. *Assessing Student Outcomes: Performance Assessment Using the Dimension of Learning Model.* Alexandria, VA: Association for Supervision and Curriculum Development, 1993.

National Center for History in the Schools, University of California. *National Standards for United States History: Exploring the American Experience, Grades 5–12.* Expanded version. Los Angeles: National Center for History in the Schools, University of California, 1996.

Shavelson, R. J., Baxter, G. P., and Pine, J. "Performance Assessments in Science." *Applied Measurement in Education 4* (4) (1992): 347–362.

Suzuki, L. A., Meller, P. J., and Ponterotto, J. G., eds. *The New Handbook of Multicultural Assessment.* San Francisco: Jossey-Bass, 2000.

Wiggins, G. "Work Standards: Why We Need Standards for the Instructional and Assessment Design." *NASSP Bulletin 81* (590) (1997): 56–64.

——. *Educative Assessment Designing Assessments to Inform and Improve Student Performance.* San Francisco: Jossey-Bass, 1998.

Yancey, K., ed. *Portfolios in the Writing Classroom.* Urbana, IL: National Council of Teachers of English, 1992.

EPILOGUE

EDUCATION IN THE TWENTY-FIRST CENTURY

The new millennium has ushered in major shifts, changes, and a reexamination of values in U.S. society and the world. As a teacher, you are now caught up in this time of change. Information and technology are growing at exponential rates, and access to information is as immediate as the World Wide Web. Relativity governs the actions of society. As the debate features in every chapter of this text showed, the pros and cons of educational issues, needs, and actions are discussed seriously by classroom teachers and educational administrators alike. New knowledge affects procedures, activities, and possibilities in technology, music, media, fashion, national and world politics, and education.

In this text we have explored and reflected on schools, students, teaching, and assessment because we believe that the teachers of this new millennium must be able to anticipate, understand, and manage change throughout their careers. As one of these teachers, you will become the agent of change.

Throughout this text you have been introduced to what we have called the big ideas of education. Those ideas were examined through the lens of each foundational area to focus on educational issues for the student and the teacher. As you continue your teaching career, those big ideas will become departure points for the future. Not only will the complexity and makeup of U.S. society change ethnographically, but so also will society in all the world, where, despite differences, we interact more and more. Schools, which once had the primary purpose of educating the masses in the fundamentals of learning, namely, "the three Rs," now additionally must focus on how to live in and protect our world. What values will enhance all peoples' lives? What ecological issues and practices must we adopt if the planet is to survive?

DEBATE

Will Public Education Survive the Next Century?

Dr. Barbara Smith Palmer is an elected member of the United Teachers of Los Angeles House of Representatives and Political Action Committee, the California Teachers Association State Council, and a UTLA delegate to the NEA Representative Assembly.

I'm excited about the prospects for teaching and learning in the 21st Century. But for public education to truly survive in the 21st Century, we will need to make some adjustments in our efforts at reform, in our philosophy, and in our teaching.

■ **Reform.** How schools are structured has complicated our attempts at innovation. The relationship between knowledge and power, within the social and political contexts for our schools, has placed burdensome external controls on teachers and students, controls ranging from excessive regulation to massive testing.

Current policies that focus on national testing and national standards are too narrow. There is no one approach that can work for all kids. Our testing and standards policies must take into account the many diverse learning styles in our student population.

■ **Learning Approaches.** Our presuppositions commonly prevent us from thinking effectively about education issues—and from committing ourselves to equity and excellence for all. We must put an end to deficit terminology and labeling. Terms like "at-risk" marginalize kids into categories and make assumptions about their learning capabilities that aren't true. Children are capable of much more than teachers and parents generally realize.

■ **Teaching.** In the school of the 21st Century, teachers will have to challenge traditional approaches to teaching and learning by modeling a collaborative form of practitioner inquiry.

Teachers need to encourage students to question answers and to express their own viewpoints. They have to provide ways for students to participate in the discourse

Cynthia Russ is a curriculum coach for Residence Park Latin Grammar Classical Studies Magnet School in Dayton, Ohio. A teacher for more than twenty-six years, Russ is an alternate member of the Resolutions Committee for both the Ohio Education Association and NEA.

As I look ahead to the next century and think about the fate of our public education system, I feel discouraged. I do not think public education will, in fact, survive the next century.

Public schools, to be sure, have always faced challenges. As public educators, we've always had to battle to make sure all children have the rights and opportunities they deserve. We had to fight to end segregation, fight for equity for Native American children schooled on reservations, and fight to get adequate funding for inner city schools.

But the opponents we face now seem tougher than ever, and we find ourselves battling on so may different fronts.

■ **Vouchers.** The increasing clamor for private-school tuition vouchers is a direct threat to public education's survival in the next century.

Vouchers siphon off much needed funding from public schools. In a voucher-friendly America, those who remain in an underfunded public system will face a vicious downward spiral of deteriorating buildings, out-of-date materials, overcrowded classrooms, and uncertified teachers. This downward spiral will only create pressure for more vouchers.

■ **Charter Schools.** Charters today are too often run by businesses out to make a buck, not educators with visions they want to try to realize. The results are predictable. Children become mere moneymakers for the companies involved. But what happens when the money runs out?

If charters continue, with little public oversight, we won't have much in our education budgets left in the next century for children to receive the education they deserve.

■ **Lack of Parental Involvement.** The absence of parents in our schools is another factor that leads me to believe that public education may not survive.

that shapes their lives. Curiosity, industry, and imagination should be encouraged and rewarded.

Teachers need more autonomy and the ability to create exciting educational experiences for students. By encouraging democratic dialogue among educators, we can empower teachers.

We can excel in the new century if teachers function as a community of scholars, engaging in collaborative diagnostic and problem-solving work to create alternative approaches for designing tasks and assessing activities.

In the classroom of the 21st Century, teachers need to involve students in interesting project based assignments so that they can learn by doing.

Students should become more engaged readers. Activities like peer-assisted reading, classroom discussions about texts, and book club projects can allow students to become leaders on their own terms.

Students will reach their personal goals through the gentle guidance of teachers, who hold themselves and their students accountable to high standards for all.

Educators joining with each other and with their students to explore a critical pedagogy of group work, collaboration, and serious individualized attention, will create a revolutionary classroom where all children learn at the highest levels.

If that happens, public education will not only survive through the 21st Century, it will thrive!

Parental support has always been the backbone for public education. With dwindling parental support, lines of communication tend to close. Schools are then left subject to gossip, innuendo, misconceptions, and bad feelings.

Schools that do not have a strong communication link with parents will not survive. We cannot survive in the next century if parents and the community do not understand what is really happening in our schools today.

If public education is to survive into the next century, we need to rebuild general public support. We must not let vouchers and other schemes take away the resources we need to help our public schools thrive.

There are problems, of course, in our public school system. But American public education—available to everyone, without regard to race, color, creed, economic status, or physical and mental ability—remains our nation's greatest contribution to democracy.

Society needs to understand that our children are our future. If we continue diluting public education, we will no longer have a viable method to educate all children. And without a focus on all children, public education will cease to exist.

WHAT'S YOUR OPINION?

Will public education survive the next century?

Go to **www.ablongman.com/johnson** to cast your vote and see how NEA readers responded.

Teachers are prepared better than ever before for their career. Students are more capable and demanding than ever before. And the school, despite constant attacks on it by critics, is better than ever before. The system is not perfect, but it has proven to be resilient and has carefully survived and adjusted to what society wants. However, schools still face tremendous difficulties associated with their readiness and continuing ability to identify and conceptualize just what it is we want for society and the schools.

Are teachers in the twenty-first century ready to take on the growing challenges for the school and the teaching profession? We believe that teachers like you are more ready today than teachers ever have been. As the U.S. school moves forward in this millennium, the education profession is in good hands. The retiring stock of teaching professionals, and there are many, is being replaced by a stronger and more capable cadre of scholars and visionaries. To you, the new teacher, we wish our very best for your successful professional endeavors.

NAME INDEX

Abraham, 399
Adams, John, 329
Addams, Jane, 333
Adler, Mortimer, 412
Alcuin, 289–290
Alexander, Herbert G., 382, 404
Alexander, Jeffrey C., 138
Alexander, Lamar, 188
Alger, Horatio, 72
Allen, Dwight, 359
Anderson, Sarah, 98
Anthony, Susan, 333
Apple, Michael W., 139
Aquinas, Thomas, 290, 300
Aratani, Lori, 173
Aristotle, 285, 286–287, 290, 389, 390–391
Armytage, W. H. G., 339
Arouet, François Marie, 294
Asp, Elliott, 567
Averroes, 290
Avicenna, 290
Ayers, William, 169

Bagley, William, 357
Banks, James A., 98, 168
Banneker, Benjamin, 328–329, 337
Barnard, Henry, 188, 310
Barnes, Donald, 369
Barr, Alfred, 358
Beane, James A., 139
Beard, Charles, 341
Beard, Joseph, 359
Beecher, Catharine, 333
Bell, George, 329
Bellah, Robert N., 98, 168
Benen, Steve, 227
Bennett, William, 188
Berman, P., 224
Bernard, Jessie, 98
Bestor, Arthur, 358
Bethune, Mary McLeod, 332, 333, 337
Binet, Alfred, 356, 360
Bloom, Benjamin S., 357, 361, 368, 461, 504, 521, 522
Books, Sue, 99
Bosetti, Lynn, 168
Bowles, Samuel, 452, 453, 458
Brameld, Theodore, 421, 452, 458
Brandt, R., 521
Brantlinger, Ellen, 124
Brennan, William, 256
Bright, Carl, 356
Brodinsky, Ben, 365
Brophy, Jere, 508
Bruner, Jerome, 357, 361
Bruschi, Barbara A., 54
Bryant, N. Z., 227
Buber, Martin, 425, 432
Buchler, Justus, 458
Burch, James H., II, 139
Burger, Warren, 265
Burr, E., 224
Bush, George, 364
Bush, George W., 173
Byngham, William, 317, 339

Carter, Jimmy, 187
Carter, Robert T., 108
Cavanagh, John, 98
Chaplin, Duncan, 138
Charlemagne, 289, 290
Charters, W. W., 357
Chavis, John, 329, 337
Chemers, Betty M., 139
Chinn, Philip C., 168
Chomsky, Noam, 357
Clinton, Bill, 173, 474, 528
Cochran-Smith, Marilyn, 165
Coleman, James, 360
Coley, Richard J., 54
Collier, Virginia P., 99
Collins, Chuck, 98
Comenius, Johann Amos, 293–294, 301
Comer, James, 482
Compayre, Gabriel, 303
Comte, Auguste, 418
Conant, James, 356
Confucius, 398
Cooper, Kenneth J., 141
Cordero, Rafael, 351
Cottom, Carolyn, 133, 139
Counts, George, 357, 421
Crandall, Prudence, 329–330, 337
Craven, Samuel M., 405
Cronbach, Lee, 357
Cross, W. E., Jr., 108
Cuomo, Andrew, 47
Curwin, Richard, 447

da Feltre, Vittorino, 292
Daley, Richard, 196
Dandridge, William L., 224
Darling-Hammond, Linda, 54
Darwin, Charles, 299
David, Samuel, 339
Degler, Carl, 365
De la Salle, Jean Baptiste, 293
Delpit, Lisa, 168
Demerer, Frank R., 277
Descartes, René, 294, 301
DeWalt, Mark W., 344
Dewey, John, 103, 138, 139, 327, 341, 357, 393, 404, 409, 419, 423, 432, 452, 458
Diggins, John P., 341, 366
Dock, Christopher, 309
Douglass, Frederick, 329, 337
Drury, D. W., 224
Duck, Lloyd, 432

Einstein, Albert, 535
Elson, William, 326

Emerson, George B., 312
Ennis, Robert, 387
Erasmus, 291, 292
Ericson, J., 224
Estrin, Elise Trumbull, 150, 168
Fassett, James, 326
Figueroa, Peter, 168
Fine, Michelle, 78
Fink, Dean, 486, 489
Flanders, Ned, 359
Flesch, Rudolph, 358
Flygare, Thomas J., 277
Franklin, Benjamin, 312, 319, 336
Franklin, Nicholas, 329
Fraser, Matthew, 265
Frederick the Great, 295
Freedman, Haskell C., 277
Freire, Paulo, 423, 432
Friedenberg, Edgar, 361
Froebel, Friedrich, 299, 301, 311
Fuller, Bruce, 173, 224
Furstenberg, Frank F., Jr., 109, 138

Gagnon, Paul, 365
Gallup, Alec M., 139
Gamoren, Adam, 481
Garber, Lee O., 277
Gartner, Alan, 99
Genesee, Fred, 169
Gerald, Debra E., 14, 15, 16, 54
Getzels, Jacob, 358
Gintis, Herbert, 452, 453, 458
Giroux, Henry A., 422, 432, 449, 458
Gitomer, Drew H., 54
Glasser, William, 446, 458
Glickman, Carl D., 416, 432, 445, 458
Goldhaber, D. D., 224
Gollnick, Donna M., 168
Good, Thomas, 508
Goodlad, John, 448, 449, 458
Goodnough, Abby, 491
Gordon, Milton M., 98
Graham Tebo, Margaret, 272
Gray, Kenneth C., 489
Greene, Maxine, 164, 169, 396, 397, 405, 450, 458
Grossman, Lynn, 227
Guilford, J. P., 357, 358
Guskin, Samuel L., 124

Hall, Primus, 330
Hall, Samuel, 319
Hammerman, Elizabeth, 427
Hannaway, Jane, 138
Hargreaves, Andy, 486, 489
Harris, Sarah, 329
Harris, Stephaan, 435
Harrow, Anita J., 521, 523
Hartman, Chris, 98
Harvard, John, 325
Havighurst, Robert, 357, 361
Hawley, Chandra, 521
Heath, Shirley Brice, 138
Helms, J. E., 108, 138
Herbart, Johann Friedrich, 298–299, 301, 311
Herr, Edwin L., 489
Hkung-tsze, 284
Hodne, Peter, 443
Hofferth, Sandra, 349
Holt, John, 361
Honeyman, David S., 224
Huerta, Luis, 173, 224
Hunt, Jean Ann, 169
Hunter, Madeline, 507–508
Hunter, Richard, 224
Hussar, William J., 14, 15, 16, 54
Hutchins, Robert M., 412

Ignatius of Loyola, 301
Illich, Ivan, 361

James, William, 419
Jefferson, Thomas, 329
Jencks, Christopher, 360
Johns, Roe L., 339
Johnson, David W., 443
Johnson, Roger T., 443
Johnson, S. M., 449, 458
Jovanovic, Jasna, 159
Joyce, Bruce, 504, 521

Kallick, Bena, 572
Kamprath, N., 224
Kandel, Isaac L., 451, 458
Kant, Immanuel, 386, 388–389, 404
Kaufman, Jonathan, 99
Kelley, M., 98
Kennedy, John F., 198
Kerzner Lipskey, Dorothy, 99
Kierkegaard, Sören, 396
King, Sally Steinbach, 159
Klein, Susan, 98
Kleiner, Carolyn, 377
Kneller, George F., 379, 404
Knight, Lucy, 277
Kniker, Charles R., 99
Kohlberg, Lawrence, 384
Kozol, Jonathan, 105, 138, 361–362
Krathwohl, David R., 521
Kreisberg, Seth, 126, 139
Ku, Leighton, 138

Labaree, David F., 139
LaBoskey, Vicki Kubler, 35
LaMorte, Michael, 277
Lang, Debbra, 489
Langdon, Carol A., 7, 8, 54
Lâo-tsze, 284
Latham, Andrew S., 54
Lebowitz, Holly J., 99
Lee, Robert E., 535
Lester, Tom, 227
Levine, Daniel U., 225
Lincoln, Abraham, 330, 542
Lindberg, Laura Duberstein, 138
Liverpool, Moses, 329
Locke, John, 294, 301, 390, 391, 404
Lofland, Gretchen D., 483
Lord, Mary, 377
Luther, Martin, 292–293, 301
Lycurgus, 285
Lyon, Mary, 331–332
Lytle, Susan L., 165

McCarthy, Bernice, 508, 521
McCarthy, Joseph, 535
McCarthy, Martha M., 489
McCullough, David, 365
McDowell, L. M., 224
McGuffey, William Holmes, 324–325
McLaughlin, Milbrey W., 138
McLuhan, Marshall, 357
McNeill, William, 365
McTighe, Jay, 486, 489, 572
Madsen, Richard, 98, 168
Majd-Jabbari, Massoumeh, 124
Males, Mike A., 120, 138, 139
Mann, Horace, 309–310, 320, 336
Marshall, Thurgood, 203
Martin, Jane Roland, 386, 389, 404
Marzano, Robert J., 521
Masia, Bertram B., 521
Maslow, Abraham, 357
Meiklejohn, J. M. D., 404
Melanchthon, 293, 301
Mendler, Allen, 447
Miller, Kathryn S., 489
Miner, Myrtilla, 329
Mohammed, 290, 399
Mohrman, S. A., 224
Mondimore, Francis Mark, 99
Monroe, Paul, 302, 303, 339

Montessori, Maria, 332, 337, 360, 368
Morphet, Edgar L., 339
Morris, Van Cleve, 409
Muhlenberg, Henry, 335
Musial, Diann, 427

Neau, Elias, 329
Neill, A. S., 425, 432
Nelson, B., 224
Nelson, F. Howard, 44
Nelson-Barber, Sharon, 150, 168
Noddings, Nel, 385, 404, 425, 428, 432
Norris, S., 387

O'Brien, Timothy, 44
Omi, Michael, 98
Orfield, Gary, 99
Osman, Howard A., 405
Ott, Paul, 227

Pai, Young, 409
Parrington, Vernon L., 341
Paul, Richard, 387
Pavlov, Ivan, 416
Pearce, Kelly, 463, 489
Peirce, Charles Sanders, 393, 419, 450
Perrone, Vito, 449, 458
Perry, R., 224
Pestalozzi, Johann Heinrich, 298, 299, 301, 311, 327
Piaget, Jean, 357, 360–361, 368
Pickering, Marvin L., 254, 255
Pierre, C. S., 458
Pinar, William, 458
Plato, 285, 286, 287, 386–388, 389
Pleck, Joseph H., 138
Plutarch, 285
Pormont, Philemon, 308
Powell, Lewis F., Jr., 203
Powell, Linda C., 78
Powell, Majorie, 359
Prichard, Dawn, 489
Prince, Henry, 206
Puryear, S., 224
Pythagoras, 285

Quintilianus, Marcus Fabius, 281, 287–288, 300, 302

Ravitch, Diane, 305, 336, 449, 458
Reed, Bobette, 224
Resnick, Lauren, 572
Rickover, Hyman, 358
Roessingh, Betty, 168
Rolfe, John, 327
Roosevelt, Franklin D., 332
Rose, Lowell C., 139
Rosenthall, Alan, 360
Rousseau, Jean Jacques, 295, 297–298, 299, 301, 311, 423, 432
Rugg, Harold, 421
Rutherford, Megan, 407
Ryans, D. G., 358

Sadker, David, 98
Sadker, Myra, 98
Sagor, Richard, 115, 138
Sanchez, George, 351
Santayana, George, 338
Sartre, Jean-Paul, 396, 405
Schmuck, P. A., 458
Schmuck, R., 458
Schoenbeit, Marian Beauchamp, 453, 458
Schurz, Margarethe Meyer, 333
Seitz, Reynolds C., 277
Seybold, Robert F., 314
Shanker, Albert, 39
Sheive, Linda Tinelli, 453, 458
Shortt, Thomas L., 499
Showers, Beverly, 504, 521
Silberman, Charles, 361
Silverman, D., 224
Simon, Syd, 384
Sizer, Nancy, 435
Sizer, Theodore, 416, 435, 480
Skinner, B. F., 361, 368, 416
Smelser, Neil J., 138
Smith, Glenn, 302
Smith, Tom W., 138
Socrates, 285–286, 386, 387–388
Solomon, D., 224
Solon, 285
Sonenstein, Freya L., 138
Spady, William, 478
Stark, Steven, 224
Stevahn, Laurie, 443
Stewart, Potter, 203
Stiggins, Richard J., 572
Stoddard, George, 358
Sullivan, William M., 98, 168
Swidler, Ann, 98, 168
Sylvester, Elisha, 330

Tan, Dali, 98
Tan, Dawei, 98
Tatum, Beverly Daniel, 108
Terman, Lewis, 356, 357
Thayer, Yvonne V., 499
Thomas, Samuel, 328
Thomas, W. P., 99
Thoreau, Henry David, 411
Tipton, Steven M., 98, 168
Tomlinson, Carol Ann, 510, 521
Torrence, E. Paul, 358
Tower, David, 326
Travis, Dennis B., 489
Trump, J. Lloyd, 358
Turk, Jane, 251
Turner, Charles F., 138
Turner, Jackson, 341
Tyler, Ralph, 464, 489

Valente, William D., 277
Vare, Jonatha W., 489
Veronesi, Peter D., 545
Vespasian, 287
Vesper, Nick, 7, 8, 54
Voltaire, 294–295, 301

Washington, Booker T., 330, 337
Watt, David L. E., 168
Webster, Noah, 324
Weil, Marsha, 504, 521
Weis, Lois, 78
Weldon, James E. C., 404
West, Cornel, 383, 385, 404
Wexler, E., 224
White, Byron, 269
White, Ryan, 247
Whitehead, Alfred North, 388, 391–392, 404
Wiggins, Grant, 486, 489, 542, 547, 548, 572, 573
Willard, Emma, 331–332, 337, 339
Williams, Nathaniel, 314
Williams, Paul, 261
Wilson, Terry P., 405
Winant, Howard, 98
Wineburg, Sam, 365
Witherell, William, 308
Wohlstetter, P., 224
Wolfgang, Charles H., 416, 432, 445, 458
Wong, Mun, 108
Wood, Craig R., 224
Worsham, Antoinette, 506, 507, 521

Yava, Albert, 401
Yeskel, Felice, 98
Yi, Daniel, 63
Young, Ella Flagg, 332, 337

Zernike, Kate, 101
Ziomek, Robert, 54

SUBJECT INDEX

Ability grouping
  class size and, 500
  homogeneous versus heterogeneous, 426, 500–501
  philosophy of, 500–503
  problems with, 501–503
  tracking and, 503
Abstraction, 381–382
Abuse, 112–113
  legal protection against, 267–268
Academic achievement as purpose of schools, 129
Academic competence of teachers and other professionals, 9–11
Academic freedom, 249, 254–256
  book banning and censorship and, 255–256
  for elementary and secondary teachers, 254–255
Academies for teacher preparation, 319
Accountability, 215–220
  expenses and, 217
  rewards for, 217–218
  roots of, 215–216
  school and school district report cards and, 218–220
  of teachers, 217–218
Accreditation of teacher education programs, 20–21
Acculturation, 69
Activity courses curriculum, 466
ADA (Americans with Disabilities Act of 1990), 246
Adaptation, change as, 451–452
Adult education, 355–356
Advanced certification, 23–24
Advertising as revenue source, 207
Affective domain of learning, 522–523
Affirmative action, 245
AFL-CIO, 39
African Americans
  education of, 327–330
  employment of, 155–156
  origins of, 77
  poverty among, 74
  segregation and. *See* Segregation and desegregation
  slavery and, 327
African education, 285
AFT (American Federation of Teachers), 39–40, 253
Age of Pericles, 285
Age of Reason, 294–295
Agostini v. *Felton,* 233, 235
Aguilar v. *Felton,* 233, 234, 235
AIDS as disability, 246–247
Alternatives for curriculum, 464
American Academy, 312
American Federation of Teachers (AFT), 39–40, 253
American Sign Language (ASL), 83
American Spelling Book, 324
Americans with Disabilities Act of 1990 (ADA), 246
Analysis of teaching, 358–359
Analytic thinking, 381–383
Anecdotal records for assessment, 544
Antiracist education, 146
Apprenticeships, teaching, 319
Asian Americans, education of, 348–350
ASL (American Sign Language), 83
Assessment
  definition of, 538–539
  of programs, 541
  reliability of, 552
  standards-based, 526–527
  of students. *See* Student assessment; Testing
  validity of, 552
Assimilation, 68–69
Assistant principals, roles and responsibilities of, 177–178
Attitudes of students, 502
Audiotapes for assessment, 546
Audiotutorial instruction, 505
Australia, education reform in, 537
Authentic assessments, 541–551
  designing, 546–551
  methods of, 543–544, 546
  for students, 427, 447
  for teachers, 18
Axiology, 380

Baby boomlet, 492
Balance, 492
Battledore, 323–324
Behavioral theory, 361
Behaviorism, 416–417
Bethel School District No. 403 v. *Fraser,* 260, 265
Biculturalism, 93–94
Bilingual education, 160–161
Black Americans. *See* African Americans
Block scheduling, 499
Blue-Backed Speller, 324–325
Board of Education, Island Trees Union Free District No. 26 v. *Pico,* 260
Board of Education of Central School District No. 1, Town of Greenbush v. *Allen,* 233
Board of Education of Kiryas Joel Village School District v. *Grumet,* 233, 234
Board of Education of Oklahoma City Public Schools v. *Dowell,* 241, 243
Board of Education of the Westside Community Schools v. *Mergens,* 237

Board of Regents of State Colleges v. *Roth,* 249, 252
Boards of education. *See* Local school boards; School boards
Books
- banning and censorship of, 255–256
- Great Books program and, 412
- hornbook, 321, 323–324
- selection of, for children, 296–297

Brown v. *Board of Education of Topeka,* 240, 241–242, 243
Buckley Amendment of 1974 (Public Law 93-380 as amended by Public Law 93-568), 268, 362
Burkey v. *Marshall County Board of Education,* 249
Busing
- growth of, 344–345
- seat belts on buses and, 346–347

Capstone assessment, 540–541
Career education, curriculum for, 472–473
Careers in teaching. *See* Teaching careers
Categorical financial aid, 189, 211–212
CD-ROMs, 517–518
Centralization, local control versus, 195–196
Certification, 248
- advanced, 23–24
- national, 25–26, 50–51
- teacher pay and, 25–26

Change, 464, 484–487
- assessing magnitude of, 484–485
- restructuring schools and, 486
- transforming schools and, 486–487

Change agents, teachers as, 451–453
Charter schools, 191–192, 463, 474–476
Chautauqua movement, 356
Cheating on tests, 554
Checkpoints for standards-based education, 561
Chemical dependency, 119
Chief state school officers, 184–185
Child abuse. *See* Abuse
Child Abuse Prevention and Treatment Act of 1974, 267
Child benefit theory, 235
China, poverty, illiteracy, and school attendance in, 81
Chinese education, 284
Chinese thought, 398
Church(es), education of African Americans by, 327–328
Church and state, 231–239
- public funds and religious education and, 232–235
- religious activities in public schools and, 235–239
- school prayer and, 227

Citizenship as purpose of schools, 127–128
City communities, 92–93
Civil Rights Act of 1964, 240, 244–245, 245, 252
Civil Rights Act of 1991, 252
Classroom(s)
- computers in, 514, 516–517
- equity in, 162
- learning centers in, 510
- world as, 455

Classroom analysis systems, 31
Classroom climate, 448–450
- space and, 450
- voice and, 449

Classroom organization, 438–439, 441–442
- lesson planning and, 439
- physical setting and, 439, 441
- student assessment and evaluation and, 442

Class size, 500
Class structure, 72–73
Cleveland Board of Education v. *LeFleur,* 249
Coalition of Essential Schools, 480
Cochran v. *Louisiana Board of Education,* 233
Code of ethics of education profession, 28–29
Cognitive development, 360–361
Cognitive domain of learning, 522
Cola companies, school contracts with, 394–395
Collage, 469
Collective bargaining, 249, 252–253, 254
Colleges and universities
- African American, 330
- colonial, 308–309, 311–312, 325
- dropping out and, 117–118
- medieval, 290–291
- state teachers' colleges, 320–321
- students bound for, 468

Collegial teams, 498
Colonial education, 307–309
- teacher preparation and, 317–318

Comer Schools, 482–483
Committee of Ten, 313
Common elementary schools, 309
Communication for standards-based education implementation, 558–559
Communities, multicultural education and, 164–165
Compensation. *See* Fringe benefits; Salaries
Competency-based assessment, 539
Compulsory education laws, 310
Computers, 512–518. *See also* Internet
- applications of, 517–518
- classroom use of, 514, 516–517
- computer labs and, 515–516
- for management, 513
- for record keeping, 513

Concrete operations stage, 360
Conflict resolution, 448
Connection, 384–385
Constants of high school programs, 472
Constitutional issues. *See* U.S. Constitution
Constructivism, 425–429
Content standards, 531–532, 559–560
Context for authentic performance assessments, 546–549
Continuing education, 355–356
Continuity of curriculum, 464
Continuous progress education, 496–497
Contract rights, 249
Control theory, 446–447
Convergent learning, 504
Core courses curriculum, 466
Corporal punishment, 266
Course offerings, 469
Court cases
- on academic freedom, 249, 254–255
- on bargaining, 249
- on contract rights, 249, 252
- on discrimination, 245, 249
- on equal educational opportunity, 205–206
- influence of, 362–363
- on public funds for religious education, 232–235

on religious activities in public schools, 236–238
on segregation, 240, 241–243
students' right to sue and, 261
on taxation and education, 203–204, 205
Court decisions, on students' rights and responsibilities, 258–259, 260
Creationism, 237, 238–239
Crime among youth, 120–121
Criterion-referenced assessment, 540
Critical pedagogy, 421–422
Critical thinking by teachers, 161–162
Cultural choice, 70–71
Cultural identity, 93–94
biculturalism and multiculturalism and, 93–94
intragroup differences and, 93
Culturally relevant teaching, 148–154
centering on cultures of students and, 149–151
cultural context and, 148–149
validation of student voices and, 151–154
Cultural pluralism, 69–70
Cultural transmission
multiculturalism and, 132–133
as purpose of schools, 131–132
Culture, 65–67. *See also* Diversity
acculturation and, 69
assimilation and, 68–69
characteristics of, 65
cultural choice and, 70–71
cultural pluralism and, 69–70
definition of, 64
dominant (mainstream), 65–66
dominant group and, 104–105
ethnocentrism and, 105–106
exceptionalities and, 88
microcultural groups and, 66–67
of schools. *See* School culture
of students, centering on, 149–151
of youth. *See* Youth culture
Current expenses, 202
Curriculum, 462–483
activity courses design for, 466
alternatives for, 464
for career education, 472–473
charter schools and, 474–476
for college-bound students, 468
Comer model and, 482–483
constructivist, 426–428
continuity of, 464
core courses design for, 466
for destination unknown students, 468
effective schools and, 477
essentialist, 415–416, 480
for exploratory education, 471–472
fused courses design for, 465
general education, 469–470
growth of, 345, 347–348
hidden, 147–148
home-based schools and, 481–482
humanist, 423–424
magnet schools and, 480–481
for nontraditional students, 468–469
outcomes-based education and, 478
perennialist, 412
private industry and, 479
school vouchers and, 478
separate courses design for, 464–465
for standards-based education, 559
for terminal students, 467–468
for vocational-technical students, 468

Dame schools, 308
Dark Ages, education during, 289–290
De facto segregation, 240
De jure segregation, 240
Delivery standards, 533
Demand for teachers, 13–18
diversity of backgrounds and, 17–18
location of school district and, 15
shortages and, 15–17
student-to-teacher ratios and, 14
Democracy
democratic schools and, 133–135
equality and education and, 122–125
multiculturalism and, 132–133
progressivism and, 420–421
purposes of schools and, 127–132
roles of schools and, 125–126
Department heads in schools, 178
Desegregation. *See* Segregation and desegregation
Diagnostic assessment, 539
Dialectic, change as, 452–453
Dialectical diversity, 83–84
Differentiated staffing, 498
Digital divide, 155
Disabilities. *See* Exceptional learners
Discernment, 384
Discipline, 445–448
conflict resolution and, 448
control theory and, 446–447
with dignity, 447–448
peer mediation and, 448
rules for, 448
Discipline-based standards, 529
Discrimination, 244. *See also* Equal educational opportunity; Prejudice and discrimination
definition of, 103
in employment, 249, 252
reverse, 245
sex, against students, 266–267
Dispositions for teaching profession, 19
Divergent learning, 504
Divergent thinking, 420
Diversity, 62–96. *See also* Culture
definition of, 64
ethnicity and race and, 75–77
exceptionalities and, 84–88
geographic, 90–93
of language, 82–84
multicultural education and, 144–145
religious, 88–90
socioeconomic status and, 71–74
student assessment and, 541
of teachers, 17–18
Domains of learning, 522–523
Domestic violence, 112–113
Dominant culture, 65–66
Dominant group, 104–105
Dress codes, 265–266
Dropping out, 117–118
Drug use among youth, 119–120
Due process, 248
students' right to, 261, 263–265

EAHCA (Education for All Handicapped Children Act) (Public Law 94-142), 245, 246, 270, 365
Early childhood education (ECE), 470
Eastern ways of knowing, 397–400
educational implications of, 399

ECE (early childhood education), 470
Economic Opportunity Act of 1964, 356
Economics, youth's outlook on, 115
Education 2000, progress toward goals of, 364
Educational malpractice, students' rights regarding, 271
Educational system, 172–222
  federal government's role in, 186–189
  financing and. *See* Financing
  foundations and, 190
  increasing complexity of, 351–357
  local control of, 195–196
  national R&D centers and, 190
  politics and, 196–200
  regional educational laboratories and, 189
  school boards and. *See* Local school boards; School boards
  school choice and, 173–174, 190–195, 196
  school districts and. *See* School districts
  school organization and, 176–177
  schools in. *See* School(s)
  state-level organization of, 182–186
Educational television, 511–512
Educational Testing Service (ETS), 356
Educational theory, 406–430
  authoritarian versus nonauthoritarian, 408–410
  behaviorist, 416–417
  constructivist, 425–429
  essentialist, 412, 414–416
  global perspective on, 429
  humanist, 423–425
  perennialist, 410–412
  positivist, 418–419
  progressive, 419–421
  reconstructionist, 421–423
Education Amendments Act of 1972, 244, 245, 266–267
Education departments, state, 185
Education for All Handicapped Children Act (EAHCA) (Public Law 94-142), 245, 246, 270, 365
Education International (EI), 42
Education reform, in Australia, 537
Edwards v. *Aguilard,* 237
Effective schools, 477
Effective teaching movement, 359
EI (Education International), 42
Eight-Year Study, 313–314
Elementary and Secondary Education Act of 1965 (ESEA), 235, 353
Elementary education
  academic freedom and, 254–255
  origins of, 309
Elementary schools, 493
  common, 309
Emergence of common man, 295, 297–299
Employment. *See also* Teaching careers
  education's relevance for, 413
  searches for teaching positions and, 49–50
Employment conditions for teachers, 248–254
Employment contracts for teachers, 250
Empowerment by teachers, 454–455
Enabling laws, 229
Enculturation, 65
English as a second language (ESL), 160
  communicating with students' families and, 84
Enrollments, increasing, 213–214, 342–343
Entrepreneurial funding sources, 207–210
Environmental education, 440–441
Epistemology, 380
Epperson v. *State of Arkansas,* 237
Equal educational opportunity, 123, 244–247, 353
  affirmative action and, 245
  under Fourteenth Amendment, 231
  states' responsibility to guarantee, 200, 205–206
  for students with disabilities, 245–247
Equality, 103
  education and, 122–125
  multicultural education and, 145–146
Equity, 143
  in classroom, 162
  information technology and, 155–157
ESEA (Elementary and Secondary Education Act of 1965), 235, 353
ESL (English as a second language), 160
  communicating with students' families and, 84
Essentialism, 412, 414–416
Essential Schools movement, 416, 480
Ethics, 380
  ethical code of education profession and, 28–29
  teaching in public schools, 384
Ethnic diversity, 76–77
Ethnic groups, 75
Ethnicity, 76
Ethnocentrism, 105–106
ETS (Educational Testing Service), 356
European Americans, poverty among, 74
Everson v. *Board of Education,* 232, 233, 235
Evolution, creationism versus, 237, 238–239
Ewing Marion Kaufman Foundation, 190
Exceptionalities, 84–88
  cultural differences affecting, 88
  disproportionate placements of, 88
  inclusion and, 85, 87–88
Exceptional learners
  education of, 245–247
  gifted, 86–87
  rights of, 270
Existentialism, 393, 395–397
  educational implications of, 393, 395–396
Expectations, for standards-based education, 561
Expenses
  current, 202
  educational results and, 217
Experimentation, 420
Exploratory education, curriculum for, 471–472
Extrinsic motivation, 466

Families, 108–113
  abuse in, 112–113
  of English language learners, communicating with, 84
  gay and lesbian, 110

homeless, 112
home schooling and, 355, 481–482
latchkey children and, 110–112
multicultural education and, 164–165
parenting and, 109–110
working with, 36–37
Federal government, 186–189. *See also* U.S. *entries*
categorical aid provided by, 189
educational programs operated by, 188–189
historical involvement in education, 316–317
increasing involvement in educational system, 352–353
leadership by, 187
spending for education by, 213
Females. *See* Gender; Women
Financing, 200–220
accountability and, 215–220
categorical financial aid and, 189
conditions of schools and, 214–215
education spending and, 210–213
entrepreneurial sources of, 207–210
by foundations, 190
gaming for, 204
increasing enrollments and, 213–214
of religious education, 232–235
state responsibility to guarantee equal educational opportunity an, 205–206
taxes and. *See* Property taxes; Taxes
First Amendment, 231
Flexible scheduling, 498–499
Folios for assessment, 543–544
Formal operations stage, 360
Foundation(s), 190
Foundation programs, 212
4Mat program, 508–509
Fourteenth Amendment, 231
Freeman v. *Pitts,* 241, 243
Free speech, students' right to, 264–265
Fringe benefits, 39, 45–46
Funding. *See* Financing
Fused courses curriculum, 465
Future of education, 574–576
Gaming as revenue source, 204
Gangs, 121
Gays, 81–82
discrimination against, 107
as parents, 110
Gender, 78–82. *See also* Males; Women
differences between females and males and, 78–81
gender identity development and, 78
performance-based science activities and, 159
sexual orientation and, 81–82
Gender-sensitive education, 157–159
General education curriculum, 469–470
Generalization, 382–383
General programs, 473
General state aid, 211, 212
Geographic location, 90–93
rural communities and, 90–91
suburban communities and, 91–92
urban communities and, 92–93
Germany
education programs in, 494–495
legal aspects of education in, 272–274
GI Bill of Rights, 365
Giftedness, number of children labeled gifted and, 86–87
Global perspectives. *See also specific countries*
on educational ideas, 283
on educational theory, 429
educational transplantation from Europe and, 310–311
Education International and, 42
on education reform, 537
on educators, 363–364
on legal aspects of education, 272–274
on Montessori schools, 332
on spending for schools, 218
on teacher training, 317
on values, 133
world as classroom and, 455
Goss v. *Lopez,* 260, 263–264
Government. *See* Church and state; Federal government; State(s)
Graded schools, 495–496
Grammar, pros and cons of correcting, 153–154
Grand Rapids School District v. *Ball,* 233, 234
Great Books program, 412
Greek education, 285–287
Griffin v. *County School Board of Prince Edward County,* 243
Grooming, 265–266
Group(s)
dominant, 104–105
prejudice and discrimination against. *See* Prejudice and discrimination
Grouping. *See* Ability grouping

Harassment
in schools, 163
sexual, by peers, 271
Hardware, 510
Hawthorne effect, 499
Hazelwood School District v. *Kuhlmeier,* 260, 268–269
Hebrew education, 284
Helena Elementary School District v. *State,* 205
Herbartian teaching method, 299, 310
Heterogeneous ability grouping, 501
Heterosexuality, 81
Hidden curriculum and, school culture, 147–148
Hierarchical team organization, 498
Higher education. *See* Colleges and universities
High schools. *See* Secondary schools
High-stakes testing, 553
Hindu education, 283–284
Hispanic Americans
dropout rate of, 118
education of, 350–351
employment of, 155–156
origins of, 77
poverty among, 74
Historical interpretation, 282
History
ability to know, 341–342
critiquing historical sources and, 314
to improve student learning, 365–366
reasons to study, 305

History of education, 279–301
aboriginal, 282–283
African, 285
for African Americans, 327–330
during Age of Reason, 294–295
aims of American education and, 313–316
Chinese, 284
colonial, 307–309
dates important in, 370–373
emergence of common man and, 295, 297–299
federal involvement and, 316–317
Greek, 285–287
Hebrew, 284
Hindu, 283–284
during Middle Ages, 289–291
private education and, 333–336
during Reformation, 292–294
during Renaissance, 291, 292
Roman, 287–288
secondary schools and, 311–312
teacher preparation and, 317–321
teaching materials and, 321, 323–327
universal education and, 309–310
for women, 331–333
Hogg Foundation, 190
Holding back students, 497
Homelessness, 112
right to education and, 259, 261
Home schooling, 355, 481–482
Homework, 349
Homogeneous ability grouping, 500–501
Homosexuality, 81–82. *See also* Gays; Lesbians
Honig v. *Doe,* 260, 270
Hope, 385
Hopi thought, 401
Horizontal articulation, 497
Hornbook, 321, 323–324
Hortonville Joint School District No. 1 v. *Hortonville Education Association,* 249, 254
Humanism, 291, 423–425
Hunter Model, 507–508
Hypocrisy, 385
Hypotheses, forming, 33

IC (innovation configuration) maps, 565–567
IDEA (Individuals with Disabilities Education Act of 1992), 246
Idealism, 386–389
educational implications of, 386
Identity
cultural, 93–94
gender, 78
racial, 78
IGE (individually guided education), 505–506
Illegal drug use, 119–120
Illiteracy in China, 81
Imagination, 382
Immigration, 77
Inclusion, 85, 87–88
Income. *See also* Salaries; Socioeconomic status
of women, 80
Income taxes, 204–205
Indentured servants, teachers as, 318–319
Independent schools, 194–195
Indian thought, 397–398
Individually guided education (IGE), 505–506
Individually prescribed instruction (IPI) models, 505
Individuals with Disabilities Education Act of 1992 (IDEA), 246
Inductive process, 506–507
Industry, involvement with schools, 479
Inflation, teacher salaries and, 45
Information age, 6
Information technology. *See also* Computers
equity and, 155–157
Ingraham v. *Wright,* 260, 266
In loco parentis doctrine, 261
Innovation configuration (IC) maps, 565–567
Institutional discrimination, 107
Instruction. *See* Teaching
Instructional materials. *See also specific materials*
evolution of, 321, 323–327
Instructional scheduling, 498–500
Instructional technology, 509–518
classroom learning centers and, 510
computers, 512–518
educational television, 511–512
INTASC (Interstate New Teacher Assessment and Support Consortium), 22
Integration, 240
Intended school outcomes, 469
Intermediate schools, 493
Intermediate units, 189
International Education Act of 1966, 353
International perspectives. *See* Global perspectives; *specific countries*
Internet, 518
access to, 155–157
impact on schools, 141
Interstate New Teacher Assessment and Support Consortium (INTASC), 22
Interviews
for assessment, 544
structured, 31–32
Intragroup differences, cultural identity and, 93
Intrinsic motivation, 466
IPI (individually prescribed instruction) models, 505

Japanese thought, 398–399
Job searches, for teaching positions, 49–50
Journals, 31
computers for writing, 517
learning, 543
reflective journaling and, 32–33
Judicial interpretive process, 229
Junior high school, exploratory education in, 471

Kellogg Foundation, 190
Kentucky Education Reform Act (KERA), 200, 206
Knowledge, professional, 18–19
Knowledge bases, 9–10
as professional knowledge, 18

Lakota thought, 400
Lamb's Chapel v. *Center Moriches Union Free School District,* 237
Language diversity, 82–84, 159–161
bilingual education and, 160–161
communicating with families of English language learners and, 84
English as a second language and, 160
Latchkey children, 110–112
Late bloomers, 468
Latin grammar schools, 287, 308, 311–312
Leaders, teachers as, 453–455

Leadership
by federal government, 187
by superintendent of schools, 182
Learning
behaviorist focus of, 417
convergent, 504
divergent, 504
domains of, 522–523
essentialist focus of, 414–415
focus on, 27, 29–30
goals for, 503–504
history to improve, 299, 365–366
mastery, 408
models of, 504–509
modules for, 498
perennialist focus of, 411–412
positivist focus of, 418
study of process of, 360
Learning journals, 543
Learning logs, 543
Lee v. *Weisman,* 237
Legal issues, 226–275. *See also* Court cases; Legislation
church and state as. *See* Church and state
constitutional. *See* U.S. Constitution
equal opportunity as. *See* Equal educational opportunity
international comparison of, 272–274
segregation and desegregation as. *See* Segregation and desegregation
teachers' rights and responsibilities as. *See* Teachers' rights and responsibilities
Legalized gambling as revenue source, 204–205
Legislation. *See also* U.S. Constitution
antidiscrimination, 244–247
on compulsory education, 310
on curricula, 347–348
early school laws, 308
enabling, 229
on funding, 200, 205–206
with greatest impact on education, 365
providing federal funding, 353
providing funding, 356
Legislatures, state, 185–186
Lehnert v. *Ferris Faculty Association,* 249
Lemon v. *Kurtzman,* 232, 233, 234
Lesbians, 81–82
discrimination against, 107
as parents, 110
Liability
governmental immunity from, 257
for negligence, 256–258
Liability insurance, 257–258
Liberal arts, 290
Licensure, 21–23, 248
alternative, 48–49
license renewal and, 50
state office websites for, 56–57
tests for, 48
Line relationships, 176
Local control, 195–196
Local school boards, 180–181
politics and, 199
powers and duties of, 181
revamping of, 196
Location. *See* Geographic location
Log(s), learning, 543
Logic, 383
Lotteries as revenue source, 204–205
Lower class, 72

The McGuffey Readers, 324–325, 326–327
Magnet schools, 191, 480–481
Mainstream culture, 65–66
Males. *See also* Gender
deviation from traditional masculine roles, 81–82
Malpractice, educational, students' rights regarding, 271
Management, computers for, 513
Manpower Development and Training Act of 1963, 353
Marriage of students, 267
Mastery learning, 408, 505
Medieval education, 289–291
Meritocracy, 122
Metaphysics, 379–380
Microcultural groups, 66–67. *See also specific groups*
Middle Ages, education during, 289–291
Middle class, 72–73
Middle Eastern thought, 399
Middle schools, 312, 493
exploratory education in, 471–472
Minorities. *See* Equal educational opportunity; *specific groups*
Modeling by teachers, 454
Modular scheduling, 498
Modules for learning, 498
Monitorial schools, 309
Moonlighting, 46
Morrill Land Grant Act of 1862, 316
Motivation, 442–445
intrinsic and extrinsic, 466
Mozert v. *Hawkins County Public Schools,* 237
Multicultural education, 140–166
culturally relevant teaching and. *See* Culturally relevant teaching
definition of, 142
diversity and, 144–145
equity and. *See* Equity
gender-sensitive, 157–159
history and, 291
information technology and, 155–157
language diversity and, 159–161
school culture and, 146–148
social justice and, 145–146
teachers as social activists and, 161–165
Multiculturalism, 93–94, 140–166
cultural transmission by schools, 132–133

National Assessment for Educational Progress (NAEP), 554–555
National Board for Professional Teaching Standards (NBPTS), 23–24
National certification, 25–26, 50–51
National Council of Teacher Education (NCATE), 20, 21
National Council of Teachers of Mathematics (NCTM), 531
National Defense Education Act of 1958 (NDEA), 347–348, 353
National Educational Research and Development Centers, 190
National Education Association (NEA), 38–39, 253
eliminating bad teachers and, 322–323
on purposes of education, 314–316
National exam, threat of, 554–555
National performance standards, example of, 533–534
National Science Foundation, 353
National Teacher Corp, 353

National Teachers' Association (NTA), 38
Native Americans, 77
employment of, 155–156
poverty among, 155
ways of knowing of, 400–402
Navajo thought, 400
NBPTS (National Board for Professional Teaching Standards), 23–24
NCATE (National Council of Teacher Education), 20, 21
NCTM (National Council of Teachers of Mathematics), 531
NDEA (National Defense Education Act of 1958), 347–348, 353
NEA (National Education Association), 38–39, 253
eliminating bad teachers and, 322–323
on purposes of education, 314–316
Neglect, legal protection against, 267–268
Negligence, liability for, 256–258
Network installations, 516
New England Primer, 324
New Jersey v. *T.L.O.,* 260
Nineteenth Amendment, 333
Nongraded schools, 496–497
Nontraditional students, 468–469
Normal schools, 319–320
Norm-referenced assessment, 499, 539–540
Northern Ireland, schools in, 483–484
North Haven Board of Education v. *Bell,* 249
Northwest Ordinance, 316
Note taking by teachers, 31
NTA (National Teachers' Association), 38

Objective testing, 418–419
Observation
for assessment, 544
systematic, 31–32
Old Deluder Satan Act, 308
One-room schools, 344
Open-space facilities, 495
Opportunity-to-learn standards, 533
Organization chart of school, 179
Outcomes-based education, 478
Parent(s). *See also* Families
teenage, 117
Parenting, 109–110
Parochial schools, 335, 354–355
Peer mediation, 448
Perennialism, 410–412
Performance assessments. *See also* Authentic assessments
for teachers, 20
Performance-based licensing systems, 22
Performance standards, 532–534
Pericles, Age of, 285
Perry v. *Sindermann,* 249, 252
Personal computers. *See* Computers
Pestalozzianism, 310
Phi Delta Kappa International, 41
Philosophy, 375–402, 434–456. *See also* Educational theory
authoritarian versus nonauthoritarian, 437–438
branches of, 379–380
classroom climate and, 448–450
classroom organization and, 438–439, 441–442
discipline and, 445–448
Eastern ways of knowing and, 397–400
existentialist, 393, 395–397
idealist, 386–389
motivation and, 442–445
Native American ways of knowing and, 400–402
pragmatist, 392–393
realist, 389–392
teachers as change agents and, 451–453
teachers as leaders and, 453–455
ways of thinking in, 381–385
Phyler v. *Doe,* 260
Physical environment of classroom, 439, 441
Pickering v. *Board of Education,* 249, 254–255
Plans of study, 469
Plessy v. *Ferguson,* 240, 243
Pluralism, religious, 88–89
Police Department of the City of Chicago v. *Mosley,* 237
Political action, of teachers' unions, 40–41
Politics, 196–200
election, volatility of, 198
school-based management and, 200
at school district level, 198–199
superintendent and, 199
Portfolios
for assessment, 543–544
development of, 33–36
of students, 510
of teachers, 22–23
Positivism, 418–419
Poverty, 73–74
in China, 81
Power, teachers' use of, 454–455
Pragmatism, 392–393, 419
educational implications of, 392
Prayer in schools, 227, 236, 238
Pregnancy, teenage, 116–117, 267
Prejudice and discrimination, 71, 106–107
definition of, 106
institutional discrimination and, 107
racial, 101, 107
sexism and, 107
Preoperational stage, 360
Principals
rewarding, 218
roles and responsibilities of, 177
Private industry, involvement with schools, 479
Private schools, 333–336
continued importance of, 354–355
importance of, 335–336
parochial, 335, 354–355
right to exist, 334–335
Problem-based learning, 428–429
Procedural due process, 248, 261, 263–264
Professional associations, 41–42
state office websites for, 58–59
Professionalization of teaching, 353–354
Professions. *See also* Teaching profession
characteristics of, 18–20
Progressive taxes, 203, 204
Progressivism, 419–421
Project Choice, 190
Project Head Start, 353
Projects for assessment, 546
Property taxes, 201–204
advantages and limitations of, 201–202
courts' perspective on, 203–204

inequities of, 203
property assessments and, 202
Prophetic thinking, 381, 383–385
Psychomotor domain of learning, 523
Publications, students' rights regarding, 268–269
Public Law 04-142 (Education for All Handicapped Children Act [EAHCA]), 245, 246, 270, 365
Public Law 93-380 as amended by Public Law 93-568 (Buckley Amendment of 1974), 268, 362
Public opinion, shifts in, 364–365
Public schools. *See also* School(s)
charter schools movement and, 475–476
religious activities in, 235–239
teaching ethics in, 384
Punishment, corporal, 266

Questions for authentic performance assessments, 549
Quintilian, 287–288

Race, 75–76
prejudice and discrimination based on, 101
racial identity development and, 78
Racism, 107
antiracist education and, 146
Rationalists, 294
Rational process, change as, 452
Realism, 389–392
educational implications of, 390
Real-world standards, 528–529
Reconstruction, change as, 452
Reconstructionism, 421–423
as role of schools, 126
Record keeping, computers for, 513
Recruitment incentives, 46–47
Reflective journaling, 32–33
Reformation, education during, 292–294
Refugees, 77
Regional Labs, 189
Regressive taxes, 203, 204
Rehabilitation Act of 1973, section 504 of, 245–246
Reinforcement, 417
Reliability of assessment, 552
Religion, 88–90
religious pluralism and, 88–89
in schools, 89–90
Religious-affiliated schools, 334. *See also* Church and state
Religious education, 354–355. *See also* Church and state
child benefit theory and, 235
public funds and, 232–235
in public schools, 235–239
Religious education associations, 41–42
state office websites for, 58–59
Renaissance, education during, 291, 292
Report cards for standards-based education, 561
Reproduction of society, as role of schools, 125–126
Research, keeping up with, 362
Resegregation, 240
Resiliency of youth, 115
Restructuring, 486
Retention, pros and cons of, 130–131
Reverse discrimination, 245
Rights. *See* Students' rights and responsibilities; Teachers' rights and responsibilities
Roman schools, 287
Rose v. *The Council for Better Education, Inc.*, 205–206
Rubrics for assessment, 546
Rules for discipline, 448
Rural communities, 90–91

Safe schools, 443
Salaries, 42–47
differences among, 43–45
inflation and, 45
low, need for extra income due to, 46
for nationally certified teachers, 25–26
recruitment incentives and, 46–47
unions and, 39
Salary schedules, 43
Sales taxes, 204–205
San Antonio (Texas) Independent School District v. *Rodriguez,* 203–204
Santa Fe Independent School District, Petitioner v. *Jane Doe,* 236, 237, 238
SAT (Scholastic Aptitude Test), 356
SBDM (site-based decision making), 191
politics and, 200
SBE. *See* Standards-based education (SBE)
Scheduling, instructional, 498–500
Scholastic Aptitude Test (SAT), 356
Scholasticism, 290
School(s)
charter, 463, 474–476
choosing, 173–174
colonial, 308–309
Comer, 482–483
conditions of, financing and, 214–215
contracts with cola companies, 394–395
criticism versus defense of, 334
democratic, 133–135
desegregation of. *See* Segregation and desegregation
dropping out and, 117–118
effective, 477
essential, 416, 480
financing. *See* Financing
graded and nongraded, 495–497
harassment in, 163
home-based, 481–482
humanist environment for, 425
increasing enrollment in, financing and, 213–214
integration of, 240
Internet and, 141–142
magnet, 480–481
monitorial, 309
need to increase number of, 343
normal, 319–320
in Northern Ireland, 483–484
one-room, 344
organization chart of, 179
organization of, 176–177, 493
parochial, 335
private. *See* Private schools
private industry's involvement with, 479
program assessment in, 541
public opinion on, 364–365
public view of, 6–8
purposes of, 127–132
recognition for, 217
religion in, 89–90
religious-affiliated, 334. *See also* Church and state
report cards for, 218–220
roles of, 125–126
safe, 443

School(s) (*continued*)
secondary. *See* Secondary schools
segregation of. *See* Segregation and desegregation
staff of, 177–180
violence in, 288
weapons in, 272
School attendance, in China, 81
School-based management. *See* Site-based decision making (SBDM)
School boards
local. *See* Local school boards
state, 184
School budgets, growth of, 345
School choice, 190–195
charter schools and, 191–192
independent schools and, 194–195
magnet schools and, 191
in public schools, 196
site-based decision making and, 191
vouchers and, 193
year-round schools and, 192
School culture, 146–148
traditions in, 147
School districts, 180–182
central office staff and, 182
consolidation of, 343–345
immunity from liability, 257
local boards of education and, 180–181
location of, teacher demand and, 15
politics and, 198–199
report cards for, 218–220
superintendent of schools and, 181–182
School enrollment, growth of, 213–214, 342–343
School outcomes, intended, 469
School programs of study, 469
School records, students' rights regarding, 268
School reform, 363
School-to-work programs, 473
School vouchers, 478
Searches, students' rights regarding, 270–271
Seat belts on school buses, 346–347
Secondary schools, 312, 493
academic freedom and, 254–255
constants and variables of programs in, 472
need for, 311–312
Segregation and desegregation, 239–244
de facto segregation and, 240
de jure segregation and, 240
present status of, 243–244
release from court orders and, 241–243
separate-but-equal doctrine and, 240
Sensorimotor stage, 360
Separate-but-equal doctrine, failure of, 240
Separate courses curriculum, 464–465
Serrano v. *Priest,* 205
Seven Cardinal Principles, 313
Seven liberal arts, 290
Sex discrimination
sexism and, 107
against students, 266–267
Sexual harassment
by peers, students' rights regarding, 271
in schools, 163
Sexuality of youth, 116–117
Sexual orientation, 81–82. *See also* Gays; Lesbians
discrimination based on, 107
Simulations, 511
Site-based decision making (SBDM), 191
politics and, 200
Skin color, race and, 75–76
Slates, 326
Slavery, 327
Smith-Hughes Act of 1917, 316–317
Social activists, teachers as, 161–165
Social development, as purpose of schools, 129, 131
Socialization, 106
progressivism and, 421
Social justice, multicultural education and, 145–146
Social stratification, 72
Society
public view of teachers and schools and, 6–8
reproduction of, as role of schools, 125–126
teachers' importance to, 6
Socioeconomic status, 71–74
class structure and, 72–73
poverty and, 73–74
social stratification and, 72
Sociological studies, 360
Socratic method, 285–286
Soft drink manufacturers, school contracts with, 394–395
Software, 510
Space, classroom climate and, 450
Special education, growth of, 348
Spending for education, 210–213
federal, 213
international comparison of, 218
state, 211–212
Spreadsheets, electronic, 517
Staff
organization of, 497–498
politics and, 199
of schools, 177–180
Staff relationships, 176
Standard(s)
differences among, reasons for, 529–530
opportunity to learn, 124
state determination of, 556–557
for teaching profession, 20
Standardized tests, teaching to, 30
Standards-based assessment, 526–527
Standards-based education (SBE), 461–462, 526–537
assessing student learning in, 560–561
conceptions of standards and, 527–530
debate of setting standards and, 535
debate over value of standards and, 535, 537
example of, 557–569
mapping implementation of, 561, 564–567
movement to, 558–560
national performance standards example and, 533–534
as paradigm change, 567–569
sources for standards and, 530–531
standards frameworks and, 534–535
types of standards and, 531–533
uses of standards and, 530–531

State(s)
education standard determination by, 556–557
lotteries run by, 204–205
organization of education at level of, 182–186
perspective on taxation, 205
responsibility to guarantee equal educational opportunity, 205–206
revenue and aid provided by, 204–205
spending for education by, 211–212
State boards of education, 184
State departments of education, 185
State legislatures, 185–186
State teachers' colleges, 320
Stereotyping, 148
Stewart B. McKinnery Homeless Assistance Act, 259
Strikes, 253–254
Structured interviews, 31–32
Structured observations, 31
Student(s)
attitudes of, 502
college-bound, 468
learning by. *See* Learning
nontraditional, 468–469
ratio to teachers, 14
rights and responsibilities of. *See* Students' rights and responsibilities
terminal, 467–468
vocational-technical, 468
Student assessment, 442, 537–557
authentic. *See* Authentic assessments
capstone/summative, 540–541
competency-based, 539
criterion-referenced, 540
diagnostic, 539
evolution of, 356–357
good, professional aspects of, 551–552
norm-referenced, 499, 539–540
objective testing for, 418–419
purposes for, 539–541
standards-based, 461–462, 526–527
in standards-based education, 560–561
student diversity and, 541
testing for. *See* Testing
Student evaluation, 442
Student fees as revenue source, 207
Student portfolios, 510
Student products for assessment, 546
Student publications, students' rights regarding, 268–269
Students at risk, 467–468
Students' rights and responsibilities, 258–272
child abuse and neglect and, 267–268
corporal punishment and, 266
court cases on, 258–259, 260
dress codes and grooming an, 265–266
educational malpractice and, 271
marriage and pregnancy and, 267
peer sexual harassment and, 271
right to due process, 261, 263–265
right to education, 259, 261, 262
right to sue, 261
school records and, 268
searches and, 270–271
sex discrimination and, 266–267
student publications and, 268–269
of students with disabilities, 270
zero tolerance and, 272
Student voices, 449
validating, 151–154
Substantive due process, 248, 261, 264–265
Suburban communities, 91–92
Suicide among youth, 121
Summative assessment, 540–541
Superintendents of schools, 181–182
board politics and, 199
leadership by, 182
staff politics and, 199
Supply of teachers, 12–13
Support staff in schools, 178
Suspending students, 262–264
Systematic observation, 31–32

Taxes, 201–205
income, 204
progressive, 203, 204
property. *See* Property taxes
regressive, 203, 204
sales, 204
state perspective on, 205
taxpayer revolt and, 214
Taxonomies, 504
Teacher(s), 5–18
academic quality of, 9–11
accountability of, 217–218
advanced certification of, 23–24
assessments for, 18, 20
bad, eliminating, 322–323
as change agents, 451–453
class size and, 14
conditions of employment for, 248, 250–254
critical thinking by, 161–162
demand for, 13–18, 343
demographics in United States, 8–9
diversity of, 17–18
educational malpractice by, 271
effectiveness of, 359–360
equity in classroom and, 162
ideal, 281
importance to society, 6
as indentured servants, 318–319
Internet and, 141–142
involvement of communities and families by, 164–165
keeping up with research and, 362
as leaders, 453–455
licensure of. *See* Licensure
moonlighting by, 46
nationally certified, salaries for, 25–26
new, 12–13
politics and, 197
public view of, 6–8
ratio to students, 14
in religious schools, 235
retention in profession, 11
returning, 13
rewarding, 218
rights and responsibilities of. *See* Teachers' rights and responsibilities
roles and responsibilities of, 178
school staff and, 179–180
as social activists, 161–165
supply of, 12–13
testing and, 555, 557
working conditions of, 47
working with colleagues and other professionals, 36
working with families, 36–37

Teacher Expectation and Student Achievement (TESA) model, 508
Teacher preparation, 317–321
 in academies, 319
 accreditation of programs for, 20–21
 apprenticeships for, 319
 colonial, 317–318
 European beginnings of, 317
 indentured servants and, 318–319
 in normal schools, 319–320
 recent, 321
 at state teachers' colleges, 320–321
Teachers' rights and responsibilities, 248–258
 academic freedom and, 254–256
 certification and licensure and, 248
 collective bargaining and, 252–253
 discrimination and, 252
 employment contracts and, 250
 liability for negligence and, 256–258
 strikes and, 253–254
 tenure and, 250–252
Teacher unions, 38–41. *See also* American Federation of Teachers (AFT); National Education Association (NEA)
Teacher voice, 449
Teaching, 490–519
 analysis of, 358–359
 balance in, 492
 for critical thinking, 387
 culturally relevant. *See* Culturally relevant teaching
 in Germany, 494–495
 goals for learning and, 503–504
 instructional scheduling for, 498–500
 instructional technology for. *See* Instructional technology
 learning models and, 504–509
 professionalization of, 353–354
 school organization and, 493
 for social justice, 163–164
 staff organization for, 497–498
 student organization for, 500–503
 teacher organization for, 492–500
 to tests, 30, 554
 variety in, 492
Teaching careers
 induction period of, 22
 job search and, 49–50
 licensure and, 48–49
 staying with, 50–51
Teaching materials. *See also specific materials*
 evolution of, 321, 323–327
Teaching profession, 1–59. *See also* Teacher(s)
 analysis of practice and reflection in, 32–33
 code of ethics for, 28–29
 developing commitments and dispositions for, 24, 26–27
 focus on student learning and, 27, 29–30
 participating in, 37–42
 practice of, 30–36
 quality assurance and, 20–24
 shortages in, 15–17
 standards for, 20
 systematic observation and journaling in, 31–32
 teacher retention in, 11
Team leaders in schools, 178
Technology. *See* Computers; Information technology; Instructional technology; Internet
Technophobia, 513
Tech-prep programs, 473
Teenage pregnancy, 116–117, 267
Television, educational, 511–512
Tenth Amendment, 230–231
Tenure for teachers, 250–252
Terminal students, 467–468
Testing, 525, 552–555, 557
 high-stakes, 553
 national, threat of, 554–555
 norm-referenced, 499
 objective, 418–419
 one-size-fits-all, 554
 preparation for, 555
 pressures to cheat and, 554
 teacher burden and, 555, 557
 teaching to the test and, 554
Thinking
 analytic, 381–383
 critical, teaching for, 387
 divergent, 420
 prophetic, 381, 383–385
Thinking skills model, 506–507
Thomism, 290
Tinker v. *Des Moines Independent Community School,* 260, 264–265
Tracking, 503
Traditions in school culture, 147
Transportation for church school students, 232
Tuning out, 470

Underclass, 72
Unions, 38–41. *See also* American Federation of Teachers (AFT); National Education Association (NEA)
U.S. Constitution, 228, 229–231, 316
 First Amendment to, 231
 Fourteenth Amendment to, 231
 Nineteenth Amendment to, 333
 Tenth Amendment to, 230–231
U.S. Department of Education, 187–188
Universities. *See* Colleges and universities
University of California v. *Bakke,* 245
Upper class, 73
Upward Bound, 353
Urban communities, 92–93

Validity of assessment, 552
Values
 transmission by schools, 132–133
 universal, 133
Variables of high school programs, 472
Variety, 492
Vertical articulation, 497
Videotapes for assessment, 546
Violence
 domestic, 112–113
 in schools, 288
 among youth, 120–121
Visions of teachers, 453–454
Vocational Education Act of 1963, 353
Vocational-technical students, 468
Voice
 classroom climate and, 449
 validating student voices and, 151–154
Vouchers, 193, 478

Waivers, 474
Wallace v. *Jaffee,* 237

WCOPT (World Confederation of Organizations of the Teaching Profession), 42
Weapons, zero tolerance policy on, 272
Wolman v. *Walter,* 233
Women. *See also* Gender *entries*
  education of, 331–333
  employment of, 156
  jobs held by, 79–80
  lesbian. *See* Lesbians
  poverty among, 74
  sexism and, 107
  sexual harassment of, 163
Wood v. *Strickland,* 260, 261
Word processing, 517
Workforce preparation, as purpose of schools, 128–129
Working class, 72
Working conditions, 47
World-class standards, 527–528
World Confederation of Organizations of the Teaching Profession (WCOPT), 42
World reformation, reconstructionism and, 423
Year-round schools, 192
Youth culture, 113–121
  dropping out and, 117–118
  drugs and, 119–120
  economic outlook of today's youth and, 115
  resiliency of today's youth and, 115
  sexuality and, 116–117
  violence and, 120–121

Zero tolerance, 272
Zobrest v. *Catalina Foothills School District,* 233, 234–235

Photo Credits

Page 5, Will Hart/Photo Edit; p. 9, 10, Will Hart; p. 11, A. Ramey/Stock Boston; p. 13, Robert Harbison; p. 17, Stephen Marks; p. 19, Jeffry Myers/Stock Boston; p. 22, L. Kolvoord/The Image Works; p. 27 (Both), Will Faller; p. 37, Donna Day/Stone; p. 38, Courtesy of the National Education Association; p. 40, Bettmann/Corbis; p. 46, 49, Will Hart; p. 68, Cindy Charles/Photo Edit; p. 70, Bob Daemmrich/Stock Boston; p. 79, Li-Hua Lan/The Image Works; p. 83, Bob Daemmrich Photography; p. 85, Brian Smith; p. 89, Robert Harbison; p. 91, Joe Bator/The Stock Market; p. 104, Laura Dwight Photography; p. 109, A. Ramey/Photo Edit; p. 117, Will Hart/Photo Edit; p. 120, Will Faller; p. 122, Robert Harbison; p. 127, Will Hart; p. 128, Robert Harbison; p. 134, Will Hart; p. 145, Mike Maple/Woodfin Camp & Associates; p. 147, Will Hart; p. 150, Jeffry Myers/Stock Boston; p. 151, Sylvia Johnson/Woodfin Camp & Associates; p. 152, Will Hart; p. 157, Bill Aron/Photo Edit; p. 165, Will Hart; p. 177, Laura Dwight Photography; p. 180, Bob Daemmrich/Stock Boston; p. 185, Matthew McVay/Stone; p. 187, Najlan Feanny/Stock Boston; p. 190, Sally & Derk Kuyper; p. 198, AP/Wide World Photo; p. 202, Phyllis Picardi/Stock Boston; p. 207, Brian Parker/Tom Stack & Associates; p. 210, Will Hart; p. 215, Roger Ressmeyer/Corbis; p. 230, North Wind Picture Archives; p. 234, Will Faller; p. 236, Rob Crandall/Stock Connection/PictureQuest; p. 242, Will Faller; p. 244, Brian Smith; p. 250, Bill Aron/Photo Edit; p. 253, Rashid/Monkmeyer; p. 257, Brian Smith; p. 261, Tony Freeman/Photo Edit; p. 264, Michael Newman/Photo Edit; p. 266, Bonnie Kamin/Photo Edit; p. 269, Steve Woit/Stock Boston/PictureQuest; p. 271, Bob Daemmrich/Stock Boston; p. 283, Will Hart; p. 286, 289, 292, 293, 294, 295, 298, North Wind Picture Archives; p. 299 (Top), Library of Congress; p. 299 (Bottom), Bettmann/Corbis; p. 310, Courtesy of the Blackwell Collection, Northern Illinois University; p. 311, North Wind Picture Archives; p. 320, Minnesota Historical Society/Corbis; p. 324 (Both), 325 (Both), 326, North Wind Picture Archives; p. 327, Courtesy of the Blackwell Collection, Northern Illinois University; p. 328, © Corbis; p. 329, Library of Congress; p. 330, North Wind Picture Archives; p. 331, © Corbis; p. 332 (Top), Courtesy of the Blackwell Collection, Northern Illinois University; p. 332 (Bottom), Library of Congress; p. 343, Will Faller; p. 345, Brown Brothers; p. 348, Courtesy of NASA; p. 350, Brian Smith; p. 352, Culver Pictures; p. 354, Greig Cranna/Index Stock Imagery; p. 355, James Marshall/The Image Works; p. 357, Robert Harbison; p. 359, Brian Smith; p. 360, © Corbis; p. 361, Lyrl Ahern; p. 363, Will Hart; p. 383, Will Hart/Photo Edit; p. 388 (Top), © Araldo de Luca/Corbis; p. 388 (Bottom), 390, North Wind Picture Archives; p. 391 (Both), 393, Courtesy of the Blackwell Collection; p. 396, Courtesy of the Special Collections, Milbank Memorial Library, Teachers College, Columbia University; p. 398, North Wind Picture Archives; p. 401, Lawrence Migdale/Stock Boston; p. 411, Will Faller; p. 415, © 1992 Terry Wild Studio; p. 417, 418, Will Hart; p. 420, Courtesy of the Blackwell Collection, Northern Illinois University; p. 422, Myrleen Ferguson Cate/Photo Edit; p. 424, Will Hart; p. 428, Will Faller; p. 438, Will Hart; p. 439, Mary Kate Denny/Photo Edit; p. 442, Brian Smith; p. 444, Charles Gupton/The Stock Market; p. 450, Will Hart; p. 451, Laura Dwight Photography; p. 452, Will Faller; p. 454, Mark Richards/Photo Edit; p. 468, Michael Newman/Photo Edit; p. 471, © Pedrick/The Image Works; p. 472, Dana White/Photo Edit; p. 473, Tom McCarthy/Unicorn Stock Photos; p. 474, Michael Newman/Photo Edit; p. 482, Robin Sachs/Photo Edit; p. 496, Oscar C. Williams; p. 498, Michael Newman/Photo Edit; p. 501, Elizabeth Crews/The Image Works; p. 506, Will Faller; p. 509, 511, Frank Siteman/Stock Boston; p. 514, Mark Lewis/Stone; p. 528, Joe Sohm/The Image Works; p. 529, Bob Daemmrich /Stock Boston; p. 530, Charles Gupton/The Stock Market; p. 533, Peter Byron/Photo Edit; p. 538, Will Hart/Photo Edit; p. 544, Mug Shots/The Stock Market; p. 549, Art Wolfe/Stone; p. 558, Oscar C. Williams.